Community Practice

Community Practice

Theories and Skills for Social Workers

Third Edition

David A. Hardcastle

with Patricia R. Powers and Stanley Wenocur

OXFORD

UNIVERSITY PRESS

OXFORD
UNIVERSITY PRESS

Oxford University Press, Inc., publishes works that further
Oxford University's objective of excellence
in research, scholarship, and education.

Oxford   New York
Auckland   Cape Town   Dar es Salaam   Hong Kong   Karachi
Kuala Lumpur   Madrid   Melbourne   Mexico City   Nairobi
New Delhi   Shanghai   Taipei   Toronto

With offices in
Argentina   Austria   Brazil   Chile Czech Republic   France   Greece
Guatemala   Hungary   Italy   Japan   Poland   Portugal   Singapore
South Korea   Switzerland   Thailand   Turkey   Ukraine   Vietnam

Copyright © 2011, 2004, 1997 by Oxford University Press, Inc.

Published by Oxford University Press, Inc.
198 Madison Avenue, New York, New York 10016

www.oup.com

Oxford is a registered trademark of Oxford University Press

Library of Congress Cataloging-in-Publication Data

Hardcastle, David A.
  Community practice : theories and skills for social workers /
David A. Hardcastle with Patricia R. Powers and Stanley Wenocur. — 3rd ed.
     p. cm.
  Includes bibliographical references and index.
  ISBN 978-0-19-539887-8 (pbk. : alk. paper)
  1. Social service. 2. Social workers. I. Powers, Patricia R. II. Wenocur, Stanley, 1938- III. Title.
  HV40.H289 2011
  361.3'2—dc22   2010038981

3   5   7   9   8   6   4

Printed in the United States of America
on acid-free paper

Preface

President Obama started his career as a community organizer on the South Side of Chicago, where he saw firsthand what people can do when they come together for a common cause.[1]

Community organizers can grow up to become presidents of the United States, but . . . on the other hand . . . he worked as a community organizer, and immersed himself in Chicago machine politics.[2]

I guess a small-town mayor is sort of like a community organizer, except that you have actual responsibilities.[3]

During the 2008 Obama presidential campaign and election season, community organization was chic with politicians and the media. It was presidential preparation, or at the least presidential campaign grounding, equivalent to machine politics to some, and an avoidance of real responsibility to others. A *Philadelphia Inquirer* political columnist argued that outnumbered House of Representatives Republicans have altered the Obama agenda because they were better community organizers than the newly elected community organizer-in-chief. The GOP out-organized the one-time community organizer on the 2009 economic stimulus legislative package: not one Republican representative voted for the stimulus package despite public pressure.[4] Although community organization and community practice are little understood within and outside the profession, let us hope community organization was not just a 2008 political campaign season fad.

Social workers need to understand social work community practice in and beyond the political arena. Of course, all social professions are political. The social component of social work is critical, though often ignored by the profession, in this new globalized millennium. Community practice is the social work professional component that helps individuals, families, groups, organizations, and communities address social forces shaping their behaviors and expanding or limiting their opportunities. Attention to the individual *in the* social environment is social work's great strength as a profession and is what distinguishes it from

other kindred helping professions. This expanded view of helping—beyond therapy—affirms social work's historic commitment to social justice: *to serve and advocate for the victims of modern industrial global society and its inherent inequalities and to develop supporting communities.* Without this social component and a commitment to social justice and community welfare, social work loses its professional authenticity.

The social commitment is particularly important during our current Great Recession, which was predicted in our earlier editions and we hope is easing by publication time, brought about by rampant individualism, greed, economic globalization and social localism, and slavish deference to an unregulated and ungoverned market—read private ownership. The economy ideology has accelerated the concentration of income, wealth, and social power at the top of the economic pyramid while increasing poverty and economic insecurity for rest of society. The global society and its political and economic power holders forgot that viable community is the prerequisite to social and individual welfare. Social workers must return to championing the diminishing middle class and increasing number of poor and work to end our social retrenchment and welfare state devolution, restriction of civil rights and liberties in the name of a false patriotism, and pathologizing of diverse human behavior, as reflected in an expanding *Diagnostic and Statistical Manual of Mental Disorders.* Revitalization of communities and social connectedness are critical fundamentals for re-establishing an ethically, socially, and economically healthy United States and world.

Unfortunately, as indicated by the National Association of Social Workers' labor force surveys, social work's interest in community practice continues to wane. Fewer social workers are opting for community organization as a career choice, and most spend little time on community tasks and social issues in their practice.[5]

The bottom line is that social work must commit to on-the-ground social work in communities rather than hooking our star to trendy notions of therapy and abstract outcome schemes. In the prefaces to our earlier editions, we observed that students generally come to schools of social work to be therapists rather than social workers. Their desire perhaps is understandable as they observe a devaluing and devolution of the welfare state, growth of contingent and contract employees in social agencies, and the increasing privatization and commodification of social services. These trends are occurring without much vocal protest from the social work profession, whether in practice or academia. Few schools of social work offer community practice concentrations. Obfuscating quasi-systems rhetoric such as "macro" and "mezzo" is used to label practice rather than community organization or community practice. Usually, the student's vision of therapy involves some sort of psychosocial counseling of dysfunctional individuals and families in individual or therapy groups with more or less regularly scheduled hourly office or clinic visits. This dream doesn't capture poverty, abuse, finding resources for client services in an indifferent society, practice management, and social justice. It is an incomplete vision of helping because it leaves out the social world in social work practice.

The inclusion of the social world and a commitment to community in the dream of really helping means being available to any group in the community, hearing what all citizens want, and providing for those most in need. It means choosing locations, hours, and staff that will make service users experience us as being there and available to them. It means providing the political support needed for programs to start, survive, thrive, and protect the vulnerable and socially marginalized. It means a devotion to social justice.

In the 1930s depression, it was hard to ignore the impact of the malfunctioning social system. Some social workers became politically active while staying in the casework trenches. Both caseworkers and community practitioners recognized the obvious relationship between private trouble and public issues that blurred the distinction between community work and casework. Social workers clearly had to attend to both. Many did. The knowledge and skills of each played a part in the creation of a new system of basic social protections and services. The same commitment is needed today in our struggles. America is declining in its quality of life for its citizens. America's Human Development Index, released by the United Nations, reveals that the United States' quality of life has fallen from second in the world in the 1980s to 15th in 2007/2008.[6] The script is written. It entails struggle, but struggle, of course, with the tools, technologies, and opportunities this era affords to construct a different and more humane social world. To the extent that this book contributes to social workers strengthening their community-building skills and allegiance to social justice, we will have positively contributed to the struggle.

As we look at the current field of social work, its future resembles past struggles. Poverty is escalating. Social divisiveness is increasing. Reactionary forces under the guise of fiscal responsibility and patriotism are abandoning and outright destroying the social safety net that has undergirded the community from the New Deal of the 1930s to 2000. As with previous "Red" scares, our current war on terrorism has led to diminished civil liberties and civil rights and increasing state police powers, secured and justified as patriotic actions necessary for homeland security. The U.S. design for the market economy subsidizes global banks and corporations and enriches the top 1% while socially and economically relegating working- and middle-class people to economic insecurity and often poverty. The new millennium's first decade has been a real recession, with record unemployment, a decline of workers' real wages and stock prices, an increase in poverty, and a loss of middle-class retirement security. It has also witnessed a continuing growth of per capita income and continuing tax cuts for the superrich. What should we do? There are no easy answers, but there are answers. Revitalization of communities and our social connectedness appears to be requisite.

The goal for this edition, as with the first two editions, is to provide readers with a comprehensive and integrated text covering community theories and practice skills necessary for all social work practitioners and others interested in community. It contains necessary topics to build a foundation for social administration, community organization, and clinical and casework practice. The text does not assume that all social workers are community organizers, but it does presume that community skills and a commitment to social justice are necessary for a true and effective foundation for all social workers in these troubled times. The theories and practice skills of communities, organizations, interorganizational practice, small groups, and individual cases are required to be effective direct service practitioners, caseworkers, case managers, clinicians, and private practice social workers.

All direct service practitioners need to be dedicated to social justice. The chapter on critical community social casework, a reformulation of case management, concentrates on the skills, knowledge, personal fortitude, and ethical commitments required of today's social workers to help their service users address and change or manage their social environments. These helping activities and skills are community practice. The concept of community captures the humanness, the passion and compassion, and the interconnectedness among people in a way that the sterile labels we often use, such as social environment, social ecology, social systems, task environment, and other borrowed physical science metaphors, neglect. As social work practice is broad and eclectic and intersects with many other fields, diverse practice theories and examples are necessary to illuminate it.

The textbook has two sections. The first part covers the ideological, ethical, emotional, theoretical, and programmatic foundation necessary for community practice. We believe professional social work practice requires this ethical, ideological, and emotional grounding as well as theoretical knowledge as foundations for the practice skills. The second section is devoted to community practice skills, such as entering communities where people live and work safely and unobtrusively, and with sensitivity to culture, to provide services effectively. These chapters cover principles drawn out of practice and the thinking of many community practitioners and theorists reflected in their literature. They address how to study, investigate, and assess communities; how to build capacity; how to help people mobilize, organize, and plan; and how to advocate. Most of the practice methods that community workers need are covered in these chapters, with guidance on how to become competent in the multiple sets of skills. The skills chapters follow what we believe is a logical order; however, instructors, students, and readers can arrange them in any order to fit their preferences. We have updated and revised all chapters, some appreciably, taking into account suggestions from students and instructors. More attention is devoted to community and community practice theories; the skills of community assessment and analysis, assets assessment and development; networking, bargaining, and negotiation. Chapter 13 delves into community organizing.

The text also encourages our belief that a social worker's personal fortitude, integrity, and dedication must accompany the use of any practice knowledge and skills. Our ideology is clear. People and their communities are fundamental to well-being. Social justice is our guiding philosophy.

Although we sometimes use terms such as *clients*, our philosophy is to view individuals, families, and community groups as collaborators and partners in change, whether the level of activity is casework, group work, or community work. We have struggled to find neutral terms to describe those whom social workers wish to assist. With clinical and casework practice, *client* has much negative baggage, yet *service user* is more awkward and unclear. At the community and societal levels, community resident seemed appropriate but doesn't capture the community practitioner's particular relationship with the community. *Citizen* is entirely inadequate given the current xenophobia. We use a mixture of labels, knowing that terminology will continue to evolve as people strive for dignity and inclusion. We hope it is not too confusing. The most recent curriculum accreditation requirements of the Council on Social Work Education were reviewed in developing the text.

At various points throughout the book, we have used the specific words of community practitioners to describe their helping practice. We have, of course, drawn upon our own and our colleagues' practice experience and theoretical and methodological knowledge. The authors' combined community and social work practice exceeds 100 years. Our experience over the past half-century includes community organization and development, social group work, administration, child welfare, aging, disabilities, consumer self-help, mental health, hunger and homelessness, fundraising, labor organizing, lobbying and political organizing, campaigning and advocacy, antipoverty work, AIDS programs, and more. The case examples come out of our professional experiences or are composites of our professional experience. We also have drawn upon the community practice experiences and contributions of other professional community practitioners and global faculty colleagues. We admire their work and thank them all.

Notes

1 *Briefing room: The blog.* (Jan. 29, 2009, 12:01 PM.). Change has come to the Whitehouse.gov. Retrieved Jan. 29, 2009.

2 Rudy Giuliani, former Mayor of New York City and Republican Presidential Nomination candidate, Rudy Giuliani Republican National Convention Speech, Sept. 3, 2008, 5:13 PM.

3 Sarah Palin, 2008 Republican Vice President Nominee, former mayor Wasilla, Alaska, and Governor of Alaska, Republican National Convention Speech. NCR Staff (Sept. 4, 2008). Palin criticized for mocking community organizing. *National Catholic Reporter.*

4 Ferris, K. (Feb. 15, 2009). Community organizing proves helpful—to GOP. *The Philadelphia Inquirer*, Section D: Currents, pp. D1, D6.

5 For two studies examining what social workers do from limited membership sample of NASW members, see Whitaker, T., & Arrington, P. (2008). *Social workers at work: NASW membership workforce study.* Washington, DC: National Association of Social Workers, and (March 2006). *Licensed Social Workers in the U.S.: 2004*, Prepared by Center for Health Workforce Studies, School of Public Health, University at Albany and Center for Workforce Studies, National Association of Social Workers.

6 See *Human Development Reports*, http://hdr.undp.org/en/statistics and Conley, D. (March 23, 2009). America is #...15? *The Nation*, 288:11.

Acknowledgments

David A. Hardcastle is the primary author of this edition. The relationship and contributions of Drs. Patricia Powers and Stan Wenocur to this project are enduring. Pat was a major contributor to the first two editions and Stan to the first edition. Their materials and contributions remain a part of this version. Both have retired from most formal social work practice and education, although they are still involved in their communities. Their counsel and professional wisdom are a part of me. For these reasons, we is used as the personal pronoun for author reference in the text, although I alone am responsible for any inclusions, omissions, or confusion.

We thank former Dean Jesse Harris of the School of Social Work, the University of Maryland at Baltimore, and our colleagues, especially those in the School's Management, Administration, and Community Organization Concentration, for their encouragement, suggestions, and criticisms. Their work has been incorporated into some of the exercises and examples. We expressly thank the students in the community practice classes over the past 35 years for their critiques of our theories. We are especially appreciative to the students over the past decades for their use and critiques of the book's material and ideas for revisions. It was their stimulation, needs, and demands for coherence in community practice as a basic skill for all social workers that inspired the book. Furthermore, we gratefully acknowledge the communities, clients, and practitioners with whom we gained our community practice experience over the past half-century and refined our theories, understanding, and skills. We appreciate the community practitioners, lay and professional, who shared with us their experience in services facilitation and advocacy for people and their communities. Their service and commitment to better neighborhoods and communities as places for people to live informed our discussion of skill building with clients, linkages with systems, and utilization of pressure points in forging change. We hope the book will continue their contribution to enhancing community practice and humane communities.

I thank Bryn Mawr College (BMC), its Provost Dr. Kimberly E. Cassidy, and BMC's Graduate School of Social Work and Social Research (GSSW&SR) and its Associate Dean Dr. Marcia L. Martin for extending me an appointment as a research associate at the College and School. This appointment enabled me to use the library and information and communication resources of BMC in completing this project. I am grateful to Susan Turkel, Outreach and Information Technology Librarian at the Canady Library, BMC, for teaching me how to use the information technologies and communication technologies. Without Susan, I'd still be searching for the dwindling hard copy of the appropriate literature. I also thank my two GSSW&SR research assistants, Lisa Couser and John Edwards. They both were a joy to work with and did yeoperson's work. Their future careers will be a contribution to social work and the community.

Maura Roessner, Senior Editor, Social Work, at Oxford University Press took me back some 40 years to my dissertation experience at Case Western Reserve University. With her constant encouragement, support, patience with elusive deadlines, and only occasional nagging, we got the project done, finally. Thank you, Maura.

I particularly thank my wife and colleague, Dr. Cynthia Bisman, Professor, Graduate School of Social Work and Social Research and Co-director, College Center for International Studies, BMC. She helped define and elaborate community practice for direct practice applications and the centrality of ethics in all social work practice. She is an insightful, persistent, and consistent helpmate, colleague, and supporter and an enduring inspiration.

I continue to salute the work of the pioneer community theorists and reformers. The profession needs heroes now. A personal hero was Dr. Harry Specht. Harry made fundamental and constant contributions to community and social justice as central facets of social work practice. His steadfast and clarion call for maintaining community and social justice as social work practice's living central tenets, while sometimes uncomfortable to many in the profession, has guided my thinking, practice, and instruction. The book reflects an effort to help Harry keep the profession faithful and bring community and social justice back into all social work practice.

David A. Hardcastle. PhD
Professor Emeritus
University of Maryland
School of Social Work
Baltimore, Maryland

Contents

I

Community Practice

An Introduction

Social: *adj*. of or relating to society or its organization.[1]

President Obama started his career as a community organizer on the South Side of Chicago, where he saw firsthand what people can do when they come together for a common cause. (Briefing Room, The Blog. Change has come to WhiteHouse.gov, Tuesday, January 20th, 2009 at 12:01 pm.)

Social work is community practice. Community is a synonym for social. It is necessary for all social workers: generalists, specialists, therapists, and activists. *The Oxford Encyclopedic English Dictionary* (p. 1377) defines social as "1. of or relating to society or its organization, 2. concerned with the mutual relations of human beings or classes of human beings. 3. living in organized communities; unfitted for a solitary life. . . ." Although usually associated with community organization, social action, social planning (Rothman & Tropman, 1987; Wells & Gamble, 1995), and other macro-practice activities, direct service and clinical social workers are community practitioners if they make client referrals, assess community resources, develop client social support systems, and advocate to policymakers for programs to meet clients' needs.

Social work's ecological perspective is about community. Whittaker, Garbarino, and associates (1983) persuasively argued that "the ecological-systems perspective . . . will compel us to do several things: (1) view the client and the situation—the 'ecological unit'—as the proper focus for assessment and intervention, (2) see the teaching of *environmental coping skills as the primary purpose of helping*, and (3) place *environmental modification* and the provision of concrete services on an equal plane with direct, face-to-face interventions with clients" (Italics added, p. 59). Indeed, as this text illustrates, social work practice is using the community and naturally occurring and socially constructed networks within the social environment to provide social supports.

This chapter provides an overview of community practice with our conception of community practice as social work practice, reviews the importance of community practice knowledge and skill for all social workers, describes the generic social work community problem-solving strategy and its use in community practice by clinical and community social workers, and critically examines the ethical imperatives and constraints of community practice.

Community Practice

Community practice applies practice skills to alter the behavioral patterns of community groups, organizations, and institutions or people's relationships and interactions with the community structures. Netting, Kettner, and

1

McMurtry (1993) conceive of community practice as part of macropractice, which they define as the "professional directed intervention designed to bring about planned change in organizations and communities" (p. 3). Community practice as macropractice includes the skills associated with community organization and development, social planning and social action, and social administration.

Community practice involves a set of cognitive, analytic, and sorting skills, plus the ability of the worker to secure commitments and establish partnerships. Think of priority setting, delegation and problem sharing, problem solving, assessment, and contracting.

- Community practice requires the abilities of looking, listening, finding, and theory building.
- Community practice entails persuasion, representation, and reframing to allow social workers to deal with different agendas when working with individuals and groups and in communities.
- Community practice necessitates organizational, management, and group skills.
- Community practice calls for interactive, responsive, and socially oriented skills of public information, collaboration, and inter-organizational tasks such as networking, social marketing, and public information.
- Community practice requires social action, evaluation, advocacy, and lobbying skills.
- Community practice *demands* a strong commitment to social justice and client and community empowerment.
- Community practice requires the ability to learn new theories and skills as needed.

Community intervention, like clinical intervention, is complex in terms of the circumstances of those needing help and in terms of professional performance challenges or use of self.

Community organization and the related community development are the practices of helping a community or part of a community, such as a neighborhood or a group of people with a common interest, to become a more effective, efficient, and supportive social environment for nurturing people and their social relationships (Butcher, Banks, & Henderson with Robertson, 2007; Delgado & Staples, 2008; Hardina, 2002; Mancini, Bowens, & Martin, 2005). Ross (1967), an early pioneer of bringing community organization into social work, conceived of community organization as "a process by which a community identifies its needs or objectives, orders (or ranks) these needs or objectives, develops the confidence and will to work at these needs or objectives, finds the resources (internal and/or external) to deal with these needs or objectives, takes action in respect to them, and in so doing extends and develops cooperative and collaborative attitudes and practices in the community" (p. 28).

Social planning, a subset of community organization, addresses the development and coordination of community agencies and services to meet community functions and responsibilities and to provide for its members. Social action, another community organization subset, involves practices and strategies to develop, redistribute, and control community statuses and resources, including social power, and to change community relations and behavior patterns to promote the development or redistribution of community resources.

Well and Gamble (1995) elaborate this basic tripartite community practice prototype into an eight-component model that combines practice acts or the *doing* with the purposes of the practice. The unifying features of their inventory are purpose and objectives. Community practice's purpose is "empowerment-based interventions to strengthen participation in democratic processes, assist groups and communities in advocating for their basic needs and organizing for social justice, and improve the effectiveness and responsiveness of human services systems" (p. 577). Community practice's objectives are to:

- develop the organizing skills and abilities of individuals and groups
- make social planning more accessible and inclusive in a community
- connect social and economic involvement to grassroots community groups
- advocate for broad coalitions in solving community problems
- infuse the social planning process with a concern for social justice (p. 577)

The model's eight practice domains are (a) neighborhood and community organizing, (b) organizing functional communities, (c) community social and economic development, (d) social planning, (e) program development and community liaison, (f) political and social action, (g) coalitions building and maintenance, and (h) social movements (Well & Gamble, 1995, pp. 580–589). Hardina (2002, pp. 2–3) expands the practice domains into more specific skills such as budgeting, grant-writing, and a wide range of research skills. Hardina (2002) also includes analytic skills of power analysis, needs assessment, and political analysis.

While these domains and skills are not mutually exclusive, the schemata expand the scope of community practice. More importantly, they specify a range of social work roles and skills necessary to fulfill the domains: organizer, teacher, coach, facilitator, advocate, negotiator, broker, manager, researcher, communicator. These are roles and skills that cut across all social work practice domains.

Our conception of community practice goes beyond macropractice as a practice arena to embrace the use of community practice skills to help individuals make use of community resources or ameliorate oppressive community structures. Community practice is broader than community organization to encompass the efforts to allow the individual to be an active community participant in the community's life. Henderson (2007) states, the processes of community practice are, as hopefully are the processes of therapy, to promote the individual's participation and engagement in community to build democratic participation in democratic community decision making and active communities.

We encourage further expanding the cross-cutting social work community practice skills for all social workers regardless of client systems to encompass campaigning, staging, marketing and social marketing, and acting as network consultant and facilitator. In our highly technological and media-driven age, these skills are essential.

Advocacy to pursue social justice is a practice task common to and required of all social work practice (Ezell, 2001; Schneider & Lester, 2001). All social workers are obliged to advocate in social and political arenas to achieve an equitable distribution of the community's physical, economic, and other social resources for social justice under the profession's ethical code (National Association of Social Workers [NASW], 2008).

The macro social worker and the direct service or clinical social worker can differ in perspective. The community organizer assumes that if the community (its organizations, institutions, and behavior patterns) functions more effectively and is responsive to its members, they will be healthier and happier. The direct service practitioner tends to view the community as a supportive or potentially supportive resource for a specific client or a class of clients, with community change efforts designed to improve the community for these clients. In attempting to improve the quality of life for individual clients, the social worker may operate from the perspective that if enough individuals can be made healthy, the community will be better for everyone. Both perspectives require knowledge of community structures and behavior and the skills to effect behavior changes in some part of the community. Both sets of social workers generally use a similar problem-solving strategy as described later in this chapter.

Social workers often engage in both modalities of practices, either simultaneously or sequentially. They work directly with clients and, at the same time, develop community resources. Social work supervisors, administrators, and social activists often begin their professional careers as direct service social workers.

The Community in Social Work Practice

Communities are always the context, if not always the content, of social work practice. Communities and community practice have been central to social work's history and development. Understanding, intervening in, and using the client's social environment as part of the helping process are skills consonant with the profession's ecological foundation. Social systems, especially communities, strongly influence the ways people think and act. Communities can be nurturing environments providing basic social, economic, and emotional supports to individuals and families. Conversely, communities can be hostile places with inequities that contribute significantly to individual and family malfunctioning (Clampet-Lundquest & Massey, 2008; Coughlin, 2004; Grogan-Kaylor, Woolley, Mowbray, Reischl, Güster, Karb, Macfarlane, Gant, & Alaimo, 2007; Mulroy, 2004). One's self-concept, at least in part, is developed through involvement in and identification with social and community groups (Clampet-Lundquest & Massey, 2008; Miller & Prentice, 1994; Sharkey, 2008; Vartanian & Buck, 2005).

Community theories help us understand what communities are, how they function, and how they influence our behavior. Often theories offer propositions to explain how communities can function to serve their members most effectively. Community theories are complex because communities are complex. Like many social science concepts, community is a slippery, intricate, ideological, and multifaceted summary concept covering a range of social phenomena. Cohen (1985) cataloged more than 90 different definitions of community used in the social sciences literature.

Communities are nonetheless real for most people, although, as will be discussed in Chapter 4, the concept of community means different things to different people. Community is a geographic space, a geopolitical or civic entity, a place of emotional identity, and a refuge in the mind. It is community's emotional identity that gives it meaning and power for most people (Bellah, Madsen, Sullivan, Swidler, & Tipton, 1985, 1991; Cohen, 1985; Grogan-Kaylor, Woolley, Mowbray, Reischl, Güster, Karb, Macfarlane, Gant, & Alaimo, 2007; Lasch, 1994).

Cohen's (1985) conception of community's reflect emotional charging, personal identification, and symbolic construction by people. He conceives of community as "a system of values, norms, and moral codes which provoke a sense of identity within a bounded whole to its members. . . . Structures do not, in themselves, create meaning for people. . . . [Without meaning] many of the organizations designed to create 'community' as palliative to anomie and alienation are doomed to failure" (p. 9). The community, Cohen continues, is "the arena in which people acquire their most fundamental and most substantial experience of social life outside the confines of the home. . . . Community, therefore, is where one learns and continues to practice how to 'be social' (p. 15)."

If we accept community's essential importance to people, it follows that community knowledge and community practice skills are necessary for all social work practitioners. Community practice calls on social workers to employ a range of community practice theories and skills to help clients contribute to use and the resources and strengths of their communities. Indeed, postmodernist social work theorists such as Pardeck, Murphy, and Choi (1994) assert that "Social work practice, simply stated, should be community based. . . . [Community] is not defined in racial, ethnic, demographic, or geographic terms, as is often done. Instead a community is a domain where certain assumptions about reality are acknowledged to have validity" (p. 345).

Community Practice Skills as Foundation for all Social Workers

Community practice is the shared foundation skill of all social workers; it is rooted in the profession's purpose and mission, its history, the policies of the two major American professional social work associations, and shared by most professional associations globally.

BOX 1.1.	Communities and Clients

1. Communities shape and limit client behavior.
2. Communities provides opportunities for and limits to client empowerment.
3. Client empowerment requires that clients have a capacity to assess, access, manage, and alter community resources and forces.
4. Clients need a capacity to contribute to, reciprocate, and affect the welfare of their communities.
5. Community involvement provides clients with a capacity to affect their communities.

Social Works Purpose and Mission

Gordon (1969), a leading social work theorist until his death in the early 1990s, stated that improving the client's social functioning is the cardinal mission of contemporary social work practice. The profession's attention is focused on the transactions between people and their social environment and the management of these transactions. "Transaction is *exchanges in the context of action or activity*" (italics added; p. 7).

Polsky (1969) in the 1960s advocated even more strongly for community knowledge and skills by the practitioner and participation by the client in community change: "Changes in dysfunctioning individuals cannot be effectuated [or] sustained unless the system in which they function also undergoes modification through client efforts" (p. 20).

The importance of the client's community is reflected in social work's dual perspectives of person in environment and person and environment, and the ecological approach to social casework practice promoted by Bisman (1994), Ewalt (1980), and Germain (1983). Bisman (1994) clarifies the complexity of the dual perspective with the community's role in social work practice: "What has been called the dual perspective of person and environment actually has three components. Person and environment means the consideration of individuals within the context of the community and its resources, societal policies and regulations and the service delivery of organizations" (p. 27).

Specht and Courtney (1994), in their critique of the contemporary profession, *Unfaithful Angels: How Social Work Has Abandoned Its Mission,* insist that:

The objective of social work is to help people make use of social resources—family members, friends, neighbors, community organizations and social service agencies, and so forth—to solve their problems. . . . Helping individuals to make use of their social resources is one of the major functions of social work practice. And just as important is the social worker's function of developing and strengthening these resources by bringing people together in groups and organizations, by community education, and by organizational development. (p. 23)

Specht and Courtney (1994), like Gordon (1969), contend that social workers should examine and facilitate the transactions between clients—indeed, between all people—in the community and inveigh against the social isolation of psychotherapy: "Social work's mission should be to build a meaning, a purpose, and a sense of obligation for the community. It is only by creating a community that we establish a basis for commitment, obligation, and social support. We must build communities that are excited about their child care systems, that find it exhilarating to care for the mentally ill and frail aged, that make demands upon people to behave, to contribute, and to care for one another. Psychotherapy will not enable us to do that. . . . to give purpose and meaning to people's lives, and enable us to care about and love one another" (p. 27).

The 21st century's first decade, with its loss of community obligation and support with globalization, reveals the wisdom in Specht and Courtney's insights.

The mission of most national and international professional social work associations reinforces social work's social context and social justice mission. NASW's 2008 Revised Code of Ethics (2008) states:

The primary mission of the social work profession is to enhance human wellbeing and help meet the basic human needs of all people, with particular attention to the needs and empowerment of people who are vulnerable, oppressed, and living in poverty. A historic and defining feature of social work is the profession's focus on individual wellbeing in a social context and the wellbeing of society. Fundamental to social work is attention to the environmental forces that create, contribute to, and address problems in living.

Social workers promote social justice and social change with and on behalf of clients.

The codes of ethics of the British Association of Social Workers (2002), the International Federation of Social Workers (IFSW, 2004), the Canadian Association of Social Workers (2005), and the emerging Russian social work association, the Union of Social Educators and Social Workers (2003), all affirm the American code's concern with social context, social justice, and community.

Emphasizing community theories and practice skills for all social work practitioners is not anti–clinical social work practice; it is pro–social work practice. We are critical of social work

---

BOX 1.2.   **Our Position on Community Practice**

Our position, theory, and set of propositions, briefly stated, on the requirement for community practice is that people best exist in social ecologies or communities. Behavior is biopsychosocial and not exclusively biopsychological. Behavior is shaped by interactions, engagements, and exchanges with the social ecology. Personal empowerment requires the capacity to develop and manage the interactions and exchanges with the social ecology. All people, including social workers and social work clients, have the capacity to develop and improve their social management skills and functioning. If all people have this capacity and if empowerment is a goal of social work, then all social workers and all people will need to develop knowledge and skill to better enable them to assist people to develop and manage supportive social ecologies or communities.

---

practice done with blinders that does not recognize social obligations to and of clients and their social context. Community knowledge and community practice skills are distinguishing attributes separating the complete social worker from the wannabe psychiatrist, a social worker who is only marginally professionally competent. Community competence is one of the properties that has historically distinguished the social work profession and effective social work practice from the profusion of other counseling and therapeutic professions (Doherty, 1995, p. 47). If social work devalues its social mission, other professions such as community psychology stand ready to pick up the mantle. Without community knowledge and skill, social workers are limited in their ability to understand and assist clients in shaping and managing the major forces that affect their lives and to help clients empower themselves to develop and manage personal and social resources. The incomplete social worker who does not recognize the importance of community apparently assumes that the client is unaffected by community, whether living in Dhaka or Des Moines.

Social Work History

Community practice skills have been an indispensable component of social work's repertoire since the inception of the profession. Beginning with its formation as a profession at the start of the 20th century, social work's professional concern has been to improve individual and collective social functioning. Mary Richmond, the American social casework pioneer, recognized the importance of community theory, the social

environment, and community practice skills for social casework in her two books *Social Diagnosis* (1917) and *What Is Social Casework?* (1922/1992). Richmond's social casework was concerned with the person in the community. The 1929 Milford Conference on Social Work, convened to specify social work's professional content and boundaries, followed Mary Richmond and went beyond counseling, advice giving, and modeling and demonstration of behavior to include the community practice skills of information gathering and referrals to other community resources (American Association of Social Workers, 1929).

The social casework Richmond and the Milford Conference championed was not deskbound or introspective counseling; rather, it involved confronting the client's problems in the community where the client lived and where the problems existed. The Charity Organization Society, Mary Richmond's principal agency and the leading casework agency of the era in Great Britain and the United States, held that community work was fundamental to casework. Bosanquet, an early leader of the British Charity Organization Society movement, is quoted by Timms (1966) as stating that "Case work which is not handled as an engine of social improvement is not . . . Charity Organization Society work at all" (p. 41).

The profession's often-reviewed cause and function strain between social action, social change, and reform, on one hand, and individual treatment and change, on the other, poses a spurious dilemma. Spurious because it is wrongly framed as an either/or choice between two mutually exclusive activities rather than uniting function with cause as two supportive and complementary social work components. Porter Lee, in his 1929 presidential address to the National Conference on Social Welfare, recognized the unity of *both* cause and function for the profession (Bruno, 1948). Lee, while credited with conceptualizing the strain in his "cause and function" address, his speech's title and the speech's emphasis were on the cause *and* function unity, not a cause *or* function division (Spano, 1982, p. 7). Lee saw no dichotomy or dilemma, nor is there one. Social work has always emphasized individual help, use of the social environment in providing help, and social action and reform (Pumphrey, 1980).

National Association of Social Workers and the Council on Social Work Education Policy

Social work's largest professional association globally, the National Association of Social Workers (NASW), and America's social work education's accrediting body, the Council on Social Work Education (CSWE), recognize the importance of community theory and skills for all social work practitioners. NASW (2008), as reviewed earlier, states that "A historic and defining feature of social work is the profession's focus on individual wellbeing in a social context and the wellbeing of society. Fundamental to social work is attention to the environmental forces that create, contribute to, and address problems in living."

NASW's Code of Ethics Preamble further notes that community and macro skills are central to the profession:

Social workers promote social justice and social change with and on behalf of clients. "Clients" is used inclusively to refer to individuals, families, groups, organizations, and communities. Social workers are sensitive to cultural and ethnic diversity and strive to end discrimination, oppression, poverty, and other forms of social injustice. These activities may be in the form of direct practice, community organizing, supervision, consultation administration, advocacy, social and political action, policy development and implementation, education, and research and evaluation. Social workers seek to enhance the capacity of people to address their own needs. Social workers also seek to promote the responsiveness of organizations, communities, and other social institutions to individuals' needs and social problems.

The professional code does not limit these obligations to nominal community practitioners. It holds all in the profession responsible. NASW's *Code of Ethics* (2008) also sets forth a set of ethical principles to which all social workers should aspire. First among the principles is that "Social workers' primary goal is to help people in need and to address social problems" (Ethical Principle 1, NASW, 2008). Additionally, "social workers recognize the central importance of human relationships" (Ethical Principle 4, NASW, 2008). This principle holds that social workers "seek to strengthen relationships among people in a purposeful effort to promote, restore, maintain, and enhance the well-being of individuals, families, social groups, organizations, and communities" (NASW, 2003).

NASW developed and advocates that social caseworkers and social work clinicians use a "person-in-environment" (P-I-E) diagnostic and classification system. Social environment in the P-I-E schema is defined as "systemic relationships that people have by virtue of being in the same location" (Karls & Wandrei, 1994, p. 3). The social environment in the P-I-E classification system is essentially the same as the conception of community just presented.

NASW's formulation of the practice methodology claimed by a majority of NASW members—clinical social work—reinforces the importance of community theory and skills. "The perspective of person-in-situation is central to clinical social work practice. Clinical social work includes intervention directed to interpersonal interactions, intrapsychic dynamics, and life-support and management issues" (NASW, n.d., p. 4). Standard 4 of the policy's 11 standards guiding clinical practice requires that "Clinical social workers shall be knowledgeable about the services available in the community and make appropriate referrals for their clients" (NASW, n.d., p. 8).

The CSWE's Commission on Accreditation (2008), the national accrediting organization for graduate and undergraduate professional social work education, charges that all social work students acquire knowledge and skill in social relations and the range of social systems (including organizations, social institutions, and communities) as part of their professional foundation. Indeed, the Commission recognizes that a basic purpose of social work is "to promote human and community well-being" (Commission on Accreditation, 2008, p. 1).

Changing Nature of the Social Work Practice Environment

The last quarter of the 20th century saw profound changes in the social work practice environment. After the 1960s and 1970s, with their emphasis on federal government involvement and services coordination, since the 1980s we have seen federal, state, and local human services policies move toward reduction, competition, divestiture, and privatization of public programs in a generally conservative era. These changes are accompanied by the rhetoric, if not always the reality, of returning power, responsibility, and control to state and local governments and the private sector for welfare and social services, and an increase in personal and family responsibility. The federal government's role and responsibilities for welfare and human services have undergone and are still undergoing their greatest transformation since the New Deal era of the 1930s. Reforms first instigated by conservative governments have subsequently been embraced and expanded by the traditionally liberal political parties (Callinicos, 2001; Deacon, 1997; Dicken, 2003; 1994; Gray, 1998; Harris, 2006; Mishra, 1999; Sennett, 2006; Tanzi, 2002; Wagner, 1997).

The national political landscape from the Reagan 1980 election to the 21st century generally was conservative. The 1995 Congressional elections saw Republicans gain control of both houses of Congress for the first time since 1958, a majority of the governorships up for election, and significant Republican gains in state legislatures (Connelly, 2000). Republicans held five of the seven presidencies since 1980 and recaptured the presidency in the 2000 election after an arduous, contentious, and still-disputed process involving dubious recounts and a legally tenuous U.S. Supreme Court ruling. The U.S. Supreme Court is the more conservative than it has been in decades (Liptak, 2010). The Republicans also retained control of the House of Representatives.

After Vermont's Senator James Jeffords dropped his Republican Party membership for Independent status and aligned with the Democrats, the Democrats controlled the Senate. The first two 21st-century elections were Democratic disasters, no matter the spin. The Republicans, after vigorous campaigns by President Bush, increased their margin of control in the House and regained control of the Senate.

Both parties have moved more to the political right since Reagan. The Democrats have become more conservative in their welfare policies generally. Since the September 11, 2001, terrorist attacks on the World Trade Center, the Pentagon, and United Flight 93 over Shanksville, Pennsylvania, ideological positions, regardless of party, are more conservative, authoritarian, and jingoistic.

From 2006 forward there were grounds for progressive optimism that the regressive tide of the past quarter century has been slowed if not halted. The Democrats gained Congressional control in 2006 largely based on voter dissatisfaction with the Bush and Republican global adventurism and domestic ineptitude and social and political intolerance. The House of Representatives increased from 46% Democratic to 53% and the Senate from 44% to 51%, with the Independents aligned with their caucus (US Census, 2009). The 2008 election offered even more progression. America elected its first African-American president with 53% of the popular vote. He is the first democratically elected president in a developed Western industrial democracy from a publically identified ethnic minority group.[2] This election also gave Democrats 59% control of the House and 59% control of the Senate with the defection of Senator Arlen Specter of Pennsylvania from the Republican Party to the Democratic Party and the continuing alignment of the Senate's Independents with the Democratic caucus. The 2010 bi-election reflects the conservative trend.

Obama's election as the first minority president is the dramatic symbol of change. He campaigned on a slogan of "Change we can believe in" and made skillful use of social marketing, community organization methodologies, and grassroots organizations such as MoveOn.org. Obama garnered 53% of the popular vote and

68% of the essential Electoral College vote (US Census, 2009). The 2010 congressional elections were not promising for Democrats. The Obama victory, historically significant as it was, reflects America's continuing challenge of ethnicity. The election occurred during America's most severe economic recession since the Great Depression of 1929 and a seemingly perpetual and increasingly unpopular war launched by a Republican administration and supported by a Republican congress. Obama's victory, while comfortable, constituted less of a popular vote received than Eisenhower in 1950, Johnson in 1964, Nixon in 1972, Reagan in 1984, and Bush I in 1988, and the margin of victory over his opponent was less than both Eisenhower elections, Johnson's, Nixon's in 1972, both Reagan's, Bush I's and Clinton's 1998 defeat of Dole (US Census, 2009). Obama's African-American identification lowered his vote total in that the political circumstances were poised to give a Democratic presidential candidate the highest margin since Roosevelt over Hoover in the midst of the Great Depression. However, in additional to Obama's political charisma and skills, the social conditions may have also allowed the election of the African-American and minority candidate.

The world and its nations are unstable. The world's economies move toward globalization with the global consequences of the continuing 2008 recession is shaking up prevailing economic philosophies. Governments have to fiscally prop up the pillars of capitalism—the financial institutions and major corporations—at the public's expense. The government propping resembles socialism without the same degree of public control. The United States, supposedly the world's only superpower, has dramatically increased military spending since September 11, 2001. However, its global military adventurism has not brought world stability or even a sense of security at home. Superpower status doesn't appear to give control. With increased military spending and dominance, the welfare state is devolving, with decreasing federal responsibility for welfare and returning greater authority and responsibility to states, localities, and the private sector. As of 2009, with the recession and its accompanying increase in poverty, unemployment, and deprivation, there

has not been a mending of the social safety net. With devolution and increased local authority, control, and responsibility for social welfare, all social workers increasingly need community practice knowledge and skills. Social workers need to assess local communities for needed resources, develop resource networks and support systems, and advocate for themselves and their clients.

Social workers have to develop their own resources in a competitive world. Clinical skills alone are insufficient for professional maintenance. With privatization, private practice, and managed care, social workers can't survive unless they are able to advocate and market themselves and their services, get themselves included on managed-care vendor lists, and access and manage networks. Privatization, contract services, managed care, and proprietary practice by social workers has become the norm. Proprietary social work, either solo, as part of a group, or with a for-profit corporation, is as extensive as public sector employment (O'Neill, 2003; Whitaker & Arrington, 2008).

The Need for Revitalization of the Community and the Social in Social Work

Despite social work's rich history of community practice, the evidence is that the importance of community practice in social work is declining. Specht and Courtney in *Unfaithful Angels* (1994) allege that social work has abandoned its historical mission of service, especially service to the poor, in the pursuit of psychotherapies, private practice and autonomy from social agencies, and increased income and status. Only 1% of licensed social workers spend 20 hours or more a week in either community organization or policy development. Only 34% spend any time in community organization and 30% in policy development (Whitaker & Arrington, 2008).

The problem is not that some individual social workers have abandoned the traditional mission of the profession and, in a sense, the historical profession, but rather that the profession itself has abandoned its customary service mission to the community and the community's most needy and vulnerable citizens.

The profession's movement away from community and social concerns is illustrated by NASW's social action and legislative agenda. NASW's major legislative efforts and successes, nationally and by state chapters, to obtain licensure and the legally mandated capacity to receive third-party vendor payments for therapies have led to a policy thrust of function over cause.

NASW's 2009–2010 (National Association of Social Workers, 2009) federal policy priorities were:

- Social Work Reinvestment Initiative: to secure federal and state investments in professional social work to meet the increasing public demand for services
- Dorothy I. Height and Whitney M. Young, Jr. Social Work Reinvestment Act: to establish a Social Work Reinvestment Commission to provide long-term recommendations and strategies to maximize the ability of social workers to serve their clients with expertise and care, to provide funding for demonstration programs in the areas of workplace improvements, research, education and training, and community-based programs
- The National Center for Social Work Research Act
- Strengthen Social Work Training Act
- Teri Zenner Social Worker Safety Act
- Legislation addressing loan forgiveness for social workers and training for child welfare workers
- Implement state and territory plans focusing on:
  - Title protection
  - Loan forgiveness
  - Establishment of social work education programs
  - Education of the public about social workers
  - Increased salary compensation

The agenda report (National Association of Social Workers, 2009) concludes with the promise that "NASW will continue its work to promote public awareness and understanding of the social work profession through public education efforts and collaboration with the Center for Workforce Studies to inform the public and policymakers about the importance of professional social workers' services."

The state NASW chapters largely focus on professional maintenance agendas and are silent in the legislative battles on welfare reform and health care. Salcido and Seek's (1992) conclusions, after a survey of the political activity of 52 NASW state chapters, still generally hold true. The chapters "seemed to act on behalf of goals related to promoting the profession and to a lesser extent on those promoting social services legislation. . . . These findings imply that the thrust of future chapter political activities may be associated with professionalization and to a lesser degree with political activism on behalf of disadvantaged groups" (p. 564). Scanlon, Hartnett, and Harding (2006) in a similar study over a decade later found similar results: "Although a majority of state chapters report working on federal policy legislation, more than one-third of chapters do not address these issues. Nearly half of all chapters also report that they do not engage in advocacy on local legislation" (p. 52). The survey also indicated that the respondents reported "that advocacy efforts by state chapters are less than effective" (p. 50).

The importance of the social—the community—is emphasized in the profession's name, *social work*. The diminishing attention directed to developing the community practice skills of all social workers, compared with the attention given to development of the more circumscribed clinical skills, is reflected in social work's and social workers' apparent lack of policy effectiveness and influence. Specht and Courtney (1994), Bellah et al. (1985), and Doherty (1994–1995) maintain that psychotherapy as therapeutic individualism can be socially amoral, isolating, and at odds with the mandate to strengthen the community and social commitments. Participating in and looking to primary social structures and groups such as the family, church, and neighborhood for guidance has often been replaced by therapy and the therapist. The therapist becomes teacher, spiritual guide, and moral arbiter without a moral base. While these roles are satisfying, they hardly allow for the building of mutual support, a sense of the common good, and a feeling for community.

Social work as a profession exists in and reflects the larger society. The decay of social work's social skills and commitment has accompanied the erosion of community spirit and social commitment in the United States. It is reflective of the "me-ism," the libertarian, self-centered philosophy currently rampant, and the social isolation and fragmentation of contemporary America (Bellah et al., 1985; Etzioni, 1993; Lasch, 1994).

Communities as unifying social institutions are declining, and this decline does not bode well for the future of the individual or the country as a whole. Strong communities enhance individual rights and individual well-being. The 1980s and 1990s—the Generation X decades—were an age of anomie and breakdown of social standards with a focus on the self and the individual. Community as a basis of identification is becoming exclusionary rather than inclusionary, socially fragmenting rather than integrating, and now rests on a negative rather than a positive base. The community has become a means for division rather than integration. In negative communities, the individual is socially isolated, and too often the reasons for community participation are individualistic, fragmented, and therapeutic.

Social workers need to integrate clients and constituencies into positive communities. Positive communities are non-utopian, cohesive communities where personal relations are captured by agreed-on communal purposes. The positive community offers the individual a shared structure of meaning, explanation, purpose, and support in both good times and bad (*The Responsive Communitarian Platform,* 1992). The Catholic theologian Hollenbach (1994/1995) asserted that both democracy and freedom require dynamic community involvement by its members: "Solitary individuals, especially those motivated solely by self-interest and the protection of their rights to privacy, will be incapable of democratic self-government because democracy requires more. It requires the virtues of mutual cooperation, mutual responsibility, and what Aristotle called friendship, concord, and amity (p. 20)."

The Social Work Problem-Solving Strategy

The social work generic problem-solving strategy is a linear planned-change process that begins with the identification of a problem—a condition that someone wants changed—and terminates with the evaluation of the change effort (Compton & Galaway, 1979, pp. 232–450; Epstein, 1980, pp. 2–5; Hepworth & Larsen, 1986, pp. 25–44; Lippitt, Watson, & Westley, 1958; Netting et al., 1993, pp. 203–220; Pincus & Minahan, 1973, pp. 90–91). The strategy, not limited to social work, is a linear, comprehensive, and rational approach to problem analysis, resource analysis and aggregation, and intervention. While the strategy's model is linear as presented in Box 1.3, in practice it consists of overlapping phases with much backfilling and looping to fill in operational gaps and modify as information and conditions change. Its social work application is constrained by the profession's values and ethics and by the preferences of the client and the client system. The client or client system can be individuals, families and other primary groups, communities, community organizations, and community groups such as neighborhoods or interest groups.

There are other models of change strategies or practice that emphasize different components of problem, task, or practice. Generally the models involve assessment and information gathering, goal setting, theory building, intervention, and evaluation (Hardina, 2002).

BOX 1.3.	The Social Work Problem-Solving Strategy

1. Recognition of a problem and establishment of the need for change
2. Information gathering
3. Assessment and the development of a case theory and plan for change
4. Intervention and the change effort
5. Evaluation and termination of the change effort

Phase 1: Recognition of a Problem and Establishment of the Need for Change

Problem-solving and change efforts begin with the recognition by an individual or a group, the initiator of the change effort, of a condition perceived as a problem that requires change. The initiator may be the client, a parent, a couple experiencing marital discord, or others, such as an individual who fears child abuse or neglect by another person and refers the situation to a protective services agency. A community group also may pinpoint problems of employment, crime, or poor treatment received from public or other social organizations. Implicit, if not explicit, in the identification of the problem and the recognition of the need for change are the goals and objectives sought. Without a statement of desired outcomes, data gathering and assessment, especially resources assessment, is hindered. This phase will be discussed more fully in later chapters.

Although the labels *goals* and *objectives* are often used interchangeably, goals will be used here as the broader, more final objective of a case plan. *Objectives* are more specific outcome events that, when accomplished, lead to the next event and eventually to the goals. Sub-objectives are the events that lead to the next level of objectives. Operational goals and objectives are set forth in a SMARRT format (adapted from *Administrative Systems for Church Management*, n.d.; Reddin, 1971). The SMARRT format criteria (Box 1.4) require goals and objectives that are *specific, measurable, acceptable, realistic, results oriented,* and *time specific.* SMARRT-formatted objectives guide case planning, case theory, and the intervention and problem-solving strategy. At the conclusion of the assessment phase, a case theory and a SMARRT case plan specifying goals, objectives, and responsibilities should be completed.

Phase 2: Information Gathering

Phase 2 in the problem-solving process is to gather information on the problem and on possible resources for intervention to achieve the SMARRT objectives.

During this phase, the social worker gathers information on the problem to develop an intervention plan. The information-gathering phase is guided and limited by the theoretical perspective of those working for the change, on the causes of the problem and the potentially available interventions. This phase includes accumulating information on the problem itself; the client system, including strengths and potential resources useful for intervention; the strengths and limitations of support and potential support systems; and any potential constraints and limitations of any change effort by the target system. Community-based practice models devote more attention to the social ecology, the environment, and the social systems in gathering information on the condition and the potential resources than do psychologically centered problem-solving strategies.

Phase 3: Assessment and Development of a Case Theory and Plan for Change

The third phase is assessment and development of the case theory and plan for change to accomplish a SMARRT objective. The case can be an individual, a group, a community, or part of a community. However, the change effort extends beyond the individual unit to include its ecology and situation. Case theory, like all theory, involves an explanation of phenomena and situation. Case theory (Bisman, 1994; Bisman & Hardcastle, 1999) is the theory or coherent explanation of a case's problem, its relevant causations, a specification of desired outcomes, selection of intervention strategies and methods of changing a condition and producing the desired outcomes, and a prediction of why and how the selected interventions will work. To refine and specify SMARRT outcomes clearly during this phase, it may be necessary to collect additional information on the availability of potential resources. Case theory is developed from the data collected in Phase 2. The data are assessed and organized according to the change agent's, the social worker's, and social and behavioral theories of choice. Examples of social and behavioral theories include systems theory, exchange theory, operant and social learning theory, and psychodynamic theories. The case theory is the social worker's construction of the problem and the model for the proposed change effort. As a case situation is both unique and complex, a case theory should avoid an overly

BOX 1.4.	**SMARRT Objective Evaluation Check Sheet**

SMARRT objectives are the desired accomplishment and results of an intervention with a client system, the change sought. Objectives are stated in empirical and behavioral language and specify changes in the client system, target system, or ecology.

1. **Specific:** Goals and objectives, as well as the words, ideas, and concepts used to describe them, are precise and not stated in vague generic language such as to "improve the condition of" unless operational meanings are given for "improve" and "condition." Specific goals and objectives need to be developed with and understood by the client and action systems.

2. **Measurable:** Goals and objectives need to contain operational and measurement criteria used to indicate their achievement. A case plan states how the goals and objectives are measured or judged. Client and action systems need to understand both the goals and the measurements used. Measurements can be quantitative and qualitative (more often both) but must always be reliable and valid.

3. **Acceptable:** Goals and objectives must be acceptable to the client system and, ultimately, to the action system and other resource providers that must cooperate with the problem-solving strategy to achieve the objectives. If the goals and objectives are unacceptable, participation is probably coerced. Acceptability implies informed consent by clients to the plan, its goals and objectives, and the intervention. The acceptability of the goals and objectives will be constrained by the mission and eligibility criteria of the social worker's agency and funding sources.

4. **Realistic:** Goals and objectives are accomplishable within the complexities of the case, time frame, resources, and intervention methodologies available. They are significant enough to be worth accomplishing. Goals and objectives are realistic if they are achievable in the best judgment of the social worker, change agent and action system, and a client or client system given the potential costs and resources available, the readiness for change of the target, and the knowledge and skills of the action system.

5. **Results Oriented:** Final goals and all objectives are expressed as outcomes, events, and accomplishments by the client and action system or changes in a target rather than as a service event or a process. The provision of service or an intervention does not constitute an objective and does not meet this SMARRT criterion. The results of the service and how it will benefit the client must be specified. If an intervention or service provides skills training, the results are not the provision of skills training or attendance at training classes but the client's acquisition of the skills.

6. **Time-Specific:** A specific time frame or target for accomplishing the goals and objectives is projected. Time limits are inherent if objectives are real and not simply desired outcomes. Time limits are based on an intervention's power, the resources available and conditions favorable to change, and the barriers blocking change and objective accomplishment. Without a time-limit criterion, it is not possible to measure accomplishments or have accountability. Without a time limit, achievement always occurs in the distant and indeterminate future. The condition can remain socially dysfunctional or a client can remain in trauma indeterminately while an ineffectual intervention is continued. It becomes "an unending war."

reductionist view of cause and effect. The causes of any problems lie in a range of phenomena. Solutions also require a complex intervention strategy and resources appropriately coordinated and managed (Chazdon, 1991, p. x).

In community practice, the concept of assessment is generally preferred over the more limited concept of diagnosis. Gambrill (1983) provides a useful discussion of the distinction between diagnosis and assessment and insight into why assessment is preferred in community practice:

The term *diagnosis* was borrowed from medicine. . . . Observed behavior is used as a sign of more important underlying processes, typically of a pathological nature. Methodological and conceptual problems connected with the use of diagnosis include frequent low degree of agreement between people in their use of a given diagnosis, and the low degree of association between a diagnosis and indications of what intervention will be most effective. . . .

Assessment differs in a number of ways from diagnosis. Observable behaviors are not used as signs of something more significant but as important in their own right as *samples of* relevant behaviors. Behavior is considered to be a response to identifiable environmental or personal events. . . . Rather than using behavior as a sign of underlying intrapsychic causes, assessment includes an exploration of how current thoughts, feelings, and environmental events relate to these samples of behavior. (pp. 33–34)

Assessment is a more inclusive and generic concept than *diagnosis,* with a greater emphasis on social and environmental factors. Agreements on an assessment, SMARRT goals and objectives, and problem-solving strategies between social worker, client, and other relevant case participants working toward change are critical for cooperative efforts.

Phase 4: Intervention and the Change Effort

The intervention is the change efforts to achieve the desired outcomes based on the case theory. Social work interventions can be categorized under casework strategies, clinical approaches, community organization, or environmental and social change, among others. Each intervention plan involves a variety of skills, techniques, and tactics; a range of people or systems, either directly or indirectly; and the use of resources. The case theory directs selection of specific intervention methodologies and technologies.

Phase 5: Evaluation and Termination of the Change Effort

The last phase of the social work problem-solving strategy is the evaluation of its effectiveness in achieving the stated goals and objectives. Depending on the level of achievement and the stability of the change, the case may be terminated, the process repeated to enhance its effectiveness or to achieve additional objectives, or the case referred to additional service resources. Evaluations also can assess interventions or processes. However, process evaluation without linking process to effectiveness is more an assessment of art than of change. Change, as Pincus and Minahan (1973) rightly asserted, whether targeted to individual or community change, is to help people, to change people, "not [deal in] vague abstraction such as the 'community,' 'the organization' or the 'system'" (p. 63). What is changed are the behaviors and interactions of the people who constitute the groups, organizations, communities, and systems.

While evaluation is generally presented in the models as part of the termination phase, it is a continuous effort and a part of all the phases. Relevant evaluation methodologies are reviewed in later chapters.

Problem-Solving Systems

The people involved in a social work problem-solving and planned change strategy can be examined, using the system's metaphors, according to what they contribute and how the change process affects them (Netting & O'Connor, 2002; Payne, 2006, pp. 142–180; Pincus & Minahan, 1973, pp. 53–64). A system, most fundamentally, connotes an arrangement of entities that interact to achieve a shared purpose or fulfil functions. The system's metaphors, as demonstrated in Box 1.5, represent functions that people fulfill in the change effort. The same people can fulfill more than one function and hence can belong to more than one system in the change process.

Although some systems and people generally are involved throughout the problem-solving strategy's change process, such as the change agent and client systems, not all systems need to be involved in each phase. Table 1.1 illustrates that the same people at the same or different phases in the process may be involved in multiple systems, and their involvement may shift as their contributions and their relationships to a change process evolve. All the systems together compose a problem-solving system.

The change agent (that is, the social worker) must anticipate and identify the people who will make up the various other systems involved in the problem-solving processes. The social worker should recognize that the people or the systems are not static. The membership and importance of a particular system's contributions vary with each phase of the change strategy.

Case Illustration of the Problem-Solving Strategy in Direct Practice: Ms. S

Phase 1: Recognition of a Problem and Establishment of the Need for Change. A working single mother, Ms. S, with two preschool-age children, ages 5 and 7, has difficulty finding a suitable babysitter. She also recognizes she is becoming more

BOX I.5.	Problem-Solving Systems in Social Work

1. *Initiator system:* The people or persons who first recognize the problem and bring attention to the need for change
2. *Support system:* The people who have an interest in and will support the proposed change and who may receive secondary benefits from it
3. *Client system:* The people who sanction, ask for, or expect to benefit from the change agent's services and who have a working agreement or contract, whether formal or informal, with the change agent
4. *Change agent system:* The people who will work directly to produce the change, including the social worker, any social action organizations and groups, clients, and the people who belong to the social worker's agency and the organization working to produce the change
5. *Action system:* The change agent system and the other people the change agent works with and through to achieve the goals and affect the target system. The action system generally includes the client as an essential component of the change process. Not all elements of an action system are part of a change agent system or need to favor the change.
6. *Controlling system:* The people with the formal authority and capacity to approve and order implementing a proposed change strategy
7. *Implementing system:* A subset of the host system composed of the people with day-to-day responsibility for implementing the change
8. *Target system:* The people who are the targets of the change effort; the people who need to be changed to accomplish the goals of the change strategy and produce the benefits for the client system. The target system can be something other than a client.

short-tempered with her children because of the fatigue and stress of working full time and raising the children alone. She worries about money. Ms. S exhausted her Temporary Assistance to Needy Families for the older child and is reluctant to exhaust it for the younger child. She is worried about keeping her job during this "Great Recession." She is distressed about the childcare arrangements. It is difficult for Ms. S to maintain her composure when disciplining her children, and she recognizes that if she loses control, she might physically abuse the children.

Ms. S is not sure what to do, as she is very tired at the end of the day after getting up at 5:30 A.M.; fixing breakfast for herself and the children; getting the children up, dressed, and fed; taking them to whatever babysitter is available; and getting to work by 9 A.M. After the work day ends, she must first pick up the children, then fix dinner and put them to bed. She has no time to play with the children or for herself. Ms. S recognizes that she is starting to resent the children and at times she feels she would be better off without them.

Ms. S saw a poster on a bus advertising the local child guidance clinic's parent effectiveness training. She goes to the child guidance clinic to obtain help in maintaining her composure while disciplining her children and training to develop effective parenting skills to reduce the need for discipline. Her job-sponsored health insurance will cover only five sessions. The social worker assigned by the agency to work with Ms. S recognizes that she is under a lot of stress and needs assistance with more than just her parenting skills.

Table 1.1. Systems Typically Involved in Phases of Problem-Solving Strategy

Problem-Solving Phase	Systems Typically Involved
Recognition of problem and establishing need for change	Initiator, client, and change agent
Information gathering	Initiator, client, support, and change agent
Assessment and development of case theory and plan for change	Client, support, controlling, and change agent
Intervention and change effort	Client, support, controlling, change agent, action, and target
Evaluation and termination of change effort	client, support, change agent, controlling, and action

Ms. S is the initiator system, as she recognized a problem, perceived a need for change, and wants to change. She and her children are the original client system as the beneficiaries of the change effort. The social worker is the change agent and part of the initiator system in recognizing the problem and helping Ms. S define the need for change.

Phase 2: Information Gathering. The social worker obtains information about Ms. S, the children, and the children's father, who is regularly employed but pays no support and only occasionally visits his children. The social worker also obtains information on possible resources in Ms. S's neighborhood and other potential social and community supports. She discovers the existence of an increasingly rare public 12-hour day-care center.

The systems most involved in information gathering are the client and the change agent systems. The information accumulated is to define and build the other necessary systems. The necessary information goes beyond describing the client, her problems, and their etiology. It includes information about potential supports for the client and her children; for example, from the absent father, the day-care center, and other potential community resources for the client that might be constructed into a support system. These potential resources make up a target system, the people who need to be changed to accomplish the goals of the change strategy and bring about benefits for the client, until they are formed into a support system for the client. The composition of the systems is dynamic over time.

Phase 3: Assessment and the Development of a Case Theory and Plan for Change. The social worker and Ms. S review the information to explain why Ms. S is stressed and fatigued and to decide what might be done to change the situation. The father has stated he will not pay support until he has regular visitation with the children. Ms. S will not allow visitation until he pays support, thus creating a standoff.

The client and change agent systems, the social worker and Ms. S, develop a case theory and plan with SMARRT objectives to resolve the

problem. The case theory is client and situation specific. Both the theory and goals are straightforward and direct. Ms. S is exhausted and stressed because she maintains a full-time work schedule in addition to the demands of being a single parent living financially on the edge. She has no social life, only the demands of work and caring for her children. Her fatigue and resentment place the children at risk. She doesn't know if she can spare the time for parent effectiveness training, although she wants the training and would enjoy the social interaction and support provided by the sessions. The goals are to achieve stable childcare, financial and social assistance from the children's father, and the use of any time gained by Ms. S from a stable childcare arrangement and the father's increased responsibility for the children for parent effectiveness training and her own needs.

The plan specifies other needed systems in the change strategy. The father and Ms. S are the target system clients, since the behavior of both must changed. The day-care center is also a target system because Ms. S's children need to be enrolled in the center. If the intervention called for by the plan is successful, the father will ultimately become part of Ms. S's support system. As an agent of the child guidance clinic, the social worker needs approval of the plan by the controlling system, the agency. The court, which must order the support payment, also is part of the controlling system. The agency is the host system, and the social worker is the implementing system. Ms. S, the social worker, and the parent effectiveness trainer are the implementing system, as they have the day-to-day responsibility for carrying out the change.

Phase 4: Intervention and the Change Effort. The intervention plan resulting from the theory of the case is a social intervention. Ms. S is to allow the children's father to have the children for one weekend a month and two evenings a week if he pays child support. A court-ordered support judgment will be obtained for the support and visitation. This should ease Ms. S's financial worries and provide help with parenting responsibilities and some time for herself. The social worker assisted Ms. S in obtaining stable day care from the public neighborhood day-care center. Ms. S. will attend the child guidance clinic's parent effectiveness training classes on one of the evenings that the father has the children.

Ms. S, the social worker, the court, and the parent effectiveness trainer form the action system to change the target systems: Ms. S, the father, and the day-care center. As indicated above, if the change effort with the father and the day-care center is successful, they become part of Ms. S's support system for subsequent changes and development.

Phase 5: Evaluation and Termination of the Change Effort. At the conclusion of the parent effectiveness training classes, Ms. S, the social worker, and the father, now a part of the problem-solving process, will evaluate the current arrangements. Single case design and qualitative research methodologies are the evaluation tools of choice (Bisman & Hardcastle, 1999).

The evaluation also is a continuous part of the monitoring of the problem-solving process. The monitoring involves Ms. S, the social worker, and often the support, controlling, host, and implementing systems. The evaluation of a problem-solving strategy before its termination can involve all of these systems through member-checking; Ms. S, the social worker, the parent effectiveness trainer, the father, and possibly the child guidance clinic supervisor.

Case Illustration of the Problem-Solving Strategy in Rural Community Development and Action

Phase 1: Recognition of a Problem and Establishment of the Need for Change. California's San Joaquin Valley naturally is a semi-desert with rainfall between 4 and 12 inches annually depending on the location. It is very fertile. With the expenditure of millions of federal and state dollars since the 1930s to bring water to the valley's communities and agriculture, the San Joaquin Valley is now the food basket of the nation. It also is the area with the lowest level of human development in the United States as measured by the American Human Development Index (HDI). The HDI was created to measure the actual experiences of people in a given country or region. Three areas are measured: health, as indicated by life expectancy at

birth; access to knowledge, measured by educational enrollment and attainment; and income, reflected by median earnings for the working-age population (Conley, 2009; United Nations Development Programme, 2008).

In the 1960s and still today, there are small rural communities populated by Chicanos, black, and poor white agricultural laborers still without a public water supply. La Colonia was one of these rural communities. Similar colonias to the one described here currently dot the southwestern United States. A colonia is a "rural, unincorporated community . . . in which one or more of the following conditions exist: lack of portable water supply or no water system, lack of adequate waste water facilities, lack of decent, safe, and sanitary housing, inadequate roads and/or inadequate drainage control structures" (Henkel, 1998, p. 18). La Colonia was a small Chicano rural farm labor village of about 100 families adjacent to a larger agriculturally based community, the Town, with about 5,000 people. La Colonia was a stable unincorporated area with a 90-year history. Its homes were generally owned by its residents. There was no formal government other than a local public utilities district (PUD) with a commission elected by La Colonia's property owners. The PUD provided no utility services because, after its formation and incorporation, it discovered that La Colonia was too small and poor to afford the startup costs of providing public services. Individual La Colonia homes received electric and gas services from the regional gas and electric utility company. The families provided their own sewage service in individual septic tanks or cesspools. Garbage and trash disposal was an individual household responsibility. The PUD and its commission basically serve as a forum to discuss community problems, mediate community disputes, and plan and conduct community events such as the celebrations of *Cinco de Mayo* and other traditional holidays. The families obtained their water from individual wells, a significant capital investment for a farm laboring family, by individual agreements with neighbors who had wells, by hauling water from the Town's public water tank taps, or from the irrigation ditches that surrounded La Colonia. The untreated water from the individual wells was often polluted by septic tank and cesspool seepage. The irrigation canal water contained agricultural field runoff with fertilizer, herbicide, and pesticide contaminants. The Town's water system was built largely by state and federal community development grants. It delivered abundant potable water to the Town's residents. The water system's mains were located less than a quarter of a mile from La Colonia. A water system connecting each home to the Town's water system could be constructed at a relatively low cost to La Colonia and the Town, as most of the cost would be paid with state and federal funds. However, the Town Council did not want to provide water to communities not incorporated into the Town, regardless of the cost. The Town Council did not want to establish a precedent and risk a possible demand from other rural communities more distant from the Town. The Town Council's policy was to restrict its provision of water to areas incorporated within its boundaries. La Colonia's PUD Commission, La Colonia's nominal leadership, did not want to be annexed to the Town, as they feared La Colonia would lose its identity, would be unable to remain a defined community with its own traditions, would simply become another Town barrio or ethnic neighborhood, and would perhaps incur a Town property tax increase. The Commission simply wanted good, affordable water.

The Commission approached the county's community action agency (CAA), a not-for-profit community development and social action organization, for help with their water problem. After a meeting of the CAA's director and the PUD Commission, the director assigned a Chicano community development worker (CDW) from the Town to work with La Colonia and the commission to obtain a potable water system.

La Colonia's PUD Commission was the initiator system and the client system. The contract was between the CAA and the commission. La Colonia was also part of the client system, as the commission was acting on the community's behalf. The change agents were the CAA director and the CDW. During this phase, the controlling system was the CAA and the commission. The CAA and the commission constituted the host system, with the CDW and volunteers from La Colonia composing the implementing system.

The client system and the change agent system saw the Town Council as the target system.

Phase 2: Information Gathering. This phase involved the action system—the CDW, La Colonia volunteers, and CAA staff— gathering information on (a) the ability and willingness of La Colonia's residents to pay their share of the water system development costs, hookup cost, and monthly water bills; (b) grant requirements for state and federal community development funds; (c) the direct costs to the Town beyond La Colonia's costs and the state and federal grants for expanding the water system to serve La Colonia; (d) potential support systems in the Town and county; and (e) procedures for placing the item on the Town Council's agenda.

Phase 3: Assessment and Development of a Theory for Change. The initial SMARRT objective for the planned change strategy was to obtain a stable, cost-effective potable water supply and system for La Colonia. The CAA also had an empowerment goal endemic to community development: to develop La Colonia's capacity as a community to work together to solve its problems and achieve greater cohesion in the process.

The theory for change, the case theory, based on an assessment of the information obtained in Phase 2, was rather simple and direct. The problem—the lack of a stable potable water system— was a result of La Colonia's lack of resources and an unwillingness of the Town to connect La Colonia to its water system under mutually tolerable conditions. La Colonia could develop the infrastructure for the water system within its boundaries if a connection with the Town's water system was made. The Town was unwilling to connect the water system for political and economic reasons. Although the Town was ethnically diverse, its Council consisted of the white establishment that largely represented the agricultural interests. In addition to the underlying racism and classism, there were the fiscal costs of expanding the water system (though minor to serve La Colonia) and the fear of a precedent that would require expansion of the water system to all surrounding rural areas, with ever-increasing, though incremental, costs, accompanying each expansion. Eventually, the council reasoned, the incremental costs would necessitate a politically unpopular property tax increase, an equally disliked water use fee increase, or both.

The case theory explaining the lack of a stable water system for La Colonia rested on the intransigence of the Town Council and La Colonia's PUD. La Colonia could petition for a property owner's incorporation vote and, if it passed, obtain water as an incorporated area of the Town. The Town could alter its policy against providing water to areas not incorporated into the Town. As La Colonia was the client system, its preferences directed the change strategy to alter the Town's policy.

The information gathered in the assessment phase indicated that (a) one Town Council member had ambitions for higher office as a county commissioner, (b) several local churches were supporting civil rights efforts in other communities and were eager to do something locally, and (3) farm labor unionizing activity was occurring in the eastern part of the county. The Town and its growers were located in the western part of the county and, as yet, were unaffected by the union organizing activity.

Phase 4: Intervention and the Change Effort. The intervention and change effort based on the case theory called for a combination of technical assistance to the Town, social action, and political persuasion and support. The intervention was both social action and "bottom-up" community development. In the process of obtaining good water La Colonia would increase its capacity to address other community needs and strengthen itself as a community (Turner, 2009). The basic political strategy was for La Colonia's leadership to target certain individuals and groups in the Town—ministers, church leaders, and a politically ambitious council member—to bring them into either the support or action system. The Town ministers and leaders were to be brought in by casting the problem as a civil rights issue. La Colonia was a Chicano community. The ministers and church leaders were first a target system, with an intent of making them part of a support system. This strategy called for

expanding the action and support systems to induce the politically ambitious council member to become a sponsor of a proposal to expand the Town's water system to serve La Colonia. In return for this sponsorship, the support system would support her county commission bid. Additionally, the CAA would assist the Town and La Colonia in developing the proposals for federal and state community development funds. La Colonia leaders would also let it be known that if the proposal did not receive favorable consideration from the Town Council, La Colonia would approach the farm labor union for assistance in developing a water system for La Colonia. This would introduce the farm labor union to the San Joaquin Valley's west side and provide the union with a local sponsor and local sanction. When the support and action systems were expanded, the Town Council (the target system) would be addressed. If the proposal to expand the water system was accepted by the Town Council, it would become the controlling system, part of the action system, the host system, and—with the Town's city manager, water department, and CAA—the implementing system to take the final step in La Colonia's water system development.

Phase 5: Evaluation and Termination of the Change Effort. Evaluation of the change effort by the client system and the CAA (as part of the action system) of the SMARRT objective of obtaining a potable water system is direct: The system was obtained. However, evaluation of the community development goals is more complex. Has the community increased its ability to continue its development? Is in more cohesive and empowered? These questions can be evaluated by participant observer methodologies. Has the number of people participating in the community increased and does it respond to other community issues?

The problem-solving approach for planned change, with its community practice skills of systems identification, community assessment, and developing and linking resources, is important whether the problem-solving strategy is used with a delimited client system such as Ms. S and her family or a larger client system such as La Colonia.

Ethics, Advocacy, and Community Practice

A discussion of professional practice in this new millennium is incomplete without attention to its ethics, the values that motivate the ethics, and ethical practice. The 20th century's last decade was and the first decades of the 21st century are soiled by a lack of ethical behavior in high and low places in the public and private arenas. We will examine the social basis for professions and the social work profession and the limitations of social work's professional ethics to provide guidance to for community practice.

Profession as Calling

A profession is more than an occupation or tradespeople with special skills (Banks, 2006, p. 130). A profession is a vocation, an avocation, and a calling. The notion of vocation comes from the religious base of most professions, meaning that the adherent will lead a certain type of life of moral behavior and service. It is a calling to care (Banks, 2004, p. 35). A profession's values constitute the service calling, not its technology; this is what distinguishes professions from occupations and contributes to their public sanction. Professions require a vision of and commitment to ends to be served and not just the techniques practiced (Bisman, 2004; Howe, 1980; Lubove, 1977).

Vocation also specifies the relationship to the community. Professions are given public protection and sanction because they are to benefit the community and the public good in addition to individual clients (Gustafson, 1982, p. 512). The mandate is to place client and public good above professional self-interest and gain. The British Association of Social Workers' *Code of Ethics* (2002) emphasizes the social responsibility of social workers with its stated principle: "Social workers have a duty to . . . humanity in their work before personal aims, views and advantage, fulfilling their duty of care and observing principles of natural fairness" (sec. 3.3.2.a.). The American Code urges social workers to elevate service to others above self-interest. Social workers are encouraged to volunteer some portion of their professional skills with no expectation of significant financial return (pro bono service) (NASW, 2008, Ethical Principles).

It is the outward service to others that provides the basic requirements of ethical conduct and the inner rewards to the professional. For example, the value of service leads to the ethical principle that "Social workers' primary goal is to help people in need and to address social problems" (NASW, 2008, Ethical Principles).

Although service as a pristine motive of a profession has been tainted and is often ignored by contemporary professionals, it is embedded in most conceptions of profession. Adherence to the outward service orientation provides professions and professionals with the community's mandate and authority to be self-regulating (Hardcastle, 1990; Howe, 1980; Vollmer & Mills, 1966).

Social Work Values

Social work ethics are derived from more abstract values. Ethics are rules to guide the social worker's conduct and behavior. Values are the motivators for the behaviors called for by ethics. Banks (2006, p. 6) somewhat tautologically defines values as "particular types of belief that people hold about what is regarded as worthy or valuable." Reamer (1995, p. 11) provides a more formal definition of values as "generalized, emotionally charged conceptions of what is desirable, historically created and derived from experience, shared by a population or group within it, and they provide the means for organizing and structuring patterns of behavior. But as Banks (2006, p. 6) reports, the concept of values is vague, with a variety of meanings.

Values have a greater emotional charging than do ethics. They motivate ethics and behavior. Values direct the nature of social work's mission—the relationships, obligations, and duties social workers have for clients, colleagues, and the broader community. Social work's basic value configuration is the result of the many forces and orientations that the profession has been subjected to and embraced over the years. Some authorities hold that social work's values base distinguishes it from other professions (Hardina, 2002, p. 17).

Professional social workers are assumed to embrace a core set of values. The NASW Code of Ethics (2008, p. 1) states that the core values of the social work profession are "the foundation of social work's unique purpose and perspective":

- service
- social justice
- dignity and worth of the person
- importance of human relationships
- integrity
- competence

Service, human relations, integrity, and competence reasonably can be assumed as core values of most, if not all, human service professions. They are not unique to social work.

The value that is most uniquely social work is an explicit commitment to social justice. Banks (2006, pp. 81–89), in her review of national codes of ethics of the social work profession globally, found that the codes of ethics of different nations draw heavily from each other. The core of most of the codes rests on the values of:

- Self-determination of client and service user
- Social justice
- Professional integrity or the notion of virtue ethics

Social Justice

Social justice is a *sine qua non*, if not the *raison d'être*, of social work. NASW (2008, p. 2) holds social justice as one of its six core values and ethical principles. It states the ethical principle in the converse: "Social workers challenge social injustice."

Social workers pursue social change, particularly with and on behalf of vulnerable and oppressed individuals and groups of people. Social workers' social change efforts are focused on issues of poverty, unemployment, discrimination, and other forms of social injustice. These activities seek to promote sensitivity to and knowledge about oppression and cultural and ethnic diversity. Social workers strive to ensure access to needed information, services, and resources; equality of opportunity; and meaningful participation in decision making for all people (p. 2).

Unfortunately, NASW compels us to deduce its conception of social justice from the indicators used: oppressed, victims, vulnerable, poor, powerless.

The IFSW (2004, 4.2) places social justice as one of the profession's foundation values: "Social workers have a responsibility to promote social justice, in relation to society generally, and in relation to the people with whom they work." Social justice requires social workers:

1. Challeng[e] negative discrimination[3] . . . on the basis of characteristics such as ability, age, culture, gender or sex, marital status, socio-economic status, political opinions, skin colour, racial or other physical characteristics, sexual orientation, or spiritual beliefs.
2. Recognising diversity . . . recognise and respect the ethnic and cultural diversity of the societies in which they practise, taking account of individual, family, group and community differences.
3. Distributing resources equitably . . . ensure that resources at their disposal are distributed fairly, according to need.
4. Challeng[e] unjust policies and practices . . . to bring to the attention of their employers, policy makers, politicians and the general public situations where resources are inadequate or where distribution of resources, policies and practices are oppressive, unfair or harmful.
5. Working in solidarity . . . to challenge social conditions that contribute to social exclusion, stigmatisation or subjugation, and to work towards an inclusive society.

The British (British Association of Social Workers, 2002, pp. 2–4), Canadian (Canadian Association of Social Workers, 2005, pp. 2-6), and Russian (Union of Social Educators and Social Workers, 2003, Sections 3, 6-7) codes hold social justice equally central for social work.

While core and omnipresent in the profession's literature, social justice is not easily defined. Banks (2006), after Rawls, holds that social justice is based on "the idea of distributing resources in society according to need (as opposed to desert or merit), challenging existing power structures and oppressive institutions and actions" (p. 39). Clifford and Burke (2009, pp. 123–124) follow an expansive view of social justice compatible with its use in social work. Social justice, like justice, has the components of:

- Fair distribution of goods and services to people based on equal opportunity
- Limitation of institutional discrimination and oppression
- All people are equally free to use opportunities without discrimination.
- Equality as the end position, with goods and services shared fairly between individuals and groups

Clifford and Burke differ from Banks in the different elements of justice. Banks separates equality from social justice. Clifford and Burke's conception poises the components as alternatives, "or's," rather than as components, with goods and services shared "fairly" rather than "equally." Equality as an end position of a fair sharing of goods and services assumes a conception of fair as being equal without consideration of need, effort, or contribution. Their conception of social justice used here varies from Karl Marx's position ("From each according to his abilities, to each according to his needs"; Marx, 1959, p. 119), which places both abilities or contribution and need as the core elements of "fairness" in a socially just distribution for consumption of goods and services.

Banks addresses the fairness issue of equality, contribution, and need by separating equality and distributive justice, although in social work these concepts often used as same. Equality means "the removal of disadvantage" as equal treatment, equal opportunity, and equality of results. Equality of treatment and opportunity are more easily achievable than results. Results require that end products, services, and behaviors be the same (Banks, 2006, p. 50).

Distributive justice means that the distribution of goods, social power, rights, and statuses is made according to specified rules and criteria. The rules and criteria specify "rights" according to criteria of deserving and of need (Banks, 2006, p. 51). But there lies the rub: who and how are the rules determined as to what constitutes need and deserving? The problems, as with any variance in rights and need, are that the criteria, the

rules of allocating, can lead to and promote inequality. With only a single kidney available for transplant, who has the greater need or is more deserving—a 25-year-old alcoholic vagrant, a retired alcoholic baseball legend, or a 70-year-old retired state governor? As Anatole France (2004) wrote, "The law, in its majestic equality, forbids the rich as well as the poor to sleep under bridges, to beg in the streets, and to steal bread."

Others, such as von Wormer (2009, pp. 107–116) and Gumz and Grant (2009), include *restorative justice* in the conception of social justice. Restorative justice is when injustice's perpetrators *restore* or compensate victims. Restorative justice can be individual, as a crime against individual victims, or collective, as when a powerful victimizer, such as a government or corporation, harms and victimizes communities of the less powerful. Restorative justice holds the victimizers accountable to victims for at least partially restoring and compensating them. von Wormer (2009) holds that it focuses on reconciliation rather than punishment, although compensation is a major component. Examples of the latter are payments by the German government to Jews and Israel; by Australia to the mixed Aboriginal Australians children comprising the "lost generations"; to victims of 1984 Union Carbide chemical gas disasters as in Bhopal, India; by France to persons in the Pacific islands harmed by nuclear tests; by affirmative action to victims of discrimination; by BP to the Gulf State residents and businesses, and by efforts to obtain restitution to descendents of African slaves in America and to American Indians. Individual compensation to individuals not part of a class includes compensation to individual victims of child abuse and medical malpractice. Affirmative action is another example of restorative justice.

A thorny problem in restorative justice is when the direct victims are not available, as the African-American slaves, to restore or compensate, but descendents suffer because of the injustice to the direct victims. The knotty tasks are is to determine what was and is the damage and to whom; how the descendents suffer as a result of the earlier acts of injustice (the damage to the descendents); how to determine, restore, and "compensate" descendents; and who is responsible to "restore" and compensate the descendents of the perpetrators (how compensation is made).

If only descendents of slaves are to be "restored," are only the descendents of slave owners and those who gained from slavery liable, or is the community as whole responsible (Gates, 2010)? If social justice is at social work's core, these are questions the profession must address.

Virtue Ethics

Virtue ethics is at the heart of social work's values of professional integrity and competence. Virtue ethics is an approach to ethics that is rooted in judgments about the character or virtue of the individual as the basis of what is ethical. Virtue ethics is about character, living well, or good. Virtue ethics represents the good life in a moral rather than a material or sensual sense. Moral virtues that a virtuous person exhibits are prudence, a sense of justice, courage, truthfulness, and compassion (Banks, 2006, pp. 55–58; Bisman, 2008, pp. 17–18; Clifford & Burke, 2009, p. 69).

There is growing academic, if not professional, interest in virtue ethics and in educating the profession about virtue. Banks (2006, p. 61) holds that virtue ethics is concerned about the social relationships people have with one another and with "developing good character and good judgment in professionals—what we might call moral education" (p. 69). The attention is more toward the character of the people than with rules of behavior. Clifford and Burke (2009, p. 103) state that virtue ethics is an approach to ethics "that concentrates on the integrity and character of the actor rather than on rules or actions."

The difficulty with the conception of virtue ethics is that it is something of a tautology: it contends that a virtuous actor's behavior is virtuous as the actor's character is virtuous. The behavior or actions of a virtuous actor cannot be otherwise than virtuous. It is like President Nixon's assertion, "If the President does it, it's legal." But is a virtuous actor virtuous regardless of his or her actions and behavior, as courage, honesty, integrity, helpfulness, and the other virtuous traits are only manifested in behavior or actions? Or is an actor virtuous in any situation when acting virtuous? Is it a duck if it walks, quacks, or behaves like a duck, or is it a duck because it is intrinsically a duck regardless of how it walks, quacks, or behaves? A virtuous or good person can't be identified except by the person's "good behavior," so the task is to learn how to chose good behavior.

Gray and Gibbons (2007) argue that teaching how to make choices for virtuous behavior is a social work education task. "The moral life must be lived morally and good prudent judgment is an individual virtue that must be cultivated. . .it is in the moment that decisions are made and social workers have to become virtuosos at 'good judgment' and always mindful that ethical action more often than not rocks the boat" (p. 235).

Virtue character and ethics provide a grounding to the forces buffeting the profession, ranging from its social justice orientation, political ideologies, religious and spiritual biases, and scientism. These are only some of the paradigms working to shape the practitioner's practice values. The movement toward scientism is perhaps the most insidious as it is presented as non-ideological. It is an amoral orientation, and there is a growing force in social work that rejects a strong value base of normative concepts in favor of an emphasis on technical, scientific knowledge as the exclusive guide to evidence-based interventions and *best practices* (Reamer, 1993; Webb, 2000).

Social Work Ethics

Ethics, as indicated above, are prescriptions and proscriptions for professional behavior. Ethics deal with the right, the good, the correct, and the rules of conduct and behavior. They address the *what*s of behavior more than *why*s of behavior. Ethics provide a basis for defining professional good guys and bad guys.

The profession's and professional's values and ethics, along with practice wisdom and experience, and technical and empirical research-based knowledge, provide the criteria for selecting actions and making judgments, choices, and decisions of intervention methods and practice behavior. Interventions are not totally a matter of empirical science, nor is the profession merely an amalgamation of technologies and evidence-based interventions. The profession and its interventions must reflect a set of coherent values and virtue ethics capturing its service orientation and social justice imperative and reflecting its ethical standards.

The codes of ethics[4] of the IFSW and NASW and the codes for national social work associations of other nations provide ethical guidelines for social workers. Many states have adopted the NASW's code of ethics as part of their legal regulations for social work (Hardcastle, 1990). NASW's code is one of the most extensive codes when compared to other codes globally (Banks, 2006, p. 86). The profession's six values enumerated above have predicated six major ethical categories: (1) social workers' ethical responsibilities to clients, (2) social workers' ethical responsibilities to colleagues, (3) social workers' ethical responsibilities in practice settings, (4) social workers' ethical responsibilities as professionals, (5) social workers' ethical responsibilities to the social work profession, and (6) social workers' ethical responsibilities to the broader society. NASW (2008) asserts the standards "are relevant to the professional activities of all social workers."

The six ethical categories have generated 51 specific ethical standards, many with numerous sub-standards. The reader is urged to consult the Code of Ethics, as there are too many for a detailed review here. For example, there are 16 separate ethical standards addressing the ethical responsibilities to clients, ranging from rules on (1.01) Commitment to clients through (1.07) Privacy and confidentiality, with 18 separate rules to (1.16) Termination of services. There also are some rather contemporary standards, such as (1.13) Payment for Services, that would not have been needed for much of the 20th century when social work was largely a public profession.

Social worker ethical responsibilities to and relationships with colleagues is regulated by 11 standards, again many with sub-standards. The standards covers a range of behaviors, including a prohibition on sexual relationships (2.07) with students, if supervised, subordinates, and sexual relationships generally with anyone over whom the social worker exercises professional authority or if a sexual relationship might produce a conflict of interest.

The IFSW and other international codes are less extensive and detailed than the NASW code. However, for all its detail, NASW (2008) contends that:

code of ethics cannot guarantee ethical behavior. … resolve all ethical issues or disputes or capture the richness and complexity involved in striving to make responsible choices within a moral community.

Rather, a code of ethics sets forth values, ethical principles, and ethical standards to which professionals aspire and by which their actions can be judged. … Principles and standards must be applied by individuals of good character who discern moral questions and, in good faith, seek to make reliable ethical judgments. … Some of the standards … are enforceable guidelines for professional conduct, and some are aspirational.

It appears that for all the detail of the NASW code, ethical behavior by social workers may be predicated more on professionally socialized virtuous social workers who fulfill their fiduciary responsibility to clients.

Ethics and Social Work's Fiduciary Responsibility

The fiduciary responsibility of a profession is embedded in its service calling and is the underpinning of all professional relationships (Kutchins, 1991). It goes beyond specific professional ethical codes. Clients have a right to expect professional competence: for professionals to be current in the valid knowledge and skills necessary to intervene in the problems of clients whose cases they accept, for professionals to know their limitations, and for professionals to adhere to *primum non nocere*—"Above all, not knowingly to do harm." The late Peter Drucker (1974), the management guru and social theorist, asserted:

Men and women do not acquire exemption from ordinary rules of personal behavior because of their work or job. . . . The first responsibility of a professional was spelled out clearly 2,500 years ago, in the Hippocratic oath . . . *primum non nocere*—"Above all, not knowingly to do harm." No professional . . . can promise that he will indeed do good for his client. All he can do is try. But he can promise he will not knowingly do harm. And the client, in turn, must be able to trust the professional not knowingly to do him harm. Otherwise he cannot trust him at all. And *primum non nocere*, "not knowingly to do harm," is the basic rule of professional ethics, the basic rule of ethics of public responsibility. (pp. 366–369)

The client has the right to expect that the professional will make an effort to know. And any potential risks the client faces as a result of the social worker's intervention are the client's choice under informed consent. The fiduciary responsibility inherent in the professional mission of service and shared with all professions is reflected in the values of *integrity* and *competence*.

Advocacy

Advocacy is a professional and ethical responsibility for all social workers. It is a part of a social worker's fiduciary responsibility. Advocacy, simply defined, is representing and supporting a client, group, organization or cause to others. The ethical codes of most U.S. and international professional social work associations call for social work advocacy (Hardina, 1993; IFSW, 2004; NASW, 2008). Case and client advocacy are inherent in NASW's ethical standard 1.01 regarding primacy of client interest and 1.02 calling for client self-determination. On a larger stage in standard 6.01, Social and Political Action, the advocacy responsibilities extend beyond a particular client, group, or cause to social and political advocacy to achieve an equitable distribution of social resources and for social justice (NASW, 2008).

Gilbert and Specht (1976) alerted social workers to guard against the seduction of the teleological position of ends justifying means in client and social advocacy. Means and ends must be within the bounds of ethical behavior. Additionally, social workers who are employed or paid by an agency or third party must be alert to any constraints to advocacy imposed by this relationship. Clients, whether an individual or a community group, under the ethical requirement of informed consent must be alerted to the worker's constraints. We discuss advocacy more fully in chapter 12.

Informed Consent

A social worker's first responsibility is not to risk the client, whether an individual or a community organization, for a greater good unless the client makes an informed decision to be at risk in the quest for a greater social, collective, and institutional good. Informed consent requires that a client has valid information on the risks, the probability level that the risks will occur and that if they occur will produce greater good, an appreciation of any personal gains and losses by client and worker, and any organizational and employment constraints placed on the worker in

the advocacy and change effort. Individuals, groups, and community organizations have the right to decide their risks (e.g., jeopardizing jobs, risking jail time, losing a home). They have a right not to be unilaterally and ignorantly placed in harm's way by a community practitioner pursuing a social, collective, or institutional good. Clients and action systems deserve the opportunity to participate or not to participate, on the basis of appraisal of the gains and risks to them. They need to be advised of the extent to which the social worker or sponsoring agency will go to protect them or to share the risks with them. Clients have a right to provide or refuse informed consent.

The social worker has a duty to warn others of the risk that a client's behavior may pose to them, and a duty to warn a client of the risks faced in any personal or social change effort. We will discuss some of the difficulties in obtaining informed consent and limitations on the duty to warn later in the text. Conflict situations, the social worker's ideological commitments, or employer interests do not remove ethical imperatives. Informed consent is necessary for worker accountability and client self-determination and empowerment.

Community Practice and the Fiduciary Responsibility

Community practice in all its forms and the use of community practice skills by direct service practitioners require adherence to the same high ethical standards of conduct as those required of any professional social work practice. Unfortunately, NASW's and the other international codes are more reflective of Howe's (1980) private model of profession, one with members who "are primarily responsible to individual clients" (p. 179). Private professions in the main are concerned with the private good of individual clients. Reisch and Lowe (2000, p. 24) contend that NASW's ethical code assumes that the ethical issues it addresses, especially in its standards 1 and 2, arise primarily within the context of a clinical relationship and the administrative and supervisory environment of that relationship. They claim that social work's code of ethics does not provide sufficient ethical guidance to community practice and that the social work literature gives little attention to the ethics of community practice. Community practice does not represent a higher form of practice exempted from ethical constraints and fiduciary responsibility. It requires the same value base with a commitment to social justice, informed consent, self-degermination, and empowerment of clients and community (Banks, 2004; Butcher, Banks, & Henderson with Robertson, 2007; Hardina, 2002, pp. 18–43). Indeed, community practice may require greater adherence to virtue ethics and the fiduciary responsibility, as both the scope of an intervention and the change's potential for good or harm often are greater. Community practice interventions can't rest on the teleological claim that moral and equitable ends can justify unethical means (Schmidtz, 1991, p. 3). Ethics governs means or practices as much as ends. Not only must the ends be ethical and just, but also the tactics and behavior used in the pursuit of the ends must meet ethical and moral criteria. No matter how well-meaning the social worker is in the search of noble ends for the client or community, the ethical constraints of informed consent and the rights of clients (albeit clients often difficult to define in community practice) inherent in ethical codes remain operative, even if these ethical standards interfere with the processes of change. Racher (2007) argues that feminist ethics should guide community practice: "Inclusion, diversity, participation, empowerment, social justice, advocacy, and interdependence are key considerations of feminist ethics from the individual to the societal level. These concepts form an ethical foundation for . . . community practice" (p. 71). Beyond feminist ethics, the core value of social justice guides the ethics of community practice (McGrath, George, Lee, & Moffatt, 2007).

The Association of Community Organization and Social Administration (ACOSA) has not developed or promulgated an ethical code for community practice. Its literature does urge proactive ethics rather than reactive ethics (Beverly, 2003). Proactive ethics focuses or preventing ethical problems rather than merely reacting to them. Beverly (2003) argues that "[i]n proactive ethics practice, one may forgo direct confrontation of the responsible individual and focus on preventing such problems in the future. For example, the social worker forms a coalition of advocates focused on the problem and/or gains appointment to the Board that governs the pertinent organization, then co-shapes policy actively aligning with the Code (p. 8)." This is similar to President Obama's decision not to investigate any misdeeds of the Bush II administration and to concentrate on moving forward. Proactive ethics, in its avoidance of direct confrontation, may also be avoiding the accountability and justice of reactive ethics, appears to require a major time investment, and, Beverly outlines, must still rely on aligning with reactive codes in the example to prevent unethical behavior.

A fundamental deficit of the private ethical codes is that they are designed to regulate professional behavior with individual clients and are not ethics for community practice. In most professions that deal with macro-practice there are not *large systems ethics* that specify standards of behavior when not dealing with the individual or collectives of individuals. The banking crisis and other major financial and corporate system practices of the early 21st century demonstrate this. It is important to also distinguish between illegal behaviors and unethical behaviors. Behaviors can be illegal and not unethical and unethical but completely legal. This will be discussed more fully below.

The Client in Community Practice

The *client* is not clearly defined in macro and community practice by traditional notions of a client relationship. Community practice shares with much of social work practice a third-party employment relationship, unwilling targets of change, and people not seeking the practitioner's service. The social worker generally is employed by and accountable to an agency rather than the service recipients. This clouds and often preempts any social worker's accountability to a client, target, or beneficiary of the professional action. In community practice the goal often is "systems change" and social justice aims not selected by the action systems.

In community practice, care must be taken not to stretch the conception of client and a client relationship beyond recognition. Most conceptions of a client in a professional relationship indicate that a client is the person who in some way engages the professional service of another. Community practice, as pointed out by Gilbert and Specht (1976), emphasizes the importance of being clear about the responsibilities to the client and to the employing agency. But who is the client? The social worker in social advocacy, social action, community development, and much of macro- and community practice is employed and engaged by a social agency or organization to produce social change. The practitioner may have no formal or even implied or informal contract with a client group, let alone the client system. Community groups are used in the action system to pursue change. The social worker is not employed by the community. The funding may come from sources outside any target or beneficiary community. The problem-solving systems discussed earlier in this chapter require careful professional attention.

Social workers, community psychologists, and similar professionals must decide and be clear about to whom they are accountable, as there are bound to be conflicting loyalties and vague mandates. O'Neill (1998, p. 234), a community psychologist, notes that we often intervene on behalf of groups who are "only vaguely aware that a professional is working to advance their presumed interests" and "who gave no consent at all." The conception and subsequent construction of a client system in situations where the practitioner is employed by a social organization other than client systems must be approached carefully. Client systems generally are the people who ask for and sanction the proposed change *and* who have a working agreement or contract, whether formal or informal, with the change agent as well as being the expected beneficiaries of the change agent's services. A meaningful conception of *client* goes beyond being a target of change, the agent of social change, or beneficiary of change to the inclusion of agreeing to the change.

As Reisch and Lowe point out (2000, p. 25), other challenges confronting community organizers include issues involving truth telling and competing interests and goals, paternalism and the limits on an organizer's interventions when there are divided professional loyalties, allocation of scarce resources between competing interests, and resolving differences between public and private interests.

The social work codes of ethics provide little guidance to the community practitioner in the client relationship, although they are more helpful in providing guidance for relationships with colleagues, employing agencies, the profession, and society.

An examination of a few of the ethical standards delineated under *Social Workers' Ethical Responsibilities to Clients* (NASW, 2008, pp. 2-5) will illustrate the point:

1.01 Commitment to Clients: Social workers' primary responsibility is to promote the well being of clients. In general, clients' interests are primary.

This raises questions as to who is the client: the community, which is rather nebulously defined, the action system, or those who may most benefit, or the social justice aim? Who is the client, and does primary commitment lie with client or with cause?

1.02 Self Determination: Social workers respect and promote the right of clients to self determination and assist clients in their efforts to identify and clarify their goals.

1.03 Informed Consent: (a) Social workers should provide services to clients only in the context of a professional relationship based, when appropriate, on valid informed consent.

Again, with 1.02 and 1.03 the community practitioner is faced with the daunting challenge of determining who is exercising self-determination and has granted truly informed consent to exercise the self-determination. Do all the problem-solving systems have the right to privacy and informed consent, or is it limited to the client system only? What about the action system? Who provides the informed consent for the community and how is it provided? Community organization as a field of practice, as separate from using community practice skills on behalf of a defined client, has a problem of "informed consent." Who gives consent: the community, agents or spokespeople of the community, or the community organizer's employer and sponsor? If the community, how does the community give it? If spokespeople or agents, how are they selected and who selected them? If the sponsor or employer, by what right and authority does it speak for the community if the client (the community) is to provide the consent after being informed? This is very similar to the question in community organization of "who is the client?"

1.09 Sexual Relationships: This standard, with its four clauses, proscribes sexual relations with current and former clients and basically with all the client's primary social networks. But how does this apply to the client systems in community practice? Is the community practitioner forced into celibacy at least in the community of practice?

Hardina (2002, pp. 28–31) argues that celibacy is hardly a viable solution. She presents a series of reasonable guidelines to govern the community practitioner's sexual relations (perhaps most relationships) with community organization participants and constituents, focusing on the nature of the power relationship between the potential sexual partners. The community practitioner should:

- Avoid sexual relationships when the partners have a superordinate–subordinate community or organizational relationship
- Not use the community organization position in any way to promote a sexual relationship or any other relationship that can lead to a conflict of interest or harm the partner in any in the community.

The difficulties in using the codes for community practice rest with the difficulties in defining client and community as client. However, the use of community practice skills by social workers working on behalf of a defined client should adhere to the codes. The community organization practitioner should attempt to be virtuous in the strict sense of the concept and adhere to the imperative of *primum non nocere*.

Whistle-Blowing and Ethics

A pragmatic challenge to an agency-based social worker or a social worker who is financially dependent on a third party is whistle-blowing. Whistle-blowing calls public attention to social and legal wrongdoing by an agency's or funding source's personnel, usually persons in authority. A whistle-blower usually does not face ethical dilemmas, although whistle-blowing generally carries with it very real personal costs, risks, and pragmatic dilemmas. No one appears to respect a snitch, even when snitching is in the public good. It can cost the whistle-blower his or her job, and potential future employers become wary. Thus, whistle-blowing should be done prudently. Whistle-blowing has become more popular as the website Leakapedia.com demonstrated, but again with costs to the whistle-blower when discovered.

Reisch and Lowe (2000) provide some guidance for potential whistle-blowers. After determining who is being accused and whether or not the accusations are fair, the potential whistle-blower should address the questions in the following guidelines.

Guideline Questions for Whistle-Blowing

1. Am I acting in the public interest and good, or for personal interests and motives?
2. Do the facts warrant this action? Have all internal alternatives been explored?
3. Does the obligation to serve the public interest outweigh my responsibility to colleagues and the agency?
4. Can the harm to colleagues and the agency be minimized? What are the least harmful methods available?

Whistle-blowing, under Ethical Standards 2.11: Unethical Conduct of Colleagues, 3.09: Commitment to Employers, and 4.04: Dishonesty, Fraud, and Deception (NASW, 2008, pp. 5–7) should be done only after exhausting all other avenues for change within the agency. Ethical Standard 2.01: Respect under 2. Social Workers' Ethical Responsibilities to Colleagues also must be weighed in the whistle-blower's decision. The use of alternative avenues for change ethically can be rejected after consideration, according to Reisch and Lowe (2000), for three reasons: (a) when no alternatives exist for the situation at hand, (b) when there is insufficient time to use alternative channels and the damage of no change or exposure outweighs the damage of premature whistle-blowing before alternatives are exhausted, and (c) when the organization is so corrupt that there is an imminent danger of being silenced or falsely refuted.

Dilemmas in Ethical Behavior

Consistent ethical conduct is difficult for social workers. The difficulty generally lies in conflicts between a social worker's pursuit of pragmatic self-interest or in meeting ethical obligations. True ethical dilemmas between two or more ethical imperatives are rare, but pragmatic dilemmas are frequent. An ethical dilemma exists when two or more ethical imperatives are equally important but require opposite behaviors. Both can't be satisfied, and satisfying one will violate other ethical imperatives, and the ethical guidelines do not give clear directions or set a clear priority as to the ethical imperatives to follow.

Pragmatic considerations frequently make ethical behavior arduous and professionally or personally risky, but the pragmatic considerations and hazards are not ethical dilemmas. The dilemmas are between ethical behavior on one hand and pragmatic consequences on the other hand.

The use of "enhanced interrogation" techniques by the Central Intelligence Agency and the military on suspected *al Qaeda* terrorists and others illustrates the point. Medical personnel were deeply involved in the abusive interrogation of overseas U.S.-held terrorist suspects, according to an International Committee of the Red Cross's secret report. The Committee held that the participation by the medical personnel was a "gross breach of medical ethics." The medical personnel functioned in the interrogation to ensure that the torture did not kill the prisoners. According to current CIA director Leon E. Pannetta, "no one who took actions based on legal guidance from the Department of Justice at the time should be investigated, let alone punished" (Shane, 2009, p. A6).

This raises the question of whether it is ethical for professionals to violate their codes of ethics and ethical standards and behave unethically simply because the behavior is sanctioned by a government. If so, all the genocidal actions of doctors and others would be okay according to the Pannetta logic if sanctioned by a government. All the Nazi behaviors prosecuted by the United States after World War II at the Nuremburg trials would be legal, as they were based on the legal guidance of the Nazi government. Or perhaps the behavior has to be sanctioned by the *winning* government. The medical personnel were not facing ethical dilemmas. Certainly they faced dilemmas between pragmatic considerations of career-ending decisions and ethical behavior. They had options. But ethical behavior is behavior mandated by ethical standards irrespective of a government's desires. Otherwise there is no need for ethics—simply do what you are told to do by the government or employer: *I was only following orders.*

There are substantial risks to pragmatic self-interests and possible conflicts between ethical behavior and pragmatic interests involved in the ethical examples discussed in the following sections.

Ethical Challenges, Example 1: Community Practice: Advocating Client Interests Over Agency Interests

A community organizer was hired several years ago by a city as a community organizer in an inner-city neighborhood known as Crabtown. The city's mayor and managers at that time believed, based on some research, that neighborhood cohesion had a deterrent effect on street crime, vandalism, and deterioration (Castro, 1997/98; Rauch, 2004). The community organizer had some success and organized a neighbor association, a neighborhood watch program, anti-drug parent patrols, and community recreation. Street crime, vandalism and graffiti, and drug-related crimes decreased in Crabtown.

Some years later, a new city administration was in power and promoted a state law to allow casino gambling in the state. The city was to get one of the casinos and planned to put it in an abandoned warehouse in Crabtown. The city's administration believed the casino would revitalize Crabtown by bring new businesses to the neighborhood, increasing jobs, reducing blight, and generating tax revenue from the casino for the city. In short, the city government viewed it as a winner for everyone. The community organizer, a city employee, was directed by the administration to *sell* the casino to the Crabtown Neighborhood Association (CNA) and other neighborhood groups and obtain their support for a casino in Crabtown.

After several community meetings held by the CNA for community input, the CNA concluded that the casino should be opposed. The reasons for their opposition were:

- Potential for increased crime and drugs with all the new people coming into the neighborhood to gamble
- Gambling being an enticement for the predominantly low-income residents and youth of Crabtown
- Disruption of the community, with increased traffic and parking demands of the casino
- Increased property taxes and property costs to Crabtown residents

The CNA saw it as a losing situation. Even the few jobs created for Crabtown residents would not be sufficient to offset the costs to the neighborhood. As one resident said, "Go to Atlantic City and walk around in the poor neighborhoods if you dare. They've had casinos for years."

The community practitioner, a social worker, believes that she faces a dilemma. The city believes the casino would be good for the neighborhood and city, and she works for the city. If she doesn't *sell* the casino proposal to the neighborhood, she could lose her job. Her clients, the CNA and the other neighborhood groups, generally opposed the casino. Doesn't the code of ethics compel her to follow her client's interests? Or is there a larger social responsibility?

1. Social Workers' Ethical Responsibilities To Clients

1.01 Commitment to Clients

Social workers' primary responsibility is to promote the wellbeing of clients. In general, clients' interests are primary. However, social workers' responsibility to the larger society or specific legal obligations may on limited occasions supersede the loyalty owed clients, and clients should be so advised. . . .

1.02 Self-Determination

Social workers respect and promote the right of clients to self determination and assist clients in their efforts to identify and clarify their goals. . . .

1.03 Informed Consent

(a) Social workers should provide services to clients only in the context of a professional relationship based, when appropriate, on valid informed consent. Social workers should use clear and understandable language to inform clients of the purpose of the services, risks related to the services, limits to services because of the requirements of a third party payer, relevant costs, reasonable alternatives, clients' right to refuse or withdraw consent, and the time frame covered by the consent. Social workers should provide clients with an opportunity to ask questions.

The preceding example need not have become an ethical dilemma or conflict if the community practitioner had adhered to the ethical standards from the beginning of the relationship. Standard 1.01 specifies that sometimes a client's interests are not primary and may be superseded. However, the client needs to be advised of these limitations at the beginning of the relationship as advised in both Standards 1.01 and 1.03. The CNA and neighborhood groups should have been advised that the community organizer works for and follows directions from the city. The risk, of course, is that the client will withdraw consent when informed of the community organizer's relationship with the city and the community.

The dilemma is more pragmatic than between conflicting ethical standards. The strain is not between two equally compelling and opposed ethical imperatives. The NASW Code of Ethics is pragmatic in that it negates client primacy and interests when they conflict with employment standards, third-party payment, and legal imperatives regardless of the moral basis of the legal imperatives, insofar as there is informed consent. The strain and the dilemma are real and important, but this is not an *ethical* dilemma. There may be a dilemma between the value of social justice and NASW's Code of Ethics that places the social worker's ultimate primary commitment to employers, third-party vendor requirements, and legal requirements rather than to clients. If she provided informed consent to the community when she first entered the community, she may have never organized it. If the social work community organizer helps CNA oppose the casino and the city, the social worker pursues the ethical principle of social justice, the spirit of primacy of client interest, and the related social action, but violates the letter of ethical standard 1 and risks her livelihood in so doing. NASW's convenient posturing on the social workers' ethical obligations to client, employer, third-party payers, and laws regardless reduces the potential for strict ethical conflicts but increases the quandary of ethics as rules for behavior versus virtue ethics as motivators for behavior.

> ### Ethical Challenges, Example 2: Casework Practice: Civil Disobedience to Maintain Ethical Behavior
>
> Public law and policy, bowing to public pressure, has been revised several times over the past years to limit services provided to illegal immigrants. City, a Northeastern community, passed an ordinance that requires that service professionals in the City report illegal immigrants to the Immigration and Naturalization Service. Should a social worker employed by a City service or voluntary not-for-profit agency adhere to this ordinance?
>
> If a social worker is discovered not reporting illegal immigrants, it, can result in the social worker's loss of employment and license, and he or she may be subjected to other civil and criminal penalties.
>
> Reporting, however, violates a series of ethical standards from the social worker's ethical responsibilities to clients through 4.02: Discrimination (NASW, 2008):
>
> "Social workers should not practice, condone, facilitate, or collaborate with any form of discrimination on the basis of race, ethnicity, national origin, color, sex, sexual orientation, gender identity or expression, age, marital status, political belief, religion, *immigration status*, or mental or physical disability".

The client is being reported not for any wrongdoing other than immigration status, so reporting appears to violate Standard 4.02. However, back to 1.01: Commitment to clients, which states that a social worker's responsibility to the larger society or specific legal obligations may on limited occasions supersede the loyalty owed clients.

This second example presents an ethical dilemma to a social worker because the ethical code presents an apparent internal inconsistency. The inconsistency is between the profession's values and its ethics. The conflict is between the profession's six ethical principles, especially the principles of service, integrity, and social justice.

Ethical Standard 1.01 presents social workers with the challenge of reconciling specific legal obligations that are assumed to supersede the loyalty owed clients and to social justice. A social worker's ethical behavior generally is a reconciliation of the often-disparate demands of personal values and ethics, professional values and ethics, and public rules of behavior called laws. Ideally they are derived from the same core values, but unfortunately, they are not always consistent. When not consistent, the social work practitioner is then challenged to adhere to the core ethical principles and values of social justice and integrity and act in a virtuous manner. History is replete with the challenges of disobeying unjust laws to behave in an ethical manner. Slavish adherence to public law in itself is not always moral, although according to the NASW's ethical standard 1.01 it is ethical. This standard negates civil disobedience in pursuit of moral goals, and historically this ethical requirement would have precluded social workers' participation in the civil disobedience to obtain full civil rights for all Americans during the Civil Rights Movement or acting as a righteous person sheltering Jews and other persecuted peoples in Nazi Germany.

The Organization of This Book

The book is divided into two parts. Part I explores the context, dynamics, and primary theories underlying community practice. This part contains three chapters that were not included in the first edition: Chapter 2, Theory-Based, Model-Based Community Practice; Chapter 3, The Nature of Social and Community Problems; and Chapter 4, The Concept of Community in Social Work Practice. Part II addresses essential community practice skills for all social workers in the 21st century and is divided into 10 chapters: Chapter 5, Assessment: Discovering and Documenting the Life of the Community; Chapter 6, Using Assessment in Community Practice; Chapter 7, Assertiveness: Using Self in Community Practice; Chapter 8, Using Your Agency; Chapter 9, Using Work Groups: Committees, Teams, and Boards; Chapter 10, Using Networks and Networking; Chapter 11, Using Marketing; Chapter 12, Using the Advocacy Spectrum; Chapter 13: Using Organizing: Acting in Concert; and Chapter 14, Community Social Casework.

BOX 1.6.	Social Work's Ethical Principles

Value: Service
Ethical Principle: Social workers' primary goal is to help people in need and to address social problems.
Value: Social Justice
Ethical Principle: Social workers challenge social injustice.
Value: Dignity and Worth of the Person
Ethical Principle: Social workers respect the inherent dignity and worth of the person.

Value: Importance of Human Relationships
Ethical Principle: Social workers recognize the central importance of human relationships.
Value: Integrity
Ethical Principle: Social workers behave in a trustworthy manner.
Value: Competence
Ethical Principle: Social workers practice within their areas of competence and develop and enhance their professional expertise.

Discussion Exercises

1. Could theories of human behavior and social work intervention be developed and used without a consideration of community influence? If so, would the theories be equally applicable to anyone in the world, without consideration of culture or community?

2. How are interventions and post-intervention successes of clients affected by the community? Do the social relations, environment, and networks of a drug user affect drug use? Will drug use be influenced by a "clean" community and a social support network of non-users?

3. Are there values that are shared by most communities regardless of culture and ethnicity? If so, what are they?

4. What are the social worker's ethical responsibilities to a client and the limits of the social worker's capacity to engage in client advocacy when employed by a social agency? Which ethical codes limit advocacy? Should the scarcity of resources limit client advocacy?

5. Are there differences between the legal requirements and ethical obligations in duty to warn, client self-determination, and informed consent? When should values supersede ethical standards?

6. Do the simultaneous obligations to clients, the community, and the employing agency and advocacy of the primacy of the client's interests present practice dilemmas? What are they?

7. In social cause advocacy, does the social work advocate owe primary loyalty to the employing organization, the social cause, or the participants? Is there a client or a client system in social cause advocacy?

8. Can there be a profession sanctioned by the community for social reform and social reconstruction? Can reform and social change be professionalized? Can a profession or occupation dependent on public funding or employed by the public sector, either directly or under contract, become a radical change-oriented profession?

9. If the first ethical rule of all professional behavior should be primum non nocere—"first of all, do no harm"—what is your position on the question, "Should the social worker risk harming an individual client in order to produce social, collective, and institutional change that might result in good for a large number of people?" Defend your position based on the social work profession's code of ethics and values.

10. Can affirmative action, a form of restorative justice, be defended as ethical by the code of ethics? How is affirmative action compatible with the code of ethics?

11. Are there ethical canons that allow law and public policy to supersede the code of ethics?

Notes

1. The Oxford Encyclopedic Dictionary. (1991). New York: Oxford University Press. p. 1371.

2. Peru elected a minority president, Alberto Fujimori, in 1990. Bolivia, another South American nation, elected Evo Morales president in 2005. President Morales claims to be an Amerindian, although critics insist he is Mestizo. Neither makes him a numerical minority but a member of a socially disadvantaged ethnic group. Neither Peru nor Bolivia is generally labeled as a developed Western industrial democracy.

3. The IFSW reports that some countries use "discrimination" instead of "negative discrimination." "Negative" is used by IFSW because in some countries the term "positive discrimination" is also used as "affirmative action" for positive steps to redress historical discrimination.

4. The complete and current Codes of Ethics are available on the Web at http://www.socialworkers.org/pubs/code/default.asp for the NASW and

http://www.ifsw.org/p38000324.html for the IFSW. All references to and excerpts from the NASW Code of Ethics were obtained from this source. Codes of Ethics for other national social work associations also generally are available on the Web.

References

Administration Systems for Church Management (n.d.), Colorado Springs. Systemation, Inc.

American Association of Social Workers. (1929). *Social case work: Generic and specific, a report of the Milford Conference.* New York: Author.

Banks, S. (2004). *Ethics, accountability and the social professions.* Basingstoke, Hampshire, UK: Palgrave Macmillan.

Banks, S. (2006). *Ethics and values in social work* (3rd ed.). Basingstoke, Hampshire, UK: Palgrave Macmillan.

Bellah, R. N., Madsen, R., Sullivan, W. M., Swidler, A., & Tipton, S. M. (1985). *Habits of the heart: Individualism and commitment in American life.* New York: Harper & Row.

Bellah, R. N., Madsen, R., Sullivan, W. M., Swidler, A., & Tipton, S. M. (1991). *The good society.* New York: Vintage Books.

Beverly, W. (2003). Reactive vs. proactive ethics in social work community practice: Does the difference make a difference? *The ACOSA Update.* 17(2), 8,15.

Bisman, C. (2008). Personal information and the professional relationship: Issues of trust, privacy and welfare. In C. Clark & J. McGhee (Eds.), *Private and confidential? Handling personal information in the social and health services.* Bristol, UK: The Policy Press, 17–34.

Bisman, C. (2004). Social work values: The moral core of the profession. *British Journal of Social Work.* 34(1), 109-123.

Bisman, C., & Hardcastle, D. (1999). *Integrating research into practice: A model for effective social work.* Pacific Grove, CA: Brooks/Cole, Wadsworth.

Beverly, W. (2003). Reactive vs proactive ethics in social work community practice: Does the difference make a difference? *ACOSA Update Online,* 17(2), 8, 15.

British Association of Social Workers. (2002). *Code of ethics.* Retrieved May 14, 2009, from http://www.basw.co.uk/

Bruno, F. J. (1948). *Trends in social work: As reflected in the proceedings of the National Conference of Social Work, 1874-1946.* New York: Columbia University Press.

Butcher, H., Banks, S., & Henderson, P., with Robertson, J., (2007). *Critical community practice.* Bristol, UK: The Policy Press.

Callinicos, A. (2001). *Against the third way: An anti-capitalist critique.* Cambridge, UK: Polity Press.

Canadian Association of Social Workers. (2005). *Code of ethics.* Ottawa, CA: Author.

Castro, B. (1997/98, Winter). Manufacturing jobs: Local ownership and the social health of cities. *The Responsive Community,* 8(1) 63–66.

Chazdon, S. (1991). *Responding to human needs: Community-based social services.* Denver, CO: National Conference of State Legislatures.

Clampet-Lundquest, S., & Massey, D. S. (2008). Moving to opportunity: A symposium: Neighborhood effects on economic self-sufficiency, A reconsideration of the Moving to Opportunity experiment. *American Sociological Journal,* 114(1), 107–143.

Clifford, D., & Burke, B. (2009). *Anti-oppressive ethics and values in social work.* Basingstoke, UK: Palgrave Macmillan.

Coughlin, R. (2004). Does socioeconomic inequality undermine community? Implications for Communitarian theory. In A. Etzioni, A. Volmert, & E. Rothschild (Eds.), *The communitarian reader: Beyond the essentials.* Oxford, UK: Rowman & Littlefield, Publishers, 117–128.

Cohen, A. P. (1985). *The symbolic construction of community.* New York: Tavistock Publication and Ellis Horwood Limited.

Commission on Accreditation. (2008). *Education Policy and Accreditation Standards.* Council on Social Work Education. Retrieved June 3, 2009, from http://www.cswe.org/.

Compton, B. R., & Galaway, B. (1979). *Social work processes* (Rev. ed.). Homewood, IL: Dorsey Press.

Conley, D. (2009, March 23). America is #...15? *The Nation,* 288:11.

Connelly, M. (2000, November 12). The election, who voted: A portrait of American politics, 1976–2000. *The New York Times,* p. wk 4.

Delgado, M., & Staples, L. (2008). *Youth-led community organizing: Theory and action.* New York: Oxford University Press.

Deacon, B. (with Hulse, M., & Stubbs, P.). (1997). *Global social policy: International organizations and the future of welfare.* Thousand Oaks, CA: Sage Publications.

Dicken, P. (2003). *Global shifts: Reshaping the global economic map in the 21st. century* (4th ed.) London: Sage.

Doherty, W. (1994–1995). Bridging psychotherapy and moral responsibility. *The Responsive Community: Rights and Responsibilities,* 5(1), 41–52.

Doherty, W. (1995, Spring). Community considerations in psychotherapy. *The Responsive Community: Rights and Responsibilities,* 5(2), 45–53.

Drucker, P. F. (1974). *Management: Tasks, responsibilities and practices.* New York: Harper & Row.

Epstein, L. (1980). *Helping people: The task-centered approach* (2nd ed.). Columbus, OH: Merrill.

Etzioni, A. (1993). *The spirit of community: Rights, responsibility and the communitarian agenda.* New York: Crown.

Ewalt, P. L. (1980). *Toward a definition of clinical social work.* Washington, DC: National Association of Social Workers.

Ezell, M. (2001). *Advocacy in the human services.* Belmont, CA: Brooks/Cole.

France, A. (2004). *The red lily.* (originally published 1894). Retrieved June 18, 2009, from http://www.gutenberg.org/etext/3922

Gambrill, E. (1983). *Casework: A competency-based approach.* Englewood Cliffs, NJ: Prentice Hall.

Gates, Jr., H. L. (2010, April 23). Ending the slavery blame-game. *The New York Times.* p. A27.

Germain, C. B. (1983). Using physical and social environments. In A. Rosenblatt & D. Waldfogel (Eds.), *Handbook of clinical social work* (pp. 110–133). New York: Jossey-Bass.

Gilbert, N., & Specht, H. (1976). Advocacy and professional ethics. *Social Work,* 21(4), 288–293.

Gordon, W. E. (1969). Basic construction for an inergative conception of social work. In G. Hearn (Ed.), *The general systems approach: Contributions toward an holistic conception of social w*ork (pp. 5–11). New York: Council on Social Work Education.

Gray, J. (1998). *False dawn: The delusions of global capitalism.* London: Granta Books.

Gray, M., & Gibbons, J. (2007). There are no answers, only choices: Teaching ethical decision making in social work. *Australian Social Work,* 60(2), 222–238.

Grogan-Kaylor, A., Woolley, M., Mowbray, C., Reischl, T. M.; Güster, M., Karb, R., Macfarlane, P., Gant, L., & Alaimo, K. (2007). Predictors of neighborhood satisfaction. *Journal of Community Practice,* 14(4), 27–50.

Gumz, E. J., & Grant, C. L. (2009). Restorative justice: A systematic review of the social work literature. *Families in Society,* 90(1), 119–126.

Gustafson, J. A. (1982). Profession as callings. *Social Service Review,* 56(4), 501–505.

Hardcastle, D. A. (1990). Public regulation of social work. In L. Ginsberg, S. Khinduka, J. A. Hall, F. Ross-Sheriff, & A. Hartman (Eds.), *Encyclopedia of social work* (18th ed., 1990 suppl., pp. 203–217). Silver Spring, MD: National Association of Social Workers.

Hardina, D. (1993). *Professional ethics and advocacy practice.* New York: Annual Program Meeting of Community Organization and Social Administration Symposium Paper.

Hardina, D. (2002). *Analytical skills for community organization practice.* New York: Columbia University Press.

Harris, P. (2006, February 12). 37 million poor hidden in the land of plenty. *The Observer,* 32–33.

Henderson, P. (2007). Introduction. In H. Butcher, S. Banks, P. Henderson, with J. Robertson, (Eds.), *Critical Community Practice,* (pp. 1-16). Bristol, UK: The Policy Press.

Henkel, D. (1998, November/December). Self-help planning in the colonias: Collaboration and innovation in southern New Mexico unincorporated areas. *Small Towns,* 16–21.

Hepworth, D. H., & Larsen, J. A. (1986). *Direct social work practice: Theory and skills* (2nd ed.). Chicago: Dorsey Press.

Hollenbach, D. (1994/1995). Civic society: Beyond the public-private dichotomy. *The Responsive Community,* 5(1), 15–23.

Howe, E. (1980, May). Public professions and the private model of professionalism. *Social Work,* 25(3), 179–191.

International Federation of Social Workers. (2004). *The ethics in social work: Principles and standards.* Retrieved May 14, 2009, from http://www.ifsw.org/p38000324.html.

Karls, J. M., & Wandrei, K. E. (Eds.). (1994). *Person-in-environment system: The P-I-E classification system for social functioning problems.* Washington, DC: National Association of Social Workers.

Kutchins, H. (1991). The fiduciary relationship: The legal basis for social workers' responsibility to clients. *Social Work,* 36(2), 97–102.

Lasch, C. (1994). *The revolt of the elites and the betrayal of democracy.* New York: W. W. Norton.

Licensed social workers in the U.S.: 2004, (March 2006). Prepared by Center for Health Workforce Studies, School of Public Health, University at Albany and Center for Workforce Studies, National Association of Social Workers.

Lippitt, R., Watson, J., & Westley, B. (1958). *The dynamics of planned change.* New York: Harcourt, Brace and World.

Liptak, A. (2010, July 24). Court under Roberts is most conservative in decades. *The New York Times.* Retrieved July 28, 2010, from: http://www.nytimes.com/07/25/usroberts.htm.

Lubove, R. (1977). *The professional altruist: The emergence of social work as a career, 1880–1938.* New York: Atheneum.

Mancini, J. A., Bowen, G. L., & Martin, J. A. (2005). Community social organization: A conceptual linchpin in examining families in the context of communities. *Family Relations,* 54(5), 570–582.

Marx, K. (1959). Critique of the Gotha Program. In L. S. Feuer (Ed.), *Marx and Engels: Basic writings on politics & philosophy* (pp. 112–132). Garden City, New York: Anchor Books.

McGrath, S., George, U., Lee, B., & Moffatt, K. (2007). Seeking social justice: Community practice within diverse marginalized populations in Canada. *Social Development Issues.* 29(2), 77-91.

Miller, D. T., & Prentice, D. A. (1994). The self and the collective. *Society for Personality and Social Psychology*, 20(5), 451–453.

Mishra, R. (1999). *Globalization and the welfare state.* Northampton, MA: Edward Elgar.

Mulroy, E. A. (2004). Theoretical perspectives on the social environment to guide management and community practice. *Administration in Social Work*, 28(1), 77–96.

National Association of Social Workers (2009). *Legislative agenda for the 111th Congress*, Washington, DC. Retrieved June 1, 2009, from http://www.socialworkers.org/advocacy

National Association of Social Workers (2008). *Code of ethics of the National Association of Social Workers [as approved by the 1996 NASW Delegate Assembly and revised by the 2008 NASW Delegate Assembly].* Retrieved May 11, 2009, from http://www.social-workers.org/pubs/code/default.asp

National Association of Social Workers (n.d.). *NASW policy statement 11, NASW standards for the practice of clinical social work.* Silver Spring, MD: Author.

Netting, F. E., Kettner, P. M., & McMurtry, S. L. (1993). *Social work macro practice.* New York: Longman.

Netting, F. E., & O'Connor, M. K. (2002). *Organization practice: A social worker's guide to understanding human services.* Boston, MA: Allyn & Bacon.

O'Neill, J. (2003). Private sector employs most members. *NASW News*, 48(2), 8.

O'Neill, P. (1998). Responsible to whom? Responsible for what? Ethical issues in community intervention. *American Journal of Psychology*, 17(3), 323–340.

Pardeck, J. T., Murphy, J. W., & Choi, J. M. (1994). Some implications of postmodernism for social work practice. *Social Work*, 39(4), 343–346.

Payne, M. (2006). *Modern social work theory* (3rd ed.). Chicago: Lyceum.

Pincus, A., & Minahan, A. (1973). *Social work practice: Models and methods.* Itasca, IL: F. E. Peacock.

Polsky, H. (1969). System as patient: Client needs and system functions. In G. Hearn (Ed.), *The general systems approach: Contributions toward an holistic conception of social work* (pp. 12–25). New York: Council on Social Work Education.

Pumphrey, R. E. (1980). Compassion and protection: Dual motivations of social welfare. In F. R. Breul &

S. J. Diner (Eds.), *Compassion and responsibility: Readings in the history of social welfare policy in the United States* (pp. 5–13). Chicago: University of Chicago Press.

Racher, F. R. (2007). The evolution of ethics for community practice. *Journal of Community Health Nursing*, 24(1), 65–76.

Rauch, J. (2004). Confessions of an alleged libertarian (and the virtues of "soft" Communitarianism). In A. Etzioni, A. Volmert, & E. Rothschild (Eds.), *The Communitarian reader: Beyond the essentials* (pp. 96–104). Oxford, UK: Rowman & Littlefield, Publishers.

Reamer, F. G. (1993). *The philosophical foundations of social work.* New York: Columbia University Press.

Reamer, F. G. (1995). *Social work values and ethics.* New York: Columbia University Press.

Reisch, M., & Lowe, J. I. (2000). "Of means and ends" revisited: Teaching ethical community organizing in an unethical society. *Journal of Community Practice*, 7(1), 19–38.

1992 #*The responsive communitarian platform: Rights and responsibilities.* (1992). Washington, DC: Communitarian Network.

Reddin, B. A. (1971). *Effective management by objectives: The 3-D method of MBA.* New York: McGraw-Hill.

Richmond, M. E. (1917). *Social diagnosis.* New York: Russell Sage Foundation.

Richmond, M. E. (1992). *What is social casework?* New York: Russell Sage Foundation. (Original work published 1922).

Ross, M. (with Lappin, B. W.). (1967). *Community organization: Theory, principles, and practice.* New York: Harper & Row.

Rothman, J., & Tropman, J. (1987). Models of community organization and macro practice perspectives: Their mixing and phasing. In F. Cox, J. Erlich, J. Rothman, & J. Tropman (Eds.), *Strategies of community organization* (4th ed., pp. 3–26). Itasca, IL: P. E. Peacock.

Salcido, R. M., & Seek, E. T. (1992). Political participation among social work chapters. *Social Work*, 37(6), 563–564.

Scanlon, E., Hartnett, H., & Harding, S. (2006). An analysis of the political activities of NASW state chapters. *Journal of Policy Practice*, 5(4), 41–54.

Sharkey, P. (2008). The intergenerational transmission of context. *American Journal of Sociology*, 113(4), 931–969.

Schmidtz, D. (1991). *The limits of government: An essay on the public good argument.* Boulder, CO: Westview Press.

Schneider, R. L., & Lester, L. (2001). *Social work advocacy: A new framework for action.* Belmont, CA: Brooks/Cole.

Sennett, R. (2006). *The culture of the new capitalism.* New Haven, CT: Yale University Press.

Shane, S. (2009, April 7). Report outlines involvement of medical workers in abusive C.I.A. interrogations. *The New York Times.* A6.

Spano, R. (1982). *The rank and file movement in social work.* Washington, DC: University Press of America.

Specht, H., & Courtney, M. (1994). *Unfaithful angels: How social work has abandoned its mission.* New York: Free Press.

Tanzi, V. (2002). Globalization and the future of social protection. *Scottish Journal of Political Economy,* 49(1), 116–127.

Timms, N. (1966). *Social casework: Principles and practice.* London: Latimer, Trend.

Turner, A. (2009). Bottom-up community development: Reality or rhetoric? The example of the Kingsmead Kabin in East London. *Community Development Journal,* 44(2), 230–247.

United Nations Development Programme (2008). *Human development indices: A statistical update, 2008.* Retrieved June 2, 2009, from http://hdr.undp.org.

U.S. Bureau of the Census. (2009). *The 2009 statistical abstract of the United States: The National Data Book, PDF version.* (Last modified March 24, 2009). Retrieved May 28, 2009, from: http://www.census.gov/compendia/statab/

Union of Social Educators and Social Workers (2003). *The ethical guideline of social educator and social worker.* Moscow, Russia. Retrieved May 13, 2009 from:http://www.ifsw.org/cm_data/russian_frome-thical.pdf

Vartanian, T. P., & Buck, P. W. (2005). Childhood and adolescent neighborhood effects on adult income: Using siblings to examine differences in ordinary least squares and fixed-effect models. *Social Service Review,* 79(1), 60–94.

Vollmer, H. W., & Mills, D. L. (Eds.). (1966). *Professionalization.* Englewood Cliffs, NJ: Prentice Hall.

von Wormer, K. (2009, April). Restorative justice as social justice for victims of gendered violence: A standpoint feminist perspective. *Social Work,* 54:2, 107–116.

Wagner, A. (1997). Social work and the global economy: Opportunities and challenges. In M. C. Hokenstad & J. Midgley (Eds.), *Issues in international social work: Global challenges for a new century* (pp. 45–56). Washington, DC: NASW Press.

Webb, S. A. (2000). Some considerations of the validity of empirical-based practice in social work. *British Journal of Social Work,* 31(1), 57–79.

Well, M. O., & Gamble, D. N. (1995). Community practice models. In R. L. Edwards (Ed.-in-Chief), *Encyclopedia of social work,* Vol. 1 (19th ed., pp. 577–694), Silver Spring, MD: NASW Press.

Whittaker, J. K., Garbarino, J., & Associates (Eds.). (1983). *Social support networks: Informal helping in the human services.* New York: Aldine.

Whitaker, T., & Arrington, P. (2008). *Social workers at work. NASW Membership Workforce Study.* Washington, DC: National Association of Social Workers.

I

Understanding the Social Environment and Social Interaction

2

Theory-Based, Model-Based Community Practice

He who loves practice without theory is like the sailor who boards ship without a rudder and compass and never knows where he may cast.
Leonardo da Vinci, artist and inventor

It is the theory that decides what we can observe.
Albert Einstein, physicist, philosopher, and Nobel laureate

A Conceptual Framework for Practice

Professional social work practice differs from nonprofessional practice in the use of social science theories and the professional values and ethics to guide professional practice. With theory-based practice, social workers will presumably use similar interventions in similar situations to produce similar results. Under the clearest circumstances, the propositions of practice theory would thus take the form "If X occurs under X_1 conditions, do Y," and professional training would primarily involve mastering the theories and their applications. So, for example, a proposition might be: "If you encounter group resistance to a new idea, then identify an opinion leader and try to persuade him or her, outside of the group context, to adopt your idea."

Circumstances, however, seldom are uniform across even similar social situations, and the complexity of human beings and human relationships means that behavioral science theories cannot be applied quite as neatly as "if X occurs under X_1 conditions, do Y." It is more likely to be "X occurs under X_1 . . . n conditions." Nor is there a single,

unified master theory of human behavior. So, in the above example, group resistance is not a simple concept; resistance can take many forms and can be explained in many different ways. A Freudian would talk about unconscious conflicts; a Skinnerian would consider rewards and punishments. Similarly, persuasion can take many different forms. Therefore, interventions to overcome resistance will vary. Discovering the kind of persuasion that works best for overcoming particular forms of resistance represents a further elaboration of theory, indeed an improvement, but one that still will not yield a simple rule.

In fact, the enormous complexity of social work practice means that often we cannot find a direct correspondence between a grand theory and practice. Basically, theory is explanation. Scientific theory, the conception of theory as generally used in science, is a set of systematic propositions to explain and/or predict phenomena according to rules of the particular scientific discipline. Social science theories rarely tell us exactly what to do.

Should social science theories be abandoned as useless? Not really. We need to develop a conceptual framework for ourselves, namely a body of related concepts that help us understand and think about the specific phenomena we are encountering and help us make decisions about how to intervene. This framework is a case theory. Case theory, as discussed in Chapter 1, is an explanation and prediction of case phenomena; the problematic conditions, the specification of desired outcomes, the selection of intervention strategies and methods to change the condition and effect the desired outcomes, and an explanation of the prediction as to why and how the interventions will produce the outcomes. Since there is no single, unified grand theory of human behavior (for which we are thankful) or of social work practice, a community practitioner case theory will necessarily draw from a number of different theories refined through practice experience. In this chapter, we will briefly outline the social science theories we believe are most pertinent to developing case theory in community practice. It must also be remembered that the community practitioner has the challenge of developing the case theory for each case compatible with the principles of social justice.

Theories for Understanding Community Practice

The theories discussed below in abbreviated fashion are meant as an introduction to those most pertinent for community practice. The reader is encouraged to pursue them in more detail from the literature.

Systems Theory and Organizations

System is a favorite concept and perhaps an overused metaphor in social work. It is inherent in most models such as "person-in-environment"

(P-I-E) and the ecological model. Indeed, the notion of theory implies system. Chapter 1 made frequent use of system concept. A system can be viewed, most fundamentally, as an arrangement of entities, things, that interact to achieve a shared purpose or fulfill functions as a whole and its interrelated parts. Its guiding principle is organization (Hardina, 2002, pp, 49–50; Netting & O'Connor, 2002; Payne, 2005, pp. 142–180). A primary assumption underlying systems theory is that a well-integrated, smoothly functioning system is both possible and desirable. Examples of systems are mechanical systems such as computers and automobiles; human or social systems such as the Baltimore Orioles, a Department of Social Services, the AIDS Outreach Service of the health clinic; or something as grand as the global economy, the ecology or, for that matter, any individual human being. Figure 2.1 presents the model of a *general system*.

For a social system to exist, it must be separable from other systems and from its surroundings. It must have boundaries. At the same time, no human system can exist without relating to its environment, a proposition that defines the essence of an open system. Systems can be open and have exchanges with their environments or closed with no interactions with their environments. Most, if not all, social systems are open. To the extent that a system can remain closed— free of outside influences—the assumption that it is well integrated is tenable. But since human or social systems are inherently open, it is more reasonable to suggest that every social system is also inherently messy and that no human system can ever be perfectly integrated. Some degree of closure is necessary for a human system to function and remain intact or coherent. At the same time, every human system must exchange information and resources with other systems and act on that information, to maintain itself

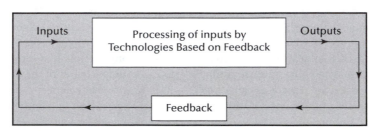

Figure 2.1. The general system model.

and flourish. In fact, the uniqueness of human systems is that they can process, create, and act on information; they can learn.

Thus we can say that every human system must negotiate its environment. Consequently, it must remain open to some degree, and it must manage some degree of uncertainty from external sources. If a human system cannot negotiate its environment, if it cannot process information well enough, then it must either exist in a protected milieu or die (Juba, 1997).

Social service agencies, like all organizations, can be viewed as open systems striving for stability. They were formed to carry out a particular mission; they are goal oriented. They also attempt to arrange their operations and decision-making rules to attain those goals. In short, they attempt to operate rationally.

Social service organizations, public, nonprofit, and proprietary, exist in an increasingly complex, demanding, dynamic, external milieu that poses a great deal of uncertainty for them. (It goes without saying that the same is true for social workers and for individual clients.) Due to such factors as the exponential growth of communication and information-processing technologies, previously unrelated elements in the environment may link up and bring about unpredictable reactions with far-reaching consequences (Emery & Trist, 1965). How do new computers and other information system technologies affect an organization's ability to compete for clients, referral sources, and revenue? How will the recession affect the demand for services and the availability of funds?

In this complex and constantly changing environment, organizational decision making can be very difficult. An organizational manager stands at the nexus of political, social, and economic streams of information and relationships, requiring new kinds of management skills (e.g., networking and coalition building), new forms of organizational structures (e.g., problem-solving teams with members from all levels of the organization), and much more familiarity with information-processing technologies than ever before. Both organizational managers and community practitioners need to learn the relevant group and organizational decision makers and how those systems operate. Social agencies will be discussed more fully in Chapter 8, Using Your Agency.

Practice knowledge of systems is essential. Systems theory postulates that systems are more than sums of their component parts. They share a common purpose, and the parts and their interaction are essential to a system fulfilling its purpose. To change a system, it is not necessary to change the entire system at once. If a part of a system is changed, the system changes. However, the system seeks quasi-stable equilibrium and will work to keep the components in their places. The practice applications of systems theory, including social systems, are discussed more fully in Part II, especially Chapter 10, Using Networks and Networking.

Social Learning Theory

Behavioral approaches to social work practice are usually identified with various forms of individual and group therapy. They are based on the work of a number of important learning theorists such as I. P. Pavlov, B. F. Skinner, Joseph Wolpe, and Albert Bandura. Social learning ideas are also useful in community-based practice, especially in understanding and influencing the behavior of individuals and groups. Social learning theory (Bandura, 1982, 1986, 1989, 1997; Payne, 2005, pp. 119–141) indicates that personal and environmental influences are bidirectional, interactional, and interdependent. Over time they can become self-reinforcing, with less need for external stimuli and reinforcements. The processes of developing effective organization leaders, satisfied staff members, and influential social action strategies can benefit from understanding and using social learning concepts and principles. It is the basis for assertive skills training.

The basic assumption of social learning theory, a cognitive-behavioral construction of human behavior, is that human behavior is learned during interactions with other persons and with the social environment. This does not deny the presence of biological or psychological processes that produce emotions and thoughts. However, little credence is given to the idea that some sort of internal personality governs behavior. Thus, learning theorists are much more interested in observable behaviors and in the factors that produce and modify these behaviors.

A shorthand way of thinking about the factors that produce or modify behavior—that is, the contingencies of social learning—is as cues, cognitions, and consequences (Silver, 1980). In Silver's words, "To understand social action, social learning looks to cues that occur prior in time, mental processes (cognitions) that mediate them, and rewarding or punishing consequences that follow. There is also feedback from consequences to cuing and thinking for future behavior. All together, these are the social learning *contingencies*" (p. 13). It follows from the old adage of *learning from experience*. Social learning and the cognitive-behavioral approaches are in tune with the contemporary emphasis on evidence-based practices.

Operant behavior, a major form of learned behavior, refers to activities that can be consciously controlled, such as talking or studying, and is influenced primarily by the positive or negative consequences that follow it in time. These consequences are commonly referred to as rewards or punishments. Reward behavior is positively reinforced and usually is maintained or increased, whereas behavior that is punished or not reinforced has a lower probability of being repeated. This is the classic stimulus–response pattern. Praise and attention are common examples of positive reinforcers; disapproval or a physical slap are examples of negative reinforcers or aversive stimuli. What constitutes positive and negative reinforcers is endless, but depends a great deal on how the individual thinks or feels about it. Pain to a sadist is a reward, not an aversion. That is to say, one's behavior is mediated by one's cognitions.

Social learning theory recognizes the importance of cognition in understanding and modifying human behavior. The human capacity to think and feel and to reflect on thoughts and perceptions, to believe, to remember the past and anticipate the future, and to develop goals— all of these affect how we behave. Social cognitive theory posits a model of reciprocal causation in which "behavior, cognition and other personal factors, and environmental influences all operate as interacting determinants that influence each other bidirectionally" (Bandura, 1989, p. 2). Thus, if I am a community worker, the manner in which I go about recruiting a prospect to join an AIDS education coalition may be influenced by how competent I think I am as a recruiter (cognition). My success may also be

affected by the prospect's prior positive or negative experiences with coalitions (consequences), as well as his or her strong belief in or skepticism about the value of coalitions for addressing a particular problem (cognition). If I succeed in forming the coalition, I will have modified the environment for addressing the AIDS problem, and this, in turn, may influence skeptics to join the effort, which may alter my perceptions of my personal competence or self-efficacy, and so on, in a continuous interactive causal chain involving behavior, cognition, and the environment.

The concepts of perceived individual self-efficacy and collective efficacy are central to social learning theory and particularly useful for community practitioners. Perceived individual self-efficacy is a self-appraisal of one's personal capacity to determine and carry out a goal-oriented course of action (Bandura, 1986, 1997). This perception stands between one's actual skills and knowledge and what one does in a given situation. It is the self-appraisal that leads to action or inaction. While a practitioner's skills may be quite good, his or her self-appraisal of the adequacy of these skills will affect how that worker performs or even responds to a challenge. A practitioner whose perceived self-efficacy is low may often avoid challenges; the worker whose self-appraisal of efficacy is high may seek them out.

Perceived self-efficacy is the foundation for belief bonding between a social work practitioner and the client. Belief bonding (Bisman, 1994, p. 79) is the shared perception, belief, and trust by both worker and client or constituent group that change is possible and they are competent and capable to bring about change. It is a bonding in the belief of their self-efficacy. Belief bonding appears to be a requisite for a committed change effort.

Individuals who have low efficacy expectations give up trying to accomplish a goal because they judge their skills to be inadequate (Bandura, 1982, 1997). Their inaction is akin to the concept of learned helplessness (Seligman, 1975), a mindset that comes about after repeated failure to exert influence over the decisions that affect one's life.

Still, some people keep on trying even after repeated failure. How can this apparent anomaly be explained? People who have high self-appraisals of efficacy and who have been successful in influencing some of the decisions affecting their lives or their external environments may develop a sense of universal hopefulness. They believe that they can succeed and that others can as well, and so they are willing to take a chance on action on behalf of change when needed. Persons with high perceived self-efficacy and low outcome expectations because of an unrewarding or unresponsive environment may develop a sense of personal hopefulness if they believe they are not personally responsible for their failures but see that the system is deficient. Such individuals are likely to mistrust the political system and, under certain conditions, will engage in militant protest to change it (Bandura, 1982). Being personally hopeful, they believe they can succeed even if the system tries to stop them. Persons who are angry at political and social injustice and who have high personal self-efficacy and personal and universal hopefulness often make excellent leaders in community planning and social advocacy efforts.

Applying the concept of efficacy to groups, collective efficacy is defined as a shared perception (conscious or unconscious) by the group members about the group's ability to achieve its objectives (Pecukonis & Wenocur, 1994). Collective efficacy includes, but is more than the sum of, the individual members' perceptions of their individual efficacy. It is a property of the group as a whole, like the notion of group solidarity. A positive sense of collective efficacy is shaped by the experiences of the members while in the group and by the group's interactions, as a group, with its external environment. At the same time, these experiences also contribute greatly to the feeling of personal self-efficacy that each member comes to hold. When the collectivity is a social action group, successful experiences will greatly enhance feelings of personal worth and empowerment. Experiential learning (connecting experiences with knowing about oneself and the world) also creates opportunities for political consciousness raising (Gowdy, 1994), an important ingredient in overcoming oppression, which will be discussed later.

Constructed Reality

Helping clients gain a greater degree of power over the organizations and institutions that shape their lives is an important goal of social work practice. In the previous section, we proposed that both clients and social workers are more likely to take a step in that direction if they see the world as potentially changeable rather than fixed. The constructed reality or social constructionism is an interpretive, postmodernist theory of understanding the world obtained from interaction with the world (Payne, 2005, p. 58). The interaction is symbolic interaction. The theory holds that reality is a construction in the minds of the observer. It is constructed from the putative information, stimuli, and data from the environment shaped by the observer's values, culture, and experiences. While the elements of a putative reality may be there, we experience it except as we construct it. Our constructions are always dependent on our history, experiences, assumptions, and perceptual filters we use to interpret the experience and world.

Meaning is the major consideration in the social construction of reality, and it rests on the propositions that:

• Physical reality may exist but its social meaning is constructed.
• Physical events may exist but the meaning is a social construction.
• This social construction reflects the self-interest and social power of those constructing it.

Symbolic interactionism and social constructionism hold that it is not the things themselves, but the meaning of the things that is important and constitutes reality. The meaning is socially constructed, defined, and transmitted (Berger & Luckmann, 1967; Blumer, 1969). Objective facts do not exist apart from the subjective meanings that people attach to them as they are being perceived. "Men *together* produce a human environment, with the totality of its socio-cultural and psychological formations" (Berger & Luckmann, 1967, p. 51). For example, in any society, people hold different kinds and amounts of riches, but the meaning of *rich*—who is rich and who is poor, what constitutes wealth and poverty—is subjectively experienced, socially defined, incorporated into individual consciousness or internalized through a process of socialization, and eventually taken as truth or reality. This latter process, "the process by which the externalized products of human activity attain the character of objectivity is [called] *objectivation* [italics added]" (Berger & Luckmann, 1967, p. 60).

The reason we need the objectivation process is that we are by biological necessity social animals. Humans must interact with other humans and with the various elements in their external environments in order to survive and grow, and to do this they need a certain degree of stability or order. Social order and interpretations of reality are created through this process as people talk with each other about their experiences and validate their understanding of them, and as they develop established ways of doing things to accomplish their goals. Objectivation allows us to create a shared reality (Bergen & Luckmann, 1967; Greene & Blundo, 1999).

For example, the family is an institution whose meaning is very much in flux in U.S. society. Different segments of society are contending for acceptance of their definitions of family. Some have a very restrictive conception and others have a more inclusive definition of family, based on new and different roles for men and women and changing social and economic conditions, and the recognition of a range of acceptable sexual orientations. The traditional nuclear family in which Mom, a female, stays home with the kids and Dad, a male, is the breadwinner, if there ever were many of these families, has given way to many different kinds of families—families in which both parents work, where one parent is absent, where divorce and remarriage have resulted in blended families, where same-sex parents and children constitute a family unit, and so on. And just as the meaning of family is changing, so is the meaning of home and marriage.

The relationship between human beings as the creators of reality and the reality that is the product of the process is a dialectical one. Thus the constructions human beings produce—for example, the language we use, the meanings we derive, the roles we develop, and the organizations we form—all influence future constructions in a continuous back-and-forth process. "Externalization and objectivation are moments in a continuing dialectical process" (Berger & Luckmann, 1967, p. 61). The social order that human existence requires and creates is an order that is constantly being recreated as we negotiate our daily lives together. For community workers

who must frequently help their clients as well as themselves in negotiating complicated bureaucratic systems to get resources to survive and perform valued social roles, reality is neither predetermined nor fixed for all time. Moreover, it is incumbent on practitioners to validate the experiences of the individuals and groups with whom they work, to understand and share their constructions, and to help them change the constructions when the constructions hinder their realities.

Symbols, especially language, represent the major currency of social interaction through a body of conventionalized signs and shared rules for their usage. Language and other symbols are the tools for constructing reality. People give meaning and structure to their experiences and share them through language and other symbols, and language, in turn, structures and limits our thinking and beliefs. Feminists, for example, have argued that language is a major source of categorical thinking and helps to sustain the patriarchal order. In this view, male is a dominant category and "whatever is *not male* is female" (Sands & Nuccio, 1992, p. 491). Similarly, ethnocentric thinking expressed in census reports has, until recently, treated whites as a dominant category, while African-Americans have been defined as nonwhites. Meaning changes if we categorize people by black and everyone else as nonblack. Thus, language does not merely convey information "but is believed to thoroughly mediate everything that is known" (Pardeck, Murphy, & Choi, 1994, p. 343). Language is not limited to the here and now. People can use it to record and pass on the past as well as construct a future.

We live in a symbolic universe, and we are defined by our symbols. What is the meaning to you, say, of the United States' "star-spangled banner," the "stars and bars" of the Confederacy's "bonny blue flag," or the black ancient Hindu symbol or swastika on a scarlet banner? Until the 20th century the swastika, an almost universal symbol, stood for life, power, the sun, strength, and good luck. Think about the struggle of the United Farm Workers and the meaning of the Aztec blue eagle to the struggling *compinsinos*. Box 2.1 illustrates different world – or perhaps post-world – views. Think about the meaning of so many of the historical *truths* Americans learned in elementary school, such as that

BOX 2.1.	**Cultural Constructions of Reality: Different Worlds**

I had two very different sets of great-grandparents. A paternal great-grandfather was a Baptist circuit rider in the Ozark Mountains and the Oklahoma Indian Territory. He was a "hellfire and damnation" preacher with a strong belief in the literal power of the "Word." Some people found great comfort and strength from his ministrations and counsel. Two of my maternal great-grandparents were Eastern Cherokee-Osage and had a quite different set of beliefs from my paternal great-grandfather. They believed that most things, especially living things, were part of a natural order and had part of the life spirit. Their shamen were able to minister to them and provide them with a sense of strength and worth even during the times of trouble.

Now how can this be? How can the same outcomes be achieved using two different sets of beliefs about of life and its purpose? How did they both produce results, and what has this to do with the art and science of social work intervention?

Both sets of beliefs have a system of propositions about the nature of things and how to explain reality and even occasionally predict and control reality. Essentially, both are theories. Both produced results, to a degree, with their respective clientele, and neither explanation was accepted as having value or worth by the clientele of the other. The systems of intervention and the explanatory theories were based on assumptions and beliefs that guided the construction of social reality.

Columbus discovered America, despite the obvious fact that people were living on the American continents when Columbus arrived, on their subsequent constructions of social realities.

Human organizations, institutions, and cultures develop their own ideologies and realities that reflect the composition of their membership and their most powerful stakeholders. Usually these constructions become reified; that is, they take on a life of their own or exist as entities apart from their human origins and makeup. The social constructions becomes reality. "Reification implies that man is capable of forgetting his own authorship of the human world, and further, that the dialectic between man, the producer, and his products is lost to consciousness (Berger & Luckmann, 1967, p. 89)." To paraphrase an old John Ford, John Wayne western movie, "When the social construction becomes reified, go with the social construction as truth."[1]

A third moment in the process of reality construction is internalization. Internalization is the incorporation of socially defined meanings, social constructions, into one's own consciousness though a process of socialization. Socialization is "the comprehensive and consistent induction of an individual into the objective world of a society or a segment of it" (Berger & Luckmann, 1967, p. 130). Primary socialization occurs early in childhood when the significant persons in a child's life basically teach the child what the world is about and how to behave in it. During this

process, the significant others necessarily filter objective reality for the child through the lenses of their own selective definitions and personal idiosyncrasies. As the child bonds emotionally with these significant persons, she or he begins to establish an identity that is partially a reflection of the socializing agents. As a child continues to grow and relate to an expanding and ever more complex universe, secondary socialization into many new sub-worlds proceeds, mainly though the acquisition of role-related knowledge and skills. Socialization provides the necessary social stability for societies. It imparts on the new member or child the rules for behavior and thinking. The stronger the socialization, the less need for external social controls (Galston, 2004).

Social construction theory is central to social work practice. "Starting where the client is" requires understanding the client's social constructions, and not reifying our own constructions. In the words of Saleebey (1994), "Practice is an intersection where the meanings of the worker (theories), the client (stories and narratives), and culture (myths, rituals, and themes) meet. Social workers must open themselves up to clients' constructions of their individual and collective worlds (p. 351)." Social phenomena such as health, crime, and normalcy cannot be defined simply in terms of empirical, objective facts. They are embedded in a "web of meanings, created and sustained linguistically" (Pardeck, Murphy, & Choi, 1994, p. 345), that make up our own and our clients' worlds. Effective social work practice requires skill in communications to understand and enter the assumptive worlds of our clients. "[C]lients are not merely consulted through the use of individualized treatment plans . . . but supply the interpretive context that is required for determining the nature of a presenting problem, a proper intervention, or a successful treatment outcome. This is true client-centered intervention" (Pardeck, Murphy, & Choi, 1994, p. 345). From a macro perspective, a constructionist approach also suggests that social workers help clients understand "the oppressive effects of dominant power institutions" (Saleebey, 1994, p. 358) and tune in to the countervailing knowledge available in their own communities (Reisch, Sherman, & Wenocur, 1981).

Social Exchange Theory, Social Capital, and Power

Exchange theory (Blau, 1964, pp. 88–114; Homan, 1958; Specht, 1986; Turner, 1982, pp. 242–273) is basic to community and interorganizational practice, networking, social marketing, and, indeed, all practice. Briefly, exchange theory's central proposition is that people act in their self-interest as they define their self-interest. The self-interest can be economic, social, sexual, or psychological. Exchange is the act and process of obtaining something desired from someone by offering in return something valued by the other person. The products can be tangible or intangible (such as social behavior), and the exchanges do not have to consist of the same types of products. Exchanges can include counseling and community organization services for money, adoration and praise for compliant behavior, information for status, political influence for PAC donations or for votes, and so forth. Whether an exchange actually take place depends on whether the two parties can arrive at the terms of exchange that will leave each of them better off or at least not worse off, in their own estimation, after the exchange compared with alternative exchanges possible and available to them (Nasar, 2001).

An example of a social exchange occurs when a securely middle-class donor contributes to a homeless shelter. The donor makes a monetary donation to receive intangible products rather than shelter. The donor does not expect to use the shelter either now or in the future but expects to receive good feelings of doing a generous deed, increased social status as a donor, and perhaps the rewards of a more humane social environment. The homeless shelter competes with all other alternative uses by the donor of the money that might provide the donor with good feelings, and a more humane social environment, or any other satisfaction. It's in the shelter's interests to see that the donor receives satisfaction in return for the donation.

Several conditions are necessary for exchanges to occur (Kotler, 1977):

1. At least one of the social units wants a specific response from one or more of the other social units.
2. Each social unit perceives the other social unit and is perceived of by the other social unit as being capable of delivering the benefits in return for the benefits it received. For transactions to occur, the involved parties require information about the products to be exchanged and a desire for the exchange product(s).
3. Each social unit communicates the capacity and willingness to deliver its benefits to the other social unit in return for desired benefits received. Given relevant information and desire, exchange theory holds that parties in a transaction select from all possible exchanges those that have the greatest ratio of benefits or rewards to costs. In social exchanges, this calculus is seldom as precise as in economic exchanges.

Social exchange theory is built on the operant conditioning aspects of social learning theory, an economic view of human relationships, and the pleasure–pain principle of behavior. People do things that reward them or give them pleasure and try to avoid things that punish or cost them or give pain.

All of the parties in an exchange field do not necessarily have direct relationships with each other at any given point in time. Two agencies, for example, might not have any direct transactions, but both might engage a common third organization. This is the network component of exchange theory. When Party A in an exchange field (be it an individual, a group, or an organization) can accomplish its goals without relating to Party B, and vice versa, these parties can be said to be independent of each other. However, as soon as either party cannot achieve its ends without obtaining some needed product or resource from the other and exchanges begin to occur, they can be considered interdependent. Usually, interdependent relationships are not perfectly balanced; that is, Party A may need the resources that Party B controls much more than B needs what A has to offer. In fact, B may not need what A can offer at all. In this extremely imbalanced situation, when A has no or few other options than B for the resources, A may be said to be dependent on B. Imbalances in exchange relationships are the basis for power and influence among members of an exchange field.

Most definitions of power in social exchanges stem from the Weberian notion that power is "the chance of a man or of a number of men [i.e., people] to realize their own will in a communal action even against the resistance of others who are participating in the action" (Gerth & Mills, 1958, p. 180). In other words, power is the ability to get what you want, when you want it, despite the opposition of other people, and in this case, the *you* is a decidedly masculine pronoun. Generally people exercise power to gain more and give less than those over whom power is exercised. Power is about gaining and losing, about control (Willer, 1999, p. 2).

Power is a function of the ability to control the resources that another party wants. Power is the capacity to produce intended and foreseen effects on others. Power has the intent of change in a particular way with the expectation of particular results (Willer, Lovaglia, & Markovsky, 1999, p. 231; Wrong, 1979).

Power is a gradient from none to total. Some social scientists use *influence* as a more inclusive and nuanced concept than power. Willer, Lovaglia, and Markovsky (1999, p. 230–231) define influence as the socially induced modification of beliefs, attitudes, or expectations without a use of sanctions and regardless of intent or effort to make change. We can influence behavior in certain directions even when it is not our intent to do so. Power and influence, as indicated in Box 2.2, rests on resources, coercion, and the willingness and capacity to use them.

Some authors therefore suggest that power can be usefully viewed as a medium of exchange, a commodity that can be invested or consumed depending upon gains or losses (Banfield, 1961). Parties who need resources that others control can engage in various power-balancing and -enhancing strategies in order to bring about more favorable exchanges. For the sake of discussion, let us consider Party A an as action organization, a community group that is trying to get resources from Party B, a target organization— say, a large private university in the area that has resources that A needs. Since the community group is in a dependent position in this situation because the university holds the resources the community group needs, the university is in the power position in the relationship. To reduce the university's power, the community group can adopt one of two approaches: either find some way to decrease its dependency or find some way to increase the university's need for the community group. These approaches lend themselves to the following power-balancing strategies: competition, revaluation, reciprocity, coalition, and coercion. Each of these strategies will now be described and will be applied more fully in the practice section.

Competition. Competition is controlled conflict when the parties in the competition recognize that they are seeking the same resource. Without recognition of the competition, conflict does not occur. Competition, as with most conflict, has the rules of the game between the competing parties (Deutsch, 1973; Kriesberg, 1982; Lauer, 1982). This strategy requires the community group to find more potential resource providers so that it can find other ways to meet its goals than making exchanges with the university. So long as the university has a monopoly on the resources that the community group needs, it will be dependent on the university. The university will have power. But if the community group can get the needed resources elsewhere, then the university's power will be reduced.

Reevaluation. In this strategy, the community group changes its immediate goals so as not to need the university's resources. If the university has any need for the community group's resources, it may try to maintain A's dependency on it by offering inducements or new advantages to sustain the exchange relationship.

BOX 2.2.	Power Theory

Propositions:
On Resources (Rewards)

1. If personal power is the ability to act in a desired manner, personal power ranges on a continuum from action in the face of no opposition to action in the face of extreme opposition, and
2. If social power or interpersonal power is the ability to have others or another act in a desired manner, the degree of power ranges from other(s) doing actions other(s) want to perform to other(s) doing actions other(s) don't want to perform, and
3. If action requires resources and different actions require different requisite resources, and
4. If everyone has some amount and kind of resources, and
5. If, resources are not equally distributed, *then*
6. Different actors have different requisite resources for different actions, *then*
7. Power, therefore, is not equally distributed across actions and actors.

Willingness to Act

1. If a requisite to power is the willingness or ability to use and manipulate resources to achieve ends and actions by other(s) to act, and
2. If requisite resources are not individually processed, *then*
3. Power rests on the ability to construct coalitions of requisite actors with the requisite resources.

On Coercion (Pain and Punishment)

1. If action can be induced by coercion, and
2. If coercion is the ability to impose physical, social, or psychological pain on others, and, secondarily, the ability to withhold essential resources, and
3. If actor(s) seek to avoid pain or require resources, and
4. If different actors and actions are vulnerable to different pain, and
5. If everyone has some ability to impose pain or withhold resources, and
6. If the capacity to impose pain or withhold resources is not equally distributed, *then*
7. Different actors have different capacities to impose requisite pain or withhold requisite resources to compel different actions, and
8. Power, therefore, is not equally distributed across actions and actors.

Willingness to Act

1. If a requisite to power is the willingness or ability to use and manipulate rewards, coercion, and resources to achieve ends and compel others to act, and
2. If requisite resources and the ability to coerce are not individually processed, *then*
3. Power rests on the ability to construct coalitions of requisite actors with the requisite resources or willingness and capacity to coerce.

Reciprocity. Reciprocity, the core of exchange theory, means that all gains and benefits carry with them obligations or a price. Reciprocity holds that each party in a social contract has both rights and responsibilities. Although the reciprocity relationship may not be symmetrical, it does require some complementarity. When a community accepts some responsibility for providing its members with a minimum living standard, it generally imposes corresponding behavioral expectations. The exact balance of the reciprocity is tempered by the power relationship between the parties in the relationship (Gouldner, 1960). Reciprocity will be explored more fully in Chapter 10 addressing Networking.

Coalition. A coalition is an alliance between individuals, groups, organizations, or even nation-states through which they cooperate in joint action, each pursuing self-interest but joining together for a common cause to achieve their individual goals. This alliance may be temporary or a matter of convenience. The individual community group may not have much influence over the university, but an alliance of community groups might.

Coercion. Coercion is the ability to impose physical, economic, social, and emotional and psychological pain on others, and, secondarily, the ability to withhold essential resources from a party to compel that party to do what another party wants. As physical threats and actual harm to persons and property are normally illegal and immoral, this falls outside the bounds of professional acceptability. However, coercion in the form of social and emotional pressure, damage to reputation, disruptive tactics, and withholding of resources often are used and are acceptable in community action. They may take the form of strikes, boycotts, sit-ins, and informational pickets. We distinguish physical coercion from political coercion and from the use of disruptive tactics that are normally legal, or sometimes illegal when faced with unfair laws. Coercive tactics were advocated by Alinsky (1969, 1971) as not only appropriate but essential in social action to get the target to bargain. We will discuss coercive tactics more fully in the practice section of the book.

Although the dynamics of power and exchange are important, many transactions in an exchange field do not carry heavy overtones of power. People are constantly relating to one another, exchanging information, and sharing resources without trying to extract advantages from the transaction. In fact, the more people exchange resources with each other, the greater the likelihood that reciprocal obligations will develop and that these will be governed by norms of fairness. As positive relationships develop, exchange partners who each obtain a desirable resource may be attracted to one another and may form cohesive associations such as support groups, networks, new organizations, coalitions, and the like.

In general, within the framework of social exchange theory, it is important to note that exchanges involving power require building relationships among people, making connections where none may have existed previously, and creating interdependencies. Since the potential for building relationships with other people is limitless, the implication is that power is neither limited as a resource nor confined to a set group of people. Rather, power can be viewed as a dynamic resource that is ever expandable. In the words of Lappé and Du Bois (1994):

Power, as it is being lived and learned, is neither fixed nor one-way. It is fluid. Based on relationships, it is dynamic. It changes as the attitudes and behavior of any party change. This understanding of power offers enormous possibilities: it suggests that by conscious attention to the importance of one's own actions, one can change others—even those who, under the old view of power, appear immovable. All this allows us to discover new sources of power within our reach (p. 54).

Social Capital

Social capital is an *au courant* concept and theory in the social sciences. Social capital is viewed as an individual and a collective and community trait. It is the glue holding communities together (Huysman & Wulf, 2004, p. 1). Unfortunately for clarity, there are a variety of social capital definitions identified in the literature stemming from the highly contextual nature of social capital and the complexity of its conceptualization and operationalization. The social interactions and connections producing social capital can range from the highly informal to highly structured and formal. Huysman and Wulf (2004) identify social capital as the "network of ties of goodwill, mutual support, shared language, shared norms, social trust, and a sense of mutual obligation that people can derive value from" (p. 1). Trust between people appears to be an, if not the, essential ingredient in social capital's connectiveness (Arneil, 2006, pp. 224–240). It is what people get from being a member of a community that non-members don't get. Putnam (n.d.) holds that "(t)he central idea of social capital, in my view, is that networks and the associated norms of reciprocity have value. They have value for the people who are in them, and they have, at least in some instances, demonstrable externalities, so that there are both public and private faces of social capital." The commonalities of most definitions of social capital are that they focus on social relations that have trust and productive benefits. Again, according to Putnam (2000), a community's social capital is the collective value of all its social networks and the reciprocity generated by these networks. The central idea of social capital "is that networks and the associated norms of reciprocity have value. They have value for the people who are in them, and they have, at least in some instances, demonstrable externalities, so that there are both public and private faces of social capital" (Putnam, n.d.). It is a key contributor to building and maintaining democracy.

Social capital is the social support and social obligations people and community acquire and owe through the norm of reciprocity. It is developed through the involvement of people in social interactions, social participation, and civic engagement. It is indigenous to social work's community development and stands with social justice as indispensable to community practice. Ross (1967), as discussed in Chapter 1, defined community organization as "a process by which a community identifies its needs or objectives, orders (or ranks) these needs or objectives, develops the confidence and will to work at these needs or objectives, finds the resources (internal and/or external) to deal with these needs or objectives, takes action in respect to them, and in so doing extends and develops cooperative and collaborative attitudes and practices in the community" (p. 28). Effectively, Ross is describing a process of developing social capital.

The British sociologists Moyser and Perry (1997) also emphasize the community development and social justice components of social capital:

One of the most urgent problems facing western democracies is that of 'exclusion'. Exclusion from group life means that a person lacks the 'social capital' which stems from participation in a 'network of civic engagement'. Interaction with others can, according to the theory of social capital, be expected not merely to promote personal interests and collective benefits, but also to generate a significant side-benefit of social trust which can be self-reinforcing. In turn social capital may be convertible into 'political capital' in the sense of collective efficacy and political trust. (p. 43)

While all participation and social interaction produces social capital (Putnam, n.d.). Ladd (1999) emphasizes that "face-to-face groups to express shared interests is a key element of civic life. Such groups help resist pressures toward 'mass society.' They teach citizenship skills and extend social life beyond the family" (p. 16). Wolfe (1998) appears to concur and in research for his book *One Nation After All* found that Americans believe the social capital and sense of community is depleting and the nation is becoming too tertiary and libertarian, with civic engagement and social participation giving way to the television set and the Internet. Rather than the neighborhood and community of residence as the center of social engagement, the workplace is. The workplace requires in addition to intellectual and physical labor social and emotional effort and obligations as well. Nevertheless, the workplace is not a community. It is built around ends other than social engagement (productivity and profit), and the status and authority hierarchy

necessary for work coordination extends to its other social interactions. Workplace relationships are transient, feudal relationships. Relationships reflecting the workplace gradient and relationships between equals have the element of workplace competition.

A community's level of social capital is generally directly associated with a range of positive social indicators (although not always true for individuals), from lower crime rates to happiness (Boneham & Sixsmith, 2006; Ohmer, 2008; Perry, Williams, Wallerstein, & Waitzkin, 2008; Putnam, n.d.; Pyles & Cross, 2008; Saegert & Winkel, 2004; Speer & Zippay, 2005).

However, some critics of the concept of social capital, such as Williams (2007), believe it is a less viable concept than social networks. It is social networks rather than social capital that produce meaningful public policy to address social injustice and structural inequities such as poverty, unemployment, and racism. This is because social capital is so vague a concept that it is difficult to operationalize compared to social networks. We will explore social capital again in our discussions of community and social networks.

Interorganizational Theory

Much community practice involves establishing and managing relationships with other groups and organizations. The selection of theoretical material thus far presented provides the groundwork for many of the ideas that help us understand these interorganizational relations. In this section, we try to understand the behavior of groups and organizations rather than the individuals who make them up. Conceptually, interorganizational relationships' unit of analysis is the organization or organizational subunit.

A proposition essential to interorganizational theory is that every organization is embedded in a larger network of groups and organizations that it must relate to in order to survive and prosper. Within this interorganizational network or exchange field, each organization must carve out a specific domain, or sphere of operation. Levine and White (1961, 1963) did the seminal work on domain theory. An agency's domain is the claim for resources the agency stakes out for itself based on its purpose and objectives. The organizational domain usually involves some combination of (a) human problem or need, (b) population or clientele, (c) technology or treatment methods, (d) geographic or catchment area, and (e) sources of fiscal and non-fiscal resources. While some of the domain may be shared and other parts may be in dispute, all parts cannot be shared or be in dispute if the agency is to maintain itself as a separate entity. For example, although there may be overlap, no two organizations serving the homeless will have identical domains. One may serve only women and the other, families. One may refuse substance abusers; another may accept all who come but require attendance at religious meetings. Geographic boundaries may vary. Some organizations may include an advocacy function and others only provide services to people.

The domain of an organization identifies the points at which it must relate to and rely on other organizations for resources to fulfill its mission. Mother's Kitchen, which provides hot meals to the needy in South Bostimore, will need serving, eating, and storage facilities, a supply of volunteers, a supply of food, health department approval, and so on. Joe's Van, which supplies coffee and sandwiches on winter weekends to homeless persons in South Bostimore, will need different kinds of volunteers, facilities, and supplies. Depending on an organization's domain, then, we can readily see that the structure and dynamics of its external environment will have a lot to do with the organization's ability to achieve its objectives. In some environments, resources are scarce; in others, they are plentiful. So, volunteers may be relatively easy or hard to find. There may or may not be a food bank to draw on for inexpensive staples. Some environments have many competitors or regulations, others few. During the economic recession of the early part of the 21st century, most resources, except for clients in need, became scarce. Complex organizations in dynamic environments have specialized positions or even whole departments to assist them in handling environmental transactions—for example, development and fundraising unit, a director of volunteers, a public relations department, and a lobbyist or governmental affairs division.

It is useful to conceptualize the set of external organizations and organizational subunits that a focal organization must deal with to accomplish its goals as a task environment (Thompson, 1967).

The task environment is the specific set of organizations, agencies, groups, and individuals with which the agency may exchange resources and services and with which it establishes specific modes of interaction, either competitive or cooperative, to achieve its goals and fulfill its mission. It is the part of the environment that can positively or negatively affect the agency's functioning and survival (Wernet, 1994; Zald, 1970). The task environment is influenced by the general environment's level of resources, the competition for resources by all alternative demands, the social ideology and philosophy of need meeting, and the socioeconomic demographics of the population (age distribution, family composition, income distribution, economic base, and so forth). A resource-rich task environment with a prevailing liberal ideology will support more social agencies than a poor environment with a conservative ideology.

The resources in the task environment do not constitute a system; they are merely a set of things until they are organized into a system to support the agency and its mission and objectives (Evan, 1963). While the concept of external environment is somewhat abstract and amorphous, the task environment concept can be delineated quite specifically. The task environment consists of six categories of components (Hasenfeld, 1983, pp. 61–63; Thompson, 1967). For any given organization, some environmental units may fit into more than one category.

1. *Providers of fiscal resources, labor, materials, equipment, and work space.* These may include providers of grants, contributions, fees for products or services, bequests, and so on. Organizations often have multiple sources of funds. Mother's Kitchen may receive federal funds channeled through the local mayor's office of homelessness services, as well as contributions from a sponsoring church. At the same time, Mother's Kitchen may receive space from a local church, office supplies from a local stationer, and maintenance supplies from a janitorial products company. The school of social work may be an important source of labor via fieldwork interns.

2. *Providers of legitimation and authority.* These may include regulatory bodies, accrediting groups, and individuals or organizations that

lend their prestige, support, or authority to the organization. The Council on Social Work Education (CSWE) accredits schools of social work. A school of social work may lend its support to a local agency's continuing education program. The dean of the school may serve on the board of directors of an agency serving the homeless, along with client representatives from the homeless union.

3. *Providers of clients or consumers.* These include those very important individuals and groups who make referrals to the agency, as well as the individuals and families who seek out the organization's services directly. The department of public welfare may be a major referral source of clients for Mother's Kitchen. Other clients may come on their own as word of mouth passes around on the streets. The South Bostimore Community Association may be a major source of referrals for a new health maintenance organization started by the local university hospital.

4. *Providers of complementary services.* These include other organizations whose products or services are needed by an organization in order to successfully do its job. Mother's Kitchen may use the university medical school for psychiatric consultations and a drug treatment center for substance abuse counseling services. The welfare department provides income maintenance for homeless families who use Mother's Kitchen.

5. *Consumers and recipients of an organization's products or services.* Social service agencies cannot operate without clients, a community organization cannot operate without members, and a school of social work must have students. Clients and consumers are critical to justifying an organization's legitimacy and claims for resources. So the consumers of an agency's services are the clients themselves, voluntarily or involuntarily, together with their social networks. Other organizations may also be consumers of an agency's products. For example, employers need to be available and willing to hire the graduates of the welfare department's employment training programs.

6. *Competitors.* Few organizations operate with a monopoly on consumers or clients and other resources necessary for them to function.

With human service organizations, other such agencies are frequently competing for the same clients or for fiscal resources from similar sources. Several schools of social work in the same city may compete for students and will try to carve out unique domains to reach into different markets to ensure a flow of applicants. Similarly, private family agencies are competing for clients with social work private practitioners and psychotherapists. Competition for funds is endemic to social agencies, and the competitors extend beyond the service sector. Resources for social services are invariably scarce, so the ability to compete successfully is a requirement for human services organization managers.

Interorganizational relations become truly interesting when we think about the concepts of domain and task environment as dynamic rather than static entities. Imagine an exchange field with multiple individuals, groups, and organizations, each of which has its own domains and task environments, but all of which are at least loosely connected, directly and indirectly. While enough order or consensus exists for these organizations to be able to get the resources they need to function (i.e., there is some level of domain consensus among the organizational players), thousands of exchanges are taking place. New organizational relationships are being formed and old ones altered, new needs and new information are emerging, new ideas are being created, available resources are shifting with political and economic developments, new players are entering the scene and old ones exiting, new domains are being carved out in response to new opportunities and constraints, and so on. No organizational domain is static. Modern organizational life, in short, is really interorganizational life, and it involves a continuous process of negotiation in a complex, constantly changing, and highly unpredictable environment (Aldrich, 1979; Emery & Trist, 1965). The power and exchange relations discussed in the previous section govern a good deal of this interorganizational behavior because the units of an organization's task environment represent interdependencies that the organization must establish and manage successfully to operate in its domain. These relationships and their will be discussed more fully in Chapter 10, Using Networks and Networking.

Conflict Theory

There is a natural tendency among humans and social systems to seek social order and stability. Hence the processes of socialization and social control that support order seem very acceptable, while processes involving social conflict often make us uncomfortable. Yet, as we said earlier, conflict and disorder is also a natural and inevitable aspect of human life. Conflict is a relationship where two or more parties want the same scarce domains, resources, power, status, or control over values, and both act on their desire (Coser, 1964; Deutsch, 1973). Like the dilemma discussed in Chapter 1, both can't be fully satisfied. The conflict can be physical, emotional and psychological, or both. Conflict that is controlled is competition.

The dialectical conflict perspective in sociology, as propounded by theoreticians such as Karl Marx (Feuer, 1959) and Ralf Dahrendorf (1959), can further inform social work practice. Although their images of society differ, Marx and Dahrendorf share some basic assumptions about the nature of society (Turner, 1982) that help us to see social systems as dynamic entities. Both believe that (a) social systems systematically generate conflict, and therefore conflict is a pervasive feature of society; (b) conflict is generated by the opposed interests that are inevitably part of the social structure of society; (c) opposed interests derive from an unequal distribution of scarce resources and power among dominant and subordinate groups, and hence every society rests on the constraint of some of its members by others; (d) different interests tend to polarize into two conflict groups; (e) conflict is dialectical— that is, the resolution of one conflict creates a new set of opposed interests, which, under certain conditions, spawn further conflict; and (f) as a result of the ongoing conflict, social change is a pervasive feature of society.

For Marx (Feuer, 1959), conflict is rooted in the economic organization of society, especially the ownership of property and the subsequent class structure that evolves. Labor's production, the means by which men and women create their daily subsistence of goods and services, is central to Marxist thought. The efforts to control this production of the workers by the propertied classes directs cultural values and beliefs, religion

to give moral justification to the control, other systems of ideas, social relations, and the formation of a class structure. Under capitalism, the means of production (factories, corporations) are owned by capitalists rather than by the workers and the community. Because workers must now depend on capitalists to be able to earn a living, they are rendered powerless and exploitable. Labor becomes a commodity and workers become dehumanized to be bought and sold at the lowest possible price, moved and shaped, as the needs of capital dictate. In the modern world, Marx would argue that the movement of corporations to different parts of the United States or to foreign countries to gain tax advantages and find inexpensive labor is a manifestation of the dehumanized commoditization process. But capitalism also contains the seeds of its own destruction (dialectical materialism) in the dehumanization and regimentation of the workers. Therefore, as alienation sets in among the workers, a revolutionary class consciousness begins to develop. The workers begin to challenge the decisions of the ruling class, ultimately seeking to overthrow the system and replace capitalism with socialism and community control of production and its rewards.

For Dahrendorf (1959), writing a century after Marx, industrial strife in modern capitalist society represents only one important sphere of conflict. Still, conflict is pervasive, having a structural origin in the relations of dominance and submission that accompany social roles in any organized social system from a small group or formal organization to a community or even an entire society. If an authority structure exists (that is, a structure of roles containing power differentials), Dahrendorf calls these social systems imperatively coordinated associations. The differing roles in these imperatively coordinated associations lead to the differentiation of two quasi-groups with opposing latent interests. These quasi-groups are not yet organized, but when they become conscious of their mutual positions, they do organize into manifest interest groups that conflict over power and resources. This conflict eventually leads to change in the structure of social relationships. The nature, rapidity, and depth of the resultant change depend on empirically variable conditions, such as the degree of social mobility in the society and the sanctions that the dominant group can impose. In the United States, the cultural wars reflect these conflicts.

The transformation of an aggregation of individuals who share a set of common, oppressive conditions into an interest group that will engage in conflict to change the situation is critical for conflict theorists and has relevance for social work advocates and community practitioners. A body of theories, collectively referred to as critical theories, address the common bond of oppression (Payne, 2005, pp. 227–315). They contain Freire's conscientisation theory (Freire, 1972), to help people understand and criticize how social institutions oppress them, and contemporary feminist theories. Critical theories are postmodernist, Foucaultian theories concerned with explaining the effects of power, social exclusion, and the prevailing constructions of knowledge (Chambon, Irving, & Epstein, 1999, p. xvi). For social work, critical theories "placed power and political considerations as central to all levels of practice" (Chambon, Irving, & Epstein, 1999, p. xvii). A main ingredient of the theories is the development of an awareness or consciousness of one's relative state of deprivation and the illegitimate positions of those in power. The National Organization for Women (NOW), in a manual on consciousness-raising (CR) groups, for example, wrote that "Feminist CR has one basic purpose: it raises the woman's consciousness, increases her complete awareness, of her oppression in a sexist society" (NOW, 1982, p. 3). Political CR is a method by which an oppressed group comes to understand its condition and becomes activated politically to change it (Berger, 1976, p. 122).

But developing this awareness is not easy. Marx argued that human beings are victims of a false consciousness born of the exploitive power of the capitalist system. For Gramsci, a neo-Marxist, an alliance of ruling-class factions maintains hegemony over the subordinate classes by means of ideology spread by the state, the media, and other powerful cultural institutions (Hall, 1977):

This means that the "definitions of reality," favorable to the dominant class fractions, and institutionalized in the spheres of civil life and the state, come to constitute the primary "lived reality" as such for the subordinate classes. . . . This operates, not because the dominant classes can prescribe and proscribe, in detail, the mental content of the lives of subordinate classes (they too "live" in their own ideologies), but because they strive and to a degree succeed in *framing* all competing definitions of reality *within their range*, bringing all alternatives within their horizon of thought. They set the limits—mental and structural—within which subordinate classes "live" and make sense of their subordination in such a way as to sustain the dominance of those ruling over them. (pp. 332–333)

Those who make the rules generally win, especially if they can make up new rules as they go along. A capitalist system thus finds myriad ways to induce people to believe that happiness lies in the pursuit and achievement of material ends, and as we have seen in the Great Recession, it changed the rules as it went along.

Marxist and neo-Marxist theory applied to the role of the state as a capitalist institution in capitalist society has special relevance for social workers because most social workers either work directly as agents of government or work in proprietary and nonprofit organizations dependent on state dollars and corporate donations. Unlike conservative political economists, who want to greatly reduce the role of the state in regulating market system activities and its human costs, and unlike liberals, who view the state as a potential leveling force for reducing income disparities and alleviating distress, Marxist analysts view the state in a more complicated fashion. In the long term, they see it as serving the interests of the ruling class by maintaining social stability (Piven & Cloward, 1971) and a low-wage workforce. On an ongoing basis, they argue that the state mirrors the contradictions in the capitalist system; hence it is an arena for ideological and practical struggles over the distribution of income, benefits, and rights (Corrigan & Leonard, 1979). In the words of Fabricant and Burghardt (1992), "class struggle is . . . an ongoing, complex, and contentious relationship among actors in the state, in the economy, and in other social groups struggling over the direction and extent of state intervention. Ultimately, this struggle will either enhance the legitimacy of social services through a combination of expansion and restructuring . . . or encourage greater accumulation and unfettered private investment—with the resultant industrialization of social services" (p. 52).

If social workers and managers of social service agencies can become conscious and critical of themselves as actors in this struggle, they can share their awareness and analysis with their clients, and they can resist treating the problems of individual clients only as private troubles rather than as systemic dysfunctions.

Additional Frameworks

Explanatory frameworks based on concepts of motivation, ecology, critique, difference, and complexity can also be applied to community practice. Key ideas will be briefly sketched here. These frameworks relate to the postmodern school, a multidisciplinary, intellectual movement highly influential since the 1980s, that challenges prior modern theories and assumptions (Butcher, Banks, Henderson with Robertson, 2007; Chambon, Irving, & Epstein, 1999; Irving & Young, 2002; McCormack, 2001; Payne, 2005). A significant component of many forms of postmodernism theories is their more explicit recognition of the political, power, and social constructionism in the formulations of social science theory.

Ecological Theories

Ecological theories draw on environmental, biological, and anthropological precepts and metaphors to highlight interconnections between social, geographic, and other factors. Ecological theories are a subset of systems theories. In social work they include the ecological approach and person-in-environment (P-I-E). Numerous illustrations make the point. Globalization has reinforced the ecological approaches. Drought in Australia increases the price of food in Mexico. Diseases are exchanged between China and New York and between Africa and the United States. U.S. movies and music influence cultures around the globe. Spicy foods from Third World countries replace blander food in Western diets. An ecological framework underscores such transactions, adaptations, and shaping (Kuper & Kuper, 1999).

Ecological theories remind us that human beings have ever-changing physical and cultural environments. Within 50 years, as some have predicted, most of the earth's people will live in areas directly challenged by the rising sea levels due to global warming. How will this change in physical environment affect our grandchildren and the relationships between nations? Cultural environments also shape things as they change. Recognitions of gay unions as marriages will alter a series of legal statutes and military regulations. Will it bring greater general tolerance? Group advocacy has created a new cultural perspective that has now made it easier for all people to exercise civil rights.

Ideas about ecology and ecosystems of human groups have influenced the helping professions (Germain & Gittelman, 1995; Pardeck, 1996). Factors that affect social functioning and a new orientation for intervention include the following:

- Viewing context to be as important as the immediate situation
- Seeing how mutuality and interdependence suggest values and obligations beyond family, neighborhood, or nation to a global society
- Examining ways communities organize to maintain themselves in given areas
- Looking for ecological, natural, and impersonal influences in addition to personal causes of human problems

Critical Theories

Critical theories, discussed earlier, have a macro-orientation, an interest in the social totality and the social production of meaning, and a focus on criticizing and changing contemporary society (Chambon, Irving, & Epstein, 1999; Payne, 2005, pp. 227–250; Ritzer, 1992, p. 149). Critical theories are conflict theories and radical in ideology. A significant component of critical theories is their explicit recognition of the political, power, and social constructionism in the formulations of social science theory. Critical theory focuses on dominating institutions and structures and how the system works and on large-scale capitalistic structures and how they exploit local environments. It prompts compelling questions such as: "How is it possible that penal systems could have expanded so rapidly and that corporate interests could have become so ensconced in punishment practices without a significant critical discourse developing?"

(Washington, 1999, p. 1). The United States has the highest incarceration rate in the world[2] and a homicide rate by firearms twice that of the next ranked country.[3] For most of the 20th century, the U.S. incarceration rate was about one-tenth of one percent, about the same as for other democratic, industrial nations. By the end of the Bush II presidency, the incarceration rate was up approximately 10 percent. Black imprisonment was over seven times higher than whites, up from four times higher in the middle of the 20th century. For both blacks and whites, the rates are higher than for any democratic nation in history (Cusac, 2009). America appears by the data to have become an exceptionally criminal nation or one with a very harsh justice system, or perhaps a bit of both. And the justice and penal systems are heavily privatized.

Critical theorists are aware of the loss of community and the need for meaningful discourse about fundamental values. They see the need for interrogation of knowledge and the received—all that comes to us as rules or givens (Swenson, 1998). Thus, rather than studying prejudice in an individual or group or legislative context, analysts also will study the role of MTV, the music cable television show watched by young people; for example, what are the cumulative effects of pro-violence, homophobic, sexist lyrics of rap musicians aired regularly on young listeners, or the growth of a proprietary society? Or, analysts might examine manipulations underlying the programming formats used by public television or by Univision and Telemundo. What does specialized television reveal about underlying patterns of culture? In social work application, professionals can seek to unmask forces in the community that perpetuate inequity and injustice or hate such as talk radio, politicians, and fundamentalist clergy.

We should challenge passivity. Here are some compelling facts on deaths in America. U.S. vital statistics reveal that the number of gun deaths for 2001 in the United States for all reasons (homicides, suicides, accidents, and reason not known) was over 29,250,[4] the number of deaths from flu was 63,729,[5] and the number of deaths from terrorism, essentially the 9/11 attack, was 3,030, with another 2,337 injuries.[6] All the deaths are tragic and the nation expended billions and reoriented itself, its government, and attitude toward foreign nationals after 9/11 to prevent another 9/11, although the deaths were less than 11% of the gun deaths and 5% of the flu deaths for 2001. The nation expanded gun availability and has done little to ensure universal flu vaccinations. Gun and flu deaths can be greatly reduced for little public and private cost. Gun and flu deaths are neither more natural nor inevitable than terrorism, and result in far more deaths to Americans than does terrorism. The reasons for the inversion of public attention compared to deaths should be explored. It can't be the number of deaths and threat to life. What are the basic motivators? At the most basic level, critical theory can help social workers grasp the connections between individual insight and societal change (Dean & Fenby, 1989).

Feminist Social Theories

Feminist social theories (there is no single feminist theory) examine the oppressive effects of power in gender social roles and relations. They are concerned with power, oppression, power sharing, consciousness raising in both genders, and social justice (Hardina, 2002; Payne, 2005, pp. 251–268). The differentiation of people, at home and abroad, that sometimes leads to "honor killings" of women and girls, dress and submission requirements for women, and increased use of date-rape drugs has traditionally been discussed as biology, customs, religion, or atrocities. Feminist theories, as critical theory, examines the gender power needs that underlie the culture and tradition. Growing out of a social movement and critical theory approach to social relations, feminist theories remain critical and activist, seeking world betterment, and may be the only theories in which those who developed them benefit so directly from the insights they provoke (Tong, 1992). Yet, they share much with other multidisciplinary, contemporary critical theories when feminist theories ask us to:

- relinquish conventional wisdom, thought categories, and dichotomies or binaries
- interrogate traditional beliefs about roles, behavior, socialization, work, conception
- examine as fundamental the use of power and oppression in gender social roles and relations.

"Where are the women?" While Marxism encourages us to see the world from the perspective of workers rather than bosses, feminism asks us to consider the vantage point of what traditionally was the invisible half of humanity. For instance, "feminist scholars reveal how gendered assumptions help to determine whose voices are privileged in ethnographic accounts" (Naples, 2000, p. 196). Among others, Hartsock (1998) introduced the idea of standpoint theory and feminist epistemology (ways of knowing). Feminist theories suggest that we question formal knowledge and core assumptions (Hyde, 1996; Kemp, 2001), since so much emanates from male-dominated scholarship.

For decades, the woman-focused perspective was considered more ideological than theoretical. Then, scholars began to realize how much had been missing from their usual scope of inquiry because women were seldom the objects of study, and their day-and-night experiences were so often ignored (Smith, 1999). Many fields have changed since addressing the question: "And what about the women?" (Lengermann & Niebrugge-Brantley, 1990). "The struggle against misogyny and for equality led to a broad array of social concerns: Social hierarchy, racism, warfare, violence [sports, domestic violence, pornography, and rape] and environmental destruction were seen to be the effects of men's psychological need for domination and the social organization of patriarchy" (Abercrombie, Hill, & Turner, 1994, pp. 162–163). In your reviewing of feminist theories, consider and compare the 2005 Roberts, 2006 Alito, and 2009 Sotomayor Kagan Senate Judiciary Committee hearings for the U.S. Supreme Court on style, tone, and content of the senators' questions to the nominees.

Insights about the role of gender have led social work to take a closer look at identity, difference, domination, and oppression. Concepts from feminist theories also have furthered an interest in experiential knowledge, personal narrative (telling your story), the actualities of people's living, and bodily being (Harris, Bridger, Sachs, & Tallichet, 1995; Tangenberg, 2000). Davis (2002) argues that the new prominence of narrative in at least nine academic disciplines relates to renewed emphasis on "human agency and its efficacy" (p. 3). He goes on to note that earlier social movement theorists seemed stuck

on "structural and interest-oriented explanations, to the near exclusion of ideational factors (p. 4)." Narrative-based theories have the goal of recognition, an emphasis on how categories shape the way we see the world, insights regarding privilege, and an affirmation of resiliency. All of these features are common to new frameworks about race, ethnicity, disability, and sexual orientation as well as gender (Weed & Shor, 1997).

The application of feminist theories is becoming more common in contemporary community practice (Handy & Kassam, 2007; Magee & Huriaux, 2008; Mizrahi, 2007; Mizrahi & Lombie, 2007). Mizrahi's (2007) examination of feminist organizers found that two related themes emerged regarding participants' styles: (1) a developmental approach that focused on the relationship between the self/individual and the group/collective, and (2) an inclusive holistic approach. Feminist theories in practice, whatever the gender of the practitioner, aspire to give voice in societal discourse to previously silenced persons.

Chaos Theory

Chaos theory and general systems theory stress mathematical interrelationships. Systems theory assumes order, integration, and logic, whereas chaos or complexity theory examines that which is less easily diagrammed. Newton's mechanical, determined universe, similar to positivist social science's view, is being replaced by one that is less predictable and more lifelike (Elsberg & Powers, 1992). Social work practice involves many components, changeable conditions, endless occurrences, and nonlinearity. Gleick (1987, p. 24) explains that "nonlinearity means that the act of playing the game has a way of changing the rules." Each client and case brings a unique twist to what may be a common situation, and the act of practice modifies the situation.

With its complexity of social environments, our profession can certainly relate to a dynamic view of reality in which seemly random events and behavior can change the whole picture. For instance, the 2000 U.S. election made a mockery of academic models predicting who would be elected president; the predictors view the result as an outlier or random shock. Chaos scientists say, hypothetically, that a butterfly in Tokyo creating Lilliputian turbulence might contribute—in combination with other events—to a storm in New York (Grobman, 1999; Ward, 1995). This notion of amplifying effects is suggested in the title of an article by Edward Lorenz: "Can the flap of a butterfly's wing stir a tornado in Texas?" By curious coincidence, the "butterfly ballots" in one Florida county helped determine the outcome of a presidential election in favor of a Texan (whose brother was governor of Florida).

The postmodern scientific mind views the universe as constituted of forces of "disorder, diversity, instability, and non-linearity" (Best, 1991, p. 194). Unlike a linear analysis that might diagram regularity, parts, and progressions, a nonlinear analysis may sketch irregularity and what interferes, cooperates, or competes. Despite its name, chaos theory is not about total disorder because "even apparently random disorder may sometimes be patterned and to some extent accessible to probabilistic prediction" (Mattaini, 1990, p. 238), especially in short-term or nearby situations. Chaos theorists are intrigued by how tiny changes in initial conditions can have major consequences (Gleick, 1987). Paradoxically, complexity theory also relates to the concept of self-organization or spontaneous emergence of order (Kauffman, 1995). Mattaini (1990) notes the relevance to social work: "This theory offers promise for practice within a contextual perspective, while suggesting the need for ongoing monitoring of results of intervention that may not be entirely predictable" (p. 237).

Complex phenomena tend to be counterintuitive and to require information not yielded by simple models. Forrester (1969) states that complex systems are counterintuitive in that "they give indications that suggest corrective action which will often be ineffective or even adverse in results" (p. 9). For example, public housing in an area can deteriorate its decline due to reduced tax revenue for services by taking property off the tax rolls, reducing property values and hence taxes, and increasing demands for services by aggregating poor people. Such ideas as counterintuition help us think about cause and effect in a more analytical way, show us how to acquire new understandings, and allow us to view chaos

as a beneficial force (Bolland & Atherton, 1999; Warren, Franklin, & Streeter, 1998; Wheatley, 2001).

The Field of Action in Community Practice

For direct service practitioners, community practice often starts with understanding the community and cultural and community influences on themselves and their clients as mutual participants in the larger system (Pardeck, 1996). It moves to community assessment for finding relevant resources, discovering or building referral and support networks, and ultimately perhaps social action. Practice interventions move to a social system focus either to address and resolve system malfunctions (e.g., to replace a local school that has become physically unsafe) or to create development opportunities. To do that, we need theories that will help us to understand the behavior of individuals as community actors; the behavior of community groups and organizations; relationships of power and exchange among individuals, groups, and organizations; and individual and group ideologies and reality constructions (Silver, 1980).

A useful way of conceptualizing community practice, then, is as a series of interventions that take place in a field of action or exchange. The important components of the field include:

- individuals, groups, and organizations or organizational subunits
- the main elements that these members exchange—namely, resources and information
- influential aspects of the relationships among the members—namely, power balances and rules of exchange, as well as individual and group ideologies, including values, beliefs, and feelings

Imagine a community practitioner addressing the spread of acquired immunodeficiency syndrome (AIDS) among adolescents in a particular community by building a coalition that will mount an AIDS education project. The social worker need to consider the potential elements of the arena in which the interventions will take place (the action field) to assess the scope of the project. Because the problem is complex, the composition of the action field will also be complicated. Elements in the field also will vary in importance at different points in the intervention process. Some of the main components of an action field in this case might be the following:

1. Adolescent groups, gangs, organizations, informal cliques or friendship networks, and individuals (by no means a monolithic group)
2. Parent groups and individuals (also not a monolithic body)
3. Groups and organizations serving adolescents, such as high schools, recreation centers, clubs, churches, and so on
4. Public health and social service organizations (nonprofit, for-profit, and governmental), such as the health department and the organization you work for, the AIDS outreach service of the health clinic, Planned Parenthood, and the department of health and mental hygiene of your state
5. Civic and community associations, such as PTAs, sororities and fraternities, neighborhood associations, and the Knights of Columbus
6. Churches and religious organizations
7. Elected officials and governmental bodies such as legislative finance committees
8. The media, including possible web networking services
9. Ideologies of these individuals and groups, including the way they view AIDS and the problem among adolescents, as well as their political, social, professional, and religious beliefs or philosophies
10. Relationships of exchange and power differentials that may exist among the members of the field, and the information and resources that the various members may control

Obviously, just knowing the potential components of the action field does not tell the worker how to go about building an effective coalition. The professional needs some theories about how this community operates to decide what to do to accomplish the task. The worker also needs to know something about how the members of the field relate to each other and how they might react to the proposed project.

Traditional Models of Community Organization

Classic Conceptual Scheme

Like numerous formulations of community practice and social change, organizing has been categorized in a variety of ways (Fisher, 1995; Mondros & Wilson, 1990). Weil (1996) holds that "A conceptual model or framework is a way of putting together concepts or ideas. It provides a design for how to think about or illustrate the structure and interworking of related concepts—a structure, a design or a system. A conceptual model is intended to illustrate the operation of a theoretical approach, and to build or demonstrate knowledge. . . . Conceptual models of community practice illustrate the diverse ways that community practice is conceived" (pp. 1–2). Weil (1996) goes on to say that models of social intervention hold an intermediate place between theory and practice skills, since they "embody theory and illustrate the actions that put theory into practice." Hardina (2002, p. 45) gives practice models a function of linking theory, intervention, and outcomes.

A word is in order regarding models as we begin to explore them. Models are not empirical reality. They are abstractions, simplifications, of empirical reality, but should contain the essential elements and structure of realty. Models are ideas with empirical referents, but they are not the empirical referents themselves. Models are complex ideas and as such they tend to be summative.

Most social workers are familiar with Rothman's highly referenced conceptual model of community practice. If not, we will briefly review it here. In 1968, Rothman devised a three-pronged model, a community practice framework that social work students everywhere have studied ever since. As mentioned in Chapter 1, the prongs are locality development, social planning, and social action. In Rothman's (1996) own words, his three approaches include:

1. the community-building emphasis of locality development, with its attention to community competency and social integration
2. the data-based problem-solving orientation of social planning/social policy, with its reliance on expertise

3. the advocacy thrust of social action, with its commitment to fundamental change and social justice (p. 71)

Application of the Model[7]

The Rothman model is easy to apply in real life. For example, Harriman, a low-income rural mountain community of about 6,000 people in Roane County, Tennessee, coal country, suffered one of the worst environmental disasters in modern America when, at about 1 a.m. on December 22, 2008, the wall of the Tennessee Valley Authority's Kingston Fossil Plant's colossal 80-acre pond, filled with fly ash from burning coal for electricity, collapsed, releasing a 1-billion-gallon sea of sludge, covering countryside and waterways. The tidal surge crumpled docks, wiped out roads and railroad tracks, and ingested a small island. The disaster was the product of all level of government's failure to do their job. Although no one was harmed, there are long-term health effects from the ash's harmful contaminants, including arsenic. In addition to property and home losses, there are the threats to Roane County's economy and culture in the beautiful Appalachian hill country.

Community intervention is imperative. Intervention modes will overlap. No single approach to organizing is sufficient, and all are necessary for social justice. The degree of use depends on how the situation unfolds.

Locality Development

A community organizer engaged in locality development would recruit Harriman residents to work together to supervise and involve

BOX 2.3.	Rothman's (1968) Community Practice Modalities and Conceptual Foundations

Concept or variable	Locality development	Social planning	Social action
Domain emphasis	Domain is the local community; development of a community domain	Emphasis on functional community domain linkages and consensus	Recognition of action group's domains, redistribution of task environment's domains
Nature of exchange	Positive, internal to community	Positive between community structures, institutions, organizations	Positive with action group and coalition, often negative with targets
Networking	Within community, across and within interest areas, broad consensus	Within functional areas, linking to a goal, consensus of core functions	Like-minded to be part of action group, movement of targets into action group, advocacy
Conception of community	Horizontal local geographic area emphasized and valued over vertical linkages.	Functional community, often beyond locality	Primarily functional within locality and emphasis on a functionally disadvantaged group
Power and empowerment	Power shared, community empowerment a primary goal	Power focused, emphasize concerting power for goals achievement, empowerment a byproduct	Power redistribution from target to action group, empowerment of action group a primary goal
Task or process emphasis	Process	Task	Task external to action group, process within
Skills most emphasized	Enabling, coordinating, mediating, teaching	Fact gathering, analyzing, facilitating, implementing	Advocacy, brokering, negotiating, bargaining, teaching

themselves in the work of range of governmental and quasi-governmental agencies from the Tennessee Valley Authority, Roane County governmental agencies, the Environmental Protection Agency, the Tennessee Department of Environment and Conservation, and the Army Corps of Engineers, among others. It is essential that community residents be involved to monitor and work with these agencies as the agencies had failed them in the past. There are also a range of voluntary agencies involved, such as Greenpeace, Southern Alliance for Clean Energy, the Southern Environmental Law Center, and, most importantly, United Mountain Defense (UMD). UMD engaged in a locality development function by engaging in door-to-door active "listening projects" to better understand the needs of the community and organizing community meetings. The locality development was necessary to build community solidarity for subsequent legal and social action.

Social Planning

The Harriman community, UMD, and the myriad other agencies engaged in social planning in their efforts to identify appropriate funding resources, such as designation as a Superfund site, Community Development Block Grants, the Appalachian Regional Commission, and the Small Towns Environment Program, and to spur local and state government to use federal stimulus funds. Harriman is faced with the task of rebuilding itself, along with the cleanup.

Social Action

It was imperative that Harriman residents become activists. Political, legal, and social action is necessary to make sure that the Tennessee Valley Authority and the other negligent agencies responsible for the disaster be held accountable. Fortunately, the community has advocates such as UMD, the Southern Environmental Law Center, Earth Justice, and Greenpeace.

Locality or Community Development

Locality development seeks to pull together diverse elements of an area by using individual and collective strengths to improve social and economic conditions. Community (locality) development and building situs is a geographically defined target area, ideally with some degree of shared social bonding and identification. It recognizes community assets, with the people being the greatest asset, and available resources as well as community needs. Locality development is an enabling and social capital building approach with community participation essential. Its process goal is collective change to empower disadvantaged citizens to more effectively define and advance their life chances. Locality development is comprehensive development to integrate economic, physical, and human development. Inevitably it requires social action.

Rothman (1987) turns to pioneer Arthur Dunham for development themes—"democratic procedures, voluntary cooperation, self-help, development of indigenous leadership, and educational objectives" (p. 5)—that are still relevant today. Community processes are to build community cohesion and social capital. Community empowerment is a primary goal. Community empowerment and collective efficacy, as well as the individual self-efficacy of the participants, are products of successful community actions and projects. New voices are heard. Difficult people must be heard and involved, and their strengths added to the community. The locality developer role calls for self-discipline, suggests Rothman (2000): "The role is complicated and in some respects runs against certain human propensities, calling on practitioners to stay in the background and neutralize their contribution; to give credit to local participants rather than to themselves; to maintain positive working relationships with opponents and vexatious elements in the community; and to refrain from proposing solutions, even when practitioners possess requisite knowledge, so that solutions will emerge from local residents themselves" (p. 103).

Social Planning

Social planning uses data, theory, history, and the present to objectively construct a future scenario of reality. Social uses available data and collects new data to define, create, and meet future social conditions efficiently. It is a systematic, task-oriented style of organizing requiring mastery of data collection and analysis, social theories, and bureaucratic complexity. Social planning's community development function often requires development and coordination of community agencies' services to meet community needs, facilitate and translate between groups with different agendas, and educate and raise the consciousness for segments of the groups not initially interested in the social problem and possible solutions. To ensure the involvement of a cross-section of the population, the social planner will become a community developer and hold meetings and hearings and secure representatives from different sectors. The social planner plays the roles of community liaison, facilitator, outreach worker, interpreter of regulations and policies, translator between groups with different knowledge bases, and consciousness raiser for groups not initially interested in the needs of the target population.

Social Action

Activists on the right and left have used tactics associated with this model. The social action approach can involve either radical, fundamental change goals or reformist, incremental goals. It can pursue social justice or a totalitarian goal, although both right and left generally use the language of social justice and civil rights. Social action organizations range from the right's Christian Coalition, Human Life Alliance, and the Institute for Justice to more centrist and leftist organizations such as Americans United for Separation of Church and State, UMD, and Southern Poverty Law Center. Social action confronts—in different degrees and with a variety of tactics—hierarchical power relationships within a community in order to benefit people who feel powerless, socially vulnerable populations, or those locked out of decision processes. Social action's aim is to develop, redistribute, and control community statuses and resources, especially social power, and to alter community behavior patterns and relations.

The adversarial methodologies of social action are used by citizen coalitions throughout the world. U.S. farmers brought their tractors to Washington to disrupt traffic, anti-abortion zealots blocked clinics and harassed potential patients, students took to the streets in Iran after its 2009 election, anti-health care reform "Astroturf" organizers yelled down Congress members at 2009 community forums, and workers held sit-ins in factories closed in the 2009 recession. The aim can be to make basic changes in major institutions or community practices (Rothman, 1987, p. 6) or in the policies of formal organizations (p. 18). Social action tactics include consciousness-raising activities, coalitions, non-violent direct action (including inaction as strikes) and civil disobedience, and political and social marketing campaigns. We will discuss these tactics more fully later in the text.

Composite Nature of Community Organization

As Rothman recognized, actual organizations and ongoing projects use all three organizing approaches combined in various forms. The efforts in Harriman by the varying groups, probably still in process, combined the three approaches. In actual practice, clinical and community work methodologies overlap, case management requires advocacy, and social action requires a locality development in its coalition development and social planning skills. The Highlander Research and Education Center outside Knoxville, Tennessee, has been combining education and training with action and community development, social planning, and social action so the people of the South can engage their environmental and social problems. Dans la Rue (On the Street) in Montreal, Canada, creatively combined locality development with social action. Initially, street kids were asked what they needed from a mobile van designed to serve them in their territory, and eventually a shelter was created that the street kids staffed and named the Bunker. Such locality development service projects led to advocacy and then to "the organization of a demonstration against the increased number of police harassment and brutality cases reported" by homeless residents of the city.

Related Community Intervention Model

Based on assessment, Rothman wanted community practitioners to fit their mode of action to the situation at hand. According to Jeffries (1996) of the United Kingdom, "Rothman's identification of three models of community organization practice has permeated the community work literature on both sides of the Atlantic" (p. 102). Reworking Rothman, Jeffries proposes a four-square model of community practice. To oversimplify, Jeffries' approach renames Rothman's first two modes and divides social action into nonviolent direct action and coalition building and campaigns.

Jeffries (1996) renames locality development "capacity and awareness promotion" because she believes "the ability is there, it just needs to be given a chance to blossom" (p. 115). This approach or mode of organizing starts with the personal concerns of neighborhood residents and moves on to "developing or giving scope for and recognition to the skills, or capacities of community groups" (p. 114). Community workers in this mode may call upon their own "interpersonal, educational and group work skills" (p. 115). She renames social planning "partnership promotion" because, rather than facilitating service delivery, the current emphasis is on collaborative planning with the community "to enable the community to act for itself" (p. 114). Ultimately, there could be "community management of services or community economic development" (p. 114) through this mode of organizing. In the third approach, having developed confidence and conviction—often from capacity and awareness promotion activities—community members can be ready to "get the attention of those in authority . . . and an unsympathetic power structure" (p. 116) using the nonviolent direct action mode of organizing. Community workers in this mode will strive to "coalesce interests into action groups" (p. 115). Such change-oriented protest work, often local or legislative in nature, can be contrasted with social campaigns:

Clearly social campaigns have long been a key feature not only of single issue organizing but also of radical, change-oriented social movements. While the former often have a more specific objective and may align themselves with organizational elites, the latter are more comprehensive in scope. They may be seeking social justice or be promoting an ecological consciousness in society. . . . These days campaign organizers can take advantage of information technology to build country-wide and international campaign coalitions. Yet to generate the mass mobilization that may be necessary to take on multi-nationals or an unsympathetic government, it is important also to have strong community level organization. (Jeffries, 1996, p. 117)

Thus, Jeffries formulates four up-to-date, relevant, and serviceable characterizations of organizing. We suggest an example for each mode (our examples are in brackets):

- Capacity and awareness promotion [Amerindian tribal gaming as economic development]
- Partnership promotion [local neighborhood–police anticrime efforts]
- Nonviolent direct action [Philadelphia voters confronting city government officials protesting library closing as cost-savings]
- Social campaigns [passing health care legislation]

British community practice theorists (Butcher, Banks, Henderson with Robertson, 2007) also have developed another related model of community practice that unites Rothman's three modalities. The model is labeled Critical Community Practice and is rooted in social justice and critical theory. Critical community practice is less a package of methodologies and more an approach to community practice. It entails an "open-minded, reflective and thoughtful approach" or a "critical consciousness" to practice with a careful attention to the context of practice. The model also embraces a strong normative dimension of values and assumptions of social justice. There are *oughts* and *shoulds* in the model, not just what works. The model requires a holistic view of goals, context, content, and values and norms (Henderson, 2007, pp. 9–13).

A Note on the Uses and Limitations of Theories and Models

This chapter has featured an array of theories and models that community practitioners should know. We now leave the reader with several caveats regarding social science, theories, and models. First, ideology is inherent in the social sciences and in their resultant theories and constructions of reality (Bisman & Hardcastle, 1999). Theories are developed not only from our observations of nature but also from the paradigms and their underlying ideologies used to guide the observations. Paradigms and their ways of finding out about nature and have, according to Kuhn (1970), strong value and ideological components. They are, in fact, largely ideology. Paradigms organize and order our perceptions of nature according to their rules. Some of the theories and models are descriptive; others are prescriptive. Some of the theories simply describe certain aspects of nature, of human behavior and interaction. Other theories and models prescribe what should be and what should be done by social workers.

The models are not empirical reality but are mental constructions of reality. Community practitioners should take care not to reify the models—not to make the models reality (McKee, 2003). Rather, they should use the models to guide, construct, and understand the complexities of reality.

Our view and construction of reality strongly reflect symbolic interactionism. Blumer (1969), a leading symbolic interaction theorist, held that symbolic interactionism "does not regard meaning as emanating from the intrinsic makeup of the thing that has meaning, nor does it see meaning as arising through a coalescence of psychological elements in the person. Instead, it sees meaning as arising in the process of interaction between people. . . . Thus, symbolic interactionism sees meaning as social products, as creations that are formed in and through the defining activities of people as they interact" (pp. 4–5).

Symbolic interaction's emphasis, similar to that of assessment and case theory in practice, is on meaning. People tend to define, construct, and give meaning to their world partly as a result of their interactions with others, as we discuss more fully in Chapter 3. A practitioner needs to understand the meaning of the interactions and the social environment to the client, the client's system, and the other systems of the change process if the practitioner is ever to understand the client's behavior. The client's constructions and meanings of reality, and hence the client's world and opportunities, can be improved with changes in the client's social interactions. A community practice task is to help the client establish new community interactions and hence to construct new realities with new meanings (Pozatek, 1994). Theory gives us a start on grasping what is happening around and within us, and practice models stimulate our imagination so we can make an effective beginning. Theory is not inherently healing, liberating, or innovative. It fulfills this function only when we ask that it do so and direct our theorizing towards this end. In summary, theories and models guide community practitioners. However, abstractions alone are insufficient. As stated earlier, in social work practice, such frameworks are melded with the political and the ideological.

Discussion Exercises

1. *"The law, in its majesty equality, forbids the rich as well as the poor to sleep under bridges, to beg in the streets, and to steal bread"* (Anatole France, The Red Lily (Le Lys Rouge), *1894, p. 89). Analyze and explain the statement from each theoretical perspective. Do conclusions differ?*
2. *Right out of our communities:*
   - *A group of affluent high school athletes takes a neighborhood girl with an IQ of 64 into a basement to sexually abuse her.*
   - *Members of a city council—citing tradition— refuse to move their town to higher ground, even with federal help. So once a decade the low-lying section, where poorer residents live, floods and the rest of the community pitches in to clean up.*

Society often discusses complex motives in actual situations like those above. But aren't the following positive stories, pulled from newspapers, equally relevant to social work?

   - *A political dissident gives up his career and easy life because of his democratic principles but, after years, emerges from disgrace as a powerful national leader.*
   - *A teenager forgoes the offer of a car and instead gives the money to a cause.*
   - *A 7-year-old collects 1,000 suitcases for foster children so they no longer have to carry their belongings around in garbage bags.*
   - *A student spends three years in high school creating a course (for credit) in peace studies.*
   - *A man sells his business and shares $130 million of the proceeds with his employees (who keep their jobs under the new management) to recognize their hard work.*

What motivates people? Do motivation theories suggest that motivations can be shaped? What can community practitioners glean from theory to understand, encourage, or stop any of the above actions? Divide into two teams. Pick two theories from the chapter. Then debate whether the 7-year-old's efforts are useless; that is, by collecting the suitcases for children in foster care, was the 7-year-old just treating the symptoms? Just making the "haves" feel better? Or is a need for dignity met by this act, so that the effort should be appreciated?

3. What is the difference between feminist theory and feminism, in your view? What do radical-right commentators such as Rush Limbaugh mean by "Femi-Nazi"?

4. Do you know a professional whose work involves locality development, social planning, or social action? How does that person's work differ from Jack Rothman's models?

5. Does your fieldwork involve any interventions described by Jeffries (capacity and awareness promotion, partnership promotion, nonviolent direct action, social campaigns)?

6. Analyze anti-globalization street protests, first in theoretical terms and then as models of organizing.

Notes

1. The movie's line given by the editor of the *Shinbone Star* Maxwell Scott to Senator Ransom Stoddard, the man who shot Liberty Valance, but didn't. "When the legend becomes fact, print the legend." John Ford's *The Man Who Shot Liberty Valance* (1962).
2. Data from http://webb.senate.gov/pdf/prison-factsheet4.html retrieved July 17, 2009.
3. Data from http://www.cdc.gov/mmwr/preview/mm wrhtml/00046149.htm) retrieved July 17, 2009.
4. Retrieved July 20, 2009 http://www.vpc.org/fact_ sht/fadeathwithrates65-04.pdf
5. Retrieve July 20, 2009 http://www.wrongdiagnosis. com/f/flu/deaths.htm
6. Retrieved July 20, 2009 http://www.september11news.com/911Art.htm
7. Information for this section primarily relies on: Campo-Flores, A. (2009, July 18). The day after: Harriman, Tenn. *Newsweek Web Exclusive.* Retrieve July 20, 2009 from http://www.newsweek.com/ id/207445; Mansfield, D., Report blasts TVA on coal ash storage after spill. *Solon.com.*, Retrieved July 22, 2009 from http://www.salon.com/wires/ ap/us/2009/07/21/D99J4V485_us_coal_ash_spill/ index.htm; No such thing as clean coal. Retrieved July 20, 2009 from http://www.unitedmountaindefense.org/and the many blogs from UMD's blog, http://dirtycoaltva.blogspot.com/

References

Abercrombie, N., Hill, S., & Turner, B. S. (1994). *Dictionary of sociology.* New York: Penguin.

Aldrich, H. E. (1979). *Organizations and environments.* Englewood Cliffs, NJ: Prentice Hall.

Alinsky, S. A., (1969). *Reveille for radicals.* New York: Vintage Books.

Alinsky, S. A., (1971). *Rules for radicals.* New York: Vintage Books.

Arneil, B. (2006). *Diverse communities: The problem with social capital.* New York: Cambridge University Press.

Bandura, A. (1982). Self-efficacy mechanism in human agency. *American Psychologist*, 37, 122–147.

Bandura, A. (1986). *Social foundations of thought and action.* Englewood Cliffs, NJ: Prentice Hall.

Bandura, A. (1989). Social cognitive theory. *Annals of Child Development*, 6, 1–60.

Bandura, A. (1997). *Self-efficacy: The exercise of control.* New York: W. H. Freeman & Co.

Banfield, E. (1961). *Political influence.* New York: The Free Press.

Berger, P. L. (1976). *Pyramids of sacrifice: Political ethics and social change.* Garden City, NY: Anchor Books.

Berger, P. L., & Luckmann, T. (1967). *The social construction of reality.* Garden City, NY: Anchor Books.

Best, S. (1991). Chaos and entropy: Metaphors in postmodern science and social theory. *Culture as Science*, 11, 188–226.

Bisman, C. D. (1994). *Social work practices: Cases and principles.* Pacific Grove, CA: Brooks/Cole.

Bisman, C., & Hardcastle, D. (1999). *Integrating research into practice: A model for effective social work.* Pacific Grove, CA: Brooks/Cole, Wadsworth.

Blau, P. M. (1964). *Exchange and power in social life.* New York: Wiley.

Blumer, H. (1969). *Symbolic interactionism: Perspective and method.* Englewood Cliffs, NJ: Prentice Hall.

Bolland, K. A., & Atherton, C. R. (1999). Chaos theory: An alternative approach to social work practice and research. *Families in Society*, 80(4), 367–373.

Boneham, M. A., & Sixsmith, J. A. (2006). The voices of older women in a disadvantaged community: Issues of health and social capital. *Social Science & Medicine* 62, 269–279.

Butcher, H., Banks, S., Henderson, P., with Robertson, J. (2007). *Critical community practice.* Bristol, UK: The Policy Press.

Chambon, A. S., Irving, A., & Epstein, Eds. (1999). *Reading Foucault for social work.* New York: Columbia University Press.

Corrigan, P., & Leonard, P. (1979). *Social work practice under capitalism: A Marxist approach*. London: Macmillan.

Coser, L. A. (1964). *The functions of social conflict*. New York: Free Press.

Cusac, A-C. (2009). *The culture of punishment in America*. New Haven, CT: Yale University Press.

Dahrendorf, R. (1959). *Class and class conflict in industrial society*. Stanford, CA: Stanford University Press.

da Vinci, Leonardo, quote, Retrieved July 3, 2009, from http://thinkexist.com/quotations/

Davis, J. E. (2002). *Stories of change: Narrative and social movements*. Albany: State University of New York Press.

Dean, R. G., & Fenby, B. L. (1989). Exploring epistemologies: Social work action as a reflection of philosophical assumptions. *Journal of Social Work Education*, 25(1), 46–54.

Deutsch, M. (1973). *The resolution of conflict: Constructive and destructive processes*. New Haven, CT: Yale University Press.

Elsberg, C., & Powers, P. R. (1992, November). *Focusing, channeling, and re-creating: Energy in contemporary American settings*. Presented at the Society for the Scientific Study of Religion, Washington, DC.

Emery, F. E., & Trist, E. L. (1965). The causal texture of organizational environments. *Human Relations*, 18, 21–32.

Evan, W. (1963). The organizational set: Toward a theory of inter-organizational relations. In J. D. Thompson (Ed.), *Organizational design and research: Approaches to organizational design* (pp. 173–191). Pittsburgh, PA: University of Pittsburgh Press.

Fabricant, M. B., & Burghardt, S. (1992). *The welfare state crisis and the transformation of social service work*. Armonk, NY: M. E. Sharpe.

Feuer, L. S. (Ed.). (1959). *Basic writings on politics and philosophy: Karl Marx and Friedrich Engels*. New York: Anchor Books.

Fisher, R. (1995). Social action community organization: Proliferation, persistence, roots, and prospects. In J. Rothman, J. L. Erlich, & J. E. Tropman, with F. M. Cox (Eds.), *Strategies of community intervention* (5th ed., pp. 327–340). Itasca, IL: F. E. Peacock.

Forrester, J. W. (1969). *Urban dynamics*. Cambridge: MIT Press.

France, A. (1894). *The Red Lily*. Doylestown, PA: Wildside Press.

Freire, P. (1972). *Pedagogy of the oppressed*. Harmondsworth, UK: Penguin.

Galston, W. A. (2004). Social mores are not enough. In A. Etzioni, A. Volmert, & E. Rothschild (Eds.), *The communitarian reader: Beyond the essentials* (pp. 91–95). Oxford, UK: Rowman & Littlefield, Publishers.

Germain, C. B., & Gitterman, A. (1995). *Ecological perspective*. In R. L. Edwards (Ed.-in-Chief), Encyclopedia of social work (19th ed.), (pp. 816–824). Washington, DC: National Association of Social Workers Press.

Gerth, H. H., & Mills, C. W. (1958). *From Max Weber: Essays in sociology*. New York: Oxford University Press.

Gleick, J. (1987). *Chaos*. New York: Viking Penguin.

Gouldner, A. W. (1960). The norm of reciprocity: A preliminary statement. *American Sociological Review*, 25(4), 161–178.

Gowdy, E. A. (1994). From technical rationality to participating consciousness. *Social Work*, 39(4), 362–370.

Greene, R. R., & Blundo, R. G. (1999). Postmodern critique of systems theory in social work with the aged and their families. *Journal of Gerontological Social Work*, 3(3/4), 87–100.

Grobman, G. M. (1999). *Improving quality and performance in your non-profit organization*. Harrisburg, PA: White Hat Communications.

Hall, S. (1977). Culture, the media, and the ideological effect. In J. Curran, M. Gurevitch, & J. Woollacott (Eds.), *Mass communication and society*. London: Edward Arnold.

Hardina, D. (2002). *Analytical skills for community organization practice*. New York: Columbia University Press.

Handy, F., & Kassam, M. (2007). Practice what you preach? The role of rural NGOs in women's empowerment. *Journal of Community Practice*, 14(3), 69–91.

Harris, R. P., Bridger, J. C., Sachs, C. E., & Tallichet, S. E. (1995). Empowering rural sociology: Exploring and linking alternative paradigms in theory and methodology. *Rural Sociology*, 60(4), 585–606.

Hartsock, N. (1998). *The feminist standpoint revisited and other essays*. Boulder, CO: Westview Press.

Hasenfeld, Y. (1983). *Human service organizations*. Englewood Cliffs, NJ: Prentice Hall.

Henderson, P. (2007). Introduction. In H. Butcher, S. Banks, P. Henderson, with J. Robertson, (Eds.), *Critical community practice* (pp. 1–16). Bristol, UK: The Policy Press.

Homans, G. C. (1958). Social behavior as exchange. *American Journal of Sociology*, 63, 597-606.

Huysman, M., & Wulf, V. (2004). Social capital and information technology: Current debate and research. In M. Huysman, & V. Wulf, (Eds.), *Social capital and information technology* (pp. 1–15). Cambridge, MA: The MIT Press.

Hyde, C. (1996). A feminist response to Rothman's "The interweaving of community intervention approaches." *Journal of Community Practice*, 3(3/4), 127–145.

Irving, A., & Young, T. (2002). Paradigm for pluralism: Mikhail Bakhtin and social work practice. *Social Work*, 47(1), 19–29.

Jeffries, A. (1996). Modeling community work: An analytic framework for practice. *Journal of Community Practice*, 3(3/4), 101–125.

Juba, D. S. (1997). A systems perspective on the introduction of narrative practice in human services organizations in the era of managed care. *Contemporary Family Therapy*, 19(2), 177–193.

Kauffman, S. (1995). *At home in the universe: The search for the laws of self-organization and complexity.* New York: Oxford University Press.

Kemp, S. P. (2001). Environment through a gendered lens: From person-in-environment to woman-in-environment. *Affilia*, 16(1), 7–30.

Kotler, P. (1977). A generic concept of marketing. In R. M. Gaedeke (Ed.), *Marketing in Private and Public Nonprofit Organizations: Perspectives and Illustrations* (pp. 18-33), Santa Maria, CA: Goodyear.

Kriesberg, L. (1982). *Social conflict*, (2nd ed.). Englewood Cliffs, NJ: Prentice Hall.

Kuhn, T. S. (1970). *The structure of scientific revolutions* (2nd ed., enlarged). New York: New American Library.

Kuper, A., & Kuper, J. (Eds.). (1999). *The social science encyclopedia* (2nd ed.). London: Routledge.

Ladd, C. E. (1999). Bowling with Tocqueville: Civic engagement and social capital. *The Responsive Community*, 9(2), 11–21.

Lappé, F. M., & Du Bois, P. M. (1994). *The quickening of America: Rebuilding our nation, remaking our lives.* San Francisco: Jossey-Bass.

Lauer, R. H. (1982). *Perspectives on social change* (3rd ed.). Boston: Allyn & Bacon.

Lengermann, P. M., & Niebrugge-Brantley, J. (1990). Feminist sociological theory: The near-future prospects. In G. Ritzer (Ed.), *Frontiers of social theory* (pp. 316–344). New York: Columbia University Press.

Levine, S., & White, P. E. (1961). Exchange as a conceptual framework for the study of interorganizational relations. *Administrative Science Quarterly*, 5, 583–610.

Levine, S., & White, P. E. (1963). The community of health organizations. In H. E. Freeman, S. Levine, & L. G. Reader (Eds.), *Handbook of medical sociology* (pp. 321–347). Englewood Cliffs, NJ: Prentice Hall.

Magee, C., & Huriaux, E. (2008). Ladies' night: Evaluating a drop-in programme for homeless and marginally housed women in San Francisco's mission district. *International Journal of Drug Policy* 19, 113–121.

Mattaini, M. A. (1990). Contextual behavior analysis in the assessment process. *Families in Society*, 71(4), 236–245.

McCormack, W. (2001, March 26). Deconstructing the election: Foucault, Derrida and the GOP strategy. *The Nation*, 272(12), 25–34.

McKee, M. (2003). Excavating our frames of mind: The key to dialogue and collaboration. *Social Work*, 48(3), 401–408.

Mizrahi, T. (2007). Women's ways of organizing: Strengths and struggles of women activists over time. *Affilia*. 22(4), 33–55.

Mizrahi, T., & Lombe, M. (2007). Perspectives from women organizers. *Journal of Community Practice*, 14(3), 93–118.

Mondros, J. B., & Wilson, S. M. (1990). Staying alive: Career selection and sustenance of community organizers. *Administration in Social Work*, 14(2), 95–109.

Moyser, G., & Parry, G. (1997). Voluntary associations and democratic participation in Britain. In J. W. van Deth (Ed.), *Private groups and public life: Social participation, voluntary associations, and political involvement in representative democracies* (pp. 24–46). London: Routledge.

Naples, N. A. (with Sachs, C.). (2000). Standpoint epistemology and the use of self-reflection in feminist ethnography: Lessons for rural sociology. *Rural Sociology*, 65(2), 194–214.

Nasar, S. (2001). *A beautiful mind: The life of mathematical genius and Nobel laureate John Nash.* New York: Simon & Schuster.

National Organization for Women. (1982). *Guidelines to feminist consciousness-raising.* Washington, DC: Author.

Netting, F. E., & O'Connor, M. K. (2002). *Organization practice: A social worker's guide to understanding human services.* Boston, MA: Allyn & Bacon.

Ohmer, M. L. (2008). The relationship between citizen participation and organizational processes and outcomes and the benefits of citizen participation in neighborhood organizations. *Journal of Social Service Research.* 34(4), 41–60.

Pardeck, J. T. (1996). An ecological approach for social work intervention. *Family Therapy*, 23(3), 189–198.

Pardeck, J. T., Murphy, J. W., & Choi, J. M. (1994). Some implications of postmodernism for social work practice. *Social Work*, 39(4), 343–346.

Payne, M. (2005). *Modern social work theory* (3rd ed.). Chicago: Lyceum.

Pecukonis, E., & Wenocur, S. (1994). Perceptions of self and collective efficacy in community organization theory and practice. *Journal of Community Practice*, 1(2), 5–21.

Perry, M., Williams, R. L., Wallerstein, N., & Waitzkin, H. (2008). Social capital and health care experiences among low-income individuals. *American Journal of Public Health*, 98(2), 330–336.

Piven, F. F., & Cloward, R. A. (1971). *Regulating the poor: The functions of public welfare*. New York: Random/Vintage Books.

Pozatek, E. (1994). The problem of certainty: Clinical social work in the postmodern era. *Social Work*, 39(4), 396–404.

Putnam, R. (n.d.). *Social capital: Measurement and consequences*. Retrieved July 12, 2009, from http://www.oecd.org/dataoecd/25/6/1825848.pdf

Putnam, R. (2000). *Bowling alone: The collapse and revival of American community*. New York: Simon & Schuster.

Pyles, L., & Cross, T. (2008). Community revitalization in post-Katrina New Orleans: a critical analysis of social capital in an African American neighborhood. *Journal of Community Practice*, 16(4), 383–401.

Reisch, M., Sherman, W. R., & Wenocur, S. (1981). Empowerment, conscientization, and animation as core social work skills. *Social Development Issues*, 5(2/3), 106–120.

Ritzer, G. (1992). *Contemporary sociological theory* (3rd ed.). New York: McGraw-Hill.

Ross, M. (with Lappin, B. W.). (1967). *Community organization: Theory, principles, and practice*. New York: Harper & Row.

Rothman, J. (1996). The interweaving of community intervention approaches. *Journal of Community Practice*, 3(3/4), 69–99.

Rothman, J. (2000). Collaborative self-help community development: When is the strategy warranted? *Journal of Community Practice*, 7(2), 89–105.

Rothman, J. (with J. E. Tropman). (1987). Models of community organization and macro practice: Their mixing and phasing. In F. M. Cox, J. L. Erlich, & J. E. Tropman (Eds.), *Strategies of community intervention* (4th ed., pp. 3–25). Itasca, IL: F. E. Peacock.

Saegert, S., & Winkel, G. (2004). Crime, social capital, and community participation. *American Journal of Community Psychology*, 34(3/4), 219–233.

Saleebey, D. (1994). Culture, theory, and narrative: The intersection of meanings in practice. *Social Work*, 39(4), 351–361.

Sands, R. G., & Nuccio, K. (1992). Postmodern feminist theory and social work. *Social Work*, 37(6), 489–494.

Seligman, M. E. P. (1975). *Helplessness: On depression, development, and death*. San Francisco: Freeman.

Silver, M. (1980). *Social infrastructure organizing technology*. Unpublished doctoral dissertation, University of California, Berkeley.

Smith, D. E. (1999). From women's standpoint to a sociology for people. In Abu-Lughod, J. L. (Ed.), *Sociology for the twenty-first century* (pp. 65–82). Chicago: University of Chicago Press.

Specht, H. (1986). Social support, social networks, social exchange and social work practice. *Social Service Review*, 60, 218–240.

Speer, P. W., & Zippay, A. (2005). Participatory decision-making among community coalitions: An analysis of task group meetings. *Administration in Social Work*, 29(3), 61–77.

Swenson, C. R. (1998). Clinical social work's contribution to a social justice perspective. *Social Work*, 43(6), 527–537.

Tangenberg, K. (2000). Marginalized epistemologies: A feminist approach to understanding the experiences of mothers with HIV. *Affilia*, 15(1), 31–48.

Thompson, J. D. (1967). *Organizations in action*. New York: McGraw-Hill.

Tong, R. (1992). Feminine and feminist thinking: A critical and creative explosion of ideas. *Anima: The Journal for Human Experience*, 18(2), 30–77.

Turner, J. H. (1982). *The structure of sociological theory* (3rd ed.). Homewood, IL: Dorsey Press.

Ward, M. (1995). Butterflies and bifurcations: Can chaos theory contribute to our understanding of family systems? *Journal of Marriage and the Family*, 57, 629–638.

Warren, K., Franklin, C., & Streeter, C. L. (1998). New directions in systems theory: Chaos and complexity. *Social Work*, 43(4), 357–372.

Washington, M. H. (1999, March). Prison studies as part of American studies. *ASA Newsletter*, 22(1), 1, 3.

Weed, E., & Shor, N. (Eds.). (1997). *Feminism meets queer theory*. Bloomington: Indiana University Press.

Weil, M. O. (1996). Community building: Building community practice. *Social Work*, 41(5), 481–499.

Wernet, S. P. (1994). A case study of adaptation in a nonprofit human service organization. *Journal of Community Practice*, 1, 93–112.

Wheatley, M. J. (2001). *Leadership and the new science: Discovering order in a chaotic world* (Rev. ed.). San Francisco: Berrett-Koehler.

Willer, D. Ed. (1999). *Network exchange theory*. Westport, CT: Praeger

Willer, D., Lovaglia, M. J., & Markovsky, B. (1999). Power and influence: A theoretical bridge. In D. Willer (Ed.), *Network exchange theory*, (pp. 229–247). Westport, CT: Praeger.

Williams, R. (2007). Moving beyond vagueness: Social capital, social networks, and economic outcomes. In J. Jennings, (Ed.). *Race, neighborhoods, and misuse of social capital* (pp. 67–86). New York: Palgrave Macmillan.

Wolfe, A. (1998). Developing civil society: Can the workplace replace bowling? *The Responsive Community*, 8:2, 41–47.

Wrong, D. H. (1979). *Power: Its forms, bases, and uses*. New York: Harper Colophon.

Zald, M. N. (1970). Political economy: A framework for comparative analysis. In M. N. Zald (Ed.), Power in organizations (pp. 221–261). Nashville, TN: Vanderbilt University Press.

3

The Nature of Social and Community Problems

Government does not solve problems; it subsidizes them.

Ronald Reagan; 40th President of the United States

[O]ur greatness as a nation has … depended on our sense of mutual regard for each other, of mutual responsibility. The idea that everybody has a stake in the country, that we're all in it together and everybody's got a shot at opportunity. … We know that government can't solve all our problems—and we don't want it to. But we also know that there are some things we can't do on our own. We know that there are some things we do better together.

Barack Obama, 44th President of the United States, Nobel laureate

We can't solve problems by using the same kind of thinking we used when we created them.

Albert Einstein, physicist, philosopher, Nobel laureate

Conceptualizing a Social–Community Problem

The generic problem-solving strategy as a linear, rational planned change problem-solving process was covered in our first chapter (also see Hardina, 2002). This chapter will examine social and community problems as social constructions of reality. Social problems don't exist until they, the social conditions, are defined as social problems (Benson & Saguy, 2005; Forte, 2004; Berger & Luckmann, 1967; Schneider & Sidney, 2009). Defining and addressing social problems involves critical thinking, values, an understanding of culture, and ideology. Diversity also is explored here in every sense of the word as we present numerous examples of challenges that social workers must meet.

A Viewpoint on Problems and Their Resolution

Communities define which of the many social conditions they will make their own as social problems. This chapter will contribute to the social worker's understanding of problems—facilitating more appropriate interventions—and will suggest applications that can lead to mutual construction and staging or framing problems and solutions and for coalition building. What determines whose definition prevails? What parts do power and passion play? From whose standpoint is a problem raised and whose worldview is accepted (Lopez, 1994)? Are there service consequences (underutilization, inappropriate interventions) to being oblivious to another group's culture or reality? Are new possibilities conceivable? Can problem solving be used to unite a community? As Rahm Emanuel, President Obama's former chief of staff, reputedly said, "You never want a serious crisis to go to waste" (Dionne, 2009). We will explore such questions and rethink the conventional wisdom regarding the nature of social problems, focusing on:

Definition—how problems are conceptualized and constructed
Meaning—how problems are experienced
Action—how problems are kept in check or solved

This requires exploring many-sided and fluctuating realities. Understanding the construction of social problems is a lesson in social constructionism and symbolic interactionism. Constructing and conceptualizing a social problem is no quixotic exercise; there are many ways to frame problems and interventions (Chapin, 1995; Mildred, 2003). The empowering thing is for community members to become part of the process of social problem construction and resolution (Butcher, 2007; Delgado & Staples, 2008).

Introduction to a Complex Phenomenon

Communities and their social constructions are complex and multi-layered. Aspiring to see the whole view of a community condition, Vissing and Diament (1995) set out to learn how many homeless teens lived in the seacoast area of New Hampshire and Maine. Social service providers kept telling them that "teen homelessness simply was not a problem in their communities" (p. 287). However, the 3,000 teenagers they surveyed conveyed a different story. Part of the difference in perception hinged on definitions, but Vissing and Diament decided that "adolescents are likely to be invisible. . . . Living with friends, floating from place to place, there is no one person to identify teens who 'live independently'" (p. 289). Thus, unveiling dimensions of community problems requires critical perception.

Professional social work assumes a social problem orientation with its professional typology of social conditions and problems for primary practice areas: addictions, aging, child welfare, health, mental health, and so forth (*Licensed social workers*, 2006; Whitaker &

Arrington, 2008). Understanding how specific clients and communities inhabit their social context contributes to problem clarification. This means "starting where the client is." Suppose a worker is told that a community has problems "related to family breakdown, drug and alcohol abuse, long-term health care, services for the elderly, equal opportunity in employment, and affordable housing" (Murase, 1995, p. 157). An experienced worker might feel perfectly confident about proceeding. However, if the community is an unassimilated immigrant community unfamiliar to the worker, specific cultural information might be needed. The same problems can take different forms within a community and between communities due to cultural variations (Greenberg, Schneider, & Singh, 1998).

Human service workers deal with a variety of human conditions reflected in the above taxonomy and some not reflected, such as poverty, crime, and maltreatment. They become social problems when seen by the community as deviations from or breakdown of social standards that the community believes should be upheld or achieved for life to be meaningful. Ginsberg (1994) says a social problem is "the shared belief that the problem represents a serious threat to a community or the larger society which provides people with the will to do something about it" (p. 41).

Distinctions Relevant to Our Profession. If social justice is a *sine qua non* if not the *raison d'être* of social work, social problems are the fuel the feeds the fire and creates the need for social justice. Social work exists to address social problems and obtain social justice for the victims of the social problems. We assume, as stated earlier, a social constructionism and symbolic interactionism perspective. Social conditions must be defined and that definition accepted by a significant part of the community to be social problems. How will the problem be defined? Organizer and policy advocate Makani Themba (1999) challenges us to think about problems in new ways:

Who are you holding responsible for social problems in this country? A strange question perhaps, but each time we choose an action to address a problem, we also assign responsibility to some group for solving that problem. . . . Youth violence? Focusing on gun policy or movie violence puts the onus on one set of players and institutions, advocating for mentoring or 'scared straight' problems targets another (p. 13).

Reaching Our Own Understandings. When people say to social workers, "Here's a social problem—fix it," we cannot take either their judgment or their command at face value. We can all agree that a condition is problematic–such as health care–but not agree on why it is problematic, let alone how to fix it. Box 3.1 asks, when does a condition become a problem? The essential component of a social problem construction is meaning to the people of the problem construction. Our theory of social problem construction, following social constructionism discussed in Chapter 2, holds that it is not the things, but the meaning of the things that is important and constitutes reality (Blumer, 1969). The meaning of things and events is socially defined Blumer, 1969, p. 2): "The position of symbolic interactionism, in contrast [ie. to the objectivists], is that the meanings that things have for human beings are central in their own right" (Blumer, 1969, p. 3).

- This view assumes that values and self-interest influence the interpretations, guide the mental constructions, and influence the methods for gathering and interpreting reality. Reality is a construction in the minds of the observer. It is constructed from putative information, stimuli, and data from the environment shaped by the observer's values, culture, and experiences.

Social workers, from this perspective, must recognize that affected individuals need to help frame social problems. To be relevant and consumer-centered (Tower, 1994) construction of social problems requires flexibility. As Castex (1993) says, "An awareness of the occasional arbitrariness of one's assumptions should lead to an openness about altering those assumptions in new situations or when more information is supplied" (p. 687).

Similarly, when everyone says a problem is impossible to solve, we cannot take that assessment at face value either. Solutions to social problems contained in social policies generally reflect the construction of the social problem. During the universal health care debate of the past quarter-century in America, it was often claimed the problem was unsolvable, even though it was "better solved" in the rest of the industrial world.

The many conceptions of problems outlined in this section reveal that a problem may be promoted on the basis of self-interest or blame. While laypeople believe they know a problem when they see it, social workers need to take a larger view. We do not want to disempower clients by adding to the chorus of those telling them, "You are the problem!"

BOX 3.1.	When Does a Condition Become a Problem?

Some Middletown residents saw a brook in their town turn red. Some workers saw their skin turn yellow. Others became fatigued and developed the "Line One Shuffle." Between 1947 and 1975, thousands upon thousands of people in this southeast Iowa town worked at the local munitions plant. Now, public health officials and university professors are attempting to locate former assembly line workers, guards, technicians, maintenance workers, and even laundry personnel.

Veiled Dimensions of the Social Condition

A deadly secret was kept through the end of the Cold War: Middletown workers had been assembling atomic weapons. Even those who were told that classified secret were not told about the dangers of radiation. Workers handled radioactive substances with their bare hands and breathed deadly fumes and powders. The U.S. Department of Energy is now providing funds so that researchers from the University of Iowa can contact everyone who might have been exposed to the bomb assembly line (Line One) processes. Public health officials are interviewing workers and holding educational outreach events.

Source: Trouble in Middleton. *Iowa Alumni Magazine*, April 2001, p. 37.

Subtle Forms of Blaming the Victim. When people unfairly attribute responsibility to individuals who have suffered harm, this pejorative practice is called blaming the victim (Ryan, 1976). This concept is cited when rapists use the victim's manner of dress as an excuse, when people with human immunodeficiency virus are blamed for acquiring their disease, or when pensioners were forced on to public assistance because of the first major fiscal crisis of the 21st century. From a blamer's viewpoint, children who ate lead paint and became ill and their parents, who "obviously" did not exercise proper "surveillance," become the problem, as opposed to manufacturers, landlords, and housing inspectors. Ryan (1976) contends that while environmental and social causes are now accepted as major factors in social problems, interventions are directed to individuals. We have yet to address the inherent deficiencies of the global market economy. Some in society, says Ryan (1976), simply dismiss victims, even in the face of "unalleviated distress," while "kind humanitarians" place blame on the environment, not on individual character.

Ryan reproaches the "kind" people who want to be compassionate while (unconsciously) leaving their self or class interests unchallenged— "charitable persons" whose mission is to compensate or change society's victims rather than change society: "They turn their attention to the victim in his post-victimized state. . . . They explain what's wrong with the victim in terms of . . . experiences that have left wounds. . . . And they take the cure of these wounds . . . as the first order of business. They want to make the victims less vulnerable, send them back into battle with better weapons, thicker armor, a higher level of morale" (p. 29).

Ryan is thinking of survival battles. Mental health practitioners focus on psychoanalytic explanations and solutions, he suggests, rather than facing with numerous clients "the pounding day-to-day stresses of life on the bottom rungs that drive so many to drink, dope, and madness" (1976, p. 30). Parsons, Hernandez, and Jorgensen (1988) add that "society is more willing for social workers to work with these victims than with other components of social problems" (p. 418). Such insights are reason enough to examine our assumptions about problem formulation and resolution.

Defining and Framing a Social–Community Problem

Before confronting community problems, it is important to understand how social workers can construct conceptions of social and community problems for intervention. We seek analytic tools that can make clear the nature of a problem and its potential relationships to its environment and solutions. However, the construction is not just, or even primarily, an analytic exercise. The construction of a social problem definition for community practice must begin with the involvement of the affected community groups. This involvement begins to counter the effects of social exclusion, increases community empowerment, allows the community to take greater control over conditions of their lives, and begins the intervention process (Butcher, Banks, Henderson, with Robertson, 2007).

As we have discussed above, social problems are socially constructed. Netting, Kettner, and McMurtry (2008) help us see the difference between a possibly problematic social condition and a social problem. A *condition* is a phenomenon present in the community "that has not been formally identified or publicly labeled as a problem." A *social problem* is a recognized condition that has been "incorporated into a community's or organization's agenda for action" (p. 83). We define a social problem similarly as social conditions defined by a significant group or coalition in the community or society, a group that has or can have social impact, as a deviation from or breakdown of social standards the definers believe should be upheld or achieved for life to have significant social meaning.

The elements in constructing social problems can be pulled together into a conceptual framework to allow the community practitioner (the initiator system and the client system, to use the rhetoric of Chapter 1) to determine (a) if the phenomena or conditions are problematic and, if so, (b) to whom they are problematic, (c) why they are problematic, and (d) the potential for social intervention. The model below eschews the assumption of universal social problems. Social conditions must be defined as social problems. While the framework presented here is not the only way to conceptualize a social problem, it provides a model for examining social problems independent of any subsequent social policy intervention, but can be used for purposes of social policy and intervention.[1] It is well suited for social work analysis because of the profession's strong normative, social justice, and ideological emphasis.

Framing a Social–Community Problem

The appropriate framing of a social condition in social problem construction is necessary to develop community acceptance of the construction. Framing is the selection and emphasis of some aspects of a perceived social condition in ways to promote the acceptance of the condition as problematic (Benson & Saguy, 2005). We will discuss framing and the related concept of staging more fully later in this section and in Chapter 11, Using Marketing. The social problem model has the six elements:

1. Definitions of normative behavior
2. Ideology and value configurations involved
3. Views of social causation
4. Scope
5. Social cost
6. Proposed mode of remediation

The framework is suited to social work analysis because of the profession's strong normative and ideological emphasis, although as an analytic vehicle the framework strives for ideological neutrality by making ideology explicitly a component. It assists us in understanding how others have come to their conceptualization, how we can come to our own, and how we can position ourselves to address problems.

Before discussing each element, an explanation of normative and deviant behavior is needed. We are not using deviation is an inherently pejorative sense. Behavior and circumstances that are regarded as desirable, acceptable, or normal within a group or a community are normative. However, a situation and behavior are defined as a deviation from the normative standards of a community, a nation, or another entity when they are significantly at variance from the entity's normative standards. The deviation, to be a social problem, needs to be different and must be defined as an unacceptable deviation from the social standards. Homosexuality is a social problem only if it is socially defined as an unacceptable deviance in sexual and social behavior. Some standards are manifest; for example, regulations are codified norms, while others are ingrained but not codified. Holding hands by men in the 1950s in American was not illegal, but in most American communities it was improper. To understand why a situation is or can be labeled as deviant, the analyst needs to search for the meaning of a particular deviance to certain community segments.

Normative and Deviant. For a condition to be identified as a problem, it must represent to the defining group an important deviation from an actual or ideal standard or norm. The norm can be statistical and the deviation quantitative, such as poverty based on deviations from standard-of-living indexes or poverty lines. The norm also can be a model or guideline and the deviation qualitative—for example, quality-of-life standards such as income security or respect. The deviation can come from shared subjective perceptions and feelings of a social collective, such as the feeling by the radical conservative right that they have "lost their country."

Social problems, the deviancies, generally are presented as needs. However, what type of needs are they? Beyond food, clothing, and shelter, most needs are social and psychological, not physiological. Freud reportedly observed that we only have the need to love and to work. Bradshaw (1977) offers a four-fold needs classification for a wider range of needs useful to social problem construction and social policy and intervention as presented in Box 3.2:

1. Normative need: Need is defined by a nominal expert or experts as deviation from a social desirable standard. A normative need conception was used by Mollie Orshansky (1965) in her food guideline or market-basket approach in developing the first generally recognized U.S. poverty lines for President Johnson's War on Poverty. Variations of this line are used by the U.S. Census Bureau and the Department of Health and Human Services. It can be argued that clergy of various religions use this approach to define sin.
2. Comparative need: Need is when a segment of the community differs appreciably from the community as a whole, or significant segments

BOX 3.2.	Social Problem Conception to Social Action

Likelihood of Social Action	Normative	Comparative	Felt	Expressed
Least likely for social problem to lead to social action	+	−	−	−
	+	+	−	−
	+	+	+	-
	−	−	+	+
Most likely for social problem to lead to social action	+	+	+	+

+ Social definition present, - Social definition not present

of the community, on social or economic variables. This approach is used whenever an "underserved" rationale is used (Silow-Carroll, Alteras, & Stepnick, 2006). Federal funding to underserved areas and populations in health and mental health and affirmation action policies use a comparative approach in constructing the social need.

3. Felt need: This need is basically a want for something based on a subjective sense of deprivation. It can be justified by normative and comparative need rationales, but felt needs are not always rooted in the other needs. When comparative data are used to justify feelings of relative or comparative deprivation, the choice of the comparison groups is critical in justifying the feeling. The lower-middle class may feel deprived when comparing themselves to the poor when they perceive the gap between themselves and the poor narrowing; this feeling was the justification for the Reagan white working-class Democrats, and we believe felt need is a motivation for the increased white conservative radicalism. But felt need alone is insufficient for community action. A task of a community practitioner is to bring the discontent of a felt need to the level of an expressed need.

4. Expressed need: This need is when the community or a segment of the community defining a social deviation as need goes beyond the study, comparison, and feeling of deprivation and discontent to taking action and demanding remediation of the deviation. A critical aspect for social problem definition and social intervention is an expression of need, although expression assumes a felt need. The social action process for social intervention requires community involvement and not just experts.

Expressed needs are most likely to be constructed as social problems by the community, although normative and comparative constructions are used to support the expressions.

Ideology and Value Configurations. Harold Walsby, in his opus on ideology, defined ideology as:

the complete system of cognitive assumptions and affective identifications which manifest themselves in, or underlie, the thought, speech, aims, interests, ideals, ethical standards, actions—in short, in the behaviour—of an individual human being (Walsby, 2008, p. 95).

Ideology is an internally consistent and integrated set of values and beliefs that reflect the social problem definer's worldview. It provides the ideals that determine how the world is and should be constructed. Ideology goes beyond limited, formal political beliefs captured by labels like conservative, liberal, or right, although an individual's ideology may contain a political set of beliefs, to encompass the holder's sense of community, community standards and acceptable behavior, belonging, and reciprocal obligations. Globalization, neoliberal capitalism, and worship of the economic market model are as much social ideologies as social science theories. Ideologies spring from religious belief, political philosophies, socialization, and life experience. The basic ideology is socialized in childhood (Berger & Luckmann, 1967). As Lt. Cable intoned in the Hammerstein and Logan musical (1949), *South Pacific,* "You've got to be taught to hate and fear."

Ideology is not inherently controversial, at least within the community where it arises and is shared. Different ideologies can cause their holders' values to range from permissive to punitive

---

BOX 3.3.   **Who Are We?**

I have a Scottish colleague in Edinburgh, Scotland, who describes his ethnic identification as:
- When in Scotland, I'm an Edinburgher.

- When in England, I'm a Scot.
- When in Europe, I'm British.
- When in America, I'm European.

---

on such issues as casual drinking, drug use, and sex. Whether a social condition is viewed as deviant and a social problem depends on perception rooted in ideology. Whether a woman should control her body and have a right to privacy and autonomy, and whether a fetus has human rights are familiar examples of different constructions rooted in different ideologies. Public participation in the 2009–10 forward national health care debate was ideologically driven and was largely unencumbered by facts. Box 3.4 and 3.6 illustrate that different ideologies and constructions of reality can frame the same condition differently.

Social Causation. The public attributes the causes of most social problems to social factors. This attribution of cause relates to the definers' perception that the condition is not totally the result of physical, biological, or natural forces, but also has social roots. The causation may represent a conflict between the physical or technological and the social, or between social elements within society. The social causes of the social problem construction commonly are the targets for intervention. Poverty's causes are usually not defined in contemporary society as the genetic inferiority of the poor, but due to social and environmental factors such as prejudice and a culture of poverty. While genetic causes usually are not attributed as the causes of poverty, there are still some archaic

theories that hold to a genetic position (Murray & Herrnstein, 1994).

Social causation does not mean that problems are exclusively social; they may have strong biological elements. Global warming is a physical, climatology condition that is primarily socially caused and is having dramatic social ramifications.

Scope. Scope is the social condition's social impact in terms of the number and proportion of the community affected by the social condition. It is the incidence and prevalence of the condition and how seriously the condition is viewed by the community. For example, while terrorism affects far fewer people in terms of deaths than does the flu (with the possible exception of the swine flu or *H1N1*), terrorism is taken much more seriously by policymakers and the public. Generally the condition has to affect more than one person to be a social problem. It represents costs to significant portions of the population. These costs can be social as well as economic, such as restricted choice, and are more than one-time costs. If a child falls into a hole or well and is rescued by a huge collective effort, that is *not* a social problem. However, the risk of predators to all children in a community is a social problem.

In framing a social condition as a social problem, the framers must be cautious not to make

---

BOX 3.4.   **What's a Problem?**

Spector (1985) captures the historical vagaries of social problems: "People who drink alcohol to excess were thought to be sinners by the temperance movement . . . regarded as criminals by the prohibition movement . . . and as diseased addicts by the medical establishment after 1940. Homosexuality used to be both a crime and a mental disorder [before] the decriminalization movement and a particularly

dramatic official vote by the American Psychiatric Association in December 1973" (p. 779).

Similarly, Gordon (1994) puts the drug problem in historical perspective, revealing how often it was promoted as a problem in the 20th century and in what forms, and showing today's resurrection of the "dangerous classes" construction (p. 225).

the scope too large as to be overwhelming or viewed as a natural state of affairs. This ominous quote is often attributed to Stalin: "One death is a tragedy; one million is a statistic." The deviation from the norm should not be framed so broadly as to appear bizarre.

Scope is concerned not only with the extent of the social problem, its incidence and prevalence, but also who specifically in the community is affected. This identification is important for targeting any subsequent remediation and for political and social action to realize remediation.

Social Cost. Social cost relates to the assumption that the condition, if left unattended, has economic, personal, interpersonal, psychic, physical, or cultural costs. It may be a real cost, an implied cost, or an opportunity cost (the cost compared to what it would be if the conditions were remediated). There is no assumption that the cost is perceived or carried equally by all members of society. The framing of the social condition uses the social costs as a way to bring community groups into the coalition endorsing the construction of the social condition as a social problem. An analytic task is to determine (a) who bears the cost, (b) what is the perceived cost, and (c) how is its distribution perceived. Defining and distributing social costs and who bears them often propels parts of the community toward intervention or remediation. The framers should strive to spread costs broadly, as well as projected benefits from addressing the problem (Schneider & Sidney, 2009). If only the poor suffer the social costs of poverty, then motivating the total community to address poverty rests primarily on ethical grounds. The case for intervention is strengthened if other social costs can be shown to the community if they don't intervene.

The definitions of social costs also may be a function of affordability. Communities tend to define social conditions as social problems as they can afford them. Conditions are defined as problematic as the interventions become affordable, resources are present or potentially so, or the costs of not intervening become greater than the cost of intervening. Examples are relative deprivation (the raising or lowering of the poverty line as the wealth of the society increases or decreases) and mental health (expansion of the definition of mental illness as technological gains

and society's abilities to treat, alter, or address the conditions expand). The social costs of intervening need to be framed as less than the social costs of not intervening.

Remediation. For intervention to be considered, the defining party must frame the social condition as a social problem amenable to change, and the target segments of the community must believe that it is alterable and remediable and the social costs of change are less than the social costs of not changing. If there is no belief, there will be no search for possible remediation. The 2009 national health care debate saw the opponents of a public option raise the costs of change beyond economic costs alone to include threats to basic morality, freedom, and even granny's life. They framed the American health policy issue as insoluble, even through national health care policy has been resolved by all other Western industrial nations.

The *levers of change*, or the things and forces that can effect change, cannot be totally out of range for the community. A means of remediation does not have to be known, only the belief that such remediation is possible. If a condition is believed to be unalterable or in the natural order of things, the condition may be defined as nonproblematic or as something that must be endured, perhaps with some attention to reducing suffering. One example is how the poor are viewed under the philosophy of social Darwinism. Or, to quote one of our mountaineer grandfathers, "What can't be cured, must be endured."

Discussion of the Social Problem Intervention Framework

If 30 of our clients share a similar condition or circumstance, this can be the start of framing a social problem. Framing will include our view and others' views of the shared condition's tractability and whether circumstances (supportive media attention, public approbation, availability of interventive technologies, and so forth) appear favorable for resolution (Mazmanian & Sabatier, 1981, p. 191). We are not presenting a formula for taking immediate action on a perceived problem but rather a means of determining what to do based on a better understanding of what needs fixing and why. Thus, if we intend to stage a problem, we figure out the factors that allow us to be most effective as interveners. We need to know the problem's scope and the community's costs if the condition remains compared with those if it is remediated. This approach thrusts the analyst toward the specification of outcomes without assuming that all of society will benefit equally from any specific outcome or alternative social state. It does not assume that everyone perceives the problem similarly or envisions the same solution. However, a careful use of the framework should enable us to determine to some degree, a priori, to whom certain outcomes will be beneficial and to whom they will be problematic. We will discuss framing and staging social problems and social interventions more fully in Chapter 11, Using Marketing.

Other Social Problem Models

While we are used to thinking of problems as being revealed by objective indicators and other measurement devices, we have seen that they are actually social constructions. The models for their constructions vary. Sociologists increasingly account for such complexity in their analyses.

Critical Theories. Critical theories analysis and framing of social problems requires us to step back, examine presumptions, and figure out who benefits from maintaining a particular problem (unemployment, vagrancy, conspiracy). A critical theories perspective, as discussed in Chapter 2, looks first at social conditions for social structural and systems inequities rather than individual psychology. The approach has an admittedly radical ideology, with a concern for social justice central (Payne, 2006, pp. 227–250). For instance, respected sociologist Herbert Gans (1971, 1973) has written cogently about functions of poverty that help explain poverty's persistence. The focus of attention in this approach is on the entire social system, in particular on the ruling class. It encompasses activist inclinations toward exposing domination and promoting emancipation. Domination reveals itself in its labels. To wit, a Salvadoran complains about the way indigenous culture is devalued and denied: "They call our art . . . handicraft; our language . . . dialect; our

religion . . . superstition, and our culture . . . tradition" (Gabriel, 1994, p. 5).

A critical approach asks us to examine societal contradictions. For instance, there's a contradiction in a commercial organization that calls its employees "associates" or a mental health program that calls the program users "members"—but then divides the lunchroom, lounge, and bathrooms between levels of associates or between staff and members. A critical approach to problems requires development of critical consciousness, or Freire's conscientisation (Chambon, Irving, & Epstein, 1999; Freire, 1994; Payne, 2006). This perspective emphasizes political activism and social change for social justice compatible with social work (Butcher, Banks, Henderson, with Robertson, 2007).

Relevance for Practitioners. Since social workers often engage in multidisciplinary work, in team practice, and within a host agency, they must be alert to theoretical perspectives about problems held by other professions. Just as the medical model shapes what should be done, a problem perspective may undergird the workings of a program with which social workers are associated. However, that perspective may not be respectful of clients or community residents.

Getting a Social–Community Problem Addressed

In this section, we continue to discuss conditions and problems from a social construction perspective.

Claims Making and Players

Once a defining group has pinpointed a troubling condition, it must get itself in a position to be taken seriously in making a demand. We call this *community organizing* (see Chapter 13). When the group works instead to position the condition so that it will be considered a social problem and to create an environment in which anyone would be viewed as having a right to make a claim because the condition is so intolerable, we call that *staging* the problem and *claims making*. We will discuss staging in Chapter 11, Using Marketing, and claims making here. Claims making is not equivalent to coalition building, where many groups find common ground; it is a competitive process that tends to favor problems with pathetic victims and groups with clout. Claims-making activities can be grassroots efforts where we can affect matters. Input is possible since we are dealing with activities of defining and demanding.

The Stages in the Claims Process. Spector and Kitsuse help us examine the claims process and how claims makers and advocates can make claims as did Gideon in Box 3.5. They stress "unfolding lines of activity" (1987, p. 158) and see the life of a social issue commonly going through four stages of development and resolution. To them, government responses are key in determining whether social problems become part of society's agenda.

1. The critical first stage occurs when a public claim is made that a problem exists and should be addressed (at this point, no formal or recognized group may even exist) with an ensuing debate.
2. A second stage of getting government engaged will follow if (a) the issue has become public, (b) the claimant has exercised power effectively, and (c) the claimant has used the various channels of recourse (such as the government and the media) well. This is the stage in which policymakers (who believe they, too, have discovered the problem) respond to the claimant and offer official recognition (if the designated agency decides to "own" the program).
3. A third stage of renewed claims may follow in which the original conditions, problems, and activities for change re-emerge. By now, these may be less of a focus for the claimant than the perceived blocked or ineffective avenues of recourse, discourse, dialogue,

and procedural resolution that had seemingly opened in Stage 2. (For further detail, see Spector & Kitsuse, 1987, pp 142–155.)
4. Finally, a stage of return to the community may happen when claimants back away from government agencies, disillusioned with their responses, and develop alternative solutions. The problem might die during or after any of these stages.

Suicides rates are much higher in elderly persons than among teens (American Association of Suicidology, 2008; 2009; Family First Aid, 2009). Although documented by organizations, scholars, and even the media (*USA Today*, *New York Times*), suicide among the elderly has not *caught on* the way teenage suicide has. In contrast, nursing home reform followed the full course. Applying the stages to concerns about quality care, the development followed this path:

1. Abuse documentation
2. Formation of resident and consumer organizations and government response units
3. Ongoing conflicts between advocates and the relevant federal agencies
4. Renewed advocacy at the community and state level

Players and States of Resolution. Who and what can contribute to recognition of a problem? Gladwell (2002) has popularized the idea that there are three kinds of exceptional people who contribute to what he calls social and word-of-mouth epidemics or the spread of "ideas and products and messages and behaviors" (p. 7). He calls them "mavens" (information collectors), "connectors," and "salesmen." A targeted push by such people can contribute to problem resolution. Blumer (1971) says that types of action (e.g., agitation and violence) may be factors. He also notes significant types of players: interest

BOX 3.5.	Gideon's Trumpet

In the morning mail of January 8, 1962, the Supreme Court of the United States received a large envelope from Clarence Earl Gideon, prisoner No. 003826, Florida State Prison.... [His documents] were written in pencil. They were done in carefully formed printing, like a schoolboy's, on lined sheets.

Source: Lewis, A. *Gideon's Trumpet*, 1966, p. 3.

groups, political figures, the media, and powerful organizations that may want to "shut off" or "elevate" a problem—or both (p. 302). Thus, many groups contribute to problem definition: those suffering from a condition, challenging groups, social movement participants, policymakers, and journalists. Helping professions can be important participants in the process (Spector, 1985, p. 780). Blumer puts professionals like social workers with others—such as journalists, the clergy, college presidents, civic groups, and legislators—who have access to "the assembly places of officialdom." We can legitimate a problem or a proposed solution through "arenas of public discussion" (Blumer, 1971, p. 303).

In what is essentially a political process, governments "respond to claims that define conditions as social problems by funding research on solutions to problems, establishing commissions of inquiry, passing new laws, and creating enforcement and treatment bureaucracies" (Spector, 1985, p. 780). In the case of maltreatment of residents by some nursing homes, for example, in the discovery stage a Nader report was published that included firsthand accounts by people who had worked undercover in several facilities. The federal government began monitoring nursing homes more closely, funded reports from the Institute of Medicine, passed the *Nursing Home Quality Reform Act*, and created the Administration on Aging's Long Term Care Ombudsman Program. (Simultaneously, the nursing home industry has fought hard to keep reform regulations from going into effect.) As one aspect of the response stage, more social workers have been hired by facilities to upgrade quality.

Concurrent with drawing attention to a condition, claims makers must interpret it. They must shape public understanding of an emerging social problem, convince the public of its legitimacy, and suggest solutions based on the new consensus and understanding (Best, 1989, pp. xix–xx). This definitional process often involves conflict, as different definitions and the solutions that flow from them compete for public favor and scarce resources (Blumer, 1971). The systems for ameliorating a problem and establishing control that result from successful staging of a problem have been studied less than the initial framing of problems. Two cases follow, in which the aftermath has been documented.

Extended Examples of Claims-Making Processes

We deliberately emphasize classic over current situations (gay marriage), so the reader can concentrate on process rather than get captured in content. Experience suggests that substantive details can distract us from seeing how a circumstance becomes a social problem. It will be productive to focus here on problems as activities.

The Rights of the Accused. A criminal justice example serves as a simple, straightforward claims-making illustration. Clarence Gideon made a claim that injustice was happening and society had a problem it should remedy immediately by paying for lawyers for the indigent in all criminal cases. Gideon was a small-town, middle-aged man who had served time. He was unjustly accused of a pool hall robbery in Florida but could not afford a lawyer and had to defend himself. He asked for a lawyer, was denied one, lost his case, and was sent to jail for 5 years. He immediately appealed, though unsuccessfully, to the Florida Supreme Court, wrote to the U.S. Supreme Court about the right to counsel, and started a legal revolution that ended with a new system of public defenders in our country. Gideon himself was acquitted at his second trial with the help of a local lawyer. He was an "average guy" who decided to make a constitutional claim and, in standing up for himself, called attention to a national social problem—the lack of legal representation in noncapital cases. Until then, only poor people facing a death sentence were provided with lawyers.

Gideon's story illustrates the sociological distinction between troubles and issues. Far more than Gideon's character and criminal troubles were at stake: values and issues of fairness at a societal level were at stake because Gideon was one of thousands of poor people whom the legal structure failed. A private matter became a public matter because of "a crisis in institutional arrangements" (Mills, 1959, p. 9).

In the first phase of claims making, prisoners from many states had petitioned for years to get redress for their perceived injustice. In the second phase, for various internal reasons, the Supreme Court was ready to consider change and therefore accepted Gideon's petition and upheld his claim, which, crucially, had been buttressed by supportive briefs filed by state officials. Claims-making analysis helps us see the important role of the Supreme Court in accepting Gideon's case, providing him, as a pauper, with top-notch lawyers at that level of the legal system, legitimizing the claims of injustice put forward by a convicted felon, and setting the stage for conclusions involving new programs at the state level. Power plays a role in the definition of problems, but so do well-positioned professionals, including social workers. So can the tenacity of one individual.

Protection of the Innocent. In our second example, the dramatization of missing and endangered children provides a complex illustration of the claims-making process. This represents another aspect of the crime and punishment saga, for it is about those who are or fear becoming victims of major crimes. The public career of this problem started with a number of sensational murders, peaked with milk carton and grocery store sacks printed with pictures of missing children, and continues with the "Have You Seen Us?" cards sent in the mail with the 800 number for the National Center for Missing and Exploited Children. The designation "missing children" combined into one broad conceptualization what had been three different problems—children kidnapped or abducted by strangers, children kidnapped or snatched by one parent, and runaway children who were missing but sometimes returned (Best, 1987, p. 104). When they were lumped together, the total number of children involved was higher. The commonly cited incidence figure for missing children became 1.8 million cases per year (inexact estimate), which got attention and led to public hearings but misled almost everyone into thinking that most of these children were abducted by strangers—by far the least prevalent circumstance (Best, 1987, pp. 106–107; Best, 2001, p. 128). In actuality, only about 100 abductions by strangers are investigated per year. By the time the advocacy campaign had lost public interest and some credibility, new organizations and television shows were attending to the problem. Many individuals were involved, but more to the point, many advocacy groups and social service organizations were part of the identification, formulation,

and promotion of this problem. Parents and child advocates sought to get "stolen" children returned and to bring flaws in the system to the attention of policymakers and the public. (A useful Web site for further information on policy concerns is maintained by the National Center for Missing and Exploited Children at http://www.missingkids.com.)

To highlight aspects of the claims-making process, Best (1989) draws on the field of rhetoric (Baumann, 1989). This approach helps us see the techniques employed to get this problem on the public agenda, such as repeated use of horror stories (atrocity tales and case histories), exaggerated use of statistics, and frightening parents into having their children fingerprinted. To stage the problem and buttress its need for attention, advocates staked out the claim that no family was exempt, as this problem was not tied to size of locale, income level, or race: "By arguing that anyone might be affected by a problem, a claims maker can make everyone in the audience feel that they have a vested interest in the problem's solution" (Best, 1987, p. 108). Rationales or justifications for focusing attention on this problem were used: the victims were "priceless" and "blameless" (in contrast, say, to drug abusers); even runaways were portrayed as abuse victims who fled, only to face exploitation on the streets (Best, 1987, pp. 110, 114). The objectives were to force more sharing and coordination of information between states and between the FBI—which handles kidnapping cases—and local police, as well as to cut down on the waiting time before children were declared missing so that the official search could begin sooner. Preventing the murder and kidnapping of children is still deemed a high priority (Amber alerts and Megan laws), but is a bit more in perspective today.

The sexual exploitation of children by Catholic priests has been part of the Church's lore for centuries and was known to the church hierarchy well before the pedophiliac behavior and its cloaking became headline news. Church officials convinced many parents and children to treat this egregious situation as a non-problem. The transition from condition to social problem took place only after large numbers of victims were documented and hidden atrocity tales were revealed through lawsuits and investigative journalism. The claims-making process involved an "innocent children" justification for the problem receiving attention and remediation. Getting a problem in the public eye does not require a consensus about causation. The sexual abuse and institutional cover-up have been attributed to many factors—for example, the church's policy of celibacy, the possibility that the priesthood may attract pedophiles because of its use of young boys in rituals, and its arrogance toward laypeople and exclusiveness of the hierarchy.

The Catholic Church's failure to discipline the pedophile priests and the subsequent claims making by the victims has resulted in very high costs to the Church. In addition to loss of moral authority, the ostensible reason for the Church's existence, it has lost millions, perhaps, billions of dollars in payouts and lost donations. In Los Angeles alone settlements with some 500 known victims have cost the Church and its insurers $660 million (Catholic Church abuse settlement, 2007).

The Politics of Claiming. Social work's participation in claims making by abused communities is part of its social justice responsibilities. Social justice requires a more socially equitable distribution of society's resources and social statuses than is currently the case. Restorative justice and its compensation, discussed in Chapter 1, requires active and vocal claims making (Clifford & Burke, 2009; Gumz & Grant, 2009; von Wormer, 2009). Social action experts Robert Fisher and Eric Shragge (2000), drawing on John Friedmann, urge social workers working with community organizations to engage in strenuous claims making, not just about social problems such as sexual abuse but also about the workings of society. Social workers should make claims for the need for the government to engage in wealth redistribution: "Claims making needs a broader strategy, which understands the fundamental importance of raising social policy, and wider political demands which critique the dominant political economy. In an era of neo-liberalism, the dominant social agenda of a relative free market with a diminished role for the state in the social and economic field cannot be accepted as inevitable. It has to be challenged" (Fisher & Shragge, 2000, p. 13). The 2008–09 Great Recession gives credence to this assertion.

Worldviews and Social Problems

Multiple Realities

Many of us know the non-Western world primarily from *National Geographic* photographs. Others know even less. Does Afghanistan border Iraq, Iran, or both? Our mental pictures of social problems in other lands are shaped by our incomplete knowledge and cultural limitation, and we have little sense of how non-Westerners who move to North America previously have lived or how they think. As the United States and many other countries become nations of immigrants, often rife with ethnic strife and anti-immigrant xenophobia , we must know intimately others'

BOX 3.6.	**In the Construction**

Cornel West has allowed plenty of time to make an important appointment, but he must catch a cab and none will stop for him in downtown New York City. West, a theology professor at Princeton, is dressed in a suit and tie. He is on the way to have his picture taken for the book cover of what will become his bestseller, named, appropriately, *Race Matters*. However, the taxi drivers do not know any of this and drive by West to pick up white passengers, only yards beyond him, instead. Ten cabs refuse him. West becomes angrier and angrier.

The observer would see this as an example of discrimination. Taxi drivers would highlight their fear not of West in his suit but of his destination. To the refused passenger, the unfairness goes deeper than the fact that the drivers—whatever their race— are violating their own regulations. The experience negates democracy, the "basic humanness and Americanness of each of us," as West (1994) puts it (p. 8), and causes achievement stories to seem like a mockery. To West, the increasing nihilism of minority groups results not from doctrine but from lived experience (pp. xv, 22).

worldviews to be relevant in interventions and to establish at least a partially shared reality. We should strive to broaden our worldviews to include the viewpoints of constituencies with whom we work and communicate and understand what they face. Events have very different meanings for our varied residents, some of whom experience foreigner discrimination and suspicion in the wake of the September 11, 2001, events. As Box 3.6 and 3.7 demonstrates that a dignified university professors and cabbies and recent immigrants in New York City, a most cosmopolitan city, have different constructions of reality.

Direct Practice and Reality Conceptions. Our field emphasizes the potential for shared meaning with clients and community members (Lum, 2003; Saari, 1991; Stringer, 1999), but some differences go deep. To be effective practitioners must become attuned to different systems of meaning. As Berger and Luckmann (1967) argue, the world and society, reality, is neither a system, a mechanism, nor an organism; it is a symbolic construction of ideas, meanings, and language. The constructions are ever-changing through human action—and they also continually change the human actors. Humans continually construct and internalize the construction of the world, which then becomes their reality, to which they must respond to as objective reality. Thus, while we are always acting and constructing and changing the world and ourselves, we do so in the context of the institutions and frameworks of meaning that we were socialized to by previous generations. Culture, with its ideology and religious assumptions about the nature of reality, shapes our construction. Normalcy is a construction.

Imagine the reality of being homeless or being born to 17th-century nobility. Both shape the realities of each. Professionals and service users cannot presume to understand each other—another reason for "checking things out"—until a common language and vocabulary, the basis of ideals and reality construction, develops. Language is a process of developing shared meanings, symbols, and constructions.

Languages are culturally bound signs and symbols. The cultures can be limited, such as particular groups, professions, and scientific disciplines. "It is imperative that social workers ensure that their manner of speaking is similar enough to the client's manner of speaking so as to be part of a shared discourse" (Pozatek, 1994, p. 399). This entails avoiding professional jargon. As Wells (1993) points out regarding emergency rooms, "Choice of words is an important consideration when dealing with a patient's family. Excessive use of medical terminology [such as *intubation*] may escalate anxiety" (p. 339). It's equally important to listen carefully and verify

---

BOX 3.7.   Separate Social Realities

The following scene extracted from recorded conversations by Erik Baard, a *Village Voice* reporter, at 9:50 p.m. on September 11, 2001, when it seemed possible that crowds would turn on neighbors and store owners as news spread of who had crashed the passenger planes into the towers of World Trade Center.

"In one of three Arab-run delis in Queensboro Plaza, a Latino boy of maybe 10 years enjoyed grilling the nervous thirtyish man behind the counter at the Plaza Deli and Grocery. The gap-toothed boy glowed the way a child does when he finds he's got one over on an adult, watching the grownup sputter silly denials, like denying a bad toupee."

"Are you an Arab?"

"No, I'm a Gypsy."
"You're an Arab."
"No, I'm a Gypsy."
"No you're not, you're an Arab."
"I am a gypsy. Next person?"

'The only Gypsy on Queens Plaza is a palm reader upstairs from the fishmongers [sic] and check cashers [sic]. The workers at the three delis studding Queensboro Plaza South are largely Yemeni. But one man already knew to hide, from even a child. (Baard, 2001, paras. 4–11)"

that key ideas are not misunderstood. During crises and commonplace activities, there are numerous and distinct realities, and no one can be "in the know" about all of them. As professionals, we can have more confidence in later actions if we first explore multiple conceptualizations about people and their situations, a step toward culturally competent practice. As the "local becomes global," this is essential.

Inside Our Heads

Problem solving requires critical thinking and reflection. Einstein's epigram quoted at the beginning of this chapter is relevant. New thinking is required. This means engaging in self-reflexivity, and being aware of possible paradigm shifts. Problem solving requires critical consciousness: practitioners should be aware of themselves, their values, their agency's values and culture, the political context and ideology of their work, and the influence of all of these on their thinking and work (Banks, 2007, p. 140). There is growing evidence that peers and neighborhoods matter as much as parents in child rearing and socialization (Eamon, 2002: Gladwell, 1998, p. 55; Sharkey, 2008; Vartanian, Buck, & Walker, 2005). Such a paradigm shift should broaden clinicians' heretofore nearly exclusive focus on matters inside the home to one that incorporates social factors such as community and peers. Community practice skills are required.

Money and Property Examples. In a rich country, it may shock us to hear that people in poor countries sell their body organs for transplant, because we lack the framework—desperate poverty—to consider it. They generally sell their organs to recipients in rich countries. Politicians could easily improve human conditions (drinkable water, health supplies) and save lives through forms of wealth sharing such as overseas aid. But ideological unthinkability stops most U.S. leaders from pursuing international or domestic sharing, even ideas considered by close allies. For example, to give young people a more promising future, Prime Minister Tony Blair persuaded the British government to set up "Baby Bonds" to guarantee that at age 18 every child will receive a fund of about $4,500 to $7,500 (a self-help

account). The poorest children receive the most money (Boshara & Sherraden, 2003).

This is not to say that ours is the only culture that finds some ideas unthinkable. In most cultures, for instance, abolition of inheritance is unfathomable. Conservatives in Congress and their allies in the media have labeled the inheritance tax a "death tax" and criticize it as if it applies to all who die.

Most Americans entertain new thoughts about money only after being exposed to ideologies other than neoliberal capitalism, to worldviews other than those held in the Western developed world, and to utopian novels and communities, or perhaps to Great Recessions. Even during the midst of the Great Recession and the mega-bank bailouts at public expense, those arguing against universal health coverage and a public option shouted that it was socialistic, communistic, and immoral and (ignoring history and the contemporary reality) that the market would eventually provide a better health care system.

Again, social workers need to be critical. Why does any of this matter in our practice? First, we must start from the premise that we have certain cognitive and ideological blinders. Second, if a way of thinking is unfamiliar—or even a bad idea or based on error—a social worker still must take notice and be able to stand in the shoes of those who use it.

Proposing a Different Thought Structure. While we often attempt to see the total picture, we rarely attempt to propose a different picture. Brandwein (1985) does just that by outlining the feminist thought structure that currently contends with the dominant Western white male thought structure. The dominant structure is rational and materialistic, while one feminist construct places value on emotional and intuitive "knowing" (p. 177). Instead of asserting a strictly gender-based conflict, Brandwein juxtaposes two philosophies and ways of seeing the world or thinking— for example, contrasting feminism's "both/and" with the dominant "either/or," and feminism's "collaborative" with the dominant "competitive." Brandwein argues that true change comes only when a new thought structure is introduced and gains acceptance and ascendancy (p. 174). Debates over pay equity do not take place so long as women are deemed to be possessions—whether as slave or wife. Brandwein is adamant that most movements, although "advocating social and economic justice," stay stuck in old thought patterns—that is, they adhere to "the dominant thought-structure in our society" (p. 169).

Thought structures can be contested (VanSoest & Bryant, 1995). For example, those in critical legal studies (a critical approach to law) ask whether it makes sense to continually take a rights approach to law reform or social change. Yet allegiance to individual rights goes so deep that it is hard for us to conceive of alternatives. The gay and lesbian movement (Tully, 1994; Warner, 1993) has challenged the way normal human behavior and development and couples counseling is taught.

Culture and Social Problems

Culture is "that which makes us a stranger when we are away from home," according to anthropologist John Caughey (1984, p. 9), who connects culture with a set of beliefs, rules, and values, with a way of life, with an outer and an inner world.

Reality in a Cultural Context

"Because we are each a product of our culture(s), culture provides the filters through which we each interpret reality," explain Kavanagh and Kennedy (1992, p. 23), but they add that approaches flowing from many cultures can have merit. Saari (1991) says, "Culture has often been referred to as if it were a singular and static thing. It is not" (p. 52). Nor is it solely about language and racial differences. Indeed, Swidler describes culture as a tool kit (Forte, 1999).

Expectations Regarding Cultural Awareness. Social workers are expected to acquire multicultural awareness and cultural competence in dealing with "discoverable" differences—for instance, that godparents are a resource in many Hispanic families (Vidal, 1988). We also must learn to interpret less obvious or apparent differences. A study of older rural African Americans found that many of them believe receiving help in old age is a reward for having lived a good life. Acquiring such cultural knowledge allows helpers to market

or program services in more appropriate ways to address problems (Jett, 2002).

To grasp the hidden, a social worker, like an ethnographer, must search for the "meaning of things" that a full participant in a separate culture "knows but doesn't know he knows" (Spradley & McCurdy, 1972, p. 34). For instance, cultural participants have a tacit understanding of the conventions and values associated with public speaking. Conklin and Lourie (1983) point out that not all speeches use the form taught in school of previews, reviews, summaries, and evaluations. An alternative form is topic chaining, shifting from one topic to the next. Moreover, many Amerindians "offer all known facts, regardless of how they apply to their own personal opinions. . . . The interactional goals of Anglo-Americans and American Indians—the one to convince the listeners, the other to submit information for their private deliberation—lead to two radically different oratorical structures (Conklin & Lourie, 1983, p. 274)."

Ethnocentrism makes us feel that our way is right because it is what we know, even though facts can give us a broader view (e.g., Americans hold silverware differently from most other Westerners). As professionals, we must know our biases, how we see the world, and how we take the measure of others. Do we grasp our own ethnic bias about what constitutes an effective speech, an appropriate or acceptable human body, or the best way to eat a formal meal? Those who must learn a new culture become more accepting of multiple traditions. For instance, Cao O. is Chinese, born in Vietnam. Now a social worker in the United States, he describes his transition as his family became more American, acquiring new habits and new wants, such as privacy: "Now what I use to eat with depends on who I am eating with. . . . At home we don't use the small rice bowls any more. We use the American soup bowls to eat with. Yet my family would use chopsticks to go with that. We don't pick up the bowl anymore. . . . Before my family all lived and slept in one big room. Now I have to have my own room" (quoted in Lee, 1992, p. 104).

It sometimes takes a jarring twist for conventional Americans to notice either different practices (such as not automatically smiling) or competing perspectives (such as thinking of oneself as "temporarily able-bodied" or "differently abled" rather than thinking of some fellow humans as "mobility impaired" or "handicapped"). Oliver (1990) describes a survey of adults with disabling conditions that included questions such as "Can you tell me what is *wrong* with you?" and "Does your health problem/disability mean that you *need* to live with relatives or someone else who can help *look after* you?" (emphasis added) (p. 7). According to Oliver, "the interviewer visits the disabled person at home and asks many structured questions. . . . It is in the nature of the interview process that the interviewer presents as expert and the disabled person as an isolated individual inexperienced in research, and thus unable to reformulate the questions" (which never focus on the environment, just the person) (pp. 7–8).

No matter how pleasant the interviewer, niceties cannot overcome his or her built-in power and control, yet the professional may not think of this or the competing realities. A disabled identity that affects the thinking of everyone with every degree of *ableness*, in Oliver's view, is constructed through medicalization, personal tragedy theory, dependency expectations, and *externally imposed* images of disability (Oliver, 1990, p. 77).

There can be rival perceptions. Many oppressed groups and persons out of the mainstream have identification considerations. Native Hawaiian children do not identify with either Japanese or white (Haole) people. African immigrants may not identify with African-Americans. With any given group, social workers must grasp whether messages from the dominant group are "accommodated, negotiated, or resisted" (Grace & Lum, 2001, p. 421).

Different Standpoints. The concept of communitarianism, discussed in Chapter 1, helps us avoid getting stuck in tribalism, balkanism, victimization, and martyrdom. However, differences and history cannot be ignored, whether one is working in a military community, with its tendency to reject homosexuals, or in a "gay" (even the language is different) community, where the 1978 murder of San Francisco city supervisor Harvey Milk and the 1969 Stonewall battle in Greenwich Village still have meaning (Duberman, 1993; Simon, 1994, p. 150). Similarly, those who want

blacks to "get over it" and quit bringing up the topic of slavery are ignoring other debasing moments in white history: hideous tortures that served as a preamble to lynchings were considered public entertainment as recently as 70 years ago (Cohen, 2000). Just as the Great Depression and September 11, 2001, still affect people, then lynchings and the *Trail of Tears*[2] also still affect people. A caseworker takes a social history; a community worker digs out a social history of a community and its people. A practitioner involved with the community in capacities such as child adoption needs to know personal and communal social histories and their accompanying worldviews.

Service users and community residents can better share their stories if they realize that we know something about their world. If a sixth grader in a self-esteem group says that she sleeps in the same bed as a parent, we do not need to presume incest when the problem may be poverty. Greif (1994) observes that "working with these parents [from public housing] has taught me to rethink many of my basic assumptions about therapy with poor families and African American families. Twenty years ago I had been trained, for example, that parents should never share a bed with children. Yet these mothers have little choice" (p. 207). Awareness of multiple realities keeps us from making premature assessments. Feminist standpoint theory takes a similar position. "Members of each group must work to understand the standpoint of others to construct views of our shared reality that are less partial," says Swigonski (1994, p. 392). For direct and indirect practice success, we must listen to and understand the voices of the community (Forte, 2004).

Different Classes. Saari (1991) asserts that "members of traditionally disadvantaged minority groups are by no means the only persons in society who must participate in more than one culture. . . . In a complex society, the individual normally participates in a number of somewhat different cultures or shared meaning systems in the course of an average day" (pp. 53–54). Some of these cultures or systems play a greater role than others. For example, it is easy to underestimate class differences if the focus is solely on race and ethnicity.

Those who are more privileged and better educated, with certain tastes, have the idea that they see things as they really are and are sure that "others" lag, without drive, stuck in their provincial or limited realities and behaviors. Less privileged and less educated people of the same heritage, with certain tastes, consider themselves down-to-earth people who see things as they really are but view "others" as fixated on striving and appearances, "uptight and stuck-up," limited by snobbish realities and behaviors. Each view is ethnocentric and cultural-centric (Berger & Luckmann, 1967). These views are internalized at quite a young age; children know about subtle distinctions, as this telling story shows: A little girl was shown a card depicting five bears who looked exactly alike, but one bear was being shunned by the other four. When she was asked what was happening in the picture, her quick reply was, "He's not our kind of bear."

Insider/Outsider Perspectives on Reality. Children gain cultural knowledge from a variety of sources, ranging from parental commands ("leave your nose alone") to peer teaching and observation of their social environments. They also develop a perspective of their own. Sixth-grade girls can "distinguish nearly one hundred ways to fool around," including "bugging other kids, playing with food, and doodling" (Spradley & McCurdy, 1972, pp. 18–19). Adults have a different perspective on such activities.

We must be aware of how the other person views experience. "The effective communicator learns to acquire and to understand, to the greatest extent possible, both insider (emic) and outsider (etic) perspectives" (Kavanagh & Kennedy, 1992, pp. 45–46). Etic analysis, which is observer oriented, gives us the ability to see similarities and differences and to compare or find commonalties across systems. Such a level of analysis might further a communitarian view by pointing out categories that all humans relate to, such as kinship. In social work, planners and organizers build on such a perspective. In contrast, emic analysis, which is actor oriented, allows us to become immersed in a worldview or lifestyle and its minutiae as a participant or a participant-observer. Emic analysis takes us into a collective, culture-specific mindset. Kavanagh and Kennedy (1992) see trade-offs: "The emic view provides

the subjective experience but limits objectivity, whereas the etic perspective is more objective, but is farther from actual experience of the phenomenon" (p. 23).

Uniting with Consumers and Community Residents. Often it seems as if there is a world of clients, communities, and causes and also a social worker world, while for practice purposes the ideal is a joint one. The core of critical community practice, indeed social work, is "a commitment *to working for social justice through empowering disadvantaged, excluded and oppressed communities to take more control over the conditions of their lives* (emphasis original) (Henderson, 2007, p. 17).

Three key ideas derived from the etic–emic discussion are as follows:

- *Those experiencing the social problem have an emic or insider view.* Therefore, "Instead of asking, 'What do I see these people doing?' we must ask, 'What do these people see themselves doing?'" (Spradley & McCurdy, 1972, p. 9). Kavanagh and Kennedy (1992) urge that we "assess from the client's perspective what the most appropriate goals are in a given situation" (p. 24).
- *Social workers and clients may not share the same context or realities during an interaction.* What we say may not be what clients hear, and vice versa. "It is essential," writes Pozatek (1994), "for practitioners to be aware of this phenomenon, and to socially construct, through dialogue with the client, a shared reality that they agree is a representation of their interaction" (p. 399).
- *Clients have reasons for what they do or decide.* We must individualize (Al-Krenawi & Graham, 2000). Green (1998) warns that if social workers view intervention modes as having universal applicability, such thinking constitutes applied ethnocentrism.

One area in which we want to build a shared reality is in constructing the story of the problem as it is told by individuals, families, groups, or community residents (Chrystal, 1999; Donaldson, 1976; Finn, 1998; Marcus, 1992; Saleebey, 1994). We may be the experts on resources and options, but our clients are the experts on their own needs and problems

(Hartman, 1992). We must convert the question "What can I as a social worker do to help out those poor people?" to a question to mull over: "What are they saying to me?"

The second way to build a shared reality is through mutual hope, mutual expectation, and a shared sense of efficacy. Saleebey (1994) sees narrative and the building of hope as connected. If only negative tales are being told (e.g., by residents in public housing), then counterstories of success or "grace under pressure" might be spread and "scenarios of possibility" might be opened up (pp. 356–357). Most individuals and advocates have such stories to tell. Since "meaning . . . can inspire or oppress," suggests Saleebey, "why not take the time to work with individuals to articulate those meanings, those stories, those possible narratives that elevate spirit and promote

action?" (p. 357). An awareness of the client's or community's symbolic associations will increase the effectiveness of the intervention (Forte, 2004, p. 522) as Asherah Cinnamon exemplifies in Box 3.8.

Social Problem Intervention: A Brief Overview

To recapitulate, we can analyze the nature of a social problem by:

- knowing our own minds and ideas, being critical practitioners, and learning how clients or consumers of services see the problem's implications for them
- figuring out which significant actors or community segments can potentially provide resources

---

| BOX 3.8. | A Problem Solver Starts a Months-Long Process |

Asherah Cinnamon is the director and sole paid staffer of the East Tennessee chapter of the National Coalition-Building Institute (NCBI), an organization that addresses intergroup tensions. This social worker, who coordinates 20 to 30 local volunteers, demonstrates sensitivity to her community:

Three days in January, though not routine for me, nevertheless represent the culmination of three years of local organizing and relationship-building. At 8 p.m. on a Monday night, I hear that a black church [and its radio station and day-care center] in our city has been burned to the ground in the early morning hours. Recovering from shock, outrage, and grief about this, I begin making phone calls to find out more about it and learn that the church is one of more than 20 that have burned to date in the Southeast USA in the past 16 months. . . . That same night, we put together a statement of support to present to the congregation of the burned-out church as quickly as possible. Calls go back and forth at 10 p.m. with the first draft of the statement, to check with the NAACP president and several chapter members to make sure that the statement is appropriate and will indeed be seen by the African community as a genuine offer of support.

Early the next morning I begin faxing the statement out to key community leaders, especially white church and synagogue leaders, for their signatures. . . . I make more phone calls to encourage other local leaders to sign the statement. . . . The vast majority

of people I speak with thank me for giving them the opportunity to show their support. Many say they did not know what to do, and their shock kept them immobile until I called.

That evening, I meet with the Methodist minister who helped me draft the statement, to attend the prayer service in the parking lot of the burned-out church. It is a freezing January night . . . and our toes feel frozen soon after we arrive. We are introduced to the presiding minister, who welcomes us and invites us to read our statement of support after the service. I do so and then list some of the community leaders who have signed. I notice the faces of the 50 or so congregants who are gathered in this place of violent destruction. As I read, I see one woman elbow her friend with an excited air as she hears the names of the signers. . . . One woman's eyes sparkle with unshed tears. . . . It is a small thing, really, to put words together and send around a statement of support. But for these people, it is a sign of hope, and a contradiction to their isolation as victims of violence and their isolation as members of a minority group in the midst of a majority culture which has too often let them down.

Source: From Cinnamon, A. (1999). Community organizing for social change. In L. M. Grobman (Ed.), *Days in the lives of social workers: 50 professionals tell real life stories from social work practice* (2nd ed., pp. 295–300). Harrisburg, PA: White Hat Communications. Copyright 1999 by White Hat Communications. Reprinted with permission of the author and White Hat Communications.

- on any issue, finding out our profession's stance, reading in other disciplines and studying the media, and reviewing past and present general views regarding solutions, as well as conservative and liberal positions
- discovering the collective definition process this problem has undergone to date and an appropriate role, if any, for our agency. If we plan to intervene, we must also look at what others have done and consider what we can do.

While the model presented in this chapter is not the only way to construct social problems, it is useful for conceptualizing social problems for purposes of social intervention and social policy. It provides a framework for determining to whom and why (costs, deviance, ideology) a social condition is problematic. The framework recognizes that different social conditions have different profiles and the same social condition can have different profiles to different groups within society and over time, although the condition may be unchanged, depending on ideology, costs, affordability, and technology.

The framework generally ignores the notion of a fundamental conception of need. Need beyond survival is a very elusive concept and is highly individualized as well as being culturally relative. Poverty in the United States is not poverty in Haiti.

The model's usefulness for social problem analysis is that it directs the analyst to:

1. determine the quantifiable nature of the condition and whether that quantifiable definition is generally shared (the basis for staging the condition as a social problem and the basis for social intervention)
2. determine specific deviations and from whose norms, standards, and ideology it deviates (the basis for coalition building and social and political support)
3. determine whether the deviation or behavior is viewed as individual and/or a social deviation; what parts are individual and what parts are socially caused
4. determine the ideological frame of reference used by definers, which shapes all other definitions
5. determine the elements, degree, and interrelationships of social etiologies while not assuming unitary causation, which provides a direction for intervention
6. determine the social costs and to whom and by what criteria the condition represents a social cost (or who pays) to form the basis of social policy decision making, remediation, and cost allocation
7. determine preferred outcomes states
8. determine protocol or procedures of interventions and remediation to lead to desired outcomes

Basically, problem identification, structuring, and staging, discussed later in the methodology section of the book, sets the perspective on intervention.

Our problem-framework components relate to intervention in social problem construction. We must work toward a shared construction of a problem. The way a condition is constructed as a problem will expand or narrow the number and variety of people who will join the action. It has become clear, for example, that the phrase "right to life" was successful as a recruitment and umbrella term for diverse constituencies, while "anti-abortion" was more limiting. In the same way, the term "pro-abortion" was problematic because abortion is not something many want to endorse, in comparison with the idea of "pro-choice." Community organizers sometimes call this "cutting the issue" (Mizrahi, 2001; Staples, 1997). If we are clear that we will be working with people of many minds, our appeals can be better directed to reach a broad group. The same holds true as we try to build an action coalition. To lobby with the community requires us to find core beliefs that unify. Problems create common denominators for citizens even while being distinctively experienced.

How does a strategic grasp of problems influence our practice? The practitioner becomes clear about what community members understand to be social problems and achieves a joint vision with them, then looks for ways to get forces in the community to work toward desired outcomes. The practitioner may strive to have defined as a problem something the community cares about or wants to change, or could strive to get something currently seen as a problem to be viewed as a non-problem or, more typically, a different kind of problem. Suppose that the current understanding of the problem is adverse to community interests or siphons off resources that should go toward solving problems in the community's interests. The effort to stop terrorists from injuring U.S. citizens is an example. A prevailing political understanding is that immigrants, foreign visitors, and men from the Middle East are potential risks See Box 3.7). Social workers who work with immigrants and refugees may be able to reframe the problem, at the community level, to protect those we serve. Certainly, all the money put into military and security programs represents money that could have been used to meet community goals and to solve social problems.

Putting Oneself in the Picture: Exercises

1. In her empowerment guide for people engaged in social action, Katrina Shields (1994) proposes ways to connect the personal and the political. We adapted some exercises she suggests:

    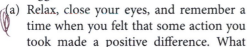

    (a) Relax, close your eyes, and remember a time when you felt that some action you took made a positive difference. What happened? Who was involved? What was the setting? Remember as vividly as possible your feelings at the time.

    Share your memory in small groups or pairs, or write about the incident in your journal.

    (b) If you were totally fearless and in possession of all your powers, what would you do to heal our world (or do about a social problem that concerns you)? With whom would you like to join forces?

    Share in a circle in pairs, or write your thoughts in your journal.

    (c) How do you "disempower" yourself? How do you perceive others as doing this? Do you have a myth, belief, or story that helps you put the current times in perspective, and to persist when the going gets rough?

    Ask yourself these questions or discuss them with others (see Shields, 1994, pp. 19, 23, 77, for original exercises).

2. Mainstream media ignore positive changes brought about by grassroots groups. Start a scrapbook of success stories about community problems and issues.

Discussion Exercises

1. *Did you disagree with any of the premises or arguments set forth in this chapter? Over which sections do you think you and your parents or you and your neighbors would have the most disagreement?*

2. *On what basis should social workers take action regarding social problems? Consider these possibilities: stopping the spread of AIDS in Africa; condemning Islamophobia in the United States; legalizing marijuana or euthanasia; replacing old, faulty voting equipment; regulating violent content in video games; rewarding never-married welfare recipients who marry; stopping abortion. Review the elements in framing a condition. What are your first three steps?*

3. *For a study of alternative realities, watch Rashomon (1951), the classic Japanese film about a lady, a gentleman, and a bandit; consider their widely differing points of view about whether there was a sexual assault and about virtues such as bravery. How can we take differing realities into consideration without losing confidence that there is any solid ground on which we can stand to practice?*

4. *Discuss similarities and differences in societal perspectives over time regarding honor and respect.* *Think about ghetto deaths resulting from "being dissed" (disrespected) and 19th century nobility deaths from dueling.*

5. *Imagine a society in which parents have their children with them for only 4 years; then the children go to live with a series of other families, randomly selected. Eventually, parents and children are reunited for 4 years. In general, children would spend about 10 of their first 26 years with their birth parents (this is based on Sandra Feldman's "Child Swap Fable" in Eitzen & Zinn, 2000, p. 547). Discuss what difference this would make in what families care about and in the U.S. budget.*

6. *Spector and Kitsuse (1987) suggest a rudimentary approach to analysis and action: cut out community newspaper clippings; put down fundamental ideas and your own beginning knowledge about a situation that should be addressed for personal or professional reasons. The requisite activities are these: (a) describe a condition; (b) tell why it is annoying, disturbing, harmful, unethical, destructive, or unwholesome; (c) identify what causes the condition; (d) describe what should be done*

about it; and (e) explain how one would begin to accomplish this (pp. 161–162). Experiment using this exercise in the field with a client. If you're working with an organization, examine an issue collectively with your group.

7. *Do not forget the importance of collecting data and obtaining a firm grasp on specifics. As a young labor organizer, Eugene Debs endeavored to protect the rights and lives of firemen on U.S. railways. To orient himself, "He set up a sheet of brown wrapping paper on one wall of his room and drew it off into squares. On the left-hand side he put the job the worker was doing; in the first column he set up the hours, in the next the wages, in the next the ratio of employment to unemployment, in the next the proportion of accidents, and what responsibility the employer took for them; and in the last column the conditions under which the men worked" (Stone, 1947, p. 44). He also learned*

the realities for the wives and children, "He knew to an eighth of a pound and half of a penny how much of the poorest grade of hock meat and bones they could buy, to the last pint of milk and thin slice of bread how much nourishment could go into each of the children; how much longer the threadbare clothing on their backs could endure" (p. 81). Find documents that pinpoint such data about a problem and about a group that are of grave concern to you.

8. *Brief research: Is rape of females viewed as a condition or as a problem in the United States, Mexico, Canada, and England? What about rape of males, especially in prison, in the same countries? Content analysis: Check to see if newspaper accounts about this act of violence use passive voice (that is, "A woman was raped last evening") or active voice ("A man raped a woman last evening) (Blezard, 2002). Does wording matter?*

Notes

1. Schneider and Sidney (2009) present a similar model, although more policy-driven.
2. Most Amerindian nations can recall their own "Trail of Tears" and ethnic cleansing imposed by the United States on them separate from the more known expulsion imposed on the Cherokee Nation.

References

Baard, E. (2001, September 11). Listening to the Arabs of New York. *The Village Voice.* Retrieved May 29, 2003,fromhttp://www.villagevoice.com/issues/0137/baard.php

Al-Krenawi, A., & Graham, J. R. (2000). Culturally sensitive social work practice with Arab clients in mental health settings. *Health and Social Work,* 25(1), 9–21.

American Association of Suicidology. (2008). *Elderly suicide fact sheet,* Retrieved August 26, 2009, from: http://www.suicidology.org.

Banks, S. (2007). Becoming critical: developing the community practitioner. In H. Butcher, S. Banks, P. Henderson, with J. Robertson, J. (Eds.), *Critical community practice* (pp. 133–152). Bristol, UK: The Policy Press.

Baumann, E. A. (1989). Research rhetoric and the social construction of elder abuse. In J. Best (Ed.), *Images of issues: Typifying contemporary social problems* (pp. 55–74). New York: Aldine de Gruyter.

Benson, R., & Saguy, A. C., (2005). Constructing social problems in an age of globalization: A French-American comparison. *American Sociological Review,* 70(2), 233–259.

Berger, P. L., & Luckmann, T. (1967). *The social construction of reality: A treatise in the sociology of knowledge.* Harmondsworth, UK: Penguin Books.

Best, J. (1987). Rhetoric in claims-making: Constructing the missing children problem. *Social Problems,* 34(2), 101–121.

Best, J. (Ed.). (1989). *Images of issues: Typifying contemporary social problems.* New York: Aldine de Gruyter.

Best, J. (2001). *Damned lies and statistics.* Berkeley: University of California Press.

Blezard, R. (2002, Fall). It takes a man: The epidemic of rape won't end until males own up to its causes. *Teaching Tolerance,* 22, 24–30.

Blumer, H. (1969). *Symbolic interactionism.* Englewood Cliffs, NJ: Prentice-Hall, Inc.

Blumer, H. (1971). Social problems as collective behavior. *Social Problems,* 18, 298–306.

Boshara, R., & Sherraden, M. (2003, July 23). For every child, a stake in America. *New York Times,* p. A19.

Bradshaw, J. (1977). The concept of social need. In N. Gilbert & H. Specht, (Eds.), *Planning for Social Welfare* (pp. 290–296). Englewood Cliffs, NJ: Prentice-Hall, Inc.

Brandwein, R. A. (1985). Feminist thought-structure: An alternative paradigm of social change for social justice. In D. G. Gill & E. A. Gill (Eds.), *Toward social and economic justice: A conference in search of social change* (pp. 169–181). Cambridge, MA: Schenkman.

Butcher, H. (2007). Power and empowerment: The foundations of critical community practice. In H. Butcher, S. Banks, P. Henderson, with J. Robertson (Eds.), *Critical community practice* (pp. 17–32). Bristol, UK: The Policy Press.

Butcher, H., Banks, S., Henderson, P., with Robertson, J. (Eds.) (2007). *Critical community practice.* Bristol, UK: The Policy Press.

Castex, G. M. (1993). The effects of ethnocentric map projections on professional practice. *Social Work*, 38(6), 685–693.

Catholic Church abuse settlement, appropriate or unjustified? (2007). *Insurancenewsnet.com*. Retrieved August 26, 2009, from http://insurancenewsnet.com/article.asp

Caughey, J. L. (1984). *Imaginary social worlds: A cultural approach.* Lincoln: University of Nebraska Press.

Chambon, A. S., Irving, A., & Epstein, L. (Eds.). (1999). *Reading Foucault for social work.* New York: Columbia University Press.

Chapin, R. K. (1995). Social policy development: The strengths perspective. *Social Work*, 40(4), 506–514.

Chrystal, S. (1999). Out of silence. *Journal of Teaching in Social Work*, 19(1/2), 187–195.

Cinnamon, A. (1999). Community organizing for social change. In L. M. Grobman (Ed.), *Days in the lives of social workers: 50 professionals tell real life stories from social work practice* (2nd ed., pp. 295–300). Harrisburg, PA: White Hat Communications. Cinnamon's contribution also appears in the revised third edition by Grobman and published by White Hat in 2005, *Days in the lives of social workers: 54 professionals tell real-life stories from social work practice.*

Clifford, D., & Burke, B. (2009). *Anti-oppressive ethics and values in social work.* Basingstoke, UK: Palgrave Macmillan.

Cohen, R. (2000, April 26). Not just "black history": Yesterday's lynchings help explain today's reality. *Washington Post*, p. A35.

Conklin, N. F., & Lourie, M. A. (1983). *A host of tongues: Language communities in the United States.* New York: Free Press.

Delgado, M., & Staples, L. (2008). *Youth-led community organizing.* New York: Oxford University Press.

Dionne, E. J. (2009). *Reports: Never let a crisis go to waste.* Retrieved August 13, 2009, from http://www.truthdig.com/report/item/20090202

Donaldson, K. (1976). *Insanity inside out.* New York: Crown.

Duberman, M. (1993). *Stonewall.* New York: Dutton.

Eamon, M. K. (2002). Poverty, parenting, peer, and neighborhood influences on young adolescent antisocial behavior. *Journal of Social Service Research*, 28(1), 1–23.

Eitzen, D. S., & Zinn, M. B. (2000). *Social problems* (8th ed.) Boston, MA: Allyn & Bacon.

Family First Aid (2009). *Teen suicide deaths, U.S., 2001.* Retrieved, August 26, 2009, from http://www.familyfirstaid.org/suicide.html.

Finn, J. L. (1998). A penny for your thoughts: Stories of women, copper and community. *Frontiers*, 19(2), 231–249.

Fisher, R., & Shragge, E. (2000). Challenging community organizing: Facing the 21st century. *Journal of Community Practice*, 8(3), 1–19.

Forte, J. (2004). Symbolic interactionism and social work: A forgotten legacy, Part 2. *Families in Society*, 85(4), 521–530.

Forte, J. A. (1999). Culture: The tool-kit metaphor and multicultural social work. *Families in Society*, 80(1), 51–62.

Freire, P. (1994). *Pedagogy of hope: Reliving pedagogy of the oppressed.* New York: Continuum Books.

Gabriel, J. (1994). Initiating a movement: Indigenous, black and grassroots struggles in the Americas. *Race & Class*, 35(3), 1–17.

Gans, H. J., (1971, July-August). The uses of poverty: The poor pay all. *Social Policy*, 2, 20–24.

Gans, H. J. (1973). *More equality.* New York: Pantheon.

Ginsberg, L. (1994). *Understanding social problems, policies, and programs.* Columbia: University of South Carolina Press.

Gladwell, M. (1998). Do parents matter? *New Yorker*, 74(24), 54–64.

Gladwell, M. (2002). *The tipping point: How little things can make a big difference.* Boston, MA: Little, Brown, & Company.

Gordon, D. R. (1994). *The return of the dangerous classes.* New York: W. W. Norton

Grace, D. J., & Lum, A. L. P. (2001). "We don't want no haole buttholes in our stories": Local girls reading the Baby-Sitters Club books in Hawaii. *Curriculum Inquiry*, 31(4), 421–452.

Green, J. W. (1998). *Cultural awareness in the human services.* Englewood Cliffs, NJ: Prentice Hall.

Greenberg, M., Schneider, D., & Singh, V. (1998). Middle class Asian American neighborhoods: Resident and practitioner perceptions. *Journal of Community Practice*, 5(3), 63–85.

Greif, G. L. (1994). Using family therapy ideas with parenting groups in schools. *Journal of Family Therapy*, 16(2), 199–208.

Gumz, E. J., & Grant, C. L. (2009). Restorative justice: A systematic review of the social work literature. *Families in Society*, 90(1), 119–126.

Hammerstein, O., & Logan, J. (1949). *South Pacific: A musical play.* New York: Random House.

Hardina, D. (2002). *Analytical skills for community organization practice*. New York: Columbia University Press.

Hartman, A. (1992). In search of subjugated knowledge. *Social Work*, 37(6), 483–484.

Henderson, P. (2007). Introduction. In H. Butcher, S. Banks, & P. Henderson with J. Robertson. (Eds.), *Critical community practice* (pp. 1–15). Bristol, UK: The Policy Press.

Jett, K. (2002). Making the connection: Seeking and receiving help by elderly African Americans. *Qualitative Health Research*, 12(3), 373–438.

Kavanagh, K. H., & Kennedy, P. H. (1992). *Promoting cultural diversity: Strategies for health care professionals*. Newbury Park, CA: Sage.

Lee, J. F. J. (1992). *Asian Americans: Oral histories of first to fourth generation Americans from China, the Philippines, Japan, India, the Pacific Islands, Vietnam and Cambodia*. New York: New Press.

Lewis, A. (1966). *Gideon's trumpet*. New York: Vintage Books

Licensed social workers in the U.S.: 2004 (March 2006). Prepared by Center for Health Workforce Studies, School of Public Health, University at Albany and Center for Workforce Studies, National Association of Social Workers.

Lopez, S. (1994). *Third and Indiana*. New York: Viking Press.

Lum, D. (Ed.). (2003). *Culturally competent practice: A framework for understanding diverse groups and justice issues* (2nd ed.). Pacific Grove, CA: Brooks/Cole—Thomson Learning.

Marcus, E. (1992). *Making history: The struggle for gay and lesbian equal rights*. New York: Harper Perennial.

Mazmanian, D. A., & Sabatier, P. A. (1981). The implementation of public policy: A framework of analysis. In D. A. Mazmanian & P. A. Sabatier (Eds.), *Effective policy implementation* (pp. 3–35). Lexington, MA: Lexington Books.

Mildred, J. (2003). Claimsmakers in the child abuse "wars": Who are they and what do they want? *Social Work*, 48(4), 492–503.

Mills, C. W. (1959). *The sociological imagination*. New York: Oxford University Press.

Mizrahi, T. (2001). Community organizing principles and practice guidelines. In A. R. Roberts & G. J. Greene (Eds.), *Social workers' desk reference*. New York: Oxford University Press.

Murase, K. (1995). Organizing in the Japanese American community. In F. G. Rivera & J. L. Erlich (Eds.), *Community organizing in a diverse society* (2nd ed., pp. 143–160). Boston: Allyn & Bacon.

Murray, C., & Herrnstein, R. J. (1994). *The bell curve: Intelligence and class structure in American life*. New York: The Free Press.

Netting, F. E., Kettner, P. M., & McMurtry, S. L. (2008). *Social work macro practice* (4th ed.). Upper Saddle River, NJ: Pearson.

Oliver, M. (1990). *The politics of disablement*. New York: St. Martin's Press.

Orshansky, M. (1965). Counting the poor: Another look at the poverty profile. *Social Security Bulletin*, 28(1), 3–29.

Parsons, R. J., Hernandez, S. H., & Jorgensen, J. O. (1988). Integrated practice: A framework for problem solving. *Social Work*, 33(5), 417–421.

Payne, M. (2006). *Modern social work theory*, (3rd ed.). Chicago, IL: Lyceum.

Pozatek, E. (1994). The problem of certainty: Clinical social work in the postmodern era. *Social Work*, 39(4), 396–403.

Ryan, W. (1976). *Blaming the victim* (Rev., updated ed.). New York: Vintage Books.

Saari, C. (1991). *The creation of meaning in clinical social work*. New York: Guilford Press.

Saleebey, D. (1994). Culture, theory, and narrative: The intersection of meanings in practice. *Social Work*, 39(4), 351–359.

Schneider, A., & Sidney, M. (2009). What is next for policy design and social construction theory? *Policy Studies Journal*, 37(1), 103–119.

Sharkey, P. (2008). The intergenerational transmission of context. *American Journal of Sociology*, 113(4), 931–969.

Shields, K. (1994). *In the tiger's mouth: An empowerment guide for social action*. British Columbia, Canada: New Society Publishers.

Silow-Carroll, S., Alteras, T., & Stepnick, L. (2006). *Patient-centered care for underserved populations: Definitions and best practices*. Washington, DC: Economic and Social Research Institute.

Simon, B. L. (1994). *The empowerment tradition in American social work: A history*. New York: Columbia University Press.

Spector, M. (1985). Social problems. In A. Kuper & J. Kuper (Eds.), *The social science encyclopedia* (pp. 779–780). New York: Routledge.

Spector, M., & Kitsuse, J. I. (1987). *Constructing social problems*. New York: Aldine de Gruyter.

Spradley, J. P., & McCurdy, D. W. (1972). *The cultural experience: Ethnography in complex society*. Chicago: Science Research.

Staples, L. (1997). Selecting and "cutting" the issue. In M. Minkler (Ed.), *Community organizing and community building for health* (pp. 175–194). New Brunswick, NJ: Rutgers University Press.

Stone, I. (1947). *Adversary in the house*. New York: New American Library.

Stringer, L. (1999). *Grand Central winter: Stories from the street*. New York: Washington Square Press.

Swigonski, M. E. (1994). The logic of feminist standpoint: Theory for social work research. *Social Work,* 39(4), 387–393.

Themba, M. N. (1999). *Making policy, making change: How communities are taking the law into their own hands.* Berkeley, CA: Chardon Press.

Tower, K. D. (1994). Consumer-centered social work practice: Restoring client self-determination. *Social Work,* 39(2), 191–196.

Tully, C. T. (1994). To boldly go where no one has gone before: The legalization of lesbian and gay marriages. *Journal of Gay and Lesbian Social Services,* 1(1), 73–87.

Van Soest, D., & Bryant, S. (1995). Violence reconceptualized for social work: The urban dilemma. *Social Work,* 40(4), 549–557.

Vartanian, T. P., Buck, T., & Walker, P. (2005). Childhood and adolescent neighborhood effects on adult income: Using siblings to examine differences in ordinary least squares and fixed-effect models. *Social Service Review,* 79(1), 60–94.

Vidal, C. (1988). Godparenting among Hispanic Americans. *Child Welfare,* 67(5), 453–458.

Vissing, Y., & Diament, J. (1995). Are there homeless youth in my community? Differences of perception between service providers and high school youth. *Journal of Social Distress and the Homeless,* 4(4), 287–299.

von Wormer, K. (2009, April). Restorative justice as social justice for victims of gendered violence: A standpoint feminist perspective. *Social Work,* 54:2, 107–116.

Walsby, H. (2008). *The domain of ideology: A study of the development and structure of ideology.* Retrieved August 21, 2009, from http://www.gwiep.net/books/obi22.htm.

Warner, M. (Ed.). (1993). *Fear of a queer planet: Queer politics and social theory.* Minneapolis: University of Minnesota Press.

Wells, P. J. (1993). Preparing for sudden death: Social work in the emergency room. *Social Work,* 38(3), 339–342.

West, C. (1994). *Race matters.* New York: Vintage Books.

Whitaker, T., & Arrington, P. (2008). *Social workers at work: NASW membership workforce study.* Washington, DC: National Association of Social Workers.

4

The Concept of Community in Social Work Practice

As we neared the end of the twentieth century, the rich were richer, the poor, poorer. And people everywhere now had a lot less lint, thanks to the lint rollers made in my hometown. It was truly the dawn of a new era.

Michael Moore, American film maker, writer

This is the duty of our generation as we enter the twenty-first century—solidarity with the weak, the persecuted, the lonely, the sick, and those in despair. It is expressed by the desire to give a noble and humanizing meaning to a community in which all members will define themselves not by their own identity but by that of others.

Elie Wiesel, writer, political activist, Nobel laureate

The American city should be a collection of communities where every member has a right to belong. It should be a place where every man feels safe on his streets and in the house of his friends. It should be a place where each individual's dignity and self-respect is strengthened by the respect and affection of his neighbors. It should be a place where each of us can find the satisfaction and warmth which comes from being a member of the community of man.

Lyndon B. Johnson, 36th president of the United States

We all have a mental image of community. Fraught with personal meaning, the word *community* conjures up memories of places where we grew up, where we now live and work, physical structures and spaces—cities, towns, neighborhoods, buildings, stores, roads, streets. It calls up memories of people and relationships—families, friends and neighbors, organizations, associations of all kinds: congregations, PTAs, clubs, congregations, teams, neighborhood groups, town meetings, and even virtual communities experienced through chat rooms. It evokes special events and rituals—Fourth of July fireworks, weddings, funerals, parades, and the first day of school. It stirs up sounds and smells and feelings—warmth, companionship, nostalgia, and sometimes fear, anxiety, and conflict as well. We all grew up somewhere; we all live in communities somewhere; we all desire human associations, some degree of belonging to a human community; we all carry around some sense of community and communities of memory within us. It goes deep into our souls.

But it is hard to imagine a more elusive concept than the idea of community. Its elusiveness comes from its multidimensionality. Cohen (1985), as cited in Chapter 1, found 90 different definitions of community in the 1985 social science literature. Community means a lot and it means different things, from the romantic and mystical to the mundane. Bellah and his colleagues define a community as a "group of people who are socially interdependent, who participate together in discussion and decision making, and who share certain practices that both define the community and are nurtured by it" (Bellah, Madsen, Sullivan, Swidler, & Tipton, 1985, p. 333). Cohen's (1985) conception of community has emotional charging, personal identification, and symbolic construction by people. Resting on its meaning, community is "a system of values, norms, and moral codes which provoke a sense of identity to its members. . . . Structures do not . . . create meaning for people. . . . [Without meaning] many of the organizations designed to create `community' as palliative to anomie and alienation are doomed to failure" (p. 9). "Community, therefore, is where one learns and continues to practice how to 'be social' (p. 15)." The British Columbia Ministry of Children and Family Development (2003), following Mattessich and Monsey (1997), define community more dryly as "people who live within a geographically defined area and who have social and psychological ties with each other and with the place where they live." Berry (1996) argued that community has no value that is economically or practically beneficial. The reasoning is that if something can't be assigned an economic value, it serves no purpose.

We take a less neoliberal economic position and argue that communities have consummate value. We have adopted Fellin's (2001) formal definition of communities as "social units with one or more of the following three dimensions:

1. a functional spatial unit meeting sustenance needs
2. a unit of patterned interaction

3. a symbolic unit of collective identification" (p. 1)

We also borrow from Willie, Willard, and Ridini (2008) with our concern for horizontal and vertical community linkages and the nature of the institutional interactions.

This conception of community is compatible with that used by other community practice authorities (Butcher, Banks, & Henderson with Robertson, 2007; Delgado & Staples, 2008; Hardina, 2002) and has the value of recognizing the spatial, interactional, and emotional components of community.

This chapter establishes the basic concepts, variables, and changes related to community life. The following two chapters examine methodologies of studying communities and methods for hearing community concerns. To change community, its parts, processes, and particularities must be understood.

The common elements in sociological definitions of community are geographic area, social interaction, common ties, and shared sentiments. While connection to a territorial base is common with neighborhoods, villages, or cities fitting the definition, functional and cultural communities or "communities of interest" without clear geographic bases (such as the social work community, the Chicano community, the gay and lesbian communities) are also included. Spatial units with clearly defined geographic boundaries are seemingly becoming less important to a sense of community because rapid electronic communication technology enables virtual communities and ease of physical mobility. We can be connected to several communities of interest because we are geographically mobile and increasingly tied together though electronic and other media. We can interact globally on collective interests. As social workers, we need to understand that our clients belong to multiple communities of identity.

Communities provide people with rich social and personal lives. They shape the way we think and act. They surround us with values and norms of behavior, explicit laws, and unwritten rules of conduct. They furnish us with meanings and interpretations of reality and assumptions about the world. They provide resources and opportunities, albeit highly unevenly—places to work, to learn, to grow, to buy and sell, to worship, to hang out, to find diversion and respite, to care and be cared for. They confront us with challenges, problems, and traumas; they intrude on our lives, and they hold out the possibilities for solutions. Communities are where we live our lives.

The social work ecological model's emphasis on person-in-environment places communities as objects of social work intervention as much as individuals, families, and groups. Social workers can build competent communities. A competent community, according to Fellin (2001), is a community that "has the ability to respond to the wide range of member needs and solve its problems and challenges of daily living" (p. 70). Community competence is enhanced when residents have (a) a commitment to their community, (b) self-awareness of their shared values and interests, (c) openness in communication, (d) wide participation in community decision making, and (e) a sense of collective self-efficacy and empowerment.

Basic Community Concepts

Community, Neighborhood, and Public Life

Community empowerment, community control, and community partnership abound in political and policy discussions. Community and grass-roots have a salient kind of social currency. They are buzzwords in politics and ideologies of the left and right. By *grassroots*, we mean a bottom-up approach, starting with the people who live in a geographic and social community. *Community* and *neighborhood* are sometimes used interchangeably to mean a local area (e.g., a section of a city or a county, where many residents develop a shared worldview). Residents can unite as indignant utility ratepayers or exuberant sports fans in ways that can facilitate shared community identity and action transcending deep differences.

Community suggests people with social ties sharing an identity and a social system, at least partially, while *neighborhood* suggests places that are grounded in regional life where face-to-face relationships are possible. See Fellin (1995, 2001) for an in-depth discussion and definition of community and neighborhood. *Public life* refers

to the civic culture, local setting, and institutional context that also are part of the "environment-surrounding-the-person" (Johnson, 2000). Your public life is available to others. Lappé and Du Bois (1994) provide a delineation of some roles in the various sectors of public life.

Geographic communities evolve in many forms and have been classified in numerous ways such as enclave, edge, center, retreat (Brower, 1996); white versus blue-collar; and boom versus bust. These descriptive structural ideas cannot substitute for the community narrative. Community is more than just local physical space, especially in urban areas, and needs social identity (Fellin, 2001). Residents can share the same geographic space and hold widely differing ideologies and particularistic religious, ethnic, and class identities. They may not constitute a community. Gays, Cuban Americans, and Hassidic Jewish Americans inhabit South Beach, Florida, without sharing the same private languages, political agenda, social interests, or social institutions. A London resident may think about himself more as a businessman or an immigrant from Pakistan than as a Londoner. People in physical proximity—that is, expatriates, international travelers, guest workers, or illegal immigrants—can still share more cultural affinity with those back home than with the new neighborhood.

People in our caseload and communities also have complex allegiances and affiliations. Think of a child who has a father in urban Michigan and a mother in rural Montana and, in either state, bounces from one relative's neighborhood to the next—bringing along clothes, attitudes, haircuts, and slang from the last school that is always one step behind and never quite fits at the new school.

We often bemoan the loss of community with its fragmentation, alienation, and increased mobility accompanied by a decline in public life, with fewer residents involved in voting and volunteering. Today, many people choose their degree of commitment to their neighborhoods and towns. Using length of stay as a variable, Viswanath, Rosicki, Fredin, and Park (2000) found four types of residents:

Drifters: Less than 5 years of stay and a high likelihood of moving away from the community

Settlers: Less than 5 years of stay and less likelihood of moving away from the community
Relocators: More than 5 years of stay but likely to move away from the community
Natives: More than 5 years in the community and unlikely to move away (p. 42)

We have added an additional type, *dreamer,* not discussed by the authors, someone who lives in a community without commitment to the community and dreams of being somewhere else, either a past community or a mystical one. Dreamers can fit into any of the above types.

Natives often blame problems on new arrivals, such as have the nativists in America and Europe blaming illegal immigrants.

Place and Nonplace Communities

The real estate agent's mantra is *location, location, location.* The community practitioner's mantra is *context, context, context.* Where do people come from? To whom do they relate and why? Where is their identity and communities of sentiment? What gives meaning to their lives? Social workers should learn about their clients' place and nonplace communities. Locational communities are a definable area, with boundaries that often constitute a political jurisdiction (Ginsberg, 1998). It focuses attention to a physical and social environment surrounding providers and consumers of services. However, within and outside such spatial and structural communities are other influential nonplace groupings based on identity, profession, religion, ideology, interests, and other social bonds that represent a more amorphous type of community. Social workers must pay attention to an individual's or family's diffuse nonplace social networks, nonplace communities, and solidarity bonds. Place and nonplace communities represent two forms of "we-ness" and identity. Box 4.1 compares the two types of communities.

A client's or case's complete social history ought to include the client's and case's community history and a client's experiences in communities as well as personal and family history—not only where was a person born, but what the person gained from living in prior locales. Social workers will want to get a complete picture of how both types of communities—place and nonplace—figure into an individual's present life.

The Changing U.S. Community

To understand the modern community as a context for social work practice, we will briefly review some important changes in U.S. life that have occurred over the past 50 years. The contemporary U.S. community has undergone significant and perhaps profound changes over the past half century. The United States has vast resources and ambitious people with the freedom and energy to invent, to explore, to develop, and to challenge. We also are a very ideological and jingoist people. Some of the changes are positive, but many, unfortunately, are not. Except for its wealth and power, in many ways the United States approaches Third World status. The United States has fallen to 15th from 2nd in 1980 on the United Nations' Human Development Indices (Conley, 2009; United Nations

| **BOX 4.1.** | **Differences and Similarities Between Place and Nonplace Communities** |

Differences

Place—Bounded Location

Collective territorial identity

Intertwined processes

Empathetic connections

Nonplace—Bounded Interest

Relationship identity and dispersion

Specialized processes

Mixed allegiances

Similarities

Traditions

Mutual constraints

Lack of absolute boundaries

Development Programme, 2008). It also ranks first among industrial nations in infant mortality rates, with a higher rate than Cuba (United Nations Development Programme, 2008). The United States has a higher incarceration rate and more actual inmates than do 36 European nations combined (Blow, 2009).

During most of the last half of the twentieth century, the U.S. economy expanded and especially boomed to end the millennium, only to welcome the new millennium with severe economic recession, corporate greed, financial system collapse, and falling in 2006 to 8th globally in gross national product per capita (United Nations Economic Development Programme, 2008). We were clear about the constellation of a good family and family values, even if we were not always faithful to them and were growing socially more intolerant. The new millennium is accompanied by threats to retirement income and Social Security, with an expanding duration of work life for an aging population. College education, seen as an American birthright until the 1980s and 1990s, has become inordinately expensive. Tuition and room and board at all four-year institutions rose in 2006-2007 dollars from an average of $2,577 for 1976-77 to $19,362 in 2007-08 (Snyder, Dillow, & Hoffman, 2009). World peace and stability, on the horizon with the end of the Cold War and the breakdown of the Soviet Union in 1991, appears to have collapsed into global ethnic strife and terrorism. And on September 11, 2001, global terrorism came to the United States.

As Bob Dylan predicted, "The times they are a-changin'" (Dylan, 1963), but not in the ways he prophesized. The social movements of the 1960s—civil rights, community action, women's liberation, peace—together with the Vietnam War did much to shake the complacency of the 1950s United States. However, the radicalism of the 1960s was followed by conservatism since the 1970s, and it's still with us.

The 1980s saw the need for two wage earners to support a family; burgeoning health care costs; expansions of unemployment, welfare rolls, homelessness, and crime; and a growing income and wealth disparity between the wealthy and the poor and middle classes. The 1990s and the beginning of the twenty-first century have reversed some of these trends and accelerated

others. Welfare, crime, and taxes decreased while income inequality, corporate power, and the influence of money in politics increased. Privatization of social welfare and public services as well as government became trendy. Prisons are a growth industry, with many operated by proprietary corporations, and the United States led the world in incarcerations (Blow, 2009). These all spoke of complex forces at work in U.S. society, seemingly unresponsive to easy fixes. Americans are no longer as optimistic about the future as they once were (Pew Data Trends, 2009). Let's now consider some of the more important forces and trends to deepen our understanding for social work practice in the twenty-first century. The changes reviewed in the following paragraphs reflect our views of what seems significant. They are not presented in any particular order of importance.

• Urbanization and suburbanization continues (Scott, 2001). Most U.S. citizens (over 83%) live in metro areas with a core city of 50,000 or more. Less than 10% live in low-density rural areas (U.S. Census Bureau, 2008). Population continues to shift from the old Rust Belt, mill towns, and smokestack cities of the Northeast and Midwest to the Sunbelt of the South and Southwest, especially California, Florida, and Texas. California and Florida had a growth slowdown with the Great Recession's burst housing bubble. Reflecting the population shift is a change in the economy from manufacturing and farming to information, personal, and entertainment services, technology, and e-businesses. Most metropolitan area growth is in the new outer ring suburbs beyond the old suburbs. Even with periodic energy crises, costs, and chronic dependence on foreign energy sources, the automobile and high-energy consuming, single-family homes still are preferred. Metropolitan area growth hasn't compelled metropolitan government to coordinate the multiple jurisdictions within the metro areas. Probably the greatest resistance to metropolitan governments comes from wealthier suburbanites' not wanting to mingle their public amenities and tax resources with the poorer neighboring core cities. The metropolitan areas are becoming increasingly balkanized and hyper-segregated with more centers of ethnic minorities and poverty, while the outer suburbs are less ethnically, economically, and socially diverse (Scott, 2002).

- Differences between rural, urban, and suburban areas will increase, with rural and city problems neglected for at least the first part of the 21st century. Poverty will continue to be disproportionately greater in rural areas than in metro areas; most of the poor counties in the United States are rural (Samuels & Whitler, 2008). Most rural poor residents are white and non-Hispanic, but poor rural counties, like poor urban areas, have a disproportionate number of poor ethnic minorities (except for the poor Southern mountain counties). Rural areas are less healthy than metropolitan counties (Samuels & Whitler, 2008), and the county in America with the lowest Human Development Indices score is a rural California county, Kings County (Conley, 2009). The natural resources and economic base of rural areas will continue to decline, with low-skill jobs largely lost to even lower-wage global competitors. The wage gap between metro and rural areas continues to widen, as does the gap in college completion rates in favor of metro areas (Snyder, Dillow, & Hoffman, 2009). Distance and a lack of sufficient density hinder rural economic development. Rural localities will continue to lose population, especially younger and more educated residents (Snyder, Dillow, & Hoffman, 2009). The proportion of the nation's population that is nonmetropolitan continues to decrease (U.S. Census Bureau, 2009a, Table 28). Agriculture is declining in the United States based on acreage cultivated, total farmland, and number of farms. Large farms (over 2,000 acres) account for 3% to 4% of the total number of farms, 52% of farm land, and 34% of cultivated land. The number, but not the size, of corporate farms is decreasing (U.S. Census Bureau, 2009b, Tables 793, 794, 796). The exceptions to these trends are the scenic, high-amenity rural areas with mild climates, which are becoming gentrified and gaining populations, and also the growing green movement in small farming slowing the decline in the number of farms (Hoppe, Korb, & O'Donoghue, 2007).

- The 1990s and beyond have seen an escalating economic inequity in the workforce. There has been an extensive loss of well-paying, stable manufacturing blue-collar jobs, with job growth in lower-paying service jobs. During the Great Recession living costs outran wage increases (Grynbaum, 2008). Unemployment in August 2009 reached 9.7%, up from 4.1% in August 2000 and the highest since the 1980s, and this trend shows no signs of abating (Andrews, 2009; Bureau of Labor Statistics, 2009). The 21st century has seen high and persistent rates of unemployment and underemployment among older industrial workers and unskilled men and women of all ages. A rising retirement age is reversing a decade-long trend of earlier retirements (Walsh, 2001). Later retirement ages will be accelerated with the decline in value of stock-based retirement plans and pensions and the increasing age requirements for Social Security retirement benefits.

Even with the Great Recession; the Enron, Lehman Brothers, and AIG fiascos; the Wall Street meltdown; the Troubled Asset Relief Program (TARP); and other corporate failures and bailouts, executive and management salaries and bonuses have continued to increase (Executive Pay, 2009). From 1983 to 2004, the median net worth of upper-income families grew by 123%, while the median net worth of middle-income families grew by just 29% (Pew Research Center, 2009). The middle class made some absolute progress but fell behind in relative terms during the economy's boon years (Krugman 2002). Inflation during this recession is rising faster than the working-class America's income (Cavanagh & Collins, 2008; Grynbaum, 2008). During 2007, CEOs of major U.S. companies collected as much money from one day on the job as average workers made over the entire year. These CEOs averaged $10.8 million in total annual compensation, according to an Associated Press survey of 386 Fortune 500 companies, the equivalent of over 364 times the pay of an average American worker (Anderson, Cavanagh, Collins, Pizzigati, & Lapham, 2007). From 1980 to the end of the century, the average pay of ordinary working people increased by 74%, while the average compensation to corporate CEOs exploded by a gigantic 1,884% (Executive Pay Watch, 2000; Executive Pay, 2002, 2009; Johnston, 2002c). The average pay for chief executives was 36 times that of the average worker in 1976, 131 times in 1993, and 369 times in 2005. In 1976, if an average worker's annual pay was $10,000 and a chief executive's was $360,000, the income differential was $350,000. In 2005, if the average worker's annual pay increased to $20,000, the CEO's compensation engorged to $7,380,000, for a $7,360,000 compensation differential (Mintz, 2007).

Studies indicate there is no direct correlation between executive compensation and corporate performance (Madrick, 2009). As the 2008 fiscal burnout indicated, many poor corporate performers continued to receive huge bonuses and severance packages (Leonhardt, 2002; Madrick, 2009; McGeeham, 2003; Mintz, 2007). The U.S. worker now works more hours a year than workers in other industrial countries. The hours in the work year are increasing in the United States but decreasing in other countries (Greenhouse, 2001).

- Unfortunately, social workers' salaries did not even keep up with inflation during the boon era (Gibelman & Schervish, 1996, p. 166), and they suffered more from the Great Recession. According to the Bureau of Labor Statistics in 2008, the average salary for community organizers was $41,790 (Bureau of Labor Statistics, 2009). Other social work practice areas had similar salaries in 2009. Social workers in mental health and drug treatment has a mean or average salary of $41,350, social workers in health care mean salary was $48,350, and all other social workers' mean was $50,470. The salary distributions were skewed with the median or midpoint social worker salaries lower than their mean salaries: $38,200 for mental health and drug treatment, $46,300 for health care, and $49,420 for all other social workers (Bureau of Labor Statistics, 2010). s. The highest mean annual social work category's salary was $50,470; this was less than 00.5% of the average CEO compensation. It will require approximately 214 years for the average social worker to earn as much as the average CEO's compensation.
- As would be expected from the earnings and compensations differences, the United States now is more income unequal, with a greater concentration of income at the top, than any other industrialized nation. The middle 60%

of U.S. society have seen their share of the national income fall from 53.6% in 1980 to 46% by 2006. The highest fifth improved their share of the national income from 46.6% in 1990 to 50% in 2008. The bottom 80% saw a decline in their share from 53.3% to 50% over the same period (U.S. Census Bureau, 2009a, p. 10). According to von Hoffman (2007), "[A] mere 300,000 people had incomes equal to the total income of the bottom earning half of the entire population." Only people at the very top made any real economic improvements during the boon years, and they saw little or no decline during the recession (Madrick, 2009). Tax policies, economic policies, the recession, and a devolving welfare state have led to increasing poverty in the first years of the new millennium. According to some economists, including the conservative libertarian economist Milton Freidman (Hamilton & Derity Jr., 2009) and an economics founding father Adam Smith (1922, p. 17), one's position in the unequal income distribution is largely a matter of birth. James Hechman, a libertarian University of Chicago economist, as quoted by Stille (2001), asserts, "Never has the accident of birth mattered more. If I am born to educated, supportive parents, my chances of doing well are totally different than if I were born to a single parent or abusive parents. . . . This is a case of market failure: Children don't get to 'buy' their parents, so there has to be some kind of intervention to make up for these environmental differences" (p. A-17).

Adam Smith, the Scottish Enlightenment philosopher and later labeled economist wrote,

The difference of natural talents in different men is, in reality, much less than we are aware of; and the very different genius which appears to distinguish men of different professions, when grown to maturity, is not on many occasions so much the cause, as the effect of the division of labour. The difference between the most dissimilar characters, between the philosopher and a common street porter, for example, seems to arise not so much from nature, as from habit, custom, and education....they came into the world...very much alike....(Smith, 1922, p. 17)

- The 1990s saw the U.S. economy and world economy globalize and the nation-states and welfare states begin to devolve. It should be recognized that globalization has been going on since humankind became more mobile than simply by walking. What makes our current globalization different is the speed that current technology allows in communication and mobility. Economic globalization aims to treats the world as a single economic system.

Globalization's intent is to reduce state sovereignty and the constraints of national borders and any social and cultural arrangements and relationships that hinder economic exchanges (Dickens, 2003; Gray, 1998; Held & McGrew, 2007; Stiglitz, 2003, 2009; Tanzi, 2002). Globalization weakens the economy's basic social partnership by shifting the balance of power to capital and corporations, and it reduces the power of labor and the state (land) (Dickens, 2003; Gray, 1998; Mishra, 1999; Stiglitz, 2003, 2009; Tanzi, 2002). Transnational corporations, especially financial ones, have reduced public regulation and responsibilities for community social welfare and any ecological agenda. As seen by the environmental unilateralism of the United States, sustainable global growth limits can be set but they need not be heeded by a single nation or global corporation (Deacon, 1997, p. 54; Dickens, 2003, Gray, 1998; Stiglitz, 2003, 2009). Competing nation-states pursuing global corporations in a global economy discard social obligations to their citizens, with a subsequent erosion and downward spiral of social provisions that can lead to the lowest social welfare denominator (Deacon, 1997, p. 196).

The economic upheavals of the globalized turbo-economy have been as dramatic as those of the industrial revolution. The Great Recession followed a global boom and with a global economic meltdown A global economy encouraged and achieved cheap labor, lower or no taxes on the rich and on corporations (Gray, 1998; Johnston, 2002b, 2002c), corporate welfare, tight money, market deregulation, protection of capital over labor and anti-labor policies, and a decline in welfare state provisions and benefits for labor as employees and as citizens of a welfare state (Freudenheim, 2002; Gray, 1998; Held & McGrew, 2007; Johnston, 2002a; Mishra, 1999; Pear, 2002; Stiglitz, 2003, 2009; Wagner, 1997). In the G7 nations, the globe's top economic powers, national marginal personal tax rates declined in all seven countries, with the greatest decline in the United States. Globalization increases aggregate national wealth, poverty, and social and income inequality within and between nations (Deacon, 1997, pp. 34–35; Halsey, Lauder, Brown, & Wells, 1997, p. 157; Room, 1990, p. 121). All suffer from the economic meltdown it causes.

With our current globalization, labor is no longer a significant force in the political economy. Labor, both as a component of production and a social institution, is weaker today than at the middle of the 20th century. Labor's decline is partially due to technological innovations, partially due to the anti-labor social policies began by U.S. President Ronald Reagan and British Prime Minister Margaret Thatcher and carried on by their successors, partially due to the successes of the welfare state (retirement, social security, health services and insurance, limited work week, publicly funded education, etc.), and partially due to the loss of community with globalization. Labor is more local as a force in the global political economy. While capital is allowed greater freedom of movement, the U.S. and European Union (EU)'s problems and resistance to free immigration indicated that labor is not seen similar to capital. Even within the EU there is debate and dissent regarding the free movement of labor between member nations, while there is far less debate regarding capital's movement (Dickens, 2003; Joppke, 1998; Tanzi, 2002). There are no true international labor unions or labor movement, but there is a profusion of global corporations. There are simply few, if any, countervailing forces to capital, certainly not labor or governments, within the global economy.

Capital has increased in power at the expense of labor, and it dominates the political economy. A global corporation can increase the market value of its stocks by terminating a portion of its labor. Capital has an inherent advantage in a global political economy over labor and land. Capital is more mobile, liquid, and global, as represented by global corporations and financial institutions. Capital is more mobile, with offshore tax havens available regardless of nation, trade within global corporations, the state's inability to tax the mobile individual or corporation, and substitution of highly mobile electronic money for hard currency (Tanzi, 2002, p. 125).

Globalization has always been accompanied by arrogance and violence, but technology now makes it more rather than less volatile. Globalization cultivates national fragmentation and a civic decay, manifested by increasing income and social inequality, poverty, fear, violence, family breakdown, fundamentalism and political and social intolerance, social and economic ghettoization, social isolation and social exclusion, political and social marginalization, and political authoritarianism (Berry & Hallett, 1998, pp. 1–12; Dahrendorf, 1995; Gray, 1998; Held & McGrew, 2007; Mishra, 1999; Pear, 2002; Stiglitz, 2003, 2009; Thurow, 1995). As the economy becomes global, people seem to want smaller niches of identity. Trends indicate a demand for social work's and community practice's community development and social justice mission to challenge the growing community fragmentation.

Globalization challenges the need for and viability of multi-ethnic nation-states such as the old Soviet Union, China, the United States, and even smaller nation-states. Contrary to historical globalization, since the advent of our current globalization 25 additional nation-states have been created over the past quarter century (Glain, 2009). We also have seen a growth of separatist movements within large and small multi-ethnic nation-states (Schaeffer, 1997).

- Welfare states, as well as the multi-ethnic nation-states, are generally devolving globally as is the United States with its regional factionalism, *Red State - Blue State* divisions, and anti-federal rhetoric (Dodds, 2001; Berry & Hallett, 1998, pp. 1–12; Gray, 1998; Held & McGrew, 2007; Mishra, 1999; Pear, 2002; Stiglitz, 2003, 2009; Thurow, 1995). We commented in Chapter 1 on the growing political conservatism in the United States. Liberal government's traditional function in a market economy—to help communities manage and protect themselves from the excesses and vagrancies of the market economy—has been reduced with global deregulation. Even after a year into the Great Recession, no significant re-regulation occurred. Universal, public option health care in the United States was

rejected in 2009 as socialistic. Globalization's logic undermines the Keynesian welfare state as a means of mutual communal support and a first line of defense against poverty. It creates downward pressures on the welfare state and its social protections supported by public taxation, undermines the ideology of social protection and community undergirding the welfare state, subverts national community solidarity, and legitimizes inequality of rewards as a necessity for economic growth. The results are welfare reform's punitive and abstemious approaches. The welfare state's devolution is to motivate the poor to accept and depend on marginal, low-wage employment, and to reduce and keep taxes low on corporations and the extremely affluent (Tanzi, 2002). First instigated by conservative government, devolution has been subsequently embraced and expanded by traditionally liberal or left political parties, especially in the United Kingdom and the United States (Deacon, 1997; Gray, 1998; Held & McGrew, 2007; Kramer & Braum, 1995; Mishra, 1999; Pear, 2002; Stiglitz, 2003, 2009; Wagner, 1997). European conservative political parties have adopted many of the welfare state policies (Erlanger, 2009).

- Privatization, proprietarization, and commercialization are currently trends and shibboleths in the welfare state's as well as the nation-state's rollback. These also are manifestations of the conservative trend. The United States has privatized prisons and war-making by widely using mercenaries (Risen, 2008). The privatization movement assumes that economic market forces serve as the best means of allocating and conducting services (Gibelman & Demone, 1998; Moe, 1987; Morgan, 1995, Salamon, 1997). The primary argument of the privatization ideology is that it forces government to be more businesslike and efficient as well as smaller—*leaner and meaner*—although just the opposite is true. Privatization reduces public sector costs and competition for money either through taxes or by borrowing. Privatization diminishes public sector involvement in enterprise decision making through deregulation (Morgan, 1995). Privatization takes the focus and political pressure off government if poor services are provided, places a buffer between the public and politicians, and transfers any onus for poor services and inefficiency to the market, resolvable by market forces. Privatization of government-financed vendor services also provides political spoils to the government's backers in terms of contingent employment and contracts (Berstein, 1997; Metcalf, 2002).

Privatization and commercial enterprises are increasing their share of education, health, and human services. In the United States, the for-profit sector has over a third of the social services market, with further growth projected over the next few years. Some of the proprietary firms involved are mammoth, vertically integrated global companies such as Lockheed Martin, Magellan Health Services, and Crescent Operating, Inc. (health and mental health), Wachenhut (corrections), and Xerox (for context, see Berstein, 1996; Fein, 1996; Freudenheim, 2002; Kuttner, 1996; Levenson, 1997; Myerson, 1997; Nordheimer, 1997; Rose, 1997; Salamon, 1997; Swarns, 1997, pp. A1, A12; Strom-Gottfried, 1997; Uchitelle & Kleinfield, 1996). The business model of social welfare transforms social workers into producers and clients into consumers. As with most public policy pronouncements, privatization's efficiency claims have not been rigorously tested and are not generally supported (Morgan, 1995).

• United Way and charitable giving in the United States has decreased, especially during the Great Recession years (Giving USA, 2009; Press, 2009; Strom, 2009a, b, c). Over two-thirds of public charities suffered a funding decrease in 2008, despite the increased needs (Giving USA, 2009). Foundations also are retaining more of their funds during the high stock market growth era of the late 1990s. With the collapse of their investments they also distributed a smaller portion of swinking endowments (Giving USA, 2009). Many charities feel abandoned by the government (Strom, 2009b); some have sought bankruptcy protection (Strom, 2009a). Corporate contributions to health and human services have dropped and constitute less of total giving than prior to the corporate and income tax reductions of the past two decades as the charitable giving deductions are less attractive (Giving USA, 2009; Marx, 1998, p. 34). Philanthropic giving largely serves the donor community's social and political ends and cultural institutions. The socially marginalized are effectively excluded from benefit (Abelson, 2000; Marx, 1998). The very affluent traditionally donate smaller portions of their income to philanthropy than do middle-income people (Phillips, 1993, p. 143; Salamon, 1997). Therefore, donations will continue to deteriorate even after the Great Recession is over as income concentrates at the top of the income distribution, a sense of a general community declines, and tax codes make giving less financially attractive (Freudenheim, 1996, p. B8; Phillips, 1993, p. 143).

• The United States is more ethnically and socially diverse and is approaching the time when no ethnic grouping will have a majority. California, Texas, and New Mexico currently have no ethnic majority (U.S. Census Bureau, 2009b, Table 18). Over a fifth of the populations of California, New Jersey, and New York are foreign-born (U.S. Census Bureau, 2009b, Table 39).

While projections are always tentative, especially with a concept as nebulous as ethnicity, Table 4.1 illustrates both the growing diversity of the population as well as the absurdity of ethnic classifications (Patterson, 2001). The total white population, including white Hispanics, remains the majority population into the next century. However, the number of non-Hispanic whites is projected to decline to less than 50% by 2060, as Hispanics increase to over a fourth of population. Non-Hispanic whites, however, will remain dominant in political and economic power.

Appiah (1997) thoughtfully observes the inconsistencies in our obsession with race, multiculturalism, and diversity:

Some groups have names of earlier ethnic cultures: Italian, Jewish . . . Some correspond to the old races—black, Asian, Indian; or to religions. . . . Some are basically regional—Southern, Western, Puerto Rican. Yet others are new groups modeled on old ethnicities—Hispanic, Asian American—or are social categories—women, gay, bisexuals, disabled. . . . Nowadays, we are not the slightest bit surprised when someone remarks on a feature of the "culture" of groups like these. Gay culture, Deaf culture . . . but if you ask what

Table 4.1. United States Population Projections by Grouping in Percentages: 2010, 2050, 2100

Population Grouping	2010	2050	2100
Foreign-born	11.2	13.3	10.9
Total white	80.6	74.3	70.9
White, non-Hispanic	67.3	51.1	40.3
Total black	13.3	14.8	15
Black, non-Hispanic	12.5	13.3	13.3
Total American Indian	0.9	1.1	1.1
American Indian, non-Hispanic	0.8	0.8	0.7
Total Asian and Pacific Islander	5.1	9.8	13.2
Asian and Pacific Islander, non-Hispanic	4.8	9.3	12.6
Total Hispanic	14.6	25.5	33.3

Note. Data in this table are adapted from *National Population Projections: I. Summary Files, Total Population by Race, Hispanic Origin, and Nativity: 1999-2100*. U.S. Census Bureau, May 16, 2008. Retrieved October 1, 2009, from http://www.census.gov/population/www/projections/natsum-T5.html

distinctively marks off gay people or deaf people or Jews from others, it is not obviously the fact that to each identity there corresponds a distinct culture. (p. 31)

An increased emphasis on the constructions of race and culture is misplaced and leads to greater balkanization, social marginalization, and challenges to a cohesive community (Appiah, 2005; Longes, 1997, p. 46). There are data to indicate that an increasing emphasis on multi-culturalism leads to less hyper-segregation and balkanization. Coffe and Geys (2006) found that ethnic diversity was inversely related to social capital accumulation in communities. Appiah (1997) again provides some insight:

To an outsider, few groups in the world looked as culturally homogeneous as the various peoples—Serbs, Croats, Muslim—of Bosnia. (The resurgence of Islam in Bosnia is a result of the conflict, not a cause of it.) . . . . [T]he trouble with appeal to cultural difference it that it obscures rather than illuminates .... It is not black culture that the racist disdains, but blacks. There is no conflict of visions between black and white cultures that is the source of discord. No amount of knowledge of the architectural achievements of Nubia or Kush guarantees respect for African Americans.... Culture is not the problem, and it is not the solution. . . . So maybe we should conduct our discussions of education and citizenship, toleration and social peace, without the talk of cultures. (pp. 35–36)

The United States is becoming more culturally and ethnically diverse. Race as a social descriptor and divider has not been made obsolete (Morning, 2008). We have done relatively well in our diversity during the past two decades when compared with the genocide, ethnic cleansing, and other types of violence that have occurred in other parts of the world. However, America has a history of all of these evils. We have seen citizens come armed to political debates in 2009. If we are to avoid these plagues in the future, we must emphasize our common community rather than our differences. As noted above, diversity doesn't promote community or the development of social capital.

- Despite advances in civil rights and the election of an African-American president, American communities are highly ethnically and economically segregated; differences are especially notable in some urban areas and between urban and suburban areas. This creates a significant barrier to upward social mobility. Poverty of women and children remains significant. Female-headed households represented 17% of all families but 48% of poor families in 2006 (U.S. Census Bureau, 2009c). Twenty-two percent of black families are poor, and black families represent 26% of all poor families. Most black families live in central cities due to historical, still extant patterns of racial segregation and economic entrapment (U.S. Census Bureau, 2009b, Table 694).

- Another product of globalization has been the increased vulnerability of the United States to terrorism, and the resultant impact of the war on terrorism and two wars we have subsequently entered. The drama and fear following September 11, 2001, was powerful, but it was often more symbolic than real for most

Americans. The United States instituted no military draft despite the two wars but did limit carry-on liquids on commercial airlines. The United States has become "the Homeland," an appellation coined for political purposes after September 11, 2001, that was rarely if ever used before then.[1] Flags and other patriotic symbolism are everywhere: in office and home windows, on cars and lapels, and especially in commercial and political advertising. Politicians wave flags at every opportunity. The political scientist Robert Putnam, based on an October 2001 poll, claimed that one positive consequence of Sept. 11 was that "whites trust blacks more, Asians trust Latinos more, and so on, than did these very same people did a year ago" (as cited in Morin & Dean, 2002). The impact, sadly, on the U.S. sense of community has been more jingoistic than profound in producing solidarity and cohesion. The increase in trust from 22% to 29%, a 7% gain, was probably a function of social desirability responses brought on by a near-universal emphasis on the concept "United We Stand." Even in the face of universal media efforts to create national unity after Sept. 11, 71% of those surveyed indicated no increase in trust.

- And other polls and indicators are less optimistic than Putnam's (Clymer, 2002). Since Sept. 11, 2001 hyper-social segregation or extreme segregation by class, income, and ethnicity has been maintained. Devolution of the welfare state, with decreasing government general welfare services and increasing privatization, continues unabated (Pear, 2002). The Pew Research Center's report *Trends 2005* indicates we remain divided along religious, political, and social ideological lines (Pew, 2005) and are less optimistic about the future (Pew, 2009). The affluent enjoy disproportionate relief from taxes and public responsibility for the nation's welfare. Corporate flag-waving is accompanied by relocations to offshore tax havens to avoid paying taxes in support of the war against terrorism and other assumed enemies of "the Homeland" (Johnston, 2002a, 2002c). Rules of secrecy are imposed and due-process protections are weakened, also in the name of homeland security, recalling a dark Vietnam War–era slogan of *destroying the village to save it* (Broad, 2002; Ignatieff, 2002).

- The United States and the world are aging. Americans are getting older and working longer. The growth of the population between 65 and 85 and the population over 85 is a significant factor in health and welfare spending (U.S. Census Bureau, 2009b, Table 33). The frail elderly, in particular, require costly in-home and institutional support, as well as more complex and expensive medical care. With a devolving welfare state and a privatization ideology, despite the political power of the elderly, Social Security's benefits and an improvement of elderly health care through Medicare or a national health insurance are at risk of cutbacks (Mitchell, 2002).

- The spiraling, pervasive, unbounded technological revolution in the United States—and our love of it—will continue. The widespread use of computers and other instant communication equipment for information access, data processing, and communication will continue to decrease the virtual time and space between people, organizations, and communities and will also reduce face-to-face interaction. As we balkanize, we are simultaneously served by national economic franchises, shaped by national and global media, and connected internationally by a high-tech information superhighway. Use of computer and electronic technologies can allow human and social services to be more widely distributed. A single professional can serve more people, and fewer professionals can serve more people. E-mails, Web pages, and tweets provide more opportunity for public information distribution, marketing, and case coordination. Internet chat rooms and social networking sites such as Facebook and MySpace are used for information sharing and emotional support groups. As everyone from the liberal political advocacy organization MoveOn.org, and the Obama campaign to the radical right have demonstrated, networks, Web sites, and online chat rooms can be used for organizing both virtual and physical communities.

Perspectives for Practice

As we become involved in developing new social work programs and services and redesigning old ones, as we provide community education and client advocacy and help structure support networks, the models that follow suggest the kinds of information, contacts, and activities we should consider in our practice.[2]

The Community as People: A Sociodemographic View

The U.S. Census Bureau collects, compiles, and distributes a huge quantity of information about the characteristics of the U.S. people and their activities. The annual *Statistical Abstract of the United States*, for example, contains aggregate information about the numbers of people, births, deaths, homeownership, occupations, income and expenditures, labor force, employment and earnings, health and nutrition, business enterprise, manufacturing, and more. In addition, the Census Bureau disaggregates information by census tract, its smallest spatial unit at the local level. The local municipal or county planning department and local libraries usually have census tract information that reveals a good deal about the composition and character of the local community. Thus, one can learn about the ages, nationalities, average income, and educational levels of people in different local areas, for example, and the data are available for comparative purposes across census tracts and municipalities. Comparisons can also be made for geographic areas over time, so that community changes can be examined. Social indicators of the relative well-being of a community can be developed, for example, by tracking crime statistics, infant mortality rates and various other health statistics, and so on. The utility of sociodemographic information to plan social programs and to understand the community is readily apparent. And, as indicated above, the way the U.S. Census Bureau chooses to divide people tells us something about the American community's perception of itself.

The Community as a Social System

The concept of a community as a social system essentially views a community as a system of interrelated subsystems that perform important functions for their members. What differentiates the community as a system from an organization that is also a system of systems is that a community's subsystems rarely are rationally organized and coordinated by a centralized authority to achieve a common goal. An American community as a political jurisdiction with a city with a mayor and a city council has important subsystems with limited or no central control, such as the nonprofit sector, the economic sector where multiple business firms produce and distribute necessary goods and services, the underground economy, and the illegitimate sectors. Communities evolve as people develop common needs, interdependencies, and sentimental bonds.

We use Warren's (1978) conception of community. It best serves our purposes of understanding community for intervention on both micro and macro levels. Following Warren's system analysis of the U.S. community, we may view the community as "that combination of social units and systems that perform the major social functions having locality relevance" (p. 9). Warren conceived of community functionally as the organization of social activities to afford people daily local access to those broad areas of activities and resources necessary in day-to-day living. A community, in this definition, has a locality but needs no well-defined and rigid geographic boundaries. Social work is concerned with where people live and, more important, with the influences of where they live on how they live. Social work is immersed in people, families, social relationships and networks for education, jobs, and values, and how people develop and maintain their social relationships and networks. Communities can be compared on the dimensions of (a) the relative degree of dependence of the community on extracommunity (vertical patterns) institutions and organizations to perform its locality-relevant functions (autonomy), (b) the extent that the service areas of local units (stores, churches, schools, manufacturing, and so on) coincide or fail to coincide, (c) the psychological identification with a common locality, and (d) the relative strength of the relationships between local, intracommunity units (horizontal pattern) (Mulroy, 2004; Warren, 1978, pp. 12–13).

Warren proposes five critical locality-relevant social functions: (a) production-distribution-consumption, (b) socialization, (c) social control, (d) social participation, and (e) mutual support. These social functions are required for survival and perpetuation of a community and its members. A community fulfills the functions through a pattern of formal and informal organizations, groups, and networks. While an organization or entities can be identified with a primary social function and are discussed in terms of the primary function, such as a school system with the socialization function, the same social units generally perform more than one function. For example, a school provides socialization and also provides jobs, opportunities for social participation, mutual support, and social control. The units that provide these functions may have local physical sites but may not necessarily be controlled by members of the community or be truly "of" the community. A supermarket can serve several different communities and belong to a regional, national, or global corporation with interests adverse to the local community. A child protective service unit may serve several neighborhoods, but the number of workers it can hire to meet the local needs, and even its conception of child abuse and neglect, are controlled by state laws, the state's child welfare department, and federal grant-in-aid funding limits and laws.

The community as a social system operates systemically, with its entities interacting and affecting one another. The entities and institutional structures interact, shape, and contribute to shared purposes and support or hinder the capacity of the others to accomplish their social functions. Each component of a system is necessary for the system to achieve its purposes. All of the social functions and social structures are interdependent and have an impact on our well-being or welfare. A school system's capacity to educate and to socialize is affected by its community's economic viability and social stability. In turn, the school system contributes to the community's economic and social viability.

A poor community has consumption needs but lacks production and has externally controlled distribution system. Its socialization structures may be weak, with community members suffering from anomie. Social control is largely externally imposed, when it exists. The poor community has greater demands for mutual support, the welfare function, but has less capacity to provide mutual support. In contrast, an affluent community has a capacity, but it may provide

mutual support only if its commonly socialized values support public welfare and voluntary giving.

Before we consider each of the five functions in more detail, we need to lay a foundation by examining the concepts of vertical and horizontal integration, reciprocity, and social exclusion. These are critical to understanding the great changes within the community's functions and to understanding community.

Changes in Communities From Horizontal to Vertical Systems. Communities are undergoing great changes in transforming from locality-focused and horizontally organized communities emphasizing primary and holistic relationships and responsibilities to vertical integrated communities and extensions of a global economy. The terms *vertical entity* and *horizontal entity* describe the relationship between the entity or organization and the local community, and not the internal structure (Willie, Willard, & Ridini, 2008). It is important to know whether an organization has a vertical or a horizontal relation to the community. *Horizontal* organizations share the same geographic domain with a community and coincide or fit within the community. Their ultimate locus of authority situs is within the community, and their relationship with the community is horizontal; they are on the same plane.

The locality limited horizontal community is a community where people live and have their needs met by structures and institutions that are contained within the same community. The hierarchical structures of authority and loci of decision making are at a community level horizontal to one another and their constituencies. The locality limited horizontal community, with ultimate decisional authority for the five community functions located in the same community, is becoming rare as community functions become global and increasingly specialized in their divisions of responsibilities; become complex in internal structures and fragmented; lack congruence with one another or with a locality; and have little or no community loyalty.

Vertical entities, organizations, and structures are characterized by hierarchical levels of authority and decision making beyond the local community to regional, state, federal and national, and global levels. The entity's verticality refers to its relationship with the local community and the community's capacity to influence its decisional authority and rule-making capacity in satisfying community needs.

In a vertical community, the decision makers for a community's social functions are beyond the local community and have little interest in it. Factories are closed regardless of community need. Decisions that affect one community social function may not correspond geographically or socially with decisions affecting another social function. This creates greater community complexity and makes decision making more remote from the individual. The local community and its welfare are unimportant to the vertical entities; a particular local community is simply one of many communities in its domain. Interests are specialized by functions, even when the vertical entity is a multifunctional entity. Economic entities are concerned with their economic interest rather than with the local community's economic and social well-being and quality of life. Vertically integrated communities have few definable geographic and social boundaries for functions, fragmented social relationships based on more explicit social contracts, extensive divisions of labor, and secondary and tertiary modes of social interaction. Individuals have a growing sense of isolation and increasing anomie, with a loss of community values to guide behavior. With alienation and normlessness comes a loss of local social control and a growth of a splintered lifestyle and social identity; special interest enclaves spring up in an effort to recreate community within the amorphous national and global social ecology (Bellah, Madsen, Sullivan, & Tipton, 1985, 1991; Etzioni, 1993).

Although our current conservative political rhetoric is for smaller, more local government and more individual responsibility, the reality is that our governmental and nongovernmental organizations are becoming larger, global, more remote in decision making from the community, more intrusive on and dominant over the individual and community, and more unregulated, uncontrolled, and uncontrollable. The community hospital and the independent family doctor have been supplanted by the proprietary and distant profit-driven national health maintenance organization operating under managed-cost principles. The few community hospitals remaining are controlled by the national insurance community and federal regulations and funding requirements. The mom-and-pop family business has been replaced by the multinational mega-corporation. The global multimedia entertainment-industrial conglomerate has deposed the local newspaper. Decision making for all these structures is distant from the local community and is based on narrowing economic self-interest rather than a consideration of community well-being.

Community practice is concerned with vertical and horizontal relationships because they influence the relationships within and between communities: cohesion, power, dependency and interdependency, community commitment, and the capacity and willingness of the organization to respond to local community needs. Vertically related structures have less community interdependence and cohesion.

As communities have become more vertically integrated, the conception of locality has expanded for fulfilling the functions. Today some functions have a global or national community. Not only is the economy global, but social welfare, socialization, and social control entities are also global. With the expansion and complexity of community, unfortunately, as Nisbet (1953, p. 52) has stated, "For more and more individuals the primary social relationships [of community] have lost much of their historic function of mediation between man and the larger ends of our civilization."

A primary criterion in assessing whether an organization or agency has a vertical or horizontal relation is the ultimate locus of authority and a local unit's decision-making ability to commit resources to local community interests. A practice task for the community practitioner, in addition to assessing whether the entity is a vertically or horizontally related entity, is to help communities develop relationships with a more horizontal character and greater power equivalency and interdependence with these vertically related entities.

Reciprocity. Community cohesion requires reciprocity and responsibility commensurate with rights and benefits, whether individuals or larger social entities. People and corporations need to give to the community on the basis of what they get from the community. This extends beyond the simplistic, though important, notion that public welfare recipients should reciprocate for the assistance received from the community. It includes obligations of the affluent to "give back" to the community for their prosperity. Global corporations have an obligation to all the communities where they operate at least equal to the gains they make. Adam Smith (1922), hardly a collectivist, advocated proportionate reciprocal community responsibilities:

The expence [*sic*] for defending the society . . . are laid out for the general benefit of the whole society. It is reasonable, therefore, that they should be defrayed by the general contribution of the whole society, *all the different members contributing, as nearly as possible, in proportion to their respective abilities. … The subjects of every state ought to contribute towards the support of the government, as nearly as possible, in proportion to their respective abilities; that is, in proportion to the revenue which they respectively enjoy under the protection of the state.* [italics added] (pp. 300, 310)

Social exclusion. The growth of the global turbo-economy and vertically structured communities has been accompanied by increasing social exclusion in the United States and Europe. Social exclusion "restrict[s] or den[ies] people participation within society. . . . Individuals or groups are wholly or partially excluded from full participation in the society in which they live . . . [and represent] a failure or inability to participate in social and political activities" (Berry & Hallett, 1998, p. 2).

Social exclusion refers to individual social marginalization and alienation. Social exclusion is the flip side of the concept of social solidarity and social capital. Social exclusion can be a trait of powerless groups that are prevented from integrating themselves within the community. The poor tend to be the most structurally socially excluded. Social exclusion is a byproduct of the globalization that excludes most of us from economic and political decision making (Room, 1990; van Deth, 1997). A critical objective of community practice is to reduce social exclusion in its pursuit of social justice and empowerment for the socially disadvantaged and isolated (Butcher, Banks, Henderson, with Robertson, 2007).

Community Functions

Production-Consumption-Distribution

Production-distribution-consumption (P-D-C) is the system of organizing individuals and other resources for the production and distribution of goods and services for consumption. P-D-C is the economy. It is the most important community function. Heilbroner (1962, p. 5) pointed out that societies and communities must meet only two interrelated needs for short-run survival:

1. They must develop and maintain a system for producing the goods and services needed for perpetuation.
2. They must arrange for the distribution of the fruits of production among their members, so that more production can take place.

A community must meet its current and the next generation's need for goods and services (until the next generation is able to provide for itself). If a generation doesn't have consumption needs met, there will be no succeeding generation of producers and hence no continuation of community. Without production and its distribution, there is no consumption. Without production there are no goods and services for mutual support. Without consumption there is no energy for socialization, social control, social participation, or production. P-D-C therefore is necessary for a community's survival, but alone it is not sufficient: communities are so much more than economic systems.

P-D-C doesn't require a particular economic system or model. Economic systems are social inventions to support the production, distribution, and consumption of goods and services by the community. P-D-C's organization is highly flexible. The models can range from a wide variety of collectivist approaches ranging from the family and clan through to nation-state collectivism on one hand to individualistic laissez-faire and wanton neoliberal corporate capitalism on the other. No particular model represents "the natural order of things" or "a higher progression of humankind" more than any another model. Laissez-faire and corporate capitalism are social inventions of fairly recent historical vintage. In Adam Smith's classic and seminal work on laissez-faire capitalism, *An Inquiry into the Nature and Causes of the Wealth of Nations,* first published in 1776, Smith's concern was with the wealth of nations as communities, not with individuals or corporate wealth. The failure of the corporate model of neoliberal capitalism in the early 21st century reveals its weaknesses, such as the fact that it is susceptible to economic bubbles. A P-D-C system exists to serve a community's needs, rather than, as it currently often appears, for a community to serve an economic system's needs. This axiom is ignored by the neoliberal economic ideology that fragments, if not destroys, community cohesion and values. New models have been proposed that will return the focus of the economic system to community well-being rather than fiscal growth (Goodman, 2009).

P-D-C's structure has become increasingly vertical, with a concurrent distancing of decision making from the community and the individual without much regard for the community's interests and needs. As we move more totally to global, highly vertical economic structures, we should keep in mind several propositions:

1. Economies are social creations and not created by nature or divinely inspired. Economics as a discipline has largely left science for ideology.
2. No economic system has greater inherent morality than other systems. Any morality is determined by how well it serves its communities, not by how well it serves itself.
3. Economies should serve communities rather than communities existing for economies. This was forgotten with TARP and the economic stimulus package in 2009.
4. While structures for P-D-C—an economic system—are necessary for community viability, economic systems alone are insufficient for a viable community. The other functions also must be fulfilled.

Socialization

Socialization is the process "through which individuals, through learning, acquire the knowledge, values and behavior patterns of their society and learn behaviors appropriate to the various social roles that the society provides"

(Warren, 1978, p. 177). Socialization is necessary for people to gain a shared set of values. It's a lifelong formal and informal process of learning social values, constructions, roles, and behaviors. It's how we learn how and what to think and do. The community is the primary arena that instructs in the particular structures and strictures of social behavior for that community.

Socialization initially was the responsibility of such primary and secondary social entities as the family, religious bodies, informal peer groups, and, more recent, the tertiary institution of schools. Research is indicating that a community's organizations and social patterns and character have a significant impact on socializing its members (Eamon, 2002; Mancini, Bowen, & Martin, 2005; Sharkey, 2008; Vartanian, & Buck, 2005). However, these primary and secondary community associations now are losing their grip on socialization. Control of socialization in the contemporary community has moved beyond the local community and its structures to becoming the province of vertical, privatized, and proprietary structures. Education, religion, entertainment, and information distribution are no longer local but national, global, and proprietary.

The commercial, monopolistic, and global media, the Web, and the Internet are now significant instruments of socialization. Young people spend more time with television, video/computer games, and the Web than with family, religious groups, or schools. The values imparted are the values of the media's proprietors and not necessarily a community's values. These values will become the community's values as young and not-so-young Americans learn them (Stein, 1993). Television and the other components of an increasingly monopolistic global media ("The Big Media," 2002) are most concerned with attracting viewers for advertisers and with shaping public opinion to support their sponsors' ideology. Cable "news" focuses less on reporting events than on shaping opinions, attitudes, and values. Socializing viewers to community values, educating them, or transmitting information has given way to tactics for luring and holding viewers. If random sex, frontal nudity, frequent violence, "reality television," erectile dysfunction ads, and entertainment "news" attract viewers, so be it, regardless of their socializing implications.

Schools sell information systems, use commercially sponsored closed-circuit television for instruction, import fast-food franchises for food service, sell sports facility naming rights to national corporations, and buy commercially packaged teaching packages and tests (Metcalf, 2002). Privatized and proprietary profit-driven school systems are touted as educational reform. The goal of public education of creating community has been replaced by pecuniary motives.

Without strong socialization to a congruent and shared set of values, there is no internal control of behavior based on these values. And without internal behavioral control, there is a greater need for external social control to regulate behavior.

Social Control

Social control represents the processes communities use to obtain compliance with their prescribed and proscribed social roles, norms, and behaviors.[3] Social control is inherent in any community and society. The concept is inherent in the notion of social living. Without social controls, there is chaos. The question is not whether a community will regulate and control its members' behavior, but how it will do so and for what reasons.

Behavioral control can be done in two ways: (a) by internal controls developed through socialization processes and (b) by external social controls, with a system of allocating rewards for acceptable behaviors and punishments for forbidden behaviors imposed by the community. Most social institutions perform some social control function. Trattner (1999) includes social work and social welfare as social control agents. Trattner sees social control as "those processes in a society that supported a level of social cohesiveness sufficient for a society's survival, including measures that enabled the needy and the helpless to survive and function within the social order—the very things we now call social work or social welfare" (p. xxvii).[3]

Etzioni's (1993) communitarianism discourse offers that when external social control is necessary, it is done best by primary groups in the community:

We suggest that *free individuals require a community*, which backs them up against encroachment by the state and sustains morality by drawing on the gentle prodding of kin, friends, neighbors and other community members rather than building on government controls or fear of authorities. . . . *No society can function well unless most of its members "behave" most of the time because they voluntarily heed their moral commitments and social responsibilities.* (pp. 15, 30, italics original)

If socialization and civic society are weakened, more demands are placed on social control structures external to the individual in an extremely heterogeneous and differentiated community. As solidarity wanes, external social controls must be maintained for social order. These controls are most often represented by the regulatory powers of the state's legal system and extragovernmental groups, usurping the power of the community. External social controls represent a failure of socialization.

The growth of external and imposed social controls is an argument for improving socialization to a common set of community values. But as we have seen, socialization by communities has weakened and they have become more vertical, more sophisticated, more interdependent, and more pluralistic. Primary societies, the *gemeinschaft* societies, had no formal contracts or separate social control organizations. Pre-Columbian Amerindian nations generally had no separate police forces. The rules of contract and law have replaced the more informal means of social control through socialization. Tertiary, vertical social control systems have led to formal limits on individual freedom and an expansion of government and corporations into people's personal lives, justified as a community good and "security." Constraints on personal freedoms and local community authority have been constrained by a national government since Sept. 11, excused by the claim that they are protecting us from terrorism and preserving "the American way of life." Again, we are burning villages to save them. The state too frequently reneges on its social responsibilities for the public good and—as a creature of the community—is abandoning its socialization responsibilities for an increased reliance on social control. It is using draconian social control approaches such as the ineffectual "three-strikes-and-you're-out" prison sentencing, a ready use of capital punishment, imprisonment for mental illness and drug use, limiting constitutional protections, and commercializing social control with the privatization of police and prisons. Law enforcement and corrections are growth industries in spite of cutbacks in education funding.

Social Participation. Social participation is the essential community function that allows—indeed, requires—its citizens to participate in the life and governance of the community if they and their community are to be socially healthy and competent. Research is replete with the importance of social participation for the individual as well as the community (Fogel, Smith, & Williamson, 2008; Ohmer, 2008; Putnam, 2009; Saegert & Winkel, 2004; Shaw, Gallant, Riley-Jacome, & Spokane, 2006; Sobeck, 2008). Social participation is necessary to develop social capital. Fellin (2001, pp. 70–71) emphasized social participation in his definition of community competence as "the capacity of the community to engage in problem-solving in order to achieve its goals." Various parts of a community collaborate, share decision making and power, and work together to address community needs. Community competence is enhanced with communitywide participation in decision making. Social participation is the core of community practice and a social component of social work practice. It is essential to participatory democracy. Social participation is indispensable to ameliorating possible adverse and arbitrary effects of a community's social control institutions and policies. It is the restorative to social marginalization. The very concept of community entails direct and unbuffered social interaction and involvement by its members to develop communal character and to transmit and implement communal values.

Social participation entails social structures that develop, maintain, and mediate regulate communal life and the other community functions of P-D-C, socialization, social control, and the next community function of mutual support. It ranges from participation in informal primary and secondary group activities to civic participation in the community's more formal tertiary rule-making governance.

Civic participation has become more remote and fragmented with industrial society's separation of work from home, extension of the community's physical and geographic boundaries, and movement to a contract society. Social interaction and participation is more complex and distant, intricate, socially isolating, and detached. Tertiary social structures of larger and more impersonal communities have replaced direct, integrating, and bonding social interactions. Town meetings and informal face-to-face discussions and debates as consensus-building modes of political interacting have been replaced by political parties, extensive media political advertising, political action committees (PACs), public opinion polls, impersonal media talk shows, and the virtual reality of Internet chat rooms, Facebook, and Twitter. As the town-hall meetings of 2009 indicated, civil civic discourse often has been displaced by gun-packing seekers of TV exposure. These techniques allow politicians and marketers to bypass the mediating structures of associations, including grassroots political parties, and appeal directly to the voters. The mass marketing approach reduces the mediating function, reciprocity, and community accountability mechanisms. Participation in these more impersonal and technological modes may be virtual, but whether they enhance the social capital and reciprocity necessary for a community's social cohesion is unclear (Beaudoin & Tao, 2008; Clifford, 2009; Everything$_2$, 2001; Kaiser, 2005; Menchik & Tian, 2008).

The current decline in social participation and engagement (other than the virtual form) within communities and an impotence of the political system contribute to contemporary social problems. Civic participation's decline, including voting, by the poor, the working class, the middle class, and the young, is accompanied by a diminished government interest in and responsiveness to the interests of the non-voting community strata. This decline enhances their social marginalization and eventually social exclusion. It has also accompanied the relative economic decline of these groups. Governments generally favor the economic interests of the elites, who control both government and the economic institutions.[4]

Full social participation requires civic participation in the governance of local and national communities. The core and necessary trait or concept is primary and secondary participation rather than just checkbook membership (Ladd, 1999, p. 16; van Deth, 1997).

Arneil (2006, pp. 210–223) argues that for diverse communities to be just communities, social capital must rest on more than simply participation. Social capital exists less in heterogeneous communities (Coffe & Geys, 2006). Trust is necessary for social capital, and trust requires connectiveness. Trust is distinct from participation. In diverse communities trust is still being negotiated, and until trust is negotiated the communities are more likely to be aggregations of individuals, or diverse groupings, than a collectivity. Diverse communities that have marginalized groups as part of their diversity have an aggregated history rather than a common history and values. In these communities, barriers to both participation and trust must be addressed. As Judt (2009) observed:

[I]t is not by chance that social democracy and welfare states have worked best in small, homogeneous countries, where issues of mistrust and mutual suspicion do not arise. ... where immigration and visible have altered the demography of country, we typically find increased suspicion of others and a loss of enthusiasm for the institutions of the welfare state. (p. 86)

The United States has the challenge of creating a common community from its diversity by making differences of color and ethnicity inconsequential.

Social and civic participation is especially important in democratic communities. Democracies, especially in a diverse mega-state, depend on their many organizations to influence policy. If people do not participate in this process, they are essentially excluded and not considered in the rule-making processes of government. In democracies, as Phillips (1990) has observed, the government's interests and policies reflect the interests of those who select the government: "Since the American Revolution the distribution of American wealth has depended significantly on *who controlled the federal government, for what policies, and in behalf of which constituencies*" (p. xiv, italics original).

Democracies respond to collective action. An individual voter exerts very little political influence in the act of voting, although an individual with great economic and social resources can have great influence in the commercialized political processes. An individual voter can share

political influence through mediating organizations. The totalitarian danger of mass society, according to McCollough (1991), lies less in a dictator's seizing control of the governmental apparatus than in atomizing effects of mass society arising from the vacuum of community where nothing stands between the individual and the state. Social and civic groups are an important influence on government. These structures and interests compete for resources. They differ in influence on a variety of factors, not the least being a willingness to develop and use influence.

Voluntary Associations. A remedy against the social atomization and social disintegration characteristic of mass societies is, of course, the active membership of individuals, especially including our clients, in all kinds of voluntary associations (van Deth, 1997, p. 5). Voluntary associations provide the opportunity to meet and network with new people, learn to work with them, expand reciprocity that integrates society, develop social and civic engagement skills, and expand social supports that reduce the impact of mass society. Participation breeds participation. People who participate tend to participate even more and have more social and political participation opportunities. Without participation on the level of association, an individual is limited in most forums of civic participation. Associations provide the individual with a network of contacts, whether or not the associations are overtly political (Foster-Fishman, Cantillon, & Van Egeren, 2007; Geoghean & Powell, 2006; Hannah, 2006; Ohmer, 2008; Nicotera, 2008; Pyles & Cross, 2008). Van Deth's (1997) meta-research led him to conclude that social participation and political behavior had a clear and direct relationship, "even when socioeconomic status or political orientation are taken into account" (pp. 13–14). Political and social participation reinforce one another (Dekker, Koopmans, & van den Broek, 1997; Moyser, 1997, p. 44).

Mediating Structures. Increasing social participation is a critical social work task. It is vital to countering complexity and size. Community-based associations are mediating structures and act as buffers between the individual and the uncongenial, complex mega-structures. They are necessary to protect the individual and

| Individual ⟺ Mediating Structures ⟺ Society's Megastructures and Institutions |

Figure 4.1. Mediating structures.

democracy from the imposition of the mega-state and mega-corporations of the global turbo-economy. They provide the individual with protective zones (Berger & Neuhaus, 1977, p. 2; Nisbet, 1953; van Deth, 1997, p. 6). Voluntary associations as mediating structures are an anodyne to the social fragmentation, atomization, and social disintegration characteristic of our mass societies. Ladd (1999) points out that "joining face-to-face groups to express shared interests is a key element of civic life. Such groups help resist pressures toward 'mass society.' They teach citizenship skills and extend social life beyond the family" (p. 16). People who participate in voluntary organizations have more civic trust (Moyser, 1997, p. 43). Examples of mediating structures are family, churches, advocacy groups, labor unions, support groups, and neighborhood associations (Fig. 4.1).

With a global turbo-economy populated and dominated by mega-transnational corporations, individual and even additional communities as independent consumers become less relevant to a market without real competition. Competition, in the classic sense of no single or few vendors or purchasers are able to highly influence or control a market, is an archaic concept. Just as an individual voter in a mega-democracy is essentially powerless to influence the political marketplace, an individual consumer has little power to influence the global marketplace. In contrast, a single multinational and multifunctional corporation has great influence. "Some are "too big to fail"." Without mediating structures, an individual is relatively powerless compared to the mega-institutional structures of government and commerce. With mediating structures, individuals can aggregate their influence and seek social justice. The organizations, associations, and coalitions serve as mediators as well as action groups in dealing with mega-corporations and the mega-state.

Mediating structures need to be as continuous as the mega-structures. They need to parallel the mega-structures both horizontally and vertically. However, there is a risk that continuous

mediating structures will follow a developmental course similar to that of the mega-structures and become impersonal, imposing mega-structures themselves (Maloney & Jordan, 1997). This seems to be the path of mediating structures such as labor unions, political parties, and large voluntary checkbook membership associations such as the Red Cross.

Social participation's relevance for social work practice is explored more fully in the practice areas of community organization, networking and coalition building, and community social casework. Social participation is imperative to social work's obligation to social justice. Clients need to be brought into civic associations and social action coalitions. Integrating clients into community-based social support networks and organizations allows them to be in contact with a range of social support resources, provides social structures for reciprocity, and provides opportunities to develop social capital for social and political empowerment. Grassroots community organizations need to coalesce and form mediating structures for individuals to survive in our global economy. Social workers need to promote local and national participation of communities/constituents as social and political actors rather than as customers, consumers, and victims. Socially marginalized clients need to be linked to local and global networks of organizations (van Deth, 1997, p. 3). Social welfare organizations and social welfare professionals hold some potential as positive mediating forces if we can develop the fortitude and skills to intervene against the excesses of the corporate and social conservatism that has captured the nation, states, and communities. As Henderson asserts in *Critical Community Practice*, if the issue is not moved to the center of the profession now, participatory democracy may be lost (Butcher, Banks, Henderson, with Robertson, 2007, p. 161).

Mutual Support

The mutual support function, the social welfare function, is the community's provision of help to its members when their individual and family needs are not met through family and personal resources. Mutual support is helping one another in time of need. Primary and secondary groups—family, neighbors, friends—traditionally provided the first line of social support and protection. As communities have become more complex, more secondary groups and tertiary formal organizations have been developed to perform the mutual support function, such as governmental agencies, for-profit and nonprofit health and welfare agencies, other proprietary organizations such as insurance companies and day-care centers, and a host of voluntary, nonprofit organizations such as burial societies, credit unions, and child-care co-ops. The helping structures may be temporary or permanent. Mutual support helps to delineate a community from a simple aggregation of people. Under this conception of mutual support, social welfare is caring for others by virtue of their membership in the community. Inherent in mutual support are the reciprocity obligations and the development of social capital.

The functional and systemic questions for mutual support relate to community membership and community cohesion. Fullinwider (1988) argues, "We almost never encounter people, even strangers, whom we think of as 'simply humans'; we encounter fellow citizens, coreligionists, neighbors, historic kinsmen, political confederates, allies in war, guests. Our typical moral judgments and responses are almost always made in the context of some connection between us and others that goes beyond being members of the same species" (p. 266).

In our current social climate, the strength of our social connectiveness may not be sufficient for adequate mutual support. During the 2009 health care debate a Bozeman, Montana, physician offered the following gloomy observation (Smith, 2009):

American culture simply has never been based on caring about what happened to your neighbor. It's been based on individual freedom and the spirit of, if I work hard I'll get what I need and I don't have to worry about [the] fellow that maybe can't work hard. … I've done my job, I've worked hard, I've gotten what I'm supposed to get. I have what I need and if the other people don't, then that's sort of their problem. And unfortunately the big picture—that our nation can't

thrive with such a disparity between the rich and the poor, the access people and the disenfranchised—that hasn't seemed to really strike a chord with Americans.

To be part of this mutual support arrangement, does a person need to be a citizen of a certain political entity (the United States, Maryland, or Baltimore), or is a member of the community defined as simply someone who identifies with and is identified by the community as "one of us"? The identity position moves the conception of community toward the ethnicity and tribal position. The concern in the conception of community is the community cohesion required for mutual support with minimum coercion. If membership requires legal citizenship of a state and not simply functional membership in or identification with a community, then coercion probably plays a part in the process of mutual support. If functional citizenship and identification in a community is required of welfare recipients, community responsibility and reciprocity is inferred. The current debates on the exclusion of illegal (and in some cases legal) aliens from public mutual support and the denial of constitutional protections to aliens emphasize the problems in defining citizenship.

We are back, again, to the importance of civic participation by all in a community, especially by the poor and welfare clients. Civic participation creates the networks and social bonding necessary for social support as well as social justice. It provides opportunity for reciprocity and gives a claim and mechanisms for exercising the claim based on reciprocity.

Trust is required to develop the cohesion and bonding between people that is necessary for mutual support. People need trust each other to avoid the "free riders and the sucker's challenge" (de Jasay, 1989). The 2008–09 California drought illustrates such a "free riders and suckers" quandary. The drought was the state's worst in several decades. California needed to conserve water. Individuals were asked to sacrifice for the sake of the community and limit all water use. This is a classic case of individualism versus the community good. It is in an individual's interest to shower daily, water the yard, and wash the car; his or her use will only marginally decrease the community's supply, and the individual is better off and no one else is appreciably worse off, *if all others follow the rules.* The individual is a *free rider* and makes no sacrifice but rides on the sacrifices of the community. If no one makes a sacrifice, then the individual is only following the behavior of the collective, and the collective made it worse. Now, if the individual makes the sacrifice but the collective doesn't, the individual is a *sucker*: the collective is better off in the short run and probably worse off in the long run, the individual conserving is worse off both in the short and long run—a sucker.

The free riders and suckers quandary is the tragedy of the commons argument made against the welfare state (Schmidtz, 1991). The tragedy of the commons argument, simply stated, is that if we all can have our needs met by doing nothing—the use of the commons or communally held resources such as water—there is little motivation for each of us to exercise restraint. We individually will be no better off. If the individual does not get his or her needs and preferences met from the commons, someone or everyone else may use up the common, thus leaving nothing for the first individual or for future generations. Personal denial ensures that our current needs will not be met, and it doesn't ensure that our future or future generations' needs will be met. Thus, the global warming conundrum. The commons can perpetuate itself only when all are in harmony and act in common. In other words, there must be strong community responsibility.

The fear of a tragedy of the commons is evident in our public health and welfare policies and programs. We do not feel responsible either as donors or as recipients. As donors, we resent the intrusion of the state on our resources and its making us share them with people who contribute little to our well-being. We have little bonding with the recipients as individuals or concern about them as fellow community members. They are not us. If recipients have little sense of communal responsibility, they are marginalized and excluded from the community. If mutual support recipients, whether from welfare, education, health, or disaster relief, fulfill no public or common good, if they demonstrate no communal responsibility and make no contributions to the commons or prudently use it, then they are free riders. And if recipients are free riders, then donors—the taxpayers and those who are communally responsible by not exploiting the commons—are suckers. If we as donors view recipients as free riders, then we must view ourselves as suckers. If we do not wish to remain suckers or to view ourselves as suckers, we must rid the community of free riders. This is called welfare reform in current political rhetoric.

Trust is imperative to avoid the free riders/suckers dichotomy and tragedy of the commons. Trust and bonding are dependent on some mutual identity. Trust stems from and builds community. It involves commitment to others (Haley, 1999). Trust and mutual identity are diminishing factors between U.S. citizens and people globally.

A welfare state exists where state or public appliances provide mutual support. The welfare state provides a public structure and resources for mutual support and community building in response to the impersonal social contract of an industrial society. When there is a reliance on state appliances for mutual support without an underlying sense of community, community cohesion, and trust, there is a general increase in using social control to implement mutual support. Vertical approaches relying on taxes and transfers instead of community cohesion are used.

Communities as Local, Global, or Virtual Networks

People have varying commitments to a variety of communities. Bennett Berger (1998) contends that people have "limited, partial, segmented, even shallow, commitments to a variety of diverse collectivities—no one of which commands an individual's total loyalty" (p. 324). We live in many communities and may feel totally a part of none. Wellman's (1999, pp. 97–100) analysis leads him to conclude that we in the Western, largely urban world live in a new type of world of loosely coupled communities with the following characteristics:

1. Community ties are narrow and specialized relationships are not broadly supportive.
2. People float in sparsely knit, loosely bounded, frequently changing networks, not traditional cohesive, tightly bound communities.
3. Communities are not neighborhood-bound, supportive, and are socially dispersed networks.

4. Private and virtual intimacy has replaced public sociability.
5. Communities have become more women-centered, although community power has become less so.
6. Political, economic, and social milieus affect the nature of communities.
7. Cyberspace supports globalized communities.

As we lose the cohesive traditional community, new models of communities are being formed, including the *virtual community*. A virtual community is a group of people "who interact primarily through computer-mediated communication and who identify with and have developed feelings of belong and attachment to each other (Blanchard, 2004, p. 55)."

Proponents argue that rather than lament fewer bowling leagues (Putnam, 2000) and a loss of a pub-culture camaraderie, we should appreciate coming together in new ways through the Web, use the Internet with its Facebook and MySpace to find each other, and recognize that we participate differently in civic and community life (Kirchhoff, 1999; Ladd, 1999; Oldenburg, 1999). Electronic linkage in a cyberspace community reduces social isolation (Clifford, 2009; McLeod, Bywaters, Tanner, & Hirsch, 2008). Internet support groups whose members are dispersed geographically but share narrow interests provide some of the functions of natural helpers and community face-to-face support groups (Beaudoin & Tao, 2008; Kaiser, 2005; Menchik & Tain, 2008; Pruden, 2006; Wellman & Gulia, 1999). While research on the efficacy of the Internet to create real community for the virtual community is mixed, it does indicate it should be pursued. The Internet can't be ignored. It has value for social contact in rural areas (Kaiser, 2005), between cancer patients (Beaudoin & Tao, 2008; McLeod, Bywaters, Tanner, & Hirsch, 2008), and between the elderly (Clifford, 2009), and within as well as between communities (Quan-Hasse & Wellman, 2004). Some research and observers indicate that its use strengthen communities beyond the virtual community (Artz & Cooke, 2007; Kaiser, 2005; Pruden, 2006; Shull & Berkowitz, 2005; Stern & Dillman, 2006-7). Quan-Hasse and Wellman, (2004) report that "people who engage in political and organizational activities tend to use the Internet as much as those not engaged. There is no strong statistical association between Internet use and active participation"in any community (pp. 124-125). On the face of it, internet usuage doesn't seem to matter.

Critics of the notion of a virtual community, such as the communitarian William A. Galston (1999), argue that the virtual community may be and contributes to many things, but it is not a community. It provide social interaction and support, communication and contact, but the virtual community does not meet the conception of community by fulfilling its varied functions. Frey (2005) argues that virtual communities suffer from being "like-minded" and homogeneous and having less density and intensity of relationships. They are less cohesive than physical communities, although they tend to be homogeneous as communities of interest, because their members can easily leave the community (by logging off), and they tend to be less authentic, because community members are limited in their information about other members and members can present themselves as they wish. Virtual communities' social capital and trust are virtual, not extant.

Procopio and Procopio (2007) concluded after an online survey of Hurricane Katrina's displaced residents about the connection between geography and the Internet that "researchers interested in promoting social capital need to recognize that the Internet is neither the panacea for building community that some suggest nor the harbinger of civil anarchy others fear" (p. 82). The authors urge that community practitioners, especially those working in crises, consider Internet connectivity issues as important as other staples.

The proponents of the loosely coupled new community conception, including the virtual community, hearken back to Nisbet, who, over a half-century ago in *The Quest for Community* (1953), argued that freedom came from multiple associations and authorities. Thus, "while the best life was to be found within community, people should not limit themselves to one community. They should experience many communities" (Brooks, 2000, pp. 244–245).

The Community as an Arena of Conflict

Viewing the community as a social system has some built-in biases that make it insufficient alone to serve as a framework for social work practice in the community. The systems perspective's basic bias assumes a set of integrated subsystems generally working together smoothly for the benefit of the whole. But there often are disagreements between powerful groups in different subsystems of the community system. We know, for example, that powerless groups' fundamental interests are not acknowledged or taken adequately into account by the powerful. The good of the system as a whole—that is, the inclusive community—does not necessarily mean the good of all of its subsystems. The recognition of community as an arena of conflict suggests that conflict and change are characteristic of U.S. communities and that the process of determining the public interest therefore involves conflict and negotiation as much as it does rational planning, collaboration, and coordination. Issues of power do not seem to enter into the systems perspective, but viewing the community as an arena of conflict brings power and politics to the fore. We are forced to ask a variety of questions: What does it mean to say that the community has a collective identity? How do we take into account community differences in values and beliefs, goals, and interests? Does the community have an overriding public interest, and, if so, how is that public interest determined? Who is influential? Is the public interest synonymous with the interests of the most powerful people in the community? To answer these questions, we must turn to conceptions of power and power structure.

Power and community. As discussed in Chapter 2, power is present in most social relationships. Power is the ability to get what you want when you want it despite the opposition of other people. As Box 2.2 indicates, power is varied. Generally people exercise power to gain more and give less than those over whom power is exercised. Power is about gaining and losing, about control and influence (Willer, 1999, p. 2) (Box 4.2).

Even for very powerful individuals and groups, however, power is rarely total. Jean Baker Miller (1983) offers a more feminist conception of power. She defines power, similar to influence, as "the capacity to produce a change—that is, to move anything from point A or state A to point B or state B. This can include even moving one's own thoughts or emotions, sometimes a very powerful act. It can also include acting to create movement in an interpersonal field as well as acting in larger realms such as economic, social, or political arenas" (p. 4).

In this view, fostering another's growth or increasing another's resources, capabilities, and effectiveness to act exercises power. People who nurture, socialize, and educate—parents, teachers, social workers—hold and can exercise a great deal of power or influence. This is quite different from a masculine conception of power, which often involves limiting or controlling the behavior of others.

Most theorists distinguish *power* from *authority,* defining *authority* as legitimated power that has been legally, traditionally, or voluntarily

---

BOX 4.2.	**Facets of Power in Our Work**

Power is the ability to control one's own destiny and the ability to form support systems that affect one's life. Power has three dimensions: personal, interpersonal, and political. The work of psychologist Robert White [enhances] and understanding of personal power. . . . [He] has suggested that all human beings have a basic drive, which he calls the effectuance drive, a drive to experience oneself as a cause, to interact effectively with the environment—in other words, to experience oneself as having power.

Interpersonal power is closely related to personal power because it carries it into the social domain.

[Inter]personal power is the ability to influence the human surround, and it is dependent upon social competence, on the ability to interact effectively with others. Political power is the ability to alter systems, to bring about some change in social structure or organization, to redistribute resources.

Source: Excerpts from a speech by Ann Hartman, then editor of *Social Work,* at "Integrating Three Strategies of Family Empowerment," School of Social Work, University of Iowa, 1990.

granted to the holder of a particular position, such as a corporate CEO, an elected governmental official, or royalty in traditional societies. In the U.S. form of democracy, authority is granted to various elected officials to enact laws; to executives to carry out the business of the state; and to the courts to interpret, arbitrate, and enforce the laws in a tripartite system of balanced powers. The distinction between authority and power notes that while authority is a form of power, not all persons in authority are powerful, and powerful persons exist apart from authorities in any social system. Other than formal authority, the sources of power are multiple, including access to and control of strategic information, economic resources, connections to other powerful people, charisma, intelligence, wisdom, age, and more.

Finally, some theorists differentiate between *reputed* or *potential* power and *actual* power. We argue that power exists in its use. Potential power is only powerful in the threat to exercise it. If a threat to use it serves to constrain the actions of others, it is power. The classic example is the labor union, which has the power to strike. The potential for a strike often acts as a stimulus to negotiation and a resolution of differences. An actual strike, should it occur, is sometimes difficult to sustain and is often costly, so in this case a threat may be more potent than the reality. Or the capacity of bosses to fire can keep a workforce docile, even though workers may rarely be fired.

Power distribution. Communities can seldom express a clear and overwhelming public interest because they are composed of competing interests for limited resources. The public policy process invariably favors some interests, those of the elites, over others. The question, though, is "Does the process always favor the same interests?"

The gist of elitist theory is that community life is dominated by a small group of people with sufficient economic and political power to control public decision making in their own interests. Citizen participation, in this conception, is limited or ineffectual, or both. Mills (1956) contends that the structure of power in the United States resembles a pyramid with three levels (Kornhauser, 1968). At the top is the power elite,

a group composed of the leaders of (a) global mega-corporations, (b) the federal government executive branch, and (c) the military. This group controls large national and multinational corporations and their corresponding public organizations. They control the means of political power, production, and destruction. They have the power, through the control of dominant institutions and the media, to manipulate public opinion and ensure that the rest of society accepts their decisions. The intervention of the U.S. Supreme Court in the outcome of the 2000 presidential election and the fact that national politicians often seem to be either part of or in the service of corporate and economic elites lend support to this version of elitist theory.

The people who make the rules and who can change them at will generally win any competition. From an elitism perspective, top leaders determine the fundamental direction of public policy and shape the public interest to coincide with their interests. In the United States, as discussed earlier in this chapter, most of the resources have aggregated to the power elite as a result of policy changes.

Surrounding this power elite is a circle of sycophants who are advisers, technical experts, powerful politicians, regional and local upper classes, and celebrities. Some eventually may be elevated to the top level.

The second tier of the pyramid, at a middle level of power, consists of a variety of special interest groups, such as labor unions, media, religious and professional associations, and farm organizations, that struggle with modest influence only within the parameters established by the power elite.

Unorganized mass society falls into the bottom level of the pyramid—the majority of the populace. This group has little power over the decision makers at the top; rather, it is those in this level to whom the top leaders send orders, information, and interpretations of events. This base is becoming more socially and economically marginalized and excluded.

A number of studies using reputational methods (Hunter, 1953) have found evidence of an elitist power structure in both smaller and larger communities, although the makeup of these structures does not strictly follow Mills' conception. Numerous studies have also found the members of this group to be related by social class (Domhoff, 1967, 1974, 1990). The reputational method essentially involves asking many people (who are in a position to know) who they think the top community leaders are. Names that frequently recur are selected as the top leaders. Then, through interviews and further community investigation, the researcher begins to sort out the extent of these leaders' influence, how they exercise power in the community, and their patterns of interaction with each other.

Pluralist theorists have strongly criticized these elitism theorists along three lines. First, they argue that the basic premise of an ordered system of power in every human institution is faulty. Researchers who begin their studies by inquiring, "Who runs this community?" are asking a loaded question because the question assumes someone or a small group is running the community, and therefore that the researchers are sure to find it. Second, they argue that the power structure is not stable over time, as the elitism theorists contend, but rather is tied to issues that can be transitory or persistent. Therefore, the assumption of a stable coalition or set of coalitions in the community is inaccurate. Third, they contend that the elitism theorists wrongly equate reputed (and positional) power with actual power: power does not exist until it is actually exercised successfully.

In contrast to the elitism theorists, the pluralist theorists propose that power is distributed among many different organized groups, with control shifting depending on the issues. Citizens participate in the public policy process through a variety of interest groups. Because individuals potentially have the freedom to organize a group and compete in the policy arena, differences can be resolved amicably. The political system therefore operates much more democratically than the elitism theorists would have us believe, the public interest being whatever comes out of the pluralistic melting pot after the process is completed.

David Riesman (1951) argued that the power structure pyramid has only two levels, corresponding roughly to Mills's bottom two tiers. There is no power elite. "The upper level of the Riesman's pyramid consists of 'veto groups': a diversified and balanced body of interest groups" (Kornhauser, 1968, pp. 39–40). Each group

mainly wants to protect its own power and prerogatives by blocking the efforts of other competing groups. There is no dominant ruling group; instead there are multiple power centers, thereby creating a much more amorphous structure of power. The lowest level of the pyramid, as with Mills, consists of an unorganized mass public, but in this case the public is pursued as an ally rather than dominated by interest groups in their struggles for power (Kornhauser, 1968). Therefore, pluralist power figures are potentially more responsive and accountable to the majority of citizens than are elitist power holders.

Elitism theories imply that democracy is at best a weak institution or at worst a sham altogether, because the public interest is basically determined by a relatively small (though not necessarily conspiratorial) group of powerful leaders. Pluralist theories suggest that the political process is complex and increasingly remote due to the large number of interest groups protecting their turf and struggling for power. Because it is so hard to get anything done, leadership is weakened and political alienation begins to set in. Whether an issue involves the community or the country as a whole, no individual or group leadership is likely to be very effective due to the presence of entrenched veto groups—consider, for example, the battles to enact health care legislation during the Clinton and Obama administrations. For Banfield (1961), this struggle leads to public decision making that is seldom the result of deliberate planning. For Lindblom (1959), it leads to "disjointed incrementalism."

There can little argument with the data. Wealth, income, and political influence have become concentrated at the top (Krugman, 2002; Mintz, 2007). Even during the Great Recession the concentration continues: wealth and income continues to move to the top 1% and 5% despite Democratic Party control of both Congress and the executive branch (Cavanagh & Collins, 2008; Executive Pay, 2009; Forbes, 2008).

There are several lines of criticism of the pluralistic approach. One main criticism is that the pluralists present a rather idealized version of the political process. Since interest groups cannot be easily organized and sustained without many resources, a large part of the community cannot participate. Furthermore, the notion that the pluralist process operates amicably and effectively by a set of institutionalized political rules does not conform to the experience of challenging groups, who have succeeded primarily by using norm-violating, disruptive tactics (Gamson, 1990).

Another main line of criticism is that pluralist theory does not recognize a hidden face of power (Bachrach & Baratz, 1962, 1963, 1970). That is, by assuming that power is played out solely in relation to concrete issues, pluralists omit the possibility that in any given community there may be a group capable of preventing contests from arising on issues that it considers important. Power may well be at work in maintaining the directions of current policy, limiting the parameters of public discourse to fairly safe issues—in short, the power elite, by controlling an increasing share of the media, can prevent some items from ever reaching the community agenda and even becoming issues. Moreover, as the pluralist methodology offers no criteria for adequately distinguishing between routine and key political decisions, by accepting the idea that in any community there are significant, visible issues, the researcher is examining only what are *reputed* to be issues. Hence, the pluralists are guilty of the same criticism they level at the elitists. Pluralism appears to exist only on less important issues than on fundamental community welfare concerns.

Although both elitism and pluralist theories talk about "groups" in the political policy process, most of the early theories tended to focus on powerful individuals rather than powerful organizations. As communities become larger and more complex and their institutions become vertically integrated, power is exercised by a loose network of compatible interests rather than a small, tight cabal. Powerful fiscal corporations, such as Goldman Sachs, with their need to maintain a stable business market, and the growing power of government in American life have led power structure theorists to focus on networks of organizations as sources of widespread and enduring power (Perrucci & Pilisuk, 1970; Perrucci & Potter, 1989). Through such arrangements as interlocking boards of directors and government/corporation executive exchanges (see Box 4.3 for some of the Goldman Sachs–government exchanges), interorganizational leaders can mobilize the resources of a network of organizations (including governmental/military/media) to influence public policy. With the

BOX 4.3.	Goldman Sachs and the U.S. Government

Name	Prior to Government Service	Government Service	Administration	Post Government Service
Stephen Friedman	Chair and CEO, Goldman Sachs	Assistant to President for Economic Policy; Director, National Economic Council; Chair, Federal Reserve Bank of New York	George W. Bush Barack Obama	Chair, Stone Point Capital (private equity company)
Robert E. Rubin	Chair and CEO, Goldman Sachs	Secretary of the Treasury	William J. Clinton	Senior consultant, Citigroup
Henry M. Paulson	Chair and CEO, Goldman Sachs	Secretary of the Treasury	George W. Bush	Visiting scholar, Johns Hopkins University
Jon S. Corzine	Co-Chair and CEO, Goldman Sachs	U. S. Senator	NA	Governor, New Jersey

Goldman Sachs in 2010 was being investigated for criminal and civil violations.

vertical structuring of society, these sorts of interorganizational arrangements operate on the local level as well as state, national, and global levels. In the final analysis, it is not the specific people who occupy the organizational linking roles that are critical; the people change. It is the elite interests that shape the interorganizational networks that represent the enduring structuring of community power.

Mediating Structures and Community-Sensitive Social Work Practice

This chapter argues that there is value in strengthening local communities and other mediating structures to meet the onslaught from larger forces outside their control. As discussed earlier, we agree with Berger and Neuhaus (1977) and propose a strengthening of mediating structures. They have great value for linking and empowering ordinary people. They stand between and protect individuals in their private lives from the alliance of global mega-corporations and the state. Berger and Neuhaus argue that "public policy should protect and foster mediating structures and wherever possible, public policy should utilize mediating structures for the realization of social purposes" (p. 6). In general, we support these propositions, but neither of them is simple to fulfill. As always, we have to find a balance between individual rights and community rights and between the protective functions of the state and the defensive functions of the mediating structures.

It is also possibly that mediating structures themselves, due to size and patterns of decision making that are not truly participatory, may have difficulty in building a strong sense of community among their participants. In a study of Baltimore's African-American community, McDougall (1993) made a potent argument for even smaller, informal community building blocks called base communities:

Mediating institutions, such as churches, schools, and community organizations, are essential to this task [of community strengthening, institution building, and networking], but small base communities of one or two dozen people, spun off from mediating institutions or growing independently, are essential to counterbalance the tendency of mediating institutions to mirror the hierarchical character of the public and private bureaucracies with which they contend. (pp. 186–187)

Conclusion

The crucial premise of this chapter is that for social workers to be effective, we need to understand how the community affects our lives and the lives of the people we work with. We live and work and play in multiple, overlapping local communities of different kinds. These communities are often culturally diverse and generally quite different from the communities where we ourselves grew up and now live. The importance of community calls for a community-based social work practice. Some examples of how community may bear on practice will help clarify this idea.

Consider the social worker employed by a church-sponsored nonprofit social work agency. In her practice she has begun to see more and more clients who are HIV-positive or who have AIDS. How should she deal with this problem? Suppose that the church has strong anti-gay sentiments and sees AIDS as "a gay problem." Suppose that the church reflects values that are prevalent in the community. What kinds of services can be provided for these new clients? How do clients themselves feel about their circumstances, given the community's values? What kinds of services are needed in the community? How might the social worker begin to address that need? (Obviously many other kinds of problems, such as homelessness, substance abuse, and teenage pregnancy, might raise similar questions.)

Take another example. Assume that, as a school social worker, you have encountered a Hispanic immigrant child, possibly illegal, who appears abused. You are obligated to involve Child Protective Services (CPS). Do you need to know how the Hispanic community views CPS workers or the nature of the relationship between the school, the Hispanic community, and U.S. Citizenship and *Immigration* Services (USCIS)? How will the situation be handled if the police become involved? Will the police refer the case to USCIS? How do the school authorities feel about CPS and USCIS and potential disruptions of the school day and possible bad publicity? How do you approach the family and the child? How can you get CPS to work with you to manage the situation in the most helpful fashion for all parties involved?

A third example. Suppose that you are a social worker in a large university hospital's department of family medicine. You suspect that the children in the family you are seeing have been poisoned by lead paint from their substandard apartment house. How can you prevent further damage? What about the children who live in other units in that building? Might there be legal or political issues that you should know about? What if the corporation owning the building is a large donor to the university and politically well connected? What are some of the different professional roles you might have to play to help your clients and their neighbors?

There are no simple answers to the questions posed in these illustrations. The answers require a sound understanding of community.

The fragmentation of some communities and the sense of distance between them and state institutions are major challenges. So too is the search by individuals for ways of acquiring a more meaningful sense of community. If these issues are not addressed then the fragility of representative and participatory democracy, …, will be threatened. Our contention accordingly, is that critical community practice needs to move to centre stage—urgently. (Butcher, Banks, Henderson with Robertson, 2007, p. 161)

Discussion Exercises

1. *How have vertical and horizontal changes in community functions affected social work practice? Give examples.*
2. *Select a client and describe the specific institutions and organizations in the client's life that are used to fulfill the five locality-relevant functions. How much do the organizations coincide in their service areas? What is the locus of decision making for the organizations? Repeat the exercise for yourself. How many of the specific structures are the same for yourself as for your client? Do any serve as mediating organizations?*
3. *In a small group discussion, consider the examples and questions posed in the "Conclusion"*

section and try to answer them. Identify the mediating structures and their roles in your answer.
4. *Identify an issue in your community relevant to the provision of social services, and try to follow it through a public policy process. Identify the stakeholders for various sides and facets of the issue. What are the roles of the media, elected officials, public agency representatives, leaders of voluntary associations, and corporation leaders in the process? Is the process democratic? Who has power? Who is left out? Is there a hidden face of power influencing the process?*
5. *What is the best community you have even lived in? Why do you select it? What made it the best? List the characteristics of this place. How can that community be made even better?*

Notes

1. An exercise: Find a reference in the political literature to the United States as "the Homeland" prior to September 11, 2001.
2. In proposing these approaches, we are mindful that the literature offers many other useful models, such as the community as a system of interaction (Kaufman, 1959), as a system of human ecology (Fellin, 2001; Poplin, 1979), as shared institutions and values (Warren, 1978), and as an ecology of games (Long, 1958).
3. For a more sinister description of social control and public welfare, see Piven and Cloward (1971, 1982).
4. For a review of the use of the state's police powers and policies to create wealth for particular classes and community interests, see Barlett and Steele (1992, 1994) and Phillips (1990, 1993).

References

Abelson, R. (2000, May 8). *Serving self while serving others. The New York Times*, p. A16.

Anderson, S., Cavanagh, J., Collins, C., Pizzigati, S., & Lapham, M. (2007). *Executive excess 2007: The staggering social cost of U.S. business leadership, 14th annual CEO compensation survey*. Washington, DC: Institute for Policy Studies and United for a Fair Economy.

Andrews, E. L. (2009, September 23). Fed to lower safety net, but gingerly. *The New York Times.com*. Retrieved January 7, 2010, from http://www.nytimes.com/2009/09/24/business/economy/24fed.html

Appiah, K. A. (2005). *The ethics of identity*. Princeton, NJ: Princeton University Press.

Appiah, K. A. (1997, October 9). The multiculturalist misunderstanding. *The New York Review of Books*, pp. 30–36.

Arneil, B. (2006). *Diverse communities: The problem with social capital*. New York: Cambridge University Press.

Artz, N., & Cooke, P. (2007). Using e-mail listservs to promote environmentally sustainable behaviors. *Journal of Marketing Communications*, 13(4), 257–276.

Bachrach, P., & Baratz, M. S. (1962). The two faces of power. *American Political Science Review*, 56, 947–952.

Bachrach, P., & Baratz, M. S. (1963). Decisions and nondecisions: An analytical framework. *American Political Science Review*, 57, 641–651.

Bachrach, P., & Baratz, M. S. (1970). *Power and poverty: Theory and practice*. New York: Oxford University Press.

Banfield, E. (1961). *Political influence*. New York: Free Press.

Barlett, D. L., & Steele, J. B. (1992). *America: What went wrong? Kansas City*, MO: Andrews and McMeel.

Barlett, D. L., & Steele, J. B. (1994). *America: Who really pays the taxes?* New York: Simon and Schuster.

Beaudoin, C. E., & Tao, C-C. (2008). Modeling the impact of online cancer resources on supporters of cancer patients. *New Media & Society*, 10(2), 321–344.

Bellah, R. N., Madsen, R. D., Sullivan, W. M., Swidler, A., & Tipton, S. M. (1985). *Habits of the heart: Individualism and commitment in American life*. Berkeley: University of California Press.

Bellah, R. N., Madsen, R. D., Sullivan, W. M., Swidler, A., & Tipton, S. M. (1991). *The good society*. New York: Vintage Books.

Berger, B. M. (1998). Disenchanting the concept of community. *Society*, 35(2), 324–327.

Berger, P. L., & Neuhaus, R. J. (1977). *To empower people: The role of mediating structures in public policy*. Washington, DC: American Enterprise Institute.

Berry, W. (1996). Does community have a value? In W. Berry & B. Castro (Eds.), *Business and society: A reader in the history, sociology, and ethics of business* (pp. 74–79). London: Oxford University Press.

Berry, M., & Hallett, C. (Eds.). (1998). *Social exclusion and social work: Issues of theory, policy, and practice*. Dorset, UK: Russell House.

Berstein, N. (1996, September 15). *Giant companies entering race to run state welfare programs. The New York Times*, p. A1.

Berstein, N. (1997, May 4). *Deletion of word in welfare bill opens foster care to big business: Profits from poverty. The New York Times*, pp. 1, 26.

The big media and what you can do about it: How the "Big Ten" shape what you think and know. (2002). *The Nation*, 272(1), 11–43.

Blanchard, A. (2004). The effects of dispersed virtual communities on face to face social capital. In M. Huysman & V. Wulf, (Eds.), *Social capital and information technology* (pp. 53–73). Cambridge, MA: The MIT Press.

Blow, C. M. (2009, August 15). *Getting smart on crime. The New York Times*. p. A19.

British Columbia Ministry of Children and Family Development. (2003). *Moving forward together: A compendium of papers presented to the provincial Child and Family Steering Committee on Community Governance*. Victoria, BC: Author.

Broad, W. J. (2002, February 17). *U.S. is tightening rules on keeping scientific secrets: Terrorist threats cited. The New York Times*, pp. A1, A13.

Brooks, D. (2000). *Boo-Boos in paradise: The new upper class and how they got there*. New York: Simon & Schuster.

Brower, S. (1996). *Good neighborhoods: A study of in-town and suburban residential environments*. Westport, CT: Praeger.

Bureau of Labor Statistics, U. S. Department of Labor. (2009). *Labor statistics from the Current Population Survey: September 4, 2009*. Retrieved September 23, 2009, from http://data.bls.gov/PDQ/servlet/Survey OutputServlet?data_tool=latest_numbers&series_id=LNS14000000

Bureau of Lbor Statistics, U. S. Department of Labor. (2010). Social work. *Occupational outlook handbook, 2010-11 Ed*. Retrieved August 10, 2010 from http://www.bls.gov/aco/006.htm.

Butcher, H., Banks, S. Henderson, P., with Robertson, J. (2007). *Critical community practice*. Bristol, UK: The Policy Press.

Cavanagh, J., & Collins, C., (2008). The rich and the rest of us. *The Nation*. Retrieved September 23, 2009, from http://www.thenation.com/doc/20080630/cavanagh_collins

Clifford, S. (2009, June 2). *Online, "a reason to keep on going." The New York Times*, p. D5.

Clymer, A. C. (2002, May 20). *U.S. attitudes altered little by Sept. 11, pollsters say. The New York Times*, p. A14.

Coffe, H., & Geys, B. (2006). Community heterogeneity: A burden for creation of social capital. *Social Science Quarterly*, 87(5), 1053–1072.

Cohen, A. P. (1985). *The symbolic construction of community*. New York: Tavistock Publication and Ellis Horwood Limited.

Conley, D. (2009, March 23). *America is …15? The Nation,* 288:11.

Dahrendorf, R. (1995). A precarious balance: Economic opportunity, civil society, and political liberty. *The Responsive Community: Rights and Responsibilities,* 5(3), 13–39.

Deacon, B. (with Hulse, M., & Stubbs, P.). (1997). *Global social policy: International organizations and the future of welfare.* Thousand Oaks, CA: Sage.

de Jasay, A. (1989). *Social contract, free ride: A study of the public goods problem.* New York: Oxford University Press.

Dekker, P., Koopmans, R., & van den Broek, A. (1997). Voluntary associations, social movements and individual political behavior in Western Europe. In J. W. van Deth (Ed.), *Private groups and public life: Social participation, voluntary associations, and political involvement in representative democracies* (pp. 220–239). London: Routledge.

Delgado, M., & Staples, L. (2008). *Youth-led community organizing: Theory and action.* New York: Oxford University Press.

Dicken, P. (2003). *Global shifts: Reshaping the global economic map in the 21st. century. 4th Ed.* London: Sage.

Dodds, I. (2001). Time to move to a more peaceful and equitable solution. *IFSW News,* 3, p. 2.

Domhoff, W. G. (1967). *Who rules America?* Englewood Cliffs, NJ: Prentice Hall.

Domhoff, W. G. (1974). *The Bohemian Grove and other retreats.* New York: Harper & Row.

Domhoff, W. G. (1990). *The power elite and the state: How policy is made in America.* New York: Aldine de Gruyter.

Dylan, Bob (1991). *The times they are a-changin'.* Special Rider Music.

Eamon, M. K. (2002). Poverty, parenting, peer, and neighborhood influences on young adolescent antisocial behavior. *Journal of Social Service Research,* 28(1), 1–23.

Erlanger, S. (2009, September 29). Europe's Socialists suffering even in bad capitalist times. *The New York Times.* p. A1,16.

Etzioni, A. (1993). *The spirit of community: Rights, responsibilities, and the communitarian agenda.* New York: Crown.

Everything2, (2001). *Definition of community.* Retrieved October 14, 2009, from http://everything2.com/title/Definitions+of+community

Executive pay: A special report. (2002, April 7). *The New York Times,* pp. 7–9.

Executive Pay: A special report (2009, April 5). *The New York Times,* pp. BU 1 7–12.

Executive Pay Watch. (2000, August). Retrieved July 9, 2003, from http://www.aflcio.org/corporateAmerica/paywatch/

Fein, E. B. (1996, July 5). *A move to hospitals for profit seems inevitable in New York. The New York Times,* pp. 1, B2.

Fellin, P. (1995). Understanding American communities. In J. Rothman, J. L. Erlich, & J. E. Tropman, with F. M. Cox (Eds.), *Strategies of community organization: Macro practice* (5th ed., pp. 114–128). Itasca, IL: F. E. Peacock.

Fellin, P. (2001). *The community and the social worker* (3rd ed.). Itasca, IL: F. E. Peacock.

Fogel, S. J., Smith, M. T., & Williamson, A. R. (2008). Creating new patterns of social and economic activity through planned housing environments. *Journal of Community Practice,* 15(4), 97–115.

Forbes 400 richest Americans list 2008: Review of the 400 wealthiest people in the United States of America, according to the Forbes business magazine. (2008). Retrieved October 22, 2009, from http://www.woopidoo.com/reviews/news/rich-list/american/rich.htm

Foster-Fishman, P. G., Cantillon, D., Pierce, S. J., & Van Egeren, L. A. (2007). Building an active citizenry: the role of neighborhood problems, readiness, and capacity for change. *American Journal of Community Psychology,* 39, 91–106.

Freudenheim, M. (1996, February 5). *Charities say government cuts would jeopardize their ability to help the needy. The New York Times,* p. B8.

Freudenheim, M. (2002, May 10). *Companies trim health benefits for many retirees as costs surge. The New York Times,* pp. A1, C4.

Frey, K. (2005). ICT-enforced community networks for sustainable development and social inclusion. In L. Albrechts & S. J. Mendelbaum. (Eds.), *The network society: A new context for planning* (pp. 183–196). New York: Routledge.

Fullinwider, R. K. (1988). Citizenship and welfare. In A. Gutman (Ed.), *Democracy and the welfare state* (pp. 261–278). Princeton, NJ: Princeton University Press.

Galston, W. A. (1999). *Does the Internet strengthen community?* Retrieved October 21, 2009, from http://www.publicpolicy.umd.edu/IPPP/fall1999/internet_community.htm

Gamson, W. (1990). *The strategy of social protest.* Belmont, CA: Wadsworth.

Geoghean, M., & Powell, F. (2006). Community development, partnership governance and dilemmas of professionalization: Profiling and assessing the case of Ireland. *British Journal of Social Work,* 36(5), 845–861.

Gibelman, M., & Demone, H. W., Jr. (Eds.). (1998). *The privatization of human services.* New York: Springer.

Gibelman, M., & Schervish, P. H. (1996). *Who we are: A second look.* Annapolis Junction, MD: NASW Press.

Ginsberg, L. (Ed.). (1998). *Social work in rural communities* (3rd ed.). Alexandria, VA: Council on Social Work Education.

Giving USA. (2009) Bloomington, IN: Giving USA Foundation, The Center on Philanthropy at Indiana University.

Glain, S. (2009). The American Leviathan. *The Nation,* 289(9), 18–23.

Goodman, P. S. (2009, September 23). *Emphasis on growth is called misguided. The New York Times,* pp. 3, 5.

Gray, J. (1998). *False dawn: The delusion of global capitalism.* London: Granta Books.

Greenhouse, S. (2001, September 11). *Report shows Americans have more "Labor Days": Lead over Japan in hours on the job grows. The New York Times,* p. A5.

Grynbaum, M. M. (2008, August 15). *Living costs rising fast, and wages are trailing. The New York Times,* p. C1.

Haley, J. (1999). Inside Japan's community controls: Lessons for America? *The Responsive Community,* 9(2), 22–34.

Halsey, A. H., Lauder, H., Brown, P., & Wells, A. S. (Eds.). (1997). *Education: Culture, economy, society.* New York: Oxford University Press.

Hamilton, D., & Darity, Jr., W. (2009, September 2009). Race, wealth, and intergenerational poverty: There will never be a post-racial America if the wealth gap persists. *The American Prospect.* Retrieved August 11, 2010 from http://www.prospect.org/cs/articles?article=race_wealth_and_intergenerational_poverty.

Hannah, G. (2006). Maintaining product-process balance in community antipoverty initiatives. *Social Work,* 51(1), 9–17.

Hardina, D. (2002). *Analytical skills for community organization practice.* New York: Columbia University Press.

Held, D., & McGrew (Eds.). (2007). *Globalization theory: Approaches and controversies.* Cambridge, UK: Polity Press.

Heilbroner, R. L. (1962). *The making of economic society.* Englewood Cliffs, NJ: Prentice Hall, Inc.

Hoppe, R. A., Korb, P., & O'Donoghue. (2007). *Structure and finances of U.S. farms: Family farm report, 2007 ed. (Economic Information Bulletin No. EIB-24).* Washington, DC: Economic Research Service, USDA. Retrieved September 21, 2009, from http://www.ers.usda.gov/Publications/EIB24/

Hunter, F. (1953). *Community power structure.* Chapel Hill: University of North Carolina Press.

Ignatieff, M. (2002, February 5). Is the human rights era ending? *The New York Times,* p. A29.

Johnson, A. K. (2000). The community practice pilot project: Integrating methods, field, assessment, and experiential learning. *Journal of Community Practice,* 8(4), 5–25.

Johnston, D. C. (2002a, February 7). *More get rich and pay less in taxes. The New York Times,* pp. A13.

Johnston, D. C. (2002b, February 18). *U.S. corporations are using Bermuda to slash tax bills: Profits over patriotism. The New York Times,* pp. A1, A12.

Johnston, D. C. (2002c, May 20). *Officers may gain more than investors in move to Bermuda. The New York Times,* pp. A1, A13.

Joppke, C. Ed. (1998). Challenge to the nation-state: Immigration in western Europe and the United States. New York: Oxford University Press.

Judt, T. (2009). What is living and what is dead in social democracy. *The New York Review of Books,* 56(20), 86–96.

Kaiser, S. (2005). Community technology centers and bridging the digital divide. *Knowledge, Technology, & Policy,* 18(2), 83–100.

Kirchhoff, S. (1999, November 20). Disability bill's advocates rewrite the book on lobbying. *Congressional Quarterly Weekly,* 2762-66.

Kaufman, H. F. (1959). Toward an interactional conception of community. *Social Forces,* 38(l), 9–17.

Kornhauser, W. (1968). "Power elite" or "veto groups"? In W. G. Domhoff & H. B. Ballard (Eds.), *C. Wright Mills and the power elite* (pp. 37–59). Boston: Beacon Press.

Kramer, D., & Brauns, H. J. (1995). Europe. In T. D. Watts & N. Mayedas (Eds.), *International handbook on social work education* (pp. 103–122). Westport, CT: Greenwood.

Krugman, P. (2002, October 20). *For richer. The New York Times.* sec. 6, p. 62.

Kuttner, R. (1996). *Everything for sale: The virtues and limits of markets.* New York: Alfred A. Knopf.

Ladd, C. E. (1999). Bowling with Tocqueville: Civic engagement and social capital. *The Responsive Community,* 9(2), 11–21.

Lappé, F. M., & Du Bois, P. M. (1994). *The quickening of America: Rebuilding our nation, remaking our lives.* San Francisco: Jossey-Bass.

Leonhardt, D. (2002, June 4). *A prime example of anything-goes executive pay. The New York Times,* pp. C1, C10.

Levenson, D. (1997, Summer). Online counseling: Opportunity and risk. *NASW News,* p. 3.

Lindblom, C. E. (1959). The science of "muddling through." *Public Administration Review,* 19, 79–88.

Long, N. E. (1953). The local community as an ecology of games. *American Journal of Sociology,* 64, 251–261.

Longes, J. F. (1997). The impact and implications of multiculturalism. In M. Reisch & E. G. Gambrill (Eds.), *Social work in the 21st century* (pp. 39–47). Thousand Oaks, CA: Pine Forge Press.

Madrick, J. (2009, August 31/September 7). Money for nothing. *The Nation*, 289(6), 5,7.

Maloney, W. A., & Jordan, G. (1997). The rise of the protest business in Britain. In J. W. van Deth (Eds.), *Private groups and public life: Social participation, voluntary associations, and political involvement in representative democracies* (pp. 107–124). London: Routledge.

Mancini, J. A., Bowen, G. L., & Martin, J. A. (2005). Community social organization: A conceptual linchpin in examining families in the context of communities. *Family Relations, 54*(5), 570–582.

Marx, J. D. (1998). Corporate strategic philanthropy: Implications for social work. *Social Work, 43*(1), 34–41.

Mattessich, P., & Monsey, B. (1997). *Community building: What makes it work.* Saint Paul, MN: Amherst H. Wilder Foundation.

McCollough, T. E. (1991). *The moral imagination and public life: Raising the ethical question.* Chatham, NJ: Chatham House.

McGeehan (2003, April 6). *Again; Money follows the pinstripes. The New York Times*, pp. 3,7.

McDougall, H. A. (1993). *Black Baltimore: A new theory of community.* Philadelphia: Temple University Press.

McLeod, E., Bywaters, P., Tanner, D., & Hirsch, M. (2008). For the sake of their health: Older service users' requirements for social care to facilitate access to social networks following hospital discharge. *British Journal of Social Work, 38*, 73–90.

Menchik, D. A., & Tian, X. (2008). Putting social context into text: The semiotics of E-mail interaction. *American Journal of Sociology, 114*(2), 332–370.

Metcalf, S. (2002). Reading between the lines. *The Nation, 274*(3), 18–22.

Miller, J. B. (1983). Women and power. *Social Policy, 73*(4), 3–6.

Mills, C. W. (1956). *The power elite.* New York: Oxford University Press.

Mintz, M. (2007). Will Congress reform wretched executive excess? *The Nation.* Retrieved September 23, 2009, from http://www.thenation.com/doc/20070212/mintz

Mishra, R. (1999). *Globalization and the welfare state.* Northampton, MA: Edward Elgar.

Mitchell, A. (2002, February 6). *Social Security pledges may haunt both parties. The New York Times*, p. 18.

Moe, R. C. (1987). Exploring the limits of privatization. *Public Administration Review, 47*, 454–460.

Morgan, P. (Ed.). (1995). *Privatization and the welfare state: Implications for consumers and the workforce.* Aldershot, UK: Dartmouth Publishing.

Morin, R., & Deane, C. (2002, January 15). *The ideas industry. The Washington Post*, p. A17.

Morning, A. (2008). Reconstructing race in science and society: Biology textbooks 1952–2002. *American Journal of Sociology, 114*, S106–S137.

Moyser, G., & Parry, G. (1997). Voluntary associations and democratic participation in Britain. In J. W. van Deth (Ed.), *Private groups and public life: Social participation, voluntary associations, and political involvement in representative democracies* (pp. 24–46). London: Routledge.

Mulroy, E. A. (2004). Theoretical perspectives on the social environment to guide management and community practice. *Administration in Social Work, 28*(1), 77–96.

Myerson, A. R. (1997, October 7). *The battle for hearts and tonsils: Hospitals specialize to enhance profits. The New York Times*, pp. D1, D4.

Nicotera, N. (2008). Building skills for civic engagement: Children as agents of neighborhood change. *Journal of Community Practice, 16*(2), 221–242.

Nisbet, R. (1953). *The quest for community: A study in the ethics of order and freedom.* New York: Oxford University Press.

Nordheimer, J. (1997, March 9). *Downsized, but not out: A mill town's tale. New York Times*, pp. F1, F13.

Oldenburg, R. (1999). *The great good place.* New York: Marlowe & Co.

Ohmer, M. L. (2008). The relationship between citizen participation and organizational processes and outcomes and the benefits of citizen participation in neighborhood organizations. *Journal of Social Service Research, 34*(4), 41–60.

Patterson, O. (2001, May 8). *Race by the numbers. The New York Times*, p. A31.

Pear, R. (2002, February 5). *Upon closer look, Bush budget cuts include risks. The New York Times*, p. A19.

Perrucci, R., & Pilisuk, M. (1970). Leaders and ruling elites: The interorganizational bases of community power. *American Sociological Review, 3*(5), 1040–1057.

Perrucci, R., & Potter, H. R. (Eds.). (1989). *Networks of power: Organizational actors at the national, corporate, and community levels.* New York: Aldine de Gruyter.

Pew Research Center. (2005). *Trends: 2005.* Washington, DC: Author.

Pew Research Center. (2006). *The future ain't what it used to be, Updated: September 9, 2009.* Retrieved September 9, 2009, from pewsocialtrends.org.pew research center.

Pew Research Center. (2009). All social and demographic trends report. Retrieved September 9, 2009, from pewsocialtrends.org.

Phillips, K. (1990). *The politics of rich and poor: Wealth and the American electorate in the Reagan aftermath.* New York: Random House.

Phillips, K. P. (1993). *Boiling point: Republicans, Democrats, and the decline of middle-class prosperity.* New York: Random House.

Poplin, D. E. (1979). Communities: A survey of theories and methods of research. New York: Macmillan.

Press, E. (2009). A perfect storm: The intensifying economic crisis slams the nonprofit world. *The Nation,* 288(12), 11–16.

Procopio, C. H., & Procopio, S. T. (2007). Do you know what it means to miss New Orleans? Internet communication, geographic community, and social capital in crisis. *Journal of Applied Communication Research,* 35(1), 67–87.

Pruden, D. (2006). Neighborhood networks: Good for residents and a good investment. *Journal of Housing and Community Development,* 63(1), 17–21.

Putnam, R. (2000), Bowling alone: The collapse and revival of American community. New York: Simon and Schuster.

Putnam, R. (2009). *Social capital: Measurement and consequences.* Retrieved July 12, 2009, from http://www.oecd.org/dataoecd/25/6/1825848.pdf

Pyles, L., & Cross, T. (2008). Community revitalization in post-Katrina New Orleans: A critical analysis of social capital in an African American neighborhood. *Journal of Community Practice,* 16(4), 383–401.

Quan-Haase, A., & Wellman, B. (2004). How does the Internet affect social capital. In M. Huysman & V. Wulf, (Eds.), *Social capital and information technology* (pp. 113–131). Cambridge, MA: The MIT Press.

Riesman, D., Denny, R., & Glazer, N. (1951). *The lonely crowd.* New Haven, CT: Yale University Press.

Risen, J. (2008, August 12). *Use of Iraq contractors may cost billions, report says. The New York Times,* p. A11.

Room, G. (1990). *"New poverty" in the European community.* London: Macmillan.

Rose, N. (1997). The future economic landscape: Implications for social work practice and education. In M. Reisch & E. G. Gambrill (Eds.), *Social work in the 21st century* (pp. 28–38). Thousand Oaks, CA: Pine Forge Press.

Saegert, S., & Winkel, G. (2004). Crime, social capital, and community participation. *American Journal of Community Psychology,* 34(3/4), 219–233.

Salamon, L. M. (1997). *Holding the center: America's nonprofit sector at a crossroad, a report for Nathan Cummings Foundation.* New York: The Nathan Cummings Foundation.

Samuels, M. E., & Whitler, E. T. (2008). *Comparative study of the status of minority populations in America's poorest counties: A pilot project, final report.* Kansas City, MO: National Rural Health Association.

Schmidtz, D. (1991). *The limits of government: An essay on the public goods argument.* Boulder, CO: Westview Press.

Scott, J. (2001, June 18). *Increasing diversity of New York is building islands of segregation: The census. The New York Times,* pp. A1, A18.

Scott, J. (2002, February 7). *Foreign born in U.S. at record high. The New York Times,* p. A18.

Sharkey, P. (2008). The intergenerational transmission of context. *American Journal of Sociology,* 113(4), 931–969.

Shaw, B. A., Gallant, M. P., Riley-Jacome, M., & Spokane, L. S. (2006). Assessing sources of support for diabetes self-care in urban and rural underserved communities. *Journal of Community Health,* 31(5), 393–412.

Schaeffer, R. K. (1997). Understanding globalization: The social consequences of political, economic, and environmental change. Oxford, UK: Rowman & Littlefield.

Shull, C. C., & Berkowitz, B. (2005). Community building with technology: The development of collaborative community technology initiatives in a mid-size city. *Journal of Prevention & Intervention in the Community,* 29(1), 29–41.

Smith, A. (1922). *An inquiry into the nature and causes of the wealth of nations* (Vols. 1 & 2; E. Cannan, Ed.). London: Methuen.

Smith, A. D. (2009). *Obama's audience speaks first. The New York Times,* p. A29.

Snyder, T. D., Dillow, S. A., & Hoffman, C. M. (2009). *Digest of education statistics 2008 (NCES 2009-020).* Washington, DC: National Center for Education Statistics, Institute of Education Sciences, U.S. Department of Education.

Sobeck, J. L. (2008). How cost-effective is capacity building in grassroots organizations? *Administration in Social Work,* 32(2), 49–68.

Stern, M. J., & Dillman, D. A. (2006). Community participation, social ties, and the use of the Internet. *City & Community,* 5(4), 409–424.

Stiglitz, J. E. (2009). *Freefall: America, free markets, and the sinking of the world economy.* New York: W.W. Norton & Co.

Stiglitz, J. E. (2003). *Globalization and its discontent.* New York: W.W. Norton & Co.

Stein, B. (1993). Work gets no respect on TV. *The Responsive Community*, 3(4), 32.

Stille, A. (2001, December 15). *Grounded by an income gap*. The New York Times, pp. A15, A17.

Strom, S. (2009a, February 19). *Charities now seek bankruptcy protection. The New York Times,* p. A17.

Strom, S. (2009b, March 5). Charities say government is ignoring them in crisis. *The New York Times*. Retrieved September 28, 2009, from, http://query.nytimes.com/gst/fullpage.html?res

Strom, S. (2009c, June 10). *Charitable giving declines, a new report finds. The New York Times,* p. A16.

Strom-Gottfried, K. (1997, Winter). The implications of managed care for social work education. *Journal of Social Work Education*, 33(1), 7–18.

Swarns, R. L. (1997, October 25). *In a policy shift, more parents are arrested for child neglect. The New York Times*, pp. A1, A12.

Tanzi, V. (2002). Globalization and the future of social protection. *Scottish Journal of Political Economy,* 49(1), 116–127.

Thurow, L. C. (1995, September 3). *Companies merge: Families break up. The New York Times*, p. C11.

Trattner, W. I. (1999). *From poor law to welfare state: A history of social welfare in America* (7th ed.). New York: Free Press.

Uchitelle, L., & Kleinfield, N. R. (1996, March 3–8). *The downsizing of America: A national headache [Series of seven articles]. The New York Times.*

United Nations Development Programme (2008). *Human development indices: A statistical update, 2008.* Retrieved June 2, 2009, from http://hdr.undp.org.U.S.

Census Bureau. (2008). Population distribution in 2005. *Population Profile of the United States.* Retrieved September 17, 2009, from http://www.census.gov/population/www/pop-profile/files/dynamic/PopDistribution.

U.S. Census Bureau. (2009a). Income, poverty, and health coverage in the United states: 2008. p. 10. Retrieved August 11, 2010, from http://www.census.gov/compendia/statabs/2009edition.html.

U.S. Census Bureau. (2009b). *The 2009 statistical abstract: The national data book*. Retrieved September 17, 2009, from http://www.census.gov/compendia/statab/cats.html

U.S. Census Bureau (2009c). POV02: People in families by family structure, age, and sex, iterated by income-to-poverty ratio and race: 2008. *Current Population Survey, 2009 Annual Social and Economic Supplement*. Retrieved October 8, 2009, from http://www.census.gov/macro/032008/pov/new02_100_06.htm

van Deth, J. W. (Ed.). (1997). *Private groups and public life: Social participation, voluntary associations, and political involvement in representative democracies.* London: Routledge.

Viswanath, K., Kosicki, G. M., Fredin, E. S., & Park, E. (2000). Local community ties, community-boundedness, and local public affairs knowledge gaps. *Communication Research*, 27(1), 27–50.

Vartanian, T. P., & Buck, P. W. (2005). Childhood and adolescent neighborhood effects on adult Income: Using siblings to examine differences in ordinary least squares and fixed-effect models. *Social Service Review*, 79(1), 60–94.

von Hoffman, N. (2007, April 4). Rich get richer, Poor get powerless. *The Nation.* Retrieved September 24, 2009 from, http://www.thenation.com/search/index.mhtml?search=April+4

Wagner, A. (1997). Social work and the global economy: Opportunities and challenges. In M. C. Hokenstad & J. Midgley (Eds.), *Issues in international social work: Global challenges for a new century* (pp. 45–56). Washington, DC: NASW Press.

Walsh, M. W. (2001, February 26). *Reversing decades-long trend, Americans retiring later in life. The New York Times*, pp. A1, A13.

Warren, R. L. (1978). *The community in America.* Chicago: Rand McNally.

Wellman, B. (1999). From little boxes to loosely bounded networks: The privatization and domestication of community. In J. L. Abu-Lughod (Ed.), *Sociology for the twenty-first century: Continuities and cutting edges* (pp. 94–114). Chicago: University of Chicago Press.

Wellman, B., & Gulia, M. (1999). Virtual communities as communities: Net surfers don't ride alone. In M. A. Smith & P. Kollock (Eds.), *Communities in cyberspace* (pp. 167–194). London: Routledge.

Willer, D. (Ed.). (1999). *Network exchange theory.* Westport, CT: Praeger.

Willie, C. V., Willard, D. A., & Ridini, S. P. (2008). Theoretical & conceptual issues in effective community action. In C. V. Willie, S. P. Ridini, & D. A. Willard (Eds.), *Grassroots social action: Lessons in power movement* (pp. 3–20). New York: Rowman & Littlefield, Publishers. Inc.

II

Community Practice Skills for Social Workers: Using the Social Environment

5

Assessment: Discovering and Documenting the Life of a Community

The undiscovered country from whose bourne no traveler returns.
William Shakespeare, poet, playwright

By mutual confidence and mutual aid, great deeds are done, and great discoveries made.
Homer, poet

We often discover what will do, by finding out what will not do; and probably he who never made a mistake never made a discovery.

Samuel Smiles, author

The Landscape of Our Lives

Overview of Chapters 5 and 6

Unless we are hermits, we generally live in communities, large and small. It is exciting to learn what makes them tick—whether a quiet town with one stop light or a "toddlin' town" like Chicago. The learning process takes us into libraries, onto the Web, and along city sidewalks and village lanes. Fortunately, it is both challenging and enjoyable. Understanding community, whether a rural crossroad settlement, barrio, hamlet, town, city, or megalopolis, is essential for community and social work practice. Like individuals, each community is unique and offers different opportunities and challenges. This chapter discusses the philosophies of and approaches to community assessment. The succeeding chapter examines the assessment methodologies.

Assessment as a Basic Social Work Process

Assessment is essential for effective social work practice. Community factors are required in any case assessment and in an analysis of the community itself. It is a professional obligation to understand client communities. Knowing the whole picture is mandatory, regardless of our intended level of intervention. Knowing the community gives us credibility with the community. Understanding a cross-section of people and their histories gives us believability and access. To appreciate the impact of the community on the individual, or on a collective of individuals, the worker must understand the community itself. Assessment serves as a means of planning or inquiry, as a vehicle for information exchange, as part of formal problem solving, and as a way to determine which services are needed by whom. Knowing the players and systems provides us with more options. Knowing what residents want offers us direction and allows us to be accountable. Learning how to do community studies will assuredly be helpful to community practitioners and organizers who will have to do community studies and direct service practitioners who need to understand communities in understand their clients. Community analysis helps us get our bearings and avoid false starts in our practice.

Understanding the life of the community by assessing the community will require the full range of qualitative and quantitative research skills.

Assessment

We understand the life of a community through an assessment process. Assessment is the first and most important practice task. Assessment is necessary before intervention, unless intervention is done either by rote or at random. Assessment's purpose is to determine the relevant attributes of a case and to gather information about the cause of the current conditions and factors necessary for change in the case.[1] Assessment, then, involves determining what is the here and now, the assets, resources, and challenges, and how it got that way and how might best get to a desired future state. Community assessment is a necessary aspect of any case assessment to understand both the content and context of the case. Assessment also is a cognitive process used with clients, situations, or problems that pays attention to uniqueness (Meyer, 1993, p. 9). Johnson (1995), in line with this approach, views assessment broadly as including (a) social study analysis and understanding and (b) resource-oriented needs assessment. Assessment is not done in a vacuum or simply to understand a community, as fascinating as that is. Assessment is done to understand a community and to use that knowledge to facilitate change for individuals and communities.

Case Theory Building

Community assessment is done to understand a community and to build a *case theory*[2] to effect change. A case theory is a coherent explanation of the case and creates a framework that will lead to the most appropriate and satisfying intervention for the case. Johnson (1995) regards it as fitting the pieces together for particular individuals or systems. To Lauffer (1982, 1984), assessment focuses on "the examination of what is, on what is likely to be, or on what ought to be" (p. 60), or a theory of change.

Case theory construction precedes development of the intervention plan. It forms the foundation for specification of desired outcomes,

definition of any problematic conditions, identification of community assets and resources, and selection of intervention strategies and approaches to achieve goals and alter problematic conditions. Case theory provides a map for intervention. Case theory is built from and makes sense of the assessment information collected. The analysis of assessment data in the case theory building helps us differentiate, comprehend, and respond to a certain population or neighborhood and determine who generally runs things in town and to grasp intangibles such as ethos, morale, and town character. Case theory constructs a framework to understand a specific community or case; it doesn't provide a general theory for classes of communities or cases (Bisman, 1994, pp. 111–121; Bisman & Hardcastle, 1999, pp. 55–61).

Individual in Society Assessment

Delineating an Individual's Ties to the Community. Until recently, social work used the label *diagnosis* to describe the investigative processes in understanding individuals, neighborhoods, and community. We prefer to denote the process as *assessment* rather than diagnosis. Assessment is a more inclusive and generic concept with greater emphasis on social and environmental factors (Gambrill, 1983). Assessment aims at understanding or knowing at a level broader than measuring and diagnosing, which are based on a medical or positivist model of linear cause-and-effect relationships. According to Rodwell (1998), the more limited approach of diagnosis "has consistently reduced to symptoms and the cause of disorders; usually in general terms that is difficult to distinguish the assessment of one situation from another" (p. 235). Classification schemes associated with assessment, such as the *Diagnostic and Statistical Manual of Mental Disorders* (*DSM*) series, often fail to individualize people and to take into account their societal context. Assessment, whatever the unit of attention, shifts from an emphasis on a need/deficiency/problem assessment to one focusing on asset/capacity/problem solving—that is, to strength assessment (Cowger, 1994; Kretzmann & McKnight, 1993; Meyer, 1995; Rosenthal & Cairns, 1994; Sharpe, Greaney, Royce, & Lee, 2000). Social work practitioners need to think of competence and assets at a community level as well as individual traits. For example, someone concerned with economic development who walks through a dusty town populated by Amerindians—or residents of a village in India—will quickly note the lack of material goods. However, someone interested in the arts might also spot sand painting in the U.S. Southwest and painted prayer decorations made by women in the villages in India. Social workers are as capable as folklorists and art collectors of seeing strengths in villages, towns, and cities.

Public health workers, community psychologists, teachers, community police officers, and social workers are expected to know how individuals and families fit into their communities and if their communities accept them (Box 5.1). The community provides resources to its members and social workers. Discovering not only the clients' internal strengths but also their "external strengths"—networks, organizations, institutions with resources—is "central to assessment" (Cowger, 1994, p. 266). There are ways and tools to determine whether someone is isolated or attached to an area or a network.

Problems in the Interface. Assessment processes should balance and synthesize person–environment relations and avoid the trap of assuming that the problem resides solely in the individual. This is important because, as health professor Gary Kielhofner (1993) insists, "We must not only seek to make members good for the social collective, but also to make the social collective good for individuals" (p. 251). Let us explore the difference between a routine assessment of an individual that takes the environment into consideration and an assessment where individual and society are given equal weight.

Sergio is 40 years old and has worked at a local plant for 4 years. Drinking beer and eating barbecue, Sergio and his buddies gripe their way through lunch. Upon his return to the floor of the factory, Sergio lurches into some equipment and is injured. Reasonable intervention objectives are to get him medical attention, any needed rehabilitation, and then back on the job.

However, Germain and Gitterman (1995) would urge us to go slower and look for interacting personal, environmental, and cultural factors. Bisman (1999) might recommend building a case theory that explains the case and creates a framework that will lead to the most appropriate and satisfying intervention for the case. A conventional diagnosis centers on Sergio's drinking. An Employee Assistance Program (EAP) professional might ask these questions: What do his supervisors say—was this an isolated incident? Has Sergio frequently been absent or late? Is his supervisor ready to fire him? Is he having other problems such as anger or credit management? Should addictions—alcohol, drugs, gambling—be explored? Does he have a treatment history?

A clinical social worker unconnected with his work might ask questions about Sergio's personal, marital, and psychiatric history, and his ethnic background and culture. Such professionals are engaged in a practical assessment to help Sergio by seeing what he is doing to himself and what services are needed. But we also need to know Sergio's personal and social assets: his education and skills and job history, community resources such as church, buddies, and other social supports.

Kielhofner would have us pay more attention to what Sergio is up against and resources available to help him meet the challenges. This means considering variables such as worker alienation (Did Sergio want to escape his particular workplace?),

BOX 5.1.	Representative Questions for Field Case Studies

- Would you show me around your [town, neighborhood, school]?
- Tell me about your typical day.
- What's the best way around here to [rent a cheap room, get a free meal, get a truck, . . .]?
- What kind of neighborhood would you say this is?
- If I needed a [passport, green card, box at the opera, . . .], what would I have to do to get one?
- Describe the sorts of things I shouldn't do at this meeting we are going to.
- What do you mean? [as a response for more elaboration]

occupational hazards (Was the machine that Sergio fell on a safe piece of equipment?), and whether the work environment is encouraging (Garson, 1994). Kielhofner thinks professionals seldom ask broad enough questions: Can the person do the work? Is the work environment a place in which any reasonable person would want to work? How do social-environmental conditions affect Sergio? According to Kielhofner (1993), "Issues of environment or workplace conditions and incentives are largely ignored. In fact, the worker who does not wish to work, or whose behavior suggests disincentive to work, is socially identified as malingering. . . . We have as much responsibility to be agents of social change and institutional transformation as we have to help persons to change" (pp. 249, 251).

Kielhofner's expertise is in functional assessment. Kielhofner (1993) believes professionals such as social workers "sit at the politically loaded juncture between the individual and surrounding institutions" (p. 248). Whether they know it or not, they exercise social control and have the power to affect rights, lives, and how the public views the "moral worth" of individuals (p. 248), in part through the assessments they write. This causes us to ask, do social workers gather information only about maladapted persons or maladaptive conditions? They should assemble information about assets and social justice. The community interface focus has us consider our angle of vision before we start an assessment. Perhaps this will result in gathering different data or connecting with different offices than usual—for example, the Occupational Safety and Health Administration as well as a consulting psychiatrist.

Two cautions are invoked in our discussion of assessments: (1) consider community context as supplying assets and opportunities and imposing constraints and (2) avoid hasty judgments. As we do our assessments, Kielhofner challenges us to transcend preconceptions and premature pigeonholing. He tells of a time when the renowned Carl Jung was asked to examine the drawings of a 50-year-old man. After making extensive negative comments, Jung concluded that the man was schizophrenic. It should give pause to all who diagnose to learn the drawings were by Picasso (Kielhofner, 1993, p. 248).

Assessment and Establishing Goals and Objectives

The first steps in community assessment involve determining the critical factors in the community, ecology, and task environment.[3]

1. What are the community's, ecology's, and task environment's boundaries? Can the boundaries be expanded if required to include more assets and resources?
2. What and where are the assets and resources available in the community? Are they adequate for objective achievement or must the community's boundaries be expanded? How can the assets and resources be accessed?
3. What factors in the community most influence behavior and opportunities? What are the communication and interaction patterns within the community?
4. What are the factors in the social environment that influence and constrain objective achievement?

Philosophies of Assessment

The act of assessment covers an astonishingly wide range of activities, from technical analyses, to preparation for massive programmatic intervention in a community, to judgments about a society itself. We must be familiar with methods and prescriptive rules. However, it would be a pity if the purposes of our profession were submerged by the practical. We must also heed the evocative in the assessment process—that is, what is indicative of what—and consider values. A listening, learning, exploring style and philosophy should guide an initial assessment interaction with an individual or a community. An assessment philosophy establishes our attitudes, organizes our approach, and directs many of our applications. It even dictates whether assessment should be a two-way process. Information gathering provides a foundation for more elaborate assessment and research.

Assessments of, in, and by the Community

Community participation as full partners is the ideal model of assessment. Community involvement in the assessment stage is critical in empowering the community and reducing any sense of social exclusion. It is a first step in helping the community take ownership of its welfare. An assessment's case theory will reflect the community's reality construction and build commitment to any subsequent realities (Butcher, Banks, Henderson, with Robertson, 2006). The bottom-up approach has been found to be effective from disadvantaged areas in London, UK (Turner, 2009), to Missoula, MT (Jacobson, 2007). In Eagle Pass, Texas, program staff ran seven focus groups to learn about grassroots health concerns. Five of the groups involved members of the community and two were with "prominent figures" who could influence the community (Amezcua, McAlister, Ramirez, & Espinoza, 1990, p. 259). The political dynamics of communities often surface during assessment and are more easily integrated into the process when local people are central to the assessment. Involvement is empowering to both communities and individual participants (Foster-Fishman, Cantillon, Pierce, & Van Egeren, 2007; Steves & Blevins, 2005).

Attitude of the Professional and Belief Bonding

The practitioner's philosophy of assessment matters because assessment is a first step in establishing a relationship with a community. The stance taken at the beginning affects all of the operations that come later. Underpinning these efforts must be the belief by the practitioner that he or she has the capacity to assist individuals and groups and the individuals and groups, in turn, have the same belief in their capacity and the practitioner's capacity. This is called *belief bonding*. Belief bonding is a shared belief by a worker and client, client system, and action system that "the worker is competent, can practice social work, and has knowledge about the problems presented by the client" (Bisman, 1994, p. 79). Belief bonding appears essential, though not sufficient, to effective social work and community practice for psychological and social interventions requiring active client, client system, and action system participation in the intervention process. Belief bonding builds on the fundamentals of the relationship component

of social work practice (Patterson, 1985; U.S. Department of Health and Human Services, 1997). As Schilling (1990) aptly observes, most people prefer to be helped by someone who believes in the efficacy of his or her intervention than someone who does not. The study of leadership generally reveals that confidence in a leader and a leader's methods and program is a critical component in successful leadership (Morrell & Capparell, 2001).

While research on belief bonding and the related therapeutic alliance is not extensive and the results are somewhat mixed, researchers generally believe that a joining between worker and client on goal and task is essential to success (Coleman, 2000; Loneck & Way, 1997; Mitchell, C. G., 1998; U.S. Department of Health and Human Services, 1997). Without belief in the capacity of the community and clients as a living system to grow and change, there is little point—besides ritual—in doing assessments at any level.

Analyzing Community Needs and Resilience

We must avoid the self-fulfilling prophecy of "you often find what you look for." By focusing only on weaknesses, social work and other professions may inadvertently create a dependency neighborhood. Human services, urban studies, and community development too often have had deficiency-oriented policies and programs responses. Consequently:

many lower income urban neighborhoods are now environments of service where behaviors are affected because residents come to believe that their well-being depends upon being a client. They begin to see themselves as people with special needs that can only be met by outsiders. . . . Consumers of services focus vast amounts of creativity and intelligence on the survival-motivated challenge of outwitting the "system," or on finding ways—in the informal or even illegal economy—to bypass the system entirely. (Kretzmann & McKnight, 1993, p. 2)

This presents a "one-sided" story of the community (O'Looney, 1996, p. 232). Meyer (1993) asks why assessment is limited to "what is the matter," in an individual or community situation, when it should also include how people are doing with what is the matter (p. 36).

Practitioners are urged to identify the capacities of local individuals, citizen associations, and institutions and to build connections and strong ties with and among them. This method of assessment looks for problem solvers, not just problems. We will return to this need in the discussion of community assets mapping.

Agency/Community Value Differences

Assessment involves points of view (e.g., a strengths perspective), how we see and construct things, and ideology and values that shape perceptions. As we discussed in chapters 2 and 3, agencies, communities, and practitioners may not share the same construction of reality because of differences in ideologies, values, and pragmatic interests. Constructed reality or social constructionism is a postmodernist theory of understanding the world obtained from interaction with the world (Payne, 2006, p. 58). Practitioners, agencies, and communities have had different interactions with the world, differences in worldviews, and different constructions.

Assessment involves mutually building with the community a shared case theory. This will require the practitioner to develop a critical practice perspective rooted in a critical consciousness. A critical practice perspective and a critical consciousness go beyond competency in technical skill to recognizing and sharing with the community value commitments and social goals. They are grounded on the premises of symbolic interactionism and social constructionism that societies and social institutions are socially constructed with the socially accepted constructions resting on social power. Social justice and community self-determination, however, requires these constructions to be arrived at through community democratic participation. Critical consciousness is necessary for critical community practice. Critical consciousness is other and community directed, reflective, and reflexive (Butcher, Banks, Henderson, with Robertson, 2007). The critical practitioner strives to become aware of philosophical and construction differences that can hamper mutual assessment. The critical community practitioner works to understand the community, oneself, and how perceptions contour the assessment.

The hardest situations are those in which professional values are in conflict with those of most community residents. Such situations require decisions about if, when, and where to substitute professional values for the values of the community, when to adhere to the community's values, and when to strive for compromise or consensus. A part of the community or the whole may feel imposed on or affronted by a program, whether it distributes condoms in schools or clean needles on the streets, arranges for birth control implants, or houses released mental patients. The critically conscious practitioner recognizes these conflicts and shares them with the community groups. This is necessary for meaningful community self-determination.

Respect and Responsiveness

We follow this principle: Respect community residents enough to seek and listen to their views (Julian, 1999). This is required for community empowerment and the imperatives of informed consent and self-determination (Butcher, Banks, Henderson, with Robertson, 2007). These are no less imperative for community assessment and practice as with social casework. In the previous chapters, we grounded ourselves in social science approaches as a means of understanding community. Here we highlight tapping current and potential service users and others in the community network as sources of information and insight into a particular community. Respect requires that we ask key informants from the community. Along with doing or reading formal studies, we must integrate intelligence gathered from the community into the assessment and case theory. We will discuss the methodologies for doing this in the following chapter.

Listening to Feedback

Feedback feeds heavily into the assessment process. Feedback can be by anonymous satisfaction-with-services evaluations, on-premise suggestion boxes, a newsletter written and controlled by clients to be read by practitioners, formal evaluation by users of services through an outside evaluator, and serious analysis of any complaints received. *Services* is used here in a broad sense, because feedback can be given on training, group therapy, oversight of homemaker services, psychodrama, and many other activities. People working in organizations of all types—businesses, government agencies, nonprofits—should "use every listening post [they] can find" (Peters, 1987, p. 152). We will discuss this more fully in the marketing chapter (Chapter 11).

Collaborative Assessments

Rothman (1984) reminds us that whatever the assessment's form, purpose, and methodology, one of the first decisions to make is who will do the assessment, how it will be done, and where it will be done:

Assessment can be a fairly technical and solitary professional activity carried out in an office surrounded by computer printouts and area maps. On the other hand, it can be conducted on a collaborative basis in neighborhood clubs, and meeting halls, with the professional and the constituency taking joint responsibility as partners. (p. 8)

Since the citizenry rarely initiates systematic assessment, such an assessment may begin with a professional, social agency, civic leader, or elected official. Unfortunately, outsiders seldom get it right, without input from residents is needed and solicited. Many residents want their preferences taken into consideration but may lack patience with the tedious, often unfathomable, time-consuming assessment exercises. When the process is meaningful, the community can be appreciative, even to celebrating the end of the experience (Elliot, Quinles, & Parietti, 2000).

Typically, community co-inquiry is modest and experimental; for example, 15 young people in Baltimore worked closely with an assessment team to help define youth health issues using photographs (Strack, Magill, & Klein, 2000). This Photovoice approach encourages people to assess their own situations and communities. Cameras are passed out to young, homeless, or mentally ill people—or to illiterate villagers—who take photographs, talk about them, look for themes, and make assessments and recommendations as a group. Program creator Caroline Wang (Wang & Burris, 1997, Wang, 2003) says, "Photovoice is a method that enables people to define for themselves and others, including policy makers, what is worth remembering and what needs to be changed" (p. 3, paragraph 2). Such a mutual learning experience can advance sound decision making and trust before action steps are taken (Abatena, 1997; Colby, 1997).

Apart from professionals, citizens must learn to deliberate with each other and express their disagreements about problems and priorities: "People who cannot choose together cannot act together" (Mathews, 1994, p. 401).

Forms of Community Assessment

Community assessments come in many forms (http://www.iapad.org/). Before launching one, we should consider such elements as collaboration, scope, focus, and purpose. We discuss the primary forms here, with the methodologies following in Chapter 6.

The Range and Flavor of Community Assessments

Social workers ought to be able to conduct full-blown community assessments and more topical status reports on such community dynamics as health status and neighborhood crime status. Community practitioners should welcome targeted questions from journalists and public officials such as, "Who will use public toilets if they are installed along sidewalks in our city, and what is the prediction for nontraditional use?" "What is the capacity of our community and its service network to absorb more refugees?" These questions provide the opportunity to interpret the community and its challenges to decision makers and opinion leaders.

Assessing the coping capacities of an individual client and of a community have much in common (see Box 5.1). For both it is a matter of aggregating assets. A group set up to assess the portable potty issue could comprise those providing direct services to the homeless; a Travelers Aid type of organization; a Women, Infants, and Children program representative; someone from a methadone clinic; and officials from the city's tourist bureau and police and sanitation departments. The refugee question could be addressed to church sponsors, job placement and housing location groups, public welfare staff, civic leaders, and representatives of (and translators for) the refugee/immigrant community already in the area.

We must organize our knowledge in a form that can be pulled together and used by others. Journalists and politicians come to the front-line worker neither for statistics nor diatribes, but rather for cases and insights that make sense of statistics. They also want easily remembered points on both sides of the question. To illustrate: If refugee wives and parents can join men already here, there might be less crime and alcoholism, but because housing in the community for large families is in short supply and there is a waiting list, tensions could be heightened if refugees are given preference. While this may seem mere common sense, it is our role to inject common sense, facts, and ethics into political decision making. We will discuss the interpretative responsibilities with our exploration of staging.

Getting Started: Familiarization Assessment

Getting started, based on available data with some firsthand data added, entails a more cursory examination of the entire community, with the goal of achieving a general understanding and becoming familiar with a community. Another example could flow from acquainting oneself with community and client concerns, such as by inviting those with similar problems to come together for a speak-out session. For instance, those from rural areas who must travel to receive radiation therapy or dialysis might share their needs and frustrations about their care or transportation. These patients could provide a more complete picture of the adequacy of their hometown supports. Follow-up assessments of rural towns could be of this type.

Comprehensive Assessment

Assessments can be comprehensive in the sense of encompassing the entire community and methodologically looking at all the components specified in chapter 4, and generating original data. To Martinez-Brawley (1990), assessment starts with abstract questions of a high order such as "How does the community rate in terms of cohesiveness, engagement and interdependence among its members?" (p. 23). Such questions

require in-depth examination. Typically, a comprehensive assessment or audit launches planning or development projects (Guterman & Cameron, 1997; Murtagh, 1999). Many communities utilize the "civic index" to systematically identify strengths and take ownership of weaknesses. Designed by the National Civic League, it facilitates self-assessment of civic infrastructure—for example, how well does the community share information? How willing is it to cross regional lines to find a solution? To illustrate results, officials in Lee's Summit, Missouri pulled together bickering interest groups to work on growth issues. Afterwards, the community stopped defeating tax initiatives and, feeling part of the agenda, voted for a dozen straight ballot initiatives (National Civic League, 1999).

What reason would we have to assess something as large as a community? Think of someone who organizes migrant farm workers—someone who has many locations from which to choose to begin work, since the workers need help wherever they live. An assessment would help the organizer to select a community where townspeople and media outlets are somewhat sympathetic, other occupations have a history of collective bargaining, unemployment is relatively low, interaction among minority groups is positive, and numerous residents speak the migrants' language.

But most assessments are more focused and examine either neighborhoods of the community or functional components.

Subsystem Assessment

Subsystem assessment examines a single facet of community life, similar to assessing a functional community or a functional component of a community, such as the business sector, religious organizations, service agencies, non-English-speaking populations, or the school system (Spradley, 1990, p. 388). A subsystem has a structure that must be demarcated and should be diagrammed. To illustrate, board and care homes are one of many subsystems on which clients rely. These care facilities are part of a multilevel provider–regulator subsystem (which is part of the long-term care system, which, in turn, is part of the health care system). The interests and concerns of immigrant communities can be assessed through analysis of print and electronic media outlets geared to ethnic groups, another subsystem. Frederick Wiseman (1968, 1994), the acclaimed documentary filmmaker, has captured internal dynamics in portrayals of multiple subsystems. Twice he has filmed high schools as a way of learning about communities. He is famous for examining without judging.

We too must initially set aside preconceived ideas to become attuned to those affiliated with whatever slice of the community we are examining (Bloom & Habel, 1998; Weiner, 1996). This often requires wide reading. We want to be able to show the operations of a subsystem, such as the world of deaf Americans, from both the participants' and our viewpoints (Box 5.2). Eventually, if appropriate, we can make judgments (e.g., for advocacy purposes).

Service Providers and Users

Assessments often involve direct service practitioners and clients and service users. A *services/ programs study* is one that looks at provision and utilization of services (affordability, suitability, effectiveness). We can examine services by observing problems and the responses to them (a) from a flowchart perspective, tracing those entities involved after the fact to those involved before the fact or vice versa, and (b) from an overview of the "quality and comprehensiveness of local services" for a problem (Koss & Harvey, 1991, p. 115). In one city, for example, a huge public housing complex was to be entirely rebuilt; therefore, residents had to relocate to other sites in town for 2 to 3 years. Part of the overall analysis of residents' needs included questionnaires and

planning sessions with social workers and housing officials to identify services and programs wanted by residents in their temporary location and in their remodeled housing complex. The degree of importance of each option—from mentoring programs to general equivalency diploma (GED) classes—was examined. An assessment of relevant service providers and other civic entities was also made to identify programs already in place at the new sites, services that could be transferred with the residents, and gaps that existed. All of this involved an elaborate assessment of organizations serving low-income people.

Box 5.3 illustrates resources a community may or may not have to use in responding to rape. This simple resource inventory can be used to assess local services, to give guidance on a range of community actions that can be taken, and to look for gaps or problems. It provides a sample assessment form that could be adapted to the reader's own subject area. (However, each community problem will require a different list.)

Assessment helps with more than research, planning, and evaluation; it gives us a quick look at areas of difficulty within the system.

In this section, we wish to focus on the realm of service resources. To *grasp a human service system*, Netting, Kettner, and McMurtry (1993) would have us inspect three types of "service-delivery units"—informal, mediating, and formal—and identify the sponsoring organizations or auspices for each. (Self- or mutual help groups and associations are examples of mediating delivery units.) Netting, Kettner, and McMurtry (1993) believe that an "astute practitioner will carefully assess all avenues of service delivery to the target population" (p. 102).

BOX 5.2.	**Walking in Their Shoes: A Community Case Study Foray**

Choose a population (teenage parents, dually diagnosed adults in group homes, immigrants) in an underserved area. Spend a day with a key informant of the group, accompanying the informant on his or her daily routine in the community. Someone who has work that takes him or her through the residential or place community of this population (if one exists), such as a pizza deliverer, meter reader, pest control employee, local transit worker, or activities

director, would be a good choice. If this is a scattered or nonplace community, ferret out members of this population whose work takes them on rounds involving this group, such as public health workers, job coaches, English-as-a-second-language tutors, and Head Start outreach workers. It is useful for a better understanding of the community and life in the community. Avoid being intrusive, be humble, and make clear your desire to understand.

BOX 5.3.	Tramping About: A Community Walk, Drive, Jaunt

The goals are to know people, places, and rituals; to build relationships with informants; and to talk with persons often avoided. Explore alleys and byways on foot or bicycle. Take your time. Main thoroughfares can be covered in several hours. By strolling through an area again and again, you become part of the community. Learn by speaking with, sitting with, and accompanying those encountered: mail carriers, shopkeepers, delivery drivers, individuals sitting on stoops. Ask them about their communities; listen to their tales. What generalizations do residents make about themselves? Learn their names. Traffic court, public benefit office waiting rooms, and blood banks can be used for resting and observing. Riding the subway in new directions makes sense; riding a bus provides an opportunity to ask passengers natural questions. Someone in a wheelchair might take an excursion through a barrier-free retirement community, spending time with many residents. Write-ups of such outings (field notes) include particulars, observations, and inferences. One might start as follows:

I live in a popular neighborhood. I walk past Rafael's Cuban restaurant—supposedly owned by militant exiles (scuttlebutt says its neon sign was used years ago to signal clandestine meetings), the grocery store, the apartment building with the circular drive, and the park. When I walk home at 6, I try to notice which parents and children are at the playground. In the mornings, I've noticed three men in the opposite corner of the park. Maybe I am seeing in new ways, because recently I observed them washing in the fountain, I realized that the park is their home.

We want to be aware of informal resources within particular communities that can be helpful. Melvin Delgado (1996) explains that *bodegas* (grocery stores) do more than sell native food in their neighborhoods. They also provide seven services:

1. Credit
2. Banking—cashing of checks
3. Community-related news and information
4. Counseling customers in distress
5. Assistance in filling out or interpreting government forms
6. Information and referral to social service agencies
7. Cultural connectedness to homeland (Delgado, 1996, p. 63)

Narrower resource assessments can be undertaken before or at the time of need. We can conduct such assessments ourselves or stay aware of others who make them and learn to interpret their conclusions. At any time, we may face a situation that requires knowledge of previously unexplored facets of the community.

Independent Assessments from Service Users

Clients and users can differ in perceptions from service providers. A separate survey of residents revealed worries not just about the continuity and predictability of services but also about the transition itself—how they would be accepted in the receiving neighborhoods. This meant that (a) the overall assessment needs to encompass residents as well as agencies, and (b) neighborhood civic associations also need to be contacted as part of the assessment.

We encourage formal consumer and community critiques of services (Stoesz, 2002) to legitimize the consumer's voice (Thompson, 1999), even if the critique is sometimes unrestrained or irritatingly insistent. Social agencies should have either consumers on the policy boards or consumer advisory boards, democratically selected, whose advice is carefully heeded during strategic planning and at other times. We must welcome the presence of advocates who often have different viewpoints and others who question actions of professional groups. This questioning may be verbal or written. Worries about accreditation, funding sources, and staying out of trouble with bureaucracies should not prevent the collection of potentially negative information and opinions, as it will provide a chance to address them before they get out of control. The trend toward independent service user evaluations such as state occupational licensing boards of practitioners such as physicians and social workers and the instant media of the Internet require service providers to be proactive. We should actively seek the information and listen.

Consumer Advocacy Recommendations

Our assessment philosophy embraces openness and willingness to integrate input from many sources because it is critical to learn what people want from service providers and their communities.

- We can encourage individuals and advocacy groups to explain, face to face, how the environment can become more responsive to their needs.
- We can use oral histories to solicit views of a service, an association, or an organization.
- We can seek out state and national publications with relevant recommendations about our area of work. Advocacy publications may be either sophisticated guides to citizen involvement or one-page flyers.

Consumer-oriented assessments of problems and their discussions of appropriate responses deserve our attention. Such discussions may focus on (a) how community life affects particular sectors or groups, (b) practical tips that might be implemented within a reasonable length of time, and (c) citizen participation or rights. For instance, older people and their advocates have suggested that communities assess their livability and make traveling easier. They argue for traffic lights to be set so that pedestrians have enough time to cross the street. They point out that bells or other sounds permit those with visual impairments to know when it is safe to cross. They also suggest the creation of large, separate paths to accommodate pedestrians and those using conventional two-wheeled bicycles and three-wheeled electric vehicles (Parker, Edmonds, & Robinson, 1989, p. 8). This illustrates how community assessments by citizen advocates may differ in emphasis from those prepared by professionals.

Ensuring Good Referral Matches

In the future, the public may be able to reach a central telephone number, 211, or an Internet site to get information and assistance regarding social, medical, housing, and other services. To date, few states provide a unified or seamless system of assistance through 211. Instead, there are dozens of unrelated service directories that lead unsophisticated people from one number to the next until they fall through the cracks.

The practitioner's job in assessing resources for a particular problem or referral starts with information sources: directories, references, and tools available in a community to locate a potential resource. It then becomes one of understanding the nature, effectiveness, and quality of its match to the needs at hand. This information is necessary for good-quality referrals and networking. For a college student in crisis, a where-and-when pamphlet listing the Alcoholics Anonymous (AA) meetings in the area is probably available from AA's local center. In most areas, the list is surprisingly long, and the meetings differ greatly in their format. Would this person benefit most from a small discussion meeting giving a strong sense of personal support, or from a less personal, lecture type of meeting that might not intimidate a shy newcomer?

Most practitioners engage in brokerage or linkage activities. When the focus is on the individual, tasks include "locating appropriate community resources; connecting the consumer to the resource; and evaluating the effectiveness of the resource in relation to the consumer's needs" (Anderson, 1981, p. 42). Kettner, Moroney, and Martin (1990, pp. 61–64) suggest developing resource inventories for a particular clientele or subpopulation. Social workers survey other providers to obtain an understanding of "what actual services are available, which services are most often utilized and why (location, quality, staff attitudes?, and different uses of key terminology" (p. 63). However, if the focus is less on "a clear statement of the consumer's need" and more on "an investigation of the nature, operations, and quality of available resources" (pp. 42–43), then we are engaged in community assessment. Netting, Kettner, and McMurtry (1993) would say that we must know not only what agencies are available but also how well they work together and if they make the linkages they should: "whether these interacting units truly comprise a system that is responsive to multiple needs" (p. 110).

Field Studies in Assessment

Community field case studies generally are studies with a holistic perspective that use methods such as informal interviewing and observation to describe from firsthand acquaintance a particular community. The community under study needs to be definable and must have boundaries that can distinguish it from other communities or units of analysis (Yin, 1984). The field investigator typically interacts face to face with the community over time in order to understand life from the community members' perspective. Eventually, the field worker should be able to write up "lived moments" that help to convey the reality of the unit to the outside world.

Such studies are closely linked with an interest in being where the action is and a willingness to meet people where they are in both the geographic and cultural senses. Field case studies have a long history of presenting and interpreting the unit as it is. They have ranged from journalist Jacob Riis' study of the underclass, *How the Other Half Lives* (1890), to the ethnographic studies of the modern corporation (Cefkin, 2009). Field-study trailblazer Robert Park's broad background familiarized him with many aspects of city life. He believed his "tramping about" helped him gain "a conception of the city, the community and the region, not as a geographical phenomenon merely but as a kind of social organism" (as cited in Bulmer, 1984, p. 90).

The field study gives us a chance to meet face to face and under better circumstances. A way social workers employ field studies today is to explain subgroups and their environments to outsiders. Once collected, the information needs to be organized to use in constructing a case theory for change. Analytical techniques for building the case theory are discussed in the subsequent chapters. These techniques organize and assess the information that is collected and also may guide the collection of information. Few of us can move into a neighborhood or retirement community or spend years hanging around a service center, but faster ways exist to enhance our understanding of neighbors, fellow citizens, and service users. We can seek out anyone who has conducted such studies in our area and ask for a briefing. We can borrow from field methods, such as observation, listening, and ethnographic interviewing, and we can embrace accepting attitudes. When we develop a deep understanding of communities, we bring fresh insights to community organizing, counseling, case management, and other interactions. More important, engaging in such studies makes us want to keep working, and in fact to do more, because the rich pastiche we discover is so intriguing, as are the individuals we meet.

Community Power Structure Studies

A community power structure study is defined by its subject—the power holders in the community—rather than by methodology. Power structure studies look at geographic or functional communities using field study and survey methodologies and available data to explore the configuration and dynamics of the system of influence and the characteristics of dominant individuals (Box 5.4). It results in a list of names and rankings of persons who are perceived to exercise power in the locality where they live or work. As discussed in Chapter 4, community

---

BOX 5.4.	Representative Questions for Power Studies

- Who runs this city? Who are the most economically powerful persons?
- Who controls the resources?
- Who determines local taxes such as real estate taxes? Who benefits?
- Tell me about the power brokers in this county that everyone knows about. Is there anyone operating behind the scenes?
- Does anyone with connections at the county or state level live in your subdivision, neighborhood, or town?
- Who is influential due to the high regard people have for him or her, or because of his or her clout with politicians?
- Do you know any family that sends their children to an excellent boarding school?

power can be exercised by a small circle or by different and sometimes competing blocs or interest groups. Power studies help us identify those who exert influence, "can produce intended effects," and affect community decision making in the political, economic, or communications sphere (Dye, 1993, p. 4).

The concepts of power and social class tend to intermingle. The very poor, poor, and working classes have no power except in numbers; they have been called everything from the *underclass* to the *silent majority*, depending on their income level. Nevertheless, others in society are very interested in the leaders of these groups. When the numbers are wisely used in social action, the disenfranchised and marginalized can have power. For instance, in 1955 Dr. Martin Luther King Jr. and Rosa Parks led a 385-day bus boycott to end the unfair seating of passengers by race (aka skin color) on the Montgomery, Alabama, bus system. Black people were seated in the rear of the bus and had to give up their seats to whites on overcrowded buses. The boycott and its related court action for equal protection resulted in fair seating on the buses on a first come–first seated basis (in any seat) and in national recognition for the civil rights movement for social justice. The marginalized had exercised power, the ability to get what they wanted despite opposition, by the use of collective economic social action and publicity, even though they were not part of the power elite (Willie, 2008).

Most individuals and families who are in power positions or who can exert power are currently upper-middle, upper, or ruling class, regardless of their original background and social standing. Power studies try to locate *the powerful, dominants, influentials,* and *elites,* labels used fairly interchangeably to describe individuals who exercise power or who are widely regarded by perceptive people as having that option (Ostrander, 1995). Admittedly, such questions as those in Box 5.3 may not elicit information about the power elite in the community; the upper class is not necessarily the ruling class, nor does the ruling class always want to be known.

Different approaches for studying the powerful include reputational, positional, and decisional (sometimes called *issue analysis* or *event analysis*) studies. These studies ask: Is this person perceived to be powerful, occupying a position that confers authority and power, or is he or she actually involved in specific decision making? As discussed in Chapter 4, the methodology of a power study often is determined by the theory of social power adopted in the study.

Applications to Our Own Work

The types of decision makers and decision making dominant in a community have obvious implications for practice. If there is a power equilibrium among competing groups, social workers need to become part of the field of exchange and to influence local policy through bargaining. If there is centralization of power and local government responds to a set of elites with a shared set of interests, workers need to bargain with elites, get elites to propose policy alternatives, and keep elites from controlling the public, which, after all, has distinct and dissimilar interests from the elites. Finally, workers can look for common interests in the community and try to link groups to expand their influence (Box 5.5).

A remote circle of people unknown to workers presents less of an opportunity than known influentials who workers have direct or indirect means of contacting. Either way, specific names are helpful. If key decision makers turn out to be generally hostile to social services, we can still find out which influential has a personal situation that may open a door or where social action may be more successful. It is imperative to know who is on the board of directors of the agency with which we are associated, as well as any parent organization, what each person's background is, and why he or she was chosen. Those working in a government agency should be similarly aware of citizen advisory boards or other influentials that might be swayed by staff concerns. We will return to these concerns in our discussion of networking in Chapter 10.

Fund-Raiser Studies. Power studies can be used to further an organization's self-interest. Knowing who the powerful persons and influentials are behind the scenes at the city and neighborhood levels can be useful for an agency's board of directors selection and recruitment process and for resource development (Useem, 1995). If power

---

BOX 5.5. **Fund-Raisers Had Better Know About Elite Power Structures: A Reputational Study Methodology**

Emenhiser's (1991) reputational method is simpler than that of most authors. He used the following steps in Indianapolis to identify and rank influentials:

1. Put together a base list of potential influentials (from research on the corporate 5% club, banks, etc.).
2. Ask seven or eight respected members of the community to review the list, to rank order the 30 most influential names on the base list, and to add names (these experts must be well connected or positioned to know).
3. Compile a new list, weight the names according to the ranks given, and reorder them.
4. Interview the 30 to 40 on the final list, asking these questions:
   a. If a project were before the community that required decisions by a group of leaders, which 10 leaders could obtain its approval?

   b. Place in rank order, 1 through 10 with 1 being the most influential, those individuals who in your opinion are the most influential in the city—influential from the point of view of their ability to lead others.
5. Weight and compile the rankings by interviewees to get the names of the 7 to 12 persons at the top.

---

studies are being undertaken for direct, obvious agency purposes such as fundraising, they probably should be contracted out and conducted by a consulting group or university—not directly by the agency—to put some distance between the requests for information and the later use of that information. Advocacy groups could do the studies themselves.

Problem-Oriented Assessment

A social problem can be a starting point to learn more about community responsiveness and how different systems interrelate. Social problems and services/programs can be studied separately or in combination. We will call a *problems study* the study needed to determine the extent and severity of specific problems or to give an overall diagnosis of the range of problems.

Social problem-oriented assessments can involve the entire community, centering on one problem, or can look functionally across communities, such as the uninsured or child abuse. Here are examples. The town of Conne River in Canada decided to assess family violence in its community (Durst, MacDonald, & Parsons, 1999). The entire community looked at one social problem. In a functional community assessment done in upstate New York, professionals assessed

poverty and social pathology in rural mobile home parks; this was an across communities social problem assessment (Fitchen, 1998). Kettner, Moroney, and Martin (1990) astutely observe that problem analysis includes "analysis of the political environment, an assessment of a community's readiness to deal with the problem, and a measure of the resources the community is willing to commit to its solution" (p. 41).

According to Siegel, Attkisson, and Carson (1987), anyone living or working in a community forms impressions about human service needs; thus, we want to obtain community residents' perspectives on the accessibility, availability, acceptability, and organization of services because their reactions give us "indispensable clues about the human service needs of the community as a whole" (pp. 86–87). In many community-oriented versions of problems and services studies, such as general population or target population surveys, the perspectives of potential and current participants in the service delivery system must be solicited and valued equally with the advice of peers, funders, professionals, and service providers (Meenaghan, Washington, & Ryan, 1982). Potential and actual service users have opinions on the types of services they want and can suggest priorities for skills they desire.

Sociologists are more likely to take a problem slant—what is breaking down society? And social workers usually take a services slant—what can reintegrate society? Some of the earliest social work endeavors involved this type of community study or social survey, obtaining necessary facts for planning and for documenting the numbers of child laborers and other social conditions or problems (Garvin & Cox, 1995).

The most common approach used by helping professions when they undertake a community problem inquiry is to spotlight a target population, a population at risk, or targets for change. The responsiveness of the community to the target or at-risk population and the community's capacity to respond often are the focus (Menolascino & Potter, 1989). These studies help bridge the gap between community and agency analysis. Such investigations may be utilized when an organization has to prove to others that a problem exists, believes some problems are unaddressed, or resolves to move toward community-based services.

Staging often is more important in the public's acceptance of social constructions than are valid data and scientifically technical theory. The sociologist Herbert Blumer (1969) indicated that social definitions and not the objective makeup of a given social condition determine the way a condition exists as presumed social reality. This has certainly been true in the national health care and global warming debates. Themba (1999) states it more emphatically:

There is only so much that information can do to improve social conditions because, contrary to conventional wisdom, information is not power. Power is having the resources to make changes and promote choices; to be heard; and to define, control, defend and promote one's interests. Many of the problems facing communities stem from the lack of power—not the lack of information. (p. 21)

… Therefore, it is not giving people information that's the key to motivating them to act, but validating their perceptions and conveying as sense that the change they dare to imagine in their private spaces is achievable and desired by a great many others. (p. 24)

Community Assets Inventory and Mapping

Assessing community resources is at the core of most community assessments (Whitworth, Lanier,

& Haase, 1988, p. 574), and community assets mapping is a strength-based community development approach to appraise community resources. Asset mapping starts with the positives available from within the community to address community issues rather than starting with a list of community deficits and problems. It focuses on community capacities rather than on problems/needs; it requires community participation; it seeks to enhance community competencies; it equalizes power between resident and professional; and it is proactive rather than reactive to community needs.

The process of asset mapping is one of discovering with a community its capacities and assets (Allen, 2005; Kretzmann & McKnight, 1993; Ridings, Powell, Johnson, Pullie, Jones, Jones, & Terrell, 2008). Assets include tangible physical resources, the people, the instrumental institutions, and the social, the symbolic, and the cultural. As Delgado (forthcoming) notes, community assets mapping requires suspension of conventional views of the limits on assets. It applies social work's strength perspective to discovering and documenting the life of the community. In asset mapping, community residents are asked to identify, inventory, and locate their community's tangible and social internal assets and resources and their relationships. Maps deal with relationships.

Although it is done before any intervention, community asset mapping can alter and ideally strengthen a community (Allen, 2005; Kretzmann & McKnight, 1993; Robinson, Vineyard, & Reagor, 2004; Yoon, 2009). It is community development because the community creates the assets inventory and guides the mapping. Through this exercise the community-mapping participants, now key informants, may look at their community in new and more positive ways by becoming familiar with their community's physical and social assets, history, and capacities. The outcomes of the process are an assets inventory, a map of asset locations and relationships, and among participants and the community a stronger sense of community, community pride and ownership, social networks, and greater social capital. Community asset mapping is about identifying and locating strengths within communities and connecting people to resources and to each other (Office of Learning Technologies, 2003).

Asset inventory and mapping is a prerequisite for the asset-focused interventions of asset building, asset claiming, and asset mobilization discussed in Chapter 13, "Using Organizing."

Participatory Rural Appraisal

Rapid rural appraisal and participatory rural appraisal (PRA) are techniques used globally to solicit views and to elicit local knowledge about cultural, social, and ecological resources. They are viewed by some authors as collaborative assessments and by others as research tools, project development methodologies, or implementation strategies. PRA is increasingly used in urban and rural social development (Bar-on & Prinsen, 1999; Berardi, 1998) because of its emphasis on community ownership of both data and the project. Reporting on efforts to involve people in remote areas of Australia who require rehabilitation and disability services, Kuipers, Kendall, and Hancock (2001) say that PRA was adopted because it had "been reported to foster the participation and decision making of community members in community projects" (p. 22). PRA epitomizes an assessment that is of, in, and by the community. However, as a process and program, it will fail if those adopting it just walk away when the communal assessment is over. For such projects to be successful, the problems identified and ranked as most important by townspeople must be those that can actually be changed at a community level (to avoid frustration and feelings of powerlessness). In addition, the PRA team must get back to community participants not only to provide the results but also to engage in active follow-through with them on their stated priorities.

Besides dialogue, PRA practitioners utilize interesting task-based methods. Community residents and an outside team (ideally multidisciplinary and gender-balanced) hold group discussions and work together on tasks. In one small village, a team worked with everyone and, in four days, inventoried social services, conducted a household census and wealth ranking, formulated a seasonal calendar, charted how men and women spent their time, and completed a territory map and a transect (Gallardo, Encena, & Bayona, 1995, p. 263). A village transect records what falls along a diagonal line drawn through the community and highlights natural resources or human activities, needs, and problems. Meitzner (2000) describes it as a quick sketch, sometimes made during a "transect walk" in which the terrain is drawn by villagers as they take outsiders on a guided tour (pp. 3–4). Other activities also encourage illiterate people to participate; for instance, a map can be drawn in the dirt with each household represented and flowers used to depict the living or the dead, or both.

PRA has found a home in applied anthropology and sociology; in the natural resource and agriculture disciplines; and in education, health, and other fields. Social workers will want to make more use of this assessment approach and program. Multiple tools can be viewed at Participatory Avenues, an electronic resource (http://www.iapad.org/).

Community Assessment Applications to Our Own Work

Agencies and organizations need the information contained in a community analysis. At a minimum, they must know community indicators in their own specialization (Mitchell, A., 1998). If we cannot conduct one, we should ask librarians and newspaper editors if they know of a community profile that has been published recently; an economic development office might also be a place to check. By doing it ourselves, we will learn more, target it more precisely to our concerns, and become known to significant people in the process. We will be on top of things and in a position to make better judgments about social service and social justice interventions.

Once we have conducted a community analysis, we will be ready for the day the mayor calls to ask our advice or the day we need a detailed understanding of several elements in our town, city, or county. This type of study also generates many ideas that allow us to do our jobs better and more easily (Cruz, 1997).

At a more mundane level, we are wise to keep abreast of even simple community developments—if only to avoid embarrassment. Can we give accurate and easy directions to clients on how to reach the office and where to park? Will we be aware when clients may be late due to a parade, baseball traffic, or a political demonstration (not to therapy resistance)? Would we realize if the buses or subways aren't operating because of a labor strike? Do we know when the school holidays occur? Do we know where clients with modest incomes can purchase cheaper medicine? The more specific we can be about resources and the more knowledgeable we are about how systems work, the easier we can make life for the users of our services—and consider their values.

An Allegorical Aside

How do we include self-reflection in community-based research (Murphy & Pilotta, 1983)? We will benefit from imaginative exploration, a willingness to face complexity, an ability to contemplate that which is not seen or heard yet still applies, and an awareness of our own mental processes. A task so nuanced, yet so audacious, is hard to describe. Therefore, we draw on the imagery of Edward Bellamy's *Looking Backward* (1960), and on Ursula K. Le Guin's short story "The Ones Who Walk Away From Omelas," with its description of an imaginary place (1975).

Bellamy and Le Guin provide us with societal extremes to consider. Bellamy, writing a novel in 1888 about the year 2000, made no pretense about neutral observation. He wrote about his vision of the perfect society of the future, contrasting it with the war and poverty of his era. In a famous comparison, Bellamy likened our society to a "prodigious coach which the masses of humanity were harnessed to," with hunger as the driver, while the rich had the seats up on top, where they could "critically describe the merits of the straining team." He continued: "Naturally such places were in great demand and the competition for them was keen, every one seeking as the first end in life to secure a seat on the coach for himself and to leave it to his child after him. . . . For all that they were so easy, the seats were very insecure, and at every sudden jolt of the coach persons were slipping out of them and falling to the ground, where they were instantly compelled to take hold of the rope. . . . Commiseration was frequently expressed by those who rode for those who had to pull the coach. . . . It was a pity but it could not be helped" (pp. 27–28). Various explanations were developed to explain why society had to operate the way it did (the innate abilities of the pullers and the pulled, etc.).

Most notions of better societies are built on the idea that we know what is right and must take the next steps to do it. Bellamy's assessment was that inhumanity grew out of failure to even comprehend what could be. Le Guin helps us look at the constant trade-offs. In her story, Le Guin paints a picture that is related to Bellamy's, but is prettier: no class of people in the fictional town of Omelas struggles in the dust and mud, pulling the rich up on a coach.

Sometimes when the macro level and the collective good are stressed, practitioners worry that the individual will get lost. Le Guin's story is one reason that social work must never lose sight of the good of the individual. Bellamy's coach metaphor reminds us, though, that if we look only at individuals pulling the coach or at those inside it or those on top of it, we may miss the big picture, the connections. We hope social workers can believe in happiness and festivals and not look compulsively for what is in the closet or cellar, but that they will do something when misery is found. Our ethics tell us that the happiness of the many must never come at the expense of even one, but if we blithely condemn the people of Omelas for their Faustian bargain, we condemn ourselves. Finally, it is to our benefit that the "narratives of humanists discuss a variety of communal, social, and psychological dilemmas" (Martinez-Brawley, 1990, p. xxiv).

We not only assess at the individual and communal levels, but we also care about the states of existence of persons and classes of persons. Despite this concern, we seldom take a planetary perspective when we assess dire human needs.

Community Reengagement: Hitting the Bricks

Certain trends are appearing, such as a requirement for community service or service-learning at public and private high schools. Bloomfield College in New Jersey requires students to take "a course called Social Responsibility and another called Society and Culture, as well as complete at least 30 hours of community service" (Sanchez, 1995). Nationwide, professors and students are being urged to become more engaged in the community around the campus, whether through work in empowerment zones, outreach, or new partnerships (Intercom, 2002; Ruffolo &

Miller, 1994). Political and community pressures drives some administrators in that direction, and a sense of obligation to assist and interact with the have-nots motivates some professors. This hitting-the-bricks philosophy tries to ensure that real listening and responsiveness, which can be byproducts of concrete experience, will inform future assessments made by sensitized citizens as well as present assessments made by professionals.

Fields from library science to engineering are taking a second look at their relationship with the communities they serve and at new modes of assessment. As one facet of an aging-in-place community support program in California, Cullinane (1993) notes that "a social worker walks a 'beat' in an inner city neighborhood. Through her contacts with merchants, bankers, pharmacists, and barbers, the social worker and the resources she represents become known to the community. In turn, she gains the confidence of the merchants, who refer their customers who need her assistance in maintaining independence" (p. 135).

In the approach known as community policing, officers who usually react to individual incidents and complaints are encouraged to become "proactive in resolving community problems," to use a problem-and-prevention approach, and to work more closely with community residents (Greene & Mastrofski, 1988, p. xii). The idea is to get out from behind a desk, even if on a part-time basis, and interact with citizens, update one's sense of the place, and experience the area's problems and struggles but also its strong points and vitality. In community or public health nursing, the focus is on the needs of populations rather than on individual psyches or ailments.

Since social work has already had community programs, this trend may not seem relevant, except that we, like the police, have begun spending more and more time indoors, in relative calm and safety, avoiding "bad weather" on the "beat." Now we need to join hands with those in social ministry and other fields that care about community.

Professions such as dentistry and psychology add a community component to the individual component in order to further the goal of promoting the common welfare or to express their fundamental concern for the collective good. Current providers of community-based services and community care are already out on the front lines, as is now being advocated for others. However, some are struggling to make a niche for themselves, so they are working more closely with community associations.

Domestic and international programs can provide models for our engagement and service delivery efforts in this direction. England had community-based programs that make legal and counseling help and review more readily available through the use of volunteers. Social benefit tribunals, dominated by lay people, are one example; Citizens Advice Bureaus, which are lay advisory agencies, are another. Rural and isolated areas are less well served by these mechanisms (Levine, 1990), but England's programs pointed a way to "tune in" to the community.

Warren and Warren (1984) put it extremely simply: "When you first arrive in a community, it's a good idea to spend a short time getting a feel for the city *as a whole*" [italics added] (p. 27). Since we want to root ourselves in the social fabric, we must go beyond the Welcome Wagon information for ourselves and those we serve

Conclusion: Unpretentious but Necessary Outings

Many federal agencies collect data on social problems and service use, and even on the quality of services. Most such studies are quantitative. We social workers must be familiar with the ongoing studies conducted in our field of interest. We also have an obligation to stay informed about events at the local level, consulting with planners and interagency task forces that prepare relevant reports. If we are unable to do studies of our own, we can seek them from hospitals, the United Way, government planning departments, urban or rural centers that specialize in social demography, and universities or colleges that do social-problem or program-evaluation studies. Our special role is our commitment to involving clients, service users, and the general public. We seek input less for magnanimous reasons and more because of our growing awareness that research alone is insufficient and that we need input from consumers, other providers, demographers, and other experts. As we shift our emphasis from broad study to focused assessment, the problems and services theme will continue to be addressed in the next chapter.

We conclude this overview of how to study and size up communities and learn more about the day-to-day realities of residents and members with these summarizing points:

- To be aware of local mores and clients' assumptions about reality, we must involve ourselves as much as possible in their worlds, with the aim of gaining putative community knowledge and the community members' construction of their reality.
- There are many ways to recognize and analyze communities; therefore, we must decide on appropriate variables (you can't find it if you don't look for it) and methodologies (how to find it) guided by the study's purposes. Our purpose ultimately is intervention for community change to promote social justice.

Notes

1. "Case" will be used to refer to the range of potential clients and the change sought. It can range from individuals through communities.
2. "Case," as with footnote 1, is the client change situation.
3. These concepts are similar and connote the social environment that influences or can influence life opportunities in positive or negative ways. We will use "community" as the referent when appropriate.

References

Abatena, H. (1997). The significance of planned community participation in problem solving and developing a viable community capability. *Journal of Community Practice*, 4(2), 13–34.

Allen, J. C. (2005). *Community asset mapping and mobilizing communities*. Coeur d'Alene, ID: Idaho Governor's 6th Annual Roundtable.

Amezcua, C., McAlister, A., Ramirez, A., & Espinoza, R. (1990). *A su salud*: Health promotion in a Mexican American border community. In N. Bracht (Ed.), *Health promotion at the community level* (pp. 257–277). Newbury Park, CA: Sage.

Anderson, J. (1981). *Social work methods and processes*. Belmont, CA: Wadsworth.

Bar-on, A. A., & Prinsen, G. (1999). Planning, communities and empowerment: An introduction to participatory rural appraisal. *International Social Work*, 42(3), 277–294.

Bellamy, E. (1960). *Looking backward*. New York: New American Library. (Original work published 1888).

Berardi, G. (1998). Application of participatory rural appraisal in Alaska. *Human Organization*, 57(4), 438–446.

Bisman, C. D. (1994). *Social work practices: Cases and principles*. Pacific Grove, CA: Brooks/Cole.

Bisman, C. D. (1999). Social work assessment: Case theory construction. *Families in Society: The Journal of Contemporary Human Services*, 80(3), 240–246.

Bisman, C. D., & Hardcastle, D. A. (1999). *Integrating research into practice: A model for effective social work*. Belmont, CA: Wadsworth Publishing Co.

Bloom, L. A., & Habel, J. (1998). Cliques, clans, community, and competence: The experiences of students with behavioral disorders in rural school systems. *Journal of Research in Rural Education*, 14(2), 95–106.

Blumer, H. (1969). *Symbolic interactionism: Perspective and method*. Englewood Cliffs, NJ: Prentice Hall.

Bulmer, M. (1984). *The Chicago school of sociology: Institutionalization, diversity, and the rise of sociological research*. Chicago: University of Chicago Press.

Butcher, H., B., Banks, S., Henderson, P., with Robertson, J. (2007). *Critical community practice*. Bristol, UK: The Policy Press.

Cefkin, M. (Ed.) (2009). *Ethnography and the corporate encounter: Reflections on research in and of corporations*. New York: Berghahn Books.

Colby, I. C. (1997). Transforming human services organizations through empowerment of neighbors. *Journal of Community Practice*, 4(2), 1–12.

Coleman, D. (2000). The therapeutic alliance in multicultural practice. *Psychoanalytic Social Work*, 7(2), 65–92.

Cowger, C. D. (1994). Assessing client strengths: Clinical assessment for client empowerment. *Social Work*, 39(3), 262–268.

Cruz, B. C. (1997). Walking the talk: The importance of community involvement in preservice urban teacher education. *Urban Education*, 32(3), 394–410.

Cullinane, P. (1993). Neighborhoods that make sense: Community allies for elders aging in place. In J. J. Callahan, Jr. (Ed.), *Aging in place* (pp. 133–138). Amityville, NY: Baywood.

Delgado, M. (1996). Puerto Rican food establishments as social service organizations: Results of an asset assessment. *Journal of Community Practice*, 3(2), 57–77.

Delgado, M. (forthcoming). *Assets management and community social work practice*. New York: Oxford University Press.

Durst, D., MacDonald, J., & Parsons, D. (1999). Finding our way: A community needs assessment on violence in native families in Canada. *Journal of Community Practice,* 6(1), 45–59.

Dye, T. R. (1993). *Power and society: An introduction to the social sciences.* Belmont, CA: Wadsworth.

Elliot, N., Quinles, F. W., & Parietti, E. S. (2000). Assessment of a Newark neighborhood. *Journal of Community Health Nursing,* 17(4), 211–224.

Emenhiser, D. (1991, Spring). Power influence and contributions. *National Society of Fundraising Executives Journal,* 9–14.

Fitchen, J. M. (1998). Rural poverty and rural social work. In L. H. Ginsberg (Ed.), *Social work in rural communities* (pp. 115–133). Alexandria, VA: Council on Social Work Education.

Foster-Fishman, P. G., Cantillon, D., Pierce, S. J., & Van Egeren, L. A. (2007). Building an active citizenry: the role of neighborhood problems, readiness, and capacity for change. *American Journal of Community Psychology,* 39, 91–106.

Gallardo, W. G., Encena, V. C., II, & Bayona, N. C. (1995). Rapid rural appraisal and participatory research in the Philippines. *Community Development Journal,* 30(3), 265–275.

Gambrill, E. (1983). *Casework: A competency-based approach.* Englewood Cliffs, NJ: Prentice Hall.

Garson, B. (1994). *All the livelong day: The meaning and demeaning of routine work.* New York: Penguin Books.

Garvin, C. D., & Cox, F. M. (1995). A history of community organizing since the Civil War with special reference to oppressed communities. In J. Rothman, J. L. Erlich, & J. E. Tropman with Fred M. Cox (Eds.), *Strategies of community intervention* (5th ed., pp. 64–99). Itasca, IL: F. E. Peacock.

Germain, C. B., & Gitterman, A. (1995). Ecological perspective. In R. L. Edwards (Ed.-in-Chief), *Encyclopedia of social work* (19th Ed., pp. 816–824). Washington, DC: National Association of Social Workers Press.

Greene, J. R., & Mastrofski, S. D. (1988). *Community policing: Rhetoric or reality.* New York: Praeger.

Guterman, N. B., & Cameron, M. (1997). Assessing the impact of community violence on children and youths. *Social Work,* 42(5), 495–505.

Intercom newsletter. (2002, Summer). *Wild Bill's Coffeeshop: A diversity initiative* (p. 7). Iowa City, IA: University of Iowa, School of Social Work.

Jacobson, M. (2007). Food matters. *Journal of Community Practice,* 15(3), 37–55.

Johnson, L. C. (1995). *Social work practice: A generalist approach* (5th ed.). Boston: Allyn & Bacon.

Julian, D. A. (1999). Some ethical standards to guide community practice and an example of an ethical dilemma from the field. *Journal of Community Practice,* 6(1), 1–13.

Kettner, P. M., Moroney, R. M., & Martin, L. L. (1990). *Designing and managing programs: An effectiveness-based approach.* Newbury Park, CA: Sage.

Kielhofner, G. (1993). Functional assessment: Toward a dialectical view of person-environment relations. *American Journal of Occupational Therapy,* 47(3), 248–251.

Koss, M. P., & Harvey, M. R. (1991). *The rape victim: Clinical and community interventions* (2nd ed.). Newbury Park, CA: Sage.

Kretzmann, J. P., & McKnight, J. L. (1993). *Building communities from the inside out: A path toward finding and mobilizing a community's assets.* Institute for Policy Research; Neighborhood Innovations Network. Evanston, IL: Northwestern University (now available at ABCD Institute).

Kuipers, P., Kendall, E., & Hancock, T. (2001). Developing a rural community-based disability service: Service framework and implementation strategy. *Australian Journal of Rural Health,* 9(1), 22–28.

Lauffer, A. (1982). *Assessment tools for practitioners, managers, and trainees.* Newbury Park, CA: Sage.

Lauffer, A. (1984). Assessment and program development. In F. M. Cox, J. L. Erlich, J. Rothman, & J. E. Tropman (Eds.), *Tactics and techniques of community practice* (2nd ed., pp. 60–75). Itasca, IL: F. E. Peacock.

Le Guin, U. K. (1975). The ones who walk away from Omelas. In U. K. Le Guin, *The wind's twelve quarters* (pp. 345–357). New York: HarperCollins.

Levine, M. L. (1990). Beyond legal services: Promoting justice for the elderly into the next century. In P. R. Powers & K. Klingensmith (Eds.), *Aging and the law* (pp. 55–79). Washington, DC: American Association of Retired Persons.

Loneck, B., & Way, B. (1997). Using a focus group of clinicians to develop a research project on therapeutic process for clients with dual diagnosis. *Social Work,* 42(1), 107–111.

Martinez-Brawley, E. E. (1990). *Perspectives on the small community: Humanistic views for practitioners.* Washington, DC: National Association of Social Workers Press.

Mathews, D. (1994). Community change through true public action. *National Civic Review,* 400–404.

Meenaghan, T. M., Washington, R. O., & Ryan, R. M. (1982). *Macro practice in the human services.* New York: Free Press.

Meitzner, L. (2000, September). Now that I'm here, how do I begin? *ECHO Development Notes,* 69, 1–4.

Menolascino, F. J., & Potter, J. F. (1989). Delivery of services in rural settings to the mentally retarded–mentally ill. *International Journal of Aging and Human Development,* 28(4), 261–275.

Meyer, C. H. (1993). *Assessment in social work practice*. New York: Columbia University Press.

Meyer, C. H. (1995). Assessment. In R. L. Edwards (Ed.-in-Chief), *Encyclopedia of social work* (19th ed., pp. 260–270). Washington, DC: National Association of Social Workers.

Mitchell, A. (1998). The rewards of getting to know the community. *Caring Magazine*, 17(4), 58–60.

Mitchell, C. G. (1998). Perceptions of empathy and client satisfaction with managed behavioral health care. *Social Work*, 43(5), 404–411.

Morrell, M., & Capparell, S. (2001). *Shackleton's way*. New York: Carlisle & Co.

Murphy, J. W., & Pilotta, J. J. (1983). Community-based evaluation for criminal justice planning. *Social Service Review*, 57(3), 465–476.

Murtagh, B. (1999). Listening to communities: Locality research and planning. *Urban Studies*, 36(7), 1181–1193.

National Civic League. (1999). *The civic index: Measuring your community's civic health* (2nd ed.). Denver, CO: Author.

Netting, F. E., Kettner, P. M., & McMurtry, S. L. (1993). *Social work macro practice*. New York: Longman.

O'Looney, J. (1996). *Redesigning the work of human services*. Westport, CT: Quorum.

Office of Learning Technologies (2003). *Community learning asset mapping: A guidebook for community learning networks*. Gatineau, Quebec, Canada: Human Resources Development Canada. Retrieved November 12, 2009, from `http://www.servicecanada.gc.ca/eng/hip/lld/olt/Resources/toolkit/mapping-guidebook.pdf`

Ostrander, S. A. (1995). "Surely you're not in this just to be helpful." In R. Hertz & J. B. Imber (Eds.), *Studying elites using qualitative methods* (pp. 133–150). Thousand Oaks, CA: Sage.

Parker, V., Edmonds, S., & Robinson, V. (1989). *A change for the better: How to make communities more responsive to older residents*. Washington, DC: American Association of Retired Persons.

Payne, M. (2006). *Modern social work theory* (3rd ed.). Chicago, IL: Lyceum.

Patterson, C. H. (1985). *The therapeutic relationship: Foundations for eclectic psychotherapy*. Monterey, CA: Brooks/Cole Publishing Co.

Peters, T. (1987). *Thriving on chaos: Handbook for a management revolution*. New York: Knopf.

Ridings, J. W., Powell, D. M., Johnson, J. E., Pullie, C. J., Jones, C. M., Jones, R. L., & Terrell, K. J. (2008). Using concept mapping to promote community building: The African American initiative at Roseland. *Journal of Community Practice*, 16:1, 39–63.

Robinson, C. M., Vineyard, M. C., & Reagor, J. D. (2004). Using community mapping in human ecology. *Journal of Family and Consumer Sciences*, 96(4), 52–54.

Rodwell, M. K. (1998). *Social work constructivist research*. New York: Garland.

Rosenthal, S. J., & Cairns, J. M. (1994). Child abuse prevention: The community as co-worker. *Journal of Community Practice*, 1(4), 45–61.

Rothman, J. (1984). Assessment and option selection [Introduction to Part 1]. In F. M. Cox, J. L. Erlich, J. Rothman, & J. E. Tropman (Eds.), *Tactics and techniques of community practice* (2nd ed., pp. 7–13). Itasca, IL: F. E. Peacock.

Ruffolo, M. C., & Miller, P. (1994). An advocacy/empowerment model of organizing: Developing university–agency partnerships. *Journal of Social Work Education*, 30(3), 310–316.

Sanchez, R. (1995, March 15). Western studies no longer sufficient: More colleges requiring education in other cultures. *The Washington Post*, pp. A1, 12.

Schilling, R. F. (1990). Commentary: Making research usable. In L. Videka-Sherman & W. J. Reid (Eds.), *Advances in clinical social work research* (pp. 256–260). Silver Spring, MD: National Association of Social Workers.

Sharpe, P., Greaney, M., Royce, S., & Lee, P. (2000). Assessment/evaluation: Assets-oriented community assessment. *Public Health Reports*, 115(2), 205–211.

Siegel, L. M., Attkisson, C. C., & Carson, L. G. (1987). Need identification and program planning in the community. In F. M. Cox, J. L. Erlich, J. Rothman, & J. E. Tropman (Eds.), *Strategies of community organization: Macro practice* (4th ed., pp. 71–97). Itasca, IL: F. E. Peacock.

Spradley, B. W. (1990). *Community health nursing: Concepts and practice* (3rd ed.). Glenview, IL: Scott, Foresman.

Steves, L., & Blevins, T. (2005). From tragedy to triumph: A segue to community building for children and families. *Child Welfare*, 84(2), 311–322.

Strack, R., Magill, C., & Klein, M. (2000, November 15). *Engaging youth as research partners in a community needs/assets assessment through the Photovoice process*. Paper presented at 128th Annual Meeting of the American Public Health Association, Boston, MA.

Stoesz, D. (2002). From social work to human services. *Journal of Sociology and Social Welfare*, 29(4), 19–37.

Themba, M. N. (1999). *Making policy, making change: How communities are taking law into their own hands*. Oakland, CA: Chardon Press.

Thompson, A. (1999, April 8–14). User friendly? *Community Care*, 14–15.

Turner, A. (2009). Bottom-up community development: Reality or rhetoric? The example of the

Kingsmead Kabin in East London. *Community Development Journal, 44*(2), 230–247.

Useem, M. (1995). Reaching corporate executives. In R. Hertz & J. B. Imber (Eds.), *Studying elites using qualitative methods* (pp. 18–39). Thousand Oaks, CA: Sage.

United States Department of Health and Human Services, National Institutes of Health, National Institute on Drug Abuse, Division of Clinical and Services Research (1997). *Beyond the therapeutic alliance: Keeping the drug dependent individual in treatment.* NIDA Research Monogram 165. Rockville, MD: Author.

Wang, C., & Burris, M. A. (1997). PhotoVoice: Concepts, methodology, and uses for participatory needs assessment. *Health Education & Behavior,* 24:3, 369-387.

Wang, C. C. (2003). Using PhotoVoice as a participatory assessment and issue selection tool. In M. Minkler & N. Wallerstein (Eds.), *Community based participation research for health* (pp. 179–196). San Francisco: Jossey-Bass.

Warren, R. B., & Warren, D. I. (1984). How to diagnose a neighborhood. In F. M. Cox, J. L. Erlich, J. Rothman, & J. E. Tropman (Eds.), *Tactics and techniques of community practice* (2nd ed., pp. 27–40). Itasca, IL: F. E. Peacock.

Weiner, A. (1996). Understanding the social needs of street-walking prostitutes. *Social Work, 41*(1), 97–105.

Whitworth, J. M., Lanier, M. W., & Haase, C. C. (1988). The influence of child protection teams on the development of community resources. In D. C. Bross, R. D. Krugman, M. R. Lenherr, D. A. Rosenberg, & B. D. Schmitt (Eds.), *The new child protection handbook* (pp. 571–583). New York: Garland.

Willie, C. V. (2008). A perfect grassroots movement: The Montgomery bus boycott. In C. V. Willie, S. P. Ridini, & D. A. Willard (Eds.), *Grassroots social action: Lessons in power movement,* (pp. 21–39). New York: Rowman & Littlefield, Publishers.

Wiseman, F. (Director, Producer, and Editor). (1968). High school [Film]. U.S.: OSTI, Inc.

Wiseman, F. (Director, Producer, and Editor). (1994). High school II [film]. U.S.: Zipporah Films.

Yin, R. K. (1984). *Case study research: Design and method.* Beverly Hills, CA: Sage.

Yoon, I. (2009). A mixed-method study of Princeville's rebuilding from the flood of 1999: Lessons in the importance of invisible community assets. *Social Work, 54*(1), 19–28.

6

Using Assessment in Community Practice

For practitioners, if assessment is not directly related to and prescriptive of treatment, it is, at best, a waste of client and practitioner time and, at worst, unethical.

Mark A. Mattaini and Stuart A. Kirk, social work scholars and teachers

The difference between the most dissimilar characters, between the philosopher and a common street porter, for example, seems to arise not so much from nature, as from habit, custom, and education....they came into the world...very much alike.

Adam Smith, philosopher, social theorist

Erin was desperate for a job. Divorced with three children to support and recovering from a car accident, she faced severe financial difficulties. Though having only a high school education, Erin wrangled an entry-level filing job from the lawyer who represented her in the accident. Like George, Erin was a curious and thinking person. She noticed incongruities in one obscure case she was filing. Her initial hypothesis was that something was wrong with the file itself.

Erin showed initiative. Besides asking her boss about those irregularities, she left the office, drove to the Mojave Desert town of Hinkley, and talked directly to the affected family. Their health and housing situation made her suspicious that the problem extended beyond this one case. Her preliminary case theory led her to believe something was wrong in the community. Gathering facts, she investigated the Hinkley area with population less than 2000 had over a forth of the residents older than five years old suffering from a disability. Pacific Gas and Electric (PG&E) maintained a gas compression pumping station for its natural gas transmission pipeline in Hinkley. The compression pumping station used hexavalent chromium, a carcinogen, as a rust inhibitor for the pumps.

Erin used ethnographic case study methodologies and available data. She gradually introduced herself and made a point of meeting everyone in the neighborhood and hearing their stories. As she attended picnics and sat in homes, she compiled evidence and learned people's strengths. She built trust because she knew that, before she could help, she and the community had to become allies. Erin rolled up her sleeves and dived in, and that was appreciated by residents and plant workers who slipped her secret documents.

Even though without legal training, Erin refused to be intimidated by technical records, and she copied what seemed relevant. She insisted on her right to use public records and gathered soil and water samples. Eventually, Erin was able to document widespread health problems caused by PG&E's hexavalent chromium contamination of the community's drinking water. Erin's investigation led to a $333 million settlement for 600 residents who sued the corporation with the help of her law firm. Erin Brockovich's determination to secure justice for these folks became the subject of a popular movie starring Julia Roberts. All this, because Erin developed skills in community assessment, advocacy, and social action to aid the community of Hinkley. (Dawson, 1993; Denby, 2000; Rogge, 1995)

Erin moved from a micro to a macro focus when she saw that the first family she contacted might be only the tip of the iceberg. Erin's use of community practice skills and community assessment took her beyond casework to community intervention. Her story illustrates that community assessment entails intensive investigation of community structures, syetems, and forces for their impact on people. By continually appraising the situation, she assisted hundreds of families who shared serious ailments and medical disorders. Her hands-on, collaborative assessment of community factors and subsequent social action brought success for the individual cases.

Assessment as a Basic Social Work Process

Assessment, as discussed in Chapter 5, serves as an umbrella term for a process that can have a wide or narrow, general or targeted focus. It builds a case theory that guides the intervention strategy. Community assessment methodologies can be employed to understand and assess any community, anywhere, anytime (see Chapter 5).

Assessment Frameworks

It is valuable to understand the community assessment methodologies for both case and community work. Whether examining the situations of clients or of community residents, relevant variables must first be identified. The assessment and case theory serve "to bring order out of the chaos of a mélange of disconnected variables" (Meyer, 1993, p. 3). To know the best approach to community work, Jeffries (1996) from the United Kingdom maintains that practitioners need to determine:

- the extent of change that is needed
- its feasibility, given the resources likely to be available in the community
- the likely resistance to or support for such change both within the community and from powerful decision makers who could be involved
- how much scope the community and the workers have to make decisions about actions needed to achieve that change, either through participation in organized decision-making processes or through community organizations—in other words, the community's state of empowerment. (p. 107)

Auspices and Context

When we assess a community or the adequacy and effectiveness of a given program, we need to be clear about our commitments. Are we a consultant for the system in question, are we employed by an agency, do we represent an advocacy group, or do we claim neutrality and disinterested status? Can we share affinities and perspectives with those who are being assessed? We should keep in mind our predispositions toward individual cases and programs. Basic decisions underlie any assessment: Whom do we listen to? Whom will we trust? How will we decide? Whose views count most? Answers can be influenced by the auspices under which we proceed—be it a county government, a nonprofit organization, a credentialing body, a university, an agency, or a grassroots community organization. We are also influenced by our education and training in our assessment constructions (Robinson & Walsh, 1999; Worth, 2001). Assessment as critical community practice requires critical consciousness (Butcher, 2007).

Assessment: Information-Gathering Methodologies

Our assessment philosophy embraces openness and willingness to integrate input from many sources because it is critical to understand the community as a place that nurtures or inhibits people.

- We can encourage individuals and advocacy groups to explain, face to face, how their communities can become more responsive to their needs.
- We can use oral histories to solicit views on a service, an association, an organization, or a community.
- We can seek out state and national publications and other available data sources with relevant recommendations and information about the community.

Consumer-oriented assessments of problems and their discussions of appropriate responses also warrant our attention. Such discussions may focus on (a) how community life affects particular sectors or groups, (b) practical tips that might be implemented within a reasonable length of time, and (c) citizen participation and perception of rights.

For instance, older people and their advocates have suggested that communities assess their livability and make traveling easier. They argue for traffic lights to be set so that pedestrians have enough time to cross the street. They point out that bells or other sounds permit those with visual impairments to know when it is safe to cross. They also suggest the creation of large, separate paths to accommodate pedestrians and those using conventional two-wheeled bicycles and three-wheeled electric vehicles (Parker, Edmonds, & Robinson, 1989, p. 8).

An assessment philosophy establishes our attitudes, organizes our approach, directs many of our methodologies, and shapes our construction of reality. Critical consciousness and critical community practice dictates that assessment should be a two-way process (Butcher, Banks, Henderson, with Robertson, 2007). Let us look briefly at some assessment methodologies.

Historical and Available Information

Gathering background and historical information is a first step in a community assessment. It provides a foundation for more elaborate assessment and research. Practitioners should inquire whether community studies have been completed by others and are available locally. This often will save time in learning about the community. Sources of historical information are readily available and include news media files, agency reports, census reports, Web pages, and social

research community study reports, as well as background social science literature on the ethnic or functional community, and local universities' and colleges' social science and professional school faculty to serve as key informants. The U.S. Census is a mother lode of data organized by census tract, although the data may be outdated when finally made available. The practitioner should decide specifically what information is needed; otherwise, the search will be overwhelming as there is so much data available (Box 6.1).

Schneider and Lester (2001, pp. 155–156) provide a detailed example of a resources directory—that is, an inventory services that are available to meet identified needs. However, such lists, directories, and other formal tools achieve their value only in combination with understanding and experience. These information sources provide basic community information on social services. Once the social agencies are identified, their service areas, eligibility requirements, and access information can be obtained.

Good data users develop their own skills and develop a network of persons who can help with selection and interpretation of this information. Internet and Google searches are also helpful in finding data. It is the combination of information from documents and computers and understanding from experience and advice that leads to the effective selection of community resources.

The advantages of using historical and secondary data are the relatively low fiscal, time, and energy costs. Using available data is essentially the only way to learn about historical events,

BOX 6.1.	Available Data Sources for Community Services

1. *Telephone book Yellow Pages* for community and social services listings by geographic area codes. Use a variety of telephone company listings, as the Yellow Pages listings require a fee for listing and are self-classified by the advertisers.
2. *Social agency registers* such as by social planning and social agency councils, Catholic Charities, Jewish Federations, United Ways, and national organizations' directories of member agencies.
3. *501(c)(3) agencies* from secretary of state for tax-exempt and donation purposes. The Internal

Revenue System has an alphabetical listing that is not coded by states or ZIP codes.
4. *Public agency and government directories* for federal, state, and local government agencies within a governmental service geographic area.
5. *State contract and vendor lists* and lists from umbrella funding agencies. State vendor lists are public.
6. *Licensure agency lists of licensed professionals.* These lists are public.

since obviously they can't be experienced first hand. This data search is similar to a researcher's literature review: it lets you know what is known about the community.

There are many disadvantages to using available data, however. The data were probably originally collected for different purposes and will not correspond exactly with the assessment information needed. There can be a lack of congruence with the boundaries of the community you are studying. The reliability and validity of the data are difficult to assess if we do not know how they were collected and developed. The information may be dated, so the researcher should use multiple data sources and supplement available data with more contemporary confirmation.

Community Field Study Methodologies

Field study means "hitting the bricks" or "being on the ground" or one of the many other expressions of immersion in the community. A scientific, ethnographic approach is central to the community field study, in part because it makes us aware of our own ethnocentrism and cognizant of the logic and wholeness of others' cultural perspectives. Yin (1984) points out that most knowledge of the world has not been developed by carefully controlled laboratory experiments, but rather by looking at the natural world. The field case study methodology is the preferred methodology when (1) "how and why" questions are being posed, (2) the investigator has little control over the event or phenomenon, and (3) the focus is on a contemporary phenomenon within some real-life context (Yin, 1984, p. 13). Community assessments fit these criteria.

How do we begin the field study? The approach, as with all field studies, combines the ethnographic with available data and quantitative methodologies.

Participant Observation

Community field studies use participant observation (P-O) methodologies. Spradley (1980), a pioneer in applying P-O methodologies to urban America noted that in P-O the researcher uses a systematic and disciplined manner to try to answer the questions of concern while participating in the community. The goal is to acquire exhaustive knowledge of a group, including its construction of reality.

Yin (1972, p. 3), in an early classic study of applying P-O to the urban neighborhood, concluded that the two roles of participant and observer often conflict. Research observation of events is objective, but participating as a part of the phenomenon is subjective. If the researcher is an active participant, then the phenomenon can be altered, and the emotional involvement of the participant can call into question the credibility of the results. Thus, researchers need to be critically conscious of their involvement. A second observer can be used to establish reliability and reduce the bias inherent in the strain of the two roles. Working and reviewing with colleagues is helpful to the observation side of P-O. Objectivity and reliability can be enhanced and bias reduced by comparing the researcher's observations to other data sources and by comparing the findings to theory and models of the community.

Social workers, whether in casework or community practice, must master these two roles and reconcile their strains in any assessment and intervention. It is difficult to maintain a balance of both roles over time: the tendency is to drift toward being a participant (over-identification with case or client, "going native") or detaching and becoming solely an observer (and hence losing the bonding with the case and some of the nuances of relationship and belief bonding).

Sometimes such qualitative P-O and case study methods are referred to as *naturalistic inquiry* (Lincoln & Guba, 1985; Rodwell, 1998), and the results are labeled *grounded theory* (Glaser & Strauss, 1967). Regardless of the label, field studies entail a humanistic approach and an empathetic stance. In order to start where the client is, one must know and understand where the client is and the client's construction of reality. To understand a community, the practitioner needs to understand a community's many constructions of reality, although not necessarily agreeing with all of them.

Wexler Vigilante (1993) elaborates on the relevance of naturalistic inquiry's constructionism for social work practice. She asks us to "assume that systematic data gathering cannot accurately reflect the complexities of human functioning. The … strategy consists of the client and worker successfully framing and reframing the client's story until coherent and shared meanings are achieved" (p. 184). In naturalistic inquiry, as with most qualitative research, the emphasis, as with assessment in practice, is on meaning. People tend to define, construct, and give meaning to their world as a result of their interactions with others.

Lamb's (1977) recommended first steps, with some Web additions, are still relevant for understanding the area of study. Buy a map, including a street directory; look up local history; review *Rand-McNally's Interntional Bankers Directory* (*http://www.faqs.org/copyright/rand-mcnally-bankers-international-bankers-directory-2/*), *Moody's Ratings Bank Credits*(http://library.dialog.com/bluesheets/html/bl0527.html), and *Standard & Poor's Register – Corporate* (http://www.standardandpoors.com/home/en/us) on the web. Hardcopies are sometimes aviable at the local library. The registers and directories will provide the names of local branches of bank and any local banks and their's and other corporation directors. Corporate, chamber of commerence, and state and local government web sites can be checked; census data reviewed, and any area studies by social workers detailing the city-wide distribution of types of cases and social problems assessed.

To study a neighborhood, Warren and Warren (1984) suggest combining key informants, available data, and *shoe leather* or *windshield* observation survey processes. First walk around city hall or central government buildings, pick up pamphlets on city services, and visit the central business district; obtain maps, the telephone book, and local newspapers; go by the library and chamber of commerce office to get a list of community organizations and their contact persons. Then drive and walk around the neighborhood, chat with people on the street, and ask them to define the boundaries of the area. After getting more settled, identify key informants and various networks and generally figure out "how the neighborhood operates" (p. 34). Again, exploration of the community's Web site, if it is a political-civic entity, is helpful.

Key Informants

Crucial sources of information in community case field studies are key informants. While any member or resident is a potential informant, key informants are those willing to initiate us into their world. Green (1995) calls them "cultural guides" (p. 102). Key informants are well-positioned insiders who can and will act as providers and interpreters of information for the outsider. They are people who are connected in the community and can provide an insider's perspective (Denzin, 1970, 202). Key informants are people who know about or have access to the information being sought. They can be indigenous people, elected leaders, or professional observers such as newspaper reporters. Cab drivers, ambulance drivers, firefighters, and police officers are familiar with various areas and with names of places. Natural leaders—people respected and listened to by others—are critical key informants.

The essential trait of a key informant is having information about the community and being willing to share it. If we can establish a working relationship with key informants, they are potentially valuable because they can "act as . . . de facto observer[s] for the investigator; provide a unique inside perspective on events . . . serve as a 'sounding board' for insights, propositions, and hypotheses developed by the investigator; open otherwise closed doors and avenues to situations and persons" (Denzin, 1970, p. 202). When selecting the first informants, Yin (1972, pp. 15–16) cautions that the participant-observer should avoid the natural biases of similar gender, age, and ethnicity. Key informants should represent a broad cross-section of the community, capturing its different segments and interests: business and commerce, public sectors, nongovernmental, not-for-profit, recreation, education, civic, faith-based, neighborhood, age differences, gender, ethnic diversity, media, social organizations, and so forth. The informants should not be just the recognized community leaders but should reflect all the community. A broad community spectrum of key informants lays the foundation for subsequent community action.

Quota, purposive, and snowball sampling techniques can be used to construct the key informant panels. In *quota sampling*, key informants are selected based on the distribution of selected traits in the sample frame. When the sample of key informants matches the sample frame on the selected traits, sampling ceases. The intent is to improve the sample of key informants' precision in representing the community's traits. Quota sampling can address only known traits. In *purposive sampling*, the researcher seeks and selects key informants based on some specific traits representing a community trait. In *snowball sampling*, a technique used in both purposive and quota sampling, the original key informants are asked to provide the names of and introductions to additional key informants who have specific traits and represent additional segments.

Obtaining an introduction to a small town can be accomplished with brief stops at the most convenient gas station, the most noticeable church, the most active real estate office, a busy pizza parlor, and a central elementary school. At this point, business owners, principals, ministers, or anyone working in a community organization or business who has time can serve as an original key informant. As Thornton Wilder's *Our Town* shows, people like to talk about their neighborhood, town, and city. Every place is different and different informants have differing constructions, so the social worker has to explore. In our exploration we might be lucky enough to run into several of Wilder's stage managers to serve as key informants. Although the community itself will take a long time to know, newcomers can quickly start familiarizing themselves with it.

Hirsch's (1998) examination of a neighborhood outside Boston exemplifies other methodologies. She secured facts from the Census Bureau and learned that a third of the households in Jamaica Plain were below the poverty line and 46% of households owned no car. She also did her homework about the community's economy. Jamaica Plain, it turned out, had these business sectors: "hardwares, bodegas, clothing, used book, ice cream and thrift shops (small-scale commercial); check cashing, real estate, restaurants (service); beer making, pretzels (light industry); small-scale agriculture" (Hirsch, 1998, p. xii). Going beyond fact gathering to observation, Hirsch discovered the following gathering places:

Lockhorn's
Bob's Spa

Costello's
El Charro
The Midway
3M Market
Old Stag Tavern
Eddy's Market
Rizzo's Pizza
Fernandez Barber Shop
Franklin's CD
J. P. Record Shop
Cafe Cantata
Black Crow Caffe (pp. xiii–xiv)

This list's variety spurs us to think more broadly about key informants and hangouts in communities. Those places, in addition to home and work, nourish social connections "where one is more likely than anywhere else to encounter any given resident of the community" (Oldenburg, 1999, p. 112). Dennis (as cited in Ward & Hansen, 1997, p. 70) suggests that gathering places be observed and monitored to keep tabs on community realities: "Learn how people live and work by observing housing. . ., neighborhoods, and primary work places. Monitor … public gathering places [such]as Laundromats, beauty parlors, restaurants, and bars. Use public transportation at various times. . ., Watch facilities such as emergency rooms, jails, and shelters for the homeless—action at these sites helps the observer understand the community's pressure points." We will explore this further in the "Community Assets Inventory and Mapping Protocol" section later in this chapter.

We can pinpoint the central area of a town or neighborhood and pick a central point, such as a key street corner, to make some instant but ongoing observations. These observations can provide a log of a community's social flavor and can help identify who might need what services. Here are notes from a community practice student's observations of a gentrified section of a large city:

Tuesday, 11 a.m. Many walking by are elderly (counted nine older people in the 5 minutes I stood here). I also noted five women pushing baby carriages—a couple looked like young mothers; the rest looked older and may have been babysitters. I saw a group of Hispanic women waiting for the bus but not any black people. I saw a handful of people, casually dressed, coming up out of the subway.

Tuesday, 6 p.m. People with briefcases and wearing running shoes pour out of subway exits—in 5 minutes, at least 50—almost everyone white adults. Bumper-to-bumper traffic.

Saturday, 2:30 p.m. From same vantage point, I saw large numbers of couples with small children, but very few older people. Again, almost everyone was white. The bus stop by the 7-Eleven appeared to be a meeting place for young people hanging out.

These findings might have program development implications. A number of possibilities can be explored if further observation reveals similar patterns. Among these are (a) potential needs of the elderly, and of house cleaners and babysitters who come into the area, such as day care for their children (or for residents' children); (b) whether play space is safe and adequate; and (c) possible discrimination in housing in the area, which could be checked out by testers.

Reviewing newspaper stories about incidents in a community of interest is another way to be observant. The idea here is to check things out: What does the community think about this incident? What is a problem for them? Observation and key informant interviews can be supplemented with available data and media reports for a more complete construction of a community.

If we begin to understand a culture well enough, we can interpret aspects of it for others (Schwab, Drake, & Burghardt, 1988). Circumstances often require social workers to make a case for client or citizen participation in decision making or for hiring a paraprofessional from the community. The more we understand, the better we can convey the worldview of another class or culture. Critical community practice and social justice require that their viewpoint be represented. It is helpful to learn to write complete description "about a specific phenomenon and its surrounding environment" (Karabanow, 1999).

Examples of Assessment

In this section, we will look at the physical and social worlds of three groups as depicted by a planner, an anthropologist, and a sociologist. Note how they use details to illustrate and give flavor to field studies. They describe their first looks at a place and a people and the means they used to conduct their studies.

Joseph Howell, the planner, portrays life on an urban block called Clay Street. His study of the blue-collar community opens with a long list of details he noticed, including "old cars jacked up on cinder blocks . . . the number of dogs and 'beware of dogs' signs . . . the chain link fences . . . the small gardens . . . old folks rocking on their porches . . . a few old, shabby houses, with excessive amounts of debris and junk out front— old toys, bedsprings, tires, and old cars. In one of these houses lived the Shackelfords" (Howell, 1973, p. 8).

Documenting lifestyles, Howell discusses this family's relationship with helpers: "Bobbi had her first visit from the caseworker. When she had been notified that the caseworker was coming to visit, she became very excited. She spent the preceding day cleaning and straightening the house, and when the caseworker arrived, Bobbi was ready. Everything was picked up and the house was very clean" (pp. 125–126).

This excerpt reveals that the family's behavior and values are complex. We cannot presume or assume after seeing one piece of the picture, like the yard. Howell assesses coping patterns and, eschewing stereotyping, distinguishes between "hard living" and "settled living" residents. He lets us hear directly from those in the area through reconstructed scenes and dialogue, which makes us care about those on the street. Such an orientation to a particular place makes us curious, rather than judgmental, about the Shackelford family and their "intense, episodic, and uninhibited" approach to life (Howell, 1973, p. 6). Thus, one purpose of a community study has been achieved—to highlight the life ways and values of a group. Of special interest to us, this study pinpoints how family events, crises, and problems can "fall outside the orbit of community service systems and how service systems are often insensitive to life situations of those they seek to serve" (p. xi). This represents a different way of examining service adequacy.

Field studies demonstrate that knowing more completely even a few families helps us better understand a community. Howell (1973) believes that participant observation consists of making friends, being where the action is, writing it all down, and pulling it all together.

Barbara Myerhoff, the anthropologist, studied a neighborhood within a community in

Venice, California, populated by Eastern European Jewish immigrants, including many elderly concentration camp survivors. The focal point for the residents was the cultural community connected with a senior citizen center, where "the front window was entirely covered by hand-lettered signs in Yiddish and English announcing current events" (Myerhoff, 1980, pp. 12–13).

Rather than looking at a community in terms of demographics or 5-year plans, Myerhoff looks through the eyes of particular individuals. The words of encouragement on the signs say a good deal about those being beckoned. Social workers can use this method, too, and learn by looking at details that accrue to become the physical environment and cultural life of those with whom they work.

Rebecca Adams, the sociologist, studied a nonplace, affinity community. For over a decade, she inquired into the lives of Deadheads, fans of the rock band the Grateful Dead who followed the band around the country and represented one element of a loose national community. Adams observed by traveling with them, and she reached the non-traveling element through questionnaires and dialogue in the Grateful Dead's newsletter and magazines. Many Deadheads stayed in touch with Adams by telephone, letter, and e-mail; for example, after the death of Jerry Garcia (the Dead's lead guitarist/singer), 150 fans wrote to Adams. Local and nearby concerts provided a setting for studying the world of fans. Adams (1998) explains, "I began my field research project by standing in line at Ticketmaster and at the Greensboro Coliseum, by spending time in the parking lot before the shows, and by attending all the shows in the run. I also interviewed police officers who were on duty at the concerts, people cleaning up the parking lot the morning after the run was over, and staff members at nearby hotels and restaurants" (p. 10). Sometimes, field researchers act as interpreters for a community that is unknown to or misunderstood by the public. In such a liaison role, Adams gave interviews to radio stations, television stations, newspapers, magazines, and independent film companies.

Like Howell, Myerhoff (1980) worked with individuals within an area. She knew 80 center members and spent time with 36. She describes her method, with the reminder that there is no

definitive way to "cut up the pie of social reality. . . . I tape recorded extensive interviews . . . ranging from two to sixteen hours, visited nearly all in their homes, took trips with them from time to time outside the neighborhood—to doctors, social workers, shopping, funerals, visiting their friends in old age homes and hospitals. . . . I concentrated on the Center and its external extensions, the benches, boardwalk, and hotel and apartment lobbies where they congregated" (p. 29).

Immersed in the lives of those who attended the center, Myerhoff spent time in nursing homes and hospitals and at funerals or memorial services. She probed for their viewpoint, asking questions such as "Do you think that being a Jew makes the life of a retired person easier or harder in any way?" (p. 46).

Some parts of any community are harder to reach than others. Like Howell and Myerhoff, Adams needed guides, but prospective key informants viewed her as unsympathetic or as an undercover police officer (a "narc"). She had to prove herself by mastering the community's special language and grasping its value system. For instance, Deadheads felt that the federal government was engaged in a "war on some drugs." Adams writes about identifying a guide: "Two groups that were particularly difficult for me to approach were drug dealers and members of a Deadhead cult known variously as the Church of Unlimited Devotion, the Family, or simply the Spinners. It was particularly important that I gain the trust of these two groups, because they tended to be the most orthodox of Deadheads. . . . [One Spinner eventually] commented on drafts of chapters, challenging my interpretations of data and steadfastly reminding me that Deadheads are not all affluent" (1998, pp. 18–19).

In a community case study, the community practitioner is first a learner, not an expert coming in. The practitioner will share and key informants will share, affecting each other and the process, so there is emphasis on interchange, "mutual learning," and "respect" (Daley & Wong, 1994, p. 18). Case studies conducted in natural settings introduce practitioners to groups and individuals who help the practitioners see life in non-mainstream communities with new eyes. The experience teaches a practitioner how to be a critically conscious practitioner and avoid being irrelevant or condescending. Such studies may assist the practitioner to "speak the same language" as the community, to obtain a clearer sense of the clients' worlds, and to share their reality constructions. Abbreviated versions of such studies may be appropriate in work with marginalized populations or before doing outreach to new communities. Even modest community case studies are valuable supplements to surveys.

Surveys

"Survey" means to look at and examine something. Survey data collection designs are frequently used in community planning and community assessment. They are generally used to gather information from a large number of respondents or subjects at a particular time point. They often involve written questionnaires or telephone interviews. Surveys are perhaps the most common design in social science research. The U.S. Census Bureau uses survey methodologies and designs in the census.

Survey Options

Common types of social or community surveys include citizen surveys, general population surveys such as the U.S. Census, target population surveys, and service provider and consumer satisfaction surveys. The time and expense involved in doing complete population surveys can be prohibitive, but using well-crafted samples and sampling methodologies can reduce expenses. A practitioner wanting to do a limited survey should consult with a trained researcher, who usually can be found at a local college. Some public service agencies have such experts in house. Practitioners using community surveys should review survey designs and methodologies, which are discussed in introductory social work research texts such as Rubin and Babbie (2007, pp. 365–389). We will focus here more on the informal survey methodologies useful in community case studies than on formal survey research designs.

Informal survey techniques are readily available to practitioners. Informal surveys are used to gather information on the life of a community or some part of it. They include ethnographic surveys and require observation, participant observation, and ethnographic and focused interviewing skills similar to field case studies; these are necessary practice skills for a community practitioner or social worker. Ethnographic interviewing is more structured than an informal conversation but is more casual and open-ended than a questionnaire survey. It is similar to focused interviewing in its features and concern for understanding the respondent's meaning (Merton, Fiske, & Kendall, 1956). The interviewer seeks to discover facts and understand their significance to the informant.

Observational survey methods include walk-arounds, drive-arounds, or shoe leather and windshield surveys. These surveys are conducted by walking or driving through a community and observing the features and behavior patterns: what is the residential pattern, what are the commercial establishments, where do people congregate, and so forth. These surveys move easily to P-O methods, with the observer talking with people, often starting with impersonal social places such as bus stops, eateries, bars, video stores, and grocery stores.

More structured P-O surveys include the use of key informants, snowball sampling, and networking. Like chain letters and pyramid schemes, the snowballing sampling process is repeated until it yields no additional informants or you are confident that the information obtained is complete and valid. It is conceptually possible through this process to reach anyone in the community ("six degrees of separation").

Mall surveys are a survey technique that falls between formally structured surveys and informal surveys. They use developed questions and criteria, but somewhat haphazard purposive sampling methodologies. However, they are relatively inexpensive and quick ways to obtain information. They are called "mall surveys" because marketers, in trying to determine consumer buying patterns and preferences, interview people at shopping malls. The survey procedure, like a quota and purposive sample, uses a profile of the traits of people from whom information is sought. Questions to determine if the respondent fits the preferred profile are asked first, and the balance of the questions are asked to those respondents fitting the profile. The technique is

BOX 6.2.	Multifaceted Assessment Vignette

To comprehend a subcommunity or network, we often must increase our knowledge of that entity. We may need to particularize our assessments as well.

A social worker in a speech and hearing clinic is about to meet with the deaf parents of a preschooler with a profound hearing loss, who are coming in to talk about the child's schooling needs. We will use this vignette to look at a subsystem. This is an opportunity to study a system and, as a byproduct, our preconceptions (reflexive assessment).

- Assessment of supportive service systems will be influenced by how professionals conceptualize persons with differences. Assessment of the educational needs of this child will be influenced by whether the worker views a disability as a personal tragedy, a variable to consider, something culturally produced by society, or a target of social oppression (Oliver, 1990, Chapter 1; Reagan, 2002).
- Cultural diversity (ethnic and other cultures viewed as existing at the periphery of our society) must be factored into the design and implementation of assessment.
- Examination of past change efforts and perceptions of the problem by others significant in the arena or subsystem will be important (Cox, 1995).

Many assessment variables exist at the societal level, where there are competing views. Talk of multiple perspectives may strike us merely as semantics or rhetoric until we apply the idea in this case and confront the huge, ongoing debate as to whether deafness is (a) a medical condition causing social isolation compensated for with signing, "a poor substitute for language," or with mainstreaming; or (b) a special culture that communicates with a different but equally rich mode of language expressed by the hands and face instead of the tongue and throat (Dolnick, 1993, p. 40; see also Sacks, 1989, p. ix). Some in the self-identified deaf community see themselves as "a linguistic minority (speaking American Sign Language) and no more in need of a cure for their condition than are Haitians or Hispanics" (Dolnick, p. 37). Describing the controversy, Dolnick points out dissimilarities to such ethnic minorities, since "90 percent of all deaf children are born to hearing parents" (p. 38). These various splits illustrate why assessments must consider social context, current theories (Cox, 1995, p. 155), and various tensions beneath the surface.

Many challenges come to the fore in a subsystem analysis. When we learn that our taken-for-granted assumptions are in question, we have no easy answers, but we can list pros and cons. The implications of these differing perspectives for treatment, schooling, and living arrangements, for medical intervention with cochlear implants or nonintervention, for identity and reality, are heightened by the fact that a decision about a baby's first language needs to be made very early. Having so much at stake in making the best decision makes the situation more pressing. One camp alleges that deaf culture has an anti-book bias and that without reading skills, dead-end jobs are common; the other camp argues that signing introduces children to language much earlier (see, for example, Dolnick, 1993, pp. 46, 51; Sacks, 1989, p. x).

An educational assessment must take note of these differing philosophies. What did the parents decide to do with their baby? How far have they gone down a certain path? Do they want to turn back or continue? How do they view their child's degree of hearing loss: (a) as a personal problem (e.g., child's temperament), (b) as a social problem (e.g., child's future), (c) as no problem at all (e.g., child can communicate satisfactorily), or (d) as affecting a decision to be made? Luey, Glass, and Elliott (1995) warn that "social workers must look at the complicated and interrelated dimensions of hearing, language, culture, and politics" (p. 178). Social workers may be dealing with the emotional upset of hearing parents who have a deaf child or the disappointment of deaf parents who have a hearing child. Just as likely, they may need to gain acceptance for a particular child or for the deaf community. Thus, this social worker must establish the family's self-definitions, listen to the "experiencer" (Oliver Sacks's word—the child in this case), and weigh community and societal factors. Practically, the community and the world beyond must be assessed for resources; the family may decide to move to a community with a public school system featuring mainstreaming, may decide on a particular bilingual approach, or may find the local deaf community and move in a different direction. The worker also must figure out what the agency has to offer. Linking this family with community organizations may be as therapeutic as personal counseling. If the problem for the child is acceptance and the clinic does not engage in advocacy, then the worker must join with those who do on the family's behalf (Harris & Bamford, 2001).

An assessment process should attune us to the realities of a given subsystem. Did the worker arrange for someone to sign or interpret whenever the deaf parents come in to talk over options? Is that service wanted by the consumer (McEntee, 1995)?

adaptable to locations where people congregate other than malls and can be conducted over the telephone. These surveys can be used to collect information for a wide variety of purposes and uses.

We may decide that we can benefit from any information about certain potential service users' needs/preferences or their knowledge of available services. For example, let's say our target group is women whose lives are actually threatened by their weight (Wiley, 1994). Doing a survey of physicians would run into confidentiality issues and would miss women who avoid doctors. We could design a mall survey questionnaire and administer it on a given Saturday in front of department stores, factory outlets, and shops selling large-size women's fashions. The challenge would be to get the stores' cooperation—they may want to screen the questions for potential offensiveness—and to select obese respondents. Surveyors would have to be trained to recognize and tactfully approach obese respondents. Our results could serve as a pretest, since responses would help us design a more relevant (and perhaps less fat-phobic) questionnaire that could be administered outside diet stores, the clothing stores again, and so on.

However, shoppers are not a representative group of all obese women. Some obese women who are self-conscious may stay at home and shop online; the obese shoppers may be more self-confident and assertive. Thus, our mall survey's sample is not a random probability sample and our findings will have limited generalizability. However, if a purposive sample is obtained, we can obtain indicative and preliminary information.

Community Information Gathering and Assessment Group Techniques

Various group methodologies lend themselves to gathering information and beginning the assessment process and fall within the scope of critical community practice. These methodologies use groups composed of community participants, similar to key informants, who represent the community or community segments. All of these techniques require some preliminary community assessment in order to structure the group and recruit participants.

Advisory groups are composed of community representatives and are used to provide a range of information on the community or other subjects. The composition is guided by the type of information sought, networks to tap, and political considerations. Advisory groups can be ongoing. They can be beneficial in terms of the advice they provide and the links they offer to various community interests. A significant weakness of advisory groups, however, is that the participants' social power often affects the group's internal processes, creates a contagion for conformity, and limits expressions of differing opinions. We will discuss advisory groups later in this chapter in the section "Community Assets Inventory and Mapping Protocol."

Nominal groups are composed of individuals with disparate interests, capacities, information, or influence to capture different parts of the community. Nominal groups can be composed of clients, potential clients, service providers, funders, or other participants. Nominal groups usually are given structured exercises in which each participant works silently alongside other individuals and then answers questions when called on until the meeting is opened to free discussion. A moderator might pose a question and ask each participant to list ideas. Each would give one answer from these lists when it is her or his turn until each participant has reported each response. Thus, 8 to 10 people sit in a group but talk in rotation as a facilitator records all ideas; eventually these will be discussed and may be ranked. The initial round-robin sharing format prevents individuals from taking over the brainstorming session (Siegel, Attkisson, & Carson, 1987) and gives an equal voice to reticent members (Alcorn & Morrison, 1994, p. 36). This technique can help to avoid disruption when the groups comprises people who hold different stakes in a particular question, such as health care financing, or who have different amounts of social power or group skills.

The processes, in summary, involve (1) individual generation of ideas in writing, (2) round-robin feedback from group members, with each idea noted in a terse phrase on a flip chart, butcher paper, blackboard, or other similar medium, (3) discussion of each recorded idea for clarification and evaluation (and bargaining),

(4) individual voting and priority setting, with group decisions being mathematically derived through rank-ordering or rating.

Nominal group meetings can also be held consecutively; for instance, landlords could give their opinions in one group and tenants in another at an earlier or later time. Nominal groups are generally task-specific and are not ongoing groups (hence the label, nominal group). The ideas generated can be the participants' ideas regarding community behavior, resource needs, patterns of interaction, or other topics where there may be diversity of representation and community interests. Specific group composition depends on the range of interests sought.

Delphi groups, a specialized form of nominal group, use reiterative but anonymous processes involving individual input and feedback. Participants anonymously provide their opinions on a question and the arguments defending their positions. Positions and arguments are collated and circulated and the process is repeated with the extreme positions (those with little agreement) eliminated after the second round. Because opinions are given anonymously, the Delphi group process allows all of the members to participate freely. However, Delphi group managers should be forewarned that participants often try to make their social power known in the expression of their opinions.

Focus groups are relatively homogeneous groups formed to give input on specific questions or topics, usually about what appeals and doesn't appeal to them about messages, ideas, and products. Sometimes this is done with a written, predetermined agenda or set of questions. Kreuger (1988) defines a focus group as "a carefully planned discussion group designed to obtain perceptions on a defined area of interest in a permissive, non-threatening environment. It is conducted with proximately seven to ten people by a skilled interviewer. … Group members influence each other by responding to ideas and comments in the discussion" (p. 18). A carefully constructed focus group representative of a specific population or part of the community can provide much information on the population's values, attitudes, and opinions, and why they think and feel the way they do. The crucial issues are whether the focus group truly represents the population, whether members of the group

believe they can reveal their true preferences in the group situation, whether social acquiesce and desirability bias will influence group members, whether "group leaders" will emerge and stifle the process, and whether the group moderator can adequately manage but not lead the group. It is assumed that because group participants do not know each other in other roles and are socially similar, open communication will be enhanced. Having a diverse group may inhibit open expression by all members. For diverse populations, different focus groups should be used for each population cluster.

Focus groups differ from Delphi and nominal groups because focus groups do not seek group consensus or any sort of group decision; rather, they are used to gather information, and group decisions are avoided. Focus groups differ from "brainstorming" groups in that no effort is made to engage in problem solving. Broadcast and print media frequently use this form of opinion gathering during political campaigns. Focus groups differ from community forums in that specific detailed information is sought, the questions are predetermined, and the participants are chosen for representativeness.

Focus Group Methodology

Protocol and Participant Selection. Agencies can conduct focus groups for assessment purposes on their own or with assistance from a facilitator. As the point is not to reach a consensus but to air many ideas, members of the group react to each other's suggestions and opinions are refined. The sessions are recorded for later study. The results must be qualified, however, because we cannot generalize from small samples.

If the researcher seeks a cross-section of the community in terms of income, race, education, and other factors, multiple focus groups are needed. Otherwise the social power of participants will enter the process and the focus group will evolve into a nominal group. The homogeneity of composition is an effort to reduce social influences within the group. Most focus group sessions meet once only for about 2 hours. Working people find it hard to arrive early in the evening. Older people prefer daytime hours and are more likely to expect to have transportation money provided. Sometimes participants are given a modest sum, but more often they are provided with a meal or refreshments because they are volunteering their time. The goal of bringing people together in this way is to encourage them to give their candid opinions. If we interrogate them or ask them questions calling for a yes or no answer, we will learn little. We are trying to create the atmosphere of a study group, not a courtroom or research laboratory.

Purpose: To Provide Valuable Information. Individual and group reactions can provide insights into issues of comprehension, suitability, and acceptable phrasing. This is why politicians test campaign themes on focus groups. Let us explore focus group methodology by understanding how a group can serve as a test audience. In the recent past, federal regulators and the apparel industry were considering voluntary warnings for sleepwear. A focus group of middle-aged and older participants was asked their preferences regarding flame-resistant fabric, warning labels, or both, to protect themselves or frail, older parents with cognitive or physical limitations. (Older people have high mortality rates associated with fires involving apparel, especially nightwear.) The meeting opened with a videotape documenting a burn hazard. The group then examined and discussed several proposed wordings for a cautionary label in sleepwear. Participants examined handouts of alternative warnings, which were also printed on big signs and displayed at the front of the room. The discussion that followed made clear a common misconception among the participants: that a labeled product must be more dangerous than an unlabeled product. Without more education, honesty might backfire in the marketplace. The advocates involved had failed in many ways to anticipate how members of the public would react, which is precisely why focus groups can be helpful.

Community forums are community meetings held either to impart information to the community or to receive information from the community. A sample forum could be titled: "Taking the Pulse: A Community Exchange to Gather Information About _____ Needs in _____ County." The forum provides an opportunity for participants to make their positions and opinions known to the forum's sponsors or other target audiences. The advantages of forums as an information-gathering technique is that they are relatively inexpensive, may allow the researcher to obtain information from a range and number of people, and also allows information to be shared with participants. Forums can help form or expand the researcher's network of key informants. Forums, however, can be easily "stacked," with biased results, and can become overtly political. Community members with strong interests, whether or not they represent significant cross-sections of community interests, can take over the forum by obtaining a large and vocal turnout, creating social acquiescence, turning the forum into a quasi-decisional group, or biasing the meeting through triangulation by strategically placing themselves in the group for group contagion. The community forums of the 2009 national health care policy debates illustrated forums often at their worst: some participants were loud and hostile and aggressive to the point of carrying firearms.

Methods of Data Gathering From Community Events

Public Participation. Critical community practice and social work ethics support civic involvement, open government, and public participation in decision making. We learn through community meetings and events. Participants will have the opportunity to talk and to hear the options, and perhaps will even read the final report. Today many open meetings are mandated public hearings (Kettner, Moroney, & Martin, 1990, p. 69). In various fields, for obligatory and democratic reasons, individuals are allowed more say. A citizen could travel from forums about cable television rate hikes to national health coverage. The researcher must remember the current competition for everyone's time when using public information-gathering and assessment methodologies.

Current and potential service users envision something tangible coming out of such interchanges and expect their recommendations to be taken seriously. To be credible and ethical, we must not falsely raise expectations, and we should want input if we ask for it. Town meetings must be accessible (transit, building, audio loops, interpreters, etc.), too.

Meeting Protocol. Suggestions for running any meeting are covered in Chapter 9. The warnings here involve only those matters that may color or cloud the assessment process. The trend to give more say to the community means that meetings can be taken over by a group with an especially obdurate agenda—such as those on either side of the abortion rights, capital punishment, gun control, health care, or immigration issues. A few people can take over or can divert the group from the agenda. The group leader must remain alert but open. For example, a meeting to discuss the perceived need for more day care might be attended by parents who oppose day care, prefer after-school care, or want help in coordinating relief time for families teaching their children at home. Genuine needs may exist, making it inappropriate to tell these parents that they came to the wrong meeting. We may not agree with or like everyone who comes to public meetings, but worthwhile information can often be obtained from unexpected or unreasonable sources.

To avoid disruption, some people who run meetings make a show of letting everyone take part but actually regulate the proceedings tightly to ward off or reject unwanted input. We should anticipate that community people will organize and try to control meetings; this is part of the process. We want to be sure that in small gatherings each person present is offered equal time, and that in big gatherings access to the microphone is handled fairly. Moderators can set time limits and establish ground rules ("Avoid arguing with someone else's statement; just make your own") without squelching participants. It is common for sensible ideas to appear garbled or self-serving in their delivery; therefore, input is properly measured by the usefulness of the suggestion, not the speaking skills and demeanor of proponents or their stance on issues.

Follow-Up Analysis After the Meetings. During a forum, an agency staffer and someone who lives in the community should take notes on each point made and who said it. He or she can then organize the notes, using tentative headings, and have the moderator check them for errors. We must sort out what we heard, using these notes and our own memories, or, better yet, listening

to a tape and noting the intensity of feelings expressed on given topics—from represented groups in particular. Next, we must separate needs from preferences and gripes, not by how participants characterized what they were saying but by customary use of the following terms:

1. *Need:* Essential, necessity, requirement
2. *Desire, wish,* or *preference:* Want, choice, longing
3. *Complaint:* Gripe, grievance, objection, protest

Despite a focus on the need for day care, say, complaints may have poured out about a particular caseworker or about how a current program is being run. This mixes needs, desires, and gripes. A useful tactic is to set aside a designated time on the agenda for participants to air their complaints and preferences, after the discussion of community needs. If this is done before this discussion, the meeting may never get to it!

Assessment Needs: Other Ways to Listen to the Community. To gather community impressions, practitioners can go to those sectors believed to have the most intense needs (whether served, underserved, or unserved to date), interview key informants, and use the target group to validate objective data (Siegel, Attkisson, & Carson, 1987, p. 93). Newer possibilities involve electronic networks and interactive media. Those interested in needs and preferences can monitor sectors of a community via Web pages and e-mail mailing lists.

Although practitioners and managers must know how to put on successful forums, they may be better off attending already scheduled community events than holding their own. We may hear better from the back rather than the front of the room when we do not have to be in charge. Getting out into the swim of things is something we know we should do, but we often lack time. Professionals shouldn't neglect community-wide celebrations and specialized events where they can gain information and exposure: Hispanic International Day, Strawberry Festival, Ice Carnival. We must look for opportunities to interact with the public and other providers. For example, if it is our turn to oversee our office's booth at the mall, then we should visit every other organization's table to gather information (to check service gaps and overlaps) and renew contacts.

Community Power Structure Studies

A community power structure study, largely using the above methodologies, explores the configuration and dynamics of the system of influence at the local level and the characteristics of dominant individuals. Its intent is to identify the names and rankings of persons who are perceived to exercise power in the locality where they live or work.

Full-blown power studies using any approach can take a year, but modest exploratory or shortcut studies can be completed more rapidly, especially if an earlier study is available. Newspaper offices and political science, economics, or sociology departments at colleges or universities are starting places to unearth such a study.

Power Study Reputational Methodologies

We can look at studies undertaken by a journalist to illustrate how successful power structure studies are conducted and what they tell us. A journalist conducted a survey of 27 community leaders (often called a panel in power structure literature) to elicit the names of "folks with real clout" in a large, mostly metropolitan county (Sullivan, 1992, p. 1). The leaders were asked to name "influential individuals . . . not necessarily those with the big jobs or titles, but the 10 people they would want on their side if they were trying to get something big accomplished" (p. 1). The runaway winner in the survey turned out to be fairly similar to county influentials in other informal studies (who are often concerned with growth), because he was a developer. His family connections also fit the picture—a father who had been acting governor and a grandfather who had run a political dynasty in the county. That the winner was also a political columnist and cable-TV talk-show host illustrates a newer route to influence. The school superintendent, county executive, and a U.S. representative were the runners-up. Public service does not equate automatically with power; in this study, not one of nine county council members was in the top 10

with real clout or sway. Influence can also be wielded by those who serve the community outside of office: the former president of the National Association for the Advancement of Colored People (NAACP) ranked eighth. Power's distribution is changing with the growing influence of media stars as the faces of power.

Almost invariably when the results of local power studies are in, we know, an acquaintance knows, or someone in our family knows an individual on the long list, if not the top 10 list, fairly well. Reading community power studies makes it clear that we have more access to influentials than we may realize. We will discuss the "six degrees of separation" in Chapter 10, "Using Networks and Networking."

Problem Studies Methodology

In any problem/services study we should first locate relevant studies conducted in our locale or in similar communities, to discover the variables that define problems and their solutions. We are looking for multidimensional and systematic studies of (a) social problems, (b) private and public sector programs addressing problems (that have been field tested) and other solutions for these problems, and (c) implementation critiques (issues, cost/benefit analyses, evidence of consumer satisfaction).

To start a community problem study, we want to check with the geography, public administration, and business departments at local universities and with police, transportation, health, recreation, and other government offices. Professionals there may have conducted research in relevant areas or may have capacities to pinpoint problems such as domestic violence by neighborhoods or wards that our organization lacks.

Numerous offices such as city planning departments have acquired a technology called Geographic Information Systems (GIS), a type of management information system that can provide new insights for community situations through sophisticated graphics and information maps (Elwood, 2001). According to Mason, Cheung, and Walker (2009), GIS provides "a powerful set of tools that captures, manages, analyzes, and visualizes spatial data" (p. 23). Their project looked at urban youth enrolled in a substance abuse program in Washington, D.C. GIS produced a "geographically specific listing of the teens' daily activity locations, as well as evaluative descriptions of various geographical environments" (Mason, Cheung, and Walker, 2009, p. 23). The GIS was able to describe and visualize 186 unique locations and was able to assign them rankings of either protective or risk location. Human service workers and organizers can use GIS to link data to the target group's environment (McNutt, 2000). Telephone complaints about rodents can be mapped so the neediest neighborhoods quickly and regularly receive rat traps and other interventions (Richards & Croner, 1999). Students in Raleigh, North Carolina, created a school archive using GIS in combination with oral histories of its graduates and discovered how the community surrounding the school had changed over time (Alibrandi, Beal, Thompson, & Wilson, 2000).

Hoefer, Hoefer, and Tobias (1994) suggest several reasons to use this new study tool:

One of the key theoretical viewpoints of social work is that the client must be viewed in the context of his or her environment. Yet, as clients' environments frequently differ from our own, we may overlook or misunderstand the effects of their environments on their problems. GIS can help us keep track of both the physical and social aspects of those environments. . . .

GIS easily addresses such questions as: Where do our clients come from? Are we accessible to our clients by public transportation? Are there geographic concentrations of particular client problems? And, if we need to change location or add satellite offices, where are the best areas to be? (p. 117)

Local Republican and Democratic parties are additional sources of GIS technical expertise. They may have created digital maps on such subjects as values or attitudes, residential density, and voting participation that could be of use. According to Novotny and Jacobs (1977), "What makes GIS so appealing to political campaigns is that it allows a small group of people to take a multitude of geographic and demographic data, from marketing and consumer research to property tax information and U.S. Bureau of the Census statistics, and render them all on a colorful multilayered map that is far more accessible to use than a mere spreadsheet of tables and numbers" (p. 268). Computer graphics can enhance community studies through the generation of

show-and-tell materials for political meetings, fundraising efforts, and so on.

In a community problem/services study, the researcher collects information according to the social problem criteria discussed in Chapter 3 to address the community problem. The following are important for constructing and staging the social problem for intervention:

- Determine the quantifiable nature of the condition and whether the quantifiable definition is generally shared (basis for staging the condition as a community problem and the basis for social intervention)
- Determine specific deviations from what and whose norms, standards, and ideology (basis for building coalitions and developing support to build significant action groups[1])
- Determine whether the deviation is viewed as an individual and/or a social deviation (what parts are individual and what parts are socially caused)
- Determine the ideological frame of reference used that shapes all other definitions
- Determine the elements, degree, and interrelationships of social etiologies, not assuming unitary causation (provides a direction for intervention)
- Determine the social costs: To whom does the condition represent a social cost? By what criteria? Who pays? (forms a basis for making remediation)

Community Assets Inventory and Mapping Protocol

Community asset inventories and maps locate a community's assets, resources, and strengths. They are the converse of problem studies. Community assets are anything that can be used to improve the quality of community life and the lives of its people. The most complete application of asset mapping literally surveys individuals within the geographic area to find out what skills, gifts, and capacities people have.

The protocols for community assets mapping are guided by the goals of the particular inventory and mapping exercise. The protocols require the range of methodologies discussed in this chapter to survey the assets and locate them in the community. While the protocols are generally linear, reiteration often is required as knowledge of the community's boundaries and composition is refined.

1. *Definition of the community and specification of the community's boundaries*

   The definition and specification of the community and clearly boundaries are essential (Office of Learning Technology, 2003, p. 9.). The boundaries determine the key informants for the assets inventory and mappings. Community unit size ultimately is determined by the intensity of the needed assets inventory and maps and the time and resources available for the process. A community development approach with maximum citizen participation is optimal. This requires some existing sense of community identity by key informants. Size of community is a critical consideration. If the community boundaries are too large, the inventorying task either is overwhelming or superficial. Smaller community units allows for intensity of assets inventory and mapping, and greater opportunities for networking and social capital development. These smaller units eventually can be aggregated to form a larger community unit. Some preliminary community assessment by the available data methodologies is advisable in setting community boundaries (Allen, 2005; Robinson, Vineyard, & Reagor, 2004; Sustainable Jersey, n.d.).

2. *Selection of key informants*

   No single person or small group has knowledge of all a community's assets. Selection of key informants should reflect the community's composition and complexity as well as the reasons for doing a community assets mapping. The key informants provide the data for the assets inventory and mappings. Different assets are important to different community segments and interest groups in the community. The asset mapping process needs to be inclusive of all community segments and interests. Asset mapping celebrates differences rather than homogeneity.

3. *Identification of asset sets for inventory*

   The objective is to get as complete an inventory as possible, whether at a neighborhood level, community-wide, or county-wide—whatever the geographic community. Within the geographic community, a functional community of interest approach can be used to organize the data. If small areas are inventoried, individual assets may also be surveyed and mapped. Sources for identifying potential asset sets include available data sources such as the phone book, preliminary reviews with key informants, neighborhood and community groups, the local media, and often "directories" that have been developed in the community. Preliminary asset sets are helpful to key informants in identifying assets.

   The assets sets provided here are preliminary and illustrative only. The sets categories

Some Preliminary Data Sets

1. Assets of individuals: individual skills of actual or potential volunteers, mentors, and community resources
2. Assets of associations: community organizations, cultural organizations, self-help and health groups, interest clubs, crime watch, friends of library, sports leagues, social action groups, labor unions, political organizations, faith-based organizations, civic and fraternal organizations, and more
3. Assets of institutions and formal organizations and agencies: public and private schools, libraries, public and civic agencies, not-for-profit social and community welfare and United Way agencies, medical and health vendors, community centers, police and fire stations, cultural organizations, not-for-profit arts and profit entertainment, religious institutions (churches, synagogues, mosques, temples)
4. Assets of economic and business organizations: Chamber of Commerce and business associations, trade groups, vendors and merchants, job training programs.
5. Assets of natural resources: parks, farms, ranches, forests, green spaces, open spaces, wetlands
6. Assets of physical structure or places: parks, schools, hospitals, places of worship, recreational resources, libraries, buildings, governmental facilities, community centers.

in any assets inventory and mapping are not exhaustive or always mutually exclusive. The sets are refined and expanded as the assets inventories are developed. The task is not to develop a clean typology of assets but an inventory of assets. It is to guide key informants in developing a comprehensive inventory of community assets. A single individual or organization generally has multiple assets. The assets inventory and map is of assets, rather than units.

4. *Selection of data collection methodologies and data collection*

Generally a steering committee composed of key informants from different community segments is formed to advise on data sets and collection methodologies that will work best in the community.[2] The approach should take into account the amount of time the key informants are willing to volunteer and the technical and organizational needs of the inventory methods. The methodologies typically involve the range of data collection tools discussed in this chapter: available data, observations, interviews, written surveys (Allen, 2005; Office of Learning Technology, 2003). The group techniques presented earlier in this chapter can be used as a data collection methodology and can help define the asset sets. The steering committee can be an ongoing advisory group or can function as a short-term nominal group.

5. *Constructing the inventory and the assets maps*

Remember, community assets inventories and mapping are about locating and inventorying strengths and assets and connecting people and organizations in the community to build community networks, cohesion, solidarity, and social capital. The inventories can catalog assets by geographic or functional asset sets used in data collection and develop new ways of classifying the assets. As a resource assessment tool, assets inventories and mapping should indicate the vertical or horizontal relationship of the asset to the community (vertical and horizontal relationships were discussed in Chapter 4). Asset mapping reveals the assets of the entire community and highlights the interconnections among them, which in turn reveals how to

access those assets. Connections to people can also become connections to resource-filled institutions. Assets location mapping can use GIS mapping in *Zagat*-type maps, probably by asset sets to reduce the "busyness" of the maps (Aronson, Wallis, O'Campo, & Schafer, 2007; Mason, Cheung, & Walker, 2009).

Eco-mapping and social network maps, discussed in Chapter 10, address the relationships and connectiveness of a community's assets to an individual or family. Eco-mapping, initially developed in family therapy, is a mapping of relationships between community assets that are part of a household's environment or ecology. The process involves asking people to list resources and to describe exchanges. For instance, they designate people to whom they can turn, such as a brother-in-law who fixes cars or a former daughter-in-law, as well as people by whom they are oppressed or drained, such as a lonely widowed mother or a brother who is becoming addicted to Ecstasy (Cournoyer, 2000, pp. 40–43). The resulting chart diagrams human relationships (for instance, a family or friendship group) and may include formal and informal resources and natural helpers (Miley, O'Melia, & DuBois, 1998, pp. 243–244).

Another way of finding out about resources and linking the community asset map to the individual or family is a social network map. The end product here is another graphic, but one that lists social supports such as neighbors, businesses, churches, self-help groups, or clubs that the individual or family does or could access (Miley, O'Melia, & DuBois, 1998, pp. 340–341). From it we may be able to see links to social institutions.

Outreach and Assessment Methods

Outreach and assessment intertwine in two ways. Community assessment may help determine the best means of outreach. Assessment can be made possible through outreach to less well-known segments of the population. Typically, outreach involves systematically contacting isolated people in their homes or wherever they reside (institutions, streets), or in the neighborhoods where they congregate, and linking them to services and financial programs for which they are believed to be eligible. Directories can be part of outreach, as can 800 or 888 telephone numbers. Outreach is also used to expand an agency's program (a) into new settings and communities, thus making a service or resource immediately and more widely available; (b) into new time periods to reach a target group, as has been done with midnight basketball; and (c) into client "linkage" with institutions, the community, or other clients to enhance "peer support" (Wells, Schachter, Little, Whylie, & Balogh, 1993).

Outreach has information-gathering and assessment potential as well as a client recruitment and case-finding strategy. It is an obligation of critical community practice. Takoma Park, Maryland, hired organizers to canvass wards full of newcomers to register people to vote in city elections but also to learn about immigrant concerns (for instance, whether illegal immigrants were being taken advantage of in their everyday transactions) (Becker, 2001). Outreach involves an interesting mix of giving and getting knowledge (Glogoff & Glogoff, 1998).

Varieties and Methods. Outreach methods vary. Some government agencies are mandated to alert potential service users or beneficiaries—for instance, regarding food stamps or Supplemental Security Income. They often perform outreach through public service announcements. In contrast, homeless shelter director Mitch Snyder (1946–1990), the legendary District of Columbia homeless advocate, used to take hamburgers and blankets out around 10 P.M. to individuals who chose to stay on the streets rather than come in from the cold. While distributing the food and blankets, he gained intelligence from those on heat grates about specific fears people had about coming indoors and which people on the streets were the sickest or most violent. A continuing education program on mental health, on the other hand, employed more conventional but equally important ways of reaching out to older people: selecting accessible community sites, allowing registration at the first class so that frail people did not have to make an extra trip, and printing materials in large type (Blackwell & Hunt, 1980). Telephone hotlines offering legal assistance to

the poor or elderly have been tried in several localities as a way to make information more available, as well as a means of collecting information on the types of requests received over time. The University of Maryland at Baltimore has a Social Work Community Outreach Service that links university resources with community groups and residents (Cook, Bond, Jones, & Greif, 2002). Support groups can be initiated, in either a public or a circumspect manner (Anderson & Shaw, 1994), as a form of outreach. Many churches and legal groups have initiated innovative outreach to immigrant groups.[3]

As shown in a newspaper story by Levine (2002) entitled "Word Gets Out on Children's Insurance," methods of outreach can be direct or indirect:

It is advertised during back-to-school nights and baseball games, in beauty parlors and liquor stores, on yo-yos and toothbrushes. The creative lengths to which state and local officials go in publicizing the Maryland Children's Health Program know few bounds. At the local bowling alley? On a Frisbee? Why not? Their work has paid off by the tens of thousands since the program began in 1998. Nearly 95,000 previously uninsured children have health coverage—a yield more than 50 percent greater than officials originally predicted and success that these days draws applause from outside policy experts. (pp. 3, 6, reprinted with permission of the *Washington Post*)

Methods of outreach can be expected or unexpected: If skywriting in Spanish were the best way to identify a service and encourage its use for a particular target group, and resources were not at issue, then it would be an appropriate mechanism. Direct, personal outreach must, of course, be made as nonthreatening and nondisruptive as possible.

Outreach can be done using the Web and the Internet in some nonthreatening ways. The Maine Department of Environmental Protection used e-mail technology as an easy, low-cost method of soliciting commitment. The outreach targeted the listserv, an e-mail distribution list, of the 420 employees of the Maine Department of Environmental Protection. The campaign focused on four behaviors: (1) checking tire pressure; (2) replacing incandescent light bulbs with compact fluorescent light bulbs (CFLs); (3) assessing refrigerator efficiency; and (4) purchasing green power (Artz & Cooke, 2007, p. 260). An introductory e-mail was sent, followed by an e-mail 2 weeks later introducing the first commitment. As the weeks followed, the other three topics were introduced by e-mail. The e-mails allowed recipients to demonstrate their commitment by replying to the e-mail. E-mails were sent again a few days later to those people who demonstrated their commitment by asking whether they followed through with the committed action. The evaluators found that e-mail "served as a viable mechanism for social marketing" (Artz & Cooke, 2007, p. 271). E-mails allowed for efficient dissemination of the campaigns and allowed recipients to provide feedback and input to the department. There are limits and cautions, however. Not all people have Internet service and can be reached by e-mails. In an era where "spam" e-mail dominates, some people may simply ignore these messages.

The philosophy is to meet people where they are in every way we can—through their own language or their own stores (e.g., botanical shops in Puerto Rican communities), accommodating them in their own environment and in ours (getting rid of barriers such as stairs), providing services or programs in a way and at a time that is convenient, and conveying messages at an appropriate level of comprehension. It is important to assess the informational requirements of the public. We can be creative in community education: comic books, for instance, can be part of adult education and advocacy efforts. The immigrant outreach networks organizations that serve non-English speakers use graphics to reach out to their target populations. We will continue our discussion of communication and outreach in Chapter 11, the marketing chapter.

The Write-Up

Once information is collected, it needs to be organized so it can be used in constructing a case theory for change. Analytic techniques for building the case theory are discussed in the subsequent chapters. These techniques are used to organize and assess the information that is collected and may guide the collection of information, but assessment does not collect information. The wind-up, if there is a final wind-up,

of any community study is the report to relevant constituencies. This is especially true for a comprehensive community study. We finish the study by writing a report and having it double-checked by our key informants. In ethnographic field studies this is referred to as *member-checking* (Bisman & Hardcastle, 1999, pp. 66–67, 220). A sample of topics to cover in a report includes:

1. Community description:
   Geographic, corporate, jurisdictional boundaries
   Demographics, statistics, subgroups
   History, community strengths today
   Political structure, governance
   Economic structure, major or key employers
   Social services structure
   Mutual aid, community action organizations
   Potential or actual civic and service problems
   Power relations

2. Description of the information-collection methodologies:
   Interviewing, "hearing" the community in new ways
   Observing, analyzing
   Collecting illuminating anecdotes, stories
   Following methods used by social scientists
   Providing orientation materials (map, photographs)
   Being aware of personal bias, limits of analysis

Communication About Need. Neuber and associates (1980) defined need assessment as "a communication medium between consumers and service providers," which can affect "the planning and evaluation of the various services to be delivered to the community and consumers" (pp. 62–63). Need assessment is also an ongoing process that involves the community in a form of continuous quality improvement (D. Menefee, personal communication, June 1995). Need assessments may be client-oriented (population at risk) or service-oriented (addressing gaps and fit).

To give an example of the latter, a graduate student thinks she has identified a need. Her dream is to start her own agency after she leaves school to provide housing for post–high-school-age youth. She wishes to find a niche in the transitional housing market and has several communities in mind, but she wants to find out if such a service is essential, in the opinion of local practitioners, and desired by decision makers in the area. The student believes a service-oriented need assessment will help her to determine in which locality there will be a positive fit and where her plan will most likely succeed.

Integrating Methods to Suit Assessment Needs

When practitioners wish to know their clients' worlds better, or when program development or another course of action is underway, several of the methodologies discussed here can be combined or their elements mixed to fit the situation. Community studies can be as personal as ethnography and as impersonal as computer analysis of available data. Approaches are mixed and matched to fit the situation and available resources. Assessment processes involve compiling available information, developing new information, or extracting relevant new information with the old. Neuber and associates (1980) urge

us to obtain data from the range of qualitative and quantitative assessment methodologies.

Disciplines usually evolve a few specialized assessment methods but adapt most of their methods from sources such as sociology, political science, or planning. In community health, for instance, surveys and descriptive epidemiological studies are common methods used to carry out an assessment (Spradley, 1990, p. 382), just as needs identification and assessment methods, including surveys, are common in social work.

Moving from Assessment to Action

What will be the outcome of all this self-scrutiny, community examination, and assessment? Using the data, insights, and community contacts gained from study and assessment, appropriate steps become more apparent. Possible action plans include:

- Finding community connections for service users
- Mobilizing community resources for clients

Illustrative Example

Your Juneau, Alaska, office has been successful at community building and has received federal stimulus money to open an office in Sitka, a town of about 9,000 residents about 70 miles away by air. You have only a tourist's superficial knowledge about Sitka. Located on Baranof Island on Alaska's panhandle, it is the state's largest port system and among the top ten ports by value in the United States. It has lumber, salmon, and halibut fisheries; tourism; a college; and a Coast Guard Air Station. But you can't see Russia from Sitka, even on a clear day.

In order to carry out the stimulus grant, you have to know Sitka better. A community study is needed. Your director asks you to move to Sitka early to start this study, which may provide guidance on hiring and programming. He gives you the names of three townspeople whom he has met: George P. of the Alaska Marine Conservation Council, Nancy F. of the nonprofit Island Institute, and Lesley A., who runs day tours for cruise ships. The director tells you to investigate the area in four ways and report back in a month.

1. Conduct a field study to learn more about the culture of any minority, low-income, fringe, or

disreputable groups in the area that might be overlooked in the community-building process. What are your first steps?
2. Conduct a field study to gain an overview and a sense of town character. Identify community assets. What are your first steps?
3. Conduct a power structure study to find out who openly and who quietly controls the community. What are your first steps?
4. Find out who has recently conducted problem-oriented community studies. Try to prioritize community concerns. What are your first steps?
5. Would you do the studies in this order or another order? Explain your rationale.

For a metropolitan, multicultural version of the exercise, use Fresno, California; Greensboro, North Carolina; San Antonia, Texas; Las Vegas, Nevada; or Nashville, Tennessee. All have multi-ethnic populations.

- Selecting appropriate community interventions (development, problem reduction, education, sector mobilization, prevention, promotion)
- Organizing sectors of the community around an issue

Look back to the beginning of the chapter to see a prime example of mobilizing legal resources and organizing a community around an issue. Erin Brockovich's story depicts the progression from assessment to action quite well.

Linking Assessment, Problem Solving, and Intervention[4]

Activating citizens and ameliorating problems are the objectives of community assessment community-building processes. As Mattaini and Kirk argue (1993), "if assessment is not directly related to and prescriptive of treatment, it is, at best, a waste of client and practitioner time and, at worst, unethical." The overriding task of the community practitioner is to help groups respond to the vicissitudes of life while keeping long-term community welfare on the agenda. A need for community problem solving usually exists when (a) there are many individuals or a class of people involved, with problems that are viewed as being large or serious enough to pose some threat, real or imagined, to the well-being of the community; or (b) the community experiences pressure due to problems in the operation of a system, such as problems in communication or socialization (see Chapter 4) (Box 6.3).

The community practitioner intervenes, on behalf of an agency or organization or as part of a coalition, in the workings of the community system and its parts. Since the magnitude, complexity, and responsibility of the task of addressing either type of problem are almost overwhelming, what is needed is a way to think about the job. A guide that points up difficulties and charts ways of overcoming obstacles is helpful.

Here are 8 ideal steps that seek to explicate the thinking, case-theory building, and behavior of a community practitioner engaging in problem solving:

1. Problem intake (identification, delineation of initiator system, preliminary assessment, delineation of a social problem and target systems)
2. Selection of potential problem-solving actors (construction, preliminary determination and location of the client, action, change agent systems)
3. Determination of desired goals and potential consensus (assessments and assets inventory)
4. Specification of types of action outcome (e.g., alleviate condition, control, rehabilitate, prevent, innovate), recruitment of change agent, action, implementing systems
5. Analysis of the facets of the anticipated intervention (case theory and implementing system)
6. Inventory and evaluation of resources (refinement of assets inventory and mapping)
7. Implementation of decisions made to reach solutions (allocation of resources, intervention)
8. Evaluation (ongoing feedback)

BOX 6.3.   Construing the Situation

When a problem or case is brought to your official notice, you must decide how narrowly or broadly to interpret it. For example, Rosenthal and Levine (1980, p. 401) point out that an individual complaint about discrimination in a local government's handling of a job promotion might be investigated in one of the following ways:

- As an individual complaint only: Did the government agency discriminate against this person?

- As a class complaint: Does the government agency discriminate against all persons in certain categories?
- As a broadly construed class complaint: Does the entire government discriminate against all persons in certain categories?

We will collect data for our organization's own use to learn what should be done and, later, after a decision is made about how to proceed, we will collect additional data to support what we want from third parties who can effect solutions. During this process, we look to agency stakeholders for insight intelligence and look to community people who have a stake in a problem and its solution for action intelligence.

Community problems, public concern for those problems, and the authority to do something about them cross institutional, geographic, and special interest boundaries (Turner, 1963a, b). This makes community work and problem solving interesting and challenging. There are no clearly detailed road maps; worse, there is an absence of well-marked roads and there are many potholes. Any guide simply specifies the points of the compass that we need to chart our daily practice excursions.

Based on community problem-solving steps (see Chapters 1 and 3), the emphasis may seem to be on all head and no heart. However, that view overlooks the emphasis on spirit found in actual practice. Belief in a cause and commitment are necessary because, in the final analysis, we must recognize that disturbances of the status quo are inherent in community organizing and planning. Resistance is to be expected. A second aspect of spirit requires that the practitioner learn to be comfortable with uncertainty. This is the companion of change and development. A third requirement is for the practitioner to master feasibility management:

practitioners must work with what is feasible at the moment they need to take action. Thus, the task of the community problem-solving practitioner is to constantly stretch the parameters of what is feasible and determine the moment for action. This, then, is the spirit of purpose and determination.

A Continuous Cycle. Assessment, problem solving, and intervention processes flow together. As a prime example, Bracht and Kingsbury (1990) conceive of community organizing in five overlapping stages: "community analysis, design and initiation, implementation, maintenance and consolidation, and dissemination and reassessment" (p. 74).

Box 6.4 illustrates the cycle of assessment, intervention, and reassessment. It provides an example of the use of a community-oriented viewpoint in planning a specific program. Note how closely the steps correspond to the fundamentals emphasized in this chapter. This section has sketched the later phases of the assessment process. Additional forms of intervention will be addressed in subsequent chapters.

Notes

1. *Significant* is defined tautologically as having sufficient social power to place the concern on the public's agenda for consideration.
2. See "Community Information Gathering and Assessment Group Techniques" earlier in the chapter.
3. Examples include the Immigration Outreach Service Center at St. Matthew Catholic Church, http://www.ioscbalt.org/; The National Immigration

---

BOX 6.4.	Steps to Establishing Successful Worksite Health-Promotion Programs

1. Build community support.
   a. Assess community norms, culture, and activities.
   b. Establish community advisory board.
2. Assess worksite culture and social norms.
   a. Capitalize on opportunities to facilitate the program.
   b. Identify and modify existing barriers.
3. Solicit top management and union support.
4. Use employee input in planning.
   a. Conduct employee surveys.

   b. Appoint employee steering committee.
   c. Appoint worksite liaison.
5. Provide ongoing programming with environmental and social supports.
6. Conduct periodic program evaluation.

Source: Sorensen, Glasgow, & Corbett (1990, p. 160). Copyright © 1990 by Sage Publications, Inc. Reprinted by permission.

Assessing Our Links as Professionals with the Community

How Engaged Am I In This Community? What Is My/Our Place In This Community?

Professionals need to make and use contacts. To analyze the contacts we already have and to find out the degree of our engagement as human service workers in our community, we can start by listing who knows us, and whom we know. For example, our agency Web page or annual report should reveal part of the local and regional professional network that we maintain. In whose newsletter is our agency mentioned? The organization chart (see Chapter 9) sketches our agency's organizational ties to governing, oversight, and funding bodies, and a task environment analysis (see Chapters 2, 4 and 11) can delineate our professional linkages with parallel and competing agencies. This process will help identify informal community partnerships. We can trace formal linkages, but personal ties are equally noteworthy; after all, social movements and other change efforts are built on networks of friends. Since a variety of people are connected with an agency, from fundraisers to secretaries, multiple informal local networks of relationships exist. One way to tap such links and explore relationships among social actors is with a social network survey (Cross, Borgatti, & Parker, 2002).

Capturing factual information about community links is a matter of becoming more systematic in identifying ties:

- Inventory community groups and organizations with which agency staffers are affiliated personally and professionally. Which of these could you call upon for assistance? For example, one social worker may have links with the National Guard, an Alzheimer's support group, and a youth gang, plus the usual memberships in professional associations.
- Look at a list of social institutions and mark those where you have some type of "in" due to knowledge, connection to staff, and so on.
- Have members of the agency's client and community boards also engage in this exercise; you may see different ties.
- List the organizational representatives in each coalition to which your agency or organization belongs.
- Do a media audit: Write down each media outlet that you rely on for information, and star the ones you could tap for coverage.
- In the above evaluations, state whether the nexus is significant or superficial.
- If staffers are willing to do a collective exercise, Mattaini (1993) suggests an eco-map, substituting your agency for the family at the center of the graphic.
- Another group exercise has everyone who is part of the agency draw individual sociograms, a picture of who is connected to whom. These will graphically display the relationships and interactions within the group of agency employees and volunteers (Johnson, 1995). Results can be revealing; weak linkages or active dislike among subgroups within the agency may reflect weak ties and subgroup tensions within the community. See Chapters 8, 9, and 10 of this volume and Valdis Krebs's "An Introduction to Social Network Analysis" Web site (http://www.orgnet.com/sna.html).

Ultimately, we seek to be in right relationship with our community collaborators. We want to be accountable to the public and to truly involve service users in decision making: that means actual input, not just ratification of staff plans (see Chapter 14).

In summary, determining whether agencies are effectively and strategically involved in community and have a community orientation requires many mechanisms and must be an ongoing assessment procedure.

Law Center, http://www.nilc.org/dc_conf/flash-drive09/Health-Care-Access-Reform/pb13; and the Immigration Outreach project of New York City's City Bar Justice Center, http://www.nycbar.org/citybarjusticecenter/projects/immigrant-justice/immigration-outreach-project/overview/

4. This section is based on work by Hardcastle (1992) and Turner (1963b). Also see Cox (1995).

References

Adams, R. G. (1998). Inciting sociological thought by studying the Deadhead community: Engaging publics in dialogue. *Social Forces*, 77(1), 1–25.

Alcorn, S., & Morrison, J. D. (1994). Community planning that is "caught" and "taught": Experiential learning from town meetings. *Journal of Community Practice*, 1(4), 27–43.

Alibrandi, M., Beal, C., Thompson, A., & Wilson, A. (2000). Reconstructing a school's past using oral histories and GIS mapping. *Social Education*, 64(3), 134–139.

Allen, J. C. (2005). *Community asset mapping and mobilizing communities*. Coeur d'Alene, ID: Idaho Governor's 6th Annual Roundtable.

Anderson, D. B., & Shaw, S. L. (1994). Starting a support group for families and partners of people with HIV/AIDS in a rural setting. *Social Work*, 39(1), 135–138.

Aronson, R. E., Wallis, A. B., O'Campo, P. J., & Schafer, P. (2007). Neighborhood mapping and evaluation: A methodology for participatory community health initiatives. *Journal of Maternal and Child Health,* 11, 373–383.

Artz, N., & Cooke, P. (2007). Using e-mail listservs to promote environmentally sustainable behaviors. *Journal of Marketing Communications,* 13(4), 257–276.

Becker, J. (2001, April 26). Activists, politicians court minorities: Changing demographics could influence elections. *The Washington Post,* p. T16.

Bisman, C. D., & Hardcastle, D. A. (1999). *Integrating research into practice: A model for effective social work.* Belmont, CA: Wadsworth Publishing Co.

Blackwell, D., & Hunt, S. (1980). Mental health services reaching out to older persons. *Journal of Gerontological Social Work,* 2(4), 281–288.

Bracht, N., & Kingsbury, L. (1990). Assessing the community: Its services, needs, leadership, and readiness. In N. Bracht (Ed.), *Health promotion at the community level* (pp. 66–88). Newbury Park, CA: Sage.

Butcher, H. B. (2007). Toward a model of critical community practice. In H. B. Butcher, S. Banks, P. Henderson, with J. Robertson, *Critical community practice* (pp. 51–76). Bristol, UK: The Policy Press.

Butcher, H. B., Banks, S., Henderson, P., with Robertson, J. (2007). *Critical community practice.* Bristol, UK: The Policy Press.

Cook, D., Bond, A. F., Jones, P., & Greif, G. L. (2002). The social work outreach service within a school of social work: A new model for collaboration with the community. *Journal of Community Practice,* 10(1), 17–31.

Cournoyer, B. (2000). *The social work skills workbook.* Belmont, CA: Brooks/Cole.

Cox, F. M. (1995). Community problem solving: A guide to practice with comments. In J. Rothman, J. L. Erlich, & J. E. Tropman with F. M. Cox (Eds.), *Strategies of community organization: Macro practice* (5th ed., pp. 146–162). Itasca, IL: F. E. Peacock.

Cross, R., Borgatti, S. P., & Parker, A. (2002). Making invisible work visible: Using social network analysis to support strategic collaboration. *California Management Review,* 44(2), 25–41.

Daley, J. M., & Wong, P. (1994). Community development with emerging ethnic communities. *Journal of Community Practice,* 1(1), 9–24.

Dawson, S. E. (1993). Social work practice and technological disasters: The Navajo uranium experience. *Journal of Sociology and Social Welfare,* 20(2), 5–20.

Denby, D. (2000, March 27). Hell-raising women: And the men who love them. *The New Yorker,* 135–136.

Denzin, N. K. (1970). *The research act: A theoretical introduction to sociological methods.* Chicago: Aldine.

Dolnick, E. (1993, September). Deafness as culture. *The Atlantic Monthly,* pp. 37–40, 46–53.

Elwood, S. A. (2001). GIS and collaborative urban governance: Understanding their implications for community action and power. *Urban Geography,* 22(6), 737–759.

Glaser, B. G., & Strauss, A. L. (1967). *The discovery of grounded theory: Strategies for qualitative research.* Chicago: Aldine Publishing Co.

Glogoff, L. G., & Glogoff, S. (1998). Using the World Wide Web for community outreach. *Internet Reference Services Quarterly,* 3(1), 15–26.

Green, J. W. (1995). *Cultural awareness in the human services: A multi-ethnic approach* (2nd ed.). Boston: Allyn & Bacon.

Hardcastle, D. A. (1992). *Social problems, needs and social policy: A conceptual review.* Baltimore: University of Maryland at Baltimore School of Social Work.

Harris, J., & Bamford, C. (2001). The uphill struggle: Services for deaf and hard of hearing people—issues of equality, participation and access. *Disability and Society,* 16(7), 969–979.

Hirsch, K. (1998). *A home in the heart of a city.* New York: Northpoint Press.

Hoefer, R. A., Hoefer, R. M., & Tobias, R. A. (1994). Geographic information systems and human services. *Journal of Community Practice,* 1(3), 113–128.

Howell, J. T. (1973). *Hard living on Clay Street: Portraits of blue-collar families.* Garden City, NY: Anchor Books.

Jeffries, A. (1996). Modeling community work: An analytic framework for practice. *Journal of Community Practice,* 3(3/4), 101–125.

Johnson, L. C. (1995). *Social work practice: A generalist approach* (5th ed.). Boston: Allyn & Bacon.

Karabanow, J. (1999). Creating community: A case study of a Montreal street kid agency. *Community Development Journal,* 34(4), 318–327.

Kettner, P. M., Moroney, R. M., & Martin, L. L. (1990). *Designing and managing programs: An effectiveness-based approach.* Newbury Park, CA: Sage.

Kreuger, R. A. (1988). *Focus groups: A practical guide for applied research.* Newbury Park, CA: Sage.

Lamb, R. K. (1977). Community life: How to get its pulse. Suggestions for a study of your home town. In F. M. Cox, J. L. Erlich, J. Rothman, & J. E. Tropman (Eds.), *Tactics and techniques of community practice* (pp. 17–23). Itasca, IL: F. E. Peacock.

Levine, S. (2002, January 3). Word gets out on children's insurance. *The Washington Post, Montgomery Extra,* p. 3, p. 6.

Lincoln, Y., & Guba, E. (1985). *Naturalistic inquiry*. Beverly Hills, CA: Sage.

Luey, H. S., Glass, L., & Elliott, H. (1995). Hard-of-Hearing or Deaf: Issues of ears, language, culture, and identity. *Social Work*, 40(2), 177–182.

Mason, M., Cheung, I., & Walker, L. (2009). Creating a geospatial database of risks and resources to explore urban adolescent substance use. *Journal of Prevention & Intervention in the Community*, 37, 21–34.

Mattaini, M. A., & Kirk, S. A. (1993). Points & viewpoints: Misdiagnosing assessment. *Social Work*, 38, 231–233.

McEntee, M. K. (1995). Deaf and hard-of-hearing clients: Some legal implications. Social Work, 40(2), 183–187.

McNutt, J. (2000). Organizing cyberspace: Strategies for teaching about community practice and technology. *Journal of Community Practice*, 7(1), 95–109.

Merton, R. K., Fiske, M., & Kendall, P. (1956). *The focus interview*. Glencoe, IL: The Free Press.

Meyer, C. H. (1993). *Assessment in social work practice*. New York: Columbia University Press.

Miley, K. K., O'Melia, M., & DuBois, B. L. (1998). *Generalist social work practice*. Needham Heights, MA: Allyn & Bacon.

Myerhoff, B. (1980). *Number our days*. New York: Simon & Schuster.

Neuber, K. A. (with Atkins, T. A., Jacobson, J. A., & Reuterman, N. A.). (1980). *Needs assessment: A model for community planning*. Newbury Park, CA: Sage.

Neuber, K. A. (with Atkins, T. A., Jacobson, J. A., & Reuterman, N. A.). (1980). *Needs assessment: A model for community planning*. Newbury Park, CA: Sage.

Novotny, P., & Jacobs, R. H. (1977). Geographical information systems and the new landscape of political technologies. *Social Science Computer Review*, 15(3), 264–285.

Office of Learning Technologies. (2003). *Community learning asset mapping: A guidebook for community learning networks*. Gatineau, Que., Canada: Human Resources Development Canada. Retrieved November 12, 2009, from http://www.servicecanada.gc.ca/eng/hip/lld/olt/Resources/toolkit/mapping-guidebook.pdf

Oldenburg, R. (1999). *The great good place: Cafes, coffee shops, bookstores, bars, hair salons and other hangouts at the heart of a community*. New York: Marlowe & Co.

Oliver, M. (1990). *The politics of disablement*. New York: St. Martin's Press.

Parker, V., Edmonds, S., & Robinson, V. (1989). *A change for the better: How to make communities more responsive to older residents*. Washington, DC: American Association of Retired Persons.

Reagan, T. (2002). Toward an "archeology of deafness": Etic and emic constructions of identity in conflict. *Journal of Language, Identity & Education*, 1(1), 41–66.

Richards, T. B., & Croner, C. M. (1999). Geographic information systems and public health: Mapping in the future. *Public Health Reports*, 114(4), 359–373.

Robinson, C. M., Vineyard, M. C., & Reagor, J. D. (2004). Using community mapping in human ecology. *Journal of Family and Consumer Sciences*, 96(4), 52–54.

Robinson, K., & Walsh, R. O. (1999). Blunders of interdisciplinary education: Our first experience. *National Academies of Practice Forum*, 1(1), 7–11.

Rodwell, M. K. (1998). *Social work constructivist research*. New York: Garland.

Rogge, M. E. (1995). Coordinating theory, evidence, and practice: Toxic waste exposure in communities. *Journal of Community Practice*, 2(2), 55–76.

Rosenthal, S. R., & Levine, E. S. (1980). Case management and policy implementation. *Public Policy*, 28(4), 381–413.

Rubin, A., & Babbie, E. (2007). *Research methods for social work* (6th ed.) Belmont, CA: Thompson Brooks Cole.

Sacks, O. (1989). *Seeing voices: A journey into the world of the deaf*. Berkeley: University of California Press.

Schneider, R. L., & Lester, L. (2001). *Social work advocacy: A new framework for action*. Belmont, CA: Brooks/Cole.

Schwab, B., Drake, R. E., & Burghardt, E. M. (1988). Health care of the chronically mentally ill: The culture broker model. *Community Mental Health Journal*, 24(3), 174–184.

Siegel, L. M., Attkisson, C. C., & Carson, L. G. (1987). Need identification and program planning in the community. In F. M. Cox, J. L. Erlich, J. Rothman, & J. E. Tropman (Eds.), *Strategies of community organization: Macro practice* (4th ed., pp. 71–97). Itasca, IL: F. E. Peacock.

Sorensen, G., Glasgow, R. E., & Corbett, K. (1990). Involving work sites and other organizations. In N. Bracht (Ed.), *Health promotion at the community level* (pp. 158–184). Newbury Park, CA: Sage.

Spradley, B. W. (1990). *Community health nursing: Concepts and practice* (3rd ed.). Glenview, IL: Scott, Foresman.

Spradley, J. P. (1980). *Participant observation*. New York: Harcourt Brace Jovanovich.

Sullivan, W. P. (1992). Reclaiming the community: The strengths perspective and deinstitutionalization. *Social Work*, 37(3), 204–209.

Sustainable Jersey. (n.d.). *Community assets mapping*. Retrieved November 12, 2009, from: www.sustainable jersey.com/listserve

Turner, J. B. (1963a, May). *The continuing debate: Community organization or community planning?* Paper presented at workshop on planning, group work, and recreation. Cleveland, OH.

Turner, J. B. (1963b, February). Guidelines to a search for a theory of priority determination. Paper presented at the Inter-Community Staff Conference, Case Western Reserve University, Cleveland, OH.

Ward, J., & Hansen, K. A. (1997). *Search strategies in mass communications* (3rd ed.). New York: Longman.

Warren, R. B., & Warren, D. I. (1984). How to diagnose a neighborhood. In F. M. Cox, J. L. Erlich, J. Rothman, & J. E. Tropman (Eds.), *Tactics and techniques of community practice* (2nd ed., pp. 27–40). Itasca, IL: F. E. Peacock.

Wells, L. M., Schachter, B., Little, S., Whylie, B., & Balogh, P. A. (1993). Enhancing rehabilitation through mutual aid: Outreach to people with recent amputations. *Health and Social Work*, 18(3), 221–229.

Wexler Vigilante, F. W. (1993). Work: Its use in assessment and intervention with clients in the workplace. In P. A. Kurzman & S. H. Akabas (Eds.), *Work and well-being: The occupational social work advantage* (pp. 179–199). Washington, DC: National Association of Social Workers.

Wiley, C. (Ed.). (1994). *Journeys to self-acceptance: Fat women speak*. Freedom, CA: Crossing Press.

Worth, A. (2001). Assessment of the needs of older people by district nurses and social work: Changing culture? *Journal of Interprofessional Care*, 15(3), 257–266.

Yin, R. K. (1984). *Case study research: Design and method*. Beverly Hills, CA: Sage.

Yin, R. K. (1972). Participant-observation and the development of urban neighborhood policy. New York: The New York City Rand Institute.

7

Assertiveness: Using Self in Community Practice

This above all: to thine own self be true,
And it must follow, as the night the day,
Thou canst not then be false to any man.

William Shakespeare, Hamlet, Act I, Scene 3

To know oneself, one should assert oneself.
Albert Camus, anarchist, author, Nobel Laureate for literature

The Negro will only be truly free when he reaches down to the inner depths of his own being and signs with the pen and ink of assertive selfhood his own emancipation proclamation.

Martin Luther King, Jr., Baptist minister, civil rights and social justice advocate, Nobel Peace Prize Laureate

Use of Self

This chapter discusses self-awareness, competency, cognition, and assertiveness as requirements for social work and community practice. Related concepts such as critical community practice, empowerment, and practitioner observation and self-observation also are reviewed. The conscious use of self is the social worker's pivotal skill, and the self is the fundamental resource. They are also traits that should be developed for clients and community participants. It is difficult, probably impossible, to pursue client self-determination without developing the client's knowledge and use of self. Identity requires self-awareness. Assertiveness is necessary for effective advocacy.

Effective Use of Self

Professional dancers, athletes, and social workers all share the need for a highly developed and

conscious use of self. Conscious use of self refers to honing and maximizing practice skills; being aware of their strengths, uses, and limitations and of when to and not to use them; and, critically important, being aware of matters and emotions that can cloud judgment. As Judith Vaughan Prather, executive director of the Montgomery County Women's Commission, put it:

Probably the most important thing they teach you in social work school is the conscious use of self; that will serve you extremely well as an administrator and as a community organizer. Whether it's with your staff, your community support, or with policymakers, you have to pose your language in ways to bring about the outcome that you want. . . . If you can put what you want them to know in ways that they are able to hear, you have a much better chance of getting them to do what you want them to do. (Powers, 1994)

Initiative and persistence are basic to any success. While ballet, modern dance, and basketball require mastery over the body and mental control, each requires specialized abilities. Similarly, social work's practice modalities draw on the same aptitudes while requiring the refinement of specific proficiencies.

The fact that social workers draw on the same core skills means that elements of practice learned in one social work modality, such as casework, are transferable to different practice modalities, such as community organizations. Interviewing and information gathering are used in all social work practice. Case workers use these skills to elicit knowledge to improve a client's condition or to run a group more effectively, while community practitioners synthesize information from interviews to undergird an exposé as part of social justice advocacy. Dealing with an upset patient or a very angry community resident by telephone requires corresponding skills.

Social workers develop competence in relating to a variety of people and build on that competence in different aspects of practice. Coordination and advocacy are as important to community practice as counseling is to casework; assertiveness and active listening are essential to all social work practitioners. The skills of coordination, advocacy, active listening, counseling, and assertiveness involve communication. Social workers must be self-aware—that is, be aware of their skills and limitations in shifting settings—and develop an intense awareness of others.

Most fundamentally, use of self implies that a social worker, while open to collegiality and teamwork, must be able to perform solo. He or she may be the only person on the scene who can and will act. Principal dancers are thrown roses or presented with bouquets at the end of performances. Championship athletes are awarded trophies. Nobody brings roses to social workers or gives them a trophy at the end of a job well done; despite that, we have used our minds, hearts, and training to change lives. Our reward comes from doing good, well (Box 7.1).

Skills for Clients and Communities. Self-awareness is a precondition for assertiveness and the foundation of empowerment (Kesby, 2005). Self-awareness, as Descartes' famous quotation holds,[1] is the thinking that is important and determines the being. Self-awareness is a conscious knowledge of one's own character, feelings, motives, desires, strengths, weaknesses, and individuality (Kesby, 2005). It's knowing what makes you tick. Without an understanding, an awareness, of one's self, a person can be aggressive but not truly self-assertive or powerful because the self is unknown.

Self-awareness is empowerment. Power, discussed in Chapter 2, is from the Weberian notion that power is "the chance of a man or of a number

BOX 7.1.	Drawing on Resources, Including Ourselves

At a respite center for parents of totally dependent children, one child was deaf, mute, mentally challenged, and in a wheelchair because of cerebral palsy. Rick's mother communicated with him through story boards. He communicated with others through squeals and jerky arm movements. A social worker drawn to this eager youth attempted to find ways in which Rick could play and express himself. Wooden puzzles were tried successfully. As Rick mastered difficult ones, the worker began to suspect that he had more cognitive ability than had been detected during years of testing and residential programs. She contacted the hospital school, which he had attended, and the public schools for guidance—but to no avail. She spoke to the founder of the respite center and recommended,

based on her observation and assessment, that a special education tutor be found for Rick. Her advice was followed. Within a year, the Rick was reading.

The worker found other ways to open up Rick's world. At home, he often sat on the porch and waved to the traffic. He was particularly pleased when a driver for Pepsi began waving back. The mother and worker contacted the company to thank the driver and ask if he would be allowed to stop and see Rick. The driver not only came to call but also brought a miniature company truck and tiny cases of bottles that fit on the wheelchair tray. Thereafter, Rick whooped and waved his truck whenever the Pepsi truck passed his corner.

of men [i.e., people] to realize their own will in a communal action even against the resistance of others who are participating in the action" (Gerth & Mills, 1958, p. 180). If so, empowerment requires the knowledge of one's will as the ability to act in the face of opposition.

Self-awareness is the source for identity. Identity is a complex concept, although its core is straightforward. A person's identity is who that person and others thinks he or she is. How the perceptions are formed is more intricate. Appiah (2005) discusses personal identity as the individual's self-awareness from a personal construction of a myriad of personal experiences, socialization, and social identities. Social identities are defined as a social grouping that can be identified by shared social and physical characteristics. The social identity is often imposed by the community's more powerful groups, although occasionally a social grouping may self-identify. Social identity has elements of labeling and assumes that all who are given the social identity share the traits. The social identities may not have existed until imposed by dominant, external groups. There were no Amerindians until after Christopher Columbus started the European conquest of the Western Hemisphere. There were no Africans until the Arabs and Europeans so defined them. Social identities are seen differently from the inside than from the outside. The phrase "Black is beautiful" changes a stigmatizing social identity to a positive one.

Personal identity as part of self-awareness is separate from social identity but contributes to it. Both are important in self-awareness and identity. Critics such as Becker (2005) and Goodkind (2009) argue that an overemphasis on developing personal identity defies the critical importance of social identities in both providing opportunities and limiting life chances. The commercialization of feminism, according to Goodkind (2009), has resulted into an overemphasis on self-esteem and personal development—"You can have it all! You can be anything you want to be!"—while ignoring the prerequisite of changing the social identity of women. Feminism as an ideology was instigated to change the social identity of women. Becker (2005) similarly argues that America's therapeutic culture, its "Oprahfication," has over-psychologized the popular construction of power and

largely ignores power's very real social, political, and economic basis. People with less powerful and marginalized social identities can't simply concentrate on personal development and identity while ignoring social change and social identities; they must develop more powerful social identities. Social identity has an element of imposition, and personal identity is constrained by the social identity's inhibitions. Social justice is about changing social identities and removing their inhibition.

Social work suffers from a social identity that it is a soft, often timid, mushy, and overly psychologized profession composed of bleeding hearts and junior shrinks. The following discussion is an endeavor to change that social identity from the inside by changing our collective personal identities. We do not, however, want to ignore the real need for changing social identities by social change for social work and our constituencies.

People integrate abilities and experiences and apply them as needed. For social workers, this is not just self-knowledge and development for personal comfort. Social workers are engaged with individuals and with the larger community. Would a ballet be meaningful if the dancers simply performed the steps without regard to creative interpretation or audience appeal? Community connections are integral to our practice, as is making the community itself a better place. To do this effectively, practitioners need certain attitudes and a broad array of abilities. Attitudinally, community social work practice calls for a vision of communal life and the collective good. It also requires knowledge of human and social problems, of the social forces that keep many of them in place, and of the interventions needed to address them. The decision to consider the community and to draw on all facets of our field does not mean a lessening of interest in or commitment to individuals. All good social work connects the personal to the social, and vice versa (Weiss, 1993). Considering community means getting a better sense of who we are, the needs not addressed, and the social justice required. We want to discover who we are not serving and form new partnerships for service delivery and advocacy. We want to be able to follow any concerns arising out of our work wherever it leads us, confident that our skills are flexible enough to meet most of the challenges of

BOX 7.2.	**Wanted: More Than Rehabilitation**

Jack lost his legs from a slate fall in the mines. . . . [At the hospital] they were trying to rehabilitate him. . . . When the disabled miners first went out on strike with the active miners, Jack was out there in his wheelchair on the picket line. The disabled miners was out to get their hospital cards and their pensions. . . . It was me and Jack that stopped the train during the strike. We didn't have a 12-gauge shotgun like some folks say. . . . We had a sign with us that said Hospital and Pension Card on it. And we just held it up. We was beside the tracks, over on the edge, we didn't really block the train. But they saw our sign and they stopped the [coal] train. They pulled it back into the company's yard.

Source: Della Mae Smith, as quoted in *Hillbilly Women* (pp. 40–43), by K. Kahn, 1973, New York: Avon.

venturing into new professional territory. We want to be able to follow clients and community residents into facets of their lives outside social services. We need to hear their pride: "It was me and Jack that stopped the train" (Box 7.2).

Expansion of Self

Political Aspects

Problems call us into the community if we allow ourselves to hear them. Hartman (1990), a former editor of *Social Work*, worries that we will use "psychic numbing to protect ourselves from the pain of seeing what is going on around us" (p. 4). She is concerned that we can tune in to one youth like Rick (see Box 7.1) but cannot deal with a school where many students are on drugs. Yet, to tune out the community is to deny our mission, our emotions, and our values from its public purpose.

Social workers must enter the political world of civic and community participation, self-governance, and responsiveness to larger problems. A social worker with a full skills repertoire has the ability not only to perform but also to sustain that performance by securing needed resources. Those in social welfare especially must be concerned with national politics and government responsibility. Barber (1984) urges universal participation in public action, politics, and the "realm of we." Social workers, clients, and community constituencies must see political and social action pursuing social justice as part of their personal and social identities. "Politics" is not something to be done by others or left to the politicians.

Achieving true community and strong democracy requires a kind of talking and listening to which social workers can uniquely contribute. Barber (1984) believes that the talk on which democracy builds "involves listening as well as speaking, feeling as well as thinking, and acting as well as reflecting" (p. 178). Talk, participation, and listening are things within social work's inventory. Barber (1984, pp. 178–179) lists "features of talking and listening in public" that are an inventory of civic interactions and obligations:

1. The articulation of interests
2. Bargaining and exchange
3. Persuasion
4. Agenda setting
5. Exploring mutuality
6. Affiliation and affection
7. Maintaining autonomy
8. Witness and self-expression
9. Reformulation and re-conceptualization
10. Community building as the creation of public interests, common goods, and active citizens

Strong democratic talk, according to Barber (1984), involves "deliberation, agenda setting, listening, [and] empathy," and strong democratic action involves "common work, community action, [and] citizen service" (p. 266).

We single out Barber's basic community activities and political talk because such civic engagement is a moral imperative. If we do not have the confidence and willingness to engage as citizens, then it is more difficult for any course of training to transform us into strong professionals.

Social workers must be concerned with Weiss-Gal and Gal's (2009) "non-take-up" challenge presented by individual clients and community constituencies. Social rights and mutual support are only real when they are used. A right not used or exercised, whether to vote or to receive food stamps, is not a right but an illusion. "Non-take-up" is when people legally and/or socially entitled to a right don't use it. Particularly disturbing is when take-up is low in programs targeted at the most vulnerable and disenfranchised social groups, often with social agency and government encouragement. Non-take-up has relevance for individuals, families, and social groups. Social workers have an ethical obligation to prevent, rather than encourage, non-take-up by individuals and communities.

New Routines—Personal Aspects

Some practitioners have limited themselves to the demands of the direct service part of their jobs, so they are untested in macro practice tasks. Too often, apprehension or inexperience restrains them from making the contributions they are capable of making at the board, association, service delivery system, neighborhood, or city level. To make the best use of one's professional self is difficult at any time, but especially when engaging in new aspects of social work or in especially challenging political environments.

Clinicians may be uncomfortable using new types of community assessment or how work in the community is discussed in the community literature. For example, a person accustomed to determining diagnoses using a manual or intuition and experience may be uncomfortable switching to weighing and calculating variables, bargaining, or engaging in social action. Some caseworkers making the transition in practice express discomfort with the analytic language of trade-offs, bottom lines, bargaining chips, and best practices because they say they value openness, empathy, and doing the right thing for its own sake. Yet social work's very emphasis on genuineness, authenticity, and getting in touch with feelings may lead us to simplify ideas and follow impulses too easily at the community level (O'Neill, 1989). Mastering a full repertoire of skills will make us more thoughtful and confident practitioners. Analyzing our anxieties and watching our behavior, we can deal with our attitudes and improve our performance (Drucker, 1999). This is the conscious use of self.

Enhanced Awareness

Cognition and Intuition. Social workers must be visionaries and risk-takers, able to formulate fresh approaches and challenge the status quo. Walz and Uematsu (1997) describe how some people, unfortunately, circumscribe themselves: "A fearful person may shut off many important interior messages and thus refrain from pursuing certain questions.... the person may lack the will or the energy to venture. In maintaining their carefully bounded existence, they will inevitably limit the range and volume of ideas, concepts, and metaphors that they would need to draw upon" (p. 24). Such professionals miss the freedom to experience the calling, the science, and the art of social work. Social workers who meld courage with creativity, on the other hand, can escape boredom and make valuable contributions to their profession and community.

Critical Thinking. We advocate in Chapter 2 a critical consciousness in social work and a critical model of community practice. Critical consciousness entails an open-minded, reflective, and thoughtful approach to critical practice with a careful attention to the context as well as the content of practice. Critical consciousness is akin to Freire's (1994) theory of conscientisation discussed earlier in Chapter 2. Critical consciousness embraces a strong normative dimension of values and assumptions of social justice. There are *oughts* and *shoulds* in critical practice above best practices. The model requires a holistic view of goals, context, content, and values and norms (Butcher, Banks, Henderson, with Robertson, 2007).

In critical community practice, self-assessment is the core. This means looking at one's community practice as from the outside, being open-minded and reflective, with a firm foundation of values and ethics and an unyielding commitment to social justice, empowerment, and anti-oppression (Henderson, 2007, p. 9–10).

The critical practice model's components are (Henderson, 2007, pp. 11–12):

- Critical consciousness by the practitioner of values, ethics, and assumptions about the nature of people, community, and society and how they shape the practice

- Critical theorizing on the scientific basis of empowerment, power, interventions of empowerment, and participatory and deliberative democracy
- Critical action on prime movers and key actors and the roles of both in achieving community empowerment and participatory and deliberative democracy
- Reflective practice (see the section on self-assessment above)

The ability to think clearly is basic to effective critical practice, service, advocacy, and public policy initiatives. Yet too often promising projects are halted or misdirected by conventional wisdom and the use of logical fallacies against them. The 2009 and subsequent health care debate was replete with logical fallacies. A logical fallacy is a misconception based on deceptive or false appearance and deceitfulness, or fraud. Gibbs and Gambrill (1999) provide us with a catalog of the most common logical fallacies:

1. *Ad hominem* (at the person): Attacking (or praising) the person, or feeling attacked (or praised) as a person, rather than examining and staying on the substance of an argument regardless of its presenter. It personalizes the position.
2. *Appeal to authority* (*ad verecundium*): An attempt to bully an opponent into accepting a conclusion by attributing the conclusion, truthfully or not, to a higher authority or recognized expert and playing on the opponent's reluctance to question the conclusion of someone who has a high status or is viewed as the expert
3. *Diversion* (red herring): An attempt to sidetrack people from one argument by introducing another argument, usually more inflammatory, so as to never deal effectively with the first position
4. *Stereotyping*: Oversimplifying about a class of arguments or the people making them by using negative labeling, profiling, and social identities. Sometime the converse stereotyping is done (see "bandwagon").
5. *Manner or style*: Believing or rejecting an argument because of the apparent sincerity, speaking voice, attractiveness, stage presence, likability, or other stylistic traits of an argument's presenter. Like the *ad hominem* fallacy, this tactic attempts to substitute the person for the argument's position.
6. *Groupthink*: The tendency for group members (e.g., of interdisciplinary teams, task groups, service-coordination groups, staff) to avoid sharing useful opinions or data with the group because they fear they might be criticized, might hurt the feelings of other group members, or might cause disunity. This ploy operates on contagion and is similar to stacking a community meeting and a bandwagon tactic.
7. *Bandwagon*: Similar to groupthink's contagion, this fallacy relies on the phrases "they say" (usually an unknown they) and "everyone is doing it or knows it" (usually an unspecified everyone)—so you had better get on the bandwagon.
8. *Either/or* (false dilemma): Stating or implying that there are only two alternative positions available and one, the opposing position, is usually untenable. This fallacy denies the opportunity to explore the true range of options.
9. *Straw man argument*: Misrepresenting a person's argument and then attacking the misrepresentation as obviously a bad choice (pp. 116–119).

Logical fallacies are used to promote or oppose change, and will often be used against the community practitioner. Advocates who encounter these logical fallacies for the first time during meetings or debates can be waylaid or deflected from the real arguments. Even national experts can be thrown off track. The nation's chance for comprehensive health reform was scuttled by television commercials paid for by self-interested insurers during the Clinton administration, and by the radical right during the Obama effort. Several fallacies were used by the typical couple, Harry and Louise, who bemoaned the overly complex bureaucracy and limited choice of doctors they said the Clinton plan would engender (West, Heith, & Goodwin, 1996). Opponents to the 2009-2010 plan used death panels, euthanasia, loss of Medicare, and loss of choice of health care providers to deflect proponents from the real arguments that the United States is the only industrial democracy without universal health care, and we pay the most for the least. Fallacies, deceit, and propaganda must be rebutted quickly and effectively, because have-nots, in this case the uninsured, are hurt by misrepresentation. Unfortunately they were not.

Praxis: Self and Others. Whether engaged in clinical, community, or management work, social workers can be even more effective when they combine the creative and critical thinking just discussed with monitoring of their cognitive and affective reactions to others. We react to others and others react to us. If the social worker is known by a nickname such as "Uncle Roy," as Royal Morales of Los Angeles was, how could that affect community practice? More factors come into play than we usually discern. Consider how universally, even if subliminally, humans react to hairstyles (e.g., pigtails, dreadlocks, "old-lady blue hair") and to hair coverings (e.g., stocking caps, yarmulkes, turbans, babushkas) that differ from their own.

Use of self includes awareness and positive use of one's experiences, background, and characteristics (Christensen, 2002; Lee, McGrath, Moffatt, & George, 2002). To explain more fully, we will examine ideas from Alvarez (2001) and Gilson (2000) about critical reflection, similar to critical consciousness and Bisman's practitioner observation, and attending to oneself as well as to the other party. Gilson suggests that we consider what will happen if we do or do not speak about our person and life. Alvarez suggests that we systematically explore—in a process-recording mode—how others perceive even our nonverbal communication.

Perceptions: How Others See Us. Alvarez stresses the "centrality of personal attributes and the perceptions of other actors, and the need to understand interactions in order to maximize personal and professional effectiveness" (2001, p. 197). Why are attributes and demographic characteristics so consequential? Because, according to Alvarez, "class, use of language, sexual orientation, religion, and physical and mental abilities influence interactions, perceptions and results (p. 199)." The way we view ourselves is not always the same as how others view us, so we must proceed deliberately. Alvarez (2001) has developed a framework called PRACSIS similar to the critical community practice model above. PRACSIS stands for Practitioner Reflection on Actions, Characteristics, and Situation, by Impact and Strategies (see Table 7.1 for parts of her grid). She urges us to pause and reflect. The method involves taking a hypothetical, historical, or actual situation and applying impact analysis. For example, suppose you are a Muslim Arab-American social worker working in a Christian Serbian-American community of first-generation refugees from Kosovo. Your religion and skin color will be more of a factor since the Sept. 11, 2001, attacks, wars and genocide in Kosovo, and the wars in Afghanistan and Iraq. Your professional identity will be shaped by the community's attribution of social identities to you. You must address these attributions and not lose your sense of personal and professional identity as a helper. The processes and skill that you use in addressing the social identity and developing a relationship can enhance

Table 7.1 PRACSIS Grid

Characteristics of Practitioner	Perceived by Practitioner	Perceived by Others (Evidence)	Effects of (+ or -)	Implications for Strategy and Practice
* Mental abilities * Sexual orientation * Religion (if any) * Ethnicity * Other (Specify)				
Actions of Practitioner	Perceived by Practitioner	Perceived by Others (Evidence)	Effects of (+ or -)	Implications for Strategy and Practice
Specify:				

Reprinted with permission of Haworth Press.
Source: From Alvarez, A. R. (2001). Enhancing praxis through PRACSIS: A framework for developing critical consciousness and implications for strategy,", *Journal of Teaching in Social Work, 21*(1/2), pp. 216–218. Reprinted with permission of Routledge.

or hinder your ability to help the community develop a new social identity for you and other social workers and Muslim Arab-Americans. Alvarez's framework is an invitation to think about how others perceive us. It can be used to anticipate or to analyze an interaction with clients or community members.

Disclosures: What We Reveal. Gilson (2000) counsels professionals to think broadly about self-disclosure and sense of purpose. Given specific circumstances, there are positives and negatives to letting others learn more about us. There needs to be general consciousness of others and of one's options, as opposed to automatically divulging or screening facts. Practitioners might ask themselves the following types of questions. If we are involved in community or advocacy organizations, do we share our experiences in a professional situation? What if our involvement stems from something of a personal nature such as having been a battered spouse? Should a professional share that his or her sexual orientation or religion? As a person who has used forearm crutches and a wheelchair, Professor Gilson believes that with an "effective use of self, I am able to address and mediate against negative biases directly and by example. Students do not study me as an object, as might occur in a less direct relationship, but are able to view a disabled person as a source of power and knowledge. This phenomenon is very unusual for people with disabilities since we are most commonly studied as in need of services" (p. 127).

Nevertheless, Gilson maintains that there are multiple issues to consider in relationships. Should social workers discuss their hidden conditions (such as epilepsy or cancer) or their family situations (such as having suicide losses in one's family or having incarcerated family members)? Is the professional overstepping boundaries or burdening others when sharing personal circumstances to a captive client or audience? Has the social worker forgotten the purpose of the relationship? How is it helpful to others to understand the professional's personal experience? Critical practice and self-awareness requires the practitioner to be aware of any impact of disclosures on the client and community. Any disclosures must be in the client's and constituency's benefit, not for the practitioner's aggrandizement (Goode, 2001).

Becoming More Mindful. We must manage ourselves in every situation in every venue. This includes being aware of our public behavior. Since we are connected to and observed by the larger world, how we come across matters. A highly successful human service professional once offered this canny advice, "Never say anything negative on the elevator. Don't grouse or whine. When people ask how your work is going, respond briefly and positively." It is especially important for professionals to be affirmative about the group they are serving, regardless of any personal frustrations. Others rarely embrace the mission, cause, or projects of practitioners who undermine their operation's reputation. Remember the importance of belief bonding. Affirm what can be affirmed and be aware of any public impressions created. Self-discipline, composure, and belief bonding are all parts of effective use of self.

Beliefs That Shape Behavior. Use of self also involves understanding belief systems, including beliefs about professional relationships (Locust, 1995), the practitioner's belief system, and the client's or constituency's belief system. A belief system is the ideology discussed in Chapter 2 is used in the construction of reality. It is a deep-seated conviction about what is true and what can happen. Ideology and beliefs involve expectations based on a construction of reality. Generally, "a placebo effect is any genuine psychological or physiological response to an inert or irrelevant substance or procedure" (Stewart-Williams, 2004, p. 198). The response or change can be either positive or negative, and it is real. Much of what is done in talking therapies depends upon belief bonding and the placebo effect. As Vroom (1964) pointed out in his classic discussion of expectancy theory, much of change is facilitated by expectation of change. Expectancy theory is one of the most popular theories of the placebo effect. In X occurs, then Y will follow as a categorical expectancy. Expectancy is the basis of the deferred gratification pattern operative in education, savings behavior, and physically working out. If people and communities expect that change is possible, they are more likely to work toward it. Conversely, if they expect that it is impossible, that they are powerless to make a change, they probably will be passive. Much of the pessimism in the United States about its youth, schools, or inner cities stems from citizens' sense of powerlessness.

Successful use of self includes a belief in one's ability to effect positive outcomes. Those with such confidence have no illusions about achieving easy victories against bureaucracy nationwide, against reactionary conservatism, against terrorism, against recession, against global warming. But those with confidence reject limiting beliefs about inability and embrace beliefs about capability for change.

Beliefs and Outcomes

Others Belief in Practitioners

Belief bonding is a shared belief by a social worker and a client, a community cadre, or another action system that "the worker is competent, can practice social work, and has knowledge about the problems presented" (Bisman, 1994, p. 79). As discussed earlier, belief bonding appears essential to effective social work and community practice. It is a necessary although a not sufficient condition for psychological and social interventions requiring active client, client system, and action system participation in the intervention process. The concept builds on the fundamentals of the relationship component of social work practice. It shares with the therapeutic alliance the importance of a partnership between client, client system, and action system in community practice and the worker in the intervention processes. It is a critical component of compliance and both the client's and the worker's willingness to participate in and follow an intervention protocol. Belief bonding and the placebo affect appear to be an element in social, mental health, and health interventions (Johnson, 1995; Judson, 2010; Luborsky, Barber, Siqueland, McLellan, & Woody, 1997; Patterson, 1985). In belief bonding, both the client and community

constituency and the worker share a belief that the client or community is worthwhile and has the capacity to change. The social worker must not only be regarded as an expert but must actually possess the expertise. "The worker and the client each need to believe that the worker has something applicable to the client, that the worker is competent, and that the client is worthwhile and has the capacity to change presented situation" (Bisman, 1994, pp. 78–79). As Schilling asserts, most people prefer to be helped by someone who believes in the efficacy of his or her intervention (Schilling, 1990, p. 256; also Patterson, 1985, p. 205). When a client sees or expects that a worker is competent, and the worker communicates self-confidence and fulfills a client's expectation, the client is more likely to fully engage with the worker in an intervention (Patterson, 1985, pp. 202–203) (Box 7.3). The study of leadership generally reveals that confidence in a leader and a leader's methods and program is a critical component in successful leadership (Morrell & Capparell, 2001).

Whether or not the client likes the worker is not at issue and may be important only to the extent that it initially allows for the formation of the bonding or relationship. The bonding is more than just a worker's empathy with a client or constituency; rather, it is an active and shared belief by a client and worker of the worker's efficacy, the rightness of both the goals and the intervention or actions taken, the division of responsibility for tasks, and confidence that accomplishment of the tasks will achieve the goals (Johnson, 1995, p. 37; Kirst-Ashman & Hull, 2008). Clients and communities can't see a social worker and intervention as their adversary.

While research on belief bonding and the therapeutic alliance is not extensive and the results are somewhat mixed, it generally supports that a

BOX 7.3.	**Belief Bonding and Successful Outcomes**

	Client's Belief Intervention Will Be Successful	Worker's Belief Intervention Will Be Successful
	High	**Low**
High	Best probability of success	Success only if the intervention can be mechanistically implemented
Low	Success only if client's involvement in the intervention is unnecessary	Least probability of success

joining, a bonding and relationship, between worker and client on goal and task is essential to success (Coleman, 2000; Kolata, 2001; Loneck & Way, 1997; Luborsky, Barber, Siqueland, McLellan, & Woody, 1997; Mitchell, 1998; Newman, 1997; Stewart-Williams, 2004). Social workers must develop competency in efficacious interventions, believe in their competency, and convey a belief to the client of the efficacy of the helping process and the client's capacity to engage in that process.

Practitioner's Belief in Others

Similarly, the professional also must believe that the client, group, and constituency with whom he or she works (whether drug addicts or people on probation) is worth the attention and capable of achieving their goals. In social work, some professionals opposed welfare reform because they believed that recipients about whom they cared very much had little capacity to obtain or hold jobs. However, we have seen the growing evidence that expectations influence outcomes. If teachers don't think that their inner-city or Indian reservation students will succeed, they probably will not. Research suggests that those who are served by teachers and other professionals achieve results only when the professionals believe the consumers of their services have potential (Furstenberg & Rounds, 1995). A teacher's beliefs can make him or her more effective, regardless of buildings, equipment, and other supports (Agne, Greenwood, & Miller, 1994). Recovering the notion that a teacher has the capacity to affect student performance has been an empowering insight (Greenwood, Olejnik, & Parkay, 1990). In comparison with belief bonding, there is less emphasis in this conceptual framework on the student, client, or recipient buying into the change process. Biddle and Biddle (1979), who write about the "encourager role," make this statement: "People respond to their perception of attitudes as these are expressed in gesture, word, and deed. If the worker acts as though he believes people are unworthy, not to be trusted, or selfishly motivated, his influence is not likely to awaken generous initiative. . . . The beliefs he holds about human beings and his intentions, stated or implied, are important to the outcome in people's lives" (p. 365).

Failure to Act

Situation:

_____

Omission (what was not done):

_____

Consequences:

_____

Discussion:

_____

Suggestions for discussion:

1. Would you act differently in the future? If so, what will you do and why?
2. What factors influenced your decision (e.g., agency policy, feared risks, ignorance)?
3. Can you think of other examples of failing to act when you think you should have acted?
4. What could be done to prevent omissions that limit opportunities to help clients?

Practitioner's Belief in Self

Anyone can be overconfident and act when he or she should not, but our earlier discussions on self-awareness, use of self, critical consciousness, and belief bonding indicate that timidity may be a prescription for failure. Gambrill (1997) suggests the following questions as a way to reflect on a failure to act (p. 47).

Barriers to Action

Belief in yourself is not conceit if it is based on knowing your strengths, and it is required for belief bonding. Persistence and knowing your strengths can be pivotal as you take action. For instance, social work pioneer Vida Scudder founded the College Settlements Association but lost heart as she saw family and social problems repeated generation after generation. Spain, a historian, states, "It may have been Jane Addams'

Experiential Pointers on Moral Courage

- "What words best describe the emotions you feel when hit with all of today's negative news?" (Lappé & Du Bois, 1994, p. 4)
- "If I were feeling strong and powerful, what I'd like to speak out about is . . ."
- "Where do you feel most capable of acting on this issue?" (Shields, 1994, pp. 8–11)

Try this visualization exercise from Shields (1994), designed for "those who want to act but are anxious or afraid of giving way under pressure" (p. 64). "The purpose is to give yourself a bodily sense of calm, groundedness and determination," (p. 64), says Shields.

"Become aware of the soles of your feet . . . aware of the sensation of contact with the ground. . . . Imagine yourself growing roots down into the earth from the soles of your feet. . . . Imagine these roots drawing strength from the earth. . . . Now let that sense of strength travel right up your spine. . . . Be aware of your backbone, feel its strength and also its flexibility. . . .

Now think of those people you are representing here whom you care for; think of their faces, names . . . perhaps also beings of the future generations. . . . Feel the presence of all these standing firmly behind you, lending strength and conviction to what you need to express. . . . Be aware that you may be their only advocate in this situation. . . .

Open your eyes and keep that feeling in your body. . . . Now you are ready to face what comes from a calm and strong position." (Shields, 1994, pp. 64–65)

prodigious staying power in the face of such adversity that propelled her rather than Scudder to the forefront of the settlement movement" (Spain, 2001, p. 118). Belief in oneself often grows with experience. A professional learns when it is helpful to be authoritative, such as during fundraising functions and when testifying in court, and when it is harmful to be authoritative, such as during community feedback forums.

At the community level, insecurity translates as "Society is in sad shape and someone else more capable than I am should do something." This is hardly a mindset to bring about change! Another limiting belief is that we or others are so deficient that nothing can change. Social workers have to prepare and be confident in their competence and ability to energize others. Only those who are confident themselves can kindle others. A first step for igniting one's own fire is to remember what energizes us—perhaps music, literature, family, exercise, mediation, yoga.

Belief in Community

Every community, every narrative needs a note of hope. Banks (2007) points out all communities have capacity for change. Practitioners and the community need to believe this. It is naïve to believe that a belief in change alone is sufficient, but without the expectancy of positive change, any change is likely to be deterioration. In our own fields and our own ways, we must convey hope, as New York City Mayor Rudolph Giuliani did after 3,000 people were killed on Sept. 11, 2001. Terrified citizens needed to believe in their mayor and themselves. Or as Mario Savio did in the 1964 Free Speech Movement (FSM) at the University of California, when he, still largely an unknown before that October day, seized leadership of the FSM by dramatic action.[2] Several thousand students were milling around a Berkeley police car on campus after the arrest of FSM student leader Jack Weinberg. They were in the process of dispersing. Savio grabbed control by shouting "sit down." Savio then took off his shoes and climbed on top of the police car, secured a bullhorn, and, with others, galvanized the students for 36 hours.

Citizens need leaders to be authentic about pain and affirmative about courage. The belief that it can be done, that we can bring about change, that people care and are capable, and that we can move forward is contagious.

Assertiveness: An Overview

Assertiveness should be a social work attribute and skill. Wakefield (1988) views it as "properly within social work's natural domain" (p. 361). It is a psychological or professional trait, like self-respect, confidence, problem-solving ability, and social skills (p. 361). Assertiveness, being assertive, is generally conceptualized as expressing yourself clearly, forcefully, and effectively, standing up for yourself and your point of view where there is some risk of a negative reaction by others, while respecting the legitimate rights of others (Australian Federation of Medical Women, 2010; Kirst-Ashman & Hull, Jr., 2008; Mayo Clinic, n.d., National Institute of Health, 1998; Williams, 2001). Assertive behavior is behavior that allows you to honestly express your desires and position without attacking or having the intent of hurting the other party. Assertion theory is based on the philosophy that every person possesses basic human rights, such as the right to be treated with dignity and respect, the right to refuse requests without feeling guilty, and the right to expression as long as it doesn't violate similar rights for others.

BOX 7.4.	Comparison of Characteristics of Passive, Assertive, and Aggressive Behavior

	Passive	Assertive	Aggressive
Emotional Characteristics	Emotionally dishonest, indirect, self-denial, inhibited, ignores own rights	Emotionally honest, direct, self-enhancing, expressive	Inappropriately emotionally honest, direct, self-enhancing at the expense of others, expressive, dominating and humiliating others
Sender's Feelings	Hurt, anxious, angry, self-depreciating, powerless	Confident, self-accepting, empowered	Righteous, superior, may be guilty later
Recipient's Feelings About Self	Guilty, superior, annoyed	Valued and respected	Hurt and humiliated
Recipient's Feelings About Sender	Irritated, pity, disgust	Generally respect, may be resentment	Anger, desire for revenge, counterattack, resentment

The basic function of assertiveness is to improve communication. As the Mayo Clinic (n.d.) notes, assertiveness is the sweet spot between being too passive or too aggressive (Box 7.4).

Assertiveness should be a characteristic and skill of practitioners, clients, and community constituencies. Assertiveness is necessary for advocacy. Advocacy in the pursuit of social justice, discussed in Chapter 1, is central to social work's fiduciary responsibility. It is contained in most international social work codes of ethics. Social workers are obligated by professional ethics to advocate in social and political arenas for an equitable distribution of the community's physical, economic, and other social resources for social justice (National Association of Social Workers, 2008). Advocacy isn't passive.

For clients, assertiveness is indispensable for self-determination, empowerment, participation, and the ability to resist injustice (Foster-Fishman, Nowell, Deacan, Nievar, & McCann, 2005). Assertiveness is empowering. Empowerment is the process whereby clients increase their self-control and ability to act in the face of opposition and gain an enhanced sense of self-efficacy. Empowerment is something that can be developed with clients (Foster-Fishman, Nowell, Deacan, Nievar, & McCann, 2005; Handy & Kassam, 2007; Kesby, 2005; Ohmer, 2008; Pearrow, 2008; Peterson & Hughey, 2003). It is enhanced through social participation in community organizations.

The history, theory, and practice of assertiveness are linked with the human potential movement, encounter groups, and sensitivity training; the women's movement and consciousness raising (Enns, 1992); business success ideas (Siress, with Riddle & Shouse, 1994); empowerment; and behavior therapy and social learning theory (see Chapter 2). Although different terms—taking charge, sticking up for yourself (Kaufman & Raphael, 1990), or empowering yourself (Harris & Harris, 1993)—are now used, ideas about assertiveness have entered into both the popular culture and the specialized training of professionals.

Assertiveness is a learned social skill and a communication style frequently discussed in terms of three response patterns: passive, aggressive, and assertive. Before discussing these frameworks, we will examine assertiveness in a more personalized way, although recognizing that its meaning is in social interaction.

The Psychology of Assertion

Assertiveness Starts With Us. Competent involvement in the processes of conflict and change, which lie at the heart of the social work enterprise, begins with articulation, with the overcoming of apprehension, with assertion.

From childhood, human beings engage in a process of sorting out the right to refuse from stubborn resistance, the desire to please from passive acquiescence, tact from timidity, circumspection from cowardice, and assertion from aggression. They learn to understand their motivations and behavior in this realm and to interpret signals and signs from family, acquaintances, and strangers. With difficulty, people learn to

Grace said we had to go get a chicken for dinner. [She] walked around in the yard, looking at all the birds, and finally spied one she liked. She chased it until she caught both the wings flat, with the chicken squawking the whole time. . . .

I didn't never think on killing nothing to eat and didn't want to do it. . . . Now Grace wanted me to kill the chicken and I didn't want to, so I tried to back away, only she said, "I know you are strong enough to do this, Jodi."

She stuck out the handle to the hatchet, but I couldn't take it. I shook my head no and said, real quiet, "I don't want to, ma'am". . . .

I ran into the barn. I climbed the ladder and went behind some hay and pulled it all over me till nobody could see me and stayed real quiet. I sucked in air and didn't give it back. Grace came and called out, "Jodi, I'm sorry if I scared you. It's all right if you don't want to help. Jodi? You don't have to hide. It's all right."

But *I was thinking on* how I told a grown-up no and didn't do what she said. I knew I was going to get whipped. Paul and Grace would send me and Brother back because I was bad. . . .

I watched Grace real good the rest of the time before bed, but she never said nothing about the chicken or me not being good. She never said nothing about it ever again.

Source: Sears, V. (1990).Grace, *Simple Songs*. Ithaca, NY: Firebrand Books., . .

stand up for themselves and others and to deal with the consequences. To be a mature, assertive person means taking risks. The story in Box 7.5 speaks to a universal challenge: standing up to adults as a child (Sears, 1990, 1993).

Assertiveness has been recommended as a way to reduce anxiety and depression and to enhance mental health (Australian Federation of Medical Women, 2010; Mayo Clinic, n.d., National Institute of Health, 1998; Williams, 2001). The Australian Federation of Medical Women (2010) notes that people who are unable to act assertively can become frustrated and resentful towards others for taking advantage of them, are often unable to express emotions effectively, and may limit their opportunities by avoiding situations in which they feel uncomfortable or lack confidence. The Mayo Clinic (n.d.) holds that "[a]ssertiveness can help control stress and anger and improve coping skills for mental illnesses." Although circumstances may require anything from saying "no" to curbing abuse, the essence is similar: "When you assert yourself, you communicate your positive or negative feelings honestly and directly" (Zuker, 1983, p. 12).

Increasing your assertiveness involves taking a more rational approach to events previously dominated by uneasiness and, often, fear. It may

Midnight. You sit in a hospital waiting room with someone who called you in a suicidal state and needs a consult and probably a prescription. The police arrive with a woman, high on drugs, who twists to get away. They handcuff her to a leg of the couch near you. She shrieks and tries to free herself. One officer slaps and kicks her. "Shut up," he yells. She makes a scene—cursing and ripping off her blouse—as the receptionist routinely goes over paperwork with the other officer. As the policeman stands over her, you are silent, sickened. You are concerned for the woman but also about the effects of all this on your client. You know things like this go on but a part of you wants out of there—you are not, after all, the woman's advocate. You try to make sense of the situation. You consider waiting things out, covering the woman up with your jacket, pointing out to the policeman that she is defenseless even though behaving obnoxiously, going outdoors with your client, telling off the brutal cop, appealing to the receptionist, and asking the other officer to simmer things down.

"There are five key steps in assessing a situation and becoming aware of what you intend to do: your sensations, interpretations, feelings, desires, and intentions," says Zuker (1983, p. 56). Thus, I see, I think, I feel, I want, I will. However, we need not act on everything we become aware of.

involve re-evaluating a lifelong stance or simply learning new scripts for specific situations. Ordinarily assertion, even assertion involving potential conflict, as in Box 7.6, is not as "dangerously risky" as nonassertive people are prone to think (Rakos, 1991, p. 66). We tend to make the other person into a dragon. Training allows us to face realistic "negative consequences" while knowing that the probability is that "appropriate" assertion will actually lessen risks (Rakos, 1991, p. 66).

The Boundaries of Assertion

Communication Response Styles

Alberti and Emmons (1990) believe that **assertive** behavior "promotes equality in human relationships" (p. 26). Those acting assertively, according to Drury (1984), "make clear, direct, nonapologetic statements" about expectations and feelings and criticize in "a descriptive rather than a judgmental way" (p. 3)—for example, "I'd like you to hear me out." They describe their own reactions to a situation. We can see that this would be important to act effectively in the waiting room incident. Assertiveness is a strong, steady style, not a formula for automatic success. When assertive people meet resistance, Drury (1984) says they persist in "following through on issues"; they also negotiate, compromise, and listen to others respectfully (p. 3). They are accountable and responsible for their behavior. Basic assertiveness skills include (Mayo, n.d.):

- Be aware of nonverbal behaviors such as animation, body language, and appropriate eye contact. Maintain a neutral or positive body stance and facial expression. Don't use dramatic gestures. It can help to practice in front of a mirror.
- Use "I" statements. "I" statements lets others know what you're thinking without sounding critical—for instance, "I disagree" rather than "you're wrong" or "I'm uncomfortable that we haven't reached a decision" rather than "why can't we reach a decision?" This does not mean that the "you" is forbidden, but rather that the response is not an attack.
- Practice saying "no" if you have trouble refusing overload or inappropriate requests. Don't equivocate, don't apologize; be direct, and

keep explanations to inappropriate requests specific and brief.
- Rehearse and role-play, with yourself or colleagues, scenarios that have been or may be challenging. It may help to write it out first, but remember it won't go as scripted, so keep the theme and your self-awareness central.

Non-assertive or **passive** behavior can result from being overly deferential to authorities and people perceived as being powerful, and lacking self-awareness and a sense of personal identity. Non-assertive behavior confuses the boundaries by hiding your real position. If the other party is concerned, it forces that party to seek out your's true position. If unconcerned, then the position is never considered. Passive people are seen as shy or easygoing, go with the group's decision, and avoid all conflict. The message, and perhaps sense of self, of the passive person is that his or her thoughts, opinions, and feelings aren't as important as other people's. Passive behavior gives others the license to disregard the passive person's wants and needs.

The passive person may believe that behaving passively simply keeps the peace and prevents conflicts. But, according to the Mayo Clinic (n.d.), what it really does is get in the way of authentic relationships. And worse, it can cause internal conflict, as the passive person's needs always come second. This internal conflict may lead to stress, resentment, seething anger, feelings of victimization, and a desire to exact revenge.

A passive person's real position is hidden by nonassertive behavior with expressions such as "I guess," "I wonder if you could maybe . . .," "It's not really important," and "Maybe I'm wrong." Such expressions aim to disarm the recipient by presenting a weakened picture of the speaker or writer. The frequent, habitual use of "like" and "like, you know" weakens and confuses assertive communication. Is the meaning the message or something similar to the message, or perhaps the listener already knows but not really? Nonverbal passive responses resulting in the same effect include don't-hurt-me stances, downcast eyes, shifting of weight, a slouched body, whining, hand wringing, a childish tone of voice, and the "poor-me" seduction of others. It is manipulative.

Aggression appears in many forms. **Aggressive** behavior is conduct with intent to dominate, hurt, demean, or diminish another. Aggressive behavior intrudes on the rights of others by demeaning the other's position, opinions, feelings, opinions. The aggressive person can be a physical, emotional, and intellectual bully who disregards the needs, feelings, and opinions of others. Aggressive people come across as self-righteous and superior. Very aggressive people humiliate and intimidate others, and may even be physically threatening and abusive. Aggressive people may get what they want, but it comes at a high cost of a loss of trust and respect, resentfulness, and aggression or passive-aggression directed back at them.

Aggressive practitioners, interested in winning and dominating, may want to prove to clients their superiority and fail to check out the client's feelings in this situation. Aggressive behavior can injure, demean, or diminish another person through words with an implied threat such as "you'd better" and through behavior such as using a raised, haughty, snickering, or snarling tone of voice or pointing a finger in the face. Some white-collar aggression is layered under propriety, disguised by parliamentary and bureaucratic procedures, or passive-aggressiveness of doing nothing (Phelps & Austin, 1987, p. 25). Extreme passivity can be an aggressive tactic.

Actors and Applications

Situations calling for assertion permeate all facets of practice and intimate life. We need assertion skills, and so do our clients.

Acting Assertively

The basics of assertiveness, to Phelps and Austin (1987), are "saying no, expressing anger, recognizing the Compassion Trap, shedding the need for approval, giving up excessive apology" (pp. 1–2). (For example, we may, out of compassion, feel that we must always be on call or helpful.) Rakos (1991) points out that "assertiveness comprises interpersonal expressiveness in both positive and negative contexts." A literature review by Schroeder, Rakos, and Moe (as cited in Rakos, 1991, p. 15) delineated seven categories of assertive responses: admitting shortcomings, giving and receiving compliments, initiating and maintaining interactions, expressing positive feelings, expressing unpopular or different opinions, requesting behavior changes by other people, and refusing unreasonable requests. For many people, the first hurdle is handling praise and criticism, not conflict. Therefore, in assertiveness groups—as in encounter groups—individuals learn to accept strokes and to give positive and negative opinions or reactions.

An assertive act may be quite simple:

- You ask questions of a lecturer.
- A colleague says you are good with protective service clients, and you respond with a "thank you" instead of disclaimers, false modesty, or a return compliment.
- Your coordinator asks you to review a paper. You thoughtfully mark up the draft to suggest reorganization.

Taking the Lead

Assertiveness is not, at heart, simply a matter of demeanor, accepting praise, or adroit handling of social predicaments. It is self-advocacy:

- A social worker with seniority on an interdisciplinary team suggests that team leadership rotate, rather than having only the psychiatric staff be leaders.
- Parents of seriously emotionally disturbed children raise the point that they need respite care, not a proposed party, during the holidays.
- A frail person says to a volunteer, "Let me hold onto you instead of you holding onto me," thus asserting a modicum of control over her life.

Assertiveness is a tool to use in our work lives (Ryan, Oestreich, & Orr, 1996). It enables a quiet staffer to ask a vocal colleague to stop talking over him at staff meetings. It helps a social worker to sell her project to the rest of the staff at a meeting. It helps supervisors. Drury (1984) asks what an appropriate assertive statement would be under these circumstances: "The group has just spent 15 minutes of a 1-hour staff meeting complaining about clients, the agency, and the newspapers. Four items need to be discussed at the meeting." Drury suggests saying, "I'm concerned because we have four items we need to discuss at this meeting. I would like to move on" (pp. 171–172).

There is no simple formula for assertiveness. Still, some people are listened to more than others—and it is important to be heard. Two people can say the same thing quite differently, according to Tannen (1994): "They may speak with or without a disclaimer, loudly or softly, in a self-deprecating or declamatory way, briefly or at length, and tentatively or with apparent certainty. They may initiate ideas or support or argue against ideas raised by others. When dissenting, they may adopt a conciliatory tone, mitigating the disagreement, or an adversarial one, emphasizing it" (p. 280).

Assertiveness can be learned. We have presented some methodologies above. Remember, learning to be assertive takes time and practice. If you've spent years silencing yourself or being too aggressive and bullying, becoming more assertive won't happen overnight.

Regardless of our background, for assertiveness or self-advocacy to be effective, we must learn to manage situations and ourselves (Lerner, 1991; Rivera, 1990; Zunz, 1998). Shoma Morita posits three principles (developed from Zen Buddhism) that appear relevant to effective assertive behavior (Morita, as cited in Clifton & Dahms, 1993, pp. 164–165):

- Know your purpose: Know what you want to accomplish, as (perhaps) distinct from what others want you to accomplish or what you want others to believe (i.e., you simply want to get through the meeting or encounter looking as though you care, not communicating information or having others adopt your position).
- Accept your feelings: Accept being angry, scared, and so on, but recognize that while you are not responsible for feelings, you are responsible for how you manage them and your behavior.
- Do what needs to be done: Put your energy into developing and using the skills needed to deal with a situation, not avoiding or being anxious over it. Actively choose the strategy for managing the situation.

More than personal communication skills are involved. Tannen's (1990, 1994) communication research reveals differences by gender, race, culture, and context. Rakos, summarizing assertiveness research, concurs that the content and style of communication will vary "according to situational, social, and cultural norms and values" (Rakos, 1991, p. 18). Attitudes of the sender and receiver influence whether someone is listened to, but we focus on the sender. Status differences and differences between social work and other professions echo gender differences. Some have no desire to move toward their opposite and defend noncompetitive stances. Similarly, no matter how assertive someone is, some hearers will experience him or her as aggressive or passive.

Regarding context, our behavior as individuals varies according to the situation (e.g., are we at the office picnic or a meeting?). Regarding diversity, there will be a continuum of assertive behavior for those of similar background or those of the same gender and striking differences between various groups. For example, one small study of faculty meetings found that men speak more often and longer than women. Tannen says that women are more likely to "speak at a lower volume, and try to be succinct so as not to take up more meeting time than necessary." In the study, the "longest contribution by a woman was still shorter than the shortest contribution by a man" (Tannen, 1994, pp. 279–280). There is no ideal length of time to talk, so long as everyone is getting a turn. "There is no a priori correct assertive response, though there are general behavioral guidelines for effective expression of feelings and desires," according to Rakos (1991, p. 24; Stevens, Baretta, & Gist, 1993).

In another study, personnel officers listened to tapes of prospective female employees—half with "unassertive speech features." Those without such features were described as "more likely to succeed in the workplace, more likely to be chosen for management positions, and more likely to be respected by coworkers" (Knotts, 1991). Examples of powerless language that makes speakers seem indecisive, tentative, and lacking in authority are tag questions ("John is here, isn't he?"), hedges ("I'd kind of like to go"), hesitations ("Well . . ."), and intensifiers ("Really . . ."). Men are perceived negatively when they use unassertive speech features. Drawing from other studies, Knotts states that "men use speech to report, to compete, to gain attention, and to maintain their position in a social hierarchy," while "women use speech to gain rapport, maintain relationships, and reflect a sense of community" (Knotts, 1991, pp. 1–32).

Tannen (1990) makes an intriguing, controversial contention along these lines: "Sensitivity training [and therapy] judges men by women's standards, trying to get them to talk more like women. Assertiveness training judges women by men's standards and tries to get them to talk more like men" (p. 297). She believes that learning each other's strategies and habits increases our flexibility as communicators. The authors of this text take the position that both men and women in social work can benefit from increasing their assertiveness. Assertiveness in its basic form, Phelps and Austin (1987) remind us, was never gender-specific but rather a way of pushing past blocks or "confronting the unpleasant or difficult without getting squashed (or squashing others) in the process" (p. 80).

Assertiveness and Class or Minority Status

Analysis or assessment of assertive behavior requires an awareness of individual, gender, and cultural differences (Lordan, 2000; Ohbuchi & Takahashi, 1994; Zane, Sue, & Kwon, 1991). Differences in what constitutes assertiveness speak to the *emic* (culturally specific) nature of assertion, according to Yoshioka (1995). She studied differences in styles and values associated with assertiveness in African-American, Caucasian, and Hispanic (mostly Mexican) low-income women living in north Florida. Contrary to her expectations, Hispanic women were found to be the most assertive by conventional and Hispanic criteria. When they had to make a request or demand of a friend, Hispanics were more likely to preface their assertive statement with a positive affirmation of the friendship.

Yoshioka (1995) makes a number of useful observations:

1. Besides linguistic differences, there may be value differences between cultures. "Mainstream" assertiveness rests on rights, individualism, personal control, and self-reliance—values not necessarily equally endorsed by other cultural communities. There are differences regarding an individual's connections and obligations to others.
2. The basic message of a response must be identified apart from the language chosen to convey it. Responses may differ in word construction and intensity of language from the way a practitioner speaks but may still be considered a culturally appropriate, assertive response within the community. Language such as "Any time you push on me, I'm going to push you

right on back" was viewed as assertive, not aggressive, by African-Americans in the study. Hispanics placed more emphasis on correctly addressing the other party and using good manners. Caucasians and African-Americans more often referred to consequences or obligations to elicit compliance from the other party.
3. There are differences within a population, just as there are between racial and ethnic groups. Individual Caucasian reactions in one role-play in the study went from inability to formulate a response to threats to kill. Individual African-Americans had fewer types of aggressive acts but used behaviors that other groups defined as aggressive. They were more direct and forthright in their strategies than were Caucasians and Hispanics.
4. People from varied backgrounds differ in where they place the boundaries between passivity, assertiveness, and aggressiveness.

Even if other studies find different particulars about these cultures, Yoshioka's conclusion is germane: Understanding specific ways a culturally different client may approach a given situation could enhance social work effectiveness. Each group of women in the study could stand up for themselves, but they acted according to different notions of appropriate personal conduct. This was particularly true when the other party in the role-play mistreated them. Would they accept an apology? Shove back?

Purposes and Benefits of Assertiveness in Social Work

Philosophy and Character

The underpinnings of assertion in practice are (1) security about ourselves and our self-awareness; (2) confidence about our facts, research, and homework; and (2) our knowledge that we developed a critical consciousness and have examined the situation carefully. Assertiveness is a particularly useful skill for integrated practice, since it is applicable in expressive therapies, casework, group work, administration, community work, and social reform. It relates to other key practice concepts—empowerment, personal power, advocacy, client self-determination, behavioral change, and ethics.

A Means to Important Ends

Assertiveness may well be a prerequisite for working in the community, an experience that almost immediately requires us to interact with strangers, officials, and competitive organizations. Assertiveness is an umbrella term for many positive attributes: initiative, persistence, poise, spunk, alertness, responsiveness, and the ability to defend oneself or being at the top of one's form. The development of assertiveness is meant to enable the social worker to:

• Identify, be in command of, and be comfortable with personal power and the assertion of basic human rights
• Provide a model for and teach assertiveness to the client and the client/citizen system, and help them realize and use their power
• Use personal power appropriately in advocacy and other interpersonal, organizational, and political situations

Although the emphasis is usually on personal assertion, the importance of examining political assertion (i.e., being the squeaky wheel that gets greased) has been urged as well. Alberti and Emmons (1990, p. 15) believe that if we become "expressive enough, governments usually respond. . . ." The growth and successes of assertive citizen lobbies—minority, homeless, children's, gay, elderly, and other rights movements, the AARP and the Gray Panthers, the various tax reform movements, including the "Tea Baggers" (aka Tea party)—are powerful evidence: assertion works and passivity doesn't!

Why Are Assertiveness Skills Important for Social Workers?

Being personally or professionally assertive is a respectful act, one implying that the other person can be (at least somewhat) trusted to behave responsibly, not to retaliate, and to remain open to a closer relationship. Lange and Jakubowski (1976) add two other aspects: respect for oneself and for the other person's needs and rights (pp. 7–8). The more difficult implementation of this philosophy focuses on interactions with involuntary clients, where respect and an awareness of clients' strengths are important but where issues of control and structure play a part in most communication transactions (Cowger, 1994, p. 263). Failing to assist clients, including involuntary clients, to be assertive rather than passive or aggressive is to deny them self-determination and social justice. As Weiss-Gal and Gal (2009) argue, a client who is not assertive in a somewhat intolerant and resistant social services world may become a "non-take-up" (someone who doesn't take up his or her legally entitled social rights). Weiss-Gal and Gal point out that it is "[p]articularly disturbing . . . that take-up is low in programs targeted at the most vulnerable social groups. Moreover, members of excluded social groups are particularly unlikely to access the services and benefit programs for which they are eligible" (p. 267). We have to be able to deal effectively with people who may oppose change and social justice.

Clients and Community. Assertiveness by social work practitioners contributes to the interests of clients and the community. Increased assertiveness benefits those with whom we interact and assist directly or indirectly. When we are stronger, there is a valuable ripple effect. We model behavior for our clients and community constituents. Assertive people are more likely to speak up to government and nongovernment operations for individual and community social rights.

Being assertive can contribute to physical self-preservation. Self-defense calls for decisive acts—running out into the street, for instance, or stopping a passing stranger. Practitioners are becoming increasingly worried about their safety in dealing with clients and the community (Box 7.7). In response to this concern, there are workshops on "Street Smarts for Social Workers" and "The Intimate Terrorist" (National Association of Social Workers—Maryland Chapter, 1995), and the *Encyclopedia of Social Work* includes an entry on "Social Worker and Agency Safety" (Griffin, 1995). A study found that social work students are more likely to be exposed to verbal or physical violence within the agency than outside (Tully, Kropf, & Price, 1993, p. 195). As more students come from suburbia, with little urban life experience, their sense of danger in field placements and on the job is heightened. Increased confidence and competence will help quell irrational fears and prevent injuries in times of actual danger (Weisman & Lamberti, 2002).

BOX 7.7.   **Personal Safety in the Field**

A thoughtful student responded to the dilemma of serving the neediest while exercising caution by taking hold of the situation; the following is her advice.

"I feel strongly that social workers (and doctors and lawyers and . . .) have an obligation to work where our clients are. If I am unwilling to visit an elderly, homebound woman because I fear her neighborhood, how can I be comfortable, as her social worker, if she continues to live in such a dangerous place? For home visiting, I take several commonsense, precautionary steps. These include:

- Bringing a second person along when I feel a need for additional support (One older woman took her Labrador retriever along for the ride);
- Always telling someone exactly where I'm going, how to reach me (if there is a phone), who I'll be meeting, and when I'll be back;

- If possible, having the client or another known person watch for my arrival and even come out to escort me into the apartment/house;
- Limiting visits to daytime hours, preferably mornings; and
- Driving to appointments, so I can park close to the place I'm going and control when I leave. (I went through a period without a car and felt more vulnerable, although nothing actually happened.)

There is recognition in the surrounding area that we are a place worth having around. Our clients are a part of the overall organization, and they are also our neighbors. My sense is that we are protected by our reputation and our role in the community."

Source: Sara Cartmill, social worker.

From the District of Columbia to Hawaii, people feel or are in peril; therefore, professionals must develop "peacemaking" skills to deal with potential violence (Colburn, 1994, p. 399). Social work training allows us to help protect others from danger—for example, in the workplace, where we can plan ahead using threat assessment teams (Masi, 1994, p. 23). Assertiveness is needed to implement precautions, as well as to continue working effectively when precautions are not possible.

Increasing Successes. Becoming more assertive in our outreach to the community includes believing that we are worth listening to, as the following experience reveals:

I was invited to a dinner of the Board of the Department of Social Services, and I was the last agenda item. The president announced that we would be finished in time for the football game. I thought by the time they got to me I'd have 10 minutes. I spoke about the local jurisdiction putting an extra fee on the cost of issuing a marriage license and using that fee to help fund domestic violence programs. By providing them with this information, I got their attention. They stayed past 9:00 and that was the vehicle they ended up using. . . . That was the beginning of a community effort and we also established a rape crisis center, so it all worked out well. (Heisner, in Powers, 1994)

Because she resisted the impulse to cut short her remarks, this social worker helped create a

new funding stream to support two additional community services.

Success may follow the discomfort associated with being invited to speak to a large or important group. Advocates can be asked to speak on their area of expertise and still be unnerved by short notice, the type of audience (highly visible leaders or unfriendly participants), or fear of failure. Many individuals dread being the center of attention. To overcome stage fright, we need to go beyond mere speaking to assertively making a case for action—or inaction.

For those of us who help with charity auctions, annual and capital giving campaigns, and phone-a-thons, a third difficult area could be asking others to volunteer or to give money. Yet success is vital to our organizational survival. Resource development requires networking and meeting with contacts and is highly reliant on using assertiveness skills (Klein, 1996).

Broader Conceptions of Assertiveness

Assertiveness involves competent communication and more. It involves self-awareness and professional competence. Beyond techniques, it involves competence in professional knowledge and skills rooted in professional values and obligations. We want to increase our competence and that of those we serve, and elevate our and their aspirations.

Becoming More Hopeful

Jansson (1990) links assertiveness with power and winning. He argues that assertiveness is "undermined" by fatalism and a victim mentality, both of which deny individual potency. These ideas are similar to the irrational beliefs that assertiveness training tries to overcome, such as that "one's past dictates one's future" (Lange & Jakubowski, 1976, p. 135). Fatalism contributes to societal cynicism and to our own passivity and submission. Jansson (1990) says it well: "The effective use of power requires people to decide in the first instance that they possess power resources, that they can use them effectively, and that they want to use them. The word assertiveness describes this proclivity to test the waters rather than to be excessively fatalistic" (p. 154).

To illustrate an assertive orientation to power within an agency, Jansson (1990) gives the example of a hospital social work administrator who learned to make repeated requests for increased funds, even though a number of her entreaties were fruitless. Her justifications educated the decision makers and sent a signal of confidence. "Unlike departments with more timid executives, her department gained in size and stature as she assertively sought resources for her department," points out Jansson (p. 155). Expectancy can replace fatalism, a sense of potency can replace a sense of victimization, and hopefulness can replace helplessness (see Chapter 2).

An assertive orientation to power outside an agency might involve governmental funding. Social workers must make regular personal contact with policymakers and test the waters by assertively stating what problems should receive priority attention, what services should receive full funding, and what cuts should be made in other sectors of the economy to protect social service resources.

Participating in social organizations and in social action by practitioners with clients and by clients has been found to be empowering and to increase assertiveness. Practitioners should mobilize clients to participate in community organizations and social action to build the capacity of the organizations and to become empowered (Foster-Fishman, Nowell, Deacon, Nievar, & McCann, 2005; Handy & Kassam, 2007; Ohmer, 2008; Pearrow, 2008).

Phelps and Austin (1987) caution, however, that while "broadscale social issues . . . [cruelty to animals, drunk driving] can be influenced with assertive attention. . . . It's also important not to regard assertion as a cure-all for every social ill or as a simplistic way to achieve personal strength and self-worth. Real problems are stubborn and significant change requires patience and power" (pp. 243–244).

As we continue our exploration of assertiveness, it is important to keep the above caveat in mind, as well as the cautions offered by Becker (2005) and Goodkind (2009) in their critiques of contemporary feminism. Much of assertive training has become commercialized and popularized as slogans (Be all that you can be, You can be anything you want) and over-individualizing and personalizing social roles. Social change is necessary as well as self-development and self-advocacy. Assertive skills need to be applied to social as well as individual benefits.

While empowering ourselves, social workers need to work with clients and community constituencies to increase their opportunities. Within health care settings, for instance, assertive people will "perform a valuable function" if they acknowledge, support, and protect patients' rights (Angel & Petronko, 1983, p. 94). Social workers can actively advocate for and abet patients in getting their rights (Weiss-Gal & Gal, 2009). Extrapolating from Angel and Petronko (1983, p. 95), social workers and other service givers can, as part of their informed consent and self-determination obligations:

- Educate clients that they have basic human rights and more specific rights as clients. Generally, they do not give up other rights when they become clients; if they do, these should be clearly detailed.
- Provide written information about rights, obligations, and appeal processes.
- Help clients evaluate the advantages and disadvantages of asserting their rights.
- Assist clients in planning for successful assertion.
- Promise and deliver support if clients decide to exercise their assertion and appeal rights.

- If required, help clients navigate through the appeal and complaint process.
- When necessary, assist clients in enlisting the help of an ombudsman and consumer advocacy or rights group, or clients rights group. (p. 95)

Becoming Open to Challenge

During the past few decades, advocates have worked to demystify law and medicine and to highlight the right to challenge lawyers, psychiatrists, and other traditional authority figures in a respectful, polite, and cordial manner. At a behavioral level, if a patient/consumer goes to another physician to get a second opinion without telling the first, that shows independence of mind and constitutes an indirect challenge (Haug & Lavin, 1983), but patients/consumers who are able to tell the original physician they are seeking a second opinion are assertive and capable of direct challenge. Assertiveness comes into play because the patient has a goal or agenda that should not have to be subordinated to the physician's personality or expectations. Those who become preoccupied with the doctor's feelings or get trapped by timidity may never get that second opinion; here non-assertiveness can have life-and-death consequences.

This trend has relevance to social work field for three reasons. First, social workers are the beneficiaries of a new relationship between professions, and between consumers and professionals, that supports us as equal players on an intervention team. Second, however, we must stay alert to ways in which our service users are "consumers" and treat them the way we like to be treated by the professionals in our lives (Tower, 1994). Third and most important, we should encourage service users and citizens with whom we work to be assertive with us, not just with others; we need to be strong enough to engage in mutual participation, with initiative coming from either party (Gutierrez, 1990; Simon, 1990). As a logical outgrowth, some social workers encourage the formation of client, resident, or user groups to play a watchdog role.

Becoming Bolder

A social worker cannot function effectively as a client advocate, a legislative advocate, or a community advocate without standing up for what is necessary in the circumstance. The right to be assertive carries with it the responsibility to be assertive. It is the take-up of the right that challenges integrity and presents the risks (Box 7.8).

Communities often hide the existence as well as the nature of problems. Close examination is necessary to deal with this and to find out what actions can be taken to eliminate the problems. Social workers may have a duty to be assertive when passivity keeps a social misery or injustice in place. Williams (1978) comments on the skills that investigative reporters need to overcome secrecy and hostility. Social workers and community practitioners need the same skills. He calls for guts and warns against gullibility. The focus is on will and willingness. "If you are afraid to argue, if you dread being shoved around, if you hate to go back after your polite requests for information have been refused—then you probably will not be a successful investigative reporter. If you believe something is true simply because a person in authority says it is true, you are in trouble" (Williams, 1978, p. 8). You probably will not be a successful community practitioner either. We may too easily condone passiveness in providers, consumers, and citizens. Then, when advocacy is required, not even the first

BOX 7.8.	In Praise of Giraffes

Chancing rejection and embarrassment, a staffer for World Vision went up to a conservative member of Congress from Virginia who was making a campaign stop in a shopping mall. She recruited him, on the spot, to take a trip to a famine site across the globe. This trip permanently committed him to eradication of hunger and misery (Harden, 1995).

Many individuals risk far more, and their valor is honored by activists of different types. The late Senator Paul Wellstone of Minnesota risked his political career to stay true to his principles. Corporate and FBI whistle-blowers have risked their jobs to tell the public about covert practices of their organizations. Giraffes are too rare when compared to ostriches.

step—assertiveness—has been mastered. Even popular magazines are beginning to reflect a broader view of bold assertiveness. Box 7.9 gives pointers on having *moxie*.

The Context and the Setting for Assertive Behavior

Limitations to Universality

Although assertive rights can and have been stated, these do not have the force of law, as do the rights of airline passengers in our country to smoke-free flights. Most "rights," perhaps contrary to Thomas Jefferson's unalienable rights, are culturally bounded. To expand rights means that culture must be expanded. Typical assertiveness training stresses rights as if they are available everywhere, but it may not acknowledge that our assertive requests will be denied more frequently, the further we get from our communities. A related criticism is that even within our own communities and culture, some assertiveness training professionals fail to alert trainees to "and/or prepare them for the possibility of retaliation or other highly negative reactions from others" (Alberti & Emmons, 1990, Appendix C).

Social Status Nuances

Success in assertiveness does not depend solely on personality characteristics; gender, race, and social status play a role, too. Political and sociological factors must be considered. Assertiveness is more likely to be "accepted from those who have traditionally had power, while it may not be accepted from those who have not had power" (Drury, 1984, p. 133). Those who are part of a dominant culture more easily master assertiveness. Yoshioka (1995) argues, "Assertiveness as it has been defined is reflective only of the dominant socio-cultural group." Others, such as Rakos (1991, p. 78), have confused social class with culture and oversimplify assertive behavior as a largely white, upper-class, well-educated mode of expressing one's preferences. (Evidently, Rakos has avoided Brooklyn or South Philly in this judgment, as the following discussion reveals!) Transactions with persons from different backgrounds require us to be adaptable, considerate of the way their preferences are expressed, and aware of power differentials between us. But, ideally, we all will be assertive.

Cultural Nuances

For practical reasons, Rakos (1991) suggests, many minorities will need and want to be "biculturally" assertive. They will benefit from knowing (1) what is considered assertive in both cultures, (2) how to function effectively in any dominant system or culture, and (3) what norms will be violated in their (sub)culture if standard

---

BOX 7.9.	**It Is Not All Right With Me!**

- Stating your needs unequivocally, with the sense that you have a right to state them, is half the battle.
- Sometimes, the truth hurts. Get used to it.
- You can be blunt without being a tactless cretin.
- When necessary, be just as ballsy on behalf of others as you are [on behalf] of yourself.
- Standing up for what you believe in isn't convenient? Sorry, you gotta do it anyway.
- Pick your fights carefully.
- Being assertive with people who can't fight back isn't being assertive, it's being a bully.
- If you're trying to make a stand just for the sake of making a stand, it'll be particularly obvious.

Source: From "Assertiveness Training," by comedian Rosie O'Donnell (*Know How*, 1995, p. 62).

Since assertiveness can take many forms and people speak in their accustomed ways, it is better to focus on intent, not communication rules. One evening in New York City, two passersby—"ordinary working stiffs en route to dinner and the tube"—see a policeman on Eighth Avenue manhandling and hurting a druggie or dealer already in handcuffs.

. . . a man in a gray suit, briefcase in hand, obviously no friend of the street drug culture, calls out: "Hey! Hey!" He hollers angrily. "Is that necessary?"

Then another voice rings out.

"You've got witnesses here," says a man who, in his manner and dress, could have been the first one's twin.

Spectators begin to gather and "getting the message, the cop finally lets up" (Springer, 1999, pp. 230–232).

assertiveness is applied without adaptation. Basically, all practitioners need to be multicultural. As Chapter 4 reveals, we are all becoming minorities.

We should not sanctify culture and multiculturalism. Cultures are social creations and change with changing social and political circumstances. Cultures, within themselves and across cultures, share values and have value differences. The "WASP culture" appears to be a myth or highly elastic if it can embrace the vast differences between the "Boston Brahmins" and the Ozarkians of south Missouri and northern Arkansas. An overemphasis on culture can lead to the identity politics that Appiah (2005) warns us against. Much wickedness is rationalized as culture, such as intolerance and persecution of gays, female genital mutilation, and the oxymoron of "honor murders." Essentially, we argue that all of us practitioners, whether or not we are nominally bicultural, in a global society must expand our cultures to become multicultural or perhaps, as discussed in Chapter 4, create an amalgam culture.

While we are all one extended community, unless nuances are recognized, true communication and bonding rarely happen. For example, the "Back-Bay Boston Brahmins" may speak in subdued ways and emphasize correct enunciation, and the guys from Canarsie, Brooklyn, speak with force and emotion and incorporate more slang. The Brahmins may perceive that language as inappropriate. Certain religious, ethnic, racial, or urban subcultures are freer in expression, and their members may argue, interrupt, criticize, or laugh loudly. Looking someone in the eye is considered a sign of honesty by many, but among some Southern mountain communities and Amerindian tribes, it's considered an aggressive and disrespectful act. We all need to increase our awareness of such nuances if we want to communicate and reach each other.

Age, gender, physical condition, and other factors affect the perceptions of those served by social workers, so we must be alert to what will be considered appropriate assertiveness. An older service user or volunteer may respond more to a commanding presence or may be more attuned to civil but declarative sentences than to direct, firm "I" messages. We need to pay attention to how others communicate as we observe service users, volunteers, community residents, and institutional residents. Apologizing is especially common among older women who grew up in another era—tentativeness, overreliance on experts, and meekness may mask a strong personality underneath—and older men may feel expected or obligated to steer the conversation. Assertive attitudes and skills of our own allow us to be more proficient and attentive, critically conscious practitioners. Regardless of cultural and social nuances and grounding, it is important to develop assertiveness skills. Unlike power, they are more readily acquired.

Modes of Assertive Communication

Being Assertive in Writing

Assertive writing, like all assertive communication, is simple, to the point, and respectful. Formal, written communication is not obsequiousness. The advocate appropriately uses forceful and powerful words, but the tone is not bullying.

Written Examples: Influencing Legislators. Letters to allies and opponents can be expressed in a positive but potent manner. Below is a sample letter offered by AARP for use by its members to urge Congress to pass financial reform legislation.[3] Assertive words, words that carry powerful images, are italicized in the copy but not the original:

> Re: Support Financial Reform
>
> Dear [Decision Maker],
>
> The *reckless behavior* of big banks on Wall Street, credit card companies, mortgage lenders and irresponsible consumers *caused a financial crisis that cost Americans millions in lost jobs, billions in tax-payer funded bailouts and trillions in lost retirement savings.*
>
> I'm writing you today to ask you to support financial reform that will rein in this behavior and *finally hold these corporations, big banks and individuals accountable* by:
>
> – *Setting limits* on pay for CEOs and executives whose companies receive government assistance;

- *Cracking down* on the *abuses and deceptive practices* of credit card companies;
- *Increasing stability* for small businesses; and
- Preventing *predatory lenders* and *irresponsible borrowers* from entering into loans they know cannot be paid back.

Financial reform will close the *loopholes* that big banks on Wall Street have taken advantage of over the past two decades, and which economists say helped cause the financial crisis.

A full 70% of voters believe America's financial system is in need of major reform. It's time to protect Americans who *play by the rules*, help small businesses, *prevent future bailouts* and job losses, and lay the foundation for a financial system that promotes stability and long-term economic growth, rather than *greed and short term-profits*.

We will return to assertive communication again in Chapter 11, "Using Marketing."

Legislative Testimony

Written or public testimony in legislative and regulatory forums involves structurally assertive communication requiring skills in written and oral communication. A shortened version of testimony is often read, and a longer version is submitted for the record. Those reading testimony stick to the script:

On behalf of [name of organization], I appreciate the opportunity to provide testimony to the Senate Business and Commerce Committee . . .

No matter how timid the writer or deliverer, by tradition the opening and closing paragraphs of testimony are strong. Testimony usually starts with an introduction of the group being represented and its organizational position on the issue at hand, such as this:

Mr. Chairman and members of the committee, I am Mrs. Alice Willer, President of L. R. Vincent Homes for Children, Inc. The L. R. Vincent Homes is a non-profit service offering substitute care for children, organized by a statewide federation of local agencies, each of which is guided by a citizens' board of directors. We thank you for giving us this opportunity to present our views on House Bill 5293.

The member agencies of L. R. Vincent Homes across the state strongly oppose in principle the practice of surrogate parenthood and strongly oppose the Surrogate Parenthood Bill. (Flynn, 1985, p. 270)

Because testimony time is limited, prepare copies of your statement and hand them out for distribution to the legislative or hearing panel. It is important to provide your testimony in written form to be entered in the record. Members may refer to testimony when later voting. Be prepared, try not to read your statement, and get to the point. Avoid weasel words and phrases and tentative or wishy-washy opinions. Do not hedge, bully, or threaten or promise anything you can't deliver. Organize your statement clearly and concisely; it is not necessary to make a lengthy, emotional exposition. Summarize your position. Don't engage in overkill. Your testimony is more effective if you speak directly and forcefully to the committee members and maintain eye contact. Members are more likely to listen attentively and to refer to your more detailed written statement later.

Be confident and cooperative, as committee members may want to hear a range of viewpoints, and even if they don't, they need to hear yours. They may challenge you or ask for clarification. Respond directly if you can; if you do not know the answer, say so.

Avoid repetition. If necessary, briefly repeat any points of agreement made by previous speakers and add your endorsement. In a long hearing the chairman may limit the time allowed each speaker and ask you not to repeat specific points already made. This may steal your thunder, but the written testimony can reinforce it.

Your tone and your choice of words are expected to be assertive, as the following excerpt illustrates:

Thank you for this opportunity to offer our recommendations regarding reauthorization of the Low Income Home Energy Assistance Program (LIHEAP). LIHEAP is extremely important to low-income older persons who are exceptionally vulnerable to extremes in weather conditions. The Association strongly supports both LIHEAP reauthorization and certain modifications that we believe will improve program administration and funding security. [testimony March 25, 1990]

No matter how angry you are, keep your language civil and respectful, in part because those calling hearings are often allies. One would never know from the following opening that women's groups had been endeavoring for over two decades to get a United Nations treaty ratified by the United States, as 169 countries had done before us:

Good morning. I am Jane Smith, Chief Executive Officer of Business and Professional Women/USA. . . . I applaud Senator Biden for holding this hearing and Senator Boxer for chairing it. I welcome the opportunity to represent the working women who are members of my organization to discuss the importance of ratifying the Convention on the Elimination of All Forms of Discrimination Against Women, often called the Treaty for the Rights of Women. [testimony by Jane Smith June 5, 2002]

Assertive Social Workers Needed: Summary

Assertiveness is an essential social work attribute. Cournoyer (1983) argues that "professional social work practice requires assertive self-expression skills of a high order" (p. 24). Assertiveness is indispensable if social workers are to fulfill their ethical imperatives of providing advocacy for social justice and for clients. Hardina (1995) provides rationales for expanded assertiveness skills: "Social workers may not be adequately prepared either to advocate on their own behalf or to improve access to services for consumers. . . . Without confrontation, it may not be possible to develop the power resources necessary to fight for social change that will benefit members of oppressed groups. Assertiveness training for social work students is an essential component of such education" (p. 13). Appendix 1 presents role playing exercises in being assertive.

Assertiveness rests on a foundation of self-awareness and critical consciousness. Clients need assertiveness skills if they are to be self-determining and empowered.

Assertiveness and advocacy highlight the theme of breaking free of conventionality and "can't-do" thinking. Practitioners need a basis for their part of belief bonding and establishing positive, "can-do" expectations of their skills and clients' capacities and strengths, whether individuals or communal, because expectations of failure will undermine the change effort.

APPENDIX 7.1: Being Assertive: Learn Through Role-Playing

Role-playing can highlight assertiveness strengths and weaknesses. Directions frequently stipulate that one person must present a claim or request an action for the other person to perform. Lange and Jakubowski (1976) emphasize that it is "OK for people to make reasonable requests and it is also OK to refuse them" (p. 102). Asking for a pay raise is a simulation with universal relevance and appeal. (In real life, a busy employer often appreciates directness.)

Employee: Thanks for seeing me.
Boss: Now what do you want?
Employee: I am here to ask for a $2,000 raise.
Boss: No one is getting one. Money is tight.
Employee: I am entitled to more money next year because of my recent contributions to the company.
Boss: We applaud your efforts. Maybe we can talk about salary in the future.
Employee: That's your call, but I'd like to talk about it now.
Boss: You still fall asleep at your desk. On the other hand, your suggestion did save the firm thousands of dollars.
Employee: Yes, that's correct.
Boss: OK, I'll take it under advisement.
Employee: That's great. I appreciate your considering the raise. When might you make a decision or contact me for further discussion?

Practitioners			
Assertiveness	Critical Consciousness	Advocacy	Self-awareness

Clients		
Self-awareness	Self-determination	Empowerment

Putting Oneself to the Test: Illustrative Examples of Assertive Comments

Example 1

Introducing oneself can reveal any of the three basic communication styles. Imagine yourself knocking on the door of the building manager to resolve a problem for a member of your organization. Imagine walking in, shaking hands, and saying: "My name is _____. I am from _____ agency. I am Mrs. Brown's advocate. She lives in your building." Your knock, walk, handshake, voice, and demeanor will convey passive, aggressive, or assertive attitudes.

Example 2

Here are varying responses to the comment, "I don't think family preservation programs work. Earlier positive research findings haven't held up." Read them all and then devise your own assertive response.

Assertive Responses

1. "I think the results are mixed, but tell me your thoughts on the subject."
2. Write one of your own: _____

Non-assertive or Passive Responses

1. Disagreeing, but not saying so
2. "Usually we agree, but not this time. I don't mean to make you mad, but I think family preservation is the way to go—not that I know the research."

Example 3

You'll find this example more demanding. Read the two questions and four types of responses.

- The head of your community advisory board prior to Christmas asks, "How do you people [meaning 'you African-Americans,' 'you Jews,' 'you Asian-Americans,' 'You Muslims,' or whatever is applicable to you] celebrate this holiday, anyhow?"
- An exasperated person says: "Why is it that you people [meaning 'you men,' 'you women,' 'you secretaries,' 'you members of the cleaning staff,' or whatever is applicable] always mess up our lunchroom?"

Aggressive Response

"That shows how little you've read about it."

Assertive Responses

1. Spoken deliberately, in response to the question about holidays: "Well, first, let's find a better phrase than 'you people.' I'd suggest _____."
2. Spoken pleasantly, in response to the comment about the lunchroom: "I won't respond to that."
3. You decide that the person is naïve or sincere, not hostile, and you answer the question in that spirit.

Non-assertive or Passive Responses

1. Smilingly changing the subject: "Don't generalize, now . . ."
2. Answering the content of the question while ignoring its form or tone: "It strikes me that the important thing about what you are asking is . . ."
3. "Not that I care about political correctness, but don't you think some people might react negatively to 'you _____ are always'? I admit that it bothers me."

Aggressive Responses

1. Coldly: "I don't appreciate your tone."
2. Some people around here think they can ask anything [or control everything].
3. "Well, you people are worse, [swear word]."

A young assembly-plant worker who considers himself hip places a call to obtain an appointment with his assigned employee assistance counselor. However, the counselor's next 2 weeks are already fully scheduled, according to the rather stuffy receptionist. Here are four possible responses to that news:

1. "Say what? I'm serious. This here appointment is important. Don't give me grief. Check that book again. Then make him come to the phone. I ain't got all day, though. What, you'll call back?"
2. "Yo, girl! Whass hapnin? Already booked! If the brother has a cancellation, my telephone number is. . . . Look, I'm not tryin' to give you attitude. I can only go to work again after I've seen the counselor."
3. "I need to see. . . . Sorry, sorry . . . my English. Maybe I not explain right. Tiempo is money.

I can't get paid—and my family needs money—until the counselor sees. . . . How you say? I beg. *Verbo, por favor?*"

4. "Tell the dude I need to bend his ear. You're damn right I'm raising my voice. Don't dog me."

Distinguish assertion from politeness and other factors in these telephone conversations. Note that assertiveness does not require a formal communication style. The same principles apply with slang, Spanglish, African-American Vernacular English (AAVE), ungrammatical English, and exaggerated examples such as those above. Which response is assertive? Passive? Aggressive? Why?

As social workers, we need to be able to state our case firmly. Yet, the recent trend toward ending sentences with a raised inflection when the person is *not* asking a question makes it even more challenging to speak in a manner that does not sound tentative. We can learn to make declarative statements and to make statements without explanation or justifications. Both the first illustrative example given previously and Example 4 below provide samples of this form of assertive communication.

Assertive training has specialized techniques. One technique is called the *broken record* (Smith, 1975). It is an accepted and easily understood

---

> *City hall employee:* Are you with the media?
>
> *Advocate:* Please direct me to a place where I can read the reports or bring them to me. Thank you.
>
> The advocate could cite a law that gives the public access, if necessary.

---

idea of persistent, calm repetition so that one's point cannot be ignored. Sometimes people feel odd practicing it because we normally do not talk that way, but exaggeration and repetition allows internalization of this technique. The repetition can vary the words used but not the meaning. The script in Example 5 can be read aloud by two individuals while a third critiques how assertive the "advocate" role-player is with regard to tone of voice and ability to convey resolve.

Example 4: Declarative Statements

Advocate: I want to look at the campaign finance records for the mayor's race.

City hall employee: Who are you? Why do you want to see them?

A nonassertive response would be: "I'm just a student. But can't I see them anyway? I'm writing a paper." But use of declarative statements would sound like the following:

Advocate: The report of contributions to each candidate's campaign is to be filed here. Are the reports kept in this office?

City hall employee: Yes, but we can't show them to just anyone.

Advocate: As you know, it is public information. I would like to see the reports.

Example 5: Broken Record Technique

Advocate: I need to speak to the principal about the Jones brothers he dismissed from school on Friday morning.

Receptionist: Mr. Furtif is busy right now. Why don't you go down the hall and speak to those boys' classroom teachers?

Advocate: Thank you, but it is the principal I need to see. Here is my card. I represent the Department of Children and Family Services.

Receptionist: Maybe the guidance counselor is around this morning. She is usually pretty busy on Mondays, but I can try to find her for you.

Advocate: Thank you for your offer. However, I must speak to Mr. Furtif himself.

Receptionist: You should have made an appointment. He never sees drop-ins off the street.

Advocate: I can appreciate that policy. I did call repeatedly Friday afternoon and was never put through to him. I'll wait until he has a break in his schedule.

Receptionist: Those boys were causing everyone headaches. I know why they were suspended indefinitely.

Advocate: Would you please call the principal and let him know their caseworker is here?

Receptionist: I couldn't bother him during a staff meeting.

Advocate: When will it be over?

Receptionist: In about five minutes, but he has other things after that.

Advocate: Please give him my card. I will wait over here until I can get 10 minutes of his time.

Left to their own devices, some would change the tone drastically. They would make friends with the receptionist and say something like this:

Advocate: Aren't you nice to suggest that? I'll bet you've been with the school for years and have seen everything. So you are probably familiar with our agency and what we need. Maybe I can sit with you and wait.

An ingratiating approach feels right but (a) risks getting caught in stalling, (b) drops the broken record strategy, and (c) loses the high ground—the emphasis on the right of the children to be in school and of the worker to deal directly with the decision maker.

Assertiveness comes into play when we have a goal or agenda, such as getting the boys back into school, and we adapt our behavior to that goal rather than to another person's personality or expectations. *Aggressiveness* arises when we subordinate the goal to a desire to respond forcefully to another person, such as the receptionist or principal. *Passivity* occurs when we allow the goal to be overridden by intimidating signals (internal or as received from another person).

Selective ignoring means that we do not have to respond to every element or nuance of a remark made to us. *Fogging* is another technique. "Like a fog bank, you remain impenetrable. You offer no resistance or hard striking surfaces" (Zuker, 1983, pp. 134–135). If those in Ian's car pool tease him about losing his hair, he may tell them to knock it off. But there are times when we must listen calmly to annoying comments and criticism—say, from a state trooper giving us a ticket. Lange and Jakubowski (1976) call fogging and selective ignoring "protective skills" to use in response to "nagging" (p. 115). A fogging rejoinder to a crack such as "Ian, you're about as bald as they get, aren't you?" is designed to dampen potential confrontation. Ian can say lightly, without affect, "I probably am" or "You could say that." Assertion is about self-control more than controlling others. See Example 6. Another fogging response would be "You have a point."

Fogging is criticized by Cotler and Guerra (1976), who view it as passive-aggressive in psychological situations. Drury (1984) uses it at work to prevent arguments: "You [agree] with the criticism in principle without necessarily agreeing with the implied judgment" (p. 227). But she limits its use: "The technique stops communication and interaction rather than uncovering and solving problems. Humor, ignoring, and fogging are all techniques that should be used only for responding to teasing or attempts to start an argument, not for cases in which someone is criticizing to solve a problem" (Drury, 1984, p. 227).

Example 6: Selective Ignoring and Fogging

Client's boss: You are wearing an earring.

Client: Yes, I am. [not "So what?"]

Boss: Why would you do that? You know what people are going to think. I'll bet your parents are upset.

Client: It's possible they are.

Boss: I don't think men should pierce their ears.

Client: _____ [Act as a coach. What should your client say here?]

What was selectively ignored? What was fogged?

Two people can read the script below, with a third person giving feedback. Notice that the social worker does not give in and does not make matters worse.

Example 7: When Fogging May Be Useful

Advocate: Hello. This is Community Action.

Hostile caller: Is this Erin/Aaron _____?

Advocate: Speaking.

Hostile caller: Are you the person who has been out looking for housing deficiencies?

Advocate: Who is calling, please?

Hostile caller: I happen to be a property owner in this community.

Advocate: And your name, sir?

Hostile caller: Name's Ross Gibson. But never mind that. I wanted you to know that we landlords don't appreciate your actions.

Advocate: I see. Do you care to be more specific? [Taking the call seriously; not sure what the problem is]

Hostile caller: You're stirring up trouble with the county for no reason without talking with me first.

Advocate: I could have contacted you personally. [Starts fogging because the caller wants to ventilate, not communicate]

Hostile caller: That group of yours is against free enterprise, you're trying to help a bunch of low-lifes, and you're going about it all wrong.

Advocate: Perhaps you're right.

Hostile caller: I checked up on you and found out you're just a student. I bet that school of yours does not even realize what you are up to.

Advocate: I am a graduate student; you're correct.

Hostile caller: I have been checking with my lawyer, and I think we can get you jailed for disturbing the peace with some of your activities.

Read the script to the end and then invent a fogging-style response (one that does not involve your supervisor, who is working under a deadline). The caller is not a client and need not be treated in the same way that a client would be treated. The idea is to avoid taking the bait, to let Mr. Gibson run down, and to get off the phone without getting an immediate return call from him.

Advocate: _____

Assertive Response Options

Standard assertiveness is a firm comeback without explanation or apology. "Assertions that contain explanations, acknowledgment of feelings, compromises and praise have been termed empathic assertions" (Rakos 1991, p. 31; Lange & Jakubowski, 1976, pp. 14–15).

Example 8: Handling a Power Imbalance Situation

The head of your interdisciplinary health team says, "You social workers always think you know better than physicians when the patient is ready to leave the hospital. Where did you study medicine?" Possible responses include the following:

- *Empathic assertion—contains an explanation:* "There's more than a medical dimension to knowing when a patient is ready to leave."
- *Standard assertion:* "You seem to like giving me a hard time, Dr. _____."

- *Fogging response:* "It's true that social workers have professional opinions about diagnostic related groups and the length-of-stay issue."
- *Timid response:* "Doctor, I don't know what to say. Maybe my supervisor should explain social work's concern to you."
- *Hostile response:* Looking up from your notes, you ask, "How do you spell anal-retentive?" (Clever, but say goodbye to your social work internship.)
- Your response: _____

Discussion Exercises

1. *Assume that you will be working temporarily with a health service delivery system on Native American land. Besides learning about tribal and federal leadership systems, you want to know this tribe's customs before you challenge anyone in your standard assertive manner. You once read a parable about an Amerindian who wanted to be on equal terms with every person he encountered, so he either brought individuals up to or down to his level, depending on their station in life. How can outsiders learn what is myth or reality regarding assertion beliefs for Native people or members of any other culture unfamiliar to us?*

2. *Our work lives are saturated with phrases about impotence, such as falling through the cracks, bogged down in the bureaucracy, and half a loaf is better than none. What is our field's equivalent to going for the gold (sports), the cure (medicine), the scoop (journalism), or the Nobel Prize (science)?*

Notes

1. "I think, therefore I am," not "I am, therefore I think."
2. One of the authors was a participant-observer at this event. It was a dramatic occurrence of *carpe diem* by Savio. He replaced us all as the face and voice of the movement.
3. Offer by AARP to membership by e-mail on Feb. 10, 2010.

References

Agne, K. J., Greenwood, G. E., & Miller, L. D. (1994). Relationships between teacher belief systems and teacher effectiveness. *Journal of Research and Development in Education, 27*(3), 141–152.

Alberti, R. E., & Emmons, M. L. (1990). Your perfect right: A guide to assertive behavior (6th prof. ed.). San Luis Obispo, CA: Impact.

Alvarez, A. R. (2001). Enhancing praxis through PRACSIS: A framework for developing critical consciousness and implications for strategy. *Journal of Teaching in Social Work*, 21(1/2), 195–220.

Angel, G., & Petronko, D. K. (1983). *Developing the new assertive nurse: Essentials for advancement*. New York: Springer.

Appiah, K. A. (2005). *The ethics of identity*. Princeton, NJ: Princeton University Press.

Australian Federation of Medical Women. (2010). *Assertiveness techniques*. Retrieved February 1, 2010, from: http://afmw.org.au/leadership/150-assertiveness-techniques

Banks, S. (2007). Working in and with community groups and organizations: Processes and practices. In H. Butcher, S. Banks, P. Henderson, with J. Robertson (Eds.), *Critical community practice* (pp. 77–96). Bristol, UK: The Policy Press.

Barber, B. (1984). *Strong democracy: Participatory politics for a new age*. Berkeley: University of California Press.

Becker, D. (2005). *The myth of empowerment: Women and the therapeutic culture in America*. New York: New York University Press.

Biddle, W. W., & Biddle, L. J. (1979). Intention and outcome. In F. M. Cox, J. L. Erlich, J. Rothman, & J. E. Tropman (Eds.), *Strategies of community organization* (pp. 365–375). Itasca, IL: F. E. Peacock.

Bisman, C. (1994). *Social work practice: Cases and principles*. Pacific Grove, CA: Brooks/Cole Publishing Co.

Butcher, H., Banks, S., Henderson, P., with Robertson, J. (2007). *Critical community practice*. Bristol, UK: The Policy Press.

Christensen, P. (2002). An eye-opening diversity assignment. *The New Social Worker*, 9(4), 13, 17.

Clifton, R. L., & Dahms, A. M. (1993). *Grassroots organizations: A resource book for directors, staff, and volunteers of small, community-based nonprofit agencies* (2nd ed.). Prospect Heights, IL: Waveland.

Colburn, L. (1994). On-the-spot mediation in a public housing project. In D. M. Kolb (Ed.), *When talk works: Profiles of mediators* (pp. 395–425). San Francisco: Jossey-Bass.

Coleman, D. (2000). The therapeutic alliance in multicultural practice. *Psychoanalytic Social Work*, 7(2), 65–92.

Cotler, S. B., & Guerra, J. J. (1976). *Assertion training: A humanistic-behavioral guide to self-dignity*. Champaign, IL: Research.

Cournoyer, B. R. (1983). Assertiveness among MSW students. *Journal of Education for Social Work*, 19(1), 24–30.

Cowger, C. D. (1994). Assessing client strengths: Clinical assessment for client empowerment. *Social Work*, 39(3), 262–268.

Drucker, P. (1999). Managing oneself. *Harvard Business Review*, 77(2), 64–74.

Drury, S. S. (1984). *Assertive supervision: Building involved teamwork*. Champaign, IL: Research Press.

Enns, C. Z. (1992). Self-esteem groups: A synthesis of consciousness raising and assertiveness training. *Journal of Counseling and Development*, 71(1), 7–13.

Flynn, J. P. (1985). *Social agency policy: Analysis and presentation for community practice*. Chicago: Nelson-Hall.

Foster-Fishman, P., Nowell, B., Deacon, Z., Nievar, M. A., & McCann, P. (2005). Using methods that matter: The impact of reflection, dialogue, and voice. *American Journal of Community Psychology* 36(3/4), 275–291.

Freire, P. (1994). *Pedagogy of hope: Reliving pedagogy of the oppressed*. New York: Continuum Books.

Furstenberg, A. L., & Rounds, K. A. (1995). Self-efficacy as a target for social work intervention. *Families in Society*, 76(10), 587–595.

Gambrill, E. (1997). *Social work practice: A critical thinker's guide*. New York: Oxford University Press.

Gerth, H. H., & Mills, C. W. (1958). *From Max Weber: Essays in sociology*. New York: Oxford University Press.

Gibbs, L., & Gambrill, E. (1999). *Critical thinking for social workers: Exercises for the helping profession*. Thousand Oaks, CA: Pine Forest Press.

Gilson, S. F. (2000). Discussion of disability and use of self in the classroom. *Journal of Teaching in Social Work*, 20(3/4), 125–136.

Goodkind, S. (2009). You can be anything you want, but you have to believe it: Commercialized feminism in gender-specific programs for girls. *Signs: Journal of Women in Culture and Society*, 34(2), 397–422.

Goode, E. (2001, 1/1). Therapists redraw line on self-disclosure. *The New York Times*, pp. D5, D7.

Greenwood, G. E., Olejnik, S. F., & Parkay, F. W. (1990). Relationships between four teacher efficacy belief patterns and selected teacher characteristics. *Journal of Research and Development in Education*, 23(2), 104–106.

Griffin, W. V. (1995). Social worker and agency safety. In R. Edwards (Ed.-in-Chief), *Encyclopedia of social work* (19th ed., pp. 2293–2305). Washington, DC: National Association of Social Workers Press.

Gutierrez, L. M. (1990). Working with women of color: An empowerment perspective. *Social Work*, 35(2), 149–152.

Handy, F., & Kassam, M. (2007). Practice what you preach? The role of rural NGOs in women's empowerment. *Journal of Community Practice*, 14(3), 69–91.

Harden, B. (1995, July 16). *A one-man human-rights crusade*. The Washington Post, pp. B1, B6.

Hardina, D. (1995, March). Teaching confrontation tactics to social work students. Paper presented at

Council on Social Work Education meeting, San Diego, CA.

Harris, C. C., & Harris, D. R. (1993). *Self-empowerment: Reclaim your personal power.* Carmel, CA: Carmel Highlands.

Hartman, A. (1990). *Family-based strategies for empowering families.* Paper presented at the "Integrating Three Strategies of Family Empowerment" conference sponsored by School of Social Work, University of Iowa.

Haug, M. R., & Lavin, B. (1983). *Consumerism in medicine: Challenging physician authority.* Beverly Hills, CA: Sage.

Henderson, P. (2007). Introduction. In H. Butcher, S. Banks, P. Henderson, with J. Robertson (Eds.), *Critical community practice* (pp. 1–16). Bristol, UK: The Policy Press.

Jansson, B. S. (1990). *Social welfare policy: From theory to practice.* Belmont, CA: Wadsworth.

Johnson, L. D. (1995). *Psychotherapy in the age of accountability.* New York: W. W. Norton & Company.

Judson, O. (2010, May 4). *Enhancing the placebo.* The New York Times, p. A25.

Kahn, K. (1973). *Hillbilly women.* New York: Avon.

Kaufman, G., & Raphael, L. (1990). *Stick up for yourself: Every kid's guide to personal power and positive self esteem.* Minneapolis: Free Spirit.

Kesby, M. (2005). Retheorizing empowerment-through-participation as a performance in space: Beyond tyranny to transformation. *Signs: Journal of Women in Culture and Society,* 30(4), 2037–2065.

Kirst-Ashman, K. K., & Hull, Jr., G. H. (2008). *Generalist practice with organizations and communities* (4th ed.). Belmont, CA: Brooks Cole.

Klein, K. (1996). *Fundraising for social change* (3rd ed.). Berkeley, CA: Chardon Press.

Knotts, L. S. (1991). *Characteristics of "women's language" and their relationship to personnel decisions.* Paper presented for departmental honors in psychology, Hood College, Frederick, MD.

Kolata, G. (2001, May 24). *Placebo effect is more myth than science, a study says.* The New York Times. pp. A1, A18.

Lange, A. J., & Jakubowski, P. (1976). *Responsible assertive behavior: Cognitive/behavioral procedures for trainers.* Champaign, IL: Research Press.

Lappé, F. M., & Du Bois, P. M. (1994). *The quickening of America: Rebuilding our nation, remaking our lives.* San Francisco, CA: Jossey Bass, Inc. Publishers.

Lee, B., McGrath, S., Moffatt, K., & George, U. (2002). Exploring the insider role in community practice within diverse communities. *Critical Social Work,* 2(2), 69–78.

Lerner, M. (1991). *Surplus powerlessness.* Atlantic Highlands, NJ: Humanities Press International.

Locust, C. (1995). The impact of differing belief systems between Native Americans and their rehabilitation service providers. *Rehabilitation Education,* 9(2), 205–215.

Loneck, B., & Way, B. (1997). Using a focus group of clinicians to develop a research project on therapeutic process for clients with dual diagnosis. *Social Work,* 42(1), 107–111.

Lordan, N. (2000). Finding a voice: Empowerment of people with disabilities in Ireland. *Journal of Progressive Human Services,* 11(1), 49–69.

Luborsky, L., Barber, J. P., Siqueland, L., McLellan, S. A., & Woody, G. (1997). Establishing a therapeutic alliance with substance abusers. In *Beyond the therapeutic alliance: Keeping the drug-dependent individual in treatment. NIDA Research Monograph #165* (pp. 233–244). Rockville, MD: U.S. Department of Health and Human Services, National Institutes of Health, National Institute on Drug Abuse, Division of Clinical and Services Research, pp. 233–244.

Masi, D. A. (1994). Violence in the workplace: The EAP perspective. *EAP Digest,* 14(3), 23.

Mayo Clinic Staff (n.d.). *Being assertive: Reduce stress, communicate better.* Retrieved February 1, 2010, from: http://www.mayoclinic.com/health/assertive

Mitchell, C. G. (1998). Perceptions of empathy and client satisfaction with managed behavioral health care. *Social Work,* 43(5), 404–411.

Morrell, M., & Capparell, S. (2001). *Shackleton's way.* New York: Carlisle & Co.

National Association of Social Workers—Maryland Chapter. (1995, March). *Violence—Caught in the crossfire—Implications for social work practice.* Program meeting.

National Institutes of Health Traumatic (1998). *Assertive skills quiz.* Retrieved February 1, 2009, from: http://www.headinjury.com/.

Newman, C. F. (1997). Establishing and maintaining a therapeutic alliance with substance abuse patients: A cognitive therapy approach. In *Beyond the therapeutic alliance: Keeping the drug-dependent individual in treatment. NIDA Research Monograph #165* (pp. 181–206). Rockville, MD: U.S. Department of Health and Human Services, National Institutes of Health, National Institute on Drug Abuse, Division of Clinical and Services Research.

National Association of Social Workers. (2008). *Code of ethics of the National Association of Social Workers [as approved by the 1996 NASW Delegate Assembly and revised by the 2008 NASW Delegate Assembly].* Author, Retrieved May 11, 2009, from http://www.socialworkers.org/pubs/code/default.asp

O'Donnell, R. (with Newman, J.). (1995, Summer). *Assertiveness training with Rosie O'Donnell. Know How,* 5(2), 60–63, 101.

Ohbuchi, K., & Takahashi, Y. (1994). Cultural styles of conflict management in Japanese and Americans: Passivity, covertness, and effectiveness of strategies. *Journal of Applied Social Psychology*, 24(15), 1345–1366.

Ohmer, M. L. (2008). The relationship between members' perceptions of their neighborhood organization and their involvement and perceived benefits from participation. *Journal of Community Psychology*, 36(7), 851–870.

O'Neill, P. (1989). Responsible to whom? *American Journal of Community Psychology*, 17, 323–341.

Patterson, C. H. (1985). *The therapeutic relationship: Foundations for eclectic psychotherapy*. Monterey, CA: Brooks/Cole Publishing.

Pearrow, M. M. (2008). A critical examination of an urban-based youth empowerment strategy: The teen empowerment program. *Journal of Community Practice*, 16(4), 509–525.

Peterson, N. A., & Hughey, J. (2003). Tailoring organizational characteristics for empowerment. *Journal of Community Practice*, 10(3), 41–59.

Phelps, S., & Austin, N. (1987). *The assertive woman: A new look* (2nd ed.). San Luis Obispo, CA: Impact.

Powers, P. (Ed.) (1994*). Challenging: Interviews with advocates and activists* [monograph]. Baltimore: University of Maryland at Baltimore, School of Social Work.

Rakos, R. F. (1991). *Assertive behavior*. New York: Routledge.

Rivera, F. G. (1990). The Way of Bushido in community organizing teaching. *Administration in Social Work*, 14(2), 43–61.

Ryan, K. D., Oestreich, D. K., & Orr, G. A., III. (1996). *The courageous messengers: How to successfully speak up at work*. San Francisco, CA: Jossey-Bass Publishers.

Schilling, R. F. (1990). Commentary: Making research usable. In L. Videka-Sherman & W. J. Reid (Eds.), *Advances in clinical social work research* (pp. 256–260). Silver Spring, MD: National Association of Social Workers.

Sears, V. (1990). Grace. In *Simple songs* (pp. 139–159). Ithaca, NY: Firebrand Books.

Sears, V. L. (1993). Grace. In P. Riley (Ed.), *Growing up Native American* (pp. 279–298). New York: William Morrow.

Shields, K. (1994). *In the tiger's mouth: An empowerment guide for social action*. Philadelphia: New Society Publishers.

Simon, B. L. (1990). Rethinking empowerment. *Journal of Progressive Human Services*, 1(1), 27–39.

Siress, R. H., with Riddle, C., & Shouse, D. (1994). *Working woman's communications survival guide: How to present your ideas with impact, clarity and power and get the recognition you deserve*. Englewood Cliffs, NJ: Prentice Hall.

Smith, M. J. (1975). *When I say no, I feel guilty*. New York: Dial.

Spain, D. (2001). *How women saved the city*. Minneapolis: University of Minnesota Press.

Springer, L. (1999). *Grand Central winter: Stories from the street*. New York: Washington Square Press.

Stevens, C. K., Bavetta, A. G., & Gist, M. E. (1993). Gender differences in the acquisition of salary negotiation skills: The role of goals, self-efficacy, and perceived control. *Journal of Applied Psychology*, 78(5), 723–735.

Stewart-Williams, S. (2004). The placebo puzzle: Putting together the pieces. *Health Psychology*, 23(2), 198–206.

Tannen, D. (1990). *You just don't understand: Women and men in conversation*. New York: William Morrow.

Tannen, D. (1994). *Talking from 9 to 5: How women's and men's conversational styles affect who gets heard, who gets credit, and what gets done at work*. New York: William Morrow.

Tower, K. D. (1994). Consumer-centered social work practice: Restoring client self-determination. *Social Work*, 39(2), 191–196.

Tully, C. C., Kropf, N. P., & Price, J. L. (1993). Is the field a hard hat area? A study of violence in field placements. *Journal of Social Work Education*, 29(2), 191–199.

Vroom, V. H. (1964). *Work and Motivation*. New York: John Wiley & Sons.

Wakefield, J. C. (1988, September). Part 2: Psychotherapy and the pursuit of justice. *Social Service Review*, 62(2), 353–382.

Walz, T., & Uematsu, M. (1997). Creativity in social work practice: A pedagogy. *Journal of Teaching in Social Work*, 15(1/2), 17–31.

Weisman, R. L., & Lamberti, J. S. (2002). Violence prevention and safety training for case management services. *Community Mental Health Journal*, 38(4), 339–348.

Weiss-Gal, I., & Gal, J. (2009). Realizing rights in social work. *The Social Service Review*, 83(2), 267–291.

Weiss, J. O. (1993). Genetic disorders: Support groups and advocacy. *Families in Society: The Journal of Contemporary Human Services*, 74(4), 213–220.

West, D. M., Heith, D., & Goodwin, C. (1996). Harry and Louise go to Washington: Political advertising and health care reform. *Journal of Health Politics, Policy, and Law*, 21(1), 35–68.

Williams, C. (2001). *Overcoming depression: A five areas approach*. Edmonton, Alberta, Canada: Arnold Publishing Ltd.

Williams, P. N. (1978). *Investigative reporting and editing.* Englewood Cliffs, NJ: Prentice-Hall.

Yoshioka, M. (1995, March 5). *Measuring the assertiveness of low income, minority women: Implications for culturally competent practice.* Paper presented at Council on Social Work Education meeting, San Diego, CA.

Zane, N. W. S., Sue, S., Hu, L., & Kwon, J. (1991). Asian American assertion: A social learning analysis of cultural differences. *Journal of Counseling Psychology,* 38(1), 63–70.

Zuker, E. (1983). *The assertive manager: Positive skills at work for you.* New York: AMACOM.

Zunz, S. J. (1998). Resiliency and burnout: Protective factors for human services managers. *Administration in Social Work,* 22(3), 39–54.

8

Using Your Agency

The trouble with organizing a thing is that pretty soon folks get to paying more attention to the organization than to what they're organized for.

Laura Ingalls Wilder, author

Meetings are a symptom of bad organization. The fewer meetings the better.

Peter F. Drucker, author, philosopher, teacher

I won't belong to any organization that would have me as a member.

Groucho Marx, comedian, actor, philosopher

The achievements of an organization are the results of the combined effort of each individual.

Vince Lombardi, football coach, author

As social workers, we will spend most of our professional lives practicing in or with human service organizations—governmental (public), nongovernmental nonprofit agencies, and proprietary organizations. Even if we go into private, solo practice, we will deal with organizations for funding and for clients. These organizations profoundly affect our personal and professional well-being. Regardless of our talents and skills, organizational structure, culture, and management strongly influence how well we are able to do the professional work for which we are trained. Work organizations affect our self-image, our livelihoods, and our sense of professional accomplishment and worth as human beings. For these reasons, understanding how organizations operate is critical. We need organizational knowledge to create a personally and professionally more rewarding and productive work milieu.

The character of human services organizations is in transition. They will look and act differently in the future. With the continuing development and

application of information technology (IT) and communication technology (CT)—smartphones, video and teleconferencing, the Internet—organizations, including the reluctant human service organization (HSO), are becoming more virtual. Employee–employer relations are becoming more fluid, with a growing use of contingent and contract employees and independent contractors. Employer and employee commitments are becoming more tenuous (Jaskyte & Lee, 2009). With the 2010 U. S. Supreme Court decision, corporations are enjoying the constitutional rights of an individual.[1] They are becoming legal people as they become less humane. Like the times, agencies are a-changin'.

This chapter is written for the front-line professional rather than the supervisor or manager. It deals with HSOs in general first, and then with the formal and informal aspects of organizational life that help and hinder practitioners in fulfilling their ethical and professional responsibilities. We also remind the reader that the social environment, the external economic, political, and institutional forces, strongly affect intra-organizational behavior. Throughout the chapter, we strive to regard social workers as organizational actors and professionals independently responsible for their professional conduct. As a prelude to this chapter, we encourage the reader to review the material on systems theory, exchange theory, and interorganizational theory in Chapter 2 and ethics in Chapter 1. Figure 8.1 presents the basic systems model.

Attributes of Human Service Agencies

Social workers practice in a very broad array of HSOs. Although these agencies vary in characteristics such as size, complexity, auspices, domain, and whether or not social work is the dominant profession in the agency, and more, as a class of organizations they are also alike in many ways. These similarities help to explain the organizational problems and opportunities that human service workers and service users often encounter. In briefly reviewing these shared attributes, we shall draw on Hasenfeld's (1992) classic work on the nature of HSOs.

HSOs are people-processing and people-changing agencies in that "the core activities of the organization are structured to process, sustain, or change people who come under its jurisdiction" (Hasenfeld, 1992, pp. 4–5). An HSO's primary purpose is to provide effective programs and services, now and in the future, to clients and the community. To provide services in the future, the HSO must persist. Organization and agency management activities—such as resource gathering, controlling and coordinating, reporting and accountability—ideally serve the ends of current and future service.

Organizations accomplish what an individual or an aggregation of uncoordinated individuals working alone cannot. If organizations simply do as well as people working alone can do, then organizations make no significant social contribution. HSO are systems. As systems, HSOs can be viewed as means–ends chains. Generally, as Figure 8.1 indicates, they are transforming systems. HSOs tend toward open systems with resources or inputs from their ecologies (people, material, ideas, knowledge, and technology) and transform or process them in some way into outputs to reach organizational objectives. Some organizational examples are job placement, information, and referral (processing), Social Security, long-term nursing home care (sustaining), counseling, school (changing).

To maximize compliance and hence control, HSOs must win their clients' cooperation and trust or have the capacity to coerce them into compliance. Social workers employed by or contracted with HSOs are agents of the HSO. Clients are first clients of the HSO and only secondarily clients of the HSO's social workers. The HSO is the principal party in the relationship with the client and supersedes the worker. The nature of this relationship is critical, and the worker and client should fully understand it. The agency frames the attachment of social worker and client. It limits such relationship components as client privacy and worker confidentiality. The organization's management control of the working relationship between workers and clients is a growing characteristic of contemporary agency-based social work practice (Thompson, 2000; Walker, 2001; Webb, 2001). This relationship is vulnerable to deliberate or unwitting abuse, since HSOs typically control some of the resources clients need. Moreover, control and standardization of the services that are delivered are difficult

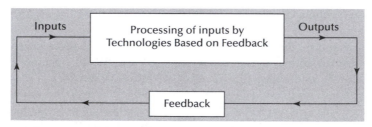

Figure 8.1. The general system model revisited.

to achieve because services, the products of professional intervention, are intangible and "inextricably bound to the person and personality of the producer" (Larson, 1977, p. 14; see also Wenocur & Reisch, 1989, pp. 9–11). Since human service "technologies" (modes of intervention) are variable and hard to reproduce (though greater reliability is the object of professional training), and since the outcomes of intervention are hard to measure and not clearly visible, HSOs, not surprisingly, have difficulty gaining support for their work.

In a turbo-market economy, HSOs are unique in that their primary funding sources are largely dwindling governmental tax dollars and declining philanthropic contributions (*Giving USA*, 2009; Strom, 2009a, 2009b), although proprietary agencies are becoming more numerous. For HSOs, often service users are not the same people as the service funders. An increase in the number of clients and corresponding services increases costs but does not automatically increase revenues. Service users generally are not service funders, they lack power over the operations of the organizations that serve them. Nevertheless, service users are valuable assets for HSOs—no clients, no organization. Agencies compete for clients as well as other resources (Greenley & Kirk, 1973). With the current privatization trend, the human services proprietary sector will continue to expand.

HSOs' funding makes them dependent on a tenuous, competitive, often turbulent and hostile political and institutional environment for legitimacy and resources. Consequently, the legitimacy and funding for human service agencies wax and wane with changes in political administrations and the ideology in vogue. Currently privatization, market models and rhetoric, and faith-based ideologies are fashionable.

Human service managers are managers of essentially political entities and need to have their political antennae up and their political hats close at hand. The political character of their work and public dependency for fiscal resources engender many challenges. The emphasis of HSOs, as well as social work, on the social environment, social interactions, and social functioning makes them inherently political. This does not imply *necessarily* a limited partisan profession consistently aligned with a particular political party, although they may reasonably align with partisan positions congruent with a profession's and an organization's mission and aims. A political profession and organization are concerned with influencing social policy or the rules that regulate social behavior and social relations. A political organization is attentive to public and civic affairs and the public or community's distribution of social statuses, privileges, and other resources that constitute the elements for the organization's well-being. Political professions and organizations are innately ideological and moral beyond the growing ideology of economic market models. They use values and ethics in selecting social theories to develop social constructions of how things ought to be as well as how things are to guide their policy behavior. Political awareness is a necessary counterbalance to escalating managerialism.

Human service work is often stressful, not only because of inadequate resources, but also because it is both "moral work" and "gendered work" (Hasenfeld, 1992). It is moral work because workers inevitably are involved in making value-laden decisions, often painful ones, that render moral judgments about the social worth of an individual or a family—for example, whether to make one more attempt to reach a difficult client, whether to cut off a service or separate a child from a family, or what kind of diagnostic label to attach. In the all-too-common situation where resources are scarce and clients' needs are strong, if not overwhelming, workers often agonize over requirements to ration services. In organizational settings where stress levels are constant and high, workers may burn out and leave or stay and find a functional or dysfunctional mode of accommodation. In public welfare agencies, such accommodations may include (a) finding a special niche in the organization that removes the worker from the firing line, (b) capitulating to agency demands to serve only "deserving" clients, (c) openly resisting agency demands, and (d) adopting a victim mentality by over-identifying with the clients (Sherman & Wenocur, 1983). With increasing use of contingent and contractual workers, option (c) is becoming less viable.

Human service work is gendered work. Women make up the majority of direct service workers, approximately 80% of licensed social workers (*Licensed social workers in the U.S.: 2004*, 2006), while men tend to hold positions of authority. Although this pattern is slowly changing, a study of NASW members and of licensed social workers indicates that most social workers are women and they largely engage in practice and for private organizations (*Licensed social workers in the U.S.: 2004*, 2006; Whitaker & Arrington, 2008). This skewed gender distribution potentially generates stressful dissonance between the assumed female workers' feminine value orientation of altruism, caring, and nurturing, which requires nonroutine activities, and the formal organization's masculine value orientation, which requires formal procedures and standardization for efficiency's sake (Dressel, 1992; Hasenfeld, 1992). This conflict, coupled with the lower pay attached to female-dominated occupations and industries, the tradition of blaming the poor for their plight, and the fact that many of the clients of human service agencies are poor women and other "undeserving" poor, devalues human service work and demeans all human service workers (Greenwell, 2010; Rich, 2009).

Organizational Auspices

Having discussed some of the similarities among HSOs, we should also attend to some of their major differences, as these also define the organization and have a strong bearing on service delivery and worker satisfaction. HSOs have three general auspices: (a) public, (b) voluntary not-for-profit, and (c) proprietary and for-profit. Auspice reflects the organization's sponsorship, control, and fundamental purpose. Social welfare agencies and HSOs are moving toward proprietary, vertically integrated, and extra-community auspices along with a managerial emphasis. The proprietary or for-profit sector has an almost 30% share of the social services market, with growth projected over the next few years. The largest proportion of proprietary HSOs are in the health and mental health sectors (Whitaker & Arrington, 2008). Immense, vertically integrated companies, such as Lockheed Martin, Xerox, and HCA, have entered and may eventually control the market. Faith-based agencies in the not-for-profit sector also are expanding and are an exception to the commercialization trend.

Public Auspice. Public or governmental HSOs are established by federal, state, or local governmental regulations and are largely supported by tax revenues. Examples include the Department of Health and Human Services, a county department of public welfare, a city mental health center, and a local high school. The fundamental intent of agencies with a public auspice is to govern. As Gortner, Mahler, and Nicholson (1987) state, "It is the business of public bureaus to administer the law. Their function is authoritarian in the deepest and most formal sense. Their role is as active and pervasive as the reach of law and government" (p. 19). Public agency accountability is broad and general, and not just to a particular group of shareholders or sponsors. While claiming community accountability, public agency accountability is to the public at large and is exercised by elected officials. Public agencies are not market-driven or directly responsive to economic forces. They are politically driven and respond to political forces that answer to economic forces and interests. Their marketplace is a political marketplace, and they respond to political actors and forces in that marketplace (Gortner, Mahler, & Nicholson, 1987, pp. 27–30).

As public organizations are established by government, the top of a public HSO's governance structure is often a politically appointed executive officer (titles may vary), such as the secretary of a department of health and mental hygiene, appointed by the governor, or the executive director of the local department of public welfare, appointed by the mayor or county executive. Other top-level administrators also may be political appointees. Below the top echelons, federal, state, and local governmental employees are hired and fired in accordance with civil service regulations that provide job classifications, salary levels, criteria, and procedures for meritorious appointments and promotions and procedures for termination. More positions in public HSOs are becoming contractual and contingent, which allows civil service rules to be sidestepped.

Some public agencies have governing boards that make major policy decisions and hire the organization's chief executive officer. Examples include elected local school boards, library boards, or the boards of regents or trustees of state universities. Some public organizations use advisory boards to assist with guiding policy, advise on top-level appointments and decisions, and serve as a network or buffer to the public. They do not have the legal authority to make the final decisions.

Frahm and Martin (2009) argue that the classic, hierarchical, bureaucratic public agencies are being replaced by a new paradigm they label as the *governance paradigm*. The governance paradigm is more a loosely coupled network of HSOs with greater flexibility and public participation. They view the governance paradigm as a synthesis of the government model and the market model. This new paradigm requires new management skills similar to those of community practice: networking, political, and marketing, with a heavy dose of IT skills.

Voluntary Not-for-Profit Auspice. Voluntary not-for-profit auspice refers to HSOs that are legally incorporated in their state as nonprofit corporations and are thereby subject to state charitable laws. Their primary function and fiduciary responsibility is to provide service to the community. In addition, these nonprofit organizations usually have been granted tax-exempt status by the Internal Revenue Service (IRS) under section 501(C)(3) or one of the other sections of the Internal Revenue Code reserved for religious, charitable, and educational organizations. They do not pay federal taxes on their corporate income. Usually nonprofit organizations also are exempt from state and local taxes, although some financially strapped local governments are challenging this policy. Nonprofits' tax exemption rests on the premise they serve public rather than private purposes and, if faith-based, the U. S. Constitution's First Amendment protections of separation of church and state.[2]

The nonprofit auspice covers a very broad range of HSOs, from huge multifunctional and global corporations such as the Johns Hopkins conglomerate and the Salvation Army, to regional family service associations, to small church-sponsored soup kitchens and everything in between.

Nonprofit organizations receive significant funding from private philanthropy (individual, corporate, and foundation donations and grants). They may also receive substantial governmental funding through purchase of service contracts, grants, and governmental insurance payments such from as Medicaid. Nonprofits frequently earn revenue from fees for services of various kinds, including third-party private insurance payments, direct fees for a service or product, and income from other related business activities, such as the operation of a health spa by a YMCA or a blood-testing laboratory by a medical school. With the relative decline in public, donor, and foundation support, fees for service are the fastest-growing funding source for social welfare (Johnston, 1997; Salamon, 1997). Private giving as a share of nonprofit revenue dropped by some 20% during the 1980s and early 1990s. This deterioration of giving is projected to continue as the national income distribution concentrates income at the top and the tax code makes philanthropic giving less financially attractive. The very wealthy customarily donate proportionately less of their income to social welfare services than does the middle class (Freudenheim, 1996, p. B8; Phillips, 1993, p. 143). Funding sources do not clearly differentiate nonprofit agencies from governmental and for-profit organizations.

The key feature distinguishing nonprofit auspices from public and for-profit agencies is that nonprofits' primary mission is service to the community rather than governance or profit. They are self-governed. Their governing boards are an all-volunteer board of directors accountable neither to nonexistent owners nor to government. They are accountable to the community. The board serves as a steward for the community. The executive officer is responsible to the board and ultimately to the community. The voluntary board is a legal requirement of incorporation as a charitable organization. Although nonprofits can earn a surplus, called a fund balance, it can't distribute the surplus over expenses to shareholders and board members. It is saved for a rainy day and reinvested in the agency. Profit is not the core of the agency's calculus.

The presence of a large nonprofit sector supports pluralistic democratic values. Nonprofits represent the essence of voluntary community action to provide citizens the services they need and want, services that government and private corporations do not provide because they are not politically or economically viable. For example, sectarian and culturally distinct groups may sponsor HSOs such as a Korean community center, a Jewish family services agency, a black mental health alliance, a group of Catholic charities, or a Hispanic community council. Moreover, because nonprofits are voluntary, self-governing bodies, they can challenge the policies and practices of private corporations and governmental agencies. Most of our important social reforms came about through nonprofit activities—child welfare, civil rights, environmental protection, women's rights, workplace safety (Salamon, 1992).

Nonprofit organizations usually provide a very different work environment from governmental agencies, one that is potentially less formal and more flexible and varied. When large and complex, both types of organizations can operate quite bureaucratically, with many policies and rules to follow, a hierarchical system of decision making, and a clearly differentiated division of labor. However, many nonprofit HSOs are not very large. A study of the Baltimore-area nonprofit sector, for example, found that in 1987, 72% of the nonprofits had expenditures of less than $500,000 (Salamon, Altschuler, & Myllyluoma, 1990). Even when they are large, nonprofits have the capacity to make decisions more quickly and to operate more flexibly than do their governmental counterparts. In part, this is a function of their system of self-governance; the executive, with the approval of the board, has great leeway to make program and policy changes. In part, it is also a function of their ability to choose whom they will serve and the nature of the services they will provide. If the market is there, a nonprofit agency can decide to provide therapy only to people with three nostrils if it is within their incorporation articles. If the market is too large, they can decide to limit their services even further or expand if they want. Governmental organizations lack this flexibility. Legally they are mandated to serve all who are eligible according to the legislation that established the organization, regardless of numbers. A child welfare agency must serve all abused and neglected children in its geographic-political service area, ultimately an indeterminate number, and any additional staffing needs are subject to political competition for scarce resources.

Not all observers hold this affirmative view of the nonprofit's organizational flexibility and

nimbleness. O'Looney (2005, p. 5) asserts: "In other fields . . ., information technologies have been applied to whole-system transformations, involving process re-engineering, job and task restructuring, expert system support, customer management, and the emergence of matrix, network, and virtual organizational designs. Far fewer of such changes have occurred as a result of the introduction of IT into organizations dominated by professional social workers."

Germak and Singh (2010, p. 79), even after the calamity of turbo-capitalism producing the Great Recession of 2008, advocate that social workers "embrace much of the straightforward business sense found in social entrepreneurship." We will discuss both IT and social entrepreneurship below.

Faith-based agencies are a particular form of nonprofit organization. They are agencies sponsored or operated by a religious organization and faith. While sharing with secular nonprofits the service mission, faith-based agencies are constrained by obligations and accountability to the tenants and dogma of the religion and its structures, whether the creed includes admonitions against abortion and homosexuality (as sins), requirements for ethnicity and religion in family relationships, and child-rearing practices. Discrimination and inequity in hiring and services to nonbelievers and persons with traits that go against the faith's doctrine—such as gays and lesbians, abortion choice, "race mixing," gender role equality—are often exercised in faith-based service agencies. Hiring discrimination is explicitly allowed in the Charitable Choice section, section 104 of the federal Personal Responsibility and Work Opportunity Reconciliation Act of 1996 (PR&WOR). The discrimination policy was allowed to continue by the Obama administration (Boston, 2010).

The question as to whether government funding of faith-based agencies does considerable damage to the Constitution's First Amendment separation and establishment clauses is best left to a social policy discussion. Over 98% of PR&WORA charitable choice funding has gone to Christian agencies, with no funding to non-Christian or Jewish agencies (Kranish, 2006). Faith-based agencies are neither more effective nor more efficient than secular agencies. The evidence does not support the claims by their advocates (Cnaan, Boddie, & Yancey, 2005) that the agencies' faith-driven zeal is more productive than the service and social justice goals of the secular agencies, especially with clients not of the agency's faith[3] (Foltin, 2000/01; Kennedy, 2003; Rosenau & Linder, 2003; Wright, 2009). A survey of social agencies in Pittsburgh, Pennsylvania (Kearns, 2007), found the secular agencies were more likely to serve poor communities than were faith-based agencies. "FBOs [faith-based organizations] are predominantly engaged in providing services to individuals and secular agencies more prominent in serving communities" (Kearns, 2007, p. 69). Service giving by faith-based agencies is often a means to proselytize and strengthen the religion's community.

Proprietary For-Profit Agencies. Proprietary for-profit auspices share the trait of having a defined ownership or proprietors—whether a single owner, a partnership of practitioners, a group of investor owners, or stockholders—and operate under the auspice of the owner rather than under public or voluntary auspices. Proprietary agencies' fundamental intent and fiduciary responsibility are profit rather than service. Service provision is a means to make a profit. Proprietary agencies provide a service only insofar as it is profitable. Someone must be willing to pay a profit margin for any services. As discussed earlier, proprietary agencies, including private practice by social workers, are a rapidly growing segment of the social work arena and social welfare field. Proprietary HSOs consist of the mega-corporations that own hospitals, home health care agencies, counseling services, residential treatment facilities, nursing homes, and the solo private social work practice, if incorporated. Proprietary HSOs are incorporated in a state as businesses and pay local, state, and federal corporate income taxes. If they are corporations, each is required to have a board of directors with a minimum of three members. These are the main administrative officers of the company. Other board members may be added because of stock ownership or special connections and expertise they bring. The chairperson is frequently the chief executive officer of the corporation. For-profit board members, unlike not-for-profit boards, expect to be paid for their services (Houle, 1989). Proprietary organizations sell their services or products at a price sufficient to cover the cost of production plus an amount for profit. Profit that is not reinvested in the organization is divided among its owners.

For-profit organizations must be extremely sensitive to the marketplace. Services often are more flexible, client-friendly, and market-responsive. The contention is that profit-seeking proprietary agencies are more performance-oriented and in tune with the latest trends and knowledge than are public and not-for-profit agencies. They allege that they are more effective and efficient, but as yet research has not supported these claims. Competition will produce advantages for clients only if there is truly competition for clients and clients have a choice of vendors, rather than the usual sole-vendor contracting. The social historian Judt (2009, p. 88), speaking on the privatization of the welfare state, argues:

So much for the theory (of privatization). The practice is very different. What we have been watching these past decades is the steady shifting of public responsibility onto the private sector to no discernible collective advantage. In the first place, privatization is inefficient. Most of the things that governments have seen fit to pass into the private sector were operating at a loss: whether they were railway companies, coal mines, postal services, or energy utilities, they cost more to provide and maintain than they could ever hope to attract in revenue.

The only reason that private investors are willing to purchase apparently inefficient public goods is because the state eliminates or reduces their exposure to risk. ... the purchasing companies were assured that whatever happened they would be protected against serious loss—thereby undermining the classic economic case for privatization: that the profit motive encourages efficiency. ... the private sector, under such privileged conditions, will prove at least as inefficient as its public counterpart—while creaming off such profits as are to be made and charging losses to the state.

The proprietary agency's disadvantages is its fiduciary responsibility: it must generate profit. Professionals in solo or group practices must operate as entrepreneurs, meet their expenses, and generate profit by generating clients or business. Flexibility gained in one aspect of practice may be offset by the time requirements of marketing and business management in another. Profit rather than service or client welfare takes priority. Large for-profit HSOs, like their counterparts in other sectors, are complex bureaucratic organizations with a highly differentiated division of labor and specialized work roles, such as marketing and public relations departments, various departments of professional services, a governmental affairs department, and so on. Individual professional authority and autonomy is lost. As businesses, proprietary agencies are organized to pursue profit.

The most intrinsic disadvantage of for-profit HSOs is that they are naturally unresponsive to the needs of poor and working-class people. Currently government, through contracts and other third-party vendor arrangements, pays and allows proprietary agencies a profit margin in the service contracts. Functionally, funders are the proprietary agency's most important constituency, not the service recipients. The health industry provides an illustration of proprietary human services. As the public sector, insurance companies, and other third-party payees reduce their market participation on behalf of the poor, proprietary agencies (including solo proprietary social workers) inevitably will correspondingly reduce their services to the poor if the poor are unwilling and unable to directly pay for the services (Sack & Pear, 2010). The poor by definition have limited capacity to purchase services. Proprietary HSOs, to survive, have gravitated to clients with a capacity to pay, and will continue to do so, when patrons such as governments continue to reduce support. When the economy is good, affluent people buy more personal services, including social work's services (Berman & Pfleeger, 1997). The poor, however, are unable to buy many services in any economy, and especially a poor economy. Profit-seeking human services ignore social work's advocacy, social justice, and social reform responsibilities.

Germak and Singh (2010) advocate social entrepreneurship as a necessary model for nonprofit HSOs in this time of shrinking resources. HSOs simply must be able to raise sufficient resources to remain operative. Social entrepreneurship is vaguely and rather broadly conceptualized as a hybrid of macro social work and business practices. Buzzwords such as "innovative" and "sound" abound in social enterprise discussions. Germak and Singh (2010, p. 81) finally settle on Paul Light's working definition of a social entrepreneur, not a conception of social entrepreneurship, as "an individual, group, network, organization, or alliance of organizations that seeks sustainable, large-scale change through pattern-breaking ideas in what or how governments, nonprofits, and businesses do to address significant social problems." This is basically a conception of good community practice.

If by "social entrepreneurship" its advocates mean good management and community practice knowledge and skills such as IT, strategic planning, market research, fundraising and product development, and responsiveness to changing client demands and needs,[4] it should be embraced. If, however, its sponsors are embracing the essence of entrepreneurship (risk and accountability), reflection is urged. An entrepreneur has the capacity and willingness to undertake development, organization, and management of an enterprise with all its attendant risks to make profit as a reward. An entrepreneur is innovative and a risk-taker (BusinessDictionary.com, 2010). Nonprofit HSOs should be innovative and accountable.[5] Profit and risk, though, are inherent contradictions to a nonprofit's fiduciary responsibility and primary mission of service to the community. The failure by a nonprofit to be prudent is a risk to clients and community as well as the agency and its employees, and rarely is there a taxpayer bailout.

Perspectives on How Organizations Function: A Brief Review

Intraorganizational Systems

Work organizations such as human service agencies or private businesses exist to do what an individual or a group of people cannot do as efficiently and effectively. The aim might be to deliver an intangible product, such as mental health services, to a needy population or to produce a tangible product, such as a smartphone. The organization's founders logically set up systematic rules for organizing the work, the division of labor and workflow, in order to accomplish their aims and then put their plans into action. In a word, they create an organization. If the founders know what they are doing, these plans work out fairly well—but seldom exactly as intended, because there are too many variables and unknowns to contend with. Organizational rationality sometimes breaks down. Some clients do not neatly fit into the image projected; some staff members do not get along with each other; some sources of funding are unexpectedly cut off; and so on. All of this is to say, as we did in Chapter 2, that organizations are open systems striving for closure. In other words, by definition, organizations always try to operate rationally, but they never can do so completely because of multiple uncertainties deriving from internal organizational sources and the external political and institutional environments that they are part of and must relate to (Thompson, 1967).

Internally, uncertainty creeps into organizations through at least three different paths: structural complexity, technological indeterminateness, and human variability. When organizations are set up to serve a large, heterogeneous population that has many complicated needs, these agencies themselves necessarily become complex systems. As mentioned previously, organizational directors and managers usually divide the work of managing the organization and producing its products or services into smaller subdivisions, a division of labor, some of which may become quite specialized. For example, a nonprofit homeless agency with a $3 million budget might have an emergency services department, a feeding program, a public policy unit, a community organizing and advocacy division, a resource development unit that includes fundraising and public relations, and an administration unit. Each unit may have additional sub-units, such as the administration's building maintenance, purchasing, and bookkeeping, and a management division that includes planning, personnel, volunteer oversight, and training. Even small nonprofits are likely to have subdivisions; large governmental or for-profit organizations can be infinitely more complex. The more differentiated the organization, the greater the difficulty in coordinating the work of the various subsystems to produce products and services efficiently and effectively. It is interesting that, at various times, both greater organizational centralization and greater decentralization have been proposed as ways to improve coordination in the interests of organizational efficiency and effectiveness. However, there is no simple answer. The

structural solution that works best depends on the goals, needs, and managerial capacities of the particular organization (Webber, 1979), as well as the organization's technology and the conditions in the external environment. An organization's technology is the things an organization intentionally does with and to the raw materials, the inputs and clients, to produce its outcomes and final products.

Technological uncertainty in HSOs comes from several sources. First, we are not always sure about how best to intervene to help deal with certain problems. What is the best approach to deal with the alcoholic, for example, or with the high incidence of alcoholism in the larger society? How about clients who are both alcoholic and mentally ill? And what about the low-income family with multiple problems? Many different technologies and belief systems may exist simultaneously in the same organization. A psychiatric hospital employs nurses, psychiatrists, psychologists, social workers, recreational therapists, and so on, each of whom may approach patients quite differently. Even within the individual disciplines, professionals may have contrary intervention practices—for example, behaviorists versus psychodynamically oriented psychologists. Secondly, we often have to rely on the cooperation of other agencies and service providers, over whom we may have little control, to provide assistance effectively. This is the governance model's collaborative approach mentioned earlier in the chapter (Frahm & Martin, 2009) Finally, since our service users are reactive, individual human beings, not inert physical materials, our interventions depend on feedback from our clients, and we cannot always predict their responses. In effect, we have to use individually customized rather than standardized technologies (Thompson, 1967) in situations where the external world often seems to be demanding mass solutions to widespread problems, such as crime or substance abuse.

Human variability, of course, also enters the organization through its employees, managers, and directors. While organizations seek rationality, all the people who make up the organization differ in personalities, beliefs and values, needs, goals, ideas, knowledge and skills, life experiences, cultural identity, and so on. They also tend to form informal groups and subgroups and develop organizational cultures that strongly influence employee and managerial behavior. The groups and subgroups can differ greatly—for example, on goals, status, and expectations—as can the culture from the official organizational governance. As various interest groups form based on shared values, norms, and predilections, some authors view the process of reaching agreements on goals and activities as an ongoing negotiation and the organization in essence as a "negotiated order," constantly in flux, rather than fixed and determinate (Cyert & March, 1963; Frahm & Martin, 2009).

One consequence of the unique characteristics of HSOs is that they tend to be structured internally as loosely coupled systems (as opposed to tightly coupled systems). In essence, the hierarchical structure of authority and clear lines of communication associated with a strictly rational system of organization do not work well in HSOs. Instead, (a) strict top-down authority is likely to be weak and dispersed in multiple authority units; (b) various subunits are likely to maintain a considerable degree of autonomy and identity, and their tasks and activities tend to be weakly coordinated; and (c) there is "a weak system of control over staff activities" (Hasenfeld, 1983, p. 150). Imagine a school system with administrators (principals), teachers, social workers, guidance counselors, psychologists, and various other specialists. Despite directives from above, ultimately the teacher runs the classroom autonomously, and necessarily so, because of the great variations among students and teaching styles. Best evidence-based practices for teaching, counseling, and social administration are limited (Briggs & McBeath, 2009; Johnson & Austin, 2006). Evaluation, even if successful counseling and social work intervention models were available, is difficult, because usually these activities are carried out even more privately and out of management's sight than is teaching. Moreover, while the principal exerts authority over the social workers, the social workers have bifurcated accountability and report to the head of the school system's social work department. The principal's authority is dissipated. Without the ability to hold staff accountable for their performance through monitoring and evaluation—and unionization and civil service requirements may add to these difficulties—the

administrator's authority is weak. One potential result of loose coupling is fragmented, disjointed service delivery system. At the same time, this arrangement may serve important functions for the organization, such as creating more potential for a flexible response to changes in the environment and buffering the organization from failures in any particular unit (Hasenfeld, 1983). Virtual organizations and management present even greater coordination and control challenges because of their dispersed nature.

Interorganizational Systems

In Chapter 2 we discussed two concepts central to understanding interorganizational relations, *domain* and *task environment*. For social service agencies and community organizations, we said that the organizational domain represents the territory that an organization has carved out in terms of the social problems it will address, the populations it will serve, and the types of advocacy or services it will provide. We want to review two points here. The first is there is generally competition for domains from other organizations, particularly when resources are scarce, a condition sometimes referred to as *domain dissensus*. Do domain consensus exists when the different actors have worked out basic agreements about boundaries and expectations about what each actor will and will not do in the task environment. We will discuss domains and the challenges of establishing and linking them in Chapter 10, "Using Networks and Networking." The second point is that an organization's domain determines the other organizations and individuals that it will have to relate to or pay attention to in order to fulfill its mission. This network of organizations, organizational subunits, and individuals forms the focal organization's *task environment*.

An organization's task environment inevitably poses uncertainty for the organization because it contains needed resources and information that the organization cannot fully control or even, in some cases, perceive. HSOs, for example, depend on having clients or members to obtain resources and legitimacy. While this is usually not a problem in public agencies, it can be a severe problem in nonprofit and for-profit organizations as needs change, populations shift, or new competitors enter the field. Interorganizational systems will be explored more fully in Chapter 10, "Using Networks and Networking."

Uncertainty and Power

Relating the concept of uncertainty to power, an inability to control the elements that an organization needs to accomplish its goals, a lack of sufficient power, creates organizational uncertainty. In today highly competitive climate for charitable dollars, nonprofit HSOs experience increasingly greater uncertainty about their funding sources. In this formulation, then, within an organization, power accrues to those individuals or groups who can resolve uncertainties for the organization (Crozier, 1964). These uncertainties may stem from internal or environmental sources. HSOs needs the capacity to process a great deal of information rapidly, so employees with computer-based information-management skills have a great deal of influence and command high salaries. The employee who can design, program, and get the system back up when it crashes may be the most powerful of all.

With the pervasive uncertainty that permeates modern organizational life, administration involves an ongoing struggle to manage internal and environmental uncertainty while keeping the organization on the path to accomplishing its goals. To succeed at this complex task, administrators and professional staff members must be able to obtain and process strategic information about every aspect of organizational life, particularly environmental trends and opportunities. A study by Menefee and Thompson (1994, p. 14) comparing management competencies of the early 1980s with requirements for the 1990s found a dramatic shift from roles and skills such as supervising and direct practice "focused primarily on internal operations to one(s) that (are) strategically oriented," such as boundary spanning and "futuring," aimed at managing a complex external environment. Thompson (1967) likens this idea of opportunistic surveillance to natural curiosity in the individual, defining this search activity as "monitoring behavior which scans the environment for opportunities—which does not have to be activated by a problem and which does not therefore stop when a problem solution has been found" (p. 151).

Opportunistic search roles take many different forms and involve both regular staff members and managers. Because they help the organization manage environmental uncertainties, they may also carry special status and influence. One important role set focuses on strategic planning. Strategic planning activities engage the organization in (a) systematically scanning its internal and external environments to identify organizational strengths and weaknesses in relation to short- and long-range trends, opportunities, and threats and (b) formulating strategies to manage the issues confronting the organization and developing a vision for the future (Bryson, 1989, p. 48). Management, staff, and volunteers may all carry out strategic planning activities. In some larger organizations, strategic planning is the ongoing business of an organizational planning department. Boundary-spanning roles encompass a large range of activities carried out by managers and staff, sometimes alone and often as parts of specialized departments, such as a public relations division, a government affairs office, an admissions department, and a discharge-planning unit.

The strategic planning activities mentioned above are also boundary-spanning functions. Boundary spanning refers to transactions that enable the organization to manage (environmental) "constraints and contingencies not controlled by the organization" (Thompson, 1967, p. 67). Boundary-spanning roles involve networking skills, the ability to develop relationships with a broad array of individuals and groups in order to exchange resources and information of value to the organization. The social worker in a hospital doing discharge planning is performing a boundary-spanning role. He or she enables the organization to respond to the constraints placed on it by the insurance companies in terms of length of inpatient stay. To do so the social worker must learn about and develop relationships with a variety of external organizations, such as home health care agencies, rehabilitation facilities, outpatient centers, and different types of nursing homes, in order to help patients continue their recovery after hospitalization. The job is sensitive and a powerful one if no one else can perform this function effectively, because the hospital is under pressure to discharge patients and, at the same time, ensure that the planning is sound so that patients recover appropriately and are satisfied with the services they have received. In one hospital where the number of non-English-speaking patients increased, a social worker developed a network of interpreters by scanning the community and reaching out to a host of immigrant groups, who were then linked to the hospital to lend their special assistance. An agency's government relations department speaks to an organizationally recognized need to be able to identify, promulgate, and influence legislation that affects the organization's ability to fulfill its mission.

Boundary spanners may develop a good deal of power in their organizations if they help the organization manage environmental contingencies that are important to it and if others cannot easily do the job (Thompson, 1967). Organizational fundraisers or resource developers, for example, can often bargain for much higher salaries than other staff members. In the growing culturally diverse environment of HSOs, social workers with skills in working with diverse populations will gain leverage. Boundary-spanning roles in organizations facing complex, competitive, and highly dynamic external environments require a great deal of personal discretion. If handled well, these positions bring influence and high compensation. In homogeneous and more stable environments with standardized boundary-spanning roles, influence will be correspondingly less.

Examining the Formal Structure and Operations

Organizational Mandates, Mission, and Goals

We need to examine both the rational and non-rational aspects of organizational life to understand the workings of an organization. On the rational side, we can begin by understanding the purpose for which the organization was formed, the mandates under which it is operating, and its operative goals. Straightforward as this sounds, such an examination moves us quickly into the tangle of organizational complexity.

Organizational mandates are what the organization is required to do according to its charter or articles of incorporation or, in the case of a public agency, as codified in laws and ordinances (Bryson, 1989). A department of child protective services, for example, may be required by statute to investigate all cases reported to it of child abuse and neglect in a particular locality. A non-profit agency may require, in its articles of incorporation, that it serve the poorest families in the county. Organizations may well exceed their mandates and provide additional services, so any search for organizational purposes should not be limited to mandates.

An organization's mission usually flows from the organization's mandate. An organization's mission statement "delineates the organization's reason for existing, usually in a short paragraph capturing the essence of what the organization is attempting to do" (Fisher, Schoenfeldt, & Shaw, 1990, p. 691). Examples of mission statements, elaborate and succinct, are presented in Box 8.1. Mission statements often appear in annual reports, agency brochures, and newsletters and provide a basis for the organization to acquire needed legitimacy and community support. Mandates and mission statements are the official goals of an organization. These are relatively easy to discover and are essential to understand for evaluating an agency's effectiveness, holding it accountable, and comprehending the underlying beliefs and values about human nature guiding the organization (Hasenfeld, 1983). However, they also tend to be rather general, vague, and grandiloquent, and do not actually tell us how the organization spends its energy and resources in the face of multiple and competing interests and pressures generated from internal and environmental sources.

To thoroughly understand an organization, according to Perrow (1961), we need to uncover the organization's operative goals. "Operative goals designate the ends sought through the actual operating policies of the organization; they tell us what the organization is actually trying to do regardless of what the official goals say are the aims" (p. 856). A corrections unit may include rehabilitation in its mission statement as one of its main aims, but if little of its budget goes into staff to provide rehabilitative services, we will have to conclude that its primary function is custodial.

Operative goals are much more difficult to discern than official goals. Firstly, any complex

BOX 8.1.	Mission Statements

The Association of Community Organizations for reform now (Acorn, 2010)

The Association of Community Organizations for Reform Now aims to organize a majority of low-to-moderate-income people across the United States. The members of ACORN take on issues of relevance to their communities, whether those issues are discrimination, affordable housing, a quality education, or better public services. ACORN believes that low-to-moderate-income people are the best advocates for their communities, and so ACORN's low-to-moderate-income members act as leaders, spokespeople, and decision-makers within the organization.

United Mountain Defense

United Mountain Defense is dedicated to protecting Tennessee's Watersheds, Air, Mountains and People.

Americans United (AU)

Americans United (AU) is a nonpartisan organization dedicated to preserving the constitutional principle of church–state separation as the only way to ensure religious freedom for all Americans.

The 2010 Nationwide Tax Revolt Tea Party

The American Tax Revolt encompasses the ideal that the only true way to rebuild the American Economy is through allowing the Private Sector to create real jobs not Government Sector jobs. We feel that through Major Tax Cuts and Major Government Cuts, the Private Sector can then be free to create jobs in a Real Market Economy. This Major Tax Cut must be accompanied by a Major Government Cut so as is [sic] to instigate this with Fiscal Responsibility.

---

organization is likely to have multiple and sometimes conflicting goals. Secondly, organizations are dynamic systems. Goals rarely are unmovable for all time; they shift as the organization loses and gains staff, board members, and resources and as the task environment changes.

How, then, are we to determine an organization's goals? This is an opportunity to apply the assessment skills discussed in the preceding chapters, included participant-observation, analysis of a sample of client case files, observations of client–staff interactions, and formal and informal interviews with the various agency constituents and key informants. Perrow (1961) says that if we know something about how the organization accomplishes its major tasks of acquiring resources and legitimacy, the skills that it marshals to deliver its services, how the staff and clients and other external agencies are coordinated, and the characteristics of the organization's "controlling elites," we can develop a pretty fair idea of an organization's operative goals. An analysis of the agency's budget to see where resources are allocated is a significant indicator of true goals. Much of this information is available to organizational insiders, and even the public, if pursued thoughtfully and systematically.

Authority and Structure

Organizations are used to do what individuals and informal groups alone can't do. This gives rise to the defining characteristics and formal structure of organizations. They are rooted in the need for efficiency and effectiveness in production, coordination of organization units, and control of behavior. The central feature of complex organizations is the scalar principle. The scalar principle is the principle of the pyramid or a hierarchy. The organization's hierarchical structure of authority of the scalar principle delineates a chain of command for decision making and a span of control for all organizational participants. This formal organizational structure is depicted graphically in an organization chart (Fig. 8.2). Its logic is that it "establishes clear lines of responsibility and accountability" for decision making, "provides for a system of controls to ensure staff compliance," and "enables the coordination of various tasks by means of hierarchical centers of responsibility" (Hasenfeld, 1983, p. 161). The scalar principle holds that higher positions in a hierarchy have greater authority and correspondingly greater organizational knowledge and competence. The flow and delegation of authority is downward from the apex, and accountability and responsibility is owed upward to the apex. Authority is delegated, and decentralization (diffusion) occurs downward and centralization (putting the organization into a whole) occurs upward (Fayol, 1987). The other significant features of complex organizations are outlined in Figure 8.2.

Organizational authority is an important form of organizational power, though not the only form, as we have seen. It derives from the formal rules and charter of the organization that legitimate the power ascribed to positions of authority by its laws. It may be supported as well by tradition, expertise, and the charismatic leadership of the authority holders. The exercise of authority depends partly on the strength of the sanctions that can be applied to produce compliance. In the final analysis, however, authority rests on the consent of the governed. Persons in positions of authority who exceed their limits or whose dictates are considered unfair will breed subtle forms of noncompliance, sabotage, or open insubordination. Box 8.2 lists the key features of a complex organization.

Leaders with rational or legal authority often are ascribed charismatic power. Staffs frequently attribute charisma to formal leaders regardless of their personal traits, especially in times of crisis. President George W. Bush was attributed charisma power for a time following the Sept. 11, 2001, terrorist attacks on the World Trade Center and the Pentagon, but it was largely lost by his second term. Mayor Rudolph Giuliani during the same period was encouraged and indeed attempted to extend his time as mayor beyond the legal term limit, on the basis of charisma but not law. His 2008 presidential campaign failed to garner enthusiasm. Charisma is often fleeting.

Charisma is particularly useful in informal organization and cultures when people are drawn to leaders based on personal traits, regardless of their organizational position. It is essential in political campaigns and organizations. Charismatic leaders are motivators. Fisher's (2009) review of motivation and leadership argues that it also is critical for social work managers: "Motivation is one side of the relationship between managers and workers. Social work managers need to understand what motivates employees, but they must also understand how to lead in order to inspire motivation" (p. 354).

The exercise of authority, leadership, and motivation depends partly on the strength of the sanctions applied to produce compliance. Compliance refers to the ways organizations

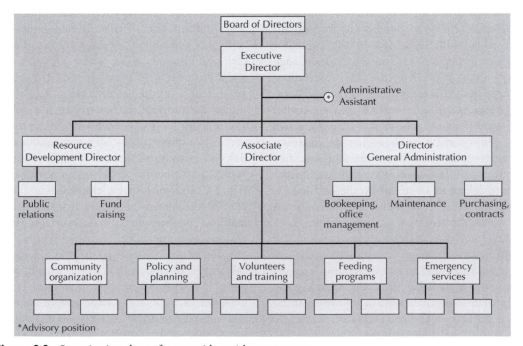

Figure 8.2. Organization chart of a statewide anti-hunger agency.

| **BOX 8.2.** | **Complex Organization's Key Features** |

1. Specialization with limited areas of authority and responsibility for each position and organization unit representing the division of labor. Each position needs well-defined authority, responsibility, and accountability (ARA).
2. Hierarchical authority structure with control and responsibility concentrated at top according to the scalar principle and delegated to subordinate organizational units and positions. Unity of command and direction is necessary for coordination, and control occurs at every level.
3. Organizational intelligence and information centralized at the top and dispersed to other units, according to need, by formal channels of communication.
4. Position specialization is rooted in the needs of the organization and requires specific expertise, authority, responsibility, accountability, and compliance with organizational job descriptions.
5. Positions are careers requiring full-time commitment, contributing to organizational stability.
6. Rules and procedures for rational coordination of activities, compliance with the complex organization's organization's division of labor, and a position's ARA established by the organization
7. Impersonality of and secondary relationship between members rather than relating by personal traits and attractions and a separation of personal lives from organizational position to contribute to the organization's stability, order, and rationality
8. Recruitment and position assignment based on merit, ability, and technical skills as required for a position, rather than on personal traits and primary relationships
9. Separation of the person's private and personal lives and primary relationships from the organizational position, to contribute to the organization's stability, order, and rationality
10. Promotion by seniority, merit, and contributions to production and organizational goals rather than because of personal relations. Seniority represents merit.

Source: Fayol, 1987; Netting, Kettner, & McMurtry, 2007.

---

obtain adherence by organizational members to organizational goals, norms, and prescribed and proscribed behaviors. There are three general types or models of compliance: *coercive* applies punishment to obtain compliance, *utilitarian* uses rewards and self-interest to obtain compliance, and *normative* bases compliance on values, norms, and ethics (Etzioni, 1987). The models are not mutually exclusive; indeed, social agencies to use all three models to obtain compliance. Employees are given raises and material rewards, are sanctioned and threatened with termination, and have their pride and professional ethics challenged. Voluntary not-for-profits (especially faith-based organizations) emphasize the normative model, while proprietary agencies are more likely to employ utilitarian approaches first.

Part of the organization's challenge is that power doesn't always correspond to the organizationally assigned formal rational or legal organizational authority. While the hierarchical structure of authority delineates a chain of command for decision making and a span of control for all of the organization's participants, it may not reflect the distribution of power. Power, discussed in Chapter 2, is the ability to act in the face of opposition to control one's self and to control or influence others. While power is rarely pure, it does exist, especially as influence or the capacity to produce intended and foreseen effects on others (Bragg, 1996; Willer, 1999; Willer, Lovaglia, & Markovsky, 1999). Influence is less than absolute power and affects the behavior of others, regardless of the intent. Influence is rooted in an ability to alter the behavior of another. Sources of power beyond the formally assigned organizational authority include control over resources needed by the organization, such as connections to networks that can be drawn upon, personal power or charisma, expert knowledge needed by the organization, and knowledge or organizational secrets (where the figurative bodies are buried). Power and influence are enhanced when others have fewer alternatives and are dependent on the resource supplier. Box 8.3 lists the various sources of the HSO's authority.

Other factors also affect the organization's authority structure. Authority seldom operates in a straight-line fashion. Confusion in the division of labor and organization design muddles up the arrangements and distribution of authority/responsibility/accountability (ARA) and creates uncertainty in an agency. Secondly, in complex organizations, authority and expertise don't always come together in a single individual sufficiently to make him or her the most effective decision maker. For example, a dean of social work school can understand social work education, social work, CSWE policy, and the university quite well and can have strong planning skills but may be ignorant of the essential knowledge and skills of resource development and fundraising. This dean will fail in our resource-starved era unless he or she can hire a development officer. To the extent that effective organizational decision making requires a unification of knowledge and authority, collective input and consultation into decision making is necessary.

Thirdly, in order to operate effectively in a turbulent external environment, organizations need flexibility more than rigid hierarchical structures to allow, both internally and externally, entrepreneurial organizational behavior. Another way of gaining flexibility is to use temporary structures. "Through independent, limited-life project, product, problem, or venture teams, specialists necessary to accomplish a mission are brought together for as long as necessary, but no longer" (Webber, 1979, p. 383).

Boards of Directors

Both for-profit and not-for-profit agencies have boards of directors, unless the for-profit or proprietary agency is not a corporation. This section primarily concerns the boards of nonprofit organizations; for-profit corporate boards may operate somewhat differently. In not-for-profit organizations, the ultimate authority for decision making about the direction of the organization rests with the board of directors or trustees, hereafter referred to as a governing board (Houle, 1989). The governing board normally works in partnership with the executive, who oversees the day-to-day operation of the organization, and with the staff, who carry out the actual work of the agency. The popular notion that boards establish policy and executives and staff carry it out does not work out that way in practice, for a variety of practical reasons. Board members serve only on a part-time basis and seldom have the professional expertise in the organization's service area or the necessary staff of their own to be able to make operating and even long-range policies. They are not in a good position to dictate policy from on high. If the board and the executive have developed a good working relationship, then, more typically, the executive will generate policy, fiscal, and programmatic recommendations for the board to consider and act on in a timely fashion. Usually these deal with general policies and large fiscal expenditures or programmatic changes, and an understanding of the meanings of *general* and *large* will need to be worked out between the parties involved. Boards ultimately have a fiduciary responsibility to the community, not to the agency or the executive director.

Of course, power struggles may arise between executives and boards, executives do not always keep their boards properly informed, or boards may try to micromanage their organizations (Kramer, 1965). In fact, in the early stages of organizational development, when an agency is starting out, board members may commonly exercise a great deal of authority over the daily affairs of the organization (Mathiasen, 1990). As the organization matures, however, governing boards evolve that recognize the need to shift from specific to general oversight.

The fiduciary responsibility for the HSO stops with the governing board and can't legitimately be

BOX 8.3.	Forms of Authority

- Traditional authority: Based on culture and customs
- Charismatic authority: Based on the personal traits and characteristics of the individual
- Rational/legal authority: Based on the organization's rules and laws and rooted in the scalar principle

delegated. Borrowing from Cyril O. Houle (1989, pp. 90–94), a governing board briefly should:

1. Keep the organization true to its mission.
2. Ensure the organization engages in long-range planning and approve all developed plans.
3. Supervise the HSO's programs to ensure that objectives are being achieved in the best fashion possible. The board needs to be sophisticated enough about programs, with the help of the executive and staff, to be able to make informed judgments.
4. Hire the chief executive officer and establish the conditions of employment.
5. Work closely with the executive and through the executive with staff to be sure the executive functions are carried out effectively. The executive has the responsibility for administering the agency, recruiting and deploying staff, developing personnel policies (along with the board), making participatory decisions, resolving conflicts, and developing effective fiscal control measures.
6. Serve as the final arbiter and mediator in conflicts between staff members on appeals of decisions of the executive and conflicts between the executive and the staff. The executive has first responsibility to resolve conflicts, with the board serving as an appeals body.
7. Establish broad policies governing the organization's program within which the executive and staff function. Policies may originate with the board, executive, or staff, but the board must adopt, modify, or reject them after due consideration.
8. Ensure that the organization's basic legal, fiduciary, and ethical responsibilities are fulfilled.
9. Secure and manage adequate financial resources to fund its policy decisions and fiduciary responsibilities. The board should not decide that the organization should move into a new program area without attending to the resources needed to operate the program. Securing resources is not solely the board's obligation, but it is one of its most important responsibilities.
10. Help the organization build and promote a positive image with the public and other institutions with which the organization transacts business. The board serves as one

of the organization's main links and boundary spanners to the task environment. These links are very important for the organization in establishing legitimacy and finding needed resources.
11. Evaluate its own performance and composition to keep its membership able, broadly representative of the community, and active. It should assess its own processes and ability to help the organization achieve its mission.

Boards of directors serve as important linchpins and boundary-spanning mechanisms. Board members help to link the agency with other agencies and give cohesion to the social agency community when board members serve on the boards of more than one agency. Agency policy and operations can be affected by influencing the board members. They also link the agency to important community constituencies such as client groups, holders of fiscal resources, and community economic and political power holders. Again, a board's fiduciary responsibility is to the community. These functions and contributions should be considered when constructing and using boards of directors.

The Informal Structure: What is Not on the Organization Chart

Let's say that a certain transitional shelter for homeless men has a formal policy of not serving drug addicts. To check on their clients, a random system of urine testing is carried out, and if the test is positive, the client is supposed to be asked to leave the shelter. A new social worker tries to follow this policy with one of his clients but is overruled by his supervisor. Unknown to the new staff member, the social work staff has developed an informal system for rating drug-addicted clients, so that some are given second and third chances after positive test results. He did not yet know the system; it's not part of any official agency policy. Analyzing why this unofficial policy developed and how it operates would provide a lot of insight into the workings of this particular organization.

This example and our experiences in organizations remind us that the formal aspects of organizational life do not tell the whole story of how organizations function. A more complete understanding requires examination of the informal structure as well—that is, the associations among members of the organization that are not part of the formal organizational chart (Scott, 1973, pp. 105–106). The members of any organization form relationships with each other for many different reasons—physical proximity on or off the job; mutual interests; personal attractiveness; similar job responsibilities; shared values, social class, status, income or other social characteristics, or because of some special issue that arises. Informal associations may take on a small-group life of their own, with unique status and communication systems, leaders, membership requirements, and norms for behavior that associational members are expected to follow. If formal relationships provide a skeletal structure for an organization, informal relationships are the glue that holds an organization together and makes it work. Jaskyte and Lee's (2009) research on organizational commitment by social workers found that the informal organization is more important than the formal organization in developing commitment: in "organizations that used informal socialization tactics, where the newcomers had opportunities to learn on the job and were not segregated from experienced organizational members, social workers tended to express higher levels of commitment" (p. 287).

Informal associations strongly influence organizational culture and behavior. Organizational culture is the aspect of organizations that functions similarly to cultures in societies. Organizational culture involves the members' basic values and constructions of reality, the ways things ought to be done, and what constitutes good citizen behavior (O'Connor, Netting, & Fabelo, 2009). Organizational culture forms a pattern of basic assumptions that have been developed by group members over time to cope with the problems of functioning in an organization; these assumptions have worked well enough to be considered valid and, therefore, are taught to new members as the correct way to perceive, think, and feel in relation to those problems. The pattern represents how things are and ought to be (Gortner, Mahler, & Nicholson, 1987, pp. 73–75; Schein, 1987, p. 385). Organizational culture has (a) observed behavioral regularities, (b) values, norms, and rules, such as "a fair day's work for a fair day's pay" or "don't be a rate

buster," (c) a philosophy, and (d) rules (or the ropes) that create (e) a feeling or climate that guides internal behavior and the ways members interact with the organizations's different publics (Schein, 1987, p. 384).

While all organizations have formal rules to guide behavior, to understand the behavior of organizational members and to understand or predict how an organization will behave under different circumstances, one must know and understand its organizational culture. Organizational culture determines the organization's symbols and reality construction. The organization's reality is influenced by its culture and its symbols and ideas that provide the way to interpret facts and data. The symbols are the emotionally charged words, phases, acts, and things that determine who gets what perks and privileges, who fits in, and who are the organizational heroes. The human relations and organizational development schools attempt to manage organizations by developing, manipulating, and managing the symbols and dramaturgy of organizational culture.

From a management perspective, informal groups and sometimes the organizational culture can "knot up" an organization by openly objecting to a new policy or program, can more subtly sabotage it, or can sometimes even make it work well. Since such associations always develop, management would do well to work with the informal organization. This involves "not threatening its existence unnecessarily, listening to opinions expressed for the group by the leader, allowing group participation in decision-making situations, and controlling the grapevine by prompt release of accurate information" (Scott, 1973, p. 107). To add to the complexities of organizational culture and managing it, a complex organization generally has multiple cultures (O'Connor, Netting, & Fabelo, 2009).

Nonmanagerial members of an organization also benefit from an understanding of its informal

A Paradigm of the Competitive Culture

- Competition is good, because it brings out the best in people and makes them more productive.
- With competition, the better, more productive people will succeed.

- The people who can't stand the pressure will fail to produce.
- If they fail, they fail because they are made of lesser material.
- If we succeed, we are better than others because we do succeed.
- If we succeed, it is because we are better and therefore deserve better treatment than those who are inferior and don't succeed.

structure and culture. The formal structure tells you who has the authority to make decisions, but when that authority is remote, the informal structure and organizational culture suggests who communicates with whom, who has influence with the decision makers, and how to gain access to them. The informal system reveals alternative sources of power in the organization. The informal system often serves as the repository of organizational tradition and history (oral history actually, because much of organizational life is not recorded). Since formal and informal values and practices do not always agree and multiple cultures can exist, organizational members can be faced with conflicting demands that are difficult to resolve. A better understanding of the informal system and some attention to organizational history may help an individual avoid these situations.

Communication, especially for coordination and control, is the lifeblood of any organization. Within the informal structure, communication tends to be oral rather than written, although the ubiquitous e-mail, smartphones, and Twitter are fast taking hold as a substitute for direct oral communication. If the memo is the symbol of bureaucratic communication, the rumor could be considered the symbol of informal communication. "A rumor is an unconfirmed message transmitted along interpersonal channels" (Rogers & Agarwala-Rogers, 1976, p. 82). If anyone can talk to anyone in the organization, rumors spread quickly through the grapevine winding under, over, and around official communication pathways, now hastened by technology. Rumors can have a kernel of truth to them, which tends to make them credible.

The organizational chart gives us some idea of the formal structure of communications.

Communication in organizations generally can be studied through network analysis. We discuss networks and network analysis more thoroughly in Chapter 10, "Using Networks and Networking." A network is two or more units (in this case people) who intentionally interact in an exchange relationship. They may interact to complete tasks, to accomplish a shared or individual goal, or to obtain mutual satisfaction. Informal analysis might involve observations of who spends time in whose offices, which groups eat together, and who regularly sits with each other at general meetings, and doing sociographic charting. Through careful observation, it should be possible to identify cliques, opinion leaders, and individuals who seem to be able to bridge different formal and informal groupings (liaisons). E-mail tracking and phone logs, if available, provide another source of network data. Further systematic analysis involves collecting sociometric and other kinds of data through surveys of the members of an organization or a subsystems.

We will explore the implications of the virtual organization on organizational culture and commitment below.

Computer Resources and Uses and Virtual Agencies

Most HSOs now use, if not rely on, computers and IT for some part of data collection, analysis, and storage, although this use is not as extensive as in the proprietary sector (O'Looney, 2005). IT and CT have increased the amount, if not the quality, of communication. Word processors have replaced the clerical staff. Smartphones are replacing landline telephones and even cell phones. Agencies are requiring social workers to learn the new technologies (O'Looney, 2005). E-mail and local area networks (LANS) have greatly expanded the speed and quantity (again, if not the quality) of intra- and interorganizational communication. The keyboard and monitor, smartphone, Twitter, and social networking venues are replacing the water cooler and coffee room as the prime means for office gossip. Computers, electronic information, communication management skills for the World Wide Web, videos, closed-circuit telenets, video bases, interactive Web sites, and virtual Internet clinics are all critical technologies and skills for managing and conducting practice. The use of the

Internet and the Web to promote social ideas and individual agencies and as a mode for therapy or counseling is an essential part of 21st-century practice. E-mails, Web pages, and social networking sites provide expanded opportunities for distributing information to the public and doing marketing and case coordination. Internet chat rooms are used for information-sharing and emotional support groups (Finn, 1996). Computerized and online library reference services such as *Social Work Abstracts* and *PsychLIT* allow more rapid and timely literature searches for developing case theory. Computers are most useful in performing repetitive tasks, in storing and retrieving huge amounts of qualitative and quantitative information efficiently, and in analyzing quantitative information. They can be used to retrieve specific information from extensive and complex data files or databases with relative speed and ease. Case records can be stored in computer files that allow for ease of retrieval and for the examination of traits and relationships across cases to develop treatment approaches. Spreadsheet software facilitates the fiscal management necessary in a competitive practice arena (Baskin, 1990, p. 6; Finn, 1988; Kreuger, 1997; Lohmann & Wolvovsky, 1997). Although sometimes employed in ways that make no real contribution in return for the effort, computers can allow access to massive amounts of information and are becoming obligatory for participation in many areas of society. Computer indexes and the Web have replaced the library's card catalogue as the go-to place to find out about problems, solutions, skills, resources, experiments, case studies, and arguments. *Google* is both a noun and a verb. However, online resources are not always reliable because opinions abound in the new electronic dialogue.

E-mail is a primary computer resource and has become an essential communications tool. It can eliminate "phone tag," although it creates stuffed inboxes, for professionals and can allow messages to be sent with documents, lists, or pictures attached. Communication systems are enhanced with e-mail and LANS of computer stations. Many individuals and small organizations have computers with Internet access mainly so they can use e-mail. Community groups can obtain free e-mail accounts using a service on the Internet and can send and receive messages from any accessible, connected computer. In our democracy, anyone can e-mail our nation's leader (president@whitehouse.gov).

Internet access is useful to social workers in several ways. General indexing services or search engines have a number of useful resources, such as nationwide telephone directories, maps and driving directions, and local directories linked to media, government, and community organizations, in addition to their primary function of finding Web pages (posted materials). State and local governments are posting detailed information about their programs and the personnel responsible for them on the Internet. A Google search on any key words will yield an abundance of information—and misinformation. Anything can and is posted on the Internet.

Community education materials about general governmental activity or particular legislative bills can be obtained by electronic means (Bourquard & Greenberg, 1996; Perlman, 2000). Knowing how to use the Internet allows anyone, including disadvantaged persons, to be in instant contact with experts—lawyers, architects, and planners—from around the country for purposes of self-education, planning, or action (Blundo, Mele, Hairston, & Watson, 1999; Mele, 1999). Caring professionals have launched projects in places such as rural Florida to ensure Internet access to low-income communities.

Like most people in society, social workers are developing skills to use computers and the Internet to communicate and gather information. A number of basic texts are available for those who want to achieve computer literacy or make better use of their computer, from finding a client who has vanished to obtaining fundraising information (Basch & Bates, 2000; Ferrante & Vaughn, 1999; Martinez & Clark, 2001; Yaffe, 2001). Local libraries may be helpful to clients, to community groups, and to us in demonstrating what can be done. Some useful Web sites are those of the Association for Community Organization and Social Administration (http://www.acosa.org); a site called "World Wide Web Resources for Social Workers" that is jointly sponsored by New York University's Ehrenkranz School of Social Work and the Division of Social Work and Behavioral Science, Mount Sinai School of Medicine (http://www.nyu.edu/socialwork/wwwrsw/); and the University of

Maryland's School of Social Work Web site (http://www.ssw.umaryland.edu) on evidence-based practice. When designing their own Web sites, agencies must make sure they are useful, interesting, and accessible to everyone (Smith & Coombs, 2000).

E-mail and Internet users should remember that they leave a trail when using agency technology. Unlike the water cooler and coffee room gossiping, e-mail leaves an electronic trail and legally is the property of the agency and can be assessed by the HSO's network managers. E-mails are not truly private: generally, office e-mails can be monitored and read by employers and LANS managers. Internet managers can follow the electronic trail of communication targets and e-mail addresses and messages.

The Virtual Agency

Most of us, unless we are excessive Luddites, have used "virtuality" and components of a virtual organization when employing IT and CT. More and more HSOs look to IT and CT to deal with critical resource scarcities, personnel concerns, and logistical issues. A typical social work student uses e-mail and cell phones or smartphones, does online literature searches, and reads articles online. The student may take online classes.

Virtual organizations are a set of units (people and departments) that rely on IT and CT across time and space to communicate, coordinate, and control the organization's production, data, skills, knowledge, and expertise. Flexibility is possible because of reconfigurable computer networks (Pang, 2001; Williams, 2007). A virtual organization does not require—indeed, it often discourages—face-to-face, personal interactions. The units participate in the collaboration and present themselves as a unified organization.

Although HSOs are becoming more virtual, according to O'Looney, they have been tardy in their transformation. The major reasons appear to be:

- They are undercapitalized and relatively small in size and can't make the initial investment in technology.
- Beyond data storage and retrieval, much of HSOs' technology, work, and production is not amenable to off-the-shelf information technologies and automation. Lack of capital prevents development of "boutique" systems.
- While networks abound between HSOs, no single agency has the capacity to impose an information and technology system, and most small-scale organizations prefer their own information management. HSO networks frequently are fractured, faddish, brittle, bureaucratic, and jealous of their limited autonomy.
- Policymakers for public sector HSOs, the politicians, do not have much interest in funding automated communication and information systems, as any benefits likely will accrue to future politicians.

Despite the obstacles and restraining forces, virtual organization components are being adapted and adopted by HSOs. In addition to the cost savings in data processing, including word processing, with a reduction or elimination of clerical staff, storage, and retrieval, there are other perceived advantages. The biggest is flexibility. Data can be recorded, shared, and retrieved simultaneously by many workers without the constraints of time and space. The movement toward outsourcing and using contingent and contract employees fits the virtual model. No elaborate physical structure and overhead are necessary for the virtual agency. Communication is virtual, not face to face. Messages can bypass the chain and go almost instantly to hundreds or thousands of employees. Networking techniques used by Facebook are organizationally adaptable. Workers are independent of a particular geographic space and can be spread throughout the community or globally and linked by the Internet and smartphones. An agency's responsibility for long-term contracts, health insurance, and physical space is removed for contract professionals who are coordinated and controlled by technology. There also is flexibility in work hours. Telecommuting and virtual commuting will be more common in the future HSO, reducing transportation costs and time and also making a positive environmental impact (the virtual organization is green!).

Unfortunately, there is little hard support for the virtual HSO beyond the data function and flexibility. Garicano and Heaton (2010), examining the relationship between IT, productivity, and organization in police departments between 1987 and 2003, concluded that the use of IT was not associated with reductions in crime rates, increases in clearance rates, or improvements in other productivity measures. Logically, CT that increases reported crime actually generates the appearance of lower productivity because of increased reports compared to clearances. IT did, however, improve productivity when used with the data-gathering and data-retrieval Compstat program.

The virtual agency faces some challenges directly related to its (dare it be said!) virtues. IT and CT tremendously increase the speed and breadth of communication, but it is not face-to-face communication. Feedback is more limited, so a common language between all units is critical. Coordination and control are reduced if, as is true of most HSOs, there are not clear, measurable performance standards. The worker reports but the manager doesn't monitor performance. The lack of face-to-face interaction and monitoring can result in the employee focusing on non-work activities. Employees need to be self-motivating, self-starting, and accountable. Virtual networks are also vulnerable to hackers (Kaser, 2007; O'Looney, 2005; Pang, 2001; Williams, 2007).

A significant disadvantage of a virtual organization is the reduction in employee commitment. Virtual networks and virtual organizations do not appear to build the social capital necessary for strong social cohesion. As indicted above Jaskyte and Lee (2009) found that informal socializing tactics and integration of new social workers with experienced workers increased expressions of commitment. In a virtual organization workers, new or experienced, are more isolated. Other observers have arrived at similar conclusions (Kaser, 2007; O'Looney, 2005; Pang, 2001; Williams, 2007).

However, commitment may not be as important to the virtual agency as to the traditional agency. Employer–employee relations are more tenuous and loose and tenures are shorter and more circumscribed.

Regardless of their strengths and weaknesses, IT and CT will continue to propel HSOs toward "virtualness." Voice-command software and natural language computers are here. They will replace the office-bound social worker as a dispenser of information, counseling, and therapy. The prudent professional will master IT and CT.

Working the System

Formal decision-making processes in organizations are necessary for action to be taken on major policies, organizational goals, and large expenditures of resources. However, within the formal policy structure, staff members and managers must make daily operative decisions using their own discretion on a wide array of significant and insignificant but necessary matters. Some of these operative decisions fall solely within one's own jurisdiction, but many also involve another's purview. An e-mail has to get out right away and your server is down; documents must be downloaded right away to complete an important client referral; a client in crisis needs immediate attention and an exception to policy to take care of it. The challenge is to get around the rules, bend the rules, or rearrange priorities to make the organization work better for yourself and your clients. In other words, how do you "work the system" to accomplish what you need to do on your own behalf or on behalf of a client?

In considering whether to work the system or change agency policy, let us first note our assumption that the worker is an active organizational professional, not merely a passive bureaucrat receiving and reflexively implementing orders from above, like Sergeant Schultz[6] in the late-1960s television series "Hogan's Heroes." A professional social worker is called on to exercise judgment in practice according to the values of the profession, not merely to act out of unquestioning loyalty to the agency. This means working the system or trying to change agency policy and practices altogether. Secondly, the question of working the system implies that organizational flexibility is necessary and desirable in the face of the myriad uncertainties that every HSO encounters.

Both working the system and changing the agency require the worker to understand its formal processes for decision making, formal and informal sources of power, and formal and informal agency rules that guide decisions. The worker needs to understand how the agency makes decisions, who makes them, and who influences the decision-making process, since persons in authority seldom act alone without input from various subordinates or others connected with the organization (Patti & Resnick, 1972). To work the system, the worker will then have to decide whether a formal decision is necessary to pursue the particular course of action in mind, or whether the course of action merely involves some organizational tinkering (Pawlak, 1976) that can be handled informally or by exercising personal discretion. If you are new in the organization, if you have not yet established your own legitimacy and influence, or if the course of action you want to take violates a basic policy or organizational tradition, you would be wise not to act without first seeking a formal decision or the approval of an administrator.

Formal and informal organizational rules beg to be manipulated. The reason is that "rules vary in specificity, in their inherent demand for compliance, in the manner in which compliance is monitored, and in their sanctions for a lack of compliance" (Pawlak, 1976, p. 377). Therefore, workers can bend or get around the rules by exercising discretion in the case of an ambiguous or general rule or by the interpretation of the rule that they choose to make. For example, an agency rule for referring homeless persons for emergency health care can be interpreted strictly or liberally. A sound knowledge of the rules can enable a worker to challenge an interpretation of a rule with another contradictory rule or to find the exceptions that can justify one's decision. Workers do need to be caution in asking their superiors to interpret a rule rather than using their own judgment, lest the authority render an unfavorable decision that must then be complied with. While official rules violations can have formal sanctions, violations of informal and cultural rules are more informally sanctioned. A last caveat here is to be careful not to impose rules that don't exist. And to paraphrase Alinsky, make the agency live up to its own book of rules.

In working or trying to change the system, we can increase our success rate as advocates and change agents by developing our own "social capital" or influence in the organization (Brager & Holloway, 1977). This involves two approaches: (a) establishing positive exchange relationships with other members of the organization and (b) establishing personal legitimacy. In the former case, by offering support, assistance, approval, or favors, the worker creates an obligation to reciprocate on the part of others, hence building potential political or social indebtedness. In a reciprocal relationship, the debt that you are owed may be used to obtain assistance, reorder priorities, or take care of a problem that you need to solve—for example, getting your letter typed right away by a busy secretary or getting some inside information. As these exchanges are made, of course, you may incur debts in turn.

In order to strengthen legitimacy in the organization, the worker needs to establish competence and expertise to deal with a particular problem area. By doing so, the worker gains influence in decisions affecting the problematic area. Remember, the sources of power in an organization are a function of controlling resources that others need or the ability to resolve uncertainties that the organization cannot tolerate. Competence in one area may help the worker to establish a reputation for competence in other areas, thereby gradually enlarging his or her sphere of influence. Building up one's social capital is a major practice task preceding a worker's attempts at organizational change.

Changing the Agency from Within

Sometimes agency rules, policies, or even entire programs need to be changed in order to prevent or correct an injustice or to improve agency programs and services. For a variety of reasons, these changes may not be initiated from the top down. Line workers and middle managers often have to act as agency change agents in their own interests or in the interests of their clients and for the good of the agency. A new staff member in a community mental health center found, in following up with clients, that many former mental patients were living in group homes near the agency that were little more than human warehouses. When she suggested to her supervisor that some group services might be extended to these homes, she was met with a negative response: "Our agency has no funds for outreach services of that sort." The matter should not end here: the worker has an ethical obligation to advocate for and to pursue social justice for her clients. She must explore and develop ways of getting them needed services. Her own agency is a reasonable place to begin. The worker ought to be a change agent. How might a worker go about acting as an agency change agent, whether in this instance or in the numerous other situations that will confront the professional social worker?

1. Viewing the agency here as the target system and the group home residents as the client system, let us consider the change process for a moment. As in other forms of professional social work practice, change, as we are considering it here, is purposeful change—that is, it is change that results from a deliberate process of intervention by the worker. Using a traditional problem-solving framework, then, the worker as the initiator will first study the problem and learn as much as possible about the agency, with special attention to the exercise of power, who exercises it, and how decisions are made.

2. Next, the worker will assess what needs to be done in order to bring about a change based on the information that has been generated, and will develop a specific change goal or goals. She will need to assess and garner potential support, action, and change agent systems.

3. The worker will develop intervention strategies, or strategies for changing the target system, and implement them. Now is the time to develop and use any support, action, and change agent systems.

4. Finally, the worker will evaluate progress or lack thereof toward achieving the goals and will make necessary adjustments.

As Box 8.4 indicates, there are ways to work the system.

While the internal agency change process mirrors other change processes, the position of the worker in this example differs. The agency ultimately is the controlling and implementing system if the change process is successful. Since the target system, the agency, did not request assistance from the worker, the worker as an agency employee is in a position of reduced power vis-à-vis the target system and is vulnerable to punitive sanctions. The risk of retaliatory sanctions depends on a variety of factors: the nature of the change sought, the culture surrounding agency decision making, the change strategies selected, and the relative power of the change agent.

The worker's potential vulnerability suggests two practical steps. Firstly, the worker, as an internal change agent, must assess the risk of punitive sanctions and consider these in planning a change strategy. Informed action always is better than ignorance. A new worker who is still on probation must obviously operate more

---

BOX 8.4.   Rules of Thumb for Working the System

1. Learn the decision-making process in the agency and for the particular course of action you are interested in.
2. Learn who has the formal authority for making decisions, as well as who has informal influence with decision makers in the organization and department.
3. Build your social capital by developing positive exchange relationships with other members of the organization and with organizational decision makers.
4. Build your social capital by establishing your expertise and competence in managing a particular problem area.
5. Learn as much as you can about the rules that can be bent or avoided safely by your course of action.
6. Search for loopholes, contradictory rules, or cases in which exceptions were made previously, as support for your action. Remember, use the rules when they are helpful.
7. Decide if your course or action requires a formal decision or whether you are better off exercising personal discretion or handling the matter informally. Avoid formalization when it's not in your favor.
8. Decide if overloading the system will be helpful. If so, overload the old protocols and have new protocols ready to replace them.
9. Use the informal system to get necessary information and compare notes (remember reciprocity).
10. If necessary, draw on your social capital to accomplish your objective (and remember to rebuild it).

cautiously than a worker with civil service longevity or longstanding influence in the agency. Strategies and tactics that are apt to provoke a strong response from the administration should be weighed carefully. Secondly, the worker should try not to act alone. Broadening the support system and developing a change agent system is helpful. The worker must develop knowledge of the informal system to identify allies who share her concerns and think strategically about how to involve influential people in the change effort. Connections to sources of power outside and inside the agency will help to decrease her vulnerability to sanctions. Box 8.5 describes a change effort by a social worker.

To operate as an internal agency planned change agent, it is almost certainly necessary to have a mental image of the organization as a dynamic system. (If you don't see the system as changeable in a particular way, you're unlikely to try to make any changes and to change it in a particular way.) Kurt Lewin's (1951) field theory helps to provide that image. Lewin looks at an organization as caught in a field of countervailing forces. Visualize an object stuck in a field made up of different kinds of forces pushing, with varying degrees of intensity, strength, and directions for change. Some are thrusting in one direction of change (driving forces), others in an opposite direction with resistance to change (restraining forces). Forces include variables ranging from external environmental factors, such as access to resources, to internal organizational factors, such as rivalries for influence or any other of the myriad variables of organizational life. When these forces are in balance with locks in place, the status quo is maintained, but when the balance of the forces is changed and the locks are removed, the resulting stress creates disequilibrium until the forces are realigned and a new dynamic equilibrium is established. With respect to a specific change, if driving forces are increased or restraining forces reduced, or some combination, change will take place.

After assessing the problem and potential risks and developing support and change agent systems, a worker can systematically analyze the force field to develop a strategy for organizational change. In this case the problem is in the agency, but the framework can be applied to an

individual, a family, a group, or a community The material that follows provides a practical set of steps for conducting a force field analysis leading to a potential organizational change strategy. Follow these steps, using the "Force Field Analysis Inventory" located at the end of the chapter. We have partially completed the inventory using the example of the deinstitutionalized mental patients warehoused in group homes. See if you can complete it, or try your own situation.

Changing the agency from within, as we have presented it here, views the organization as a target of change (a target system). This perspective does not assume cooperation from management at the outset, although it by no means eliminates that possibility. Collaborative strategies to help change the organization are usually preferable to conflict-oriented strategies, as they create more impetus, more driving forces, for change. They are most appropriate in situations in which there is good communication between the action system and the target system, with basic agreement that there a need for change, and the direction of the proposed change is desirable (Brager, Specht, & Torczyner, 1987). The agency's administration, as we have pointed out, ultimately will be the implementing and controlling system.

When the change agent is an outside consultant brought into the agency by management to help solve an agency problem or to create a particular change, such as more receptivity to an emerging client population, the agency is a client system. The agency is the management consultant's client. Many management consultants use organization development strategies, which are always "cooperative, collaborative, and consensus building in nature" (Resnick & Menefee, 1993, p. 440), to achieve their aims. The interventions that are part of this discipline include such methods as "team building, intergroup activities, survey feedback, education and training, technostructural activities, process consultation, grid organization development, third-party peacemaking, coaching and counseling, life and career planning, planning and goal setting, and strategic management" (Resnick & Menefee, 1993, p. 439). Staff members who are acting as change agents and who have had some organizational development training can use

BOX 8.5.   Changing an Agency from Within: Chainie Scott

Quiet and attractive, Chainie Scott is an MSW with the foster care system in the District of Columbia. In 1990 she took part in a sustained effort within the agency to draw attention to huge caseloads and subsequent neglect by the system of children entitled by law to receive help from the city. First a foot soldier going to meetings and sharing her horror stories, Ms. Scott gradually became more involved and was eventually one of only two agency workers to testify against the system in the case the American Civil Liberties Union brought against the city. As a result of her leadership and as part of their change tactics, Ms. Scott was featured in several stories in the *Washington Post*. The social action in which Ms. Scott participated resulted in mandates for new policies for the foster care system. (In 1995, the courts placed the system in receivership.)

Ms. Chainie Scott-Jackson, largely an unsung social work hero except to those who knew her, died of leukemia and lymphoma, December 5, 2002, in Lanham, Maryland. Chainie Scott was interviewed November 6, 1992, by Brenda Kunkel, graduate student at the University of Maryland School of Social Work for *Challenging: Interviews with Advocates and Activists* (1993), a monograph edited by Dr. Patricia Powers.

"The whole process we went through, myself and other social workers, I don't think we put a title to it in any set category of social activism or anything. It was a reaction of professionals. The kind of thing you do for your clients all the time, we needed to do for ourselves. It was a natural progression of events. The situations we faced were so difficult: large volume of cases, inability to visit clients, lack of basic resources like cars, and telephones that didn't work.

I had gone to meetings, had voiced concerns, but I didn't spearhead the action that went on. I was a soldier rather than a leader, which was good because everyone needed to play their role. Working with the agency for about three years, I was very frustrated; 99 percent of the people were feeling frustration. I had reached the point where I decided it didn't matter—there wasn't anything they could do to me. It didn't seem fair, because I thought I deserved better than this as a professional. I have a graduate degree, and so I assume I should have a better working environment. Most importantly, it didn't seem fair to the children. It seemed like such a lie. Here we are, an agency that is supposed to protect and serve children, and we weren't doing either. To see the kind of suffering that happened. There was a lot of hesitancy on my part. I figured, 'What the hell, what do I have to lose?' [Jokingly] Fire me! Fire me!"

Q: "Can you describe the social action involved in confronting the injustices in the foster care system?"

A: "There was definitely a plan. There were social workers who spearheaded the whole thing. Everyone else made their contribution either by comments or by coming to meetings or helping draft memos that would be sent upstairs. There was fear, too. No one wanted to risk their job, or their reputation, or their career or whatever. We tried to go through the chain of command. All the memos went to the right people. All the meetings were checked with the right people. The newspaper—Everything started gradually. There were some studies going on by the Child Welfare League looking at foster homes. The climate for foster children in the District of Columbia was such that they were not being provided the services mandated by Public Law 2-22. How not to run a child welfare system! The American Civil Liberties Union became involved. From reviewing records, they focused on the cases of Leshawn A., a child in foster care, and seven other plaintiffs, all foster children. The ACLU also began to see the problems that the system was having.

It was, for me, a feeling like somebody had to do something. There was a meeting with an ACLU attorney. The word was out that this person from the ACLU needed to talk with line-level social workers to see what's going on. I went to the meeting. I listened. There were a couple of people there, and they were saying things that didn't hit home. They weren't getting at the meat of it. So, I just started talking. I said, 'Wait a second, what about this? What about that?' They, I don't know, I guess they were impressed. They kind of said, 'Oh, yeah, she'd be good. Get her.' [Laughing]

They asked if I wanted to do it. I said no at first. Then after some thought, I said, 'Okay, I'll do it.'

As a result, the ACLU decided it was appropriate to bring suit against the District of Columbia on behalf of Leshawn A. and seven other foster care children. The suit talked about the lack of continuity of care for the children, children remaining in homes that were inappropriate, children who didn't have appropriate permanency plans. The suit named all the defendants: the mayor, a director of human services, the commissioner, the administrator, and the family services division chief. We had to go to court.

It was scary! There was only two of us who gave testimony in Federal Court, Judge Hogan's courtroom. It was just matter-of-fact questions, but it was someone who was on the front line answering those questions with answers that you wouldn't get from the administration. The order came down from

Judge Hogan that our child welfare system is unconstitutional to the children. After the Leshawn hearing ended and the ruling came down, we did interviews for the radio. That was still a part of the process.

I'm not sure what the process is going to be in the post-Leshawn days. I don't know how active I'll be. I'll be there, but I may not be in the front. We said early on we should be part of the remedy for change. It never happened. I read through the plan, and it's a good plan. But I think it could have had a different tilt to it had line-level social workers been involved. There's this callousness beyond the line-level social worker. Maybe as you move up and become more of the policy part of it, you're so far removed you don't feel it—because you don't see it. That's why we're having so many problems now with the plan.

That's been real difficult. Here we are now, 2 years later, and people are still leaving. The big thing our agency keeps talking about now is, we have hired 90 new social workers. I say you need to ask how many have left and why did they leave? I can bet you, they left for the same reasons that came out at the court hearing—lack of cars, lack of support, lack of resources, lack of direction, too many cases, overwhelmed. They're leaving for the precise reasons that folks like myself and all the others have been complaining about and crying and screaming and saying, 'Hey, help us!' Nothing has changed for it! How could that possibly be?"

After the lawsuit had been won and reforms were slowly underway, Ms. Scott has had time to reflect on the process and the outcome.

"Professionally I say the court win was good. Personally, I say I don't think it really made a difference. Professionally it was good because it was something you have to do as a social worker. You have to be the one that says, 'Oh, wait a second, this is wrong, this is not right, we're not doing this right.' You have to not allow yourself to get brainwashed by your system, whatever that system is—private or government. If it's not right, then you have to say something or do something to make it different. Personally, I don't think it made a big difference because I just don't think our administration has the stomach for it, the courage, or the commitment to do it. They talk good talk, but they're not walking the walk.

When I started in 1987, we were getting cases on our unit, mommy on crack, mommy selling food stamps, mommy leaving child alone, leaving child with unwilling caretaker, child left alone, electricity about to be cut off, mother facing eviction. Every single case. Now somewhere along that line, somebody in a position of policy, of administration, should have said, 'Now what kind of cases are we getting? What's going on here? Is there a trend going on out there?' There was no forecasting, no planning, no sense of how the population changes or what kinds of things we are seeing. It didn't have

to get as bad as it was. What could have qualified as social action is if one of the administrators had said, 'Wait a second. We have a problem here. Let's stop this.' If commitment was there, why are we still where we are? I don't want to hear that it takes a while to turn the system around. I know it takes a while to turn the system around. How did it get this way? Why didn't someone do something, rather than taking the posture of business as usual?

I feel real changed by what happened in that I'm not afraid. I was afraid of them. It was like treading on water. But now, I think I have a better sense of the process. When you speak out, and if you have the commitment, you have to figure, 'What can they do?' If they do something, what difference does it make so long as the change that you want comes about?

Inside themselves, social activists have to know where their commitment lies. They need to know what that battle is for them; if they have the resolve to do it; if they end up becoming a sacrificial lamb, whether that's okay with them. This is something you have to go through and not feel bitter about in the end. In the classroom you have to learn what it is to organize, how to communicate what those concerns are that you're dealing with and how you want to see those issues resolved. You certainly have to have a frame of reference. You need to understand why people didn't want to change. You bring all your knowledge together. In the process of change, you have to continue to be part of the remedy. You just can't bring it on. You have to be there to help devise the rules.

[Laughing] It was a fun process. You get all psyched up! 'Yes, let's go! Oh, yeah, that's what you want to do? Grrr!' It's very exciting! I have no regrets about anything I did. As a matter of fact, I feel proud of myself. I have a sense of principle. I thought testifying, etc., was the right thing to do. Now, I want to leave district government. I can make a much more positive impact outside of a system that's restrictive and bureaucratic and censorized. So, while I'm still feeling some of those frustrations that led to wanting to change the foster care system, I made my mark when it was appropriate for me to make my mark. I don't want to continue being on the front line anymore. I have enough experience and ammunition and that thing that gets in you when you've been through a lot—that 'we can't let this happen again because I've lived through it.' It would be a natural progression to do advocacy for a group. I always find myself looking at *this big picture. I see myself staying in social action in some capacity or another.*"

A caveat is needed: The situation in the agency is still problematic. Change of any large organization is complex, whether internally or imposed externally. It requires a persistent effort if the change is to endure, and unfortunately, persistence in Washington, DC, public agencies is a rare commodity. Policymakers are remote and transient, and funding is stingy.

Force Field Analysis Steps and Inventory.

Step 1

Describe, succinctly, the problem you want changed. Record this on the Force Field Inventory (FFI).

Step 2

Specify the Specific, Measureable. Acceptable, Realistic, Results-Oriented, Time-Specific (SMARRT) goal or objective to be achieved. In doing this, you begin to break the problem down into smaller parts. Be as operationally specific as possible. Your goal or objective should be stated so that it can be measured. Record your goal on the FFI.

Step 3

Identify all of the restraining forces—those that contribute to the problem or work against goal achievement. Record these forces on the FFI.

Step 4

Identify all of the main driving forces—those that currently or potentially support and work for changes to achieve the goal. Record these forces on the FFI.

Step 5

Estimate the amenability to change of each force. Designate each as H (high), L (low), or U (uncertain). Place the appropriate letter in the column to the left of the restraining forces and to the right of the driving forces.

Step 6

Identify the crucial actors and facilitators whom you feel will be best able to influence the forces you have identified as amenable to change. Record them on the FFI.

Step 7

List the driving and restraining forces that are amenable to change and identity the actors who can influence these forces. Record them on the FFI.

Step 8

Select two or more restraining forces from your diagram and outline a strategy for reducing their potency. The forces should be both important and changeable. Record your plan on your FFI.

Step 9

Select two or more driving forces from your diagram and outline a strategy for increasing their potency. The forces should be both important and changeable. Record your plan on your FFI.

Force Field Analysis Inventory

Definition of Terms

Critical Actors: Individuals or groups with the power to make a change. Their support or approval is necessary for your SMARRT objective to be achieved.

Facilitators: A critical actor (1) whose approvl must be obtained before the problem can be brought to the attention of other critical actors and (2) whose approval, disapproval, or neutrality has a decisive impact on the critical actors.

Driving Forces: Forces that when increased change behavior and conditions in a desired and planned manner toward achieving SMARRT objectives.

Restraining Forces: Forces that when increased or static reinforce the status quo or move conditions away from the SMARRT objective.

Potency or Strength: The strength of a restraining force to inhibit or a driving force to promote change. Potency can be rated as high (H), low (L), or uncertain (U, unable to be assessed).

Amenability of Conditions to Change or Influence: Potential to change the potency of a force: ability to increase a driving force's or decrease a restraining force's potency.

Problem Situation or Need	SMARRT Objective
Support group services needed for mental patients in the Green Street group home	Have an operational support group service for the mental patients in the Green Street group home by January 30, 20xx.

Restraining Forces against establishing support group (Rate Potency or Strength: (H) high, (L) low, (U) unable to decide)	**Driving Forces** for establishing support group (Rate Potency or Strength: (H) high, (L) low, (U) unable to decided)
• Tight budget and fiscal situation ( ) • Transient caseload ( ) • Clinical staff opposes ( ) • No group worker on staff ( )	• New program director wanting to establish herself ( ) • Social group work interns available ( ) • Patient interest in support group ( ) • Media coverage of warehousing mental patients ( )

Critical Actors (CA) and Facilitators (F)

1. Program director (CA) to approve group and reduce clinical opposition

2. Social work field practicum director (CA) to assign group work student intern to agency
3. Agency director (F) to approve project operation
4. Media beat reporter (F) to do story on the facility after support group begins
5. School of social work faculty (F) to serve as field instructor for student intern and provide legitimacy to the project
6. Others (based on your agency experience, speculate as to possible critical actors and facilitators)

Based on your agency experience, speculate as to what other forces, critical actors, and facilitators might serve as driving forces and as restraining forces.

Change Strategies

- Strategies to reduce potency of restraining forces and to influence conditions to be amenable to change
- Strategies to increase potency of driving forces and to influence conditions to be amenable to change

these methods of intervention when collaborative strategies are appropriate.

When the action system and the target system agree that a problem exists but disagree strongly on what should be done about it, change agents may have to use campaign tactics to influence the organization (Warren, 1969). "Campaign tactics include political maneuvering, bargaining and negotiation, and mild coercion" (Brager, Specht, & Torczyner, 1987, p. 353). Political maneuvering is involved in internal (and external) change efforts. It takes many forms, from persuading uninvolved influential people, from inside or outside the agency, to join the change effort to trading bargaining chips. Once a campaign moves to formulating demands as the basis for bargaining and negotiation, as well as more disruptive, conflict-oriented strategies and tactics, it requires a well-organized action system; intensive, careful planning; and a strong commitment to objectives. All these strategies are usually time-consuming and are likely to provoke angry, hostile responses from management. For these and other reasons, staff rebellions occur relatively

infrequently, though t... important values are a...

On the other hand, ... negotiation frequently ... staff is unionized. U... structure and process... to act collectively. So... history of participati... ment, past and present (Alexander, 1987; Wenocur & Reisch, 1989), so unionization is a viable option for agency change by professional social workers.

Lastly, whistle-blowing (calling public or a higher authority's attention to agency or management wrongdoing) is a change option. Whistle-blowing frequently carries with it very real personal costs, with no guarantee of organizational change. Agencies, including the whistle-blower's fellow employee and colleagues, tend to rally to the flag and protect their own. The potential whistle-blower should apply the guidelines set forth in Chapter 1 to be sure the action is fair and in the public interest and is the least harmful to colleagues and the agency of the available alternatives (Reisch & Lowe, 2000).

In sum, organizations are necessary and important because they enable people to accomplish collectively what individuals acting on their own cannot accomplish. Complex industrial societies are inconceivable without the existence of large and small organizations (Aldrich, 1979, p. 3). They need to be developed, maintained, and monitored by their constituencies and employees to serve the public's good.

Notes

1. The Court rejected the argument that political speech of corporations or other associations should be treated differently under the First Amendment simply because such associations are not "natural persons." See: Supreme Court of the United States. Syllabus. Citizens United *v.* Federal Election Commission Appeal from the United States District Court for the District of Columbia, No. 08–205. Decided January 21, 2010.
2. The First Amendment states, "Amendment I (1791) Congress shall make no law respecting an establishment of religion, or prohibiting the free exercise thereof; . . .."

f your agency needs a change in client services, how will you go about making the
change?
2. If clients are being harmed by an agency
policy or operation and management is
unwilling to alter the program or operation,
what is your ethical obligation? What should
you do? How will you go about it?

3. See earlier discussions in chapter 7 of *belief bonding*.
4. The first edition of this text (1997) urged social workers to develop these skills throughout the text as good community practice without the label.
5. With the Troubled Asset Relief Program (TARP) and the bailout stimulus package, there may be few accountable and risk-accepting entrepreneurs left in the business sector.
6. Sergeant Schultz was a German prison guard in the World War II prisoner-of-war comedy (an oxy-moron) who coped with the inanities of his job by uttering the catch phase "I know nothing" as he just followed orders.

References

Aldrich, H. E. (1979). *Organizations and environments*. Englewood Cliffs, NJ: Prentice Hall.

Alexander, L. B. (1987). Unions: social work. *Encyclopedia of social work* (Vol. 2, 18th ed., pp. 793–798). Silver Spring, MD: National Association of Social Workers.

Basch, R., & Bates, M. E. (2000). *Researching online for dummies*. Foster City, CA: IDG Books.

Baskin, D. B. (Ed.). (1990). *Computer applications in psychiatry and psychology*. New York: Brunner/Mazel.

Berman, J., & Pfleeger, J. (1997). Which industries are sensitive to business cycles? *Monthly Labor Review*, 120(2), 19–25.

Blundo, R. G., Mele, C., Hairston, R., & Watson, J. (1999). The Internet and demystifying power differentials: A few women on-line and the housing authority. *Journal of Community Practice*, 6(2), 11–26.

Boston, R. (2010). Church, state, and Obama: A one-year report card. *Church and State*, 63(1), 7–9.

Bourquard, J. A., & Greenberg, P. (1996, March). Savvy citizens. *State Legislatures*, 28–33.

Brager, G., & Holloway, S. (1977). A process model for changing organizations from within. *Administration in Social Work*, 1(4), 349–358.

Brager, G., Specht, H., & Torczyner, J. L. (1987). *Community organizing* (3rd ed.). New York: Columbia University Press.

Bragg, M. (1996). *Reinventing influence: How to get things done in a world without authority*. Washington, DC: Pitman.

Briggs, H. E., & McBeath, B. (2009). Evidence-based management: Origins, challenges, and implications for social service administration. *Administration in Social Work*, 33(3), 242–261.

Bryson, J. M. (1989). *Strategic planning for public and nonprofit organizations*. San Francisco: Jossey-Bass.

2010 *BusinessDictionary.com*. Retrieved Feb. 18, 2010, from: http://www.businessdictionary.com/definition/entrepreneurship.html

Cnaan, R., Boddie, S. C., & Yancey, G. I. (2005). Rise up and build the cities: faith-based community organizing. In M. Weil (Ed.), *The handbook of community practice* (pp. 372–386). Thousand Oaks, CA: Sage Publications, Inc.

Crozier, M. (1964). *The bureaucratic phenomenon*. Chicago: University of Chicago Press.

Cyert, R. M., & March, J. G. (1963). *A behavioral theory of the firm*. Englewood Cliffs, NJ: Prentice Hall.

Dressel, P. L. (1992). Patriarchy and social welfare work. In Y. Hasenfeld (Ed.), *Human services as complex organizations* (pp. 205–233). Newbury Park, CA: Sage.

Etzioni, A. (1987). Compliance, goals, and effectiveness. In J. M. Shafritz & J. S. Ott (Eds.), *Classics of organizational theory* (2nd ed., pp. 177–187). Chicago: Dorsey.

Fayol, H. (1987). General principles of management. In J. M. Shafritz & J. S. Ott (Eds.), *Classics of organizational theory* (2nd ed., pp. 51–81). Chicago: Dorsey.

Ferrante, J., & Vaughn, A. (1999). *Let's go sociology: Travels on the Internet* (2nd ed.). Belmont, CA: Wadsworth.

Finn, J. (1988). Microcomputers in private nonprofit agencies: A survey of trends and training requirements. *Social Work Research and Abstracts*, 24(1), 10–14.

Finn, J. (1996). Computer-based self-help groups: On-line recovery for addiction. *Computers in Human Services*, 13(1), 21–41.

Fisher, C. D., Schoenfeldt, L. F., & Shaw, J. B. (1990). *Human resource management*. Boston: Houghton Mifflin.

Fisher, E. A. (2009). Motivation and leadership in social work management: A review of theories and related studies. *Administration in Social Work*, 33(4), 347–367.

Frahm, K. A., & Martin, L. L. (2009). From government to governance: Implications for social work administration. *Administration in Social Work*, 33(4), 407–422.

Foltin, R. T. (2000/01, Winter). Rethinking charitable choice. *The Responsive Community*, 11(1), 92–95.

Freudenheim, M. (1996, February 5). Charities say government cuts would jeopardize their ability to help the needy. *The New York Times*, p. B8.

Garicano, L., & heaton, P. (2010). Information technology, organizations, and productivity in the public sector: Evidence from police departments. *Journal of labor economics*, 28:a, 167-201

Germak, A. J., & Singh, K. K. (2010). Social entrepreneurship: Changing the way social workers do business. *Administration in Social Work*, 34(1), 79–95.

2009 *Giving USA*. (2009) Bloomington, IN: Giving USA Foundation, The Center on Philanthropy at Indiana University.

Gortner, H. F., Mahler, J., & Nicholson, J. B. (1987). *Organizational theory: A public perspective*. Chicago: Dorsey.

Greenley, J. R., & Kirk, S. A. (1973). Organizational characteristics of agencies and the distribution of services to applicants. *Journal of Health and Social Behavior*, 14, 70–79.

Greenwell, M. (2010). America's proud tradition of blaming the poor. *Poverty in America*. Retrieved February 22, 2010, from: http://uspoverty.change.org/blog/view/americas_proud_tradition_of_blaming_the_poor?utm

Hasenfeld, Y. (1983). *Human service organizations*. Englewood Cliffs, NJ: Prentice Hall.

Hasenfeld, Y. (1992). *The nature of human service organizations*. Newbury Park, CA: Sage.

Houle, C. O. (1989). *Governing boards: Their nature and nurture*. San Francisco: Jossey-Bass.

Jaskyte, K., & Lee, M. (2009). Organizational commitment of social workers: An exploratory study. *Administration in Social Work*, 33(3), 227–241.

Johnston, D. C. (1997). United Way, faced with fewer donors, is giving away less. *The New York Times*, pp. 1, 28.

Johnson, M., & Austin, M. J. (2006). Evidence-based practice in the social services. *Administration in Social Work*, 30(3), 75–104.

Judt, T. (2009, December 17). What is living and what is dead in social democracy? *The New York Review of Books*, 56(20), 86–96.

Kaser, D. (2007). Virtuality. *Information Today*, 24(3), 14.

Kearns, K. P. (2007). Faith-based and secular social service agencies in Pittsburgh. *Journal of Community Practice*, 14(4), 51–69.

Kennedy, S. S. (2003). *Charitable choice: First results from three states*. Indianapolis: Center for Urban Policy and the Environment, School of Public and Environmental Affairs, Indiana University–Purdue University Indianapolis.

Kramer, R. M. (1965). Ideology, status, and power in board–executive relationships. *Social Work*, 10, 108–114.

Kranish, M. (2006, December 4). Democrats inspect faith-based initiative. *Boston Globe*. Retrieved February 24, 2010, from http://www.boston.com/news/nation/washington/articles/2006/12/04/democrats_inspect_faith_based_initiative

Kreuger, L. W. (1997, Winter). The end of social work. *Journal of Social Work Education*, 33(1), 19–27.

Larson, M. S. (1977). *The rise of professionalism*. Berkeley: University of California Press.

Licensed social workers in the U.S.: 2004 (March 2006). Prepared by Center for Health Workforce Studies, School of Public Health, University at Albany and Center for Workforce Studies, National Association of Social Workers.

Lohmann, R. A., & Wolvovsky, J. (1997). Natural language processing and computer use in social work. *Administration in Social Work*, 3(4), 409–422.

Lewin, K. (1951). *Field theory in social science*. New York: Harper & Row.

Martinez, R. C., & Clark, C. L. (2001). *The social worker's guide to the Internet*. Needham Heights, MA: Allyn & Bacon.

Mathiasen, K. (1990). *Board passages: Three key stages in a nonprofit board's life cycle*. Governance Series Paper. Washington, DC: National Center for Nonprofit Boards.

Mele, C. (1999). Cyberspace and disadvantaged communities: The Internet as a tool for collective action. In M. A. Smith & P. Kollock (Eds.), *Communities in cyberspace* (pp. 290–310). London: Routledge.

Menefee, D. T., & Thompson, J. J. (1994). Identifying and comparing competencies for social work management: A practice-driven approach. *Administration in Social Work*, 18(3), 1–25.

Netting, F. E., Kettner, P. M., & McMurtry, S. L. (2007). *Social work macro practice* (4th ed.). Boston: Allyn & Bacon.

O'Connor, M. K., Netting, F. E., & Fabelo, H. (2009). A multidimensional agency survey. *Administration in Social Work*, 33(1), 81–104.

O'Looney, J. (2005). Social work and the new semantic information revolution. *Administration in Social Work*, 29(4), 5–34.

Pang, L. (2001). Understanding virtual organizations. *Information Systems Control Journal*, 6. Retrieved February 15, 2010, from: http://www.isaca.org/Template.cfm

Patti, R. J., & Resnick, H. (1972). Changing the agency from within. *Social Work*, 17(4), 48–57.

Pawlak, E. J. (1976). Organizational tinkering. *Social Work*, 21(5), 376–380.

Perlman, E. (2000). Chief of tomorrow: Focused on digital government. *Governing*, 14(2), 36.

Perrow, C. (1961). The analysis of goals in complex organizations. *American Sociological Review*, 26, 854–866.

Phillips, K. P. (1993). *Boiling point: Republicans, Democrats, and the decline of middle-class prosperity*. New York: Random House.

Powers, P. (Ed.). (1993). *Challenging: Interviews with advocates and activists* [Monograph]. Baltimore: University of Maryland at Baltimore, School of Social Work.

Reisch, M., & Lowe, J. I. (2000). Of means and ends: Teaching ethical community organizing in an unethical society. *Journal of Community Practice*, 7(1), 19–38.

Resnick, H., & Menefee, D. (1993). A comparative analysis of organization development and social work, with suggestions for what organization development can do for social work. *Journal of Applied Behavioral Science*, 29(4), 432–445.

Rich, F. (2009, September 19). Even Glenn Beck is right twice a day. *The New York Times*. Retrieved February 22, 2010, from: http://www.nytimes.com/2009/09/20/opinion/20rich.html?

Rogers, E. M., & Agarwala-Rogers, R. (1976). *Communication in organizations*. New York: Free Press.

Rosenau, P. V., & Linder, S. H. (2003). A comparison of the performance of for-profit and nonprofit U.S. psychiatric inpatient care providers since 1980. *Psychiatric Services*. Retrieved February 22, 2010, from: http://psychservices.psychiatryonline.org/cgi/content/full/54/2/183.

Sack, K., & Pear, R. (2010, February 18). States consider Medicaid cuts as use grows. *The New York Times*. Retrieved February 25, 2010, from: http://www.nytimes.com/2010/02/19/us/politics/19medicaid.html

Salamon, L. M. (1992). *America's nonprofit sector: A primer*. New York: Foundation Center.

Salamon, L. M. (1997). *Holding the center: America's nonprofit sector at a crossroad. A report for Nathan Cummings Foundation*. New York: Nathan Cummings Foundation.

Salamon, L. M., Altshuler, D. M., & Myllyluoma, J. (1990). *More than just charity: The Baltimore area nonprofit sector in a time of change*. Baltimore: Johns Hopkins University, Institute for Policy Studies.

Schein, E. H. (1987). Defining organizational culture. In M. Shafritz & J. S. Ott (Eds.), *Classics of organizational theory* (2nd ed., rev. & exp.). Chicago: Dorsey.

Scott, W. G. (1973). Organization theory: An overview and appraisal. In F. Baker (Ed.), *Organizational systems: General systems approaches to complex organizations* (pp. 99–119). Homewood, IL: Richard D. Irwin.

Sherman, W. R., & Wenocur, S. (1983). Empowering public welfare workers through mutual support. *Social Work*, 28(5), 375–379.

Smith, M. L., & Coombs, E. (2000, Spring). *Could Stevie Wonder read your web page? The New Social Worker*, 21–23.

Strom, S. (2009a, March 5). Charities say government is ignoring them in crisis. *The New York Times*. Retrieved September 28, 2009, from, http://query.nytimes.com/gst/fullpage.html?res

Strom, S. (2009b, June 10). Charitable giving declines, a new report finds. *The New York Times*, p. A16.

Thompson, J. D. (1967). *Organizations in action*. New York: McGraw-Hill.

Thompson, N. (2000). *Understanding social work: Preparing for practice*. London: Macmillan.

Walker, S. (2001). Tracing the contours of postmodern social work. *British Journal of Social Work*, 31(1), 29–39.

Warren, R. L. (1969). Types of purposive social change at the community level. In R. M. Kramer & H. Specht (Eds.), *Readings in community organization practice* (pp. 205–222). Englewood Cliffs, NJ: Prentice Hall.

Webb, S. A. (2001). Some considerations on the validity of evidence-based practice in social work. *British Journal of Social Work*, 31(1), 57–79.

Webber, R. A. (1979). *Managing organizations*. Homewood, IL: Richard D. Irwin.

Wenocur, S., & Reisch, M. (1989). *From charity to enterprise: The development of American social work in a market economy*. Urbana: University of Illinois Press.

Whitaker, T., & Arrington, P. (2008). *Social workers at work*. NASW Membership Workforce Study. Washington, DC: National Association of Social Workers.

Williams, R. (2007). Moving beyond vagueness: Social capital, social networks, and economic outcomes. In J. Jennings, (Ed.). *Race, neighborhoods, and misuse of social capital* (pp. 67–86), New York: Palgrave Macmillan.

Willer, D. (Ed.). (1999). *Network exchange theory.* Westport, CT: Praeger.

Willer, D., Lovaglia, M. J., & Markovsky, B. (1999). *Power and influence: A theoretical bridge.* In D. Willer (Ed.), *Network exchange theory* (pp. 229–247). Westport, CT: Praeger.

Wright, D. J. (2009). *Taking stock: The Bush faith-based initiative and what lies ahead.* Albany, New York: The Nelson A. Rockefeller Institute of Government, State University of New York.

Yaffe, J. (2001). *Social work on the net.* Boston: Allyn & Bacon.

9

Using Work Groups: Committees, Teams, and Boards

The well-run group is not a battlefield of egos.
Lao Tzu, philosopher, founder of Taoism

We must remember that one determined person can make a significant difference, and that a small group of determined people can change the course of history.
Sonia Johnson, excommunicated Mormon, feminist, activist, educator

Meetings are indispensable when you don't want to do anything.
John Kenneth Galbraith, economist, social critic, statesman, author

Meetings are an integral part of all social work practice. There are staff meetings, team meetings, interagency meetings, board and committee meetings, professional association committee meetings, advisory committee meetings, and community meetings. There are meetings to make decisions and meetings to stall action. These are not clinical group meetings. None involves direct group work with clients—for example, running a support group for returning Iraq and Afghanistan military personnel. Nevertheless, they are a professional social worker's obligation. All the meetings involve work with task groups of some kind—committees, boards, teams, coalitions, task forces, planning bodies. Task groups are working groups established to achieve some specific purpose or goal. The specific purpose goal or goal is usually external to the group and does not focus on changing the traits of individual group members (Kirst-Ashman & Hull, 2009, pp. 93–100; Payne, 2000).

Effective work with task groups is an important aspect of all social work practice and essential

for community practice. The task group is one of the main mechanisms for community practice. Organizing groups and committees and participating as chair, member, or staff facilitator are the means by which social advocacy, interagency and interprofessional planning and coordination, and community development are accomplished. Although we often participate as members of a task group, in this chapter the social worker is conceived primarily as leader, chair, or staff member. The tasks can be adapted to participation as a member in work groups if we keep in mind why task groups are used. We participate in work groups because we want to get something done and need a group to get it done. If not, participation is recreation. Regardless of our formal position in the task group, we should assume leadership when necessary to enhance the group's effectiveness. Leadership and decision making in task groups and organizations, including social agencies, are rarely democratic with everyone having equal authority and say but should be *consultative-participatory*.

A Case Example

Besides the task groups in direct service agencies, social action organizations are sustained by task groups. These may be temporary, ad hoc groups internal or external to the organization. Organization or agency members, staff, or leaders can serve a part of outside groups formed by other organizations. Organizations can support task groups without members serving on the task group or controlling the task group by providing other resources, including legitimacy. Organizations also have to fight the work of task groups formed by opponents. A distinctive and critical feature of macropractice and social action task groups is community involvement. Community involvement and participation is the crux of the community's empowerment and self-determination (Henderson, 2007).

Task groups are used to recruit and train leadership, develop and tailor participation for subgroups of community members, further program objectives, and empower the community members. Very small organizations use work groups to build networks and alliances by involving contributors from other organizations, and huge organizations use groups to create more intimacy for participants and get to the grassroots level. Progressive organizations use these work groups to enable members to run the organizations. They are essential to critical community practice and community empowerment (Butcher, Banks, & Henderson with Robertson, 2007).

Some established community organizations have an enormous national reach that extends into the local networks of institutional members (churches, unions, schools, and other community organizations). This requires an organizational structure and process that can keep association and individual members of the alliance engaged. Sociologist Mark Warren has studied southwestern Industrial Area Foundation agencies. He provides an organizational map of the units constituting one Fort Worth affiliate known as ACT (Table 9.1). The task groups that make up the organizational apparatus were permanent by design, even as their membership changes. ACT was formed to bring together African Americans, Anglos, and Mexican Americans in united social action on pressing issues (Warren, 2001, Chapter 4). As Warren (2001) explains, "ACT leaders from different

Table 9.1 Teams and Other Ways to Involve Organization Members

Organizational Unit	Composition and Involvement
Co-chairs	2 or 3 top leaders, including Strategy Team chair and The Organizing Council (TOC)
Strategy Team (Executive Committee)	16 key leaders representing three ethnic groups that make up TOC. Meets bimonthly to plan strategy, sets agenda for TOC, co-opts its members from TOC.
The Organizing Council (TOC) Steering Committee	About 45 attendees, usually 2 or 3 leaders from each member church decision-making body, meets monthly
Delegates Assembly	Size varies from 30 to 80 members, meets occasionally, usually every 3 months, to ratify important decisions
Action Teams	5 to 7 members, usually from the three ethnic groups, leaders drawn from different churches
• Job training • Health care • Parental empowerment (schools) • Education reform • Neighborhood strategy project • Utility reform • Money campaign (fundraising)	
Member Church Committees	Address church/neighborhood concerns, implement ACT-wide campaigns in the church
Annual Convention	Network of all leaders (1,000–2,000 depending on year), stages ritual events that endorse agenda and leadership; conducts business with public officials

Note. Adapted from *Dry Bones Rattling,* by Mark Warren, 2001, p. 115. Copyright 2001 by Princeton University Press. Adapted with permission.

communities have the opportunity to build bridging ties with each other through working together on action teams and on organization-wide leadership bodies. Action teams work on a variety of campaigns, like job training. . . . [A]bout 45 leaders, drawn from all member congregations, meet monthly as the organization's central decision-making body. The Strategy Team brings about 16 leaders from the three racial groups in the organization together to act as the executive committee" (p. 114).

We have emphasized the importance of community and constituency participation in our discussions of social justice, belief bonding, empowerment, and self-determination. Community participation on the boards, committee, and task groups in HSOs and community organizations is a necessary ingredient of community development. Community organizations and HSOs can further community participation by creating structures that are designed to be inclusive and democratic (again, see Table 9.1). The structures can be very functional for sustaining alliances involving the socially marginalized. Community development for HSOs to build and bridge social capital entails an array of processes. Community organization and service efforts that build on community participation and involvement tend to be successful (Anderson, Zhan, & Scott, 2006; Delgado & Staples, 2008; Foster-Fishman, Cantllon, Pierce, & Van Egeren, 2007; Jacobson, 2007; Patterson & Panossa, 2008; Turner, 2009). Conversely, those not encouraging participation are less successful (Geoghean & Powell, 2006; Silverman, 2005). Community participation is critical in service development and delivery, perhaps contributing to the community's belief bonding with the service and agency.

Social work practice with task groups is a deliberate process of intervention to accomplish a goal. Community social workers use themselves consciously and deliberately in meetings to further the aims of the task group. *Social workers participating in a task group, whether as staff, leader, or regular member, should approach a meeting prepared.* The task group is an *action system* for the social worker. Members of a task group usually participate as citizens, colleagues, or representatives of larger network constituencies who come together to achieve an external

purpose. It is not a therapy group. They have not sought the social worker's help with an interpersonal or intrapsychic problem. The social worker's preparation is for helping them work on the task and achieve its goals. Even when the task group comprises agency clients, the aim of the group, as a working group, is external, not internal. Clients change roles and are part of an action system.

The worker does have an implicit or prescribed contractual relationship with the group as with a client system. The agency board hires a social worker to coordinate its fundraising efforts, or the agency staff members hire a consultant to help them improve their skill in serving a population with special needs. A written job description can form the basis for a working agreement, and direct negotiation about roles and boundaries will usually take place before any substantive work begins. Frequently the contract is implicit, as when a school social worker organizes a parents' group to develop a mentoring program. Here the social worker's and the members' understanding of their respective roles and responsibilities evolves out of their shared interaction and out of the worker's explanations or interpretations of the different roles in the group.

Teams

Teams are a specific type of task group. A team generally is a number of people working together, with each member or position on the team having a fairly unique, complementary, and essential contribution that forms a whole necessary to achieve the common and shared goal. Although each team member's contribution may not be equal, all are necessary. There is interdependence. Success or failure is defined as a collective achievement. Individuals do not achieve success without the whole team's achieving success (Payne, 2000, pp. 5–7, 55–59). Members with contributions not truly needed are not truly team members. And, unlike the National Football League, there are no all-stars on losing teams.

Teams can be used to coordinate different expertise or to form networks. They are used in social services as *linchpin structures* to unite the resources of different organizations, or intraorganizationally to coordinate resources of different units in the same agency. A linchpin structure connects a network of units with its members as representatives or linking units to bring the constituencies to the team's task.

Teams, whether linchpins or composed of individual expertise, require certain qualities for effectiveness and accountability (Payne, 2000):

- Boundaries between each member's expertise and contributions, and authority/responsibility/accountability (ARA) are clearly understood by all team members.
- With ARA clarity, each member knows the contributions and the roles of other team members and the policies, rules, and procedures for coordination.
- The team builds on the strengths inside the team and uses the members to link to resources outside the team.
- The team emphasizes the use of consensus and a consultative-participatory leadership for team decisions. Consensus is operationally defined as "everyone can live with it" rather than "everyone thinks it's the best thing to do."
- The team respects, extends, and works with each member's skills. While maintaining some flexibility for reorganization and recognizing that it is sometimes necessary, it avoids frequent reorganization, as it confuses ARA, weakens cohesion, and complicates coordination.[1]

Teams are specific types of work groups, and *task forces* are special subsets of teams (Gersick, 1988). Task forces are working groups that are goal- and action-oriented, time-limited, and formed administratively to deal with problems that cannot be resolved by routine methods (Johnson, 1994). Their particular nature, it is argued, makes them prone to a development pattern of "punctuated equilibrium" whereby the group alternates between fairly long periods of inertia and bursts of creative energy. Task forces should be used where there are especially clear, reasonably unique, and time-limited SMARRT objectives—or to develop the objectives.[2] SMARRT objectives are operational goals that can be translated into specific actions to achieve them. They have saliency and acceptability to members. SMARRT objectives emphasize a task

orientation rather than a process of gradual development as proposed in most models of group development.

Boards of Directors and Trustees

Boards of directors and trustees are a special kind of agency task group. Boards of directors govern not-for-profit organizations and are responsible for the overall performance and the ultimate achievements of the organization (Iecovich, 2005). The board legally is the responsible body for the HSO fulfilling its fiduciary responsibility to the community. They are the trustees and stewards of the agency for the community. They are responsible to the community just as the board of a proprietary corporation is responsible to the shareholders.

Boards have several critical stewardship responsibilities:

- Establishing the agency's policies and program priorities and overseeing their operation. The board sets policies and sees that they are followed by agency staff.
- Fundraising and resource raising for the agency. Resources include fiscal resources and legitimacy.
- Annual budget allocation and oversight. The board determines how resources are to be spent and oversees the spending.
- Developing responsibilities of, recruiting and hiring, and supervising the agency's top management
- Linking with critical resources and advocating for the agency in the task environment, including local, regional, and national relations and lobbying

The agency staff's, especially that of the top management, responsibility to their board is to assist the board in fulfilling its responsibilities and not to usurp them. The board bears the ultimate fiduciary responsibility. Much of the failures of the financial institutions leading to the Great Recession of 2008 forward can be placed on the boards for not fulfilling their fiduciary responsibilities and allowing executive staff assuming board functions. Nonprofit groups over the years have had their own set of scandals involving such venerable agencies as the United

Way and the Red Cross (Mead, 2008; Storm, 2007). Much of the reason for the failures was board irresponsibility.

Boards need to be diligent to develop and maintain a community orientation and not succumb to an agency groupthink mentality. This orientation may not always be easy for staff, but it is better for the agency and community.

Group Development and the Role of the Social Worker

Task and Process

Professional practice with task groups requires good listening skills and keen observation of behavior. The worker is truly a participant-observer, but what should the worker attend to? The answer is that all group interactions have a *task* and a *process* dimension. *Task groups of all kinds must attend to both in order to succeed.*

A group's *task dimension* refers to the subject or content of the group's interactions. For example, when parent volunteers begin to meet with a school social worker to plan a mentoring program for their children's school, the different ideas they discuss about mentoring programs and how they are established represent the task dimension of that interaction. In the course of the meetings, the worker will listen to alternative proposals and help the group to assess clarity, see connections between ideas, consider their merits, determine what information may still be needed, and make decisions that will eventually lead to agreement on a plan and its implementation.

A group's *process dimension* deals with the nature and dynamics of the interactions and relationships that develop within the group. In the words of Philip Hanson (1972): "Process is concerned with what is happening between and to group members while the group is working. Group process, or dynamics, deals with such items as morale, feeling tone, atmosphere, influence, participation, styles of influence, leadership struggles, conflict, competition, cooperation, etc." (p. 21).

While task and process dimensions of group interaction are conceptually distinct, operationally they are inseparable. Task groups are to complete tasks related to influencing the world external to the group rather than merely to engage in a process. Process has consequence in that it can contribute to or distract from task achievement. Process is about task. And success on group tasks enhances process, bonds members, and makes the group more rewarding. A good process in task groups contributes to task accomplishment and is concerned with the satisfaction group members obtain from participating in successful group task accomplishments. Member morale generally is more a function of task success than process. When the members of a mentoring group become angry at a member (Mrs. Smith) who monopolizes meetings, arguments begin to break out, and attendance begins to wane. These are manifestations of the group's process dimension disrupting the group's task dimension. In observing a group for task and process, Hanson (1972) suggests that a worker think about the following questions: What signs of feeling do I see in the group members? How do the members feel about each other? Are there any cliques that seem to be forming? What is the energy level of the group? Are all of the members getting a chance to participate? How does the group make decisions? In the course of the meetings, the worker will try to facilitate interaction that strengthens the members' bonds to each other and their commitment to the group as a whole. The worker, of course, is also mindful of keeping the group on task.

In the above example, where Mrs. Smith arouses the ire of the other group members, the arguments that take place may well be about the proposals someone has offered or the procedures for reaching a decision. So, both content and process issues emerge at the same time. Or suppose that a member asks the group to review how a particular decision was made—that is, to consider the process that the group went through. For analytical purposes, we can generally assign interactions centered on issues of communication to the process dimension, and interactions centered on issues of goal implementation to the task dimension.

Stages of Group Development: When Is a Group a Group?

People who meet for the first time to do some work together, whether as a committee or a team or planning body, will vary greatly in the amount of energy they want to invest in the task and in their commitment to working with other people to do it. Yet they have come together because the task is either too complex or too difficult to do alone; it will take a group to do it. This tension between *differentiation* (going it alone, doing it one's own way) and *integration* (collaborating with others, giving up some of one's autonomy) captures the essence of the struggle involved in forming a group (Heap, 1977). *Until that collection of autonomous individuals begins to feel some allegiance to the collectivity and finds some way to work together on a common goal, a group has not yet fully formed.*

Stage theories of group development exhibit a remarkable degree of similarity despite variations in the number and names of the stages. They are useful in that they reinforce the simple but important idea of *group development over time*. Groups can do different things at different points in the course of group formation. This knowledge gives workers a frame of reference for their interventions in the group and helps them set realistic objectives for group meetings.

A few cautions are necessary before we consider the stages of group development in more detail. First, the stages of group development, presented discretely in theory, cannot be neatly separated from each other in the real world. The stages represent a continuum, perhaps a pleated continuum, with overlapping and spiraling stages. A group can sometimes loop back to a preceding stage if it was previously unsuccessful in completing that stage or if its membership changes. A group with a significantly changed composition becomes a new group for group development purposes. One phase runs into another; groups take two steps forward and one step backward, and so on. Nor can we define an exact length of time for a given phase. We cannot say, for example, that it takes a group three meetings or 3 hours to get through the formative stage. Nor does the notion of stages make group life as predictable as it might seem. In the same way that each of us is unique even though we all pass through similar stages of growth and development, groups are unique. The dynamics of any group are influenced by many different variables—size, purpose, sponsorship, context, composition, nature of the task (complexity,

emotionality, etc.), stage and more. To practice effectively with task groups, we need to know the theories about groups in general and about task groups. We also need to know our task groups. Group behavior is not simply a function of the group's stage of development.

With these cautions in mind, let us review the stages of group development. Tuckman (1965) synthesized a great deal of research on small groups into a developmental model that links group task (instrumental) and process (socioemotional) dimensions with stages of development. His easy-to-remember lyrical stages are *forming, storming, norming, performing, and adjournment* (Tuckman, 1965; Tuckman & Jensen, 1977). Table 9.2 presents a comparison of the main features of each stage, the characteristic behaviors one might expect along the task and process dimensions, and the role of the worker. We have amplified Tuckman's ideas with information from other models (Bandler & Roman, 1999; Toseland & Rivas, 1995) and community practice experience.

Stage 1: Forming. In this stage, prospective group members try to determine what the group and other group members are all about. They are getting oriented. They are wondering what the group will be like, what will be expected of them, whether they will be accepted, and whether or not to make a commitment. They are rather dependent on the leader, organizer, or chair to provide an orientation. They ask orienting questions and sometimes exhibit testing behaviors. Members are ambivalent about commitment and often are unwilling to volunteer for tasks. They joke around, and if not convinced of the group or task's importance, may attend irregularly. In this formative phase, the worker, either directly if there is no chairperson or working through the chairperson if there is one, helps to establish the group climate (accepting, business-like, formal, informal, open, etc.). Leadership, whether by the formally recognized leader such as a chair or by others assuming leadership, also helps the group establish or clarify its goals into SMARRT objectives and ground rules.

SMARRT objectives and operational goals need to be distinguished from a group's inoperative goals. Inoperative goals can't be translated into action. They are generally used as part of

Table 9.2. Stages of Group Development

Stages of Development	Main Features	Task Dimensions	Process Dimensions	Worker's Role
Forming	Ambivalent about commitments, dependence on leaders	Orientation to task and content, search for ground rules	Testing behaviors in performance due to ambivalent commitments	Orienting members, contracting, setting goals and rules, working through members' dependency issues
Storming	Conflict, struggles for power and group roles, structure development	Obtaining agreement with content and substance	Heightened emotions, hostility, struggles for control, resistance to work	Constructive conflict resolution, fostering participatory democratic structures
Norming	Development of group cohesion, harmony	Open exchanges of opinions, Task-focused, emergence of solutions	Acceptance of members' peculiarities, development of bonding and "we-ness"	Keeping group focused on task rather than just socializing, guarding against groupthink
Performing	Structuring participation for task accomplishment	Obtaining agreement on decisions and accomplishments	Functional role relatedness, interpersonal issues temporarily set aside	Structuring tasks and process to lead to outcomes, evaluating efforts, celebrating success, developing broad group leadership, guarding against groupthink
Adjourning	Regression to earlier patterns of behavior, nostalgia		Emotional resistance to ending work and ending group, nostalgia, especially if high bonding	Discussion of winding down, rewarding and staging closing as success, orienting group members to future task accomplishments and successes

(Bandler & Roman, 1999; Toseland & Rivas, 1995, Tuckman, 1965)

staging or as public relations window dressing to enhance group acceptability, either internally or externally, and to promote morale (Zastrow, 1997, pp. 58–61).

In addition, a group needs to develop ground rules for interaction and to work through any issues of dependency by accepting responsibility for its functioning. Competition in a work group needs to be recognized and managed. While competition can be productive between groups, it is generally not productive within groups. It interferes with group cohesion, coordination, and a unity of resources and effort. Overly competitive members whose competitive needs can't be directed outward generally disrupt internal group processes.

The roles of the work group are negotiated, established, assigned, and accepted. Leadership needs to know these roles and their allocation. The group is preliminarily structured during this phase. Considerations in structuring a group's work include agendas and seating arrangements. Agendas are the formal agendas that lay out a group's purpose and work. *Hidden agendas*

reflect goals of a single individual or small clique, a cabal, in a committee or board that are often unrelated and sometimes at variance with a group's purpose and unknown to all group members. While any member of a work group can have unique reasons for participation, hidden agendas generally are destructive since their promoters manipulate the group for private, secret ends, often ones that are contrary to the group's goals. A leadership task is to discover and manage any hidden agendas to limit their destructiveness to group task and process.

Seating arrangements are one way to help manage hidden agendas and facilitate group process to foster the group's work. Students of history will recognize the importance of seating arrangements. During the preliminary stages of the negotiations to end the Korean War in the 1950s and America's involvement in the Vietnam War of the 1960s and 1970s, months were spent negotiating the shape of the table and seating arrangements prior to starting the actual peace negotiations. Seating arrangements often indicate and confer status within a group. The arrangements can facilitate or hinder oral and visual communication, focus or diffuse attention, reduce or promote member distractions, and reinforce or weaken cliques and side discussions. These are all part of developing a working contract in a group.

Stage 2: Storming. As the group members begin to invest their emotions and energy in the group, they initiate a stage of development often characterized by conflict and struggles for power and control. The newness of the group has worn off. Emotions may run high; disagreements over substance and procedure arise. Although conflicts may be difficult to manage, the fact that they are going on indicates that a group has formed. Members care enough about the group and each other to fight over it. This is a crucial period in the life of the group. The group members are moving toward some resolution of the tension between differentiation and integration, between having their own way and giving in to the requirements of the group. The worker or leader must help the group to resolve conflicts in a constructive manner and to foster a democratic structure for decision making. Alternatively, the group is at risk of developing an authoritarian structure or of falling apart.

Stage 3: Norming. Having found a workable resolution to the conflicts created in the previous stage, the group begins to gel. A sense of cohesion emerges, characterized by greater acceptance of the unique traits of each member and a willingness to express views openly. The members feel comfortable with each other and begin to get down to doing the work necessary to accomplish the group's goals. The group needs to avoid too much socializing and to keep on task.

Stage 4: Performing. In this stage, the interpersonal structure that has developed becomes the functional instrument for dealing with task activities. Roles become flexible and functional, and group energy is channeled into task completion. Structural issues have been resolved (e.g., who plays what role, rules for decision making), so that the structure can now support task performance. The group can make decisions efficiently. This period is characterized by an emergence of solutions. The work of the group is structured in order to lead to outcomes and help the group to evaluate and celebrate its accomplishments. If the group's mission is completed, it prepares for adjournment.

Stage 5: Adjournment. As the group begins to recognize that its work is reaching a conclusion, members often feel ambivalent about ending—pleased about accomplishments, but sad about ending relationships and coming to a conclusion. During this period, groups often express their ambivalence by regressing to earlier forms of unconstructive behavior and patterns of relating. Meetings may be missed; emotions may run high again; old conflicts can break out. The group reaches a successful conclusion (a) if it encourages its members to talk openly about their feelings about ending; (b) by planning for group-appropriate closing rituals or events such as parties, testimonial dinners, and the like; and (c) by focusing on plans and life beyond the group.

Some Caveats on Groups

Virtual Groups

As discussed earlier, HSOs are becoming more virtual. Task groups, committees, and boards also are adopting virtual technologies. Meeting by video-conferencing, Internet, and teleconferencing saves time and related member costs such as transportation. After the startup costs and IT staff time, it saves the agency resources.

However, there are costs associated with *virtual groups* (VG). Aside from the startup, maintenance, and operating costs of the hardware and software, VGs have less social cohesion and build less social capital than do face-to-face groups. Completed forming, storming, and norming stages of group development are essential for social cohesion. These stages for the VG can be cursory and information can be limited. VG members are more hidden than are face-to-face group members. Henderson (2009), after a review of VG literature and research, concluded that VG members become more abstract in their judgments, are more likely to stereotype, and make topical judgments rather than specific judgments to group tasks and objectives. They perceive fewer differences between members and are more likely to believe that other members share their positions. VG members don't as readily deal with nuances as do face-to-face group members. A corrective measure to deal with the limitations of the VG's cohesion is to have face-to-face forming and norming stages and periodic face-to-face reinforcement.

Groupthink

Groupthink, a term coined by Janis (1972, 1982) is when group contagion, pressure, and self-deception allows individuals in a group to ignore or forego their independent judgment and conform to group judgments and will. It is a form of political correctness and *to get along, go along*. It is a potential and dangerous side effect of group cohesion. Groupthink occurs when group members become so focused on the search for consensus that it overrides any realistic assessment of deviant or unpopular views. It represents deterioration in an individual's mental efficiency and reality testing because of group pressures.

Groupthink is an important consideration for work groups as it impedes the group from considering the full range of opinions and option. The classic groupthink illustration is President Kennedy's Bay of Pigs invasion, when his best and brightest advisors succumbed to groupthink in their invasion planning. Groupthink is heavily influenced by charismatic and dominant members to whom the group attributes greater knowledge and abilities (Anderson & Kilduff, 2009).

According to Janis (1972, 1982) and our observations, groupthink is promoted by:

- Homogeneity and isolation of group members: Members are the same in terms of background, values, and orientation and operate in isolation from a diverse social environment.
- Illusion of invulnerability: We are right because we are the best and the brightest.
- Belief in group's inherent morality: The option is right because we are moral and right.
- Collective rationalization: If information doesn't support the groupthink option, discard the information rather than the option.
- Outgroup stereotypes: We can't consider any option they present as they are always wrong. This is the bane of a partisan political process.

- Self-censorship: Members are afraid or reluctant to question the apparent group consensus, feeling that because the group is right, they must be wrong.
- Illusion of unanimity: It must be the right option because we all think it is the right option (and those disagreeing are reluctant to share their disagreements).

Groupthink weakens the task group's work and processes by:

- Limiting its discussion to the few politically correct options
- Not fully examining the favored option for its weaknesses
- Not fully examining minority positions
- Uncritically adopting the dominant members' positions
- Never seeking outside expert opinion
- Accepting only information that supports the favored option
- Not considering contingency plans

The task group can guard against the deleterious effects of groupthink in several ways:

- Select and construct groups with internal diversity.
- At the beginning of the process, appoint a gadfly or devil's advocate, someone to critically examine any group proposals independent of the group.
- Encourage everyone to be a critical evaluator.
- Follow the model of the most junior member stating preferences first rather than leaders or dominant members.
- Set up subgroups to independently consider each option.
- Consult with experts or others outside the group.
- Invite outside experts ignorant of the group's position(s) to present fresh ideas and information.
- Use modifications of Delphi Group methodologies to allow group members to independently and anonymously consider options.

Groupthink is contrary to the need for and purposes of a group. If a group is to think as one, there is no need for a group, only for one. Again, social workers need to use critical practice skills in the group.

Effective Meetings

How many times have you gone to a meeting and left with the feeling that it was a waste of time? Frequently this happens because whoever was responsible for running the meeting did not think through the specific decisions to be made at the meeting or could not facilitate the decision-making process effectively. If you can miss a meeting and never feel that you've been gone, this is an indication of poor task and process. *Task group meetings all share a common purpose: making decisions or completing a task.* Whatever the larger purpose of the group, when a task group holds a meeting, it does so to make decisions that will help the group move toward achievement of its goals. The fact that meetings may also provide opportunities for socialization, networking, and education does not alter their decision-making function. Therefore, effective meetings require both planning and chairperson skills. (Members of a group who are not chairing a meeting also have responsibility for advance planning and for helping a meeting accomplish its tasks by their interventions, both verbal and nonverbal.) Let us look at the planning aspect first.

Meeting Planning: Footwork and Headwork

An effective meeting is *the culmination of a prior planning process* (Tropman, 1980). The planning process begins before the first meeting and occurs thereafter with the follow-up work after the meeting, thereby beginning the planning process for the next meeting. Box 9.1 indicates

some of the necessary pre-meeting tasks. Tropman (1980) provides some guidance to plan for good task group decision making:

- Personality is not as important in the decision-making process as are the roles of the participants.
- The formal meeting itself is an endpoint in a long series of pre-meeting activities leading to decisions rather than the beginning point in decision making. Once a meeting begins, events have largely been determined.
- The pre-meeting phase provides the most opportunities for influence, bargaining, and coalition structuring and agenda setting. (The importance of the pre-meeting phase increases with a group's size and diversity and constituent diversity.)
- The purpose of a meeting of a decision-making group is to make good decisions, not just decisions (p. 15).

Enough attention should be paid to administrative chores and decision-making requirements ahead of the meeting so effective decisions can result. Since there are many different kinds of task groups (e.g., staff groups, coalitions, treatment planning teams, boards), and since meetings vary in their degree of formality, pre-meeting planning activities will vary as well, but in all cases pre-meeting planning should go on. In advance of a meeting, the chair (and the staff member for the group, if assigned) should have thought through the following:

1. The dynamics of the group in light of its development
2. Task and process objectives
3. Decisions that need to be made at the meeting
4. Information the group must have in order to make decisions

---

BOX 9.1.	**Pre-Meeting Meeting Administrative Chores**

1. Preparing meeting minutes
2. Getting out meeting notices
3. Reproducing agendas and other informational materials and getting them to members before the meeting

4. Arranging for and setting up meeting space
5. Arranging for refreshments, water, notepads.

5. The various roles of the participants and how the work of the group can be carried out
6. The actual meeting agenda

In formalized groups, such as a social service agency team meeting, a board meeting, a neighborhood association community meeting, or a working coalition strategy session, typically the chair and possibly some other members plan the agenda and consider the decision-making process sufficiently in advance of the meeting so members can get the agenda and meeting materials early enough to review them before the meeting. If the group has a staff member assigned, such as with a board of directors or with a community group that a social worker is forming (e.g., to do a neighborhood needs assessment), then the worker and the chair and other members would meet and plan in advance of the meeting. If a group is meeting monthly, the members should receive the agenda and materials at least a week in advance of the meeting. Every item on a meeting agenda will not necessarily lead to a decision, as for example with progress reports of a committee or subcommittee or an informational briefing by an expert in a particular substantive area. Getting member input and feedback about the business of the group and its process is important. Also, some agenda items may take more than one meeting to complete. However, for every task group meeting that is scheduled, the worker and chair (and members, too) should be asking themselves what decisions should be made at the meeting that will advance the purpose of the group. The agenda should reflect these prospective decision items. If no decisions are necessary, other, less time-consuming virtual venues of information sharing should be considered.

In agenda planning, the worker and chair will consider how various agenda items can be disposed of during the meeting in light of the group's needs and dynamics. For example, to foster group participation, preplanning may include asking particular members to take responsibility for reporting on or handling an agenda item. If members have been doing work in preparation for a meeting, they must be given the opportunity to report back. Otherwise you will discourage future voluntary action. Many prospective agenda items will emerge during a meeting, with insufficient information for the group to make a decision. Usually these items need to be assigned to an existing committee for work outside the meeting, leading to recommendations for group action in the future. Critical agenda items should not be scheduled at the end of a meeting. This will limit debate and possibly any decision.

Of course, sometimes the best-laid meeting plans, as those of mice and men *gang aft agley*, may go astray by a critical but unplanned issue that suddenly arises. In this situation, modifying the agenda may be a necessary and appropriate course of action. However, these issues will often have to be assigned to an existing or newly formed committee in order to bring them to resolution at a later meeting.

The worker and chair, as Box 9.2 emphasis, must also pay attention to the process or socioemotional dimension of the group in meeting planning. Members who make an emotional investment in a group seldom go through the group experience without being aroused by the way a decision is handled, or the way some members behave, or the lack of opportunity to present their own points of view. For example, observations of unexpressed or expressed anger may be

BOX 9.2.	Effective Task Group Decision-Making Rules

- Give members opportunities to participate and equalize member participation to enhance cohesion and avoid exclusion and marginalization.
- Give members opportunities to express preferences and positions.
- Seek expression of diversity of opinion and interest within the group to avoid groupthink and to create cohesion from the diversity.

- Start with the least-powerful members of the group in seeking member expressions of opinions, to promote a full expression of opinion.
- Structure the agenda to promote good decisions, because the purpose of the group is to encourage good decision making.
- Emphasize consensus, with good decisions being what everyone can live with.

cues for follow-up phone contact to help members manage their feelings or find a way to express them constructively at the next meeting. Other pre-meeting contacts may be important for any number of reasons, such as to encourage participation, to bridge communication gaps, to lend support, or to try to understand a member's reactions. In addition, groups have the wonderful capacity to be able to reflect on their own process. When emotions run high, a chair needs to plan for some time in a meeting for the group to look at its process and take corrective action.

The Meeting Itself

Members come to meetings of a working group to do business during a specified time, usually between 1 and 2 hours. Effectiveness tends to diminish if meetings last longer than 2 hours. Although there is no guarantee that members will come to a meeting properly prepared, *if* the agenda and other materials have reached them in advance and *if* the meeting stays on track so that the agenda is dealt with in the allotted time and decisions are made, the probability for meeting effectiveness increases (Tropman, 1980). If not, effectiveness decreases.

Staying on track means beginning and ending a meeting on time and covering the items on the agenda. If meetings begin late, members will start to arrive late. Time for conducting the group's business is limited, and meetings will run over the agreed-on time of closing. Inevitably some members will arrive late, so it is usually a good idea to begin on time with the lighter part of the agenda, such as approving minutes and making announcements. Save roughly the middle third of the meeting for the weightiest agenda items, when the members' attention is most focused and everybody is ready to get down to business. The final portion of the meeting can then be more relaxed. This is a good time to generate new agenda items, talk about the process and progress of the group, pull together the decisions that have been made, and remind the group of the next meeting date (Tropman, 1980).

The structure for decision making that task groups adopt varies on a continuum from formal to informal. Many groups fall somewhere in between. At the formal end of the continuum, the group adopts formal rules and procedures

for reaching decisions based on a vote. Some agreed-upon meeting protocol is necessary. Usually this process is guided by *parliamentary procedure*, a fair and orderly process for reaching decisions. *Roberts' Rules of Order*, developed over a hundred years ago, is used extensively. Revised editions are available in any bookstore or library on and the Web.[3] Short versions are regularly published. Social workers regularly involved in task group work should become familiar with the basics of parliamentary procedure.

A formal structure for decision making is invaluable with groups too large for easy decision making (e.g., a meeting with 25 or more community members, as compared with a committee of less than 8 to 10 people).[4] The bigger the group, the more important the procedures for reaching decisions. Formal decision rules, such as those of parliamentary procedure, have the advantages of preventing a minority from controlling the group and ensuring that group decisions are clearly ratified. The disadvantages are that discussions can easily become bogged down in rules and in competitive parliamentary strategizing to gain advantage; a positional minority group can be abused; and the procedures can be handled so rigidly and mechanically that the process dimension of group life is totally ignored.

An informal decision-making structure, at the other end of the continuum, usually involves a consensus-seeking process, which can but often does not culminate in a vote. Consensus-seeking behavior tends to emphasize careful listening, the broad expression of different viewpoints, constructive conflict over ideas, and a search for creative solutions that have wide member input and approval. It places a premium on process. An informal structure tends to be most useful when the group is fairly small, when member trust is high, when creative problem solving is needed, and when time for reaching decisions is not a problem. Remember, the consensus sought is not that everyone thinks the same thing is the best thing, but that a decision is reached that everyone can live with (Payne, 2000, p. 211). The disadvantage of seeking consensus, in comparison with the *dictatorship of the majority* or a majority vote, is that it is often a time-consuming and overly complicated process, and

BOX 9.3.   Guidelines for More Effective Committee/Board Meetings

1. Agenda integrity
   a. DO always have an agenda and a reason for the meeting.
   b. DO always have necessary agenda items and address all necessary items.
   c. DO always make all necessary decisions.
   d. DON'T discuss items not on the agenda.
   e. DON'T make unnecessary, unneeded, or premature decisions.
2. Temporal integrity (time management)
   a. DO always begin and end meetings on time.
   b. DO always have and keep the meeting to an agenda time schedule.
   c. DO always have a committee/board long-range schedule with preplanning to allocate agenda items to relevant meetings when decisions are needed.
3. Rule of halves
   a. DO prepare agenda items by priorities and schedule discussion and decisions by the priorities.

   b. DON'T place an item on the agenda unless it is submitted by the time one half of the period between meetings has elapsed.
4. Rule of thirds
   a. DO place and deal with the most important items in the middle third of the meeting, when group energy is highest.
   b. DO have a break at the two-thirds point, for a distraction.
5. Rule of three quarters
   a. DO make the agenda available to members sufficiently in advance to allow members time for preparation.
   b. DO avoid last-minute surprises.

(Tropman, 1980, pp. 25–31)

can allow for a *dictatorship of a minority* as seen in the health legislation debates of 2009–2010, especially if a minority is allowed to control the group. Box 9.3 lays out some *do's* and *don'ts* of meeting management.

As we stated earlier, many task groups fall somewhere along the formality–informality continuum. Many groups use a modified version of parliamentary procedure to formally consider an agenda item and reach a decision through voting; at the same meeting, some decisions will be reached by consensus—a nod of the head from the participants, signifying agreement. Some meetings benefit from the best of both worlds: strict parliamentary procedure with an allotted period of consensus-building time in the meeting. For example, a very formal meeting may also set aside time for a brainstorming session on a difficult agenda item, with no censorship of ideas—in fact, encouragement of even the wildest notions—and a conscious attempt to avoid reaching any decision.

There are no explicit rules on how task group meetings must be run. Much depends on group size, the leader and staff's skills, the group's task and process needs, and the group's saliency for its members. Box 9.4 identifies why committees and task groups don't always work well. It's a

responsibility of leadership to address these issues.

Chairing Meetings

The chairperson role is complex. Meetings are public space. Whatever happens at a meeting is available to all of its participants. If a participant is treated unfairly, for example, by being insulted or cut off prematurely, all other participants observe and experience that treatment in some way. If a bully dominates a meeting, the members are bullied. For meetings to be effective, therefore, it is incumbent on the chair to act as a neutral, objective arbiter of the group's business and to insist on sensitivity and fair play by and to all members. The chair sets the tone for the meetings. If the chair in a formal meeting has very strong feelings or opinions about an issue and wants to express them, he or she usually asks someone else to preside until that agenda item is resolved.

Issues of distance arise in other ways as well. In general, the chair must be involved enough in the substance and process of a meeting to be able to engage the ideas and the people, yet uninvolved enough to be able to step back and guide the interchange to fruitful decisions. The chair

BOX 9.4.	Why Committees/Boards Don't Always Work Well

- Activities have low saliency and importance for members. Missing a meeting does not make a difference to the committee's decision making, absent members, or the unit that the member represents.
- Committee has decision overload and spends too much time with trivia that doesn't contribute to or crowds out real decision making.
- High inertia in group's and meeting's structure because of poor agenda planning, lack of pre-meeting work, lack of agenda clarity on needed decisions, and poor time management.
- Group's culture and history involve ineffectiveness, irresponsibility, not following through, and other behaviors not conducive to decision making. The group is unable to overcome its history and culture of ineffectiveness and irresponsibility.

(Tropman, 1980, pp. 19–20; Zastrow, 1997, pp. 58–61)>

generally should not guide the group to a particular decision. The chair should guide the group to complete its work. The chair is not a group worker. The good of the meeting occurs outside the group as a result of its work. *The chair operates with a split vision or dual consciousness, one aimed at understanding the ideas being expressed and the meaning of the interaction, the other aimed at using the group process to help the group members make sound decisions in which they are also invested.* This duality comes together in the various roles that the chairperson plays in a group meeting. We have identified these as *presider*, *facilitator*, and *administrator*.

Presider. The chair, as presider, ensures that the business of the meeting is accomplished in a democratic fashion. The chair controls the flow of interaction in a meeting so that the agenda is dealt with effectively. The chair convenes the meeting, calls on the members to start the work (calls the meeting to order), and closes the meeting at its conclusion. Between the start and the finish, the chair regulates the discussion by calling on people to express their feelings and viewpoints. By summarizing, clarifying, repeating, and reminding the participants of the topic under discussion and the time available, the chair keeps the meeting agenda on track. The chair often synthesizes ideas for the group and determines when the group is ready to make a decision. When the group is ready to act, the chair clarifies the decision that is being made and ratifies the action by taking a vote or a reading of the degree of consensus. (Group members, of course, may also help to keep meetings on track, synthesize ideas, and clarify decisions.

These roles are by no means limited to the chair, nor would you want them to be.)

Facilitator. As group facilitator, the chair observes and interprets the way relationships are developing among the members, and the development of the group as a whole. The chair must intervene so that the group process supports the group's task objectives. This involves the chair in many different kinds of interventions. Four important types of intervention are the following (Sampson & Marthas, 1981, pp. 258–259):

1. *Providing support* (e.g., "That's really an interesting idea") helps to create a positive "climate for expressing ideas and opinions, including unpopular and unusual points of view," and to "reinforce positive forms of behavior" (p. 258).
2. *Mediating conflict* (e.g., "Let's see if we can get to the bottom of this disagreement") helps the group members communicate more openly and directly with each other to relieve tension and to reduce disruptive behavior.
3. *Probing and questioning* (e.g., "I wonder if that idea could be enlarged") helps the group "expand a point that may have been left incomplete" and "invites members to explore their ideas in greater detail" (p. 259).
4. *Reflecting feelings* (e.g., "The group seems to be having a very hard time coming to grips with that decision") "orients members to the feelings that may lie behind what is being said or done" (p. 259).

Perhaps it should be emphasized again here that group members also can and should help to facilitate the group process. That role is not limited to the chair.

Administrator. Without staff support, the chair, as administrator, basically coordinates the work of the group before, during, and after meetings. The chair, for example, attends to many of the pre-meeting tasks mentioned earlier, such as ensuring that information the group needs for making decisions is available in a timely manner. Before and during the meetings, with the help of other group members, the chair generates agenda items for future meetings. During the meeting, the chair usually assigns tasks and delegates responsibilities—for example, assigning a particular agenda item to a committee or subcommittee for follow-up work. The chair also makes sure that the particular agenda item returns to the group at an appropriate future date. The chair also serves as spokesperson for the group when the group needs to be represented (Tropman, 1980).

Staffing a Task Group

Many social workers provide staff support to task groups, as with boards of directors or board committees, community development associations, interagency teams, planning bodies, and long-term coalitions. In these instances, the role of the professional is to enable the group to function effectively by providing assistance to the group, mainly through the chair, in handling administrative tasks and coordination, preparing for meetings, and serving as process consultant and, in some cases, as strategy and substantive expert. The main point here is that the professional staff person plays a critical, but *behind-the-scenes*, role, assisting the leaders of the group (the chair and various other members who accept responsibilities) in performing their functions effectively. The staff person thus primarily carries out a *leadership development* role.

Although the paid staff person clearly has responsibility for the group, he or she is normally not a voting member of the group. In many cases, the staff person is directly hired and can be fired by the group. In other instances, the employment relationship with the task group is much more indirect, although the group still has influence over a staff member's status. A direct service worker who is organizing a community group to sponsor a health fair would serve as staff to the health fair steering committee and would not typically be a voting member of that body. Or, for example, in an organization such as United Way, the staff person is a member of a larger professional staff responsible to the organization's executive director. This professional staff works with a host of volunteer planning and fundraising committees but is not a voting member. The executive is responsible to the board of directors and serves as its professional staff. The executive here is usually an ex officio board member (a board member by virtue of the office held), but again without a vote.

In working with chairpersons and other group leaders, staff must gauge the chair and group's experience and sophistication and adapt the assistance provided accordingly. In general, staff should help a chair prepare for meetings by jointly developing and reviewing the agenda, the tasks to be accomplished, and a plan for accomplishing them. The plan may include preparing some group members for roles they might play in the meeting; planning how to break down a complicated agenda item into smaller decisions; considering process snags and how to handle them; and, in some cases, considering how to reach an acceptable decision in the face of the political machinations of various subgroup factions. Inexperienced chairs may need help in role-playing parts of a meeting. More sophisticated chairs may need other forms of assistance, such as sensitization to process concerns.

At community meetings, professional staff are, of course, visible and have a good opportunity to talk to the group members and get to know them better, and vice versa. Once the formal meeting begins, though, staff take a back seat to the chair directing the meeting. Since the staff member has already had input into the meeting by virtue of pre-meeting preparations with the chair and other members, during the meeting the staff person carefully observes the group process while following the substance of the discourse. Sitting beside the chair, the staff person can share comments, suggestions, and observations discreetly with the chair. This is not to say that the staff member must be totally silent. Sometimes the chair or a member will ask the staff person directly for observations or suggestions. Sometimes a meeting may be getting out of hand or off course, and the staff person may judiciously make a corrective comment or ask a question. Sometimes it may be apparent that the chair does not know how to handle a particular situation, and the staff member may have to intervene. *A principle to keep in mind, however, is that while leadership, group development, task and process balance, and decision making are staff goals, staff must be careful not to usurp the authority and leadership of the chair.*

Since professional staff tend to spend more time on the business of a task group than do the chair or other leaders, they often tend to take over a group or at least to dominate it. Sometimes this is not even a conscious decision; staff just find it easier to act for the group than to work through the group. This approach retards the group leadership and the group as a whole in developing fully. While the group is forming to reach some specified set of goals, the bottom line is that the *members of the group have to own the group if it is to succeed.* For ownership to occur, staff have to enable the group members to make their own decisions about the nature and direction of the group and to take responsibility for its work. Enabling involves a delicate balance between holding back advice and hands-on assistance and offering them at various critical points to guide a group over a rough spot. There are no simple guidelines for managing the balance, but if a group does not seem to be developing, staff members at least need to ask themselves whether they have done too much for the group. Perhaps more holding back would be appropriate.

Dealing with Group Problems

All groups experience problems; these come with the territory. For example, task groups commonly experience difficulties getting started, handling conflict, reaching decisions, dealing with disruptive behavior by an individual member (the meeting monopolizer, the angry challenger, the bully, etc.) or by a subgroup (negative bloc voting), and more. Common as these and other group problems may be, however, there is no standard recipe for how best to deal

with them. Because groups differ in so many ways and because the circumstances surrounding any problem are unique, in working with groups, just as in social work with individuals, families, or communities, we prefer a general approach to problem solving rather than a set of fixed solutions. Let's look at the framework first and then apply it to some group problems one might encounter.

A Problem-Solving Framework

The now-familiar problem-solving framework used in this book has four general steps: (a) study, (b) assessment, (c) treatment or intervention, and (d) evaluation or reassessment. The framework is a useful guide, a kind of mindset, for dealing with group task and process problems. The time frame involved in these steps can range from instantaneous to prolonged. As a problem arises in the group, the social worker as leader, member, or staff person may respond then and there, based on observations and some conclusions about the meaning of the behavior. Or the social worker may choose not to intervene, but instead to continue to observe and consider the nature of the problem and what to do about it, saving the intervention for some later date. Since a group is a public space for all participants, a decision for nonintervention sometimes is a form of intervention. Whenever the intervention has occurred, the social worker should assess its effect and make a decision about whether to respond further, and what kind of intervention to make and when. The transition from thought to action and back to reflection, sometimes referred to as *praxis, is part of critical practice*; it can be seamless or spaced out.

Problem Definition. The study section of the problem-solving framework, then, is the period for defining and clarifying the nature and extent of the problem in the group. When a problem arises, we need to ask ourselves the following questions: What is the actual problem? What are the observable behaviors indicating that there is a problem? How is the group affected? How serious is the problem?

Assessment. Assessment is done to clarify and complete the case theory construction of the problem. We connect our observations to our theoretical knowledge and construct a case theory in order to intervene effectively. Assessment is an information-gathering process to understand a problem, a situation, a case, to effect a future change (Bisman, 1994, pp. 111–121). Assessment questions are: Why is this problem occurring? What's going on outside the group or in the group that may be contributing to this problem? Am I contributing to the problem in some way? Where is the group developmentally? What role do subgroups or factions play in this problem? What part do the individual needs and personalities of the participants play in this problem? Is there any pattern to the behavior I am observing? What is my understanding of the problem?

Intervention. This is the point of action. The worker needs to say or do something in the group, or sometimes outside the group, to help the group deal with the problem. When intervening, the worker may think about the following kinds of questions: How can I get the group to start to handle the problem? How will my reaction to an individual member or to the group as a whole facilitate the group process and keep the group on course? How will my intervention be perceived by the group? Are there specific techniques I can use to affect the problem?

Evaluation. Having intervened to try to deal with the problem, the worker now needs to observe the impact of that intervention. The main questions, then, are as follows: What effect did my action have on the group? What effect did my intervention have on specific individuals and/or subgroups? Does my diagnosis seem to be correct, or do I need to modify my understanding of the problem? Do I need to take any follow-up action?

Three Common Group Problems

As we turn to some examples of problems and interventions, we should keep in mind, once again, that the responsibility for dealing with problems does not rest with the leader/chair or staff person alone. All members of a group share responsibility for helping the group to function effectively, and any member may be instrumental in helping the group address problematic behavior. Since this chapter is written from the perspective of the chairperson or leader and staff person, and since these individuals often do intervene to deal with group problems, we shall adopt that stance in the illustrations that follow. As we go through these examples, consider your own analysis of the problem and possible interventions.

The Meeting Monopolizer. Scenario. Imagine the third meeting of a treatment planning team of staff members on an acute illness unit of a large psychiatric hospital. The unit leader, who is a social worker with many years of seniority, is also the team leader. The other members of the team include a psychiatrist, a head nurse, a nursing assistant, a psychologist, an occupational therapist, and a recreational therapist. Team planning on the unit is not new, but this particular team, with three new members, represents a new team configuration. The team meets weekly. The newcomers are the psychiatrist, the head nurse, and the nursing assistant. Although the social worker, Karen Jones, chairs the meetings, the meetings have increasingly been dominated by the psychiatrist, Dr. Matthew Maton, who has a lot to say about each case before the group. Other team members have had difficulty interjecting their ideas. Some group members are beginning to grumble outside the group about their inability to be heard, and it is becoming difficult to arrive at treatment plans that everyone can accept. So far, the team leader has taken a laissez-faire approach to chairing the group, but now the time has come to intervene more directly. In this third meeting, when the second case is put before the group for discussion, Dr. Maton immediately takes the lead in explaining the nature of the patient's illness. How might the chair intervene?

Study. At each meeting, Dr. Maton monopolizes the discussion of the cases. He usually does a lot of teaching about the nature of the illness and reviews current research before getting to his own recommendations. While the information is interesting, other members are forced to sit and listen passively. The doctor is not good at picking up cues that others want to contribute their observations. He does not maintain good eye contact with other group members. He also discounts input from other disciplines. Group members have begun to resist coming to agreement on treatment plans and are often restless. Two members have come late to the third team meeting and have expressed some resentment to the leader outside the meeting. Dr. Maton's behavior is threatening the effectiveness of team planning.

Assessment. The case theory can posit a number of factors that can contribute to this problem. The team leader has not dealt with the fact that the team has several new members who may not be familiar with the ground rules the old team had established. Her laissez-faire approach thus has not provided the group with a sufficient orientation to the team's expectations and norms. The psychiatrist is new and is trying to find his niche in the group. Other new members have a similar challenge, while older members are used to their particular format for team meetings. Dr. Maton's previous experiences as team leader himself may have led him to adopt a dominant leadership-teaching pattern. His behavior may reflect discomfort with his status on the unit and in the group. Also, Dr. Maton appears not to be a good listener, at least as far as the staff is concerned. Monopolizers often are bullies.

Intervention. The group leader has a number of options. Some possibilities include the following:

1. She could confront Dr. Maton directly about his behavior. "Dr. Maton [firmly until she has his attention], you seem to have an awful lot to say about each case before the group. Although your points are informative, I'd like to stop your discourse at this point so that other members have a chance to express their views on the case. Thank you."
2. She could reflect the group's behavior back to the group and solicit their feedback. After Dr. Maton finishes his discourse, or after politely interrupting, the leader might say, "I'd like to stop the discussion of cases for a few minutes to consider our process. As I look around the group, I see a lot of restlessness and dissatisfaction. I wonder if we could talk about what's going on."
3. She could reflect back her own behavior to the group as a means of inviting clarification

of ground rules. After Dr. Maton finishes his discourse or after interrupting him politely, the leader might say, "Before Dr. Maton finishes his explanation, I need to interrupt the group for a few minutes to take care of some important business that I realize I neglected. As I've been observing the group, it seems that I never took the time to orient this team from the outset about expectations for team functioning. Since we have three new team members, maybe we could take some time now to make some decisions together about how we want to handle our cases in the group meeting."

Evaluation. The first intervention offers Dr. Maton limited support but also lets him know directly that his behavior is not acceptable, sets limits on it, and lets the other team members know that their participation is valued. Other group members may also feel freer to interrupt Dr. Maton in the future. Dr. Maton, however, may find the confrontation surprising and irritating, laboring under the notion that he was doing what he was supposed to do as team psychiatrist. He may feel that he has lost face in the group.

The second intervention potentially allows the group to express their dissatisfaction with Dr. Maton's monopolistic behavior, as well as their own expectations for participation. Since this is only the third team meeting, the members may not be willing to take Dr. Maton on. If they are willing, the leader risks a session that deteriorates into an attack on the psychiatrist.

The third intervention recognizes the group's formative stage of development, directs some of the group's anger back to the leader rather than the psychiatrist, and opens the way for the team to establish its ground rules in a constructive fashion. Once the members have negotiated the rules of the game, monopolization will be less likely to occur and will be easier for the team leader and other members to limit, since the group has guidelines for participation.

Group Conflict. Scenario. You are serving in your first year as an associate director of a moderate-sized nonprofit family services agency. Your responsibilities include supervising the professional staff and chairing monthly agency staff meetings. Along with the director and another associate director, who is also new, the agency staff consists of 12 professional social workers, 2 immigrant resettlement workers, and 4 case aides. The agency is departmentalized into four divisions: family and children's (six social workers), single adults (two social workers), senior adults (two social workers), and immigrant services (two social workers and two resettlement workers). One case aide works in each division, handling arrangements for in-home services, transportation, respite care, and the like. Staff turnover in the agency is generally low, so that these staff members know each other quite well. Half of the professional staff members have been with the agency for more than 10 years. The agency has been trying to work out a policy on home visiting. Currently, the only staff members who regularly make home visits are the nonprofessional workers and the two social workers handling adoptions in the family and children's division. This division is within your purview. The other new associate director, Hector Gravas, has proposed that every client seen by the agency have a home visit, with the exception of single adults, unless there is severe contagious illness. The professional staff is split on the policy. One faction, led by Molly Black, the head of the family and children's division and a senior staff member, is adamantly opposed. Although a subordinate of Hector Gravas, she is vocal in opposing the home visit proposal. She states that for professionals "to be gallivanting around the city making home visits" is a poor use of professional time. The other faction, led by Felice Navidad, head of immigration services under your direction and also a senior staffer, strongly favors home visits by professionals. The nonprofessional staff members, feeling caught in the middle, have tried to stay out of the line of fire.

After going round and round for nearly an hour and making no headway, rational discourse has deteriorated into simmering anger that can split the work units. How might you intervene to begin a process of constructive conflict resolution?

Study. Groups frequently experience conflict, especially as part of their development. The task is to manage the conflict effectively so that group cohesion can be enhanced rather than destroyed and an appropriate decision for the agency made.

When the group has a strong sense of trust and commitment to group goals, when the conflicts represent substantive disagreements over ideas, procedures, or priorities, and when the group has a history of productive problem solving, constructive resolutions are easier to achieve. When conflicts erupt due to struggles in the group over status and power, when attacks become personalized and hostile, when there is a win/lose competitive atmosphere and the members begin to take sides, the group deteriorates into destructive conflict. With two relatively new associate directors and passed-over staff, cohesion is lacking. Constructive resolution is much harder to achieve. In the family services staff group, conflict seems to have taken a destructive turn following competitive lines that split work units into factions. The group has not been able to make any progress on coming up with an acceptable policy. Anger is running high. The professional staff has polarized into two factions. The nonprofessional staff are not participating so as not to be subjected to personal attacks or retribution from more powerful group members. The atmosphere has degenerated into a win/lose situation.

Assessment. A quick analysis and case theory conjectures that a number of factors may be contributing to this destructive climate. The members of the family and children's division, under Molly Black, see themselves as highly professional therapists with neither the time nor the resources to do extensive home visiting. Hector Gravas is viewed as something of an upstart trying to shake things up just to exert power. In addition, Molly wanted but did not get his associate director's job. Instead, an outsider was hired for the position. Her division feels slighted. Hector Gravas is aware that Molly was a candidate for his position, but as her supervisor, he has never discussed this matter with her. Felice Navidad, the senior professional staff member in charge of immigration services, already spends a lot of time seeing immigrant families in their homes. She believes the proposed policy will eventually generate more resources for her department. Her vocal support has not sat well with the family and children's division and gives the impression that you, as her supervisor, support this position. A number of other staff members do support Hector's proposal, and they maintain that prevention, social support, and resocialization should represent the major professional goals of the agency. The nonprofessional staff have mixed feelings about the policy. Some believe that if all members of the professional staff did home visits, the nonprofessionals' contribution would be recognized and more greatly appreciated. Others fear that if all staff members did home visits, there would be less need for their services, potentially leading to cutbacks in nonprofessional positions.

Thus, a shift in agency policy could upset the existing tenuous group equilibrium. The new associate directors are being tested. Your honeymoon periods as new staff leaders are over; staff members no longer feel they have to be polite and deferential. They can take more risks in expressing their feelings and ideas and find out how the new group leader/authority figure will react and what your limits are. Will you understand them? How will you and Hector deal with anger and internal competition? He did not recognize the potential ramifications of his proposal and therefore made no moves before the meeting to get feedback on his idea and to reduce the anxiety that often accompanies change. Neither did you. Had either or both of you recognized the potential for conflict ahead of time, the staff might have been prepared more effectively before the meeting. The most important time is the pre-meeting time. Hector also has avoided dealing with Molly's competitive and hurt feelings about his receiving the associate director's job over her.

Intervention. The following are some possible interventions:

1. You try to legitimate differences of opinion and defuse the situation a bit. Ideally you will recognize that you, as well as Hector Gravas, are being tested, and you will not overreact. You do not want a win/lose solution or to contribute to the conflict by undermining either Hector Gravas or Molly Black. You want a win/win solution that still deals with the task—that is, the proposed policy change. In an effort to achieve this, you might propose a cooling-off period that will allow for less visible and emotion-charged negotiations. It will also allow Hector Gravas to address and work out his administrative relationship with Molly Black in a less public and volatile environment. "After an hour of hot and heavy debate, let's recognize that there are legitimate differences of opinion. I don't think there is any right or wrong solution here. Why don't we think about the policy and come back to it next week with some ideas about how to blend the different positions?"

2. You recognize that more is evidently at stake than a substantive difference over a policy option. You try to get at the underlying anger and fear by reflecting back the group's behavior. "After listening and watching the interchange about this policy, I've noticed that several people have not said anything for almost an hour, while others have taken sides without fully listening to and hearing each other. I'd really like to understand what's going on."

3. You acknowledge that the conflict goes deeper than the policy itself and try to get at this by reflecting back the group's feelings. "I think we need to stop for a minute and try to understand the anger and fear that this policy suggestion seems to have aroused. I don't think we'll make much progress if we're this tense about the proposal, and I would like to make some progress."

4. You adopt a structural approach to defuse the conflict that also incorporates a cooling-off period. "We seem to have hit an impasse on this policy for now. One group is strongly opposed, one group is strongly for, and another contingent seems stuck in the middle. I'm going to ask two members from each subgroup to meet during the week and see if they can work out a compromise proposal that everyone can live with. I'll meet with the group afterward to see what has been worked out, and we'll discuss it at the next staff meeting." This, as with as the first approach, provides time for you to act as a mediator.

Evaluation. Not every conflict that a group experiences has to be processed by the group. Otherwise, the group might spend all of its time doing that and nothing else. When a conflict has destructive qualities, as was the case in this scenario, the group probably does need to look at it in more depth. Nor are these responses necessarily mutually exclusive. For example, the fourth alternative, or something like it, might well follow a discussion generated by the second or third alternatives. The interventions identified above also are not the only possible responses. Sometimes a group may even need the assistance of an outside facilitator to get at their difficulties and resolve them.

In the first response, you recognize that the group is tired and has gone as far as it can for now. Legitimizing differences is generally a constructive approach, and allowing for a cooling-off period may be helpful. It sets a tone of calm acceptance, in contrast to the group's turmoil. In this situation, it seems unlikely that the group will come up with a compromise policy on its own without some specific structure in place for doing the work. Since the conflict has some destructive properties, the chair needs to be sure that the situation will not be dropped, lest it fester and surface again and again in different ways. Before the next meeting, you as chair need to talk with Molly and other staff members individually to get a clearer sense of their feelings and concerns. You might want to informally mediate a discussion between Hector and Molly. You then will be more prepared to lead a discussion of the policy at the next staff meeting.

In the second intervention, you feed your observations of their behavior back to the group. In effect, you hold up a mirror and show them how their behavior appears, with the aim of opening up the discussion about their underlying concerns and feelings in a manner that can lead to some resolution. Again, the tone is calm and accepting.

In the third intervention, you openly recognize the strong feelings that the proposal has aroused and legitimate discussion of feelings and concerns. Again, the aim is to move beyond the policy itself, because the staff's anger and fear are blocking effective progress.

In the fourth alternative, you try to defuse the staff's anger by taking time to explicitly deal with the policy outside the group. This is like the first alternative, except that here you set up a structure for working on the compromise. You still have work to do between meetings in eliciting the staff's feelings and concerns.

Group Silence or Nonparticipation. Scenario. The six-member steering committee of a local homeless service provider coalition is meeting to decide on an activity that will mobilize support for a bill requiring the city to provide 24-hour mobile emergency aid teams to reach out to the homeless on cold days. The mayor has come out publicly against the proposal due to budgetary constraints. The group has met six times, and the members generally know each other because of their common work with the homeless population in the city. The discussion, chaired by the organizer/leader, has gone on for about an hour, without much enthusiasm or focus. The members don't seem to be able to come up with viable ideas or to take hold of the issue. The mayor's position has reduced the issue's saliency for the committee. Finally, the group leader, Mary Brown, enthusiastically proposes a dramatic activity to get media coverage on the issue—a demonstration in front of the mayor's private home. Nobody responds. There is an uncomfortable silence.

Study. The group has shown signs of apathy throughout the meeting. The discussion has been unenthusiastic and unproductive. The feeling tone of the meeting has been apathetic. The leader has tended to carry the discussion, until finally her last proposal has been met with silence.

Assessment. There are many reasons why a group may behave apathetically or withhold participation. Some common reasons may apply to this group. Among the first possibilities a group leader must consider are reasons related personally to the leader. The leader may be out of tune with the interests and experiences of the members. Or the leader may have been monopolizing the group, creating a dependent relationship in which the members' level of participation is low. In this case, we have a group of service providers who are not accustomed to social action. Social action is outside their professional experience but not outside of the leader's interests and experience. The leader is out of step with her group.

Some members' reluctant participation may be due to a variety of unspoken fears. As homeless service providers, each member's organization receives some city funding. They are afraid that political action may result in funding cutbacks to their agencies. In this light, the proposal to challenge the mayor is particularly threatening.

Some members do not believe that social action is the purpose for the group's formation. Their primary interest and not-too-hidden agenda is better service coordination and networking with other providers. The group has never discussed its goals in SMARRT language and arrived at a consensus on the group's purpose.

The task of mobilizing support for passage of a bill in the city council may be too daunting. The providers are up to their ears in work just to keep their services operating. Even if they are interested, they may not have the time or energy to devote to this sort of project.

The leader herself is a highly respected, long-time advocate for the homeless. Some group members are uncomfortable about opposing her openly and perhaps being viewed as anti-the-homeless.

Intervention. Again, a variety of interventions are possible, depending in part on the leader's diagnosis of the problem.

1. If the leader has had a flash of insight about being out of step with the group, she might say, "Judging from the unenthusiastic discussion over the last hour and your silence, maybe I've been pushing for social action too hard. What do you think?"
2. The leader might tune in to the lack of clarity about the group's purpose. "I can see that there is not too much excitement about a campaign to pass the city council bill. I guess this is pretty different than the other work the group has done. Maybe we should go around the room and check on what we see as the purposes of the group. John, could you start us off?"
3. The leader might open up further discussion about the group's purposes by zeroing in on the underlying fears of the members of exposure and loss of funding. "Since nobody is saying anything, I'm guessing that the idea of going after the mayor is pretty scary. How do you all feel about our coalition getting involved in social action?" She can also explore social actions that don't directly embarrass the mayor or work through intermediaries.

Evaluation. In the first intervention, the leader reflects back the behavior of the group and tries to solicit feedback, starting with responses to the direction of her leadership. In the second intervention, the leader is direct about starting the feedback process. She is also beginning a process of negotiating a contract that did not take place previously. In the third intervention, the leader tunes in to the feelings of inadequacy about a social action campaign that she senses in the members. This approach can also lead to further clarification of the group's purposes and negotiation of the group's contract. With some expression of feelings on the table and a chance to look at the project, the group might be more ready to engage in action, but something appropriate to their level of experience and available time.

Conclusion

The group problems and interventions we have illustrated in this chapter are only a few of the many typical and atypical problems and challenges that task groups encounter. As should be apparent, although task groups are about decision making, group behavior and feelings sometimes interfere with the best-laid plans and require a leader to facilitate the group process. In this chapter, we have advocated a systematic approach to problem solving that is transferable to all kinds of group practice situations you may encounter. A critical practice approach is indispensable. As members, leaders, chairs, organizers, or staff, social workers invariably participate in task groups and, as in other aspects of professional practice, they need to use themselves consciously to enable a group to achieve its goals.

Discussion Exercises

1. The state's foster care review board's director has appointed you to chair an interagency foster care review team of eight members. You are preparing for the first meeting. The team reviews cases of children placed in foster care by the city child protective services agency to be sure that the placements are appropriate.
   (a) Identify your process and task goals for the meeting.
   (b) Write out an agenda for the meeting.

(c) Identify the tasks you will attend to before the group convenes.

(d) Explain how you would start the meeting and how you would end it.

2. The foster care review team is having its fifth meeting. In a carryover discussion from the previous month's meeting, the group has gotten bogged down in figuring out how to handle the large volume of cases most efficiently. Two main proposals have been identified: adding extra meetings and dividing up the cases between two subcommittees. At this point, one of the committee members, Connie Williams, who missed the previous meeting, introduces a third alternative: adding more members to the committee. Mae Harris supports this new proposal. The other members get upset.

(a) Explain what may be going on, in terms of your knowledge of group development.

(b) Indicate what you would do in this situation.

3. This is the first meeting of a group of seven representatives from local public and private agencies who are trying to develop a citywide referral system. The staff person from the department of social services has worked hard in pre-group contacts and discussions to help develop an acceptable agenda and get the group going. She is chairing the meeting. About halfway through the meeting, a respected agency director asserts loudly, "This meeting isn't getting anywhere and I have to leave. I sure hope the next meeting is more productive!" And with that, he packs up and walks out. The members look a bit stunned and turn to you for the next move.

(a) How would you explain what is going on?

(b) What would you do?

4. Near the end of the first meeting of the above group, someone suggests that the group appoint a chair to conduct the meetings. The idea is received enthusiastically. When you ask for nominations, no one responds.

(a) How would you explain what is going on?

(b) What would you do?

5. It is the fourth meeting of a planning committee in an agency. One staff person comes in 15 minutes late. Although she has done this before, no one says anything about it, including the chairperson of the group. The late arrival is also the highest-status member of the group, representing a large department in the agency.

(a) How would you explain what is going on?

(b) What would you do?

6. The fifth meeting of the above agency planning committee begins with silence. Although the agenda has been prepared and members received it in advance, no one says anything. It is beginning to seem that the silence might continue for some time.

(a) How would you explain what is going on?

(b) What would you do?

Notes

1. "We trained hard . . . but it seemed that every time we were beginning to form up into teams we would be reorganized. . . . I was to learn later in life that we tend to meet any new situation by reorganizing; and a wonderful method it can be for creating the illusion of progress while producing confusion, inefficiency, and demoralization" (attributed to Petronius Arbiter, 210 B.C.).

2. SMARRT objectives are specific, measurable, acceptable, realistic, results oriented, and time specific. See Chapter 1 for discussion.

3. For example see: http://www.rulesonline.com/

4. We will discuss the impact of group size in the networking chapter.

References

Anderson, C., & Kilduff, G. J. (2009). Why do dominant personalities attain influence in face-to-face groups? The competence-signaling effects of trait dominance. *Journal of Personality and Social Psychology*, 96(2), 491–503.

Anderson, S. G., Zhan, M., & Scott, J. (2006). Developing financial management training in low-income communities. *Journal of Community Practice*, 13(4), 31–49.

Bandler, S., & Roman, C. P. (1999). Group work: Skills and strategies for effective intervention (2nd ed.). Binghamton, NY: Haworth Press.

Bisman, C. D. (1994). *Social work practices: Cases and principles*. Pacific Grove, CA: Brooks/Cole.

Butcher, H., Banks, S., Henderson, P. with Robertson, J. (2007). *Critical community practice*. Bristol, UK: The Policy Press.

Delgado, M., & Staples, L. (2008). *Youth-led community organizing: Theory and action*. New York: Oxford University Press.

Foster-Fishman, P. G., Cantillon, D., Pierce, J., & Van Egeren, L. A. (2007). Building an active citizenry: The role of neighborhood problems, readiness, and capacity for change. *American Journal of Community Psychology*, 39, 91–106.

Geoghean, M., & Powell, F. (2006). Community development, partnership governance and dilemmas of professionalization: Profiling and assessing the case of Ireland. *British Journal of Social Work*, 36(5), 845–861.

Gersick, C. G. (1988). Time and transition in work teams: Toward a new model of group development. *Academy of Management Journal*, 31, 9–41.

Hanson, P. G. (1972). What to look for in groups. In J. W. Pfeiffer & J. J. Jones (Eds.), *The 1972 annual handbook for group facilitators* (pp. 21–24). La Jolla, CA: University Associates.

Heap, K. (1977). Group theory for social workers: An introduction. New York: Pergamon Press.

Henderson, M. D. (2009). Psychological distance and group judgments: The effects of physical distance on beliefs about common goals. *Personality and Psychology Bulletin*, 35(10), 1330–1341.

Henderson, P. (2007). Introduction. In H. Butcher, S. Banks, & P. Henderson with J. Robertson. *Critical community practice* (pp. 1–15). Bristol, UK: The Policy Press.

Iecovich, E. (2005). Environmental and organizational features and their impact on structural and functional characteristics of boards in nonprofit organizations. *Administration in Social Work*, 29(3), 43–59.

Jacobson, M. (2007). Food matters. *Journal of Community Practice*, 15(30), 37–55.

Janis, I. L. (1972). *Victims of groupthink*. New York: Houghton Mifflin.

Janis, I. L. (1982). Groupthink: Psychological studies of policy decisions and fiascoes (2nd ed.). New York: Houghton Mifflin.

Johnson, A. K. (1994). Teaching students the task force approach: A policy-practice course. *Journal of Social Work Education*, 30(3), 336–347.

Kirst-Ashman, K. K., & Hull, G. H., Jr. (2009). *Generalist practice with organizations and communities* (4th ed.). Belmont, CA: Brooks/Cole.

Mead, J. (2008, March). Confidence in the nonprofit sector through Sarbanes-Oxley-style reforms. *Michigan Law Review, 106 Mich. L. Rev. 881.*

Paterson, B. L., & Panessa, C. (2008). Engagement as an ethical imperative in harm reduction involving at-risk youth. *International Journal of Drug Policy*, 19, 24–32.

Payne, M. (2000). *Teamwork in multiprofessional care*. Chicago: Lyceum Books.

Sampson, E. E., & Marthas, M. (1981). *Group process for the health professions* (2nd ed.). New York: Wiley.

Silverman, R. M. (2005). Caught in the middle: Community development corporations (CDCs) and the conflict between grassroots and instrumental forms of citizen participation. *Community Development*, 36(2), 35–51.

Storm, S. (2007, September 29). Firing stirs new debate over Red Cross. *The New York Times*. retrieved March 25, 2010, from: http://www.nytimes.com/2007/11/29/us/29cross.html

Toseland, R., & Rivas, R. B. (1995). *An introduction to group work practice* (2nd ed.). Boston: Allyn & Bacon.

Tropman, J. E. (1980). *Effective meetings: Improving group decision-making*. Beverly Hills, CA: Sage.

Tuckman, B. W. (1965). Developmental sequence in small groups. *Psychological Bulletin*, 63, 384–399.

Tuckman, B. W., & Jensen, M. A. C. (1977). Stages of small group development revisited. *Group and Organizational Studies*, 2(1), 419–427.

Turner, A. (2009). Bottom-up community development: Reality or rhetoric? The example of the Kingsmead Kabin in East London. *Community Development Journal*, 44(2), 230–247.

Warren, M. (2001). *Dry bones rattling*. Princeton, NJ: Princeton University Press.

Zastrow, C. (1997). *Social work with groups* (4th ed.). Chicago: Nelson-Hall.

10

Using Networks and Networking

Call it a clan, call it a network, call it a tribe, call it a family: Whatever you call it, whoever you are, you need one.

Jane Howard, feminist, novelist

We are caught in an inescapable network of mutuality, tied in a single garment of destiny. Whatever affects one directly, affects all indirectly.

Martin Luther King, Jr., Baptist minister, civil rights and
social justice advocate, Nobel Peace Prize laureate

Everybody on this planet is separated by only six other people. Six degrees of separation. Between us and everybody else on this planet.

John Guare, playwright (Six Degrees of Separation)

What is a Network? What is Networking?

We are all caught in a web of networks. The social and physical world is a maze of interconnected networks. People are nodes in multiple networks from the loosely coupled, to the virtual, to the cohesive and dense (Albrechts & Mandelbaum, 2005). The major challenge for social workers and clients is to manage existing networks and construct new ones. Whittaker, Garbarino, and associates (1983) and others (Payne, 2000; Travillion, 1999) hold that assessing, developing, and managing social networks and assisting clients in their assessment, development, and management of social networks is the crux of social work practice. Networks and networking are inherent in social work's emphasis on the client's social ecology, service coordination, and the holism of social work's person-in-environment (P-I-E) perspective.

Client needs generally do not coincide with a single agency's service packets. The sheer number of agencies with varying service arrangements and regulations and a client's informal social supports generates management complexity for the individual client and social worker and demands commensurate network management skills. Clients, like all of us, need to develop and manage social support networks. The more important form of networking for clients, community residents, and all of us, is with primary and secondary social supports. Family, friends, and neighborhood organizations often provide more help than tertiary or formal social agencies, especially for the elderly, immigrant groups, and ethnic minorities (Garcia, 2005; Lincoln, 2000; Lindsey, Browne, Thompson, Hawley, Graham, Weisbart, Harrington, & Kotch, 2008; Mason, 2009; McLeod, Bywater, & Hirsch, 2008; Payne, 2000; Phillips, Bernard, Phillipson, & Ogg, 2000; Tsai, 2006; Uttal, 2006). Networks are the substance of macro community practice, which largely consists of building and managing social networks. This chapter will review social network theory and its underlying social theories, the dimensions of social networks, client social supports as networks, and the application of networking to social work practice.

Social networks are social arrangements of peoples, groups, organizations, or other social units that interact and engage in exchanges to achieve their purposes. Social support networking occurs when people seek others who can or may be able to help them or whom they may be able to help. Social networking involves building and maintaining social relationships with others. Social networks are support networks when they provide a structure for social exchanges. A social action coalition of neighborhood organizations is an example of a social network common in community work. While systems have shared objectives or purposes (Anderson & Carter, 1984, pp. 1–23; Hearn, 1969; Martin & O'Connor, 1989), a social network's units can have objectives or purposes different from each other. What the units share is a belief that their individual objectives or needs will be improved by the network relationship (Knoke & Yang, 2008; Whittaker, Garbarino, & associates, 1983, p. 4). Nohria and Eccles (1992) maintain that social networks are not the same as electronic and mechanical networks. Social networks require social and human interaction for bonding and cohesion, although it can be argued that social but not face-to-face interaction does occur in electronic social networking (Clifford, 2009; Kaiser, 2005; Prudent, 2006). McIntyre (1986) holds that networks and support systems exist in any situation involving an exchange of resources. The resources exchanged can be tangible, such as money and clients, or intangible, such as information, emotional support, or legitimization.

Networks can be personal, professional, and organizational. Networking can be interpersonal between individuals and interorganizational between organizations and agencies. A network doesn't require that all network units are in direct contact with all other network units or even aware of them. MacKay (1997, p. 6) proposes that a network is an organized collection of contacts and the contacts' contacts. Client referral systems between agencies and service coordination agreements between two or more agencies are examples of interorganizational networks.

Interorganizational networking exists when people in a network bring organizational resources and commitments beyond their personal resources to a network.

Networking is the assessment, development, and maintenance of networks. It involves the actual exchanges. It is the creation of conditions for and the actual exchanges of material and instrumental and affective resources. Mackay (1997, p. 61) defines interpersonal networking, although applicable to other forms of social networking, as "finding fast whom you need to get what you need in any given situation and helping others to do the same." Inherent in networking is sustaining reciprocity and interdependency, not complete dependency.

Why Networks and Networking?

Network involvement for an agency or an individual means a potential loss of autonomy and a necessity to invest some resources in developing and maintaining the network. Agencies and people are involved in networks because they expect to make gains over their expenditures of resources sufficient to compensate for their loss of autonomy. Research (Galaskiewicz & Wasserman, 1993; Woodard & Doreion, 1994) indicates that networks are developed and maintained under the following conditions:

- Network units need other units for the resources to fulfill their functions and achieve their goals. The network provides a structure, a marketplace, for exchanging resources.
- The units need other units to respond to an external problem or cope with stress, opportunity, or mandate because the resources necessary to respond are available only through networking. The network provides a structure for aggregating resources and for coordinating domains politically and functionally.
- Network units that compete for domains need to regulate competition and conflict. The network provides a structure and mechanism for politically regulating competition, negotiating domain consensus, and legitimating the domains of competing network members.

Social Exchanges and Networks

Networks are established and maintained through social exchanges. Social exchange theory, as discussed in Chapter 2, is the basic theory underlying networking. *Social exchanges* occur when network units recognize the domains or control of desired resources by other participating network units and *trade* or *exchange* domain recognitions and resources. Exchanges are present when governments exchanges resources for commitments and programs compatible with the government's prevailing ideology. For reviews of ideological exchanges between the government and various constituencies on the social and political left and right, see Moynihan (1969), Murray (1984), and Pivan and Cloward (1971).

The potential exchange partners for a network usually are not limited to bilateral exchanges between two participants. Instead, there is an *exchange set,* delineated as the number of potential partners in the task environment or community. There is a field of potential exchange partners in the task environment. The number of potential partners in the exchange set determines the prevailing value of each participant's resources in likely exchanges. *Value* is the reward or gratification to the recipients of the resources or products received. The more potential exchange partners with the desired resource there are in the exchange set, the more easily realized and less costly are the exchanges for the party seeking the resource. *Costs* are the rewards, products, and resources traded and foregone in the exchange or the punishments incurred in order to obtain the desired resource. Each participant in the exchange relationship defines the value of the products received and compares this value to the cost of the products traded in the exchange.

Network Dimensions

Networks differ on several related structural and relational dimensions that shape unit behavior. It is critical that social work practitioners understand the terminology, concepts, principles, theories, and research of networks to successfully practice social work. Nohria and Eccles (1992, pp. 4–7) contend that the actions, attitudes, and behaviors of people can be best explained in terms of their positions in networks. Knoke and Yang (2008, pp. 4–6) maintain that the structural relations between people in networks are often more important in explaining their behavior than are gender, ethnicity, values, and ideology. Particular behaviors exist only in terms of specific structural and time/place relationships such as student–teacher in a classroom and lay community leader in a community meeting. Network relations determine status and role. Secondly, social networks affect perceptions, beliefs, and actions through a variety of socially constructed structural mechanisms and relations between entities. Thirdly, network relationships are dynamic processes, with the changes in structure and interactions changing the units. Networks constrain and shape the actions of people in their interdependency and reciprocity. We will consider 12 basic network dimensions, ranging from domain recognition and agreement of network members to the locus of authority of networks for their members.

Domain Consensus

Domain consensus is the recognition of and agreement by network members or units and potential network partners of a person, agency, or unit's domain claim on the task environment. Recognition and some degree of domain consensus are necessary for interpersonal and interorganizational relations and networking. Recognition of domains by network partners is required if exchanges are to occur. Domain recognition is prerequisite to domain consensus. The degree of domain consensus can vary on all or some of the domain variables, but the higher the agreement on a wider range of variables, the more likely it is that a network unit or agency will find network partners for resource exchanges.

Size

Network size can vary from only two units or to an almost infinite number of units, such as in a telephone network, Twitter, and the Internet. Network size, even in social support and mutual aid networks, is no longer geographically limited to a specific community, with contemporary communication and transportation technology. Virtual networks, including online social networks such as MySpace and Facebook, are global. The parlor game "six degrees of separation" speculates that no more than six people separate everyone from anyone else in the world. Milgram (1967) tested this assumption in a field experiment and found it convincing. The average number of links was five, not six. Of course, the challenging practice task is to identify and connect (or network) the relevant five or six people in the chain, convince them to pass back and forth relatively unchanged the exchanges between you and your target, and eventually shorten the chain of separation between you and your target to reduce your dependency on the chain. The chain can be constructed only if the final target is known.

Larger networks potentially have greater resources and more exchange partners than do smaller networks. Larger networks, however, generally are more inefficient, with resource redundancy. They require more management to regulate exchanges, depending on the network's construction, and can suffer from lower cohesion (Burt, 1992; Nohria & Eccles, 1992, pp. 288–308). Implications and relevance of size will be discussed under the dimensions of power, influence, and dependency; density; coordination and control (management); and cohesion.

Reciprocity and Exchanges

Networks are exchange mechanisms. Reciprocity is inherent in exchanges. It is both the act and obligation of returning value for value received. Individuals or network units who supply rewarding services to another obligate the receiving unit. To discharge the obligation the receiving must furnish benefit to the first. Balanced reciprocity (fairer exchanges) and trust enhance network cohesion, stability, and use (Blau, 1964). If exchanges are viewed as unfair, then it is more likely that other exchange partners and networks will be sought and used. Research with social support networks discussed in chapter 2 of this text and in Beeman (1997) has found this to be true). Reciprocity in social support is associated with greater psychological well-being than when an individual unit is only a giver or only a recipient (Dalton, Elias, & Wandersman, 2001, p. 240; de Jasay, 1989).

Power, Influence, and Dependency

Power, as we have discussed it in this text, is an ability to act and get one's way, generally in the face of opposition. Power is a continuum, and one's power is rarely absolute. Power in networks is an ability to get resources, to gain influence, and to get things done in the network (Bragg, 1996; Willer, Lovaglia, & Markovsky, 1999, p. 231). Influence (less than absolute power) affects the behavior of others regardless of intent. Influence is rooted in the ability of a network member to alter the behavior of another network member by providing or withholding resources. Dependency is reliance upon others or another for support and desired resources. Dependent units in a network are usually subordinate to, are highly influenced by, and have less power than units providing them support.

Power, influence, and dependency in a network are functions of resource distributions within the network. Box 10.1 lays out the Power Equation described here. If one unit is the sole or primary possessor of a resource highly desired by a number of other potential network trading partners, the demand for the resource is likely to

BOX 10.1.	**Power Equation**

Influence of Network Unit A over Network Unit B is a function of B's dependency on A for a resource or resources and the number of Bs competing for A's limited available resource:

$(IA/B \text{ [Function of]}(BDA) + (B_nDA)$

A will have influence on all Network Bs that are dependent on A for the resource.

Symbols: I = influence; n = number; / = over or on; D = dependency

be high and the gains, power, and influence of the valued resource holder should be great. The holder of a highly desired and limited resource will gain influence over other network units dependent on it for resources. The strength and vulnerability, the ability to influence and be influenced, of a network member results from the potential number of exchange partners for its resources and its competitors for a desired resource. The more the likely exchange partners or options a network member has within a network or accessible in its task environment for future networking, the less dependent it is on a single trading partner or a few trading partners. If a network member has a scarce resource, a resource in great demand such as leadership ability, and there are limited options for this resource to a network and other network units except for the resource holder, the fact that the member has many options to exchange the resource puts the holder in a position of strength, influence, and relative power in network exchanges. The network is asymmetrical. Many potential exchange partners in a network reduce vulnerability and dependency for members of the network but can increase potential obligations and network maintenance costs. These costs are mitigated, according to Knoke (1993), by keeping networks flexible, informal, and decentralized.

Balanced exchange relationships, with all sides dependent on the other and having mutual and reciprocal influence, create countervailing power relationships. This is *interdependency*. Interdependency, with its balance, enhances stability and offers a sense of fair exchange to a network. A goal of network management for social work practitioners is balanced interdependency and countervailing power relationships by empowering clients.

Network units can engage in exchanges directly or through other units in a network. Indeed, intermediate units create networks beyond a dyad. Exchanges and networks can be regulated by a third party with a capacity to mandate and monitor exchanges between network participants. Mandated referrals and exchanges of resources occur when a third party requires two network units to interact. This is often the case when a superordinate agency requires referrals or particular types of exchanges among subordinate units. Health maintenance organizations and managed care direct and mandate exchanges between other health care network units consisting of health care providers and patients. The managed care agency is the superordinate network unit. It maintains its superordinate position and the responsiveness of health network units by controlling scarce fiscal resources.

The amount and desirability of a network unit's resources are important in a social network's exchanges and the unit's network influence. However, resources alone do not determine all influence in a social network. According to Mizruchi and Galaskiewicz (1993), resource control and dependency's importance as a critical variable in determining influence likely is nested in variables such as social class and the networking skills of network actors. Bargaining skills also contribute to a social network unit's influence. This is important for social work practice, as workers and clients often have to compensate for a dearth of resources with networking skills.

Cohesion

Cohesion is the internal bonding strength of a network. It helps the network remain a network. Cohesiveness is operationally defined as anything that attracts people to join, participate in, and remain in a dyad, group, organization, or network. Fair exchanges and reciprocity encourage cohesion, and network cohesion encourages more subsequent exchanges among network participants. Cohesion is also more likely to be higher in networks with primary and secondary group characteristics with more face-to-face interaction than with tertiary, limited-interest networks (Nohria & Eccles, 1992; Travillion, 1999, pp. 22–25).

Social networks are more cohesive and stable with *homophily*, or composed of units with like characteristics. Social networks with face-to-face interaction are more often likely to be composed of people with same socioeconomic status and interests, rather than different classes. Social networking as a social mobility strategy requires a high level of networking skills (Coughlin, 2004, pp. 120–125). Practitioners seeking cohesive networks need to create opportunities for fair exchanges, broad interest among participants in each other, and face-to-face, more personalized interactions.

Network cohesion is affected by the network's symmetry and interdependence. Blau's (1964) *superordinate–subordinate power relationship principle*, introduced with our network power discussion, elaborates this network relationship. Superordinate and subordinate refer to the distribution of power and resources in a social exchange. If a relationship is too imbalanced, network cohesion is adversely affected. The theory and principle holds that:

- The more exchange relations between superordinate and subordinate become imbalanced, the greater the probability of opposition to those with power.
- The more the norms of reciprocity are violated by the superordinate, the less fair the exchanges and the greater the imbalance.
- If networks are composed of many subordinates and few superordinates, the more subordinates experience collectively relations of imbalance with superordinates, the greater the sense of deprivation, and the greater the probability of opposition by the subordinates to the superordinates.
- In short, dependency breeds resentment, opposition, and instability. Interdependence and fair exchanges foster network cohesion and solidarity.

The superordinate–subordinate power relationship principle underlies social action in community and labor organizing. Activist-organizers often help community groups, action systems, and client systems recognize and understand the imbalance of power and their subordinate positions. Lee's (1994) empowerment social work practice uses this principle in discussing the importance of helping clients assume a holistic approach in their problem analysis. They should assume a critical theory perspective, *conscientisation,* and recognize social oppression rooted in class and ethnicity in the deconstruction of their problems. Similarly, in the construction of interventions and solutions, social oppression based on class and ethnicity must be recognized. We believe that the reactionary political, religious, and social right's opposition to President Obama's health care legislation had as much to do with his identity as an African-American and the House leadership on the legislation from a woman and a gay as with the content of the policy. We will discuss the political nature of client problems more fully in our chapter on community social casework practice (Chapter 14).

Symmetry

Each network unit has some resources to exchange. This is the reason for their being in the network. However, the resource distribution among network units is frequently not symmetrical. Not all units have equal resources or power and make equivalent gains and losses in exchanges. Network symmetry is the degree to which resources are evenly distributed and exchanges balanced. It is a function of the availability and distribution of network resources and the network units' skill in bargaining. If resources are aggregated and only a few of the network's units have bargaining skills, the network's exchanges will be asymmetrical. Woodard and Doreion's (1994) study of community service networks found that less than half of the exchanges were symmetrical.

Symmetry enhances network stability and cohesion. Symmetry is promoted by and promotes fair exchanges and reciprocity cohesion. Socially marginalized clients are unlikely to have symmetrical networks. Individual clients generally have limited social resources. They have little symmetry in their network relations with community agencies and other tertiary social organizations. This lack of symmetry and its impact on power, dependency, and interdependency highlights a need for collective, countervailing mediating organizations and coalitions of clients and allies in networking with a largely vertical tertiary social services and welfare system. Social workers have a similar need for countervailing power organizations, because they deal with the same organizations. It is logical, therefore, for social workers to partner with their clients to achieve greater symmetry in networking with these tertiary systems.

Density and Structural Complexity

Network structures can be simple, with few units and relationships, or dense, with complex structures. Density is the number of actual relationships in the network, as compared with the possible number of relationships (Dalton, Elias, & Wandersman, 2001, p. 252–255; Specht, 1986). Potential density increases exponentially with the addition of each new network member. The addition of a single new unit to a six-unit network increases the potential number of relationships by six, the number of prior network units, rather than one. In simple structures, all network units relate to each other. Simple structures are potentially dense.

Large networks can have high or low density, depending on their structure. A network with 100 units has a potential density of 4,950 individual links. With increased size of a network, the density and the potential cohesion of the network become more difficult to manage, given the number of possible relationships between units. Each member potentially has 99 separate relations. If the actually density doesn't reach the potential density, network cohesion is reduced and certain units are marginalized and do not interact with other network units:

$$PD = NU(NU-1)/2$$

with PD = potential density and NU = number of network units.

The network management task is to reduce potential density without marginalizing members. A complex structure can reduce density by reducing the number of relationships. It essentially breaks the network into smaller sub-networks or departments. This allows for easier management. Formal organizational models, the bureaucratic models, with channels of communication, chains of command, and decentralized structures of sub-networks, reflect this design. Sub-networks and network segments are network patterns within a network where interaction and density are greater within the segments than across segments. The sub-networks are linked into an overall network rather than a linking of individual people into one network. Segments creating smaller networks and networks of networks deal with the challenges of size and density (Dalton, Elias, & Wandersman, 2001, p. 252–255). We will will examine structure more fully under the network dimensions of centrality and coordination and control.

Centrality and Reachability

Centrality and "reachability" are two critical variables contributing to network power and influence. They are also critical in leadership of community interventions. Centrality is present when other network positions have to go through a network position and unit in order to communicate and reach others in the network. Centrality provides a thermostatic function. The central unit's position in the flow of exchanges gives it power. The central unit can regulate the network and alter exchanges that pass through it. Centrality is inherently, positively, and significantly related to power in networks (Bass & Burkhardt, 1992, p. 210). Reachability is necessary for a network position to have centrality. Reachability is a network unit's accessibility to other network units (Woodard & Doreion, 1994). A participant's power in a network is enhanced with centrality and reachability by other network units (Knoke, 1993).

In Figure 10.1, a chain network of five positions, position 3 (other things being equal) is in a position of greater influence than other network units because interactions must always go through it to reach the other end. The centrality of positions 2 and 4, while not as great as 3's, is greater than that of 1 and 5. The capacity for influence is enhanced by centrality, as exchanges must pass through the more central positions.

The chain network also has low density. In effect, it has four overlapping segments composed of positions 1 and 2, 2 and 3, 3 and 4, and 4 and 5. With its low density, there is less likelihood for cohesion and stability and greater likelihood for marginalization of 1 and 5. Positions 1 and 5 are isolated and have no direct interaction with 75% of the remaining network units. Units 2 and 4 are critical to maintaining 1 and 5 in the network. Position 3 is literally pivotal for any exchanges between 1 and 2 to and from 4 and 5.

1 ⟷ 2 ⟷ 3 ⟷ 4 ⟷ 5

Figure 10.1. Chain network.

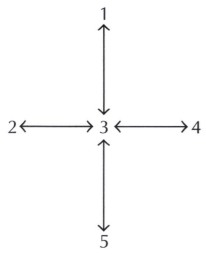

Figure 10.2. Star network.

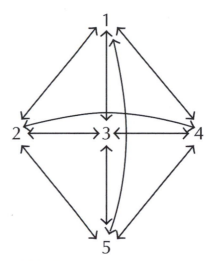

Figure 10.3. Group network.

It should be the most powerful, although it has no more direct linkages than do positions 2 and 4.

In Figure 10.2, a star network, position 3 has greater reachability by more network participants than do the other network positions. All participants must go through the "star," position 3, to reach an exchange partner. Position 3's network influence should be the greatest, as all exchanges between any network positions must go through it. This network has low density and has four segments: 1/3, 2/3, 4/3, and 5/3. With centrality and power potentially come greater network management and maintenance capacity and responsibilities. The stability of a star network depends on the star.

In Figure 10.3, position 3's influence based on network position has no greater centrality or importance in the network. In the group network all positions have equivalent reachability and centrality, with no power advantage based on position. This network is dense, with all network participants having direct access to all other network participants. If the density is maintained, it can be a more stable network than the other two. As group network size increases, density may become unstable or require structural centrality and segmentation.

Figure 10.4 shows a segmented network of 9 positions. Position 5 is central and has the greatest reachability. Structurally, position 5 is the most powerful. The segmentation reduces density and the number of linkages from 36 if a

group network to eight links. Cohesion may be reduced with any non-central segment breaking off.

Coordination and Control

A network's need for coordination and control is a function of its size, density, segmentation, frequency and types of exchanges, and need for stability. The capacity for coordination and control inherently resides in network positions with centrality and reachability. Loosely coupled networks (Weick, 1976) are composed of loosely connected units with a capacity to act independently on most matters but still capable of exchanges and joint actions when needed. Loosely coupled networks often reconcile the strains between autonomy and interdependence for their members.

Network coordination in loosely coupled networks is informal between participants, with any dominance resting with the coordinators who serve as the linchpins, as Figures 10.1 and 10.2 illustrate, or, in the case of Figure 10.3, through

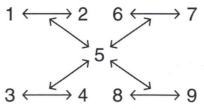

Figure 10.4. Segmented network.

group mechanisms. Group mechanisms lend themselves to more equality but suffer from the expense of maintaining multiple interactions and duplication.

As networks become larger and if stability is needed, they become more formal, with set protocols, rules, and procedures to coordinate and control the management tasks and the interaction density. They become bureaucratic. Individual discretion and variation are reduced and the formal protocols and structured positions govern the interaction. Individuals lose autonomy corresponding to the network's size and the need to control and coordinate density. Without management and maintenance, *entropy* (a characteristic of systems) begins (Van de Ven, Delbecq, & Koenig, 1976). Figure 10.4, a segmented network, has a management position, position 5, to control interaction between segments.

Practitioners in constructing and managing networks should be aware of the importance of structural positioning in the network and its influence on the flow of information and the management of exchanges. When tighter control is necessary, network design should have a position with centrality. Practitioners needing network influence should seek to hold central positions.

Network Unit's Social Status

People and other social units come to social networks with different social statuses. Agency's networks and networking vary by the individual participants' hierarchical level within the agency and social status in the community. Agency administrators network on the policy and programmatic levels. The management-level networking is concerned with exchanges of population and problem information, fiscal and material resources exchanges, and management and domain information exchanges (Woodard & Doreion, 1994). Line-level staff can network as part of formal agency service agreements or more informally with personal networks. Line-service staff engage more often in exchanges involving client referrals, services coordination, and information exchanges for specific clients. Line-service staff often are ignorant of management's networks exchanges (Woodard & Doreion,

1994). Woodard and Doreion's (1994) research found that line-level staff networks were not always symmetrical but were more symmetrical with frequently used network partners when exchanges were viewed as fair exchanges. Generally, line-level networks were more symmetrical than were management interagency network exchanges. Healy's (1991) research on line-staff services coordination found that they preferred service coordination through informal rather than formal networks. Informal networks may develop as a response to the difficulty of participating in the large, complex, and formal networks. Informal networks can indicate either a beginning for formalization or entropy of formal networks.

The social status a participant brings to a network affects network status. Participants who bring high social status to the network tend to have high status, power, and influence in the network (Bragg, 1996; Willer, 1999, p. 2).

Locus of Authority

Networks also can vary by the locus of authority. The locus of authority is where the authority for creating, defining, and maintaining the network's objectives and tasks resides. The locus of authority can be within or outside the network. The locus of authority is the foundation of and where the organization derives its authority. Both networks and the units can have internal or external loci of authority. If the local administrator of an agency in a network reports to or must obtain permission from a decisional authority outside the local agency, the networked unit has an external locus of authority. It is important to determine network and network partners' loci of authority because these are the centers of influence. The viability of domain and network agreements rests with the loci of authority. Decentralized structures of large complex organizations are often part of extra-community organizations called vertical structures. The decentralization is an attempt to reduce many of the negative attributes of the behemoth organization and to assume more locally responsive structure and relationships. However, the primary criterion of a decentralized structure's ability to engage in community networking is the capacity of local decision makers in the decentralized unit to commit the decentralized unit's resources to local community interests.

Networks composed of voluntary participants have internal loci of authority for the network, although the unit may have an external locus of authority, while mandated networks have external network loci of authority. The managed care networks described earlier, and interagency coordinating groups required by funding sources such as the federal government or United Way, are examples of networks with external loci of authority. The objectives, goals, structure, and rules of exchange within the network are determined not by network members but by a superordinate external authority.

The locus of authority's effects on network performance is unclear. Schopler (1994), after a review of the research literature, speculated on the types of tasks for which each locus might be best suited. Mandated networks with their externally proscribed rules should be best suited for clearly defined, standardized, and limited tasks, as the external mandating authority usually has reasons for creating a network. Voluntary networks with internal loci of authority should respond better to tasks requiring innovation and creativity, although they may be less efficient in operation. Morale is often higher and cohesion stronger in networks with internal loci of authority. Unlike the mandated members, no external authority holds the network together.

Horizontal and Vertical Network Relationships

Network units sharing the same geographic domains, having the same task environments, existing within the same community, and having a similar locus of decision making, have *horizontal* network relationships. Horizontal networks (networks primarily composed of units with horizontal relations) are more likely to be decentralized, informal, fluid, and—at times—competitive and market-like.

If a network unit's geographic domain and service or market area encompasses several communities and its locus of authority rests outside another network unit's community, the relationship to that unit is *vertical*. Vertically related

structures are generally superordinate and have less network interdependence. The vertical or superordinate unit's interests, responsibilities, and accountability extend beyond the local community. The superordinate unit's perception of its best interests may be different from the community's good. Local concerns simply are not a priority in the superordinate unit's decision equations. As mutual support, social welfare, and health provisions become part of national and global corporations, and providers adopt proprietary models and behaviors, the relationships to local communities and the networks become vertical. As these agencies follow the profit-driven decisions and emulate other vertically controlled and economically driven organizations, the local community's well-being is not paramount to the extra-community mega-structures. National organizations are horizontal to other national organizations; they tend to respond in their interorganizational relations in a formal fashion. For an extensive review of the growing importance and impact of vertically related organizations and their decisions on local communities, see Barlett and Steele (1992).

Vertical and *horizontal*, as used here, describe the relationship between the network units, the network linkages in the network, and the network to the community (Alter, n.d.). The viewpoint is from the network's relationship to the community. It is important for social workers in assessing agencies, organizations, and network units to determine if the relationships are vertical or horizontal. This will affect the bargaining and negotiation, influence and interdependency, the exchange agreements, the authority of local administrators and agents to make decisions responsive to community needs, and the capacity of the organization to respond to local community change. Vertical units and networks inherently have less community commitment and linkages than do horizontal units and networks. Community social work practitioners develop network relationships with a more horizontal character of power equivalency and interdependence with the vertical agencies in the network through organizing the horizontal entities into a countervailing power network relationship. Critical community practice emphasizes horizontal relationships.

Establishing and Maintaining Domains and Networks: The Practice Challenges and Tasks

Network units generally seek domain consensus to reduce domain conflicts and competition. Domain consensus maximizes resources and reduces the amount of energy and resources expended in bargaining to obtain resources, to protect domains, and to engage in and manage competition and conflict. Domain consensus promotes stability and predictability. Domain conflicts and competition occur whenever a social entity attempts to establish itself in or to obtain all or part of another entity's domain. The conflict and competition can be for any of the domain's tangible or intangible resources (Chetkow-Yanoov, 1997; Coser, 1964). Establishing domain consensus, developing and coordinating networks, and managing networks depend on the resources available in the task environment, the dimensions listed earlier, and the skills of the participants. Social agencies have missions and objectives related to the environment, whether the objective is to increase the economic self-sufficiency of Temporary Assistance to Needy Families (TANF) mothers, to improve the social functioning of mental patients, or to reduce child abuse and neglect. Each agency seeks domains and resources and generally must network with other agencies and organizations to achieve their objectives and fulfill their mission. Agencies seek to maximize autonomy and resources. This is also the charge to social workers in client empowerment and self-determination—to maximize client autonomy. However, neither agencies nor clients operate in social isolation: maximizing autonomy and resources requires interaction with the social environment or the task environment. The task in both establishing and maintaining networks is to facilitate interdependency rather than dependency. Box 10.2 lists the basic steps for determining needed network limits.

Competition

Competition is controlled conflict, when the parties in the competition recognize that they are seeking the same domain or resource. Without recognition of the competition, conflict does not occur. Competition can occur between network units and between networks. It generally requires some type of propinquity. Competition, as with most conflict, has rules of the game between the competing parties (Deutsch, 1973; Kriesberg, 1982; Lauer, 1982). Governments have devoted much time and energy to developing and managing the rules for national and international marketplaces, such as the North American Free Trade Agreement (NAFTA) and the Geneva Convention's "Rules of War." Electoral campaigns with their campaign rules represent rules of conflict for changes of government in a democracy. The rules of the game are adhered to in conflict, competition, and change only if the competitors see the rules as fair, if others are seen as playing fairly by the rules, and if competitors believe that violating rules produce costs exceeding any potential

---

BOX 10.2.   Protocols for Determining Needed Network Units

1. Determine total scope of the technology, tasks, and resources required to accomplish objectives.

2. Determine agency's (or client's) current domains of technology, tasks, and resources.

3. Compare agency's (or client's) existing domain with total scope of technology, tasks, and resources required to accomplish objectives. If a gap exists, agency (or client) needs to expand either its domain or network with resource providers—fiscal, non-fiscal, client, legitimizers, technology holders, and other complementary agencies (or social supports)—to achieve objectives.

4. Assess community and task environment, for domains and holders, in terms of the needed resources and their exchange preferences.

5. Negotiate exchanges with resource providers based on resource exchanges required by the resource holder as social support. Recognize in negotiations and networking the importance of size, complexity, dependency, cohesion, centrality, reciprocity expectations, competition, and the other network dimensions.

gains. As Alinsky's (1971) fourth rule counsels, make your competitors live up to their own book of rules. If they can't—and they often can't—this provides a rationale for going outside the rules with them. But remember, those making the rules usually win.

Network participants are vulnerable to internal competition and conflict when other network participants think they are not fulfilling their network responsibilities and hence not allowing other network units to maintain their domain obligations. Ideological differences between network units often lead to conflict as different ideologies shape different perceptions of reality, domain responsibilities, and what constitutes a fair exchange (Chetkow-Yanoov, 1997, p. 47; Lauer, 1982, p. 182).

Conflict and competition can have value for a network. Network conflict with outgroups (nonnetwork units) increases internal cohesion and collective network identity. This "us against them" situation is useful in developing team spirit and patriotism. It can generate energy and a sense of purpose. Conflict with outgroups, and sometimes even with the network, can release emotional steam and reduce tension. Networks that survive internal conflict often are stronger, as the conflict served to clarify values and commitments (Coser, 1964; Kirst-Ashman & Hull, 2009, pp. 91–95; Kriesberg, 1982, pp. 69–108). Conflict often is necessary for the socially marginalized in changing the status quo.

Conflict Resolution Strategies

Coser (1964) has asserted that, as the world becomes interdependent and closer, there will be greater need for rules of conflict and for conflict resolution. Without rules, society will disintegrate. Tannen (1998/1999, p. 48) argues that conflict is a function of our market ideology. The United States' culture, especially its political culture, is increasingly argumentative, confrontational, and adversarial. By casting everything in *either/or* dichotomies, win/lose terms, we lose nuances, middle ground, and the possibility that there are a range and variety of viable positions. Everything becomes a market model of competition and clash of ideas, with necessary winners and losers. The winner/loser ideology is reflected in the pop-culture reality television shows such

as *Big Brother* and *Survivor,* and the Republican Party during President Obama's first term as well the burgeoning "Tea Party" movement. Survival by any particular social entity, whether a client group, an agency, or a social worker, in this environment will depend on the entity's skills in using the rules and its participation in making fair rules to be used.

Conflict requires that one or both sides recognize the conflicting areas of means or outcomes, that one or both sides are dissatisfied with the status quo, and that one or both sides have a belief that it is not the "natural order of things" and believe that conflict will change and improve conditions. Much of social action is directed toward increasing the action system's dissatisfaction with the status quo and helping the action system accept that conditions can be changed by social action. Creating a collective identity is critical for conflict strategies based on a sense of grievance and deprivation. Conflict is more likely when the social environment is neutral. If the social environment or significant parts of it are aligned with one or the other side, the momentum necessary for conflict is unlikely, as there is little environment support for the minority side. Such momentum is more likely if one or both sides believe they will get support from the social environment that will enable them to inflict and sustain punishment (Coser, 1964).

Conflict can have several outcomes, as shown in Table 10.1. One outcome is the maintenance of the status quo, where neither party gains or loses resources other than those expended in the conflict. If the conflict is on fundamental issues, maintenance of the status quo is only a temporary resolution of the conflict. Maintenance of the status quo, however, is an unacceptable

Table 10.1. Conflict Outcomes

Conflict Resolution	Unit A Change	Unit B Change
Status quo	No change	No change
Zero–sum gain	+	-
Zero–sum gain	-	+
Win–win non–zero–sum	+	+
Lose–lose non–zero–sum	-	-

conflict outcome for most social work change efforts.

The second set of outcomes is a zero–sum solution. A zero–sum solution (a win–lose solution) exists when the gains of one side are offset with equivalent losses by the other side. The distribution of total domains and resources between contestants is changed, but the total amount of domains and resources is unchanged. This resolution generally involves the use of the various forms of social power. The side with the greater social power or one that is more skilled in applying its social power usually wins.

Strategies in conflict resolution include the following (Coser, 1964; Kirst-Ashman & Hull, 2009; Strom-Gottfried, 1998):

- *Retreat* is an outcome that occurs when one party leaves the conflict and the opponent wins by default. Retreat is acceptable only as a short-term strategy to preserve resources for later conflict re-engagement; otherwise, retreat is defeat.
- *Accommodation* is a variant of retreat and consists of one party's giving in and letting the other party win, to preserve the peace. It may be acceptable as a short-term solution if one side of the conflict judges that it cannot carry the contest.
- *Bargaining* is the compromise strategy and involves give-and-take: winning some and losing some. Bargaining and negotiation is the most frequently used strategy unless one side has sufficient social power to essentially ignore the other side. We will discuss bargaining in detail below, as it is the practice skill most useful for our conflict situations. Bargaining skills can overcome, to some degree, deficits in other forms of social power. Conflict and social action tactics such as embarrassment, loss of community support, and financial loss (such as with strikes and boycotts) and the disruption tactics of picketing and sit-ins are often used to bring the opponent to the bargaining table. Bargaining (Hardina, 2000) often tries to reframe the conflict as a non–zero–sum game involving positive exchanges, with both sides winning. A *win–win* strategy involves using *collaboration* and *cooperation*, where focusing on

similar contestant needs and sharing of resources becomes a means of conflict resolution. A positive exchange relationship in which both sides make gains is a non–zero–sum game. Assessing the task environment for new resources and other new domain possibilities as yet unclaimed can lead to a non–zero–sum game or allying with other domain holders to add to the domains of the previously competing parties from domains not claimed by network units. The trades and gains do not have to be in the same type of resource.

- *Subjugation* is a strategy that calls for tactics to force an opponent to accommodate or retreat from the conflict. Subjugation defeats an opponent and generally involves causing the opponent to expend the resources that are the sources of the opponent's power and then isolating the entity from additional resources.

Bargaining

Bargaining and negotiation skills are crucial to social work advocacy and practice. Bargaining is a "process whereby two or more parties attempt to settle what each shall give and take, or perform and receive, in transactions between them" (Rubin & Brown, 1975, p. 2). The conflicting parties, at least temporarily, come together in an exchange relationship, a bargaining relationship, regardless of any prior or future relationships. Bargaining concerns (a) the division or exchange of one or more specific resources or (b) the resolution of one or more intangible issues among the parties or among those whom the parties represent, or (c) both. Bargaining usually involves the presentation of demands or proposals by one party, and evaluation by the other party, followed by concessions or counterproposals or both. The activity is thus sequential rather than simultaneous (Rubin & Brown, 1975, pp. 6–18). It requires clarity of communication between the parties, a willingness to compromise and seek areas of agreement and middle ground, and a mutual recognition of the legitimacy of the parties to bargain. Bargaining typically is a process with several components (Deutsch, 1973; Kirst-Ashman & Hull, 2009; Rubin & Brown, 1975, pp. 6–18; Rubin & Rubin, 2001, pp. 328–335; Strom-Gottfried, 1998; Tannen, 1998/1999):

- Prior to directly bargaining, establish a BATANA (best alternative to a—or to any—negotiated agreement) (Fisher, Ury, & Patton, 1981; Strom-Gottfried, 1998). A BATANA is the best alternative available that appears possible without negotiation. The BATANA provides a basis for comparison of any negotiated gains or losses to what might be gained and lost without bargaining. This provides a basis on which to determine whether negotiations should be done at all.

- Partialize or break down your position in its parts and place in priority order your areas of concern and your positions. Positions should reflect interests and areas of concern and should not be too rigid and narrow so that you can be flexible in the give-and-take of negotiation. You may have to leave out some low-priority issues to prevent overwhelming the process. Fragmentation of issues is always possible and doesn't preclude future negotiation on the omitted issues. Inclusion of some throwaway issues may help in the bargaining—a throwaway issue is an issue that you are willing to give up rather easily, as a sign of concession, or readily trade off for a real gain. It is used to persuade the other party to make similar (and ideally real) concessions.

- Attend to the *rules of engagement* before substantial bargaining. Future gains and losses in bargaining are affected by the rules of engagement. These rules govern where the bargaining will occur; the length and nature of the sessions; the format, agenda, and procedures; whose position will be presented first; and even the shape of the bargaining table. The rules of the game or engagement determine the fairness of the process. If biased criteria are used to evaluate the fairness of proposals, positions, and solutions, the outcomes will be biased. When establishing procedures and protocols, avoid adversarial win–lose procedures, as they harden the opposition's position. It is important to have the criteria and rules of engagement in place, agreed upon, and agreeable, prior to proposal presentation and consideration of solutions. The rule maker usually wins, and if both sides make the rules at least the field will be level.

- Encourage your opponent to present his or her position first. This will allow you to tailor your responses and prevent you from prematurely conceding too much. If there are areas of agreement or near-agreement with your opponent, work on these areas first and be willing to make apparent concessions that don't fundamentally jeopardize your position. In establishing common ground, co-opt part of your opponent's position that doesn't fundamentally conflict with yours and treat it as your own. Your opponent then must bargain against the original position or accept it. If the opponent accepts it, the tactic helps to establish empathy and your image of flexibility. You also can use it as a throwaway issue.

- Seek mutually accommodating agreements that allow both sides to satisfy fundamental principles if possible. Try not to challenge your opponent's deepest moral convictions, but negotiate from your convictions. Don't give them up in the desire to reach accommodation. Communicate your empathy with your opponent's perspective, that you can understand it but not necessarily accept it.

- Avoid rigid premature positional bargaining and try to keep your opponent from doing the same. Move from interests rather than rigid positions. Talk less of rights, which are nonnegotiable, than of needs, wants, and interests, which are negotiable. Separate your feelings, likes, and dislikes for the opponent from the problem. Do not demonize your opponent in the bargaining stage, because eventually you will have to join in agreement. The bargaining is on interests and issues, not on interpersonal relationships. The line from the *Godfather* movie saga is applicable: "It's not personal, it's business."

- Don't rush to premature solutions, conclusions, and closure without seeking areas of mutual gain. This is critical to a win–win approach and vital if there is future bargaining, cooperation, and collaboration. However, do not be so reasonable and conciliatory that you lose touch with your core beliefs, passions, and needs that compelled the bargaining originally. Be clear on the areas of agreement and continuing areas of disagreement.

- If bargaining has not produced results favorable to your position, keep bargaining. Again, don't rush to premature conclusions, and don't accept them. Keep the communication and bargaining process going until it is more satisfactorily concluded.

- Prepare for future negotiation regardless of the outcome of the current bargaining. If satisfactory, the task is to maintain the gains. If unsatisfactory, the challenge is to reopen negotiations to arrive at conclusions that are more favorable. Emphasize and maintain communication if you wish to change your relationship with your opponent from that of a competitor to that of a network partner.

Mediation and Arbitration

If through direct bargaining you can't arrive at mutually agreeable accommodations, then having a third party act as an observer, mediator, or arbitrator is a less costly option than other forms of conflict. Nonpartisan observers often keep the process moving, and if one side is capricious, they help to build public support for the other side. Rubin and Brown (1975) claim that observers make the process more trustworthy: "The mere presence of an audience (including the psychological presence) motivates the bargainers to seek positive, and avoid negative, evaluations—especially when the audience is salient to the bargainers" (p. 44). Observation can also make the bargainers more cautious and conservative, as tentative positions are often prematurely frozen.

Mediation is a process that uses a third party (a neutral party to the conflict), the mediator, to clarify communicate between the parties on their positions. A mediator's effectiveness rests on whether he or she is seen as fair by all parties in the dispute. Mediation helps to reduce irrationality, provides opportunities for face saving, facilitates communication by lowering its tone or tension, and can regulate costs regarding third-party interests and information and evaluations of alternative solutions. Mediators and mediation can be formal or informal. Mediation helps the parties comply with the bargaining processes and protocols. The mediation and mediator's goal is accountability to the process of bargaining rather than the decisions and bargaining outcomes. In addition to formal mediators, mediators can be clients or representatives of the public or other constituencies.

If mediation is unsuccessful, arbitration is another option before coercive action. A side to a dispute generally seeks arbitration only if (a) it appears to be losing, or (b) its position is most likely to be adopted by the arbitrator, or (c) both. Arbitration is the use of a third party, superordinate to the conflicting parties for purposes of the conflict resolution, to find and dictate a solution. Arbitrators generally hear both positions and apply the rules of the game to the dispute to arrive at a solution. The rules of the game can be public law, when applied by the courts as arbitrators, or may be privately agreed-upon rules, as used by major league baseball arbitrators. Arbitrators can be agencies such as the United Way with its superordinate funding position over member agencies, or they may be agencies such as the courts or other third parties with authority over all sides to the dispute. Arbitration does present dangers to all parties in the conflict, because they all surrender autonomy to the arbiter, which becomes a superordinate authority for dispute resolution.

Establishing and Maintaining Domains

A final task in domain conflict resolution is to establish mechanisms to maintain and protect domain boundaries to reduce the amount of resources necessary to wage future domain conflicts. Establishing new domains is promoted by resource richness and dispersion in the task environment and the instability or weakness of existing domain agreements and networks. If there is consensus and stability among network units, units seeking to establish new or expand existing domains will need to engage in conflict and competition to create instability and turbulence. This will allow them to claim domains and resources and establish new linkages by breaking down existing networks. Conversely, once a unit has an established domain, it should secure it by working toward network and task environment stability and placidness. However, the richer the resources of the task environment, the more all domains and networks are likely to be sustained.

Table 10.2. Task Environment Conditions to Establish and Maintain Domains

Establishes Domains	Maintain Domains
When task environment is unstable, turbulent, heterogeneous	When task environment is stable, placid, homogeneous
When task environment resources are dispersed, rich	When task environment resources are concentrated, rich

The 1960s and 1970s—an era of resource richness with an abundance of federal funding for social agencies—saw the establishment of many new social agencies and service networks. Since then, with the growing fiscal resource stinginess, social turbulence, and competitive market ideology entering the social service arena, social service agencies are paralleling the proprietary sector and new social work skills are needed (Germak & Singh, 2010; Menefee, 1994). Many social agencies are looking for ways to "grow their brands" by finding new growth opportunities. Table 10.2 lists conditions beneficial to establishing and maintaining domains. The importance and usefulness of the rules of the game, and the techniques, mechanisms, and structures for competition and exchanges, have become more important for social work and its clients in this era of resource scarcity. Networking and bargaining are essential skills in this turbulent and competitive world.

Virtual Networks and Networking

The virtual or online network opportunities are ubiquitous. Wikipedia, the online encyclopedia, lists websites for literally hundreds of social networks for people interested in developing software, cats, cooking, or parenting (List of social networking websites, 2010). There are worldwide and involve literally millions of users. Facebook, Twitter, MySpace, YouTube, and LinkedIn are just some of the online social networking sites that keep users connected. There are dating services for all segments of the population, including cat lovers, gay or straight cat lovers, and probably cat detesters. There are sites to help you create your own social network site. Networks and chat rooms abound. With a computer, or one of many new IT devices, and the Internet one never needs to be lonely or leave home again.

The virtual network is an important tool in social work practice and social agency function. Like the commercial sector, the HSO can develop online networks. It provides a means to communicate quickly and relatively inexpensively with staff, clients, and community. Listservs of clients can provide general and individualized follow-up information and contact with discharged patients. E-mail allows for efficient dissemination of information and provides a means for feedback (Artz & Cooke, 2007; O'Looney, 2005). Agencies can use the Internet to communicate and share data between them as well as advertise their services. Some research has found that IT use has a positive effect on agency operations and resources (Kaiser, 2005; O'Looney, 2005).

For developing social support networks, the Internet has demonstrated great value (Kaiser, 2005; O'Looney, 2005; Stern & Dillman, 2006):

Like many older people, Paula Rice … has grown isolated in recent years. Her four grown children live in other states, her two marriages ended in divorce, and her friends are scattered. Most days, she does not see another person. Paula Rice, 73, had been "dying of boredom" before discovering social networking sites. … Housebound after suffering a heart attack two years ago, she began visiting the social networking sites Eons.com, an online community for aging baby boomers, and PoliceLink.com (she is a former police dispatcher). Now she spends up to 14 hours a day in online conversations. (Clifford, 2009, p. D5)

A virtual network's virtues are easily demonstrated, but its limitations and shortcomings must also be recognized. As discussed earlier, the Internet allows anyone to be whatever he or she wants to be. Sometimes a social support can morph into a social predator. Presentation of self and the development of trustworthiness are limited because of the limitations of the communication (Van Ark & Edeleubos, 2005), although this is changing with the growing video and audio capacity of computers. Virtual networking, as discussed earlier, does not appear to build the social capital necessary for strong social cohesion. Loosely coupled Internet networks have no space or time dimension. Virtual networks are less intense and dense, and cohesive (Albrechts & Mandelbaum, 2005, pp. 2–4). Virtual networks tend to be composed of more like-minded people, such as cat-lover sites. Their capacity to develop trust, which is essential to voluntary networks, is less than face-to-face networks (Frey, 2005; Van Ark & Edeleubos, 2005). The Internet as a communication venue is limited to people with Internet access; low-income and marginalized communities are more likely not to have such access or to have only limited access (Kaiser, 2005).

The Internet is a valuable organizing tool (Stern & Dillman, 2006). It allows reaching and maintaining contact with an almost unlimited potential. Both progressive and reactionary social organizers have used it. The Obama presidential campaign, MoveOn.org, and the "Tea Party Bagger" movement have used it to the benefit of their organizations and social causes. For instance, the "Tea Party Bagger" activists use a variety of Internet sites to communicate with and organize their followers (Barstow, 2010). We will return to the use of the Internet in marketing and organizing in subsequent chapters.

Clients and Social Support Networks

Clients exist in a web of social relations and primary and secondary, informal social support networks. Empowerment and social capital have been linked to participation in natural social support networks, social networks, and self-help groups across different populations (Beeman, 1997; Blau & Alba, 1982; Beaudoin & Tao, 2008; Dalton, Elias, & Wandersman, 2001; Garcia, 2005; Heller, 1990; Lincoln, 2000; Lindsey, Browne, Thompson, Hawley, Graham, Weisbart, Harrington, & Kotch, 2008; Magee & Huriaux, 2008; Mason, 2009; McLeod, Bywater, & Hirsch, 2008; Payne, 2000; Moynihan & Pandey, 2007; Ricketts & Ladewig, 2008; Tsai, 2006; among others). Client empowerment means increasing a client's capacity to take control of his or her life to improve it. Empowerment, like power, is in the ability to act (Lee, 1994). Empowerment is the cornerstone of social work practice and social work's value of client self-determination (Butcher, Banks, Henderson with Robertson, 2007). Empowerment requires action and is not done in isolation. It needs collective and individual actions. Empowerment requires social networks and social support networks.

Social support networks are social networks with some special qualities. Whittaker, Garbarino, and associates (1983) specify the special qualities as "the relational structure through which people request support and make demands. . . . a series of communication links. . . . a set of interconnected relationships among a group of people that provides enduring patterns of nurturance (in any or all forms) and provides contingent reinforcement for efforts to cope with life on a day-to-day basis" (pp. 4–5).

While social networks can either support or detract from the individual's social functioning, social support networks are limited to social networks that provide supports. The community psychologists Dalton, Elias, and Wandersman (2001, pp. 234–235) state that social support is not a simple, unitary concept. It represents a collection of social, emotional, cognitive, and behavioral processes occurring in social relationships that provide help and promote adaptive coping. Social support can take the following forms:

1. *Generalized social support*—Ongoing support involving a general sense of belongingness, acceptance, and being cared for. Generalized social support promotes social integration and emotional support. Social integration provides a sense of belongingness to social groups, communities, friendships, and workplace relations. Emotional support gives comfort and caring within personal relationships, often a result of social integration.

2. *Specific social support*—Limited and direct problem-focused support for coping with specific stressors, often in a particular setting. Specific social support can be any of the following:

   (a) *Esteem support* or encouragement—Support bolstering a sense of personal competency for dealing with specific challenges. It is task-focused rather than deep, enduring emotional support and can come from a range of people. It is often more empowering when it comes from superordinates.

   (b) *Informational support*—Cognitive advice and guidance, usually tailored to specific situations rather than generalized emotional support.

(c) *Tangible support*—Concrete assistance, material aid, and things.

Streeter and Franklin (1992) and Shumaker and Brownell (1984) provide similar social support categories in their review of social support network research. Streeter and Franklin (1992) defined six social support categories:

1. Material supports in physical things
2. Behavioral assistance with tasks
3. Intimate interaction such as listening, caring, expressing understanding for self-esteem and emotional gratification
4. Guidance by giving specific advice, information, and instruction
5. Feedback that provides reaction to and assessment of thoughts, behaviors, and feelings to help enhance identity
6. Positive social interaction for fun and relaxation that aids identity and esteem (p. 83)

The types of social support are not mutually exclusive, and a particular network can provide more than a single social support. For instance, a boss can provide encouragement and praise on current performance, with advice and guidance on future career opportunities (informational) as a mentor, and can provide tangible rewards with a raise. What makes something a social support, according to Streeter and Franklin (1992, p. 82), is that it is embedded in actual connections, trust, and a sense of belonging that people have with significant others (family, friends, colleagues, and others in their environment) rather than isolation and alienation. To have and use social supports, people must perceive them as social supports. This requires that others in the network provide the actual behaviors of support and assistance.

Social support networks vary in size and density. While research indicates mixed findings, a midrange size is typically most supportive. The effects of density, the number of possible relationships, and the amount of cohesion depend on the type and amount of support needed. Less dense networks are more conducive to emotional supports.

Social support networks differ by gender traits as well (Lin & Westcott, 1991). Patterson, Germain, Brennan, and Memmott (1988) found

that female natural helpers in support networks were more dependent on bonding, more expressive, and more effective with friends and family than they were with neighbors and less-close contacts. Male natural helpers were more effective instrumentally, with neighbors, and less so on personal and emotional or expressive concerns.

Access to social support networks differs across societies, communities, and individuals (Walker, Wasserman, & Wellman, 1993, p. 75). As with the social agency networks, proximity and the ability to make contact (reachability) are important for individual social support networks. Although proximity correlates with reachability, the telephone, the Internet, and other modern transportation and communication technologies greatly reduce the need for physical proximity for contact and connectedness. Proximity is important but not necessary for the social support of companionship and is less important than reachability for some of the other types of social and emotional supports.

Social Support Network Benefits

That social support networks are beneficial appears to be uniformly supported in the research cited earlier. Social support networks provide mutual support and help with living, coping, and integration and reintegration in the community for immigrants, discharged mental patients, the elderly, and drug abusers. Network members learn skills to help themselves as they are receiving help or helping others. The clinical and therapeutic effects of social support networks are positive, with benefits literally ranging across the spectrum. They reduce the need for institutional and social agency help. Before we review some of the specific research, we need to keep Specht's (1986) cautions in mind. Specht concluded, after his review of the research in 1986 (and his conclusion appears valid after our more recent review), that the concepts of social support and social support networks are often vaguely and broadly used. Often the labels have been used for different phenomena. The directions of the relationships between the social support networks and the behavior or comparison variable are imprecise. The research is cross-sectional and inconclusive, with the relationships being more association than causation. The questions of whether social support networks promote well-being or whether well-being allows greater social support network involvement are not resolved.

The cohesive and integrating effects of social support networks act to reduce social isolation and alienation, especially when networks serve as mediating structures. Zimmerman and Rappaport (1988), in a cross-sectional study of community participation, concluded that greater involvement was positively associated with individual psychological empowerment and inversely associated with alienation. Psychological empowerment was described as the "connection between a sense of personal competence, a desire for, and a willingness to take action in the public domain" (p. 746). Schore and Atkin (1993) reported on 1960s U.S. Department of Labor data that the incidence of depression declined to 12% among workers in workplaces with high levels of social support, from almost 27% in workplaces with low social supports. These conclusions were supported by Moynihan and Pandey's (2007) later research. Social supports are positively associated with mental health and mental health gains (Lin, Ye, & Ensel, 1999; Lindsey, Browne, Thompson, Hawley, Graham, Weisbart, Harrington, & Kotch, 2008), stable marriages and child rearing (Volling, Notaro, & Larsen, 1998), community integration on the part of immigrants (Garcia, 2005; Tsai, 2006), school performance (Rosenfeld, Richman, & Bowen, 2000), and reduced rates of homelessness (Letiecq, Anderson, & Koblinsky, 1998).

Social Networks and Globalization

Social networks and social support networks, always critical in representative and participatory democracy, are especially important in the vertically dominated communities of the global economy (Wessels, 1997). People and communities in a global economy need a variety and multiple levels of organizations to mediate between them and the global mega-corporations (van Deth, 1997, pp. 1–25). Market competition, in the classic sense of no vendor or purchaser having the capacity to highly influence or control the market, is archaic. Individuals as consumers have no influence, whereas a single

multinational and multifunctional corporation can have great influence on the political economy and control markets. Social fragmentation accompanies industrial and global society, with its separation of work from home and often community, a functional extension of the community's physical and geographic boundaries to a global scale, movement to formal, contract society from organic society, and a predominance of secondary and more often tertiary social interactions. An individual voter has little political influence in the act of voting, although an individual with great economic and social resources may have influence in other ways. Just as a voter can have shared political influence through mediating organizations, an individual consumer can have shared influence in mediating consumer organizations.

However, one of the most urgent problems facing Western democracies is that of the social exclusion of citizens. Social exclusion from group life means that a person lacks the social capital derived from participation in a network of civic engagement. Interaction with others can, according to the theory of social capital (Moyser & Barry, 1997; Putnam, 2000), be expected not merely to promote personal interests and collective benefits, but also to generate a significant side benefit of social trust that can be self-reinforcing (Frey, 2005; Ricketts & Ladewig, 2008; Stern & Dillman, 2006; Van Ark & Edeleubos, 2005). In turn, social capital may be convertible into the political capital of collective efficacy and political trust (Parry & Moyser, 1992, pp. 44–62). Social capital is inversely related to diversity, and globalization has increased the diversity of many communities (Coffe & Geys, 2006).

A remedy against social exclusion and the social disintegration characteristic of mass societies is, of course, the active membership of individuals in all kinds of voluntary social networks (Dekker, Koopmans, & van den Broek, 1997). Voluntary social networks provide the opportunity to meet and network with new people, develop social supports, develop civic and social engagement skills and contacts, learn interpersonal skills, and develop reciprocity and the cohesion that integrates society and reduces the impact of mass society. These networks act as a buffer between the individual and the ongoing modernization of industrial society. Participation in civic and voluntary associations is inversely correlated with economic and social inequality (Wessels, 1997). Participation in voluntary associations, especially mass political associations, serves to mediate the negative impact of globalization. Civic engagement must be multi-ethnic to help overcome diversity's limiting effects on trust. Communication technology can facilitate community and social action organizing (pp. 198–201). The core and necessary trait is primary and secondary participation, social networking, rather than just "checkbook membership" or writing a check rather than socially participating.

Politically and as the vehicle for civic participation, associations serve as interest groups in the social mix to determine social policy. Without the associations and participation on the micro level of the association, the individual is limited in macro participation. The associations provide the individual with a network of contacts. Associations (the networks) are political whether or not they are overtly so (Almond & Verba, 1963; Dekker, Koopmans, & van den Broek, 1997). They are political because they develop social skills, involve social interaction, and interlink social networks.

Membership in associations, whether or not politically motivated, leads to a politically more competent citizenry. Van Deth (1997), after a review of the literature on social participation, concluded that social participation and political involvement are correlated. "Voting behavior (turnout), [has] a clear and direct relationship with social participation … in most analyses, even when socioeconomic status or political orientation are [sic]taken into account" (p. 13). Joining organizations and participating in politics reinforce one another. A similar correlation was found for other conventional modes of political behavior and social participation. Groups are not only cooperative endeavors toward mutual ends but are also a means to a shared life, a civic life, and this makes for political capital.

Large-scale membership subscription or checkbook organizations as tertiary networks (e.g., AARP, National Rifle Association, MoveOn. org, Greenpeace) reduce some of the civic benefits and skills of direct participation (Maloney & Jordan, 1997, pp. 107–124). Decision making in these large-scale organizations is anticipatory democracy rather than participatory democracy: one anticipates the nature of the decisions by virtue of joining rather than by participating in the decision-making processes of the network. The networks are anticipatory oligarchies, with decisions made by a few at the top. Participation is financial in terms of membership fees, especially for the broad base of members, rather than broad-based participation. This allows the oligarchies to function and pursue the anticipated actions. Like the virtual network, anticipatory checkbook organizations do not provide the complete benefits and qualities of direct participation and face-to-face networking. The influence is less mutual and flows more from the mass organization to the individual.

These tertiary organizations are called "new social movements." They have replaced the traditional political party structure as a means for encouraging direct participation in the political process. Political party sizes decline as these new social movements increase. The managerial-dominated new social movements expend a great deal of effort and resources on getting members to join, as many lose interest and drop out after a year or so.

Reciprocity

If they are to endure, social support networks require interdependency and reciprocity rather than dependency. Informal, voluntary, and primary groups need internal interdependency. Their maintenance depends on their member satisfaction. Meta-research by Walker, Wasserman, and Wellman (1993), also supported by Maton (1988), concluded that unilateral support is a myth. Social support is not one-dimensional or unidirectional. If there is true reciprocity, there must be a balancing of provider and recipient roles. Reciprocity or mutual obligation is inherent in social supports networks because "providing support to someone in the same network increases the probability that one's own needs will be met in the future" (Shumaker & Brownell, 1984, p. 29). Reciprocity, as expected from the propositions of exchange theory, tends to match the recipient's view of the value of the resources supports received. When reciprocity is absent, the social support network entropies and cohesion is lost (Shumaker & Brownell, 1984, pp. 24–29; Walker, Wasserman, & Wellman, 1993). Trust that there will be reciprocity is inherent in viable social support networks (Frey, 2005; Van Ark & Edeleubos, 2005). Reciprocity in self-help groups and social support networks enhances members' sense of well-being; the sense of well-being is higher when members give as well as receive (Dalton, Elias, & Wandersman, 2001, p. 240; Maton, 1988). Also, activities beyond the self-help group, where members have other networks, are a key component of self-help group efficacy. The extra group involvements may lower demands on the self-help group. Kelly and Kelly's (1985) research on natural helping, a form of social support, found that social support networks may be focused and that helpers tend to be respondent- and network-specific; they are not generalized helpers serving a wide number of respondents. The helped often became helpers as payback or reciprocity for help that they received from the current respondent or others.

Costs of Social Networks

Social workers, in assisting clients with social support networks, should be aware that social networks could have detrimental effects. Not all self-help and support networks are socially helpful to a client or community, although the client may receive some generalized or specific benefit. They may drain resources from the client in reciprocity obligations or make social and emotional demands harmful to the client—like "bad companions" (Heller, 1990). Shinn, Lehman, and Wong's (1984) exploration of social support networks discovered that the reciprocity demands (the current and future demands for resources by the provider of current resources) on the recipient can be pernicious. If the recipient fails to reciprocate because the obligations exceed his or her resources and capacity, this failure creates stresses on both the provider and recipient. The provider may come to view the recipient as a free rider. The recipient has the stresses of unmet obligations and a sense of dependency and loss of autonomy, especially if he or she is constantly a recipient and never a helper. The situational and compliance requirements to receive continuing unilateral supports are harmful to the recipient's sense of self-efficacy.

Social support networks can be simultaneously beneficial and detrimental, but different kinds of relationships can also provide different kinds of supports in emotional aid, material aid, information, and companionship. The exchanges between social support network participants are not always rational or intentional, with the actual effects sometimes differing from the intended effects. Parties may differ in terms of perception and evaluation of benefits and helpfulness, with differences in evaluations reducing cohesion (Shumaker & Brownell, 1984, p. 21). Social supports can have harmful effects, even when the intents are beneficial. The short- and long-term coping effects can differ, with beneficial effects in the short term and negative effects in the long term, especially if the social supports lead to long-term dependency, future obligations, and reciprocal claims for future resources. For instance, the Ku Klux Klan and other ethnic supremacist groups, no matter what ethnic group they consider to be superior, can provide esteem and tangible support, but the group does not assist a member in socially developing or contributing to the total community's well-being. Antisocial youth gangs may be a social support to their members by providing affinitive support, protection, and often material rewards for participating in gang activities, but the reciprocity requirements (current and future) and the requirement to engage in violent, antisocial, and self-harming behavior will inhibit the youth's social functioning. To counter this, alternative sources of social supports should be devised for the youth. The "Tea Bagger" (aka. Tea Party) movement reduces members' alienation and sense of powerlessness, but it weakens community integration and mutual support beyond the movement.

Similar to interagency networks, personal social support networks, including those used by clients, demand maintenance and can consume time, energy, and even finances. Networks that are too tightly integrated, dense, and cohesive can be socially isolating and limiting. Barth and Schinke's (1984) examination of social supports for teenage mothers found that tight family networks can actually cut the mother off from other potential social supports. Nonetheless, network participation usually is associated with enhanced social, interpersonal, and parenting skills.

Primary, Secondary, and Tertiary Social Support Networks

All social support networks can reasonably be conceptualized as falling somewhere along the primary, secondary, to tertiary continuum. These concepts refer to the nature of the relationships between units in the network. *Primary* networks or networks with primary relationships have members with broad interests in each other's lives. Most typical primary networks are composed of family, kinship, and close friends. *Secondary* networks have a more narrow interest in their members than do primary networks but have broader interests than do tertiary networks. Secondary support groups are those with broad interest in and meaning to the individual, such as informal friendship groups and more formal groupings, still with broad and personal interest in the individual, such as church and religious groups, fraternal groups, unions, and other similar associations. Secondary networks and relationships are typically neighborhood organizations, social clubs, or membership benefit organizations such as labor unions, churches, and support groups. *Tertiary* network relationships are generally more formal, with a specific and limited interest in their members' lives than the other two types. Tertiary supports include therapy and formally constructed support groups, as well as special interest associations such as the Sierra Club. The common feature of all of these groups is their more limited interest in the individual. As Putnam (1995) says, their ties are to common ideas or issues shared by the membership but not to the individual members. Although more secondary relationships can grow out of the tertiary associations—even primary ones if some members become close friends—the individual member does not turn to the formal association to provide a wide range of social supports. The tertiary support groups provide a forum for individuals to focus on themselves, generally only certain parts of their life, such as alcoholism or sexual abuse, in the presence of others. Bonding between members as individuals is not required. Any group of like others is sufficient. The bonding is to the group as a whole and to its idea. It is often relatively unimportant who the others are in the audience; the audience can be transient, as long as there is an audience. The member bonding is not between the members as people but between the members and the collective and the idea. They tend to be tertiary, vertical to the community, but often can serve as countervailing forces to other vertical structures.

The criticism of tertiary groups is not so much on what they do, but what they don't do. The intimacy of the tertiary network is low and these networks may usurp more encompassing primary and secondary associations. In their packaging and limiting of relationships, tertiary groups can drive out the time, energy, and effort required for the bonding and reciprocity of more primary and secondary associations and hence reduce social supports and a general sense of community not falling within their purview.

Research findings repeatedly show that people who have primary social supports—spouses, family members, and friends—who provide psychological and material support have better physical and mental health than do people who have fewer social supports (Lincoln, 2000). Most people receive most of their help through primary social relationships (Streeter & Franklin, 1992; Whittaker, Garbarino, & associates, 1983). This appears to be especially true for lower-income and working-class people. A British study (Phillips, Bernard, Phillipson, & Ogg, 2000) of working-class Bangladeshi and white elderly people in the U.K. demonstrated that they felt relatively marginal to the welfare state and its resources. Middle-income elderly people had more connections to and success in obtaining and using the formal services for the elderly offered by the welfare state. Generally, most care given to the working class and elderly was by primary (family, kin) and secondary (neighbors, neighborhood groups and organizations) rather than by tertiary or formal agencies. Primary social networks can have negative consequences, however, if they drain resources from the individual and support aberrant behaviors.

Practitioners need to know a client's actual and potential primary supports and possible secondary supports. Social workers, when assessing a client's social support networks, should not assume uniformity of networks across clients. The client's functional social supports will vary by culture, integration into the community and isolation from a primary community, and the richness of the client's task environment. Primary and secondary social support networks should be explored before turning to the often more accessible tertiary supports.

Developing and strengthening of primary networks is akin to primary prevention (intervention given to a population not yet at risk with the intent of reducing potentially harmful circumstances). Strengthening of primary supports can lead to lessening of tertiary relations and dependency. Conversely, an overreliance on the tertiary leads to a weakening of the primary. The tertiary is better suited for instrumental resources. Networks rich in both expressive and instrumental resources are better for social supports.

Agencies, Volunteers, Primary and Secondary Social Networks

Research by Haski-Leventhal and Cnaan (2009) and Hustinx and Handy (2009) and a review of research by Musick and Wilson (2008) has led them to conclude that volunteers are beneficial to agencies and clients as well as to the volunteers themselves. They can add efficiency if they enable agencies to serve more clients, increase visibility in the client community, and link agencies with community groups and networks. Volunteers legitimize an agency in a community and link it to community networks. They can be effective in media relations as they are viewed as laypeople and not staff. Volunteers can link clients to natural primary and secondary social support networks and other community resources and can reduce the isolation of clients as well as the agency from the community. Social agencies need to be a part of the community with active support constituencies. Volunteers are good boundary-spanning mechanisms for both the agency and the community.

Volunteers do not come in "one size fits all." Agencies need a carefully planned strategy of recruiting, training, and selecting volunteers to fill their particular needs, train them appropriately, and allow them the responsibility of their work if the volunteer experience is to meet agency needs and be a rewarding experience for the volunteers (Haski-Leventhal & Cnaan, 2009). Volunteers are more likely to obtain satisfaction and continue to volunteer based on the work they actually do rather than from abstractions and mission statements. Using experienced and satisfied volunteers with new volunteers is a good way to socialize and train the new volunteers (Haski-Leventhal & Cnaan, 2009; Hustinx & Hardy, 2009).

Who will make the best volunteer is still unsettled. Musick and Wilson (2008) say that volunteers tend to be more politically active and better educated than the general population. They are not likely to be socially isolated, although the use of CT does allow more opportunities for shut-ins to volunteer. Hustinx and Hardy (2009) caution that the more highly educated are frequently more skeptical of mission statements and more critical of their volunteer experiences. Older volunteers also are less likely to be satisfied with their volunteer experiences. Volunteers tend to be satisfied if they have a meaningful volunteer job.

Some guidelines gleamed from the literature for working with volunteers are:

- Select from a range of resources to ensure a variety of community linkages and networks.
- Use existing, seasoned volunteers to recruit, train, supervise, and socialize new volunteers to the agency's volunteer culture, as they probably already have some bonding.
- Recruit volunteers from groups; then recruit the group.
- Train volunteers in groups when possible, as this promotes bonding and social control and responsibility within the group.
- Do as much on-the-job training as possible and responsible, as the volunteer *volunteered* to work. That is where the volunteer's satisfaction comes from.
- Use real normative rewards of status and praise, and provide work feedback. Allow the volunteer to take ownership of the job.
- Develop meaningful tasks for the volunteers—"meaningful" being defined by the volunteer. If the volunteer doesn't see the job as meaningful, the experience will not be positive, and the agency will lose its volunteer.

Social Work Practice in Networks

Social work practice is network practice (Payne, 2000; Travillion, 1999; Whittaker, Garbarino, &

associates, 1983). We argued that development and use of primary and secondary social support networks is preferable and more conducive to client empowerment than a dependency on tertiary social supports and social agencies. Stated plainly, social workers should work first with clients to establish or re-establish primary support systems and work with clients and communities to create and use community-based secondary social support systems. Reciprocity is more likely to be balanced in the support network. Clients should develop and use their strengths and the strengths of their families and communities for empowerment. While we underscore the obligations of the larger community, the state, and the nation to provide mutual social supports, we recognize the tenuous nature of their tertiary social supports in this era of welfare state devolution. Empowerment needs to be client- and community-centered.

Protocols and techniques for developing and managing client social support networks are discussed more fully in the exploration of community-based practice in chapter 13. Developing and helping clients manage their social support networks require client and community assessment skills. Community assessment techniques, discussed in greater detail in chapters 5 and 6, the assessment chapters, include using key informants, community forums, social indicators and demographics for cultural indicators, and field surveys. The techniques are more effective when used in combination (Davenport & Davenport, 1982; Humm-Delgado & Delgado, 1986). We will focus here on assessing the community for client social networking.

Social mapping techniques are used to assess social support networks. Social maps are also called *eco-maps* when used with individual clients. They collect and organize information into a social map of a client's community, indicating potential and actual social supports, social structures, and linkages. The map provides the actual and potential ecological relationships between the client and other primary, secondary, and tertiary groups and organizations. These groups can either positively or negatively affect the client. The client's current and actual social network is analyzed and compared to the networks needed to attain the case objectives. Social mapping starts with case assessment (Bisman, 1994; Lukus, 1993). The assessment's intent is to understand

the case's reality and meaning to the case. The first steps in community assessment involve determining with the case the critical factors in the case's community, ecology, and task environment. What is it we need to know in order to achieve the case's objectives? This requires information on the client's current social networks, a formulation of the needed network, and knowledge of the primary, secondary, and tertiary groups and organizations in the community and the linkage and reciprocity requirement. The groups and organizations are analyzed and categorized by functions (see assets mapping in chapters 5 and 6). Assumptions underlying eco-mapping are set forth in Box 10.3.

Social work practitioners require skills in assessing and establishing or re-establishing primary and secondary social support networks, as most help will come from these types of networks. Practitioners need to know the client's primary supports, the secondary supports within a neighborhood area, and the formal services in a particular catchment area (Phillips, Bernard, Phillipson, & Ogg, 2000, p. 851). Community assessment is critical in direct service practice. Community assessment skills are required, as different communities have different patterns. Box 10.4 specifies the basic questions to be answered with community assessment.

Community assessment in direct service practice requires an ethnographic approach, which is discussed in the assessment chapters. Ethnography and an ethnographic approach stress "the importance of understanding the perspectives of the people under study, and of observing their activities in everyday life, rather than relying solely on their accounts of this behavior or experimental simulations of it (Hammersley & Atkinson, 1983, p. ix)." Meaning or a client's cognitive appraisal is critical to the understanding of a client. Cognitive appraisal is the emotional and cognitive meaning of a person's relationship to his or her social environment. A variety of social support assessment measurement tools are available to assist in the assessment. Streeter and Franklin (1992) describe a number of the social support network assessment and data-organizing instruments (pp. 86–95). However, caution is advised when using these tools: they were most often developed for research uses rather than practice. They need to be reliable, valid, practical, and usable in the

---

BOX 10.3.   Eco-Mapping Assumptions

- Clients are not social isolates but are in social networks that can support, weaken, substitute for, or supplement the helping efforts of professionals. These networks compose the client's ecosystem and can be assessed, mapped, and managed.
- Comprehensive ecosystem assessment and mapping requires data to be collected on all components of the ecosystem—family, home, community—that influence the client's behavior. Information includes the number of components or units and their dimensions.
- Data are collected from a range of sources, including the client, significant others, the

worker's direct observations and interactions with the ecology, and available data and history.
- Assessment involves gathering data on all critical variables to describe the person-in-situation and the person-in-environment.
- The data are integrated into a comprehensive and coherent case theory to explain person-in-situation.
- Ecosystem assessment and resultant case theory direct the repertoire of intervention strategies. Practitioners must have person- and environment-changing interventions.

---

practice situation. While validity generally means that an instrument measures what it is designed to measure, in practice the question is how well the instrument measures what needs to be measured in practice (Bisman & Hardcastle, 1999, pp. 96–102). Triangulation, the use of multiple measurement approaches, is encouraged to enhance validity.

Social Support Network Assessment

Eco-mapping and eco-matrices can be done for any social unit or case. Eco-matrices are tools that lay out the relationships, the matrices, of resources in the environment. Eco-mapping and eco-matrices consider three sets of relationships involved in a change effort: (a) the supportive social relationships, (b) the additional social supports required, and (c) the social relationships that hinder change.

The mapping and matrices organize information gathered from the assessment on the following questions:

1. What are the compositions of the case's networks? How do the network units relate to the case? Can new units be networked?
2. What are the existing networks' strengths, capacities, and limitations? How might the network be altered to reduce limitations and improve strengths (see assets mapping in chapters 5 and 6)?
3. What are the current network exchanges and reciprocities? Are the exchanges balanced? What new resources are needed? Can the resources for the exchanges be made available? If not, can the case or network obtain the resources needed for exchanges? What are the obstacles to obtaining the resources, and can they be removed or reduced?

BOX 10.4.   Community Assessment and Direct Practice

---

1. What are the case's community, ecology, and task environment's boundaries? Can these boundaries be expanded to include more opportunities?
2. What factors in the case's social environment influence the case's behavior and opportunities? What are the case's behavior and interaction patterns with the community? What are the community's communication and interaction patterns?

3. What factors in the social environment influence and constrain objective achievement?
4. What resources are available to the case from primary, secondary, and tertiary sources? Are they adequate for objective achievement, or must the ecology be expanded? How can the case obtain needed resources?

Eco-mapping starts with a client or case's perspective. Streeter and Franklin (1992, p. 82) offer three dimensions to capture this perspective: social embeddedness, perceived support, and enacted social supports. *Social embeddedness* is the actual connections people have to significant others in their environment and the direct and indirect networks that tie people with family, friends, and peers. It is a sense of belonging as opposed to isolation and alienation.

Perceived support is a person's cognitive appraisal of his or her connections with others. To use social supports, a person must perceive social supporters as supporters. *Enacted social supports* are the specific behaviors of the supporters as they support a person by listening, expressing concern, lending money, or provide other supports; it is what the supporters actually do for the recipient. Box 10.5 provides an eco-mapping protocol.

BOX 10.5.   Eco-Mapping

Eco-Mapping and Matrices (See Assessment Chapters): Requires determining (a) existing primary social supports, (b) potential primary social supports available but not currently used by the client, (c) barriers to use, and (d) theory of how to overcome barriers. The process is completed for primary, secondary, and tertiary social supports and for networks harmful or not supportive of the client. Steps (c) and (d) for harmful networks involve how to create barriers to interaction and a theory to disengage client from these networks.

1. Data sources to triangulate for mapping:
   a. Client
   b. Significant others and key informants knowledgeable about the client, community, or both
   c. Available data, such as family records
   d. The worker's observations, including "windshield" and "shoe leather" surveys
   e. Community assessment tools such as directories, agency directories, and community surveys
2. Ecosystem units to assess the client's existing networks and community:
   a. Primary units such as family and friends
   b. Secondary units such as neighbors, neighborhood and other organizations and groups, churches, labor unions, and other membership benefit organizations
   c. Tertiary or formal organizations such as schools, employers, voluntary and public agencies, and relevant proprietary organizations

Dimensions of Mapping Social Support Networks. Assess the following:

1. Network size—Number of units in client's social support networks
2. Network's unit lists and description of units—Names of each network unit and description as to whether the network relationship is primary, secondary, or tertiary; unit type such as individual, group, formal or informal organization

and auspices, and other salient characteristics of network units
3. Multidimensionality of network units—Amount of resources provided, number of exchanges, and number of roles fulfilled by each network unit with, to, and for the client. Primary social supports are more likely multidimensional.
4. Network segments—Sub-network patterns within the network where interactions are more within segments than across segments.
5. Density—Network ties between all network members. Density is ratio of actual number to possible number of network ties. Size, a reason for segmenting, can reduce density.
6. Network map—Graphically lays out relationships and connectedness or density of all network units

Perceived Availability of Resources of Network Units. Assess by:
1. Type of resource
   a. Material and concrete resources
   b. Behavioral assistance
   c. Intimate interaction, feedback, and emotional support
   d. Guidance, advice, provision of information

Assess whether the resource is available always, almost always, rarely, or never.
1. Importance of resource—Whether the resource is critical, somewhat important, or only marginally needed
2. Closeness—Proximity and availability of the network unit to the client
3. Reciprocity—Expectation of resource reciprocity, exchange expectations network units for its resource, and when expected
4. Directionality—Primary direction of support; from or to client, or symmetrical and bilateral between the client and the network unit
5. Stability—Length of time of network relationship
6. Frequency—How often exchanges and contacts between the client and the network unit occur

Eco-matrix (Resource Exchanges Between Client and Other Network Units)

Network Unit Name 1st Unit, . . ., Last Unit	Type* and Social Area**	Concrete Support: Always, Almost Always, Occasionally, Rarely, Never	Emotional Support: Always, Almost Always, Occasionally, Rarely, Never	Information/ Advice: Always, Almost Always, Occasionally, Rarely, Never
Unit Name 1st Unit, . . ., Last Unit	Type* and Social Area**	Guidance: Always, Almost Always, Occasionally, Rarely, Never.	Importance of Resource: Very, Somewhat, Marginal. Proportion Unit Provides: High, Moderate, Low	Closeness: Very, Somewhat, distant

Unit Name
1st Unit, . . .,
Last Unit
	Type* and Social Area**	Reciprocity
		    Requirements:
		High,
		Moderate,
		Low
			Reciprocity Time
			    Expectations:
			Immediate,
			Extended
				Exchange
				    Directionality:
				From Unit,
				To Unit,
				Balanced

Unit Name 1st Unit, . . ., Last Unit	Type* and Social Area**	Relationship Duration: Record Time Length	Exchange Frequency: Record Number of Exchanges	

*Indicates whether primary, secondary, or tertiary.

**Description of unit type, such as individual, group, organization, whether formal or informal, auspices, and other salient characteristics of functional areas.

Discussion Questions

1. *Develop the network of six people between you and the President of the United States and the President of the People's Republic of China. Now develop the same network for a client.*

2. *Take a client from your caseload and list what the client can provide in exchange in a social support network.*

3. *What are your primary social support networks? Compare the units in your social support networks to those in a client's network. What can a client provide in exchange in one of your social support networks? Use the eco-matrix.*

References

Albrechts, L., & Mandelbaum, S. J., (Eds.). (2005). *The network society: A new context for planning.* New York: Routledge.

Alinsky, S. D. (1971). *Rules for radicals: A pragmatic primer for the realistic radical.* New York: Random House.

Almond, G. A., & Verba, S. (1963). *The civic culture: Political attitudes and democracy in five nations.* Princeton, NJ: Princeton University Press.

Alter, C. F. (n.d.). *Casebook in social service administration* (2nd ed.). Iowa City: University of Iowa School of Social Work.

Anderson, R. E., & Carter, I. (1984). *Human behavior in the social environment: A social systems approach* (3rd ed.). New York: Aldine.

Artz, N., & Cooke, P. (2007). Using e-mail listservs to promote environmentally sustainable behaviors. *Journal of Marketing Communications,* 13(4), 257–276.

Barlett, D., & Steele, J. B. (1992). *America: What went wrong?* Kansas City, MO: Andrews & McMeel.

Barstow, B. (2010, February 15). Tea party lights fuse for rebellion on right. *The New York Times.* Retrieved Feb. 17, 2010, from: http://www.nytimes.com/2010/02/16/us/politics/16teaparty.html

Barth, R. P., & Schinke, S. P. (1984). Enhancing the social supports of teenage mothers. *Social Casework*, 65, 523–531.

Bass, D. J., & Burkhardt, M. E. (1992). Centrality and power in organizations. In N. Nohria & R. G. Eccles (Eds.), *Networks and organizations: Structure, form, and action* (pp. 191–215). Boston: Harvard Business School Press.

Beeman, S. (1997). Reconceptualizing social support and its relationship to child neglect. *Social Service Review*, 71(3), 421–440.

Bisman, C. D. (1994). *Social work practice: Cases and principles*. Pacific Grove, CA: Brooks/Cole.

Bisman, C. D., & Hardcastle, D. A. (1999). *Integrating research into practice: A model for effective social work*. Pacific Grove, CA: Brooks/Cole–Wadsworth.

Blau, J. P., & Alba, R. D. (1982). Empowering nets of participation. *Administrative Science Quarterly*, 27, 363–379.

Blau, P. M. (1964). *Exchange and power in social life*. New York: Wiley.

Beaudoin, C. E., & Tao, C-C. (2008). Modeling the impact of online cancer resources on supporters of cancer patients. *New Media & Society*, 10(2), 321–344.

Bragg, M. (1996). *Reinventing influence: How to get things done in a world without authority*. Washington, DC: Pitman.

Burt, R. S. (1992). The social structure of competition. In N. Nohria & R. G. Eccles (Eds.), *Networks and organizations: Structure, form, and action* (pp. 57–91). Boston: Harvard Business School Press.

Butcher, H., Banks, S., Henderson, P., with Robertson, J. (2007). *Critical community practice*. Bristol, UK: The Policy Press.

Chetkow-Yanoov, B. (1997). *Social work approaches to conflict resolution: Making fighting absolute*. New York: Haworth.

Clifford, S. (2009, June 2). Online, "a reason to keep on going." *The New York Times*, p. D5.

Coffe, H., & Geys, B. (2006). Community heterogeneity: A burden for creation of social capital. *Social Science Quarterly*, 87(5), 1053–1072.

Coser, L. A. (1964). *The functions of social conflict*. New York: Free Press.

Coughlin, R. (2004). Does socioeconomic inequality undermine community? Implications for Communitarian theory. In A. Etzioni, A. Volmert, & E. Rothschild, (Eds.), *The communitarian reader: beyond the essentials* (pp. 117–128). Oxford, UK: Rowman & Littlefield, Publishers.

Dalton, J. H., Elias, M. J., & Wandersman, A. (2001). *Community psychology: Linking individuals and communities*. Belmont, CA: Wadsworth.

Davenport, J., & Davenport, J., III. (1982). Utilizing the social networks in rural communities. *Social Casework*, 63, 106–113.

Dekker, P., Koopmans, R., & van den Broek, A. (1997). Voluntary associations, social movements and individual political behavior in Western Europe. In J. W. van Deth (Ed.), *Private groups and public life: Social participation, voluntary associations, and political involvement in representative democracies* (pp. 220–239). London: Routledge.

de Jasay, A. (1989). *Social contract, free ride: A study of the public goods problem*. New York: Oxford University Press.

Deutsch, M. (1973). *The resolution of conflict: Constructive and destructive processes*. New Haven, CT: Yale University Press.

Fisher, R., Ury, W., & Patton, B. (1981). *Getting to yes: Negotiating agreements without giving in*. Boston, MA: Houghton Mifflin.

Frey, K. (2005). ICT-enforced community networks for sustainable development and social inclusion. In L. Albrechts & S. J. Mandelbaum, (Eds.), *The network society: A new context for planning* (pp. 183–196). New York: Routledge.

Galaskiewicz, J., & Wasserman, S. (1993). Social network analysis: Concepts, methodology and directions for the 1990s. *Sociological Methods and Research*, 22, 3–22.

Garcia, C. (2005). Buscando trabajo: Social networking among immigrants from Mexico to the Unites States. *Hispanic Journal of Behavioral Sciences*, 27(1), 3–22.

Germak, A. J., & Singh, K. K. (2010). Social entrepreneurship: Changing the way social workers do business. *Administration in Social Work*, 34(1), 79–95.

Hammersley, M., & Atkinson, P. (1983). *Ethnography: Principles in practice*. New York: Tavistock.

Hardina, D. (2000). Models and tactics taught in community organization courses: Findings from a survey of practice instructors. *Journal of Community Practice*, 7(1), 5–18.

Haski-Leventhal, D., & Cnaan, R. A. (2009). Group processes and volunteering: Using groups to enhance volunteerism. *Administration in Social Work*, 33(1), 61–80.

Healy, J. (1991). Linking local services: Coordination in community centres. *Australian Social Work*, 14, 5–13.

Hearn, G. (Ed.). (1969). *The general systems approach: Contributions toward an holistic conception of social work*. New York: Council on Social Work Education.

Heller, K. (1990). Social and community intervention. *Annual Review of Psychology*, 41, 141–168.

Humm-Delgado, D., & Delgado, M. (1986). Gaining community entree to assess service needs of Hispanics. *Social Casework*, 67, 80–89.

Hustinx, L., & Handy, F. (2009). Where do I belong? Volunteer attachment in a complex organization. *Administration in Social Work*, 33(2), 202–220.

Kaiser, S. (2005). Community technology centers and bridging the digital divide. *Knowledge, Technology, & Policy*, 18(2), 83–100.

Kelly, P., & Kelly, V. R. (1985). Supporting natural helpers: A cross-cultural study. *Social Casework*, 66, 358–386.

Kirst-Ashman, K. K. & Hull, G. H., Jr. (2009). *Generalist practice with organizations and communities* (5th ed.). Belmont, CA: Brooks/Cole.

Knoke, D. (1993). Networks of elite structures and decision making. *Sociological Methods and Research*, 22, 23–45.

Knoke, D., & Yang, S. (2008). *Social network analysis* (2nd ed.). Thousand Oaks, CA: Sage Publications.

Kriesberg, L. (1982). *Social conflict* (2nd ed.). Englewood Cliffs, NJ: Prentice Hall.

Lauer, R. H. (1982). *Perspectives on social change* (3rd ed.). Boston: Allyn & Bacon.

Lee, J. A. B. (1994). *The empowerment approach to social work practice*. New York: Columbia University Press.

Letiecq, B. L., Anderson, E. A., & Koblinsky, S. A. (1998). Social support of homeless and housed mothers: A comparison of temporary and permanent housing arrangements. *Family Relations*, 47(4), 415–421.

Lin, N., & Westcott, J. (1991). Marital engagement/disengagement, social networks and mental health. In J. Eckenrode (Ed.), *The social context of coping* (pp. 213–237). New York: Plenum.

Lin, N., Ye, X., & Ensel, W. M. (1999). Social support and depressed mood: A structural analysis. *Journal of Health and Social Behavior*, 40(4), 344–359.

Lincoln, K. D. (2000). Social support, negative social interactions, and psychological well-being. *Social Service Review*, 74(2), 230–2542.

Lindsey, M. A., Browne, D. C., Thompson, R., Hawley, K. M., Graham, J. C., Weisbart, C., Harrington, D., & Kotch, J. B. (2008). Caregiver mental health, neighborhood, and social network influences on mental health needs among African American children. *Social Work Research*, 32(2), 79–89.

List of social networking websites. (2010). *Wikipedia, the free encyclopedia*, retrieved April 2, 2012, from: http://en.wikipedia.org/wiki/List_of_social_networking_websites

Lukus, S. (1993). *When to start and what to ask: An assessment handbook*. New York: W. W. Norton.

Magee, C., & Huriaux, E. (2008). Ladies' night: Evaluating a drop-in programme for homeless and marginally housed women in San Francisco's mission district. *International Journal of Drug Policy*, 19, 113–121.

MacKay, H. (1997). *Dig your well before you're thirsty*. New York: Currency Book.

Maloney, W. A., & Jordan, G. (1997). The rise of the protest business in Britain. In J. W. van Deth (Ed.), *Private groups and public life: Social participation, voluntary associations, and political involvement in representative democracies* (pp. 107–124). London: Routledge.

Martin, Y. M., & O'Connor, G. G. (1989). *The social environment: Open systems application*. New York: Longman.

Mason, M. (2009). Social network characteristics of urban adolescents in brief substance abuse treatment. *Journal of Child & Adolescent Substance Abuse*, 18, 72–84.

Maton, K. I. (1988). Social support, organizational characteristics, psychological well-being and group appraisal in three self-help group populations. *American Journal of Community Psychology*, 16, 53–77.

McIntyre, E. L. G. (1986). Social networks: Potential for practice. *Social Work*, 31, 421–426.

McLeod, E., Bywaters, P., Tanner, D., & Hirsch, M. (2008). For the sake of their health: Older service users' requirements for social care to facilitate access to social networks following hospital discharge. *British Journal of Social Work*, 38, 73–90.

Menefee, D. (1994). *Entrepreneurial leadership in the human services: Trends, implications, and strategies for executive success in turbulent times*. Unpublished manuscript, University of Maryland at Baltimore, School of Social Work.

Milgram, S. (1967). The small world problem. *Psychology Today*, 1, 60–67.

Mizruchi, M., & Galaskiewicz, J. (1993). Networks of interorganizational relations. *Sociological Methods and Research*, 22, 46–70.

Moynihan, D. P. (1969). *Maximum feasible misunderstanding: Community action in the war on poverty*. New York: Free Press.

Moynihan, D. P., & Pandey, S. K. (2007). The ties that bind: Social networks, person-organization value fit, and turnover intention. *Journal of Public Administration Research and Theory*, 18, 205–227.

Moyser, G., & Parry, G. (1997). Voluntary associations and democratic participation in Britain. In J. W. van Deth (Ed.), *Private groups and public life: Social participation, voluntary associations, and political involvement in representative democracies* (pp. 24–46). London: Routledge.

Murray, C. (1984). *Losing ground: American social policy 1950–1980*. New York: Basic Books.

Musick, M. A., & Wilson, J. (2008). *Volunteers: A social profile*. Bloomington, IN: Indiana University Press.

Nohria, N., & Eccles, R. (1992). Face to face: Making network organizations work. In N. Nohria & R. G. Eccles (Eds.), *Networks and organizations: Structure, form, and action* (pp. 288–308). Boston: Harvard Business School Press.

O'Looney, J. (2005). Social work and the new semantic information revolution. *Administration in Social Work*, 29(4), 5–34.

Parry, G., & Moyser, G. (1992). More participation—more democracy. In D. Beetham (Ed.), *Defining and measuring democracy* (Sage Modern Political Series, No. 36, pp. 44–62). London: Sage.

Patterson, S., Germain, C. B., Brennan, E. M., & Memmott, J. (1988). Effectiveness of rural natural helpers. *Social Casework*, 69, 272–279.

Payne, M. (2000). *Teamwork in multiprofessional care*. Chicago: Lyceum.

Phillips, J., Bernard, M., Phillipson, C., & Ogg, J. (2000). Social support in later life: A study of three areas. *British Journal of Social Work*, 30(6), 837–859.

Pivan, F. F., & Cloward, R. A. (1971). *Regulating the poor: The functions of social welfare*. New York: Pantheon Books.

Pruden, D. (2006). Neighborhood networks: Good for residents and a good investment. *Journal of Housing and Community Development*, 63(1), 17–21.

Putnam, R. D. (1995). Bowling alone. *The Responsive Community: Rights and Responsibilities*, 5(2), 18–33.

Putnam, R. D. (2000). *Bowling alone: The collapse and revival of American community*. New York: Simon & Schuster.

Ricketts, K. G., & Ladewig, H. (2008). A path analysis of community leadership within viable rural communities in Florida. *Leadership*, 4(2), 137–157.

Rosenfeld, L. B., Richman, J. M., & Bowen, G. L. (2000). Social support networks and school outcomes: The centrality of the teacher. *Child and Adolescent Social Work Journal*, 17(3), 205–226.

Rubin, H. J., & Rubin, I. S. (2001). *Community organizing and development* (3rd ed.). Boston: Allyn & Bacon.

Rubin, J. Z., & Brown, B. R. (1975). *The social psychology of bargaining and negotiation*. New York: Academic Press.

Schopler, J. H. (1994). Interorganizational groups in human services: Environmental and interpersonal relationships. *Journal of Community Practice*, 1(1), 7–27.

Schore, L., & Atkin, J. (1993). Stress in the workplace: A response from union member assistance programs. In P. A. Kurzman & S. Akabas (Eds.), *Work and well-being: The occupational social work advantage* (pp. 316–331). Washington, DC: National Association of Social Workers.

Shinn, M., Lehmann, S., & Wong, N. W. (1984). Social interaction and social support. In A. Brownell & S. A. Shumaker (Eds.), *Social support: New perspectives in theory, research, and intervention* (pp. 55–76). New York: Plenum.

Shumaker, S. A., & Brownell, A. (1984). Toward a theory of social support: Closing a conceptual gap. In A. Brownell & S. A. Shoemaker (Eds.), *Social support: New perspectives in theory, research, and intervention* (pp. 11–36). New York: Plenum.

Specht, H. (1986). Social support, networks, social exchange and social work practice. *Social Service Review*, 60(2), 218–240.

Stern, M. J., & Dillman, D. A. (2006). Community participation, social ties, and the use of the Internet. *City & Community*, 5(4), 409–424.

Streeter, L. L., & Franklin, C. (1992). Defining and measuring social supports: Guidelines for social work practitioners. *Research on Social Work Practice*, 2(1), 81–98.

Strom-Gottfried, K. (1998). Applying a conflict resolution framework to disputes in managed care. *Social Work*, 43(5), 393–401.

Tannen, D. (1998/1999). The rules of engagement and the argument culture. *The Responsive Community*, 9(1), 48–51.

Travillion, S. (1999). *Networking and community partnership* (2nd ed.). Aldershot, Hants, UK: Ashgate Arena.

Tsai, J. H-C. (2006). Xenophobia, ethnic community, and immigrant youths' friendship network formation. *Adolescence*, 41(162), 285–298.

Uttal, L. (2006). Community caregiving and community consciousness: Immigrant Latinas developing communities through social service programs. *Community Development: Journal of the Community Development Society*, 37(4), 53–70.

Van Ark, R. G. H., & Edeleubos, J. (2005). Collaborative planning, commitment, and trust: Dealing with uncertainty in networks. In L. Albrechts & S. J. Mandelbaum (Eds.), *The network society: A new context for planning* (pp. 271–283). New York: Routledge.

van Deth, J. W. (1997). Introduction: Social involvement and democratic politics. In J. W. van Deth (Ed.), *Private groups and public life: Social participation, voluntary associations, and political involvement in representative democracies* (pp. 1–23). London: Routledge.

Van de Ven, A., Delbecq, A. L., & Koenig, R. (1976). Determinants of coordination modes with organizations. *American Sociological Review*, 41, 322–338.

Volling, B. L., Notaro, P. C., & Larsen, J. J. (1998). Adult attachment styles: Relations with emotional well-being, marriage, and parenting. *Family Relations*, 47(4), 355–367.

Walker, M. E., Wasserman, S., & Wellman, B. (1993). Statistical models for social support networks. *Sociological Methods and Research*, 22, 71–98.

Weick, K. (1976). Educational organizations as loosely coupled systems. *Administrative Science Quarterly*, 21, 1–19.

Wessels, B. (1997). Organizing capacity of societies and modernity. In J. W. van Deth (Ed.), *Private groups and public life: Social participation, voluntary associations, and political involvement in representative democracies* (pp. 198–219). London: Routledge.

Whittaker, J. K., Garbarino, J., & associates (Eds.) (1983). *Social support networks: Informal helping in the human services.* New York: Aldine.

Willer, D. (Ed.) (1999). *Network exchange theory.* Westport, CT: Praeger.

Willer, D., Lovaglia, M. J., & Markovsky, B. (1999). Power and influence: A theoretical bridge. In D. Willer (Ed.), *Network exchange theory* (pp. 229–247). Westport, CT: Praeger.

Woodard, K. L., & Doreion, P. (1994). Utilizing and understanding community service provision networks: A report of three case studies having 583 participants. *Journal of Social Service Research*, 18, 15–16.

Zimmerman, M. A., & Rappaport, J. (1988). Citizen participation, perceived control, and psychological empowerment. *American Journal of Community Psychology*, 16, 725–250.

11

Using Marketing

It is the necessary, ... the propensity to truck, barter, and exchange one thing for another....It is common to all men, and to be found in no other race of animals, ... Man is an animal that makes bargains: no other animal does this—no dog exchanges bones with another.

Adam Smith, philosopher, social theorist

A market is the combined behavior of thousands of people responding to information, misinformation and whim.

Kenneth Chang, science reporter, The New York Times

Love is often nothing but a favorable exchange between two people who get the most of what they can expect, considering their value on the personality market.

Abraham Lincoln, president, philosopher, martyr

- In a much-anticipated 2010 Super Bowl commercial, Pam Tebow faced the camera holding a picture of her son Tim as an infant (Tim would grow up to become college football's 2007 Heisman Trophy winner). "I call him my miracle baby. He almost didn't make it into this world. I remember so many times when I almost lost him. It was so hard. Well he's all grown up now, and I still worry about his health. Everybody treats him like he's different, but to me, he's just my baby. He's my Timmy, and I love him." Tim appears on screen, looks adoringly at his mother, and hugs round her neck. "Thanks mom. Love you too." The screen then goes to a message encouraging viewers to visit the Web site of Focus on the Family, with the slogan: Celebrate family, celebrate life.[1]
- A full-color, full-page advertisement ran for several weeks in May and June 2010 in most major newspapers, proclaiming in bold type: We will get it done. We will make it right. In standard type was a narrative taking up two thirds of a page presenting BP's efforts to stop the Gulf of Mexico oil spill and a promise to "make things right." A color photograph of a boat laying a boom in front of a marsh topped the page.[2]
- The Maine Department of Environmental Protection targeted the e-mail distribution listserv of employees and sent a series of e-mail messages regarding how they could save energy in their daily lives. The e-mails allowed recipients to demonstrate their commitment by replying to the email. E-mail allowed for efficient dissemination of the campaigns and allowed recipients to provide feedback and input to the marketers (Artz & Cooke, (2007).
- Nottingham, UK, implemented an anti-smoking campaign using geodemographic methods to identify target segments composed of low-income people over 40 years old. To shape and refine the campaign's

303

message, qualitative interviews were conducted with community members who were actively smoking or who had quit. A marketing agency developed materials with the theme *Listen to Reason* that presented reasons for quitting smoking (such as health or for family members). Mass media was used to get the campaign's message out (De Gruchy & Coppel, 2008).

Neither the Super Bowl commercial nor the full-page BP advertisement was promoting a specific tangible product or an immediate service. Rather, they were promoting social ideas to influence people's perceptions, values, and attitudes. Their intent was to alter people's social constructions and behaviors to make them more favorable toward the ad's sponsors. Focus on the Family was trying to show that even difficult pregnancies and births could lead to Heisman Trophy winners. BP was presenting itself as a responsible, caring, and good corporate citizen. Likewise, Maine and Nottingham were not selling a product. They were trying to change individual behavior by using information and communications technology and marketing methodologies. These are examples of social marketing and marketing applied to social concerns.

Agencies and social workers engage in marketing as they make themselves more usable to their clients and communities. They are adapting their service provision to reach new users, making their services known, doing market research, and staging social problems in ways that they can address. This chapter presents an overview of and an introduction to strategic marketing of social services, social marketing and staging of social issues, and applications of

essential concepts, theories, and methodologies of marketing to the social and human services. The chapter also analyzes some of the characteristics of nonprofit agencies, whether voluntary or public, and the social work profession that present particular challenges to the strategic marketing of social and human services.

Markets and Marketing

A *market* is a set of people who have an actual or potential interest in the exchange of goods, products, services, and satisfactions with the others in the set and the ability to complete the exchange (Enis, 1974; Kotler & Andreasen, 1987; Kotler & Lee, 2008). Markets are composed of people who have some need, desire, or preference and are willing to exchange something in order to satisfy that need, desire, or preference (Table 11.1). A *target market* is that part of the public whom the marketer perceives as having the resource the marketer wants and who is capable of making an exchange. A target market has tangible or intangible resources sought by the marketer as necessary or useful to achieving the marketer's objectives.

A *preference* is a need or, more accurately, a desire of the target market or a target market segment (TMS). A TMS is a more precise, finite portion of the target market with shared traits and preferences. TMS preferences are not decided by the marketer but by a TMS: buyers, users, clients, exchange partners. *Preferences* and *needs* mean the same thing in this chapter. Needs beyond a survival level are difficult to define and distinguish from preferences. Needs are shaped by culture, and an individual's decisions in defining needs are shaped by individual and cultural preferences. In market exchanges, the concern is

Table 11.1. A Market

Potential Exchange Partners	Resources Needed	Available Resources for Exchanges
Mental Health Center	Fiscal resources; mentally impaired clients needing improved social functioning; public sanction	Services to improve the social functioning of mentally impaired citizens; concerned image for county government
County Government	Improved social functioning for mentally impaired citizens; public image of concern for citizens	Fiscal resources; mentally impaired citizens in need of improved social functioning; public sanction
Mentally Impaired Citizens	Assistance in improving social functioning	Behavioral resources to mental health centers; legitimacy to center

with social preferences and effective demand, to use an economic concept. An *effective demand* occurs when people express a need or preference and are prepared to back that expression with resources and behavior (Bradshaw, 1977). Exchanges represent behavior and effective demand. The people may be called *buyers* and *sellers*, *customers* and *vendors*, *consumers* and *producers*, *service providers* such as social workers and *clients*, *doctors* and *patients*, or *fund seekers* and *fund providers*. However, in order to form a market, the people must be real, reachable by others, and interested in an exchange.

Marketing, formally defined, is the analysis, planning, implementation, and control of carefully formulated programs designed to bring about the voluntary exchange of values by one part of the market with another part of the market (the target market or markets), for the purpose of achieving the objectives on the part of the market seeking the exchange. It is the active processes of the market (Kotler & Andreasen, 1987, p. 61). Kotler (1971) defines marketing as "the set of human activities directed at facilitating and consummating exchanges" (p. 12). Enis (1974) provides an even more encompassing definition of human behavior in his conception of marketing: "Marketing is a fundamental human activity. . . . Marketing encompasses exchange activities conducted by individuals and organizations for the purpose of satisfying human wants" (p. 21).

Social marketing is a subset of marketing that is most important for social welfare. Social marketing is the application of marketing principles and techniques to produce, communicate, and deliver value to influence the behaviors of TMSs that benefit the targets and the community (Andreasen, 2006; Kotler & Lee, 2008). Andreasen (1995, p. 3) defines social marketing as "the application of marketing technologies developed in the commercial sector to the solution of social problems where the bottom line is behavior change." Its intent is to influence the voluntary behavior of target audiences or people in the community to improve their personal welfare and the community's. Stead, Gordon, Angus, and McDermott (2007, p. 127) state that there are four key features of social marketing: (1) voluntary behavior change as distinct from manipulated or coerced behavior change; (2) the principle of exchange with a clear benefit for the TMS that changes behavior; (3) the use of standard marketing techniques; and (4) an end goal to improve individual and/or community welfare. In short, social marketing is the application of marketing methodology for creating behavior change (Boehm & Itzhaky, 2004; De Gruchy & Coppel, 2008; Darrow & Biersteker, 2008; Stead, Gordon, Angus, & McDermott, 2007). Success or failure is judged essentially by what the TMSs actually do.

Marketing, including social marketing, is more than a set of techniques and technologies to promote exchanges. It is a philosophical perspective to look for what can be done to provide value for others in order to get the marketer's needs met. Marketing is an exchange of value: what a TMS values that the marketer has or can produce for what the TMS has that the marketer values or needs. Both sides are better off, in their own estimation, after the exchange.

Marketing Challenges for the Social Services and the Social Work Profession

Markets and marketing, as are social exchanges and need meeting, are intrinsic to human behavior, to human services, and to social work practice. Historically marketing was not generally accepted or explicitly practiced by social workers, but its knowledge and skills are essential for today's social workers in our turbulent, resource-competitive, overly commercialized, attention-deficit world. Services to promote human and social well-being are becoming commodities offered by a growing number of competitive nonprofit and proprietary vendors promoting their brands. To successfully engage in marketing, social workers and not-for-profit agencies, including public agencies, must meet challenges often not faced to the same degree by their proprietary competitors.

Product Orientation

Perhaps the greatest challenge is that many nonprofit agencies and social workers have a product orientation. A *product orientation*, according to Kotler and Andreasen (1987), "holds that the major task of an organization is to put out products that it thinks would be good for the public" (p. 38). A product orientation is an inward-looking orientation and a belief by the agency and professionals that they know best, that they know what is good for clients, and that their products and services are intrinsically good.

Social workers and not-for-profit agencies tend to be wedded to what they do, while proprietaries are wedded to profit. They are more likely to change products as TMS preferences change in order to make a profit. A product orientation is a tendency to view markets as homogeneous, satisfied by one or a few products determined by the producer. The diversity of consumers and their preferences is ignored. To paraphrase a quote attributed to Henry Ford with the introduction of the mass-produced automobile: *The public can have any color car it wants, as long as it's black.*

Organizational Orientation

An organizational and bureaucratic orientation is similar to a product orientation. An organizational and bureaucratic orientation is a preoccupation with rules, norms, and policies of the agency because it is unique. This orientation is an *organization-centered mindset* and believes the agency's mission is inherently good (Andreasen, 1995). The organizational orientation is a passion for the agency and its particular products and service rather than a fervor to be of service to clients and the community. If the agency and its services and products are not valued by a community or clients, it is because of client and community ignorance, lack of motivation, or insensitivity. Clients are problems rather than resources. Marketing is limited largely to promotion, public relations, advertising, and getting the agency's story out. If the public knows the agency, they will love it. There is an aversion to discovering what client and user prefer. Clients are perceived and treated as a homogeneous mass and not as individuals with different preferences and needs.

Often agencies and people with this orientation make the fatal mistake of ignoring the competition (Andreasen, 2006). The organizational orientation limits competitors to agency clones. Competition is ignored because the agency or

professional sees itself as unique, precious, and peerless, so competitors can't really exist. If the public is not supporting it or clients are not flocking to their doors, it is due to public and client ignorance. Eventually, competitors replace the myopic holders of this orientation.

Professional Orientation

Professionals, including social workers, are socialized to assume a stance of professional expertise. Professions rightly are concerned with professional autonomy and authority. However, when this mindset produces rigidity to change because the professional knows best and a particular service, a particular therapy, or a particular theory serves all clients, that professional has the blinders of a professional orientation (Rothman, Teresa, Kay, & Morningstar, 1983, pp. 62–78).

Assumption of Consumer Ignorance

Assumption of consumer or client ignorance is a necessary correlate assumption to product, organizational, and overdeveloped professional orientations (Andreasen, 1984, p. 133; Germak & Singh, 2010). This assumption holds that clients do not really know what they need, what is good for them, and the services required to meet their needs. The professional, by virtue of education, training, expertise, and experience, and the agency, drawing upon a variety of professions and professional wisdom and experience, are in a better position to determine the client and community's true needs and service requirements. After all, the public's sanction given to the professional and the agency is based on their superior knowledge and skills.

Marketing Is Selling

For agencies and professionals with a product orientation and who view consumers or clients as ignorant, the rational and logical approach to marketing is production and selling (Andreasen, 1984 & 2006; Kotler & Andreasen, 1987, p. 39). Convince an ignorant public that the product is good for them. If the product is good, the public and the clients will be better off with more of it. If the public will be better off with more of the product, the agency should produce more of it. If the agency produces more of it, the marketing task is to convince an ignorant consumer or public to use more of it. A *selling orientation* occurs when marketing is seen as convincing ignorant consumers that they need the agency's products. A selling orientation has an overemphasis on promotion and packaging. Communication will flow out from the agency and professional to the client, rather than both ways in and out, between the agency or professional and client (Andreasen, 2006; McNamara, n.d.). Marketing is narrowly viewed as selling, public relations, advertising, and persuading.

Professional Antipathy to Entrepreneurial Approaches

Professions and nonprofit human service agencies often have an antipathy to the idea of competition among professional and social agencies and an aversion to entrepreneurial approaches to meet the demands of competition (Germak & Singh, 2010; Kotler & Andreasen, 1987; Shapiro, 1977). Marketing is viewed as unprofessional, unseemly, and inhumane. Adherents to this position are repelled by the apparently self-interested nature of market transactions, the ideas of a buyer and a seller, of marketers and markets, in what should be a social welfare or altruistic activity. This partly may be due, as Kotler (1977) indicates, to a low level of consciousness and ignorance of marketing.

Declining Prestige of Social Services Agencies

Secular not-for-profit and public social service agencies suffer in public prestige compared to their proprietary and faith-based competitors. Privatization is a shibboleth. If done by the proprietary and faith-based sectors, it is assumed done better and more efficiently than if done by government. The pinnacle is the proprietary auspice rather than not-for-profit agencies. The projections are for more privatization, commoditization, and proprietarization of social services. Privatization, proprietarization, and private property are basic tenets of faith in the United States.

Another tenet of faith in the United States is the political perception that faith-based charities should be a major vehicle for publicly financed social services delivery. This political conviction was made public social policy by the charitable choice provision of the inelegantly and murkily titled *Personal Responsibility and Work Opportunity Reconciliation Act of 1996* (PL 104–193), more commonly called *welfare reform*. The charitable choice provision encourages states to contract with faith-based organizations to deliver social services. Republican and Democratic presidents have supported it. Our intent is not to analyze and debate the claim's veracity for faith-based agencies compared to secular agencies, but to point out that there is no reliable evidence that they have greater efficacy than secular nonprofit and public social services (Kearns, 2007; Kranish, 2006; Kennedy, 2003; Wright, 2009). The acceptance supports our assertion that secular nonprofit and public agency are suffering from decreasing prestige. This decline presents a marketing challenge for public and secular nonprofit agencies.

Government Regulations

Although politicians and policymakers use marketing to develop and promote themselves, their brands, and their ideology, local, state, and federal policies often restrict social agencies to limited marketing activities. The complexities of the tax codes under the Internal Revenue Code's Section 501, the section of the tax code that confers tax-exempt status, limit the ability of nonprofits to use certain promotional strategies and engage in some political and entrepreneurial activities available to competing proprietary, for-profit agencies (Bryce, 1987; Kotler & Andreasen, 1987; Lovelock & Weinberg, 1984). Section 501(c)(3) states:

Corporations, and any community chest, fund, or foundation, organized and operated exclusively for religious, charitable, scientific, testing for public safety, literary, or educational purposes, or to foster national or international amateur sports competition (but only if no part of its activities involve the provision of athletic facilities or equipment), or for the prevention of cruelty to children or animals, …, *no substantial part of the activities of which is carrying on propaganda, or otherwise attempting, to influence legislation (except as otherwise provided in subsection (h)), and which does not participate in, or intervene in (including the publishing or distributing of statements), any political campaign on behalf of (or in opposition to) any candidate for public office* (emphasis added). (Retrieved June 11, 2010, from http://www.fourmilab.ch/ustax/www/t26-A-1-F-I-501.html)

Many nonprofits avoid other legitimate marketing activities out of fear that they may lose their tax-exempt status (Kotler & Andreasen, 1987, p. 13). The constraint of government regulations on nonprofits should not be overdrawn. Governments have intruded into the proprietary sector with environmental, health, safety, employment, and product regulations.

Social Regulation

Nonprofits face significant social regulations beyond those generally faced by proprietary enterprises and often beyond any formal governmental regulations. Activities of nonprofits with clients sometimes involve controversial behaviors by clients and occasionally the agencies themselves. Occasionally the products appear counterintuitive. Services oriented toward birth control and safe sex for adolescents, for example, are often assumed by conservatives to promote promiscuity. Similarly, clean needle programs for addicts to reduce the spread of AIDS and condoms for male-on-male sex are often viewed with disgust (Darden, 2006; Darrow & Biersteker, 2008).

Using funds donated for services and charitable purposes on marketing activities, such as product advertising and promotion, or market research, is seen by critics as improper (Kotler & Andreasen, 1987, p. 21). The critics are assuming a product orientation that marketing is unnecessary if the services and other products are truly needed. They assume that money spent for market research reduces the money spent for services, is a waste, and is unnecessary. If the agency and the professionals are competent, they ought to know, probably intuitively, what their clients need; if they do not know or if their services are not used, then they're not needed. The agencies and professionals should not try to develop new products or services to meet new needs. After all, aren't nonprofit human service agencies and professional social workers trying to work themselves out of a

job? Of course, none of these arguments is applied to proprietary enterprises entering the human services marketplace as both types of agencies struggle for resources.

Another reason that the public more freely regulates nonprofits is that nonprofit agencies operate as public trusts. There are no owners who bear the risks, nor are revenues directly dependent on satisfying the preferences of consumers. Boards of directors act not for owners or users of the agency's services: they are stewards acting for the public and for the public's good (Anthony & Young, 1988, pp. 59–60). Public sector agencies belong to the public, with elected policymakers serving as stewards. And if nonprofit and public sector agencies are owned by everyone, everyone sees himself or herself as having a say in their operations.

Difficulty in Measuring Success

Proprietary enterprises generally have two clear criteria that are useful in measuring success: profit and return on the investment and market share. Nonprofits do not have comparable clear measurements of success as profit and market share. There is no direct imposed market discipline—that is, survival does not depend on product demand and the ability to satisfy that demand as well as or better than competitors (Bryce, 1987; Kotler & Andreasen, 1987; Lovelock & Weinberg, 1984).

The nonprofit agency is more limited in its ability to use market measures to judge success. Firstly, as discussed earlier in this text, coordination and market restrictions to prevent service duplication are valued more by public and nonprofit agencies than are competitive markets. Without competition and if there is no recognition of competition, market share is inconsequential as an indicator of client preferences. An agency's market share demonstrates its success compared with alternative choices available to the market. Profit is inherently not a benchmark for not-for-profit agency success, nor should fund balances, beyond those prudent for survival, be a mark of good performance and sensible management even in our entrepreneurial era of proprietary emulation. However, the social agency is not without a *bottom-line* measurement of performance. The bottom line for most social service agencies is behavioral change by clients or community (Andreasen, 1995, 2004, 2006; Kotler & Lee, 2008; Stead, Gordon, Angus, & McDermott, 2007) and public use of their services, market share, when choices are available.

Multiple Goals

A challenge to nonprofit agencies is in the nature of their products. Nonprofit agencies generally produce services and intangible products rather than physical commodities. The quality and even the quantity of services and other intangible products are generally harder to measure than the quantity and quality of tangible physical products. With services, the measurements tend to assess the characteristics of the service providers, their education and credentials, or the effects of the services on the users. The actual services dispensed and the interactions between service providers and recipients often are hidden from observation and measurement. Judgments of quality generally rely on vendor self-reports, the service effects on recipients, although infrequently measured, and inputs such as the average amount of time spent with the recipients, and the staff-to-recipient ratios. Meaningful measurement and fiduciary responsibility require a substantial commitment to a bottom-line criterion of client or user behavioral change.

Public welfare agencies, typical of nonprofit agencies, commonly have multiple and often conflicting goals. Is a public assistance agency successful if recipient rolls are reduced, if recurring pregnancy rates of mothers receiving Temporary Assistance to Needy Families (TANF) are down, if the average length of time that recipients are on assistance is reduced, if families raise socially productive children, if the poverty of children is ameliorated, or if public assistance spending is reduced? Is the agency successful if it meets some goals but not others? Does meeting some of the goals preclude meeting other goals? Reducing poverty of children may be counterindicative to reducing the public assistance rolls and the average length of time on welfare.

Multiple Publics

Nonprofit agencies have multiple publics or TMSs (Andreasen, 1984; Lovelock & Weinberg, 1984). There is generally a separation of clients and service recipients from the sources of revenue for the agency. The nonprofit agency's product–revenue relationship often is indirect. Consumers or users of the services usually are not the agency's major sources of revenue. TANF recipients, for instance, do not provide the revenue for public assistance or the services offered by the public assistance agency.

Multiple publics for nonprofit agencies go beyond clients and funding sources to include a range of constituencies and publics in the task environment and support systems relevant and critical to the agency: professional associations, public and professional regulators, licensing and accrediting unions, legislatures, employee associations and groups, collaborating and complementary agencies serving as sources or recipients of client referrals, and volunteers, to name only a few. Multiple publics also is becoming more characteristic of proprietary businesses with the growth of government regulations and regulators, consumer advocate groups, environmental advocates, employee unions and associations, and so forth. However, proprietary businesses have a range of influencers, such as lobbyists, to deal with the regulators and competing publics.

Lack of Market Data

The challenges, especially the product orientation and the assumption of consumer ignorance, have often resulted in and from nonprofits' lack of sophisticated market data on the target market's characteristics, wants, and needs required to facilitate product development and exchanges. Agencies with product, organization, and professional orientations assume it is unnecessary to develop information on the target market.

A Market Orientation for the Profession

Social workers and nonprofit agencies need to develop a market and consumer orientation. Market and consumer orientations are compatible with professional functioning and values. Although nonprofits face greater challenges in marketing than do proprietary agencies, marketing and its techniques are compatible with social work, nonprofit agencies, and social services. A market orientation, or Andreasen's marketing mindset (1995, p. 37, 2004, 2006; also McNamara, n.d.), requires that all decisions emanate from a regard for target clients and target systems. Social work and the human services industry should be equipped by training to adopt a marketing orientation and constructively practice marketing to the benefit of their public and themselves. Marketing requires knowledge of the behavioral and social sciences to assess, understand, reach, and engage people. The basic means of achieving improved social welfare is through influencing behavior. The ultimate objectives of the behavior change are benefits to the client systems, the community, or society and not to the marketer. A market orientation has several essential components.

> CLIENT EMPOWERMENT AND SELF-DETER-MINATION require providing a client with the maximum information on product, prices, place, and benefits so the client can make an informed decision and give TRULY INFORMED CONSENT.

Adopt a Client and Consumer Orientation

A market orientation's core is clients' views of their needs, satisfactions, and preferences and an accounting for these preferences in program design and service delivery. A consumer orientation, or in social work's case a client orientation, lies at the opposite end of a true continuum from product and agency orientations (Fig. 11.1).

A client orientation assumes that clients as a market are experts on their needs and preferences. Consequently, it compels market assessment to gather client information to design and deliver products in ways that meet the preferences of the market as defined by the market. A client orientation goes beyond being *client-focused* and *having a concern about clients* to the involvement individually and collectively of clients in the decision-making processes on service design and delivery. The client is someone with unique perspectives, perceptions, needs, and wants. Assessment and market research is vital.

The marketer gathers knowledge about clients individually and collectively through client and community assessment. The bottom line of a client orientation is client behavior change by meeting needs and wants (Andreasen, 2004, 2006; LeFebvre, 2007; Moulding, 2007; Stead, Gordon, Angus, & McDermott, 2007).

Behavioral Change as the Bottom Line

The marketing orientation for human services recognizes the bottom line as target market, target system, and client behavior change. This is true whether the targets are clients in family therapy or the community power structure in social action. Intervention efforts and devotion to an intervention model are important only if they produce the desired behavioral change. Advertising, persuading people to use or fund a service, public education, and public relations are marketing tactics to produce behavioral change. The people with behavior to be changed are resources because the bottom line can't be reached without them. They are resources to social workers or agencies in reaching their missions and achieving objectives. For instance, the reduction or elimination of child abuse requires change in abusive behavior. This requires access to child abusers. The abusers are resources, because changes in their behaviors are necessary for an agency to achieve its objective of eliminating or reducing child abuse. Detection, investigation, treatment, or full caseloads are relevant only if they lead to behavioral change.

Competition

Every choice, every action by the target system and client involves giving up some other choice or action. The alternative choices and actions perceived by the target are the competitors. Competitors are not clones of the service provider or change agent, or even limited to other service providers. Competitors are the alternative uses of the resources sought by the marketer. There is always competition for the client's and target market's resources even when a social

Product   Consumer
Orientation   Orientation

Figure 11.1. Product orientation/consumer orientation.

agency has a service monopoly for a particular service to a particular segment of a community. In social services, including gratis services, clients have alternative uses of their time, energy, and effort. The TMS, including clients and potential clients, determines the alternatives and makes the decision on the alternative uses of the resources. As Andreasen states (1995), "Consumers [i.e., clients] always have choices—if only to continue their existing behavior. This can be very compelling competition" (p. 80). He further observes that "competition is always there, and it is typically always changing" (p. 54). Social workers must develop market and consumer orientations and understand all forms of competition. They need to assess what they provide to the target.

There is no question that social workers, the human services, and the nonprofit sector are marketing. Markets exist. The appropriate query is not "Should we market?" or "Are we marketing?" but rather "How can we market more effectively in an increasingly competitive and turbulent world?"

Marketing and Community Practice

A market, as discussed earlier in this chapter, is a set of people who have an actual or a potential interest in the exchange of tangible or intangible goods, products, services, and satisfactions with others, and the ability to complete the exchange. The American Marketing Association (n.d.) defines marketing as:

the activity, set of institutions, and processes for creating, communicating, delivering, and exchanging offerings that have value for customers, clients, partners, and society at large. (Approved October 2007)

The determining feature of a market is that the sets of people must be actually or potentially in an exchange relationship. This requires that the people be real, interested in making exchanges, and capable of making exchanges with potential trading partners. Marketing is a continuing, planned process. It involves how transactions are created, stimulated, facilitated, valued, and completed (Andreasen, 2004 & 2006; Kotler & Lee, 2008).

Marketing is voluntary rather than coercive (Andreasen, 2004, 2006; Kotler & Lee, 2008; McNamara, n.d.; Stead, Gordon, Angus, & McDermott, 2007). The ethics code of the American Marketing Association (n.d.) forbids coercive marketing: "Avoid using coercion with all stakeholders." The capacity of one party to impose or force its will on the other party, according to Fine (1992, pp. 23–24), is not marketing but coercion. Good marketing rests on allowing potential trading partners to choose whether to engage in the exchange.

Marketing is advocacy. It is not merely the advocacy, or promotion, of particular products but rather the commitment that the TMS (the particular clients, customers, and other exchange partners) will get their preferences met.

Last, and most important, marketing is change. In social marketing and social services marketing, the ultimate objective is behavioral change to benefit clients, the community, and society. Marketing is appropriate for all organizations that have publics, not just consumers, with whom they make exchanges.

Exchange Theory and Marketing's Propositions

Exchange theory, discussed in Chapter 2, is basic to community and interorganizational practice. It also is the explicit theory underlying marketing. To review briefly, exchange theory's central proposition is that people act in their self-interest as they define it, whether that self-interest is economic, social, or psychological. Exchange is the act and process of obtaining a desired product from someone by offering in return something valued by the other party. The products can be tangible or intangible (such as social behavior), and the exchanges do not have to consist of the same types of products. Exchanges can include counseling and community organization services for money, adoration and praise for compliant behavior, information for status, political influence for PAC donations or for votes, and so forth. Whether an exchange actually take place depends on whether the two parties can arrive at the terms of exchange that will leave each of them better off or at least not worse off, in their own estimation, after the exchange compared with alternative exchanges possible and available to them.

An example of a social exchange occurs when a securely middle-class donor contributes to a homeless shelter. The donor makes a tangible monetary donation to receive intangible products from the shelter. The donor does not expect to use the shelter either now or in the future but expects to receive good feelings of doing a generous deed and perhaps the rewards of a more humane social environment. The donor also may want to avoid encountering the homeless. The marketer (that is, the homeless shelter) competes with all other alternative uses by the donor of the money that might provide the donor with good feelings, a more humane social environment, or any other satisfaction. If the donor continues to encounter the homeless, the donor may not believe the reciprocity is sufficient and contribute elsewhere.

Several conditions are necessary for markets to exist and exchanges to occur in addition to those found in other social network exchanges (Kotler, 1977):

1. At least one of the social units wants a specific response from one or more of the other social units. The social unit seeking the response is the *marketer* and the social units from whom a response is sought is the *target market*. The response sought from the target market is acceptance in the short or long run by the market of the market's product, service, organization, person, place, ideology, and/or social idea. The marketer wants the market to respond with the resources and behaviors sought by the marketer.

2. Each social unit perceives the other social unit and is perceived by the other social unit as being capable of delivering the benefits in return for the benefits received. Each social unit communicates the capacity and willingness to deliver its benefits to the other social unit in return for desired benefits. A function of advertising is to convince the target market that satisfaction can be delivered by the marketer.

3. Each social unit can accept or reject the benefits of the other social unit in the exchange, although if the social unit withdraws from the exchange relationship, it forgoes the benefits

and may pay an opportunity cost. Marketing exchanges are voluntary.

4. Marketing's indispensable activity is the marketer's creation and offering of value to the target market as the target market defines value. Effective marketing is the marketer's choice of actions calculated to produce desired responses, exchanges, from the target market in behaviors and resources desired by the marketer.

5. Marketing assumes that the marketer can alter the target market's response. Marketing is a process to alter the target market's responses. The marketer wants to produce a desired, voluntary response by creating and offering desired products with value to the target market. The indispensable activity is the marketer's creation and offering of value as defined by the market. Effective marketing consists of actions that are calculated to produce the desired response from the market.

6. Both social units gain and pay in an exchange. The value of the exchange above its cost, or profit, is determined by the value of benefit received less the cost of the resource exchange for the benefit.

Profit = Benefit received – Cost of resource exchanged or lost

Each social unit in an exchange relationship estimates the cost of the resources given and the value of the resources or benefits received.

Let us illustrate these axioms with a case example. A community mental health agency (the marketer) is trying to develop and implement a counseling service for adults who were abused as children and who are suffering from adult anxiety. These adults, not all adults suffering from anxiety, constitute potential clients (the target market). The agency has examined the research on various forms of therapy on adults abused as children and suffering from adult anxiety and the findings of a small focus group from the target market to determine the most effective service. The projected service (product) is a combination of individual counseling, offered in 30 sessions of 50 minutes once a week in a given calendar year, and social support groups and networks. The sessions will be offered in the evenings and on weekends, because most of the adults are employed. The number of sessions is limited by the requirements of the third-party payers. The agency has to respond to two sets of actors in the community: the potential clients and the third-party payers.

The agency is seeking specific responses from potential clients and third-party payers. It wants potential clients to become actual clients, for clients to reduce and effectively manage their anxiety, a value to clients, the agency, and community, and for third-party payers to pay for the service.

Potential clients' responses are not fixed; they may or may not become clients. The agency (the marketer) wants them to become clients and tries to achieve this by offering the therapy at convenient times. The likelihood that the potential clients will become actual clients can be altered by the agency's actions in terms of outreach, public information, recruitment, and referral networking; by ensuring that the design, location, and timing of the service meet the potential clients' preferences; and by ensuring that the service is effective. However, service effectiveness—the ability of counseling and support to reduce the anxiety of these persons—is relevant only if the potential clients use the service.

Using continuous marketing, the agency will try to design its products to meet the needs and preferences and give value to potential clients, and demonstrate to them how the products will help and give value to them. The responses of the potential clients (the market) are voluntary; they are neither obliged nor coerced to become clients. They will engage in exchange with the agency—that is, become clients—because the agency's services meet their needs better than other options available to them.

Social Marketing

Social marketing is a specialized form of marketing with the marketer offering social ideas to obtain a behavioral response from the market. Fox and Kotler (1987) define social marketing as social cause–oriented marketing. It is "the design, implementation, and control of programs calculated to influence the acceptability of social ideas" (p. 15). In most conceptions of social marketing (Andreasen, 2006; Jenkins & Scott, 2007;

Kotler & Lee, 2008), it is clear that its *sine qua non* is the target's behavior change in ways desired by the marketer. Social marketing is behavior influencing, as is all marketing, trying to get people to behave in specific predetermined ways. Andreasen focuses on behaviors that constitute social problems (2006, p. 15). Social marketing is the application of marketing concepts, theory, and techniques to promoting social ideas rather than physical commodities and services. The social ideas can be progressive or reactionary.

Andreasen's (1995, 2006) emphasizes the social marketer's motives rather than technology as paramount in establishing whether a marketing effort is social marketing. Its ultimate objective is to benefit target individuals or society and not the marketer. Social marketing is used, however, in social causes, fundraising, lobbying, and campaigning for political candidates promoting social ideas of the left or right. This concept of social marketing is similar to our concept of staging discussed below.

Staging

Staging, also called *framing*, is fundamental to social marketing. Staging also is crucial to any social acceptance of a social problem construction and the perception of social realty. It is part of the claims-making process discussed in Chapter 3. Staging is the presentation of a social issue, cause, or policy to the community and target decision makers, using the marketer's construction of social reality as presumed reality. Staging presents a social condition as a challenge to the public's welfare, and generally proposes interventions, behaviors, and services contributing to the public good. Successful staging captures the broad range of the community standards, interests, and ideology. Staging's goal goes beyond just informing the targets to seeking their acceptance of the marketer's social constructions. It builds on as well as shapes the public's values and ideologies. Staging is done by both proprietary and nonprofit organizations.

Staging pertains to the promotion of a social idea and not to the marketer's auspice or motives. Staging's analytic market approach is used for an array of social ideas, products, and policies. A range of political and proprietary for-profit organizations use staging to promote social ideas congenial with political and profit-oriented concerns. The Tebow Super Bowl commercial and the BP ad are part of a staging campaign by the respective nonprofit and proprietary organizations. We are all familiar, in our media-driven culture, with the marketing tactics of political campaigns. Newman and Sheth (1987) discuss the penetration of marketing into political campaigns when potential voters are treated as consumers rather than as participants in the political processes. Campaigning is marketing to a *voter market*, using marketing tools of assessment and research through polls and focus groups, differentiation and positioning a candidate as product design, and a range of promotion techniques to sell the candidate.

Staging often is more important in the public's acceptance of social constructions than are valid data and scientifically technical theory. The seminal sociologist Herbert Blumer (1969), discussed in Chapter 2, indicated that the social construction, and not the objective makeup of any given social condition, determines the presumed social reality (also see Krosnick, 2010). Themba (1999) states it more emphatically:

There is only so much that information can do to improve social conditions because, contrary to conventional wisdom, information is not power. Power is having the resources to make changes and promote choices; to be heard; and to *define, control, defend and promote one's interests* [emphasis added]. Many of the problems facing communities stem from the lack of power—not the lack of information. . . . it is not giving people information that's the key to motivating them to act, but validating their perceptions and conveying a sense that the change they dare to imagine in their private spaces is achievable and desired by a great many others. (pp. 21–24)

Our position, word by word . . .

Courtesy

At Philip Morris, we believe that common courtesy and mutual respect are still the best ways for people to resolve their differences.

By respecting each other's rigts and preferences, both groups can easily work things out.

Source: The New York Times, November 1, 1994, p. A9

Economic corporations and the political right (Lewin, 2001, p. 20) have long understood the

importance of staging. Examples are the "Harry and Louise" TV commercials that health insurance companies sponsored during the 1994 national health insurance debates and fear-mongering about so-called death panels by Republicans during the 2009–2010 national health insurance debates. The opposition claimed that its beliefs were rooted in the American values of freedom of choice and protection of liberties rather than in profits. With the U.S. Supreme Court's decisions on corporate political involvement,[3] corporate staging in public policy will increase both directly and through Potemkin and Astroturf fronts (discussed below) (Liptak, 2010).

Staging helps a marketer's image and social position with potential exchange partners. GTE, an electronics firm, sponsored collegiate academic All-Americans in the 1990s; this helps with the positive acceptance of the firm's other products. The spokespeople used in social marketing are critical. Pharmaceuticals and other marketers use recognizable, likeable, and sympathetic faces with a high "Q-rating" (Dowie, 2002): Focus of the Family used Tim Tebow and his mother; GlaxoSmithKline has used Kelsey Grammer; and Michael J. Fox serves as the unpaid face of Parkinson's disease (Kuczynski, 2002). A social worker visibly promoting the social idea of gender equality, women's rights, might help obtain women clients.

Language is critical. In the 2000 presidential election, the Republican Party successfully staged the idea that conservatism is compassionate and caring (Brooks, 2003). The art and technology of selling conservatism as compassion, caring, and fair ideology is taught at the Leadership Institute, a conservative training school for young politicians. The training school teaches how to palatably present conservative ideas and to network and place young conservatives in political, governmental, and media jobs (Harden, 2001, p. A8). Candidates also were taught by Republican Party consultants how to sound "green" as well as compassionate (Lee, 2003a).

The creation and use of *Potemkin* and *false-front* interest groups and organizations is helpful in staging (Pollack, 2000; Rubin, 1997). Potemkin organizations are hollow organizations that give an impression of representing a broad community or the public interest. A dozen or so people can create several organizations with the same overlapping memberships. False-front organizations are organizations with names that disguise their real interests, indicate broad membership, and convey a positive public interest. An example of a conservative Potemkin organization is FreedomWorks, a sponsor or channel for corporate funding to the Tea Bagger movement and other more extreme reactionary organizations. Corporations fund FreedomWorks,[4] which can feed funds to other political action organizations, giving the corporate sponsors a "beard" or cover for their support.

The aim of Potemkin and false-front organizations is to take a narrow, self-interested position and make it seem to the public to be a broad public interest and good position. Selling cigarettes or protecting insurance or energy company profits is not the stated goal; rather, the goal appears to be the preservation of choice, freedom, and security. The selection of a name should capture a target's view of the public interest and a social good: FreedomWorks, Citizens for Better Medicare, SeniorsUSA (Goozner, 2002; Hogan, 2003; Lee, 2003b; Pollack, 2000; West & Francis, 1996). A coalition of social workers in the 1980s advocating for the extension of third-party vendor payments to cover only clinical social workers used the name *Coalition for Patients' Right to Choose.* The name disguises a coalition that is almost exclusively composed of social work organizations and agencies. The patients' right to choose is expanded by adding a single profession, social work, to the eligible vendors list. The coalition's name indicates a broad concern for patients' rights and choice—a public good—but the intended change is rather narrow.

Staging and social marketing's products are the social ideas and the value received by the market as satisfaction in upholding the social ideas, such as respect for the environment, concern for future generations, and money savings in energy conservation, health, and the preferred behaviors and satisfaction the social ideas allow the market to pursue and receive (Andreasen, 2004, 2006; Artz & Cooke, 2007; Fox & Kotler, 1987; Kotler & Lee, 2008; LeFebvre, 2007; Moulding, 2007; Newton-Ward, 2007). While other incentives may be added to manipulate the market's response and increase satisfaction, such as the giving *goody bags* give-away (Cork, 2008) or in fundraising by National Public Radio and public television stations, the social idea is the basic product. In public radio, the programs can be listened to regardless of the listener's contributions to the radio station. The programs are free to the individual listener. The fund appeals generally address listeners' values in the social ideas promoted by public radio and television; the specific commercial-free programs; and the provision of more tangible products such as CDs, tote bags, and coffee mugs to encourage the marginally committed listener to donate. The tangible items also have value in conveying the user's public image of concern and providing free publicity to the marketer, especially if they have appropriate logos, as well as any utility to the user of the CD, tote bag, or cup.

We will discuss the media and staging later in this chapter.

Strategic Marketing and Market Management

Successful marketing requires developing and implementing a market plan or strategy (Andreasen, 2004, 2006; Stead, Gordon, Angus, & McDermott, 2007). Lauffer (1986) defines *strategic marketing* as "a comprehensive and systematic way of developing the resources you need to provide the services that others need. By responding to the needs of the consumers, providers [of resources], and suppliers, it becomes possible to minimize some of the disruptions in supply and demand that otherwise play havoc with agency programs" (p. 31).

Effective strategic marketing involves an outside-inside marketing approach (McNamara, n.d.). This marketing strategy begins with the consumer's or target market's needs and preferences (the outside), not with the organization's product (the inside). The product is developed to meet the preferences of the consumers, clients, and targets of the proposed exchange.

Stoner (1986) asserts that strategic marketing is a planning strategy that involves developing answers to the questions: Where are we? Where do we want to be? How do we get there? Strategic planning and implementation of the plan answers these questions. Strategic planning is a social planning model similar to social work's generic problem-solving model, reviewed in Chapter 1. The essential tasks are to determine the primary markets, those central to the agency's core functions, resources, and achievement of its mission, and the secondary markets, those important but not essential to the agency's mission. The primary and secondary markets include all the social entities in the task environment: the individuals, groups, organizations, and support systems from which resources and exchanges are sought.

Andreasen (2004) makes extensive use of three conceptual frameworks in his social marketing campaign model: (1) stages of target market change: precontemplation, contemplation, preparation and action, and maintenance; (2) the BCOS factors: benefits, costs, influence of others, and self-efficacy; and (3) competition: what is working against the change, including the target's behavior patterns, social and physical environment, and ideology. The social marketing plan needs to address each component.

Market Positioning

Determining and locating primary and secondary markets is market positioning. *Market positioning* consists of the processes by which an agency selects its markets. It involves determining the market's location, assessing its preferences, estimating the competition for the target market, and appraising the potential for exchanges (Lauffer, 1986, p. 37). The processes of determining primary and secondary target markets and market positioning are discussed later in the chapter under "Purchasers," addressing the development of target market segmentations and exchange partners.

The marketing literature (Fine, 1992; Kotler & Andreasen, 1987; Kotler & Lee, 2008; Lombardo & Leger, 2007; Winston, 1986) presents the components of a strategic marketing plan with varying precision by a series of related *P*s. Although the number and conceptualization of the *P*s vary with the authority, we use the following six:

1. *Probing:* the market research to determine the preferences and needs of relevant publics (clients, donors, etc.) or market segments

2. *Purchasers:* the TMS, the relevant publics or the exchange partner sought
3. *Products:* the goods and services offered to the purchasers and market segment
4. *Price:* the cost of the products to the purchasers and market segment
5. *Place:* the locations for exchanges with the purchasers and market segments and the paths by which the segments get to the places for exchange
6. *Promotion:* the communication of the anticipated values and prices of the products and places for exchange to the purchaser and market segment

Fine (1992, pp. 4–5) uses an additional *P* for *producer*, for the source of the promotional message and products. Winston (1986, p. 15) uses *people*, for all people involved in the organization, including volunteers, if they affect the exchange. Fine's producer and Winston's people are our marketers. Moore (1993) separates *path* from *place*, with path being the processes potential exchange partners (purchasers, clients, or customers) use to get to the place of the exchange. Lombardo and Leper (2007) add *public* and partnerships, similar to Winston's *people*, *policy* or the rules, and *purse strings* or the source of the marketer's resources.

Probing

Probing is the generic *P* for market research. *Market research* consists of the formal and informal processes and methods used to determine the TMSs, the potential and actual exchange partners, their preferences, and how these preferences can be met. The TMS's needs and preferences are the outside of strategic marketing, and developing products to meet these preferences is the inside. Community assessment, discussed earlier, can be adapted to be a market research methodology. Functional target market segmentation is discussed later in the chapter under "Purchasers."

Market studies include *surveys* of clients' and potential clients' needs and preferences; *community assessments* to determine community needs and resources; *focus groups* to determine potential clients' needs or preferences; *case and client studies* and analysis; *follow-up studies*; and *client satisfaction studies*, with the intent of answering questions on resources available, targeting market preferences, and gaining knowledge of conditions conducive to or inhibiting exchanges with the target market segments, and *marketing audits* that do it all.

The market research answers the key set of questions listed below (Winston, 1986, pp. 9–12). Direct service practitioners, whether independent or agency-based, can use the same set of questions to study their target markets by viewing themselves as the marketer. The nominal *clients* are used here as the illustrative exchange partner or TMS. However, as is discussed a little later, a TMS is any part of the task environment, any potential partner, with whom the marketer seeks an exchange. Potential exchange partners and TMSs in addition to clients include potential funding sources, client referral sources, and volunteers. They vary with the resources wanted.

- What is the marketer's practice mission and purpose? What does the marketer want to achieve with what parts of our task environment? What are the behaviors sought?
- What resources are needed to achieve the marketer's goals and objectives and fulfill the mission? Where are the resource holders located? Are they accessible? What are their social, behavioral, and demographic characteristics that can or will affect the exchanges? Market studies and community assessments are done to determine the location of target markets, their preferences, and how those preferences affect product design and delivery, how the target markets communicate, and whether the target markets requires additional segmentation.
- Are the needed resources general or specific? Are resources generally distributed evenly across the target market or clustered around specific traits of the TMS? Is the target market's capacity uniform in ability to pay the price for our products and meet our expectations? Resources that are clustered indicate additional target market segmentation to expedite exchanges. If the capacity to provide the exchange is not essentially equivalent across the market, then additional segmentation is indicated.

- What are the most effective and efficient ways to obtain the resources? Is a single approach sufficient or are multiple stratagems necessary? Will different product designs, delivery systems, and pricing strategies enhance exchanges? If multiple approaches (different approaches to different parts of the target market) facilitate exchanges, then greater market segmentation is indicated.
- How does the target market get its information? Is it uniform across the target market, or are there different patterns of communication and information getting? What are the optimal marketing approaches to communicate and facilitate exchanges with the TMSs? How can the value and price of the products compared with those of competitors in meeting the TMS's preferences and the place for exchanges be best communicated to the TMS? What things interfere with effective communication? Greater segmentation is indicated when communication patterns differ.
- How does each TMS define its preferences and needs? How does it determine value? Are the presences, products desired, and values uniform or different across the market? For instance, a family services agency offers family therapy to families suffering from discord. Family therapy is the agency's product. The segment's preference, however, is a reduction of family discord and stress rather than family therapy. The family might be happier to avoid therapy if their stress can be reduced in other, less costly ways. The therapy is a means to achieve the family's preference. Value is rooted in how well the product meets preferences.
- What product prices and places for exchanges most encourage exchanges by the TMSs? How can the price be kept lower than the value to the TMSs but above the marketer's costs?
- Who are the competitors? What other organizations and entities are trying to meet the TMS's preferences? What are the alternative ways the TMS can use its resources? Remember, a competitor is any alternative way a TMS can use its resources that we are seeking, including the resource of its behavior.
- What are the marketer's strengths and competencies? Has the marketer built it or can

the marketer build from strengths and competencies in designing new products to meet potential TMS preferences?

- What are the marketer's weaknesses that require attention? Can the weaknesses be corrected? Weaknesses requiring attention are deficiencies that interfere with exchanges and place the organization at a competitive disadvantage in the TMS's assessment for its resources use.

Market Study and Market Audit Methodologies. Market research's methodologies and techniques are similar to community assessment discussed earlier in the text. The first step is defining the market segmentation, discussed under "Purchasers" below. The market research and audit should be completed before the marketing plans are developed and revised as needed. Some of the methodologies of market research are as follows:

1. *Case studies* (Lovelock & Weinberg, 1984; Yin, 1986) of similar marketing efforts by the agency or other agencies. Case studies look at how successful marketers design, develop, and deliver services that meet the preferences of the TMS or similar market segments, with the intent of replicating the successful efforts. Unsuccessful cases also should be scrutinized to avoid their failures.

2. *Surveys* of particular TMSs for their needs, preferences, and capacity and willingness to make the exchanges—pay the price—and preferences for the location of exchanges can be done by client exit interviews or other "opinionaires" and evaluations; surveys of TMSs such as consumer and client satisfaction surveys; or surveys of potential donors. Surveying the TMSs reveals why the segment uses or would use the agency, makes a donation, becomes a volunteer, accepts the social idea, and so forth. Surveys, while a potentially powerful assessment tool, have several limitations. Not the least are the costs of developing, pretesting, distributing, and administering them, and analyzing the results. Meaningful surveys of the TMS require a representative sample—that is, a sample containing all the important traits and characteristics related to the market segment's preferences for products, prices, and places. If the people who respond to the survey do not represent the TMS, the survey's results do not reveal the true preferences of the TMS and will not be helpful in the design and delivery of the products.

3. *Focus groups* are a less costly approach to market research and are now widely used. A carefully constructed focus group representing a specific TMS can provide much information on the segment's preferences. Focus group construction and operations were discussed in the assessment chapters.

4. *Advisory boards and panels* can provide information similar to that of focus groups by sharing their opinions on product design, service delivery, and similar agency concerns. However, advisory groups differ from focus groups in that they often represent diverse constituencies or TMSs.

5. *Mall surveys*, using quota and purposive sampling techniques, are frequently used in market research. The mall survey takes its name from the market researcher's practice of going to a shopping mall and asking shoppers what they look for in products, what they buy, and where they shop. The collected data are analyzed according to a predetermined profile of preferred consumer characteristics. The social service agency or practitioner can use similar techniques in other areas, where samples of its target market segments are located. If an agency is interested in developing a program for hard-to-reach adolescents, it can send someone to the places where they congregate—in this example, it may indeed be the mall. The mall survey is relatively inexpensive and easy to conduct. Its weaknesses are the weaknesses of all surveys, especially those conducted with samples of convenience: whether the sample represents the target population, the willingness of the target to participate in the survey, and the truthfulness of their responses. As with the focus group, participants in a mall survey are not truly anonymous, and this may bias their responses.

6. *The market audit* is the most complete and powerful approach to market research. The audit incorporates most of the above

methodologies. Market audits address the questions presented in the previous section and collect information on the agency's task environment, including competitors for resources, the agency itself, and the *P*s of the purchasers (TMSs): product, price, place, and promotion. The audit helps the marketer learn its weaknesses and deficiencies, its strengths, and where it is dominant and deals most effectively with its competition. The audit report contains recommendations and proposals to improve the organization's market access and share. A sample audit guide is included at the end of the chapter.

7. A *market matrix* is a simple approach to market research and analysis. In filling the cells, the market researcher has to specify for relevant TMSs the product, price, place, and promotion. The market matrix addresses the *P*s of purchasers (TMS): product, price, place, and promotion (Table 11.2). The sixth *P*, probing, is audit and analysis necessary to complete the matrix's cells. Of course, each TMS indicated above will require greater segmentation. Rarely are clients, funders, political influencers, legitimizers, or volunteers homogeneous groupings.

Purchasers

Purchasers as resource suppliers, especially clients, are the most important TMSs. Purchasers are those parts of the task environment that control or represent resources necessary for the agency to achieve its objectives. Purchaser market segmentation determines and establishes the TMSs essential to effective product development and exchanges.

Market Segmentation

Market segmentation involves obtaining the precision necessary to facilitate exchanges by allowing specificity in product, price, place, and promotion strategies for each TMS. For-profit businesses have different TMSs for different product lines. A cereal company may produce a variety of breakfast cereals to meet specific preferences of each TMSs. An automobile manufacturer sells luxury gas-guzzlers, SUVs, and hybrids to different target market segments. Nonprofit agencies have different TMSs with different preferences. They should not attempt to have one product line for all segments or assume the target market is homogeneous. The mental health agency that has only one form of therapy, designed and offered in the same way, during the same hours in the same places to all potential clients, regardless of demographics or other circumstances, almost certainly is not meeting the preferences of all potential market segments. The agency will lose clients. Market segmentation, as demonstrated by Table 11.3, is compatible with social work's admonition to *start where the client is*.

A TMS is a smaller part, a subset, of the target market, sharing some traits with the general target market but also possessing some unique characteristics and traits setting it apart and affecting the exchange (Conner, Takahashi, Ortiz, Archuleta, Muniz, & Rodriguez, 2005; Jenkins & Scott, 2007; Powell, Tapp, & Sparks, 2007). Segmentation is needed unless all people in the target market have the same preferences satisfied by the products, place, and promotion in the same ways. Appropriate market segmentation requires knowledge of the traits, characteristics, and preferences of a target market and any

Table 11.2. Market Matrix

Target Market Segments, or Purchaser (Describe each TMS, such as those listed below.)	Product (What is the product(s) desired by and for the TMS?)	Price (What is the price of each product for the TMS?)	Place (What is the place of exchange for each product and for each TMS?)	Promotion (What promotion best reaches and communicates value to each TMS?)
Client (TMSs, fiscal resource suppliers, political influencers, volunteers, legitimizers, other segments)				

Table 11.3. Market Segmentation and Social Work Values

... starting where the client is: Who are the clients? Where are the clients? What do they prefer? Market segmentation makes exchanges easier by requiring the marketer to design products more precisely, with benefits, places of exchange, and prices to meet the preferences of specific types of people.

Target markets	That part of the task environment or community with the necessary resources sought by the marketer to achieve objectives and with whom the marketer seeks exchanges.
Target market segments (TMSs)	Those parts of a particular target market sharing specific traits of behavior, values, and preferences that influence exchanges. TMSs share some traits with the total target market but differ on some traits with other parts of the target market. A particular target market generally has more than a single segment.
When to segment?	When traits of the potential target market are diverse and diversity will affect exchanges and product design and delivery. The target market is segmented for greater homogeneity within each segment.
How to segment?	Cluster the traits of the target market that might affect exchanges: for example, education, values, preferences, capacities, motivation.
How much segmentation?	Additional segmentation is indicated when exchanges with target market are low. The marketer is not obtaining resources and behavior changes from target market segmenting used.

subgrouping's clustering of traits and preferences. Probing or market research and community assessment is a prerequisite for viable segmentation. Box 11.1 lays out the segmenting protocol.

A product line can mean different things to different constituencies (clients, funding sources, and so forth) and therefore, in effect, represents different products. The nonprofit agency's perception of its products delivered may differ from the perceptions of these products by different constituencies. Nonprofit agencies need to recognize how different market segments perceive the products, even in the same product line. These perceptions may be very different from those of the agency.

The degree of market segmentation needed is determined by (a) the specificity of resource exchanges that the marketer wants from the task environment (i.e., whether the resource desired is homogeneous and general or diverse and specific), (b) the nature of the potential trading partners or target market (homogeneous or diverse), (c) the distribution of the resources sought (concentrated in a few trading partners or widely distributed in the task environment), and (d) the products desired by the potential trading partners (uniform or diverse).

As a guideline, the variables can be summed using the numbers 1 or 2 preceding the subvariables. The higher the sum, the greater the need for market segmentation. If the resource

---

BOX 11.1.	**Segmenting Protocol**

1. Marketer determines resources and behaviors necessary to achieve objectives.
2. Marketer assesses task environment (community assessment) to determine who has resources and behaviors and where they are located.
3. Marketer assesses target market's preferences.
4. Marketer assesses whether resource holders' product and benefit preferences are homogeneous or heterogeneous across target market.
5. If resources, behaviors, and preferences are homogeneous, then segmentation is now complete;

if heterogeneous, then additional segmentation is needed until resource, behavior, or product preferences holders are clustered into reasonably homogeneous segments.
6. Marketer assesses where exchanges can occur and preferences can be met.
7. If a single place for exchange exists, then no additional segmentation is needed; if a single place for exchange does not exist, then additional segmentation is needed until sufficient places exist.

desired is homogeneous (I.1), there are many potential trading partners who have the resource (II.1), the potential trading partners are similar on important traits (III.1), and their product preferences are uniform (IV.1), the summed score is 4 and little segmentation appears necessary. By contrast, if the resources desired are specific and diverse (I.2), held by a few potential trading partners (II.2), who have diverse characteristics (III.2) and desire diverse products in exchange for their resources (IV.2), the summed score of 8 represents a complex market and the need for greater segmentation to assist exchanges.

Guidelines for Target Market Segmentation

  I. Resource desired from the task environment
   1. Homogeneous and general
   2. Diverse and specific
 II. Number of potential trading partners
   1. Many
   2. Few
III. Nature of potential trading partners
   1. Homogeneous
   2. Diverse
IV. Products desired by potential trading partners
   1. Uniform
   2. Varied

Benefits and Place

If the benefits, value, and behavioral outcome of job training are to enable the client to be employed with sufficient income, the intervention must consider where the client's life occurs. Is the place conducive to realizing the intervention's benefits of employment with a living wage? Or must changing place, relocation, be part of the intervention?

In market segmentation, physical, psychological, attitude, demographic, economic, and other social diversity; use patterns; cost efficiencies of segmenting; neglected segments; and preference differences are considered. Each segment should have relatively homogeneous traits in terms of its product response. If part of the segment responds differently to the product, it probably represents another TMS. The final target market segmentation represents a balance of the market's diversity and the economy or the affordability of more finite segmentation. Segments should be large enough to be served with a product economically and specific enough

to allow the product to be differentiated and individualized.

Technology is available to assist in segmentation. Geodemographic mapping data, discussed in the assessment chapters, allows for segmenting of target markets. Powell, Tapp, and Sparks (2007), after their examination of the technology's use, concluded that the use of geodemographics allows social marketers to tailor campaigns and interventions to segments of the population at "country, city, towns, ward, neighbourhood and street levels. . . . The first premise of social marketing is that these barriers must be understood before attempting to influence change. From a practical standpoint, geodemographic tools allow precise targeting of particularly vulnerable groups, which means resources can be precisely deployed to areas of most need" (p. 186).

Product

Products are tangible goods such as food, services such as counseling, and ideas such as non-discrimination or healthy lifestyles, developed by the agency or the professional (the marketer) and offered in exchange for the resources needed from the TMS (Andreasen, 2006; Bull, Posner, Ortiz, Beaty, Benton, Lin, Pals, & Evans, 2008; Fine, 1992; Kotler & Lee, 2008; Mbilinyi, Zegree, Roffman, Walker, Neighbors, & Edleson, 2008; Magill, & Abele, 2007). Product development seeks product mutability rather than immutability. Product *mutability* means that products are designed and adjusted to meet preferences of specific TMSs. The TMS is not forced to fit the product, but products are designed to meet the TMS's preferences. This is marketing's outside-inside philosophy, discussed earlier.

The product, as discussed earlier, may be an intangible, such as an opportunity for the TMS to fulfill a certain ideology or value. The aim of the promoter of the idea, such as conservation or good parenting behavior, is the adoption not only of the idea but also of the behaviors resulting from it. The product for the target market is the end results of the behaviors flowing from the idea—a better environment or safer, healthier children (Cork, 2008; Kotler & Roberto, 1989, p. 140). Even more tangible products, such as counseling services, training, or case management, are designed to produce behaviors from the TMS. However, as has been constantly emphasized, the primary consideration of product design is the product's capacity to provide value to a TMS, as judged by that segment.

Product Management. After market segmentation, the agency or professional must engage in *product management.* This entails selecting the criteria by which target segments and consumers will be selected, designing the products, positioning the products in the market, and providing an appropriate mix of products for different segments.

The product design component should consider and balance the following criteria (Fine, 1992, pp. 40–41):

Specificity: Products are designed to meet the needs and preferences of a specific TMS. Generic product labels such as *counseling* or *psychotherapy* are too broad and assume little differentiation in the TMS's needs and preferences.

Flexibility: Product designs are adaptable to changing markets and TMS preferences.

Attainability: Products are designed within the limits of an agency's or professional's assets and strengths.

Competitive advantage: Products are built on strengths and emphasize that the marketer's qualities are not possessed by the competitors.

Care must be exercised in product development to avoid the pitfalls of a product orientation discussed earlier. If we become enamored of our products at the expense of consumers' preferences, we may not gain the resources desired

from the TMS. A consumer orientation and awareness of what consumers prefer and are actually receiving facilitates marketing. What an agency believes it is delivering may differ from the products it really produces and delivers. An example is an agency dealing with unruly behavior of students. The agency may believe that the product is counseling and therapy to provide the students with insight into their unruly behavior. However, the product received by the student is rooted in the student's satisfaction with it and its value to the student. If the student neither seeks nor receives insight, the product received by the student is different from the one the agency seeks to deliver. The product received by the student may be an hour spent with the counselor out of the classroom or playground and gaining a reputation as a tough guy or girl. The student will appraise this hour's gains and loses compared to alternative uses and costs of the time.

The product delivered is defined by the providers; the product received is defined by the preferences of, use by, and value to the recipient. In the case of mandatory therapy for spouse abusers, the court, the agency, and the professional therapist may view the product delivered as therapy to help abusers alter their behavior. However, the abusers may view the product received, especially if they do not want to alter their behavior, as a way to avoid imprisonment and meet any requirements set by the court to continue a relationship with their spouses. These spouse abusers will expend only enough resources to achieve their preferences. Exchanges are more likely to occur, as Box 11.2 indicates, when both sides get their preferences met.

Product Positioning. Product positioning is the location, or position, the marketer seeks for its

---

BOX 11.2.	Marketer and Target Market Segment Exchanges

ARE PROMOTED WHEN: The resources and behaviors that the marketer wants from the TMS match the resources of and behaviors within the TMS's capacity, with the TMS's benefits sought and value preferences matching the marketer's product benefits better than competitors as evaluated by the TMS.	ARE IMPEDED WHEN: The resources and behaviors wanted by the marketer from the TMS don't match the TMS's resources and behaviors are not within its capacity, or the benefits wanted and value preferences don't match the marketer's product benefit better than competitors as evaluated by the TMS.

products in terms of the TMSs: intended consumers, clients, or users. The market position is the niche the product occupies in satisfying some segment of the range of potential TMSs. The community mental health agency, discussed earlier, that is trying to develop and implement a therapeutic service to adults abused as children and now suffering from anxiety, is positioning itself in the market. It is pursuing a particular TMS and has designed a particular service to meet the preferences of this segment. The design of its services and the hours offered will not meet the preferences of all adults or even of all adults who want mental health services, but these need to meet the preferences of a particular TMS.

The TMS's *image* of the product and the marketer (the producer) is an important ingredient in market position. *Image* is the way a product is viewed by the TMS in meeting its preferences. A marketer may view the product as meeting certain needs, but if the segment does not share that image, there will not be exchanges. An agency's personnel may believe its counseling is helpful and not stigmatizing, but the critical image is the TMS's (potential clients) view of counseling. Their view, or product image, will determine the exchange (Stern, 1990; Table 11.4).

Marketing Mix. The *marketing mix* is the number and kinds of products matched to the number and kinds of TMSs and prices charged to the TMSs. Weinberg (1984) describes the marketing mix for nonprofit agencies as the "maximization of the amount of products or services which are consumed or utilized, subject to the amount of revenues and donations being at least equal to the cost of providing the service" (p. 269). The marketing mix results from determining the product preferences of the selected TMSs, designing the products, and pricing them appropriately.

Price

Price is a significant factor in product management. *Price* is the total contribution and cost required of the TMS in money, time, energy, effort, psychic costs, social costs, and lifestyle changes in exchange for the product and its benefits. The price needs to be competitive with the prices of alternative products and benefits available to the TMS. Although the marketer determines price, to a degree, the TMS, not the marketer, decides the value received. *Value received*, the satisfaction received relative to price compared to competing commodities and their value and price, will guide the TMS in product selection. The marketer must, in the long run, keep the monetary price equal to or above the costs of producing, promoting, and distributing the products, and the value above the price to the TMS in comparison to alternative uses of the price by the TMS. It's the value the TMS receives that ultimately will regulate product exchange and use. A TMS's willingness to *pay a price* is a function of its capacity to pay and the price compared to benefits. It is this subjective meaning of price that is important and will determine completion of the exchange.

> Value = Benefits – Price

An exercise video has a fiscal price, but it also has a social and personal price if its benefits are obtained. The monetary price may be a few dollars, or it can be borrowed from a library or from a friend, but the benefits are not free and depend on paying the social and personal price of devoting time, effort, and energy and altering a lifestyle to the exercises. There is a psychic price of admitting that one needs to exercise and the risk to self-image of not exercising after recognizing the need. A healthy diet has a fiscal price, often lower than the price of an unhealthy diet, but the

Table 11.4. Product Image and Position

Marketer's Questions for Target Market Segment's (TMS) Image of Agency (Marketer) and Product
1. How does the marketer wants its image to be seen by the TMS?
2. What is the TMS's image of each?
3. How can we determine the images held by the TMS?
4. How satisfied is the marketer with the images held by the TMS?
5. How do the images held by the TMS promote exchanges?
6. What factors help or hinder changes in the images held by the TMS?
7. What are strategies for changing the images held by the TMS?

Table 11.5. Mental Health Counseling Benefits and Costs

Benefits	Costs
• Healthier self-concept • Improved social functioning • Potentially greater longevity • Possible improved status, depending on view of therapy • Attention of a concerned, caring person • Possibly pleasant activity	• Monetary cost of therapy process • Time expended in preparation for and going to, from, and in therapy and in any behavioral change processes • Energy and effort of going to, from, and in the therapy and behavioral change processes • Lifestyle changes of any effects of therapy • Possible stigma associated with therapy

social and personal price may often preclude its benefits. The enjoyment and benefits of a healthy lifestyle and a healthy diet are evaluated by the potential consumer in comparison with the prices of giving up the fatty foods with their stronger, more satisfying tastes and ease of preparation. Similar costs-to-benefits comparisons can be made with mental health counseling (Table 11.5).

A marketer needs to appraise prices and meanings to potential users and look for ways to reduce price or improve benefits. Again, market research is critical here. Remember, value is a function of price as well as benefits. Increasing benefits or lowering price or both can add further value to the TMS and produce exchanges. The mental health counseling marketer needs to ensure delivery of counseling's benefits, not just the counseling, and devote attention to lowering costs in order to increase value for the user.

Pricing is a critical component of regulating demand. For example, a long waiting list may indicate underpricing of an agency's services, while idle time for the service providers indicate overpricing or no market. With pricing and the target market, it is generally more attractive to the target market to lower price than to raise it, especially in a competitive market. Fine (1992) states, "The key to pricing is to build in value into the product and price it accordingly" (p. 42).

Nonprofit social agencies and their staffs often view their products (services) as "free goods" to their clients if the clients do not pay a monetary price. Donors or the government rather than clients customarily pay the monetary costs of the agency's services. However, the clients pay a social price. A *social price* is the non-monetary price paid by the purchasers (the clients). Social prices are common in the use of

social agency and professional services and products even when there are no direct monetary costs, and the marketer should consider them in developing a pricing policy. There are four common types of social price: time, energy or effort, lifestyle, and psyche (Fine, 1992).

Types of Social Prices. Time prices include the time the user spends in receiving, using, and obtaining the benefits from the product. It is the time the purchaser devotes to making the exchange and receiving the product's value. There are four elements of time price:

1. *Direct time price*, or the time spent going to and from the place of the exchange and the time spent there waiting to make the exchange. Examples of direct time price in a counseling situation include the time spent getting to the counselor's office, waiting for the counselor, and the participating in the counseling session.

2. Beyond the direct time price, such as the time spent in counseling or training, there is the *performance time*, the time required to learn and carry out the desired social behavior. This might include stress reduction exercises or other behaviors that are part of the intervention.

3. Another element of time price is the *flexibility/fixity of time*, or whether the exchange and the behavior can be carried out when the client prefers or must be done on a fixed schedule. Other aspects of flexibility/fixity relate to frequency (how often the social behavior must be performed to be effective), the regularity of the social behavior required, and how long it must be performed.

4. The last factor is *disruption/simultaneity*, or to what extent the social behavior requires the

TMS to rearrange its current time preferences. Can the social behavior be done at the same time as other behaviors, in conjunction with other behaviors, or with little disruption to other preferred behaviors?

Services and products that have little time flexibility and high time demand compared with alternative uses of time and alternative products carry a higher price and may not be used by clients. This is especially true if the clients, such as those in a particular form of therapy, perceive little value received from the time investment compared with alternative uses of time in meeting their preferences. The time price of therapy to a client includes the time spent in therapy sessions, the time required to get to and from the therapist's office, the time spent waiting there, the rigidity of the therapy hours, how convenient the sessions are for the client's schedule, and the time demanded outside the therapy to receive its benefits. The client's evaluation of benefits compared with price will include the time price. We make other exchange decisions, such as the selection of our bank or grocery store, based partially on time price, so it is reasonable to assume that clients consider time in their evaluation of social work interventions.

Effort and energy prices include the effort, both physical and emotional, required by the TMS to obtain benefits from the products compared with alternative available products, including doing nothing. For a client in therapy, the investment includes the effort and energy spent in the therapy, getting to and from the therapist's office, and energy demands outside the therapy to receive its benefits. The client's evaluation of benefits compared with price will include the energy price.

For those of us in poor physical shape, our physical condition generally is not a result of ignorance of how to get into shape or its potential physical and emotional benefits. It is not a function of money. It depends on our willingness to devote time and energy to getting into shape and making certain lifestyle changes. We remain flaccid and lethargic because it is less expensive, at least in the short run; it has a lower price in time, effort, and energy.

If the TMS or the individual exchange partner can obtain the same results—the same or

equivalent value as he or she perceives it—with little energy expenditure, exchange theory indicates that the more energy-saving alternative will be used. If a training program enrollee believes he or she will remain unemployed after conclusion of a training program or perceives no greater benefits from employment than from unemployment, the enrollee probably will not pay the price of time and energy to succeed in the training program. The expected value (no job) is similar whether the enrollee participates with either a high or low expenditure of time and energy. Rationality urges the enrollee to save the time and energy.

Lifestyle prices are the changes the TMS must make in lifestyle to use and receive value from the products. Lifestyle price recognizes that in the exchange, the TMS is required to give up certain aspects of life that are rewarding in order to use the product and produce the desired effects. Willingness to pay the lifestyle price is related to the value placed on the gains received by using the product or engaging in the service and the belief that the product or services will produce these gains. Older persons returning to college for a graduate social work degree must alter their lives when they re-enter school. They must give up time with family and friends for classes and study and often must lower their standard of living as they cut back on work to allow class and study time and to pay for tuition and books. Their willingness to do so is predicated on the belief that it is the price they must pay to receive the future benefits of a master's degree in social work. Clients often must make lifestyle changes that may represent costs to them in order to receive benefits from the intervention. Their willingness to pay the price is a function of their valuation of the current or future benefits received from the lifestyle change.

Psyche price is any emotional cost in self-esteem and self-image the TMS pays in using the products. The older social work graduate student is now back in a student role after perhaps having been a competent professional, perhaps a supervisor or administrator, a parent, and a mature, responsible adult. This return to the student role may impose psyche costs. To take another example, if a client believes that mental illness is a weakness and a stigma, and that mental health treatment is a public recognition or assignment of the stigma, the use of treatment carries a psyche price and will be considered in the client's valuation of the treatment. It is the client's valuation that determines the psyche price, not the agency's or the public's. If the client perceives no greater stigma with treatment than he or she currently suffers, there is no increase in psyche price.

Agency marketers wanting to increase product demand can look for ways to reduce the social prices. Conversely, an increase in social prices will reduce demand and clients' use of a service.

Social price needs to be distinguished from *social cost* and *public price. Social cost* is the cost imposed on the community by the product and the exchange. It is the externalities of the exchange beyond the costs and benefits to the marketer and the exchange partner. A homeless shelter or community-based psychiatric housing center can be perceived by the surrounding neighborhood as having a social cost that the neighborhood, rather than the center, its staff, and clients, pays (Zippay & Lee, 2008). *Public price* is the price paid by the public for the product.

Market Segmentation Approach to Social Pricing

1. Identify relevant publics or TMSs, such as clients, funders, and legitimizers, from the community assessment, market research, and probing.
2. Identify social marketing approaches and mechanisms to bring about social exchanges and social change (products) for the TMS.
3. Assess the perceived prices, including the social prices of time, energy, lifestyle, and psyche, paid by the TMS using market research.
4. Construct a segmentation matrix of product, price, place, and promotion for the TMS.
5. Rank the TMS on its acceptance of the price using market research.
6. Examine possible ways to reduce perceived price and increase value of the product to the TMS by altering the product to meet the TMS's preferences, reduce time demands, increase time flexibility, and reduce effort, lifestyle, and psyche costs.

7. Determine specific pricing programs and strategies to encourage the TMS to replace his or her present behavior or products with the marketer's products.

Place

Successful market strategies require developing viable mechanisms and places for exchanges to occur. *Place* includes the social characteristics of the physical location where the exchanges occur, along with the associated social prices, convenience, credibility, and legitimacy of the place to the TMS (Shapiro, 1977, p. 110). The physical facilities, immediate environment, and, as Moore (1993) indicates, the paths and routes consumers and exchange partners take to get to the products, access services, and make exchanges are factors associated with place. Winston (1986) states, "The place component . . . consists of the characteristics of service distribution, modes of delivery, location, transportation, availability, hours and days opened, appointment (requirements), parking, waiting time, and other access considerations" (p. 15).

Place is intimately related to price, especially social price, and to promotion. The marketer (agency or professional) should try to facilitate exchanges by making the place for exchange—the physical facility and its environment, its ease of access, and its comfort level—compatible to the exchange partner's preferences. Does it add to the TMS's financial, time, effort, lifestyle, or psyche prices or to the sense of benefits received? Can the prices associated with place be reduced? A central location can make exchange easier; a more remote one can affect client flow.

Place has a series of prices or costs to the marketer: The facility has a price such as rent, taxes, equity costs, utilities, and maintenance. There is a cost of delivering services to clients in their location. Place also has a range of prices to the TMS in fiscal and social prices: location, treatment by staff, dignity of service, safety of the social and physical environment, confidentiality.

> Benefits of place to TMS – Prices of place to TMS = Value of place to TMS

Place, however, in the social services exchanges goes beyond a narrow conception of place as an office or service facility. As with social products and social goals and objectives—goals beyond a fiscal profit—the conception and meaning of place expand. The purpose of the social work exchange is (a) for the marketer to obtain resources from the TMS, (b) for the marketer to achieve behavioral objectives other than profit, and (c) for the TMS to obtain benefits beyond the tangible or intangible services received in an office, and this is more complex than just the office or physical facility. The concept of place includes where the bottom-line behaviors occur. For a TMS, place is both where the segment exchanges its resources for the product's benefits and values and where the segment receives any benefits and value. The marketer's evaluation of place and its impact on product consideration of place appraises the product's benefits received within a particular TMS's social environment.

If the place where the client is to demonstrate the bottom-line behaviors inhibits the behaviors or requires too high a price in the client's estimation, the likelihood of achieving this objectives is low. Drug treatment in high-drug-use environments is notoriously unsuccessful. The practitioner/marketer needs to alter the place to be conducive to achieving the behavioral objectives.

The marketer can influence the value of place to a TMS and individuals constituting a TMS by (a) determining the price and benefits of the place as perceived by a TMS and (b) working to lower the price and improving the benefits as perceived by a TMS. This will increase the TMS's estimation of value.

Place, when possible, should add to rather than distract from the product's value. The place also communicates to the potential exchange partner the marketer's evaluation of the partner. Dingy waiting rooms where clients' confidentiality is not respected and where clients are kept waiting for hours add to the product's price. The value of the product has increase to compensate for the price of place.

Promotion

Promotion, marketing's last *P* task, is the agency's or professional's communication of information to the appropriate TMSs. Promotion information conveys (a) the product's qualities, (b) how the product will meet the market segment's preferences, (c) its price, and (d) the places and processes of exchange. Promotion goes far beyond advertising: it includes *all* messages, verbal, visual, and social, that the marketer, agency, and professional communicate to a TMS regarding their views of a TMS and the value and benefits of a TMS to the agency and professional.

Effective promotion motivates its targets "to take specific action and promises a desirable benefit if they do" (Stern, 1990, p. 74). An agency's or professional's office and waiting room, behavior toward clients, and the demeanor of all those in contact with clients all communicate the value the agency or professional assigns to clients, the agency's products, and the products' capacity to meet clients' preferences.

Communication involves language and its meaning, symbols and their meaning, the medium of communication, and all the formal and informal ways of receiving and sending information used by clients and potential clients. It helps a TMS construct the marketer's vision of a TMS's reality. Effective promotion requires "de-massification" of U.S. culture in formal and informal communication and the use of symbols (Halter, 2000). The targets of promotion need to understand the meaning of the message. This, in turn, necessitates that the marketer understands what defines and determines meaning to a target market, both in content and context of messages. Context shapes the meaning of content. The same message in terms of words, construction, and syntax, heard over the radio while commuting home from work or from a telemarketer interrupting dinner, is received differently and probably has different meaning.

Different TMSs require different communications and venues shaped to carry the desired message to each market segment. Rothman and his colleagues (Rothman, 1980; Rothman, Teresa, Kay, & Morningstar, 1983) consider the need for differences in communication and promotion in their discussion of the diffusion of the results of social research and development (social R & D). Diffusion, in Rothman's social R & D model, is basically promotion and dissemination of the products—the findings of the social R & D—such as new knowledge or skills in ways that the Social R&D consumer can evaluate and use the findings. Social R & D itself is an outside-inside marketing strategy, because it starts with a client's problem or need.

Promotion can be mass promotion with low or high intensity. An example of low-intensity diffusion and promotion is advertising to a general, unsegmented target market. High-intensity promotion is targeted, individualized, personalized, and often with direct contact with the recipients of the communication.

Communication strategies and techniques used to reach potential clients include feeding information into client networks and support systems, providing key informants with information and using other word-of-mouth techniques, and holding community forums and special events for target client groups. Once clients or other TMSs begin the exchange process, communication is generally high intensity.

Information and Communication Technology. TMSs use a variety of information resources. Information technology (IT) and communication technology (CT) are increasingly becoming major information sources, although television, radio, and television are still the larger sources. Newspapers often are read over the Internet or on electronic devices (Loechner, 2010; Pew Research Center, 2006). Technologies such as social networking, listservs and e-mails, and Web sites and blogs have successfully been used in social marketing. The IT and CT use needs to be part of an overall promotion campaign and targeted to appropriate user audiences (Peattie, 2007). Some potential target markets segments, such as the elderly, the isolated, and socially marginalized, are still offline and use IT and CT to a limited degree or not at all. Others may simply prefer to lead non-technological lives.

Promotion and Client Empowerment. *Client empowerment* and *self-determination* require providing the client with the maximum information on product, prices, and potential benefits and risks to enable the client to make a truly informed decision (Box 11.3). This is the essence of good promotion: communicating with the client and potential clients and other potential stakeholders so they can make informed decisions. It is a requisite for genuine informed consent.

Public Relations and Public InformationAny time the agency or professional (the marketer) deals with any actual or potential TMSs, it is engaging in public relations. The publics can be clients, prospective staff, donors, potential or current supporters of the agency, legitimation sources, and potential volunteers. Kotler and Andreasen (1987) define public relations as the image-building function that evaluates the attitudes of important publics, identifies the policies and procedures of an individual or organization with regard to the public interest, and executes a program of activities to earn understanding and acceptance by these publics. Sometimes a short definition is given, which says that PR stands for *performance* plus *recognition* (pp. 576–577).

While recognizing the overlap between the concepts, Brawley (1983) distinguishes public relations from public education. Public relations are "efforts intended to interpret the characteristics, functions, and activities of human service workers to the general public or particular segments of it" (p. 12). Public education, as Brawley uses the concept, has less precise targets and is more akin to staging, general image building, and educating on general social condition: "Public education is . . . the provision of information to the general public or a given audience about social issues, social problems, categories of people with special needs, appropriate and inappropriate collective or individual responses to particular problems or needs, the functions of specific human service programs, and needs for new or changed social policies or programs" (p. 12).

BOX 11.3.	Questions for True Informed Consent in Promotion

1. How should different cultural, ethic, and socio-economic TMSs affect the content and context of messages?
2. Does informed consent require communication of all benefits, all prices (including all social pric-

es), and all risks?
3. Should social and psychological interventions require the same warning labels about possible risks and side effects as do physical and pharmacological interventions?

Developing and Assessing Communication

1. What is the specific public or TMS with which the agency or professional wants to develop an exchange relationship? Are there any special circumstances and traits—location, demographic characteristics, boundaries, other factors—that affect communication?
2. What is the exchange—the benefits offered to and responses sought from the TMS? What specific actions or responses are sought from the TMS?
3. How does the TMS obtain its information? What are the information sources and venues—specific print media, television (specific programs and times), IT and CT technologies of internet, Twitter, Internet, word of mouth, information and opinion leaders—used by the TMS? What level and intensity of information is sought or required in order to make an exchange?
4. What information is needed by the TMS to make a decision? What specific information is required by the TMS to perform the desired behavior and engage in the exchange? What are the specific benefits to the TMS? What is the price to the TMS?
5. How will the agency or professional know that an exchange has occurred—that is, that the TMS has received the desired product and the agency has received the desired behavior and resources in return? What are the feedback mechanisms?

Public relations and education are exercises in communication. As with all communication, the message sender's tasks are to determine whether (a) the message reached the intended target (b) in the manner intended, (c) in a way that the target can understand and respond (d) in the way the sender intended, (e) to produce the outcome behavior desired by the sender, and (e) in a way that will allow the sender to know that the desired outcome behavior by the target has occurred. The communication management task is to have the message reach the target in a timely fashion in the manner intended with the content intended.

Good formal communication as part of promotion has the following characteristics: (a) brevity—it is only as long as needed, (b) appeal—it focuses on the possible positive outcome in the exchange, and (c) honesty—it provides honest information about the product, price, and place. Messages and communication, to repeat the earlier discussion, go beyond advertisements and formal communication to include all the interactions between the TMS and the agency or marketer.

Readability. A challenge in developing written and verbal messages is assessing the educational level required to understand the message. A message's educational appropriateness is important if a message is to convey meaning.[5] There are several ways to assess readability. Perhaps the best way is to field test the message with a representative sample or focus group of a message's target audience. These methods suffer from the expense of developing the inventory of the target population, constructing the sample or focus group, field testing a message, and repeating the process until an appropriate message level is developed.

There are many computer and Internet readability software programs to calculate the readability level of written messages.[6] The message is entered into the software or program and then assessed for the readability grade level [6]necessary to comprehend it. The basis for the readability calculation programs is contained in a do-it-yourself methodology, the SMOG Readability Formula (Office of Cancer Communication, 1992, p. 77).

SMOG Calculation

1. Take the beginning, approximate middle, and last 10 sentences of the message, for a total of 30 sentences, and count the number of polysyllabic words (words with three or more syllables). A sentence occurs when the phrase ends in a period, question mark, or exclamation mark, even though it may not be grammatically a complete sentence. The intent is to obtain a representation of the total message. Random sampling to obtain the 30 sentences from all sentences can be done, although this is probably spurious precision.
2. Consider numbers, whether written or numeric, abbreviations such as *etc.*, and hyphenated words to have their spoken number of syllables. For example, *192* has six syllables and *etc.* has four syllables. Hyphenated words are counted as one word.

3. Compute the square root of the number of polysyllabic words in the 30-sentence sample to the nearest whole square root. For example, the square root of 193 is 13.89 and the nearest whole square root is 14. The square root and nearest whole square root of 9 is 3. The square root of 10 is 3.16, and the nearest whole square root is 3.

4. Add a constant of 3 to the square root, and the sum is the minimum educational level, within 1.5 grade levels, necessary to understand the message. The 1.5 grade levels is the possible error range.

For example, if a 30-sentence message contains 60 polysyllabic words, the computation of the readability level is as shown in Box 11.4.

This message would be appropriate for someone with an 11th-grade reading level, although the error range indicates that it might be readable by someone with as low as a 9.5 grade reading level or would perhaps require a reading level of 12.5 years (that is, graduation from high school and some college). With a TMS that has a general reading level of 10.0, given the error range, the marketer probably should lower the readability level. This can be done by lowering the number and ratio of polysyllabic words per sentence.

Messages with fewer than 30 sentences can be converted into a format appropriate to SMOG by dividing the total number of polysyllabic words by the total number of sentences in the message and multiplying the results by 30. This will provide the adjusted number of polysyllabic words. The adjusted product is then entered into Step 1 of the calculations and the remaining steps are completed. For example, if a communication has 15 polysyllabic words in eight sentences, the

following calculation converts the data into a format appropriate for a SMOG calculation:

$$\text{Total number of polysyllabic words used} = 15/8 = 1.875 \times 30 = 56.25 \text{ adjusted number of polysyllabic words}$$

The 1.875 is multiplied by 30 and the product is the likely number of polysyllabic words the message would have if it were 30 sentences. The adjusted total number of polysyllabic words is entered into the computation procedures as shown in Box 11.5, with a resulting estimated readability level of 9.5 to 11.5.

SMOG, as all the readability calculations, provides a rough approximation of readability level. Complexity and hence readability are judged by the complexity of words, with polysyllabic words assumed to be more complex, and sentence structure. SMOG assumes that a message with long, complex sentences is likely to contain more polysyllabic words than are ten short declarative sentences. These messages generally require more education to understand them. If a message yields a score above the minimum education level targeted, it probably is a good idea to rework the communication to use shorter declarative sentences and to avoid polysyllabic words where possible. For communication, it is better to have the message too simple than too complex.

SMOG's advantage is that it requires little time and expense when compared with alternative methods. No representative panels of the TMS are required. The time and expense of field testing are eliminated. No computer expertise is required. The costs for this assessment method are the costs of a calculator to compute the square roots (less than $10), the ability to count and recognize polysyllabic words and

BOX 11.4.	Readability Test Calculation Steps

Total number of polysyllabic words	60
Square root	7.75
Nearest whole square root	8
Addition of constant	3
Approximate minimum grade level	11
Approximate appropriate grade level range (1 or 2 1.5 grade levels)	9.5 to 12.5

BOX 11.5.	Readability Test Calculation Steps for Less Than 30 Sentences	
Total number of message sentences		8
Total number of polysyllabic words		15
Average number of polysyllabic words per sentence		1.85
Calculation adjustment $1.85 \times 30 =$		56.25
Adjusted number of polysyllabic words		56
Square root		7.5
Nearest whole square root		8
Addition of constant		3
Approximate minimum grade level		11
Approximate appropriate grade level range (1 or 2 1.5 grade levels)		9.5 to 12.5

sentences as defined by SMOG, and the time needed to count the sentences and polysyllabic words. SMOG's disadvantage, as with all readability calculation procedures, is that it provides only a crude approximation of the readability grade level.

The Use of Media. The media is used to reach TMSs, although the particular venue and media may differ for each segment. Newspapers and television are more viable for older TMSs and the IT and CT for young targets. When the media are used, they become exchange partners, and their needs, preferences, and operating procedures must be considered unless the exchanges are purely commercial. As with all exchanges, the marketer needs to increase the value and decrease the price for the exchange partner. The media respond to promotional efforts when they see gains.

The previously discussed general communication issues apply to the use of media. Communication should be focused, brief, and honest, with information provided in a manner to present the least work and cost to the venue (the reporter). The marketer should be available to the venue for any follow-up questions or if the reporter wishes to do a follow-up story. The journalistic criteria of the five Ws (*who, what, when, where,* and *why*) and sometimes the *H* (how) are reflected in the message and media releases (Rose, 1995):

1. *Who* are you; *who* is interested in the information (a TMS)?

2. *What* is the newsworthy event or occurrence of interest? *What* will be expected of a TMS? *What* will be the TMS's benefits?
3. *When* will the event occur?
4. *Where* will the event occur?
5. *Why* is the event and information important to a TMS?
6. *How* did the event come about?

Articles and releases should be written in a manner that involves the least work and cost to the venue. Venues should be surveyed and relationships developed with the appropriate editors and reporters to discover their preferred length, timing, style, and format.

Keeping a media information file on your computer or in a Rolodex or file box can be helpful (Rose, 1994). The file should contain the following information:

1. Names, addresses, and telephone numbers, including fax numbers and e-mail addresses, of the main media outlets and contacts in each outlet. If contacts are personalized, exchanges are helped.
2. Names, addresses, and telephone numbers, including fax numbers and e-mail addresses, if any, of the media outlets' decision makers, such as the editors and producers. Again, contacts in each outlet should be personalized.
3. Specific information about each outlet's news, information, and entertainment interests; special features; when published, circulated, or broadcast; target audiences, and which of

the marketer's TMSs this medium reaches, as well as the geographic audience radius.

4. Deadlines for news stories, feature stories, and columns in the print media, differing program types in radio and television, and blog connections and links.

5. A brief analysis of the successes and failures for each contact and venue.

Information on specific media venues can be obtained from the white pages and yellow pages of the telephone directory, media directories, and the Internet. Many outlets provide media kits. Rose, the *NASW News* columnist on marketing, emphasizes the use of smaller media outlets, "such as local weekly papers or community radio or television stations or programs. These are usually in need of material and may use just about anything you send them. They reach a smaller audience, but the coverage is free . . . this way is gravy" (Rose, 1994, p. 5). It is also often beneficial to hold media events such as press conferences, if there is significant timely news, and media receptions. Bloggers, the Internet, IT, and CT are an important part of the mix. The marketer needs to develop a focused blog and link it to other blogs and virtual social networks to get the message out. However, the success of media use is measured by whether the coverage communicates the intended message to the intended target audience and not by the amount of coverage or range of distribution.

Media Outlets. The following five media outlets are most useful:

1. *Print media:* Op-ed pieces, press releases, letters to the editor, feature stories, and information contacts with reporters and columnists are ways to use the print media as outlets. Human interest stories and case studies that grab the reader's attention and tell a compelling story are often preferred over statistics, although statistics may supplement the story. Magazines are often useful outlets for feature stories. Multiple letters to the editor by different writers stressing the same subject and message have a better chance of being published than a single letter. They generate media interest. Most newspapers and magazines publish only a small fraction of the letters they receive; *The New York Times*, for instance, publishes less than 5% of the letters it receives (Zane, 1995).

2. *Television:* Talk and interview shows, tabloid shows, cable and public access TV, news shows with visuals and sound bites, and public service announcements provide opportunities for communication through television.

3. *Radio:* Using call-in and talk shows, public service announcements, interview shows, buying radio time or having a regular time-slot show on a problem area (all it takes is a sponsor), news shows, and crafting sound bites are tactics for radio use. Multiple calls and callers will probably be required for the call-in and talk shows. Generally the talk shows screen calls and limit repeat callers within a given time period. The producers also screen calls to be supportive of the host or sometimes serve as a convenient foil.

4. *Electronic bulletin board, blogs, and social networks:* These emerging venues are gaining wider use as communication approaches. They are useful in reaching particular target audiences, especially, but not limited to, younger audiences (Antz & Cooke, 2007; Barstow, 2010; Lin & Huffman, 2005).

5. *Volunteers:* Volunteers, in addition to providing personnel resources, are a promotional and linking mechanism, as described in Chapter 10. They link the marketer to a range of networks (Musick & Wilson, 2008). Sources of volunteers include business firms, service clubs, "helping hand" programs in schools, and student internship programs in college departments such as business, journalism, communications, and social work. These volunteers talk about their positive and negative experiences in other aspects and networks of their lives. A popular Baltimore radio columnist and commentator on business investments and financial matters regularly volunteers at a homeless meals center and often talks about his volunteer experiences on his radio show. After his radio talks, donations and volunteers to the center increase for a short time. This is valuable free promotion for the center.

Media and Social Marketing. It is risky to rely solely on journalists and the media as intermediaries to get information out, for staging, and for public education and social marketing for any cause and organization. Reporters and bloggers are professional skeptics, gadflies, and can't be counted on to convey a particular message in the way intended by the marketer. Generally political conservatives are more advanced in applying staging techniques, strategies, and tactics: they have more corporate monies to sponsor staging campaigns, their corporate base has a history in the use of unethical marketing tactics, and their sense of moral righteousness has persuaded them that their ends justify any immoral means; also they have greater media control through increasing direct ownership and through advertising monies. The right often uses religious and patriotic rhetoric and values in the pursuit of material and political goals. Compare the new coverage of the ACORN's scandal with that of the *reporters* who helped create the scandal and subsequently broke into a U.S. senator's office.

The print media, television, and radio broadcasting are becoming more consolidated under a handful of corporate owners, some, like Fox News, with active conservative agendas (Carter & Ruterberg, 2002; Miller, 2002; Wyatt, 2010). The media use of polling is suspect: many of the polls fall into the category of "push-polls," which direct the respondent to an "acceptable" answer. Forced-choice wording, preselected questions and answers, and limited response categoriesemphasize reliability as *scientific*, and sacrifice validity. Often polls shape opinion as much as they reflects it (Blow, 2010; Mooney, 2003; Krosnick, 2010). Greenberg (1999) prophetically wrote on the Clinton health care proposal:

[P]ublic opinion research in the hands of political consultants is a tool for shaping public opinion. Sophisticated measurement techniques tap core values, prejudicial fears, and optimistic hopes, in an effort to discover how to sway, persuade, and convert. … The decline in support for health care reform is instructive in this regard. The invocation of "more bureaucracy" and "more government" by Republican policymakers and other opponents of (health care) reform contributed to a rightward shift away from the Clinton plan. … rather than reflecting the public's shallow commitment, declining support for health care reform rested precisely on the calculated understanding by the Republicans and the insurance industry that Americas are ambivalent on whether the government should be involved in health care—and, if so, to what degree. Public opinion, therefore, reflects the preferences and biases of the political class as much as it reflects the public's own desires. (p. 57)

However, media coverage advocacy has an impact on policymakers and the public (Box 11.6). Many social marketers supplement their media efforts with advertisements and purchased media space and time. This increases the marketer's control, although it doesn't have a news article's or TV spot's credibility (West & Francis, 1996).

Marketing: A Summary. Marketing is a philosophy and strategy of service development and delivery and an approach to expediting exchanges. Marketing starts and ends with the TMSs and attempts to promote exchanges by meeting the preferences of these segments. Marketing is compatible with social work ethics and the values of client self-determination, starting where the client is, client and community empowerment, and client advocacy.

Marketing in the social and health services is effective. The literature is replete with success stories in health (Jenkins & Scott, 2007; Kohr, Strack, Newton-Ward, & Cooke, 2008; Meyer, Brun, Yung, Clasen, Cauley, & Mase, 2004; Moulding, 2007; Newton-Ward, 2007), AIDS (Conner, Takahashi, Ortiz, Archuleta, Muniz, & Rodriguez, 2005; Darden, 2006), drugs (Powell, Tapp, & Sparks, 2007), and a range of other behavior changes (Boehm & Freund, 2007;

BOX 11.6.   Media Advocacy in Staging

Media reporting and advocacy ⟹ Influence on policymakers ⟹ Media reporting policymakers' response ⟹ Public opinion shaped by reports ⟹ Policymakers respond to public opinion ⟹ Media report policymakers' response ⟹ Public opinion shaped ⟹ Policymakers respond with social policy.

Boehm & Itzhaky, 2004; Cork, 2008; Evans, 2008; Kirkwood & Hudnall, 2006; Zippay & Lee, 2008). When marketing success was limited, it was attributed to inadequate market research and marketing strategy, lack of segmentation, poor choice of venue and promotion methods, and lack of resources for adequate follow-through (Bull, Posner, Ortiz, Beaty, Benton, Lin, Pals, & Evans, 2008; Darrow & Biersteker, 2008; De Gruchy & Coppel, 2008; Olshefsky, Zive, Scolari, & Zuniga, 2007; Timmerman, 2007).

The Marketing Audit Guide[7]

1. **Mission Review** Does the organization have a written mission statement or bylaws that detail its mission? What are the mission and objectives? Are objectives stated as measurable, behavioral outcome terms? If no written mission statement and objectives exist, does the agency convey a mission and objectives to staff and other relevant publics? How does the organization determine success?

2. **Resources** What are the resources the agency needs to achieve its mission and objectives: fiscal, mandate and legitimacy, support systems' sanction, personnel, volunteers, tangible facilities, supplies, and equipment?

3. **Task Environment** Has the agency determined the resources it needs from its task environment to achieve its mission and objectives? What are the TMSs that have the necessary resources (publics, groups, organizations, agencies, and others)?

4. **New Markets** Are new TMSs needed for the agency to achieve or expand its mission? What are they? How can the agency locate and assess these TMSs for resources and preferences? Have other community-wide surveys been conducted by either the agency or some other group that can be used to assess the market?

5. **Communication** How does the agency communicate with each TMS? List the publics or markets that have known barriers to effective communication. What are the barriers? How are the needs and preferences of each TMS assessed? What is the agency's image with each TMS? Is the image the one desired by the agency?

6. **Referral Sources** List all organizations or individuals that refer patients/clients to the agency, starting with those that refer most often. Is the agency satisfied with its communication and with the results of the referral network? How does the agency provide feedback to referral sources? Are they satisfied with the feedback? What is the annual turnover, if any, of referral sources? Are the reasons for this turnover known? What changes or shifts in clients/patients have affected referrals?

7. **Clients** What are the products for each client TMS? What are the services, broken down into the smallest complete components? What is their value to the TMS? What client preferences do they meet? What is the price to the TMS? What do clients exchange for the products? How does the agency obtain information on the TMS? What does the agency do with the information it receives from clients or patients? Is the agency satisfied with its communication with clients and potential clients? What is the agency's image with clients? Is the image different from the agency's intended image?

Which current services and products bring the agency the most income and other resources? The least? How do the resources exchanged by the client TMS help the agency meet its objectives?

8. **Competition** List all known and potential competitors of the agency by resources sought; include size of staff, ownership, services, service area, fees, caseload, size, and annual growth rate. Describe the one agency or group that is thought to be the chief competitor. How can this competition be met? Compare the agency's fees and other social prices with those of similar organizations; are they comparable and competitive, higher or lower?

9. **Market Management** Does the agency have a spokesperson? If yes, who is that person and what is the position's title? Is there an agency public relations director or a person responsible for public relations? Is there an agency marketing director or a person responsible for overall marketing direction? Do all agency staff members understand their functions as agency representatives, spokespeople, and marketers? Is there

a board public relations committee and a marketing committee? Do all board members understand their functions as agency representatives, spokespeople, and marketers? If the agency has not had marketing research or planning, how have user needs been determined in order to expand existing services or add new ones?

10. Promotional and Public Information Strategies Does the agency have a written press relations policy? Where is it located and how is it used? Do all agency members understand it? How has the policy benefited the organization in the past 2 years? How were benefits determined? Does the agency have a brochure or other written information for distribution that explains the agency's mission, objectives, and services? When was the material last revised? Which TMSs get the material? Is it adapted to meet the needs, interests, and preferences of the specific TMSs that get the brochure? Does the agency have an internal newsletter or publication, an external newsletter or publication, direct-mail operations for fundraising and information distribution, a regular news release program, a newspaper clipping service, a radio or television news recording service, radio and television public service announcements (PSAs)? Which benefits and products are covered in the radio and television PSAs? To which publics are the radio and TV PSAs directed? Are representatives of any TMSs consulted in preparing the public information program? Which TMSs are consulted and why?

Does the agency have policies and protocols for press releases? Which of the following do press releases address: new personnel (particularly managers or department heads), new services, new equipment, revised policies, procedures, special events, recruitment of employees and volunteers, financial and statistical data, and feature and human interest stories promoting the successes of the agency and its clients? How does the agency determine how well its purposes, objectives, problems, mission, and news distribution policy are understood by the news media?

Are annual reports published? If not, how does the agency direct the flow of information that normally is found in an annual report?

Does the agency have a speaker's bureau? Which publics are addressed in activities or promotion of the bureau? Which main messages are the agency's speakers conveying to audiences? What and who determines the subject matter of speeches? Does the agency hold community seminars, symposia, or lectures? Are volunteers, board members, and other auxiliary personnel used in community relations? How has the agency benefited from their activities?

Does the agency use print, radio, and television advertising? To which TMSs are these messages addressed? Do the ads bring the agency new clients or patients or other new markets? How is this determined?

Are all staff members involved in, or do they have the opportunity to participate in, promotions and make suggestions for improvement? Does management consider the suggestions?

11. Locating New Markets How does the agency find new TMSs—clients, fiscal and non-fiscal resource providers, other resources? Who is (are) designated to find new clients, referral sources, employees, and sources of funding? Is case finding an agency practice? Do auxiliary members or volunteers perform community relations, resource location, and case-finding functions for the agency? Does the organization attract or encourage walk-in users? If yes, how do such users discover the organization?

12. Agency Fees Does the agency have a fee structure? How do clients characterize the fee structure (acceptable, unacceptable, no opinion)? How is this determined? How is the fee structure communicated to current and potential clients? Does the agency convey an image that it can provide more free or reduced-fee care than it actually can deliver? How is this determined? What questions about fees do referral network representatives ask? How does the agency communicate the main points of its fees to its key TMSs? How often in the past 2 years has the agency raised its fees? How was this received by key TMSs? Was increased value perceived by the segments?

Notes

1. Retrieved February 17, 2010, from: http://www.huffingtonpost.com/2010/02/07/tim-tebow-super-bowl-ad-v_n_436383.html

2. For example: *The New York Times* (June 4, 2010), p. A11. Factually the disaster in the Gulf of Mexico was not a spill, but a malfunctioning offshore oil well.

3. See: SUPREME COURT OF THE UNITED STATES Syllabus: CITIZENS UNITED *v.* FEDERAL ELECTION COMMISSION APPEAL FROM THE UNITED STATES DISTRICT COURT FOR THE DISTRICT OF COLUMBIA No. 08–205. Decided January 21, 2010.

4. See: http://www.freedomworks.org/ for board of directors and sponsors of FreedomWorks.

5. Educational level is the comprehension capacity and not the formal education of a message's recipient. Comprehension can be above or below the formal education level of a recipient.

6. For example, see: http://www.standards-schmandards.com/exhibits/rix/, http://www.addedbytes.com/code/readability-score/, http://www.micropowerandlight.com/, http://www.editcentral.com/gwt1/EditCentral.html, among numerous others.

7. See Rubright and MacDonald (1981) for a more complete market audit form, questions, and discussion.

References

American Marketing Association (n.d.) MarketingPower. Retrieved June 11, 2010, from: http://www.marketingpower.com/AboutAMA/Pages/Statement%20of%20Ethics.aspx

Andreasen, A. R. (1984). Nonprofits: Check your attention to customers. In C. H. Lovelock & C. B. Weinberg (Eds.), *Public and nonprofit marketing: Cases and readings* (pp. 131–135). Palo Alto, CA: Scientific Press.

Andreasen, A. R. (1995). *Marketing social change: Changing behavior to promote health, social development, and the environment.* San Francisco, CA: Jossey-Bass.

Andreasen, A. R. (2004). A social marketing approach to changing mental health practices directed at youth and adolescents. *Health Marketing Quarterly,* 21(4), 51–75.

Andreasen, A. R. (2006). *Social marketing in the 21st century.* Thousand Oaks, CA: Sage Publications, Inc.

Anthony, R. N., & Young, D. W. (1988). Management control in nonprofit organizations (4th ed.). Homewood, IL: Richard D. Irwin.

Artz, N., & Cooke, P. (2007). Using e-mail listservs to promote environmentally sustainable behaviors. *Journal of Marketing Communications,* 13(4), 257–276.

Barstow, D. (2010, February 15). Tea Party lights fuse for rebellion on right. *The New York Times.* Retrieved February 17, 2010, from: http://www.nytimes.com/2010/02/16/us/politics/16teaparty.html

Blow, C. (2010, June 5). Gay? Whatever, Dude. *The New York Times,* p. A21.

Blumer, H. (1969). *Symbolic interactionism: Perspective and method.* Englewood Cliffs, NJ: Prentice Hall.

Boehm, A., & Freund, A. (2007). How using a marketing approach helps social work students to develop community projects successfully. *British Journal of Social Work,* 37(4), 695–714.

Boehm, A., & Itzhaky, H. (2004). The social marketing approach: A way to increase reporting and treatment of sexual assault. *Child Abuse and Neglect,* 28(3), 253–265.

Bradshaw, J. (1977). The concept of social need. In N. Gilbert & H. Specht (Eds.), *Planning for social welfare* (pp. 290–296). Englewood Cliffs, NJ: Prentice Hall.

Brawley, E. A. (1983). *Mass media and human services: Getting the message across.* Beverly Hills, CA: Sage.

Brooks, R. (2003). A nation of victims: Bush uses well-known linguistic techniques to make citizens feel dependent. *The Nation,* 276(25), 20–22.

Bryce, H. J., Jr. (1987). *Financial management for nonprofit organizations.* Englewood Cliffs, NJ: Prentice Hall.

Bull, S. S., Posner, S. F., Ortiz, C., Beaty, B., Benton, K., Lin, L., Pals, S. L., & Evans, T. (2008). POWER for reproductive health: Results from a social marketing campaign promoting female and male condoms. *Journal of Adolescent Health,* 43, 71–78.

Carter, B., & Rutenberg, J. (2002, November 13). Fox News head sent a policy note to Bush: back and forth on newsmen and advice to presidents. *The New York Times,* p. A12.

Conner, R. F., Takahashi, L., Ortiz, E., Archuleta, E., Muniz, J., & Rodriguez, J. (2005). The SOLAAR HIV prevention program for gay and bisexual Latino men: Using social marketing to build capacity for service provision and evaluation. *AIDS Education and Prevention,* 17(4), 361–374.

Cork, S. (2008). Beating the barriers to social marketing. *Social Marketing Quarterly,* 14(1), 37–49.

Darden, C. (2006). Promoting condoms in Brazil to men who have sex with men. *Reproductive Health Matters,* 14(28), 63–67.

Darrow, W. W., & Biersteker, S. (2008). Short-term impact evaluation of a social marketing campaign to prevent syphilis among men who have sex with men. *American Journal of Public Health,* 98(2), 337–343.

De Gruchy, J., & Coppel, D. (2008). "Listening to Reason": A social marketing stop-smoking campaign in Nottingham. *Social Marketing Quarterly,* 14(1), 5–17.

Dowie, M. (2002). A Teflon correspondent. *The Nation*, 274(1), 36–39.

Evans, W. D. (2008). Social marketing campaigns and children's media use. *The Future of Children*, 18(1), 181–203.

Enis, B. M. (1974). *Marketing principles: The management process.* Pacific Palisades, CA: Goodyear.

Fine, S. H. (1992). *Marketing the public sector: Promoting the causes of public and nonprofit agencies.* New Brunswick, NJ: Transaction.

Fox, K. A., & Kotler, P., (1987). The marketing of social causes: The first ten years. In P. Kotler, O. C. Ferrell, & C. W. Lamb (Eds.), *Strategic marketing for nonprofit organizations: Cases and readings* (3rd ed., pp. 14–29). Englewood Cliffs, NJ: Prentice Hall.

Germak, A. J., & Singh, K. K. (2010). Social entrepreneurship: Changing the way social workers do business. *Administration in Social Work*, 34(1), 79–95.

Goozner, M. (2002). Drug money: How PhRMA's front groups buy elections. *The American Prospect*, 13(19), 12–13.

Greenberg, A. (1999). Defending the "American People." *The Responsive Community: Rights and Responsibilities*, 9(4), 52–58.

Halter, M. (2000). *Shopping for identity: The marketing of ethnicity.* New York: Schocken Books.

Harden, B. (2001, June 12). In Virginia, young conservatives learn how to develop and use their political voices. *The New York Times*, p. A8.

Hogan, B. (2003, February). Pulling strings from afar: Drug industry finances nonprofit groups that claim to speak for older Americans. *AARP Bulletin*, 3–5.

Jenkins, M. W., & Scott, B. (2007). Behavioral indicators of household decision-making and demand for sanitation and potential gains from social marketing in Ghana. *Social Science & Medicine*, 64, 2427–2442.

Kearns, K. P. (2007). Faith-based and secular social service agencies in Pittsburgh. *Journal of Community Practice*, 14(4), 51–69.

Kennedy, S. S. (2003). *Charitable choice: First results from three states.* Indianapolis: Center for Urban Policy and the Environment, School of Public and Environmental Affairs, Indiana University–Purdue University Indianapolis.

Kirkwood, A. D., & Hudnall, S. B. (2006). A social marketing approach to challenging stigma. *Professional Psychology: Research and Practice*, (5), 472–476.

Kohr, J. M., Strack, R.W., Newton-Ward, M., & Cooke, C. H. (2008). The use of programme planning and social marketing models by a state public health agency: A case study. *Public Health*, 122, 300–306.

Kotler, P. (1971). *Marketing management* (2nd ed.). Englewood Cliffs, NJ: Prentice Hall.

Kotler, P. (1977). A generic concept of marketing. In R. M. Gaedeke (Ed.), *Marketing in private and public nonprofit organizations: Perspectives and illustrations* (pp. 18–33). Santa Maria, CA: Goodyear.

Kotler, P., & Andreasen, A. R. (1987). *Strategic marketing for nonprofit organizations* (3rd ed.). Englewood Cliffs, NJ: Prentice Hall.

Kotler, P., & Lee, N. R. (2008). *Social marketing: Influence behavior for good* (3rd ed.). Los Angeles, CA: Sage Publications.

Kotler, P., & Roberto, E. L. (Eds.). (1989). *Social marketing: Strategies for changing public behavior.* New York: Free Press.

Kranish, M. (2006, December 4). Democrats inspect faith-based initiative; 2 call for probe to determine use of taxes. *The Boston Globe.* Retrieved February 24, 2010, from http://www.boston.com/news/nation/washington/articles/2006/12/04/democrats_inspect_faith_based_initiative.

Krosnick, J. A. (2010, June 9). The climate majority. *The New York Times*, p. A21.

Kuczynski, A. (2002, December 15). Treating disease with a famous face. *The New York Times*, Section 9; 1, 15.

Lauffer, A. (1986). To market, to market: A nuts and bolts approach to strategic planning in human service organizations. *Administration in Social Work*, 10, 31–39.

Lee, J. F. (2003a, March 2). A call for softer, greener language: G.O.P. adviser offers linguistic tactics for environmental edge. *The New York Times*. p. 18.

Lee, J. F. (2003b, May 28). Exxon backs groups that question global warming. *The New York Times.* Retrieved June 6, 2010, from: http://www.nytimes.com/2003/05/28/business/worldbusiness/28EXXO.html?

LeFebvre, R. C., (2007). The new technology: The consumer as participant rather than target audience. *Social Marketing Quarterly*, 13(3), 31–42.

Lewin, T. (2001, May 20). 3 conservative foundations are in throes of change. *The New York Times*, p. 20.

Lin, C. A., & Hullman, G. (2005). Tobacco-prevention messages online: Social marketing via the web. *Health Communication*, 18(2), 177–193.

Liptak, A. (2010, June 9). Justices block matching funds for candidates in Arizona. *The New York Times*, p. A16.

Loechner, J. (2010). News right now drives newspaper readers to WEB. *MediaPost.* Center for Media Research. Retrieved June 17, 2010, from: http://www.mediapost.com/publications/?fa=Articles.showArticle&art_aid=121607

Lombardo, A. P., & Leger, Y. A. (2007). Thinking about "Think Again" in Canada: Assessing a social marketing HIV/AIDS prevention campaign. *Journal of Health Communication*, 12, 377–397.

Lovelock, C. H., & Weinberg, C. B. (1984). Public and nonprofit marketing comes of age. In C. H. Lovelock & C. B. Weinberg (Eds.), *Public and nonprofit marketing: Cases and readings* (pp. 33–42). Palo Alto, CA: Scientific Press.

Magill, J., & Abele, F. (2007). From public education to social marketing: The evolution of the Canadian Heritage Anti-Racism social marketing campaign. *Journal of Nonprofit & Social Marketing*, 17(1–2), 27–53.

Mbilinyi, L. F., Zegree, J., Roffman, R. A., Walker, D., Neighbors, C., & Edleson, J. (2008). Development of a marketing campaign to recruit non-adjudicated and untreated abusive men for a brief telephone intervention. *Journal of Family Violence*, 23, 343–351.

McNamara, C. (n.d.). *All about marketing*. Retrieved June 9, 2010, from: http://managementhelp.org/mrktng/mrktng.htm.

Meyer, C. L., Brun, C., Yung, B., Clasen, C., Cauley, K., & Mase, W. A. (2004). Evaluation of social marketing efforts designed to increase enrollment in the Children's Health Insurance Program (CHIP). *Journal of Nonprofit & Public Sector Marketing*, 12(2), 87–104.

Miller, M. C. (2002). What's wrong with this picture? *The Nation*. 274(1), 18–22.

Mooney, C. (2003). John Zogby's creative polls: And a closer look at his methods. *The American Prospect*, 14(2), 29–33.

Moore, S. T. (1993). Goal-directed change in service utilization. *Social Work*, 38, 221–226.

Moulding, N. T., (2007). "Love your body, move your body, feed your body": Discourses of self-care and social marketing in a body image health promotion program. *Critical Public Health*, 17(1), 57–69.

Musick, M. A., & Wilson, J. (2008). *Volunteers: A social profile*. Bloomington, IN: Indiana University Press.

Newman, B. I., & Sheth, J. N. (1987). *A theory of political choice behavior*. New York: Praeger.

Newton-Ward, M. (2007). North Carolina's social marketing matrix team: Using social marketing concepts to institutionalize social marketing capacity in a state health department. *Journal of Nonprofit & Public Sector Marketing*, 17(1–2), 55–82.

Office of Cancer Communication, National Cancer Institute. (1992). *Making health communication programs work: A planner's guide*. (NIH Publication No. 92–1493). Washington, DC: U.S. Government Printing Office. Retrieved June 13, 2003, from http://cancer.gov/pinkbook.

Olshefsky, A. M., Zive, M. M., Scolari, R., & Zuniga, M. (2007). Promoting HIV risk awareness and testing in Latinos living on the U.S.-Mexico border: The *tu no me conoces* social marketing campaign. *AIDS Education and Prevention*, 19(5), 422–435.

Peattie, S. (2007). The internet as a medium for communication with teenagers. *Social Marketing Quarterly*, 13(2), 21–46.

Pew Research Center for People and the Press. (2006). Online papers modestly boost newspaper readership: maturing internet news audience broader than deep. *Survey Reports*. Retrieved June 17, 2010, from: http://people-press.org/report/282/online-papers-modestly-boost-newspaper-readership

P.L. 104–193, Personal Responsibility and Work Opportunity Reconsideration Act of 1996. (August 31, 1996). Retrieved July 18, 2003, from http://www.lexisnexis.com/congcomp

Pollack, A. (2000, November 4). Protecting a favorable image: Biotechnology concerns in quandary over drug giants. *The New York Times*, p. B1.

Powell, J., Tapp, A., & Sparks, E. (2007). Social marketing in action—Geodemographics, alcoholic liver disease and heavy episodic drinking in Great Britain. *International Journal of Nonprofit and Voluntary Sector Marketing*, 12, 177–187.

Rose, R. (1994, October). Marketing: To build clientele, build a media file. *NASW News*, 39, 5.

Rose, R. (1995, February). Marketing: Hook editors with a pro-caliber release. *NASW News*, 40, 5.

Rothman, J. (1980). *Social R & D: Research and development in the human services*. Englewood Cliffs, NJ: Prentice Hall.

Rothman, J., Teresa, J. C., Kay, T. L., & Morningstar, G. C. (1983). *Marketing human service innovations*. Beverly Hills, CA: Sage.

Rubin, B. R. (1997). *A citizen's guide to politics in America: How the system works & how to work the system*. Armonk, NY: M. E. Sharpe.

Rubright, R., & MacDonald, D. (1981). *Marketing health and human services*. Rockville, MD: Aspens Systems Corp.

Shapiro, B. P. (1977). Marketing for nonprofit organizations. In R. M. Gaedeke (Ed.), *Marketing in private and public nonprofit organizations: Perspectives and illustrations* (pp. 103–115). Santa Maria, CA: Goodyear.

Stead, M., Gordon, R., Angus, K., & McDermott, L. (2007). A systematic review of social marketing effectiveness. *Health Education*, 107(2), 126–191.

Stern, G. J. (1990). *Marketing workbook for nonprofit organizations*. St. Paul, MN: Amherst H. Wilder Foundation.

Stoner, M. R. (1986). Marketing of social services gains prominence in practice. *Administration in Social Work*, 10, 41–52.

Themba, M. N. (1999). *Making policy, making change: How communities are taking law into their own hands*. Oakland, CA: Chardon Press.

Timmerman, G. M. (2007). Addressing barriers to health promotion in underserved women. *Journal of Family and Community Health*, 30(1S), S34–S42.

Weinberg, C. B. (1984). Marketing mix decisions for nonprofit organizations: An analytical approach. In C. H. Lovelock & C. B. Weinberg (Eds.), *Public and nonprofit marketing: Cases and readings* (pp. 261–269). Palo Alto, CA: Scientific Press.

West, D. M., & Francis, R. (1996). Electronic advocacy: Interest groups and public policy making. *PS: Political Science & Politics*, pp. 25–29.

Winston, W. J. (1986). Basic marketing principles for mental health professionals. *Journal of Marketing for Mental Health*, 1, 9–20.

Wright, D. J. (2009). *Taking stock: The Bush faith-based initiative and what lies ahead*. Albany, New York: The Nelson A. Rockefeller Institute of Government, State University of New York.

Wyatt, E. (2010, May 20). F.C.C. begins review of regulations on media ownership. *The New York Times*, p. B10.

Yin, R. K. (1986). *Case study research: Design and method*. Beverly Hills, CA: Sage.

Zane, J. P. (1995, June 19). A rivalry in rabble-rousing as letter writers keep count. *The New York Times*, p. D5.

Zippay, A., & Lee, S. K. (2008). Neighbors' perceptions of community-based psychiatric housing. *Social Service Review*, 82(3), 395–417.

12

Using The Advocacy Spectrum

I . . . present the strong claims of suffering humanity. I . . . place before the Legislature of Massachusetts the condition of the miserable, the desolate, the outcast. I come as the advocate of helpless, forgotten, insane men and women; of beings sunk to a condition from which the unconcerned world would start with real horror.

Dorothea Dix, social reformer, educator, nurse, advocate for the mentally ill

Which side are you on?

Florence Reece, folk songwriter and singer, social activist, union organizer's wife

Making Change Happen

Advocacy is the heart of social work. Social workers are advocates. Its part of our ethical code, values, and history and is inherent in almost all practice. As Florence Reece wrote in 1931 in her iconic labor movement anthem *Which Side Are You On?* social work has chosen a side. A part of a social worker's fiduciary responsibility, advocacy, simply defined, is presenting, representing, and supporting a client, group, organization, or cause to others. Advocacy, whether for an individual or a cause, case, or class, means championing, speaking, and acting for the interest of clients or citizens. Social work managers, for example, often promote causes involving service users with officials and decision makers (Donaldson & Shields, 2009; Menefee & Thompson, 1994, p. 18). Advocacy has a role in transforming private troubles into public issues or personal problems into social issues. It has a responsibility in challenging inhumane conditions at a micro or macro level. In direct service work, advocacy is often part of client support and representation and, if possible, involves client self-advocacy. Case advocacy emphasizes ensuring service delivery in one's field of practice and securing resources and services for particular clients in one's caseload (Donaldson & Shields, 2009; Grosser, 1976; Hardina, 1995; Johnson, 1995). Cause and class advocacy involves groups, institutions, and modification of social conditions (Donaldson & Shields, 2009; Johnson, 1995).

Donaldson and Shields (2009, p. 90) hold that what separates social work advocacy practice from other advocacy professions is that social work "meaningfully engages and partners with clients and other marginalized groups for social change." It is the partnership, with and not just on behalf of, that distinguishes social work advocacy. This style of advocacy, integral to critical practice, grew from social work's settlement house history of community engagement. As advocacy is a public putting forth of self, assertiveness and critical consciousness are requisites of effective advocacy, and empowerment is a product of successful advocacy.

Ethics and Values

Our review of the ethical codes of most U.S. and international professional social work associations in Chapter 1 revealed their call for social work advocacy. Case and client advocacy are inherent in NASW's ethical standard *1.01, Regarding primacy of client interest* and *1.02, Calling for client self-determination*. Standard *6.01, Social and Political Action*, requires social causes be transformed into social and political advocacy to achieve an equitable distribution of social resources for social justice. Chapter 1 also presented the ethical keystones of social work practice.

Social justice is a *sine qua non* of social work's advocacy obligations locally and globally. American social workers are obliged to advocate in social and political arenas to achieve an equitable distribution of the community's physical, economic, and other social resources for social justice under the profession's ethical code (NASW, 2008). Social work has chosen a side. Our values compel us to work to end or at least alleviate acute, chronic, and seemingly unfixable misery.

Process

Although often associated more with social action, advocacy is generally inherent in most community practice that pursues social justice, from community development (Jacobson, 2007) to social marketing. Advocacy is a change process promoting a client's, a case's, or a community's interests or a cause or ideal that involves directed, purposive, and intentional change. Advocacy change strategies can vary widely, from direct social action and political action through education (Wandersman, Clary, Forbush, Weinberger,

Coyne, & Duffy, 2006) and consciousness raising.

Advocacy and social action are strategies or means to an end. Such strategies are employed by progressive professionals and by a wide variety of concerned citizens (Lewis, 1998) and organizations that vigorously oppose the status quo. Advocacy can be micro, such as self and individual, client and case, and group advocacy, or macro, concerned with institutional and social cause advocacy (Weiss-Gal & Gal, 2009). Cause or class advocacy is a form of social action and may be a part of a social movement. The Birmingham Bus Boycott was class advocacy, social action, and part of the civil rights movement (Willie, 2008). These concepts are similar. The list in Box 12.1, based on Panitch (1974), suggests the variety of techniques used by social workers engaged in advocacy and social reform. In addition, the new communication and information technologies greatly expand the audience for and participants engaged in advocacy (Lohmann & McNutt, 2005; Hick & McNutt, 2002). The major difference is that case or individual advocacy, while often leading to larger social action, is individually focused rather than intentionally seeking larger social change. Class and cause advocacy is social action.

Social Action and Advocacy

What is Social Action?

We have defined social action, a subset of community organization, as practices and strategies

---

BOX 12.1.	**Advocacy and Social Action Tactics**

1. Build coalitions with other agencies and community organizations, grassroots, Astroturf, false front, Potemkin coalitions (see Chapter 10).
2. Organize client, consumer, and citizen groups.
3. Organize petitions and letter-writing, telephone, e-mail campaigns.
4. Appeal to review boards. Make the targets follow their rules.
5. Threaten or initiate legal action.
6. Threaten and engage in nonviolent direct action and civil disobedience (e.g., boycotts, strikes, sit-ins, rallies, forums, teach-in, pickets, leafleting).
7. Embark on legislative and political action campaigns.
8. Use social marketing, blogging, letters to the editor, talk-show call ins, and public education.
9. Be visible, interesting, persistent, and unpredictable.
10. Whether you win or lose, prepare for the next struggle. You can be sure the other side is.

to change community relations and behavior patterns to promote the development, allocation, redistribution, and control of community statuses and resources, including social power. Social action is a collective endeavor to promote a cause or make a social change in the face of opposition. It usually brings together people who feel aggrieved to take direct action. The critical component is the feeling of being aggrieved, whether or not there is a factual basis for the feeling. Alinsky (1989, pp. 116–117) wrote that the organizer must "stir up the discontent, *rub raw the resentment of the people*, and *fan the latent hostilities*."[1] The social action mobilizes the discontented, resentful, and hostile and provides a channel to be self-advocates, as well as cause-advocates, to release the discontent, resentment, and hostilities. The social action can be calm but often is disruptive (Ehrenreich, 2009; Perelman, 2009). Whether peaceful or troublesome, the action needs to be carefully staged to capture the public's and media's attention. As social action, it has to be visible. Although often claimed by progressives, social action is used by progressives and radical conservatives to promote social change (Barstow 2010; Ehrenreich, 2009; Ferris, 2009; Perelman, 2009).

While social action can be used to address real grievances and injustice, it is built on emotion, feelings, and perception as much as factual and comparative data. Alinsky's admonitions emphasize emotion. Wallerstein (1993, p. 219) views social action as leading to community empowerment as it "promotes participation of people, who are in positions of perceived and actual powerlessness [italics added] towards goals of increased individual and group decision-making and control, equity of resources, and improved quality of life." For instance, the Tea Party movement (aka Tea Baggers) capitalizes on its adherents' feeling of loss, deprivation, and resentment. However, polling of adherents in 2010 discovered that "the 18 percent of Americans who identify themselves as Tea Party supporters tend to be Republican, white, male, married and older than 45" (Zernike & Thee-Brenan, 2010, p. A1). They also are more affluent and educated than most Americans (Zernike & Thee-Brenan, 2010, p. A17).

Social action is broader than case advocacy. It is usually more systemic and aims at policy and

community behavior. Social action can entail changing an agency from within, working with mobilized populations, or conducting community-controlled participatory action (Alvarez & Gutierrez, 2001; Wagner, 1990). Human services agencies can engage in social action, although they rarely use disruptive tactics (Donaldson & Shields, 2009).

Social action emphasizes an internal change through consciousness raising and changing as well as the external social change. The internal change is the empowerment and capacity for new social constructions (Butcher, 2007). As discussed in Chapter 2, thought patterns and constructions of reality can encourage or discourage involvement. Part of social action is raising the consciousness—the rubbing raw—of possible action systems. Gamson (1992) has analyzed what facilitates involvement. He describes three collective action frames—injustice, agency, and identity—used by the mind to justify action. The *injustice* component is the moral indignation that is summoned as part of political consciousness. The *agency* component refers to the belief that something can be done and we can do it through collective social action. The belief that we can do something to produce change was reviewed in our Chapter 3 discussion of social problems. The *identity* component creates a mental adversary, a "they"—human agents—who can be affected or turned around, and as agency declares, "we" will prevail.

Social action has been part of social work since the settlement house and social reform era in the United Kingdom and the United States (Herrick & Stuart, 2005; Reisch & Andrews, 2002; Trattner, 1998). We have had the Abbott sisters and Jane Addams. It has been concerned with challenging power-holders because social action promotes insurgency, reform movements, reform, and third-party traditions. Social action has been with us even before Moses. Today, social action manifests itself in media events involving the Tea Baggers, MoveOn.org, and campaigns for all manner of reforms. Social action is used internationally with demonstrations and protests around the world for a variety of causes, from the liberation of Palestine to slowing the pace of corporate and political globalization. Social action is multifaceted, occurring on the streets and on the Internet.

Recapping Social Action

Social action works to promote change, ranging from reformist, incremental change to radical, fundamental change. It is used by progressives and reactionaries. Generally social action's purpose is to redistribute community resources, especially social power, and social relationships. Tactics embrace social marketing campaigns to educate and raise consciousness about social conditions, coalition building and networking, direct action of coalitions (including public demonstrations, disruption, and nonviolent civil disobedience), and political action. Usually more than one tactic is employed.

Ensuring Individual Rights. Advocacy and social action from a progressive standpoint pursue fairness in individual and collective rights. They seek social justice. Sometimes this requires creating new legal rights to ensure a level playing field for everyone. Individuals and groups fighting for their own rights contribute to the rights of all members of the community. Ensuring civil rights and promoting social equality for African-Americans, the civil rights movement, provided the impetus for civil rights and equal opportunity for women and gays. This mode of change influences our practice in many ways. Social workers sometimes help secure or create new rights—such as the right to treatment or to die—and often help implement or enforce existing rights.

The rights we are discussing fall into three categories: (a) due process (a concept of fairness) or procedural rights, (b) substantive rights, and (c) basic human rights. The first two flow from the Bill of Rights (the first 10 amendments to the Constitution of the United States) and other provisions of the Constitution, legislative directives, or court orders. Due process rights require agencies and authorities to play by the rules—to give the process due. Substantive rights are those that apply to everyone (free speech), to those in a certain category (the right to Medicare benefits if criteria are met [Weiss-Gal & Gal, 2009]), or to those in a particular group (e.g., compensation for past discrimination). Some are remedial, such as special education for special needs children. Basic human rights are promoted by the United Nations and include freedom from arbitrary government restrictions and a right to food. Immigrants lacking citizenship rights have humanitarian appeals rights and a right to human treatment, although these rights are not always honored by nations. Our profession adds client rights to self-determination and participation (Butcher, Banks, Henderson with Robertson, 2007). Since the terrorist attacks of Sept. 11, 2001, in the United States some of these substantive rights have come under attack in the name of patriotism.

Wood and Middleman (1989) make an interesting point with regard to obtaining benefits for an entitled client: "We value the positive experience which people can have as they work together and take action in their own behalf, even if they do not succeed. . . . But when [rights] are at stake, we do not value the psychological experience above task accomplishment. . . . we believe that the positive feelings associated with accordance of one's rights are more real and more lasting, irrespective of the extent to which one has obtained it through one's own efforts" (p. 145). Pressing needs may not wait for empowerment.

Rights won at a societal level on behalf of a class, such as affirmative action, discussed in Chapter 1, are implemented on an individual level. Social work practitioners can *aid individual clients* by informing them of their rights as a class member and monitoring to ensure that their rights are respected in receiving services (Weiss-Gal & Gal, 2009). Simon (1994) warns that it "would be a grave error to assume, without inquiring, that one's client has good knowledge of his or her rights as a citizen and as a consumer of services," since few of us know our own "rights and entitlements" (p. 20).

Advocacy Spectrum: Spanning People and Policy

Along the Spectrum

Advocacy aims to bring about change in order to benefit people in a variety of circumstances. Advocacy ranges from putting forth the interests of oneself, another individual such as a client, to helping a definable group such as a community group or tenants, to a defined community, to social and institutional change to help society and communities now and in the future.

Advocacy can be carried out directly with a client or indirectly on behalf of a client or group or for the public good. An advocate can operate at different points along the advocacy spectrum, or people working in different areas of the same field can address problems simultaneously. The construction of a problem, as discussed in Chapter 3, shapes the advocacy tactics and targets.

Consciousness raising is inherent in all advocacy. It is inherent to empowerment and fundamental to most clinical social work goals. Hyde (1994) believes clinical and social action approaches can be blended since the "caseworker is in an ideal position to help a client begin to consider new life goals. As part of that exploration, the possibility of participation in a macro change effort should be included" (p. 61). Walz and Groze (1991) call for a new breed of clinical activists who might also serve as advocacy researchers; such clinicians would gather data, analyze connections between individual situations and social forces, and measure their success through "multiples" who had been helped (p. 503). Moreau (1990) singles out "unmasking power relations" (p. 56) as pertinent to direct practice—that is, being open with clients about power relationships (Hartman, 1993; Sherman & Wenocur, 1983). The worker will promote individual awareness and a belief in human agency or instrumentality. Workers and clients, as "co-investigators," can explore reality, critical thinking, and liberating action (Freire, 1971, p. 97). This Freire style of dialogue involves "reducing unnecessary social distance between worker and client . . . sharing information and demystifying techniques and skills used to help," according to Moreau; it means that clients can see their files and that no "case conferences concerning them are held without their presence" (Moreau, 1990, pp. 56–57). Many believe that numerous individual transformations contribute to a collective metamorphosis.

Box 12.2 presents a simplified example of how social workers might respond to a question from a service user in accordance with all three philosophies of change.

Self-advocacy. Self-advocacy is elemental to any form of advocacy. It involves self-awareness, critical practice, and assertiveness. Without raising one's own consciousness, it is difficult to raise the consciousness of others. A practitioner who wants to start a client group must believe in the project and his or her ability to carry it out, convince the agency of both, and then bond with group members.

BOX 12.2.   Response Styles

Client: Why aren't our benefits higher? We can't live decently on income way below the poverty level.

Conventional responses:

It'd be nice if they were higher. Can we make a list of your expenses to see if I might have any suggestions to help you make ends meet with the check you receive?

I wish I could get you more money, but we have to work with what we've got—given the cutbacks and today's politics.

(Goal: to avoid being personally blamed, and to express empathy)

Rights-oriented response:

Perhaps you aren't receiving all you are entitled to. Want me to review your finances with you? Maybe we can appeal.

(Goal: to secure rights collaboratively)

Public interest advocacy response:

A coalition is trying to influence the governor to supplement the amount the feds provide. Do you want some information about this fight to raise benefits?

(Goal: to involve the client, increase civic skills, and secure the client as a witness or letter writer)

Transformation or critical consciousness responses:

What do you think the reason is?

If a family with more money traded places with yours for a week, what would they learn?

Does it ever make you angry?

Who, in your opinion, decides who gets government benefits?

(Goal: to start a dialogue and raise consciousness about income and power distribution, sociopolitical and economic forces)

Maggie Kuhn's story exemplifies self-advocacy. When a certain retirement age was mandatory, traditionally men were given gold watches and some women, including Kuhn, received a sewing machine. Today, mandatory retirement is illegal except in a few circumstances. Kuhn (1991, pp. 130–131) recounts her retirement and her consciousness raising to self-advocacy and empowerment:

In the first month after I was ordered to retire, I felt dazed and suspended. I was hurt and then, as time passed, outraged. . . . Something clicked in my mind and I saw that my problem was not mine alone. Instead of sinking into despair, I did what came most naturally to me: I telephoned some friends and called a meeting. Six of us, all professional women associated with nonprofit social and religious groups, met for lunch. . . . My office at work was next to a Xerox machine, so it was easy to slip over there and whip out copies of a notice for a [large] meeting. . . . We agreed we should all band together to form a new social action organization.

Kuhn founded and headed the Gray Panthers for 25 years, until her death. Her story epitomizes Gutierrez's point: "Empowerment can transform stressful life events through increasing self-efficacy, developing a critical consciousness, developing skills, and involvement with similar others" (1994, pp. 204–205).

Self-advocacy in social work includes self-help and, as with Kuhn, helping others to help themselves. Workers can provide the knowledge and encouragement that clients need to act personally and collectively on their own behalf. A goal of client advocacy is to help the client be an advocate. This can be done through administrative and technical assistance, such as clerical and volunteer help and providing meeting rooms. Practitioners help by offering encouragement, acknowledging the worth of the endeavor, and giving it legitimacy. Another vital support is organizing, again as Kuhn did, by bringing together people concerned with the same issue and sharing information. Self-advocacy also occurs in low-income groups and groups concerned about specific issues such as drunk driving or AIDS. We can learn from self-advocates with organizational skills. We should always be on the lookout not only for indigenous leaders, but also for clients who make progress in self-advocacy in a less public way.

Individual, Case, and Client Advocacy

NASW's ethical standard 1.01, *Commitment to Clients*, calls for a primacy of client interest by the social worker:

Social workers' primary responsibility is to promote the wellbeing of clients. In general, clients' interests are primary. However, social workers' responsibility to the larger society or specific legal obligations may on limited occasions supersede the loyalty owed clients, and clients should be so advised (NASW, 2008).

Although riddled with caution, the standard's intent is reasonably clear: advocate for the client. Client advocacy means helping clients in self-determination, helping them to obtain their rights within the agency and the community, supporting their empowerment, and raising consciousness. Case advocacy is central to Lee's (1994) empowerment practice: "Empowerment is both the journey and the destination" (p. 207). Case advocacy for the worker entails promoting social justice, raising the consciousness of the client, and teaching and modeling assertiveness and advocacy (Weiss-Gal & Gal, 2009).

Advocacy challenges arise in working with clients who have circumstances that restrain or prevent their desire or ability to act. For these cases client support and advocacy groups are useful. They provide clients with advocacy, emotional support, a recognition that they are not in this alone, and some cover against individual retribution from target systems. "Advocacy in this context becomes a form of personal self-assistance, based on self-identified needs, that unfolds within the context of a very supportive interpersonal relationship with an advocate" (Moxley & Freddolino, 1994, p. 96).

An exciting example of self-advocacy is the growth of the mental health consumer movement. It was started 30 years ago, according to *U.S. News and World Report*, by groups such as Network Against Psychiatric Assault, Mad Pride, and the Insane Liberation Front. "Although it began with a marginalized collection of former mental patients demanding the closure of state hospitals, today it's a national, mainstream movement, representing the entire array of psychiatric diagnoses and challenging psychiatrists and other 'helping professionals'" (Szegedy-Maszak,

BOX 12.3.   **Get Me Out Of Here!**

A mother declared her teenage daughter incorrigible and in need of protection by juvenile services. Since the emergency shelter was full, Theresa was placed at a holding facility in a room where unfortunate youngsters stayed until foster homes were available. The matron soon had Theresa babysitting for 10 young children housed at the facility. When the teenager rebelled after a week and refused to babysit, she was locked up behind bars. Her worker was stunned when she came to visit, for there had

been no hearing, nor had she or Theresa's family been contacted. The worker was so indignant that she told her supervisor she wanted to write a letter to the judge in charge of Theresa's case. The supervisor expressed doubt that anything would be done but agreed to humor his young supervisee. The worker wrote a letter to the judge requesting Theresa's release. The teenager was released from her cell the day the judge received it.

2002, p. 55). Thus, individual desires for self-determination led to a collective effort. Today, some formerly homeless, brain-disordered people are employed by or in charge of mental health associations.

Working With Rather Than For. Where clients are jailed, ill, or unable to act for themselves, such as the one described in Box 12.3, the advocate honors their expressed wishes and acts on their behalf. When people cannot advocate for themselves or participate jointly in advocacy with the practitioner or the advocacy or support group, the advocate-practitioner must guard against taking a "benefactor" or "liberator" stance (Simon, 1994, p. 7). Client self-determination is a guiding ethic: we want to create situations in which individuals can develop into their own heroes rather than becoming dependent on an advocate-practitioner.

Advocacy and Respecting the Client. Individual and family-level case advocacy frequently involves efforts to influence organizational or institutional decisions or policies on behalf of a third party. Once a practitioner agrees to serve as an advocate, he or she cannot countenance or condone having clients demeaned, whether or not the clients are present in an interaction. The ethical principles of respect for and the dignity of clients and the inherent worth of the individual are operational whether or not a client is physically in attendance (NASW, 2008; Weiss-Gal & Gal, 2009). These principles are basic. There are many opportunities to practice them, but they are not easy to follow because so many clients interact with an array of officials who make a

practice of belittling them or treating them as objects. Box 12.4 provides an example of a caseworker's efforts to make the bureaucracy respect the clients' rights.

Group Advocacy

Group advocacy can arise from case advocacy, it can be part of a particular reform effort, or it can be a component of an ongoing community organization and development process or a social movement. For instance, parents of children who are both physically and mentally challenged and thus cannot use existing group homes might band together to get facilities modified or built to meet their children's needs. The practitioner-advocate's task is help the parents develop consciousness and a collective consciousness and the knowledge and skills to self-advocate. They could make demands of an individual worker or of a county or state agency. In our classification scheme, this is group self-advocacy.

In assessing a problem, we may start with individuals and end up advocating for a group. A social worker troubled that classmates are teasing a boy in speech therapy about his stuttering might talk to his teacher. This same concern, writ large, might lead that advocate to write to a television show that pokes fun at a character who stutters. A worker with a mentally ill client in jail, as a result not of a crime but of his symptoms, should tend to that person's needs but can also note other ill inmates. The worker can then find out what is happening and how to aid such prisoners. Sometimes we work on behalf of people who are scattered and are never seen by each other or the worker, as with the macro advocacy modalities.

BOX 12.4.	Making Them Live up to Their Rules

An Alinsky (1989) dictum is to make the enemy or target of change live up to his or her own rule book. In California's agricultural counties in the 1960s, it was a general practice to discontinue one-child families from Aid to Needy Children (ANC) during the summer and agriculture harvest months. This practice was rooted in agriculture's need for cheap labor and the assumption that the mothers could fill the need. This was done automatically regardless of childcare arrangements or the mother's ability to find transportation, and contrary to state policy that required childcare plans to be in place before any work-based discontinuance. The county administrators assumed the mothers could find childcare or could take the children to the fields, a common practice before the farm labor union was organized, and ride to the fields, often some distance from the barrios, on the labor contractors' buses. Most public assistance workers disagreed with the practice but felt helpless.

One worker decided to make the county play by the rules. ANC was a federal–state–local program; most of the funds were provided by the federal and state governments but it was run by county administrators. The counties were required to state on the back of all official forms (it was usually in small print) that if clients disagreed with a decision, they could appeal to the state department at the address provided. The worker dutifully advised all one-child cases, about 60 cases (as caseloads were generally over 100), that in accordance with county policy their ANC aid was to be discontinued from June through September. They could reapply in September. The worker pointed out the clause on the back of the form alerting the clients to their right of appeal and offered suggestive wording.

The state office received almost 200 appeals of the county's policy because the workers and other clients networked with the worker's clients. This was a record number of single-month appeals for any county, and the state did not have sufficient hearing officers. The state, prior to any hearing, requested the county review its policy for compliance. The county did, repealed the policy before the state review, and reinstated the aid until suitable childcare and transportation could be arranged. If the state found the county out of compliance, the state could assume administration of the program at the county's expense and penalize the county.

The county's welfare department director called the worker in for a dressing down and possible disciplinary action. The worker innocently asked what rule he violated by rigorously following procedure? The director was helpless, recommended the worker for a state MSW educational stipend, and sent him on his way.

A practitioner-advocate wants to ensure that maximum benefits are delivered to the greatest number of people, but not at the expense of the original client's position. A client is never sacrificed for the greater good except at the client's urging after fully informed consent. Bringing together many persons who have been harmed in the same way or who seek the same remedy to a common problem helps define the parameters of a problem. Having more people involved increases the availability of information, provides documentation of a pattern of abuse, and aggregates social capital for empowerment. Evidence that 10 apartment building tenants have no heat and hot water is more credible than a similar complaint from a single resident.

Support groups may be empowered by advocating for one of their own. Box 12.11, at end of this chapter, describes the success of a worldwide virtual mental illness discussion group whose members became advocates for a delusional woman, whom they did not even know personally, who had attempted to pay for coffee with a quarter and a packet of cocoa. Few people participating in support groups have training in advocacy. However, experience teaches support group members, who are willing to go public, to formulate their thoughts carefully. To use our example in Box 12.11, an appropriate statement might be, "This victory on behalf of a mentally ill person who was jailed after not paying properly for a cup of coffee affects all of us with this disease by showing that we can act to help each other and challenge the rigidities of society." Legal immigrants and citizens sharing their ethnic identify may say the same thing about the denial of basic rights to illegal immigrants.

A group may already exist, such as a tenants' organization, or one can form after the advocate starts with one individual and finds others.

In either case, the advocate must get to know each member of the group, understand the group dynamics as the process unfolds, and be accountable to the group, which is equally true in the next situation. Practitioner-advocates often work with groups whose members cannot easily communicate their concerns. The advocate has to work through ethical and authority issues. When representing groups with inarticulate and passive members, all the various sub-interests within the group must be considered; otherwise, only the members who are present and articulate will prevail. The issues presented in Chapter 9 such as interpersonal conflicts and positive allegiances will affect group cohesion and the ultimate agenda for action and must be addressed by the practitioner-advocate. When members want to organize for self-government or to fight discrimination or hardship, the practitioner-advocate must fully inform the group of any potential risks, and then encourage the group's self-determination and follow its lead.

Community Advocacy

Community advocacy has many facets and bridges the micro and macro advocacy modalities

of the spectrum. Community advocacy requires community consciousness raising and education about tactics challenging the status quo. Community advocacy most often arises from situations that dishearten, disadvantage, aggravate, or harm a segment or segments of a community. The seminal social work example of advocacy occurred in 1889, when Jane Addams and House advocated on behalf of a marginalized neighborhood in West Side Chicago (Addams, 1910) (Box 12.5). It is continued today by the adherents of Alinsky. Community residents can advocate on their own and use non-residential advocates such as social workers. Social workers have an ethical obligation to raise a professional voice on behalf of the unorganized, subgroups, and pressing community needs. Collective advocacy and social action is dealt with in other places in this textbook, along with the methodologies of community assessment, networking, coalition building, bargaining and negotiation, and social marketing; these are all community advocacy tools. Here we discuss what an individual can do to advocate for and with residents of a given community. The La Colonia case in Chapter 1 illustrates community advocacy.

BOX 12.5.	Jane Addams Improves an Alley

We began a systematic investigation of the city system of garbage collection . . . and its possible connection with the death rate in the various wards of the city. . . . Twelve [Woman's Club members] undertook in connection with the residents, to carefully investigate the condition of the alleys. During August and September the substantiated reports of violations of the law sent in from Hull House to the health department were one thousand and thirty-seven. . . . In sheer desperation, the following spring when the city contracts were awarded for the removal of garbage, with the backing of two well-known business men, I put in a bid for the garbage removal of the nineteenth ward. My paper was thrown out on a technicality but the incident induced the mayor to appoint me the garbage inspector of the ward. . . . Perhaps our greatest achievement was the discovery of a pavement eighteen inches under the surface of a narrow street [after the removal of eight inches of garbage]. . . .

Many of the foreign-born women of the ward were much shocked by this abrupt departure into the ways of men, and it took a great deal of explanation to convey the idea even remotely that if it were a womanly task to go about in tenement houses in order to nurse the sick, it might be quite as womanly to go through the same district in order to prevent the breeding of so-called "filth diseases." . . .

The careful inspection, combined with other causes, brought about a great improvement in the cleanliness and comfort of the neighborhood and one happy day, when the death rate of our ward was found to have dropped from third to seventh in the list of city-wards and was so reported to our Woman's Club, the applause which followed recorded the genuine sense of participation in the result, and a public spirit which had "made good."

Source: Addams (1910), pp. 200–205.

Let's consider another case to illustrate rural and urban community advocacy activities (Rankin, 2000). Brookburg, a composite of three actual towns, is a country town of 500 in a county of 12,000 residents. While community-wide advocacy may be needed anywhere, the construction of the community boundaries must consider the community's resources, social capital, and potential social power.[2] Compared to a large metropolitan neighborhood, what can be accomplished in a village with a post office, a cemetery, one gas station, three parks, one combination fire, police, and government hall, two churches, and two restaurants?

Firstly, the advocate might organize events that enhance or sustain the quality of the community. Even small towns surrounded by farms or ranches can have street festivals or fairs that draw people from neighboring areas. Money raised can pay for streetlights and upkeep of parks. Yearly events such as a Halloween parade can draw in rural families. All will help build community consciousness and identity.

Secondly, advocacy often involves efforts to maintain the status quo for a community resisting the tides of modernity. In some areas, there is advocacy for zoning ordinances, for restrictions on development, or for establishing a bypass around the town to keep traffic from destroying the quality of life—or for blocking a bypass to maintain traffic for business. If the Brookburg post office were under threat of relocation, an advocate could try to keep a place where people may see each other and connect. If the Brookburg cemetery were endangered by development, an advocate would explore how to protect the place (Perlman, 2000).

Thirdly, advocates may demand public access to resources. The village of Brookburg is 10 miles from the nearest supermarkets and medical clinics and 50 miles from the nearest city. Some neighborly volunteer projects can help, but transportation needs might require a service plan and appeals to the state government.

Fourthly, advocates strive to become accountable to the community. If residents are increasingly afraid because officials ignored several unusual incidents, accountability is needed. After the beautification association put up new welcome signs, the signs were destroyed. No thorough investigation was conducted and no one was apprehended;

officials wrote it off as a prank. Then a number of mutilated animals were found in empty lots and the parks. It was beyond a prank stage. Yet, when townspeople call Brookburg's part-time officials, they feel they are starting from scratch each time. No cumulative record is kept. In this case, the advocate can document the incidents, go to see officials, establish a reward fund for information, call a town meeting, and consider whether to ask for assistance from outside Brookburg.

All these tactics result in social inclusion that provides community citizens with justice and dignity. Frontline public-sector advocates can be another force for community change. Of course, only practitioners who truly do their jobs and are fearless about repercussions are embraced by citizens as their advocates—as people who place the community before governmental and business interests. This is critical to community practice's belief bonding. Such determination creates local heroes.

Political leaders and elected city officials and managers can serve as, and often are, community advocates. But too often, they are lacking. Michael DiBerardinis, a community organizer who was appointed Philadelphia's Commissioner for the Department of Recreation, is described as a model for officials as advocates. He brought an uncommon commitment to community development and enhanced citizen participation (Perlmutter & Cnaan, 1999).

Community advocacy can spring from case advocacy. Messinger (1982), a social worker and city official, describes the ways in which she provides constituent services: she pinpoints individual advocacy, then empowerment, then community advocacy:

Many people . . . [contact a] politician because they need something done. . . . I or my staff . . . give them an address, make a phone call, track down a check, do whatever is necessary, but we try, always, to notify the people we assist about whom we are calling, what the most useful telephone number is, how they might do the same thing for themselves, and what to do if they do not get help.

Sometimes, too, it is necessary for my staff to intervene to rescue individuals from becoming victims of the system. We recognize that it takes a mass effort by many people to make systems work better, but we do not . . . turn every problem with the bureaucracy into a cause. Nevertheless, we look for patterns in this work with constituents and for areas in which it is of mutual advantage to organize a lobbying and advocacy force rather than just to give help. (p. 216)

Public Interest, Political, and Cause Advocacy

Public interest, cause, advocacy, expands the beneficiaries of the advocacy. It involves societal responsibility and "getting a place at the table" for the socially marginalized to enable them to participate in the community's decision making. Giving voice to the voiceless entails representing general and dispersed, often disorganized, interests (in contrast to concentrated special interests) and underrepresented views. Those interested in keeping public schools strong are dispersed, compared with the parents of children in private and charter schools, who argue collectively for vouchers and subsidies. Middle-class taxpayers seeking tax relief are dispersed, in contrast to the business community with its myriad of national and local lobbying and self-interest associations that secure tax loopholes.[3] Low-income people are the most marginalized by a lack of resources and the most underrepresented in the public debate. Promoting *pro bono* (for the public good) work is important for the poor and for the public. Public interest advocates "strengthen the position of weak, poorly organized, or unarticulated interests in society" (Handler, 1978, p. 4).

Unlike the rights approach, in which an individual may be part of an observable and protected class (such as classes based on gender, race, and so on), many who benefit from public advocacy are part of an indistinguishable public, such as is the case with environmental advocacy. Reform helps current and future publics. Thus, efforts to protect the environment epitomize public interest advocacy.

Public interest advocacy declares to social work: "We have to be public citizens and wherever there is a need we must work to meet it" (Mikulski, 1982, p. 18).

Citizen civic action and democratic policy-making are associated with public interest advocacy. This approach uses:

- Social/legal reform to promote pluralism and to gain an entry to government by strengthening outsider groups (Handler, 1978, p. 4)

- Access and investigative methods to force accountability in the private and public sectors (Powers, 1977)
- Community education to develop life skills and civic skills in the populace (Mondros & Wilson, 1994)

While the rights approach often focuses on government wrongs and remedies, the public interest approach challenges corporate abuse as well. Even with the dalliance of Congress and the misuse of the Trouble Asset Relief Program (TARP), corporate executive pay has declined over the past two years in the face of negative public opinion (Leonard, 2010). Three out of five American felt in 2008 that businesses are too powerful and profitable, while almost 80% believed that too much power was in the hands of large corporations (Pew Research Center for the People & the Press, 2008). Executive pay does reflect public opinion, among other variables, and public interest advocacy affects the private sector (Kuhnen & Neissen, 2010). This advocacy—for classes of citizens who can rarely defend their own interests—relies on citizen evaluation, expertise, awareness of pressure points, freedom of information statutes, and the media.

Political and Policy Advocacy

Public policy and political advocacy offers an opportunity for system change. Political advocacy is practiced across the ideological gamut. Paul Wellstone, the late U.S. Senator from Minnesota, was a one-time community organizer who championed many social work policy issues. He voted his principles about poverty or peace above politics, even if the vote was 99 to 1. Prairie populist Wellstone started out as a tireless, tenacious advocate for rural residents and ordinary people and fought for causes as a political science professor. Just before he died in a plane crash in 2002 (an event that is still contentious), Wellstone risked his re-election to vote against a resolution authorizing force against Iraq. In this way, Wellstone was like social worker Jeannette Rankin (1880–1973) of Montana, the first woman elected to the U.S. Congress, who voted against U.S. entry into both world wars.

Political advocates seek change at any level of government through electoral and political processes. For instance, numerous social work advocates have been active in the campaigns of, among others, Georgia Representative John Lewis, social work senators Barbara Mikulski of Maryland and Debbie Stabenow of Michigan, and Senator Ron Wyden of Oregon. The advocates often had worked with the elected official on issues before he or she ran for office. Most maintain their policy commitments after their election. Social workers work in many governmental jobs that involve full-time advocacy, including county commissions, state staff positions, or even legislative directors in the U.S. Senate. Some participate in media and political campaigns that involve field organizing.

Most social work and progressive policy and political advocates, however, are grassroots citizen advocates and not elected officials. Some are "hired guns" or paid political advocates and lobbyists. Increasingly, the advocates run field operations for campaigns, lobby, and create and maintain information and voter databases. Salcido and Manalo (2002) involved social work students in state electoral campaigns in California through "a voter registration drive, an absentee ballot drive, a student rally/forum, and a 'get-out-the-vote' drive" (p. 55). In addition, initiative campaigns and campaigns for third-party candidates afford great opportunities to gain political advocacy experience. At any level of government, someone who designs, enacts, defeats, or changes ordinances, acts, regulations, and other policies is a policy advocate.

Some advocates can mobilize whole districts and large populations, educate the base, and form policy proposals. If you are on the e-mail lists of MoveOn.org, Campaign for America, Organizing for America, or one of the emerging Tea Bagger organizations, you know what it is like to be barraged with pleas to contact your legislators on behalf of specific policy positions. If only a small fraction of the list respond, legislators are deluged with policy advocates. While the legislators rarely read the messages, staff do count the positions and view the senders as activists. Policy advocates can prevail despite unfavorable political odds, although the past few years have seen a largely deadlocked Congress. For example, under a Republican administration, policy advocates were successful in convincing Congress to restore funding to community medical centers.

More recently, reactionary policy advocated delayed and weakened health care and financial reform legislation, despite Democratic control of the House, Senate, and Executive branch.

Policy and political advocacy overlap. Politicians make policy. Advocacy involves pressure tactics from giving or withholding financial support to disruption. Advocates on the right and left have used disruptive tactics. A social work professor, students, and other advocates forced a governor to reverse an action he had taken that harmed people with disabilities (Soifer & Singer, 1999). In France, activist held " wild picnics." Activists from the New Anticapitalist Party protesting both the cost of food by large global food corporations and the government inattention to the plight of workers during the Great Recession set up tables in supermarkets and had picnics from food on the shelves without paying (Perelman, 2009). The Irish have a saying: "You can accomplish more with a kind word and a shillelagh, than you can with just a kind word."

Policy and political advocates influence decision makers through their constituents and persuasion tactics (e.g., advocacy advertising, field trips to see conditions), knowing that politicians and civil servants may be as concerned with their personal images as with issues.

Legislative Advocacy and Lobbying

Lobbying's purpose is to influence policy decision makers. Lobbying can be direct or indirect (Box 12.6). Indirect lobbying involves the staging and social marketing of social ideas by generating public and media support for a position to encourage policymakers to adopt it to maintain their constituency support. Direct lobbying is when lobbyists directly engage and communicate with policymakers.

Lobbyists are professional or civilian, volunteer lobbyists. Professional lobbyists are of three types: hired guns, administrative, and cause.

Hired guns work for a fee based on the amount of time they devote to the contract. They advocate similar to attorneys for their client with legislators, the executive branch, and administrators. They often conduct indirect lobbying using social marketing and "Astroturf" or bogus grass-roots organizations. They do not necessarily

BOX 12.6.	Direct and Indirect Lobbying

Direct Lobbying	Indirect Lobbying (Shaping Public Opinion)
• To legislative bodies • To legislative committees • To party platforms • Political elections • Agency regulations • Policymakers at social events • Key decision makers' staff positions • Decision makers' information networks • Political action committees (PACs) • Agency regulation decision makers	• Influence organization and agency agenda and priorities • Use of grassroots, client, false-front, Astroturf, Potemkin organizations • Influencing media: letters to editor, op-ed., TV, call-in talk shows, blogs, chat room postings • Influencing opinion polls • Paid advertisements • Books, pamphlets • Social marketing and educational campaigns

have a social commitment to their clients or causes, and they have multiple clients. The administrative lobbyist is usually a professional who works for a particular agency, corporation, or association and lobbies exclusively for that organization. The cause advocate lobbies for particular causes or interests. He or she can have a single employer, but the commitment is to the cause.

Regardless of the type, to professional lobbyists, the policy process is a game they play every day. Their value is that they know the policymakers and the other players, have access to and personal relations with policymakers and their staffs, know the thinking of policymakers, and know their way around the policy arena for access and monitoring. Like an attorney advocating for a client, lobbyists will cut deals with other lobbyists and policymakers for support while offering their support to others. The nominal policymakers, legislative committees and executive branches, often merely act as judges to ratify these plea bargains or deals. They also help each other in policy monitoring and often form transient coalitions to pursue mutual interests.

The civilian lobbyist is a nonprofessional lobbyist who lobbies part-time for legislation supportive of grassroots causes. Grassroots relates to a policymaker's constituency. They bring zeal, dedication to the cause, and an appearance of representing the people and the electorate. The popularity of grassroots lobbyists has led professional lobbyists and their clients to create "Astroturf" and "Potemkin" organizations to provide them with a similar aura of populism.

While many civilian lobbyists are quite knowledgeable, a general weakness of civilian lobbyists is a lack of knowledge of the legislative process and players and inadequate time to monitor the process. They often do not have relationships with legislators and staffs to obtain access and information critical for monitoring and projecting actions. They also do not have the perspective on the process and may clog up the works in their belief that their bill is the most important.

The most effective lobbying approach generally is to combine the civilians with strategy and tactics managed by professionals.

Effective lobbying is a year-round job and is done best when done by grassroots activists in the home districts of policymakers. There were in 2009 over 13,694 registered lobbyists in Washington, DC (OpenSecrets.org, 2010). This averages something like 26 registered lobbyists for each legislator. The fundamental resources that lobbyists bring to policymakers, all verbiage aside, in exchange for their policy support are money, time, popular support or voters, and knowledge. Money is the most muscular of the resources in that it is fungible and is used to generate the other resources. The health care industry alone spent over $250 million in 2009, over $466,000 per legislator, for lobbying, and overall lobbying from all sources totaled over $3.45 billion, or over $6 million per legislator (OpenSecrets.org, 2010). Most progressive civilian or even professional lobbyists can't compete with conservative and reactionary interests on money, so they must develop other resources.

| BOX 12.7. | Lobbying the Legislative Process |

- Start Early
- Identify the goal to be achieved.
- Research the issue. Is existing law adequate if properly administered? Is administrative rather than legislative action necessary?
- Build a support coalition. Start indirect lobbying and staging the issue and legislation.
- Learn and know the legislative processes, including leadership, key committees and leadership, legislative calendar.
- Start early with legislators and key committee members in their home districts. In communicating with legislators:
  * Be specific. Always identify yourself and your group, especially if you are constituents.
  * Know what it means for the legislator, the constituency, the district.
  * Be constructive, be courteous, don't threaten (it's implied, and you'll have to deliver).
  * Be concise.
  * Be persistent.
  * Keep in regular contact
- Get a bill introduced pre-session, preferably sponsored by leadership of both parties and the key committee, ideally by respected and effective legislators who are knowledgeable about the issue (or educate them and their staffs). Provide a draft of legislation. Most passed legislation is pre-filed for that session.
- Consider possible support or opposition. Be prepared to promote the idea and provide estimates for cost and anticipated effect.

- Follow the bill in committee. Bills are referred to committee on basis of subject; usually all related bills go to the same committee.
- Lobby the hearing committee, preferably by their constituents; recruit members of your organization who live in their legislative districts. Concentrate your efforts on those legislators who seem undecided rather than strongly in favor or opposed.
- Testify at a committee hearing (see Box 12.8).
- If not favorable reported out of committee with a recommendation to pass the legislation, try to have the bill held over for the following year's legislature.
- Monitor the bill through the session and the governor's approval. The executive will also need to be lobbied.
- Monitor the rules and regulations and implementation processes. Remember, it's not policy until it's implemented.
- If you aren't successful, repeat the process. It can take multiple years to pass legislation.
- Make sure to thank legislators, coalition, and others whenever help is given.

Resources: This and Box 12.8 were developed using the authors' professional experience, DeVries and Vanderbilt (1992), Florida PTA (2010), League of Women Voters (1983), Mater (1984), Rubin (1997), and many other Web sites.

Analyze your lobbying successes and failures (Box 12.7). There are more failures than successes. Most legislation introduced never becomes law. Less than a third of introduced legislation in the states passes (Pew Charitable Trusts, 2004). Members of the 110th Congress, 2007–08, introduced nearly 14,000 pieces of legislation but passed only 3.3%, and much of the passed legislation, about 25%, was ceremonial, such as naming post offices, buildings, and recognition days (Singer, 2008). Learn from your successes and failures. Why didn't the bill pass? Was it lost in the logjam of legislation in the final days of the session? Was it killed in committee? Did it make it to a floor vote only to be defeated? To understand why your bill failed, analyze voting records in committee and on the floor. Legislation is generally voted on more than once

in each legislative body, and most of the time authority is separate from appropriations: policymakers often give authority for something without providing the capacity. Killing a bill is easier than passing one.

Lobbying as Marketing. Lobbying involves exchange and social marketing, especially indirect lobbying. The theory and discussion of communication is important here. The lobbyist will stage presentations and events to present a visual representation of support for the issue. Staging is important in attracting and holding the public's attention in our short-attention-span era.

Staging frequently uses Potemkin, Astroturf, and false-front interest groups. Potemkin organizations are hollow organizations that give the impression of representing a large number of people (broad community interests). False-front organizations are organizations with names that disguise their real interests and convey a positive connotation: for instance, Americans for Prosperity is a corporate-sponsored front organization opposed to public regulation, and FreedomWorks is corporate front bankrolling the Tea Bagger movement. The Coalition for Health Insurance Choices, which sponsored the "Harry and Louise" commercials against the Clinton health care proposals, was solely sponsored by the Health Insurance Association of America. The aim of these types of organizations is make them appear to have broad public interest and support rather than being motivated by narrow economic self-interest. The selection of name should capture the target's view of the public interest.

An example closer to home has been social work's efforts to obtain professional licensure social workers. Advocacy coalitions were often formed with names such as "The Coalition for Patients' Right to Choose." Usually it was not mentioned that the coalition was almost exclusively composed of social workers and that choice was limited to adding social workers only to the eligible vendors. The name, however, indicated a broad concern for patients' rights and choice—the public good.

When holding public rallies, forums, and other events, the advocate must consider presentation in terms of where and how to hold the event when policymakers and the media are invited. A rally that no one attends is not a viable influence technique! At legislative hearings and policymakers' town meetings, cover them, triangulate, and make scattered presentations, and use later presenters to counteract and respond to opposing positions.

Social workers can enter the policymaking process part-time and succeed. Richan (1996), Haynes and Mickelson (2002), the literally thousands of Web sites that can be found available under the search word *lobby* or *lobbyist* (including www.moveon.org and www.fcnl.org), and this text give ready guidance for beginning social policy advocates.

Using Clients as Witnesses. Direct service practitioners, of all the players in the political arena excepting one, are most likely to provide examples of the suffering that has been or will be caused by social welfare cutbacks and other punitive policy decisions or to find examples of people overcoming or successfully "coping with barriers" (Chapin, 1995, p. 511). That exception is the clients. However, it probably will be traumatic, even in this age of reality TV, for clients to bare their personal lives in a possibly hostile arena. Their impact may not live up to their potential. Many might be not be telegenic or convincing at hearings. To describe their lives in a concise and intriguing manner requires preparation, rehearsal, and role-play. If someone's privacy is protected with a pseudonym during the initial publicity, advocates must be able to prove the person exists, has the problem in question, and actually will be affected positively or negatively; reporters can check out such stories.

Protecting Clients and Citizens. It is unethical and unwise to thrust already vulnerable individuals into public view without first having their trust and permission and providing fully informed consent. Rehearsal and role-play should be done to prepare them to cope with hostility and embarrassment. Clients must be informed of and prepared for the risks inherent in *any* type of advocacy, including testifying. The risks go beyond exposure at hearings and may include retaliation, reduction or loss of benefits, the anger of family members, and anger from the community. Social workers can aid, if not fully protect, witnesses by accompanying them and handling the technical aspects of testifying to allow them simply to tell their stories. Both expert and human-interest witnesses are often prepared for the same hearing. Witnesses should dictate or write their own statements for easy grasp of the facts and easy oral presentation (Box 12.8).

Structural and System Change Advocacy

Advocacy for structural change is more fundamental in terms of the ends sought, it is more ideologically driven, and it is more revolutionary than is advocacy concerned with an individual's rights and interests (Ackerman & Alstott, 1999; Fabricant & Burghardt, 1992; Wagner, 1990). It can be promoted by either the political left or

BOX 12.8.	Guidelines for Legislative Testimony

- Know the legislation and review with sponsors any issues with the legislation.
- Coordinate testimony with sponsors and other coalition advocates to complement but not duplicate other advocates.
- Obtain the fiscal note from the Department of Fiscal Services that estimates the proposed legislation's cost to the state.
- Use the most informed and effective speakers to present testimony.
- Have facts and information well developed and rehearsed. Role-play and rehearse some more. Substantiate and validate your facts with logic, reason, and evidence. Use true personal testimony and cases.
  - Find true stories of real constituencies that relate favorably to the legislation's position. Use cases to stress your issue.
  - Keep it simple; it will be easier to tell and understand.
  - Be specific about what you want.
  - Tell the story in direct, strong, declarative sentences and structure.
  - Don't lie. Avoid hypothetical cases and find real ones.
- If you use statistics and numbers:
  - Put the numbers in human terms: "every man, woman, and child," "Three out of 10 children in your district."
  - Simplify the numbers by using examples of people.
  - Avoid percentages; use ratios such as "2 of 5" rather than "43%."
  - Use numbers sparingly
  - Use a reference or base for numbers dear to the policymakers.
  - Know your numbers and how they were developed. Be prepared to cite your source (ideally more than one).
- When testifying, be thoroughly prepared.
  - Identify yourself and your organization. Mention its location, especially if covers the relevant legislative district. If your organization is small, do not give its size.
  - State your position for or against the proposed bill.

- First, summarize your recommendations; then, develop each point. Organize your statement clearly and concisely. It is not necessary to make a lengthy, emotional exposition of a situation that needs correcting or a service that is needed; the members have probably heard it all before. Summarize and document your position but don't indulge in overkill. Avoid clichés, wordiness, vague generalities, and undue flattery.
- If possible, include the costs and savings of the proposed bill.
- Summarize your position at the end.
- Don't read the testimony. It is more effective to speak directly and forcefully to the committee members and maintain eye contact. Members are more likely to listen attentively and to refer to the written statement later.
- Be confident and cooperative. Committee members want to hear other viewpoints. They have no reason to embarrass or challenge you, but they may ask questions to clarify points you make. Respond directly if you can; if you do not know the answer, say so.
- Use experts only if they are effective speakers. Otherwise, submit the testimony as written testimony.
- Coordinate your testimony with that of other coalition supporters. Schedule, if possible, with the coalition supporter to open testimony and end testimony so that you can rebut the opposition.
- Prepare copies of your testimony and distribute them to the secretary or designated legislative staff person. Many members will not be present at the hearing, so be sure to have sufficient copies. Often others at the hearing will want copies.
- Do not let testimony inhibit other lobbying tactics. Hearings are frequently only show-and-tell exercises.
- If you cannot present oral testimony, send written statements to the committee chair and members.
- Follow up with committee members after the hearing.
- Report back to the coalition, grassroots group, and sponsors, and advise them on the next steps.

right, including faith-oriented networks that work to change the structural causes of poverty and injustice or to make the community a theocracy. The goal is not improving conditions for some, but fundamentally altering the community's structure. Institutional change implies "widespread and basic alteration" despite strong resistance (Brager, 1967, p. 61). Think of the long fight to overcome tobacco interests and end Jim Crow segregation, and the fight still going on to provide for adequate health care for all. Many systems affect our clients and society in general, and we want to be able to influence them. Those who would transform themselves and their environment must be able to construct a vision and convince the action and target systems as to how the community can be.

Transformative structural and systems change results in profound alteration or revitalization of society, although overthrow of an existing government or economy is not essential or even sufficient. Governments can change peacefully or violently without the community changing. The American civil rights movement transformed American society. Although not completely successful and at risk of regression, the United States has in 2010 an African-American president and a woman speaker of the House of Representatives, and the last four secretaries of state, America's ambassador to the world, have been a woman, an African-American, or both. These things were only imaginable in 1960 and have become reality thanks to the civil rights movement.

The community in structural change is both the action and target system. Alinsky (1972) says, "History is a relay of revolutions; the torch of idealism is carried by the revolutionary group until this group becomes an establishment, and then quietly the torch is put down to wait until a new revolutionary group picks it up for the next leg" (p. 22). Social work's capacity to carry the torch spotlights the contesting, but not contradictory, social ideologies of service and justice (Van Soest, 1994).

Systems Advocacy and Change

Individual, state, and national economic investment and boycotts are effective tools for system change. For instance, making socially responsible domestic investments or conducting boycotts can help develop grassroots, community-oriented, and self-help organizations. They were used in the American civil rights struggle and the South African campaign to end apartheid and are being used in the current immigration wars. As part of the advocacy spectrum, we have discussed the political system. However, the insurance system, the medical system, and the media as an institution also affect the average American. Campaigns are being waged to reform each.

Many attempts have been made and are being made nationally and internationally to transform various societal systems, including the economic system, the patriarchal family system, and gender roles. Community or neighborhood change might be provoked in a year or two, but major challenges to the social order take longer. Individual advocates are important in social movements for change. Imagine the American civil rights movement without Dr. Martin Luther King Jr. or the decades-long struggle to end apartheid in South Africa without Nelson Mandela. Individual actors and action do count, along with group and collective action. Elizabeth Cady Stanton and Susan B. Anthony toiled to abolish slavery, restrict liquor, and obtain property, marriage, and voting rights for women. Mother Jones started organizing coal miners at age 47 and continued for 40 years (Jones, 1980). George Wiley gave up a career as a celebrated chemistry professor at age 33 to fight for the down-and-out in civil rights and welfare rights struggles (Kotz & Kotz, 1977). James Chaney, Andrew Goodman, and Michael Schwerner gave their lives in the Mississippi Freedom Summer of 1964 and became the face of the movement for many young Americans. The first social workers, and early ones such as Harry Hopkins and Frances Perkins, were involved in many progressive battles for change, such as workers' rights, honest government, and Social Security. We have all been rewarded by the actions of these champions and the sacrifices of many unsung heroes. Goodwyn (1978) captures what is important about social movements and change endeavors to the people who are part of them (Box 12.9).

These words describe the aims of many of today's movements and embryo political parties. Today's protestors resist the latest version of a giant industrial engine. The International Monetary Fund and the World Bank, debtors and donors, have been brought to public attention. Globalization and extreme poverty have become part of our public discourse because of the insistence of advocates for systems change.

Large-scale social change endeavors often have tendrils reaching into community advocacy, political advocacy, and systems change.

BOX 12.9.   The Hope of Concerted Action

[Populism] was, first and most centrally, a cooperative movement that imparted a sense of self-worth to individual people and provided them with the instruments of self-education about the world they lived in. The movement gave them hope—a shared hope—that they were not impersonal victims of a gigantic industrial engine ruled by others but that they were, instead, people who could perform specific political acts of self-determination. . . . the men and women of the agrarian movement [were]

encouraged and enhanced by the sheer drama and power of their massive parades, their huge summer encampments, their far-flung lecturing system. . . . Populism was, at bottom, a movement of ordinary Americans to gain control over their own lives and futures, a massive democratic effort to gain that most central component of human freedom—dignity.

Source: Goodwyn (1978), pp. 196–197

The civil rights and women's movements are good examples (Hahn, 1994; Ryan, 1992). After working for years to achieve political change through suffrage and the Equal Rights Amendment (a failed constitutional amendment), women turned back to their communities and outward to larger systems, seeking other types of equality—in terms of jobs, education, insurance rates, and even public sanction regarding the sharing of domestic chores. After winning important gains in the judicial and legislative areas for years, African-Americans have experienced community setbacks tied to street crime and institutional setbacks tied to standardized testing and persistent incarceration. In short, progress is uneven and is undercut in insidious ways or occurs in unexpected ways; both the attack and the defense interweave multiple advocacy approaches. Yet victories continue. We have ethnic minorities, women, and gays in high elected office where previously they were not allowed.

Advocacy's Relevance to Direct Practice. Social workers who are in direct practice, the majority of social workers, have an advocacy obligation. Lee (1994) holds that the role of direct practice is to help clients develop self-advocacy skills by developing self-control, self-efficacy, and a self-construction as victors rather than victims, and assisting them in their empowerment. Practitioners can use their skills to link clients and assist them in making connections through social networks and community organizations. They can similarly encourage participation in the process when a need arises to engage in community intervention. Mondros and Wilson

(1994) make explicit the tie between organizing techniques and direct practice tasks, stating that a "clinician who works with a group of homeless mothers used these techniques to help them organize for repairs and police protection in a park where they frequently took their children. She saw this work as a natural extension of her clinical work with her group" (p. xvii).

The relationship between types of advocacy is clear. Past struggles influence much about our lives today—our work, our legacy. Our professional work frequently pertains to rights and programs that were won earlier through systems reform, which indicates that there truly is "give" in the system. In response to events such as elections, we often feel under siege from those opposed to what we value. Perhaps, though, reading history, we can more appropriately say, "Let's celebrate" because much has been won by and for progressives and social work. If there is ever any question as to whether we have allies or as to the existence of a flourishing spectrum in action, all we need do is look at the extensive inventory of national liberal advocacy groups.[4] There is, however, an equal list of conservative advocacy organizations.[5]

Change Modalities Relevant to Direct Service. Advocacy that melds with direct practice falls into three modalities:

- Ensuring individual rights: pursuing actual delivery of what everyone should have
- Public interest advocacy: participating in society's decisions and sharing benefits, power, and responsibilities

- Transformation: perceiving the possibility of a better, and profoundly different, society and working to bring it about

All three manifestations of change make members of marginal and invisible groups more central and visible, address social isolation and disenfranchisement, link individuals to social resources and contribute to their social capital, and promote empowerment, confidence, and optimism. Wandersman and his associates (Wandersman, Clary, Forbush, Weinberger, Coyne, & Duffy, 2006), after researching mentoring programs, concluded that they "have the potential to contribute to positive youth development, yet that potential is not always realized (p. 781)." The researchers propose a direct service model that "incorporates roles for both community organizing and advocacy" (p. 789). Pearrow's (2008) review of urban youth empowerment programs concluded that uniting youths to work together in social action is an essential component of Team Empowerment, and addressed skills development at both the individual and group levels. Engaging in community organizing and critically examining community issues provide young people with the experience, self-efficacy, and social connections to continue to work for community-based change.

Client Advocate and Practice Roles. To accomplish the important work of client advocacy, the professional's work extends from supportive personal advocacy to confrontations to help clients. Advocacy tactics are determined by the involved client or client system's preferences and the action system's (clients, agency, community organizations) operational comfort level with tactics ranging from education and consciousness raising to disruption. A task for the advocate-practitioner often is to help the action system expand its comfort level to include the most effective and efficient interventions.

To return to our early example of crowded schools, we can think of many types of advocacy with which to address the problem. The parents could advocate for themselves as taxpayers on behalf of their children. A social worker could write a letter to the board of education or lobby an influential alumnus to call for improvements. A worker could take the concerns of parents from several schools to the media and help the parents give interviews. A worker could organize a campaign to get local firms to forego their annual holiday parties one year in order to buy textbooks, or could organize parents and neighborhood churches to boycott the school until their demands for improvement are met. A worker could drive a group of parents to meet with their legislator regarding equity in education. A worker could build a coalition to overturn school funding that is based on property taxes.

With an ongoing and complex issue, it is common—though not always necessary—to begin with individual advocacy and progress to institutional change. Consider an addictions worker who counsels individuals and then becomes involved with Mothers Against Drunk Driving (MADD). Initially, the worker helps support the members' personal feelings and provides community education, and later engages in joint efforts with the organization to secure tough yet humane sentencing. This advocacy finally leads the worker to oppose the advertising of alcohol. Activities along the spectrum can be conducted consecutively or simultaneously. Parts of the spectrum interrelate and the process, even for a single advocate, is dynamic. As the advocate engages in advocacy, consciousness is raised.

Box 12.10 reminds us that client and community advocacy can transpire in ways other than heated controversy. Schneider and Lester (2001) recommend the use of the general practice model when attempting to influence powerful people whose decisions will affect clients:

1. Identify issues and set goals.
2. Get the facts.
3. Plan strategies and tactics.
4. Supply leadership.
5. Get to know decision makers and their staff.
6. Broaden your base of support.
7. Be persistent.
8. Evaluate your advocacy effort.

Supporting the Spectrum: Job Descriptions and Advocacy Postures

Some workers are hired advocates. Others, like the late Dorothy Height, a social worker and

BOX 12.10.	Advocates Confront Myriad Problems with Clients

Setting: Office of Customer Relations Representative

Advocate: I am a community service worker with the Neighborhood Center. Our office provides assistance in housing and utility issues. This is Mrs. Edna Gardner. We requested an appointment because she received a telephone call stating that her service would be terminated today due to nonpayment of bills.

Utility Rep: Yes, I am aware of Mrs. Gardner's bill. (To client) Mrs. Gardner, you are two months in arrears, plus the current bill for June is due. We have received no payment. You did not contact us to say when we could expect payment, so we have no alternative but to discontinue your service.

Client: Look, I have three children at home. There has to be another way. Don't turn off the gas.

Utility Rep: There is another way. Pay your bills on time like any other good citizen.

Advocate: That is exactly why we are here today. To work out an arrangement so Mrs. Gardner can pay her bill. Mrs. Gardner and I have discussed the situation and feel a deferred payment plan might be a solution.

Utility Rep: In some situations deferred payment is a solution. When we feel there is a strong likelihood that individuals will live up to their obligations to make installment payments, we agree to such a plan. Quite frankly, Mrs. Gardner, you don't appear to fit into that category.

Client: (Angry) What do you mean? I have tried very hard to pay all my bills and it's not easy. Have you ever tried coping as a single parent?

Advocate: (To client) Just a minute, Mrs. Gardner. (To utility rep) Let me explain that Mrs. Gardner moved in March, so she did not receive a bill in April. Therefore, her bill in May was over $175. She did try to explain her inability to pay to your office, but unfortunately a payment agreement was not proposed at that time. Also, Mrs. Gardner had not received written notification that her service was to be terminated and did not realize how serious the situation was until today. Mrs. Gardner is prepared to make an initial payment on her bill right now.

Utility Rep: Well, we require at least half of the amount in arrears, which would be approximately $85 to $90.

Advocate: We are prepared to pay $60 today.

Utility Rep: I just told you we need at least half of the amount in arrears.

Advocate: I've worked with your office before, and the policy has been to accept initial payments as low as one-third of that amount.

Utility Rep: $80.

Advocate: Let me check with Mrs. Gardner (talks to her quietly, then to the utility rep). $70 is the most we can pay today, but we'll assure you of three installment payments of approximately $35 to pay the rest.

Utility Rep: How do you expect to make the payments if you can't even come up with $80?

Advocate: We will manage that aspect of our agreement. What we need to do now is put the terms of this agreement in writing, in Mrs. Gardner's file, and issue the stop order on the turnoff.

Utility Rep: You'll pay $70 today and $35 for 3 months?

Client: Yes.

Utility Rep: However, since Mrs. Gardner's service was scheduled to be turned off today, the service men are probably at the house now.

Advocate: We just mutually agreed to a plan.

Utility Rep: Well, it's all right by me, and if we had entered into the plan yesterday or before the truck started on its rounds. . . . Now, once the reconnect charge is paid, our arrangement will go into effect.

Advocate: Your company policy has been not to terminate service once a payment plan has been set up. There can't be a reconnect charge either under the circumstances. You must be able to stop the shutoff.

Utility Rep: You came too late. There is no way I can reach the men now.

Advocate: Someone must have contact with the service truck.

Utility Rep: I don't.

Advocate: Then let me speak to your supervisor.

Utility Rep: You'd like to speak with my supervisor?

Advocate: Yes, we would.

Source: National Public Law Training Center script in Advocacy Spectrum manual. Some of the material on authority figures is taken from a videotape and manuals by the National Public Law Training Center (NPLTC), a former advocacy training organization. Robert Hoffman and Pat Powers produced the video. George Hacker, William Fry, Barry Greever, Cathy Howell, and Pat Powers, among others, contributed to NPLTC's Advocacy Spectrum training manual. Advocacy Spectrum (n.d.). Manual developed by the National Public Law Training Center, a nonprofit organization. Washington, D.C.

crusader for social justice, undertake advocacy as a professional and personal obligation (Fox, 2010). till otherssocial workers, like all clinicians, must engage in case advocacy to fulfill their professional obligations. As a social worker commented on a computer bulletin board, while discussing a mistreated patient, "I was developing a pretty strong hankering to do some serious advocacy work here, even though it is not my job as a clinician." To paraphrase Rick (Humphrey Bogart) in *Casablanca*, the clinician was misinformed.[6] Clinicians *are* case advocates for their clients. Social workers need to act as advocates or obtain more effective advocates, if available.

Advocate and Ombudsperson. The advocacy role and the ombudsperson role are frequently confused. An *advocate* pushes the interests of a person, group, community, a point of view, a cause, or a social and political philosophy. An *ombudsperson* serves more as a go-between, an interpreter, and a problem solver, untangling various points of view, and sees if rules, procedures, and contracts are honored. An ombudsperson is not a conventional mediator or alternative dispute resolution player but rather an effective criticizer who tries to "set right" the government system that is "out of gear." The ombudsperson's powers are "to investigate, criticize, recommend, and publicize" (Davis, 1975, p. 286). Advocate most frequently work outside government or the target organization, while ombudspersons normally work as grievance handlers and red-tape cutters within agencies or targets. Ombudspersons often have license to constructively critique their employers, even publicly, although they usually function quietly, providing information, referrals, and complaint resolution. Others in human services, such as patient advocates/ombudspersons in hospitals, creatively combine the seemingly incompatible roles. The important quality is adequate authority, since the job involves questioning professionals about their actions or inactions and ruffling feathers. Tower (1994) argues that client-centered social service agencies should "establish ombudsmen or other client assistance programs to resolve conflicts between the agency and its consumers" (p. 196).

Internal Advocates Advocacy can arise inside or outside an agency. An *internal advocate* makes changes for the client through vigilance and intervention inside the agency, using decision-making channels, where possible, and informal influence systems. Schneider and Lester (2001) believe, "Internal advocates can be very effective in carrying out their role of representing the needs of those who cannot speak out or who do not have natural advocates within a service delivery system" (p. 307). More than supervisors' temperaments, the organizational culture may dictate constraints. Tower (1994) urges administrators who care about their clientele to "support and enhance the advocacy efforts of their frontline workers. After all, they are the ones most acutely aware of the client's unmet needs. It is likely that the main reason that more practitioners are not currently involved in consumer movements is fear of repercussion, primarily from their employers" (p. 196).

Mounting a major change effort in a system that serves as one's employer is obviously a challenge. Usually one can rely on some colleagues to help, but it may require "keeping community groups informed of agency developments that go against their community interests" (Galper, 1975, p. 205). We discussed internal advocacy and its perils in Chapter 8.

Best Interests Versus Stated Wishes of Client. The question as to whether a practitioner-advocate follows the stated wishes of the client or pursues the client's best interests is more apparent than real. Self-determination and client empowerment argue that a client, not a practitioner-advocate, should decide the client's best interests. Practitioner-advocates are not savants best able to determine the client's best interests. The practitioner-advocate's responsibility is to provide the client with his or her best judgments of the consequences of pursuing the client's wishes. He or she can argue with the client. But a client's capacity to make the decisions is a question for guardians or the courts, not the practitioner-advocate. Clients have the right to self-determination. However, the practitioner-advocate does not have an obligation to assist a client in foolish, unethical, illegal, or self-destructive behavior.

The practitioner-advocate can withdraw from the relationship.

Conciliatory Versus Adversarial Strategies. How long to cooperate, coerce, or compromise before becoming adversarial is a critical consideration. Wood and Middleman (1989) warn against escalating too soon on behalf of powerless clients, who, unlike the worker, will suffer the consequences if the action fails. They insist that the roles of broker and mediator must be tried first (p. 142). On the other hand, Patti and Resnick (1972) urge workers who want to change their agencies to consider both collaborative and adversarial strategies, depending on the circumstances. One consideration should be whether or not the target of change is "rational, open to new ideas, and acting in good faith" (Patti & Resnick, 1972, p. 224). We must carefully consider with clients and colleagues whether a combative or a facilitative stance will be most productive in a given situation.

Key Advocacy Skills

This final section briefly reviews four basic skills used in advocacy processes. They have been discussed elsewhere in this text.

Basic Skills

Persuasion. Persuasion is a key interpersonal skill used in both micro and macro interchanges. It involves promoting, marketing, working for favorable interpretations for a client or a cause, and changing minds (Mondros & Wilson, 1994). Persuasion is part of many practice situations— for example, during program development, case conferences, discharge planning, and many others. It is a pivotal skill in policy situations, which require knowing the pressure points and how to use them (Flynn, 1985). Persuasion can take many forms; an advocate may win a public argument by using a dramatic story that can "unify and energize community and reinforce values and inspire collective action" (Felkins, 2002, p. 50).

As Ezell (2001) states, "Many times the success of advocacy is reduced to one's ability to persuade another person in a certain way [using] logic, emotion, or values" (p. 184). Having personal persuasiveness (Burghardt, 1982) and projecting "personal authoritativeness" (Jansson, 1990, p. 201) combined with a solid command of the facts can be compelling.

Rules of thumb for persuading others are:

- Know what you want.
- Know the facts and have them available.
- Understand your source of power.
- Rehearse, and then rehearse some more.
- Use clear, simple language and visuals.
- Appeal to both emotions and logic.
- Make eye contact if culturally appropriate.

Representation. As societal transactions grow increasingly complex, it becomes more difficult for individuals to have the knowledge and capacity to conduct all of their affairs directly. Consequently, most of us need an experienced person to lead us through certain areas. Just as we turn to instructors to teach us first aid or how to drive a car, others request our help to obtain public housing, credit counseling, or union job protection during pregnancy. Representation begins when one person asks another person and the second person agrees to become a spokesperson. To represent someone is to take that person's view (or to work out a meeting of the minds together), to advocate, while being forthright about the person's chances and prospects—and when nothing can be done. Adeptness is required in communication, finding out the client's real wants and needs (his or her construction, not just ours) and educating and motivating the client to become a self-advocate.

Representation often involves a forum such as a meeting or session or assembly (Schenider & Lester, 2001, p. 96) where the advocate and person seeking help together make a case. Non-lawyers can act as authorized representatives, if requested, by an eligible person or recipient for federal programs including Social Security, Medicare, SSI, veterans, and public housing. Here is an example of the type of representation form that is used by some agencies to formalize the relationship.

AUTHORIZATION AND WAVER OF CONFIDENTIALITY

To _____ [agency]:

This is to notify you that I, _____ [client's name], residing at _____ [client's address], hereby authorize _____ [representative's name] of _____ [advocate's agency] to act as my representative regarding _____ [program]. You are authorized to release any and all records and information relating to me and/or my case, including confidential information, as my representative may request.

_____ [client's signature]

Rules of thumb for representation include:

- Discover and check out what your client wants and how he or she views the need for representation.
- Establish whether someone besides the affected party needs to be involved.
- Assess the need and share your assessment with the client.
- Lay out options and let the client decide the desirable ones and their order of importance.
- Determine the formality of the contract and process.
- Agree upon the division of labor, encouraging the client to increase his or her level of self-advocacy.
- Coordinate with each other and become an action system, guarding against divide-and-conquer tactics.

Allow the client to hire and fire you and celebrate the success of the client's becoming empowered and no longer needing you.

Negotiation and Bargaining. Community practitioners negotiate and bargain informally and formally to build networks (as discussed in Chapter 10), on behalf of neighborhoods, programs, and projects, and during issue campaigns. Kahn (1991) uses this definition: "Negotiations occur when the two sides (or three or four) sit down together and try to come up with a resolution that is acceptable, if not completely satisfactory, to all parties concerned" (p. 175). It is important to know your position and to learn quickly whether the negotiator has decision-making authority. Bargaining is a "process whereby two or more parties attempt to settle what each shall give and take, or perform and receive, in transactions between them" (Rubin & Brown, 1975, p. 2). The major approaches to negotiation are bargaining and problem solving. Negotiation and bargaining are also covered in Chapter 10 and we have included negotiation exercises at the end of chapter..

Bargaining and Problem Solving. The negotiation literature on agreement building dichotomizes bargaining and problem-solving approaches. Those who emphasize bargaining (Halpern, 1999; Kolb & Williams, 2000) are more likely to stress control and tactics: where to sit at the table, timing, reading the opposition, and so forth. To know how to bargain during the actual negotiation, negotiators engage intensively with those they represent. Those who emphasize problem solving (Gibelman & Demone, 1990; Sebenius, 2001) are more likely to stress the big picture, understanding, and what-if questions.

Problem solvers work toward reaching a collaborative solution that concludes in a workable agreement. Ideally, each party leaves the negotiation feeling that it has attained something it wanted.

Interest-based negotiation stresses the following elements of a successful, principled negotiation (Field, 2000):

1. *Interests* (each party's needs, desires, concerns, and fears)
2. *Options* (potential solutions parties can take together)
3. *Alternatives* (each party's independent choices)
4. *Criteria* (established standards for legitimacy and fairness)
5. *Communication* (organized thinking, addressing misunderstandings, questioning, listening)
6. *Relationships* (establishing trust, working relationship)
7. *Commitment* (clear, feasible agreements)

Skills and Rules of Thumb Reaching a successful negotiated agreement and bargaining is not easy, but the good news is that negotiation is a learnable skill. There is a procedural and psychological process to negotiation—give and take. Kaine (1993) believes that one controls a negotiation by questioning, not arguing. Kaine gives invaluable advice on how to steer negotiations, be clear, and make the other side more receptive: "For example, before making a point, the expert negotiator says, 'I would like to make a point.' He then makes his point. He says, 'May I ask a question?' and then asks a question. If he has a concern, he will say, 'I have a concern,' and then states it. . . . Good negotiators do not label their disagreements. They do not say 'I disagree with you because . . .' [They might say] 'I have this point I would like to discuss with you. It is . . ., and as a result, I disagree'" (p. 40).

In their book on making deals, Gottlieb and Healy (1990) recommend that negotiators prepare to deal effectively with an adversary by doing the following: (1) take an inventory of the adversary's assets and liabilities; (2) make thorough preparations by knowing the needs of the adversary and his or her end goal; (3) don't underestimate the amount of strength the adversary possesses in this process; (4) project a belief that your offer is the best available alternative (BATANA), and (5) rely on your expertise as a problem solver. Negotiators should remember they can decide to walk away and should exercise patience and self-control because many concessions take place late, close to a deadline.

To engage in successful negotiation, Gottlieb and Healey (1990, pp. 38–44) also say to:

- Explore possible options and alternatives and closely examine areas of conflict to help establish a creative, problem-solving climate where people collaborate rather than compromise.
- Use "trading off," the process of sorting, evaluating, and deciding which options would work most effectively for your party and the other side. Be sure and analyze how a trade-off affects the other variables in your equation and what you get for what you give.
- Try to control the pace of communication. Don't be rushed into agreement. Continually

assert that issues are open until agreement. Issues are interrelated and changes in one will affect the others.
- Maximize your impact as a negotiator by personalizing yourself and the situation.

Interacting with Authority Figures

An advocate must know how to contend, how to insist, how to negotiate, how to bargain, and how to leave. This means defending and protecting an individual, getting those who have authority and hold power to change their minds or behavior, and holding one's ground with intimidating people. The requisite is knowing what to do and doing it in the face of opposition.

Those in Key Positions Rational/legal authority, as discussed in Chapter 8, is the legitimate power to influence or command thought, opinion, or behavior. A rational/legitimate authority figure is a person in command who has legitimate power to make decisions. Any practitioner-advocate wanting to help others or make changes in a community must deal with authority figures. The way authority holders are dealt with is a major determinant of the results. There need be nothing sinister or malevolent about authority figures. They can exercise discretion. They may mistake authority for power and be intimidating in their bearing, demeanor, or tone of voice. Simon (1994) entreats us to "interrupt contempt" (p. 189). The practitioner-advocate must anticipate a variety of responses from the authority figures involved because each has a different personality.

In negotiating and confronting authority holders, learn what rules and policies a given authority holder is subject to or must abide by, as well as those that he or she controls. Hold the authority holder to his or her rules; if the rules are not followed, get a trade-off. Advocates must know the chain of command in any situation. In bureaucracies, "the power of the advocate is the potential power to escalate the problem, to raise it to higher levels in the hierarchy" (Wood & Middleman, 1989, p. 142). The situation presented in Box 12.10 illustrates this. It also highlights how frequently technical jargon unfamiliar to the layperson is used, whether in a business or social services agency. Note these other points as well:

- Do not let others shift the burden of responsibility on every point to you.
- Don't assume that a person who has the authority to make a certain decision can decide all things.
- Do not waste time and effort in small talk, trying to appease, ingratiate or bully, or over-explaining or excusing the client's situation.
- Do keep focused.

Years ago, Grosser (1965) argued that advocacy was necessary because arbitrariness and discretion can create an uneven playing field:

Often the institutions with which local residents must deal are not even neutral, much less positively motivated, toward handling the issues brought to them by community groups. In fact, they are frequently overtly negative and hostile, often concealing or distorting information about rules, procedures, and office hours. By their own partisanship . . . they create an atmosphere that demands advocacy on behalf of the poor. . . . If the community worker is to facilitate productive interaction between residents and institutions, it is necessary . . . to provide leadership and resources directed toward eliciting information, arguing the correctness of a position, and challenging the stance of the institution. (p. 18)

While these words are equally relevant today, confrontation is not inevitable. Many situations are resolved amicably. It is important for practitioner-advocates to be aware that those in key positions view their reputations or jobs as being on the line, much as we feel about our clients and our jobs. We should respond to antagonism with firmness. "The impulse to obey authority and the reluctance to confront it are deeply ingrained in the human psyche" (Bell, 1994, p. 136). Transactional analysts might say that many over-adapt and become passive-aggressive. Workers and clients are likely to react similarly to those who have the power to influence outcomes—with awe, avoidance, and anger. Professionals who make themselves interact anyway go on to become effective advocates.

Rules of thumb for dealing with authority include the following:

- Know the system being confronted.
- Know the facts.

- Be ready to demonstrate that you have done your part.
- Know what you want (and BATANA).
- Consider all options about the time, place, and manner of engagement.
- Have materials organized in serviceable fashion for use under pressure.
- Speak in an even tone.
- Listen carefully and take notes.
- Look for a clear decision.

Virtual Advocacy Virtual advocacy, or more accurately the use of the Internet to advocate, is a widespread and growing phenomenon. Advocacy groups can rally their supporters to e-mail political policymakers and provide the supporters with links to the decision makers' e-mail boxes. MoveOn.org has used this tactic for what it labels *virtual marches* on Washington and Wall Street, as well as massive e-mail campaigns.

Blogs are posted for any cause, issue, or candidate (Box 12.11). A Google search on April 29, 2010, using the search words *virtual advocacy* generated 3,080,000 sites. Virtual pro-life advocacy produced over 65,000 sites, and prochoice a lesser number of sites, 38,400. The blogs can be used for public education, persuasion, social marketing, developing virtual networks and mailing lists, and rallying and communicating with supporters (Confessore, 2006; Galst, 2009, Wildman, n.d.). It is widely used in political campaigns to generate money (Luo, 2008) and voter support (Lyall, 2010). When combined with Facebook, YouTube, Twitter, and the other networking sites, virtual advocacy has the potential to be powerful. The challenge is to break through the clutter and not become spam or end up at the bottom of the list of sites. This will require a *hit strategy* and links with a variety of other sites.

As Lohmann and McNutt (2005) point out, virtual advocacy has not been rigorous evaluated. It has been used extensive by cause and political organizations. Some claim success for virtual campaigning in fundraising (Luo, 2008), as by the Obama campaign, and in rallying voters (Lyall, 2010). In any case, as with the other components of community practice, it is a crucial skill for advocacy.

| **BOX 12.11.** | Advocacy and Empowerment via Internet |

The schizophrenia discussion group (SCHIZOPH) is an open, unmoderated group composed of approximately 250 individuals at any given point in time. They come from all over the world and their main interest is in discussing about issues related to severe mental illnesses, in particular schizophrenia. The members of this forum are consumers, parents, and professionals from various disciplines . . .

It all started with a simple posting by one member of the group to the listserv.

Are you familiar with the 44-year-old woman with schizophrenia who has broken into David Letterman's house on more than one occasion, and had delusions that she was his wife?

Well, it seems this same woman had a cup of coffee in a diner in Fond Du Lac, Wisconsin, yesterday. She tried to pay her 79-cent bill with a quarter and a package of instant hot cocoa mix. The diner called the police, and they arrested her.

She refused to have her mug shot taken and fingerprints taken because she believes that the government can eliminate her from the human race if they are allowed to take these things from her. She is being held in the city jail until she consents to the photographs and fingerprints.

Pretty big deal over a cup of coffee, I'd say.

This posting generated many responses from the group.

What's the name of the restaurant? I'll send them their money with a (nice) letter attached.

I certainly would write a letter and send the rest of the bill. How much was it?

Hi. Thanks for your words of support and encouragement. The bill was only 79 cents, but I figure if everyone sends the money and a letter, it would make quite a statement, don't you?

Yes, I think we should send letters and $.79 to the restaurant and a copy of the letters to the police.

If you call the TV station, you may be able to find out the name of the restaurant. However, it might have a greater impact to send the 79 cents plus letters to the TV station rather than the restaurant, anyway!!!

I SECOND THAT MOTION!!!

On Thursday, 20th of March 1997, less than a week after the first posting of the incident, the group got the news that someone was listening to their voice.

That evening the WBAY news carried the whole story explaining what had occurred and had interviews with psychiatrists and others involved. The group felt that they had made their point and affected the community.

The arrest of a woman in North Fond Du Lac last week touched a nerve nationwide . . . Action 2 News has since received numerous letters containing 79 cents—the cost of the coffee—as well as e-mail.

. . . All expressed dismay that someone with a mental illness was arrested for not paying for a cup of coffee. (WBAY News)

The judge in the case decided that the 17 days the person served in jail was adequate punishment and ordered her release. The members of SCHIZOPH were euphoric about the success of their campaign.

Source: From "The 79-Cent Campaign: The Use of On-Line Mailing Lists for Electronic Advocacy" (pp. 75–79), by G. M. Menon, 2000, *Journal of Community Practice*, 8(3), Copyright 2000 by *Journal of Community Practice*. Used with permission of Routledge.

Discussion Exercises

1. *Read the works of Pertschuk (1986), Tower (1994), or Courter (1995) included in the reference list below and discuss the attributes of an individual advocate.*
2. *George Wiley was admired by social workers who worked with him in the welfare and civil rights movements. His belief was that he should use himself fully. His biographers (Kotz & Kotz, 1977) describe him as:*
   - *Well organized, energetic, and uninhibited*
   - *Committed to obtaining information and data*

   - *Able to present information clearly and powerfully*
   - *Able to link diverse, strong-minded allies*
   - *Able to get others involved.*

   Wiley's biographers portray him as someone who:
   - *Believed he could convince others—even foes*
   - *Juggled myriad tasks but kept his eye on the target*
   - *Applied heady ideas in practical ways*
   - *Made and kept lists (e.g., resources, contacts)*
   - *Listened well*
   - *Sought out mentors and fundraising help*
   - *Wanted to achieve concrete gains.*

Pick someone you know who is successful at community practice. What traits and skills does he or she have?

3. *Read Bombyk's (1995) Encyclopedia of Social Work article on progressive social work. Bombyk challenges us to name a current social worker with a national reputation for championing the interests of underdogs. Who were the past champions?*

4. *Music is an emotional stimulus—think of We Shall Overcome for the civil rights movement and Joe*

Hill and Which Side Are You On? for the labor movement. What songs and music have you incorporated into practice? What songs are appropriate for social justice, gay rights, women's rights, immigrant's rights?

5. *As a research project, trace the legislative and advocacy history of the health care reform bills of 2010. Find out the names of the key individual lobbyists (social workers and others) who advocated for the mentally ill. Who was most effective and why?*

Appendix 12.1: Illustrative Exercises

An Actual Negotiation

Officials finally cracked down on slum landlords. They condemned an apartment building that had hundreds of housing code violations and announced that the owner would receive criminal penalties as well as fines. However, the city insisted that the building had to be emptied for repairs. Community advocates argued the plan was unfair to the tenants who, after living in lousy conditions for years, now would be forced to find scarce affordable housing. The advocates entered into negotiations with city officials, the owner-landlord, and the owner's lawyer. A compromise was achieved. The building was sold to the tenants for one dollar. Social workers and tenant leaders coordinated the cleanup and rehab of the building. The property owner paid for extensive repairs to the building. He was not jailed but was prohibited from owning any more residential property in the city.

Explain how this example illustrates a win–win negotiation. What leverage was used to achieve this result? Were the advocates negotiating with one, two, or three parties?

Putting Oneself to the Test

The following scenario will allow you to practice negotiation skills. Decide if you will take a bargaining or a problem-solving approach.

As director of your county mental health program, you have been handed a hot potato assignment. Bordering your headquarters is a parcel of land and a boarded-up county mental hospital, a relic of an earlier era. The county has decided to sell the land and building, with half of the proceeds going to your program's group homes and transitional housing program. Zoning regulations permit the property to be used for a variety of purposes. However, concerns about appropriate uses have been debated for months in the press. The worth of the property has also been the subject of intense speculation. County Council Head Beverly Basey once asserted the land is worth at least $3 million.

Today, you receive a copy of a fax addressed to the Council from a prospective buyer, Douglas Younger, the head of the Ballet and Modern Dance Academy. *Their organization has unexpectedly received a huge bequest that will enable them to purchase the land and make massive renovations to the building. On behalf of the Academy, Younger offers a total purchase price of $4 million to be paid in two segments three years apart, plus an annual payment of $75,000 for 20 years in lieu of property taxes. Since he wishes to immediately launch a capital campaign, Younger concludes:*

"I request an immediate meeting with you, Madame Chair, or your authorized designee to negotiate a mutually acceptable purchase agreement, in order that this important project may see fruition."

You get a follow-up e-mail from Chairperson Basey asking you to represent the county in negotiations and to quickly respond to Younger. County lawyers will be involved after you have resolved any initial sticking points.

What should your primary consideration be in preparing to handle the County Council's directive? Are there creative ways to negotiate benefits for your client group?

Notes

1. These statements apparent has produced the apocryphal task attributed to Alinsky that the organizer-agitator "rubs raw the sores of discontent."

2. Assets inventory and mapping are discussed in the community assessment chapters.

3. Adam Smith on business: "People of the same trade seldom meet together, even for merriment and diversion, but the conversation ends in a conspiracy against the public, or in some contrivance to raise prices. . . . But though the law cannot hinder people of the same trade from sometimes assembling together, it ought to do nothing to facilitate such assemblies; much less to render them necessary" (Smith, 1922, p. 130).

4. For a list of progressive organizations see: http://www.startguide.org/orgs/orgs00.html.

5. For a list of 527s organizations see: http://www.opensecrets.org/527s/527grps.php

6. Rick Blaine, café owner: "My health. I came to Casablanca for the waters." Captain Renault: "The waters? What waters? We're in the desert." Rick: "I was misinformed." *Casablanca* (1942), Michael Curtiz, Director. Warner Brothers Pictures.

References

Ackerman, B., & Alstott, A. (1999). *The stakeholder society*. New Haven, CT: Yale University Press.

Addams, J. (1910). *Twenty years at Hull House*. New York: Macmillan.

Alinsky, S. D. (1989). *Rules for radicals: A pragmatic primer for realistic radicals*. New York: Vintage Books.

Alvarez, A. R., & Gutierrez, L. M. (2001). Choosing to do participatory research: An example and issues of fit to consider. *Journal of Community Practice*, 9(1), 1–20.

Barstow, D., (2010, February 15). Tea Party lights fuse for rebellion on right. *The New York Times*. Retrieved February 17, 2010, from: http://www.nytimes.com/2010/02/16/us/politics/16teaparty.html

Bell, D. A. (1994). *Confronting authority: Reflections of an ardent protester*. Boston: Beacon Press.

Bombyk, M. (1995). Progressive social work. In R. L. Edwards (Ed.-in-Chief), *Encyclopedia of social work* (19th ed., pp. 1933–1942). Washington, DC: National Association of Social Workers.

Brager, G. (1967). Institutional change: Parameters of the possible. *Social Work*, 12(1), 59–69.

Burghardt, S. (1982). *The other side of organizing*. Cambridge, MA: Schenkman.

Butcher, H., B., Banks, S., Henderson, P., with Robertson, J. (2007). *Critical community practice*. Bristol, UK: The Policy Press.

Butcher, H. B. (2007), Power and empowerment: The foundations of critical community practice. In H. B. Butcher, S. Banks, & P. Henderson, with J. Robertson (Eds.), *Critical community practice* (pp. 17–33). Bristol, UK: The Policy Press.

Chapin, R. K. (1995). Social policy development: The strengths perspective. *Social Work*, 40(4), 506–514.

Confessore, N. (2006, April 16), Virtual army of bloggers battles a development. *The New York Times*. Retrieved April 30, 2010, from: http://query.nytimes.com/gst/fullpage.html?res=9C07E7DF173FF935A25757C0A9609C8B63

Courter, G. (1995). *True stories of a child advocate: I speak for this child*. New York: Crown.

Davis, K. C. (1975). *Administrative law and government*. St. Paul, MN: West.

DeVries, C. M., & Vanderbilt, M. W. (1992). *The grassroots lobbying handbook: empowering nurses through legislative and political action* (ANA publication GR-4). Washington, DC: American Nurses Publishing.

Donaldson, L. P., & Shields, J. (2009). Development of the Policy Advocacy Behavior Scale: Initial reliability and validity. *Research on Social Work Practice*, 19(1), 83–92.

Ehrenreich, B., (2009). Foreclosure fightback. *The Nation*, 288 (5), 11–15.

Ezell, M. (2001). *Advocacy in the human services*. Belmont, CA: Brooks/Cole.

Fabricant, M., & Burghardt, S. (1992). *Welfare state crisis and the transformation of social service work*. Armonk, NY: M. E. Sharpe.

Ferris, K. (2009, February 15.). Community organizing proves helpful–to GOP. *The Philadelphia Inquirer*, D1, D6.

Felkins, P. K. (2002). *Community work: Creating and celebrating community in organizational life*. Cresskill, NJ: Hampton Press, Inc.

Field, C. G. (2000, December). *Description of principled negotiations*. Handout at workshop on Interest-based negotiation held in Baltimore, MD.

Florida PTA (2010). *Lobbying techniques*. Retrieved April 28, 2010, from: www.floridapta.org.

Flynn, J. P. (1985). *Social agency policy: Analysis and presentation for community practice*. Chicago: Nelson-Hall.

Fox, M. (2010, April 21). Dorothy Height, largely unsung giant of the civil rights era, dies at 98. *The New York Times*, p. A25.

Freire, P. (1971). *Pedagogy of the oppressed*. New York: Herder & Herder.

Galper, J. H. (1975). *The politics of social services*. Englewood Cliffs, NJ: Prentice Hall.

Galst, L. (2009, November 12). Campaigning for a cause (and customers). *The New York Times*.

Retrieved April 30, 2010, from: http://green.blogs. nytimes.com/2009/11/12/campaigning-for-a-cause

Gamson, W. A. (1992). *Talking politics*. New York: Cambridge University Press.

Gibelman, M., & Demone, H. W., Jr. (1990). Negotiating: A tool for inter-organizational coordination. *Administration in Social Work*, 14(4), 29–42.

Goodwyn, L. (1978). *Democratic promise: The populist movement*. New York: Oxford University Press.

Gottlieb, M. R., & Healy, W. J. (1990). *Making deals: The business of negotiation*. New York: New York Institute of Finance.

Grosser, C. F. (1965). Community development programs serving the urban poor. *Social Work*, 10(3), 15–21.

Grosser, C. F. (1976). *New directions in community organization: From enabling to advocacy* (2nd ed.). New York: Praeger.

Gutierrez, L. M. (1994, June). Beyond coping: An empowerment perspective on stressful life events. *Journal of Sociology and Social Welfare*, 21(3), 201–219.

Hahn, A. J. (1994). *The politics of caring: Human services at the local level*. Boulder, CO: Westview.

Halpern, R. G. (1999). Opening a new door to negotiation strategy. *Trial*, 35(6), 22–29.

Handler, J. F. (1978). *Social movements and the legal system: A theory of law reform and social change*. New York: Academic Press.

Hardina, D. (1995). Do Canadian social workers practice advocacy? *Journal of Community Practice*, 2(3), 97–121.

Hartman, A. (1993). The professional is political. *Social Work*, 38(4), 365–366.

Haynes, K., & Mickelson, J. (2002). *Affecting change: Social workers in the political arena* (5th ed.). New York: Longman.

Herrick, J. M., & Stuart, P. H. (Eds.) (2005). *Encyclopedia of social welfare history in North America*. Thousand Oaks, CA: Sage Publications.

Hick, S., & McNutt, J. G. (Eds.). (2002). *Advocacy, activism, and the Internet: Community organization and social policy*. Chicago: Lyceum Books.

Hyde, C. (1994). Commitment to social change: Voices from the feminist movement. *Journal of Community Practice*, 1(2), 45–64.

Jacobson, M. (2007). Food matters. *Journal of Community Practice*, 15(3), 37–55.

Jannson, B. S. (1990). *Social welfare policy: From theory to practice*. Belmont, CA: Wadsworth.

Johnson, L. C. (1995). *Social work practice: A generalist approach* (5th ed.). Boston: Allyn & Bacon.

Jones, M. H. (1980). *The autobiography of Mother Jones*. Chicago: Charles H. Kerr.

Kahn, S. (1991). *Organizing: A guide for grassroots leaders*. Silver Spring, MD: National Association of Social Workers.

Kaine, J. W. (1993). Don't fight—Negotiate. *Association Management*, 45(9), 38–43.

Kolb, D. M., & Williams, J. (2000). *The shadow negotiation: How women can master the hidden agendas that determine bargaining success*. New York: Simon & Schuster.

Kotz, N., & Kotz, M. L. (1977). *A passion for equality: George Wiley and the movement*. New York: W. W. Norton.

Kuhn, M. (with Long, C., & Quinn, L.). (1991). *No stone unturned: The life and times of Maggie Kuhn*. New York: Ballantine.

Kuhnen, C. M., & Neissen, A. (2010). *Is executive pay shaped by public attitudes?* AFA Meeting, 2010. Retrieved April 16, 2010, from: http://papers.ssrn.com/sol3/papers.cfm?abstract_id=1328572.

League of Women Voters of Maryland. (1983). *Lobbying the Maryland General Assembly: A practical guide for the citizen lobbyist*. Annapolis, MD: Author.

Lee, J. A. B. (1994). *The empowerment approach to social work practice*. New York: Columbia University Press.

Leonard, D. (2010, April 2). Bargain rates for a C.E.O.? *The New York Times*. Retrieved April 16, 2010, from: http://www.nytimes.com/2010/04/04/business/04comp.html

Lewis, B. A. (1998). *The kid's guide to social action* (2nd ed.). Minneapolis, MN: Free Spirit.

Lohmann, R. A., & McNutt, J. (2005). Practice in the electronic community. In M. Weil (Ed.). *The handbook of community practice* (pp. 636–646). Thousand Oaks, CA: Sage Publication.

Luo, M. (2008, February 20). Small online contributions add up to huge fund-raising edge for Obama. *The New York Times*. Retrieved April 30, 2010, from: http://www.nytimes.com/2008/02/20/us/politics/20obama.html

Lyall, S. (2010, April 8). Courting the U.K. women's vote, online and unrelenting. *The New Times*. Retrieved April 30, 2010, from: http://www.nytimes.com/2010/04/09/world/europe/09britain.html.

Mater, J. (1984). *Public hearings procedures and strategies: A guide to influencing public decisions*. Englewood Cliffs, NJ: Prentice-Hall, Inc.

Menefee, D. T., & Thompson, J. J. (1994). Identifying and comparing competencies for social work management: A practice driven approach. *Administration in Social Work*, 18(3), 1–25.

Menon, G. M. (2000). The 79-cent campaign: The use of on-line mailing lists for electronic advocacy. *Journal of Community Practice*, 8(3), 73–81.

Messinger, R. W. (1982). Empowerment: A social worker's politics. In M. Mahaffey & J. Hanks (Eds.), *Practical politics: Social work and political responsibility* (pp. 212–223). Silver Spring, MD: National Association of Social Workers.

Mikulski, B. A. (1982). *Community empowerment and self-help strategies*. In *Social Welfare Forum, 1981* (pp. 11–23). New York: Columbia University Press.

Mondros, J. B., & Wilson, S. M. (1994). *Organizing for power and empowerment*. New York: Columbia University Press.

Moreau, M. J. (1990, June). Empowerment through advocacy and consciousness-raising: Implications of a structural approach to social work. *Journal of Sociology and Social Welfare*, 17(2), 53–67.

Moxley, D. P., & Freddolino, P. P. (1994). Client-driven advocacy and psychiatric disability: A model for social work practice. *Journal of Sociology and Social Welfare*, 21(2), 91–108.

National Association of Social Workers. (2008). *Code of ethics of the National Association of Social Workers [as approved by the 1996 NASW Delegate Assembly and revised by the 2008 NASW Delegate Assembly]*. Retrieved May 11, 2009, from http://www.social-workers.org/pubs/code/default.asp

OpenSecrets.org. (2010). *Lobbying: Top industries*. Center for Responsive Politics. Retrieved April 27, 2010, from: http://www.opensecrets.org/index.php

Panitch, A. (1974). Advocacy in practice. *Social Work*, 19, 326–332.

Patti, R. J., & Resnick, H. (1972). Changing the agency from within. *Social Work*, 17(4), 48–57.

Pearrow, M. M. (2008). A critical examination of an urban-based youth empowerment strategy: The teen empowerment program. *Journal of Community Practice*, 16(4), 509–525.

Perelman, M. (2009). Vive la revolution? *The Nation*, 288(19), 22–24.

Perlman, E. (2000). Rest in place: Development is endangering many rural cemeteries. *Governing*, 14(2), 18.

Perlmutter, F. D., & Cnaan, R. A. (1999). Community development as a public sector agenda. *Journal of Community Practice*, 6(4), 57–77.

Pertschuk, M. (1986). *Giant killers*. New York: W. W. Norton.

Pew Charitable Trusts. (2040). *Pew initiative analysis finds checkerboard of state legislation*. Retrieved April 27, 2010, from: http://www.pewtrusts.org/news_room_detail.aspx?id=22764

Pew Research Center for the People & the Press (2008). *Public attitudes toward government and business*. Retrieved April 16, 2010, from: http://people-press.org/report/?pageid=1400

Powers, P. (1977). Social change: Nader style. *Journal of Education for Social Work*, 13(3), 63–69.

Rankin, T. (Ed.). (2000). *Local heroes: Changing America*. New York: W. W. Norton and the Center for Documentary Studies.

Reisch, M., & Andrews, J. (2002). *The road not taken: A history of radical social work in the United States*. New York: Brunner–Routledge.

Richan, W. C. (1996). *Lobbying for social change* (2nd ed). Binghamton, NY: Haworth.

Rubin, B. R. (1997). *A citizen's guide to politics in America: How the system works & how to work the system*. Armonk, NY: M. E. Sharpe.

Rubin, J. Z., & Brown, B. R. (1975). *The social psychology of bargaining and negotiation*. New York: Academic Press.

Ryan, B. (1992). *Feminism and the women's movement: Dynamics of change in social movement ideology and activism*. New York: Routledge.

Salcido, R., & Manalo, V. (2002). Planning electoral activities for social work students: A policy practice approach. *Arete*, 26(1), 55–60.

Schneider, R. L., & Lester, L. (2001). *Social work advocacy: A new framework for action*. Belmont, CA: Brooks/Cole.

Sebenius, J. K. (2001). Six habits of merely effective negotiators. *Harvard Business Review*, 79(4), 87–95.

Sherman, W., & Wenocur, S. (1983). Empowering public welfare workers through mutual support. *Social Work*, 28(5), 375–379.

Simon, B. L. (1994). *The empowerment tradition in American social work: A history*. New York: Columbia University Press.

Singer, P. (2008). Members offered many bills but passed few. *Roll Call*. Retrieved April 27, 2010, from: http://www.rollcall.com/issues/54_61/news/30466-

Smith, A. (1922). An inquiry into the nature and causes of the wealth of nations (Vols. 1 & 2; E. Cannan, Ed.). London: Methuen.

Soifer, S., & Singer, J. (1999). The campaign to restore the Disability Assistance and Loan Program in the state of Maryland. *Journal of Community Practice*, 6(2), 1–10.

Szegedy-Maszak, M. (2002, June 3). Consuming passion: The mentally ill are taking charge of their own recovery. *U.S. News & World Report*, 132(19), pp 55–57.

Tower, K. D. (1994). Consumer-centered social work practice: Restoring client self-determination. *Social Work*, 39(2), 191–196.

Trattner, W. I. (1998). *From poor law to welfare state: A history of social welfare in America*. New York: The Free Press.

Van Soest, D. (1994). Strange bedfellows: A call for reordering national priorities from three social justice perspectives. *Social Work*, 39(6), 710–717.

Wagner, D. (1990). *The quest for a radical profession: Social service careers and political ideology*. Lanham, MD: University Press of America.

Wallerstein, N. (1993). Empowerment and health: The theory and practice of community change. *Community Development Journal*, 28(3), 218–227.

Walz, T., & Groze, V. (1991). The mission of social work revisited: An agenda for the 1990s. *Social Work*, 36(6), 500–504.

Wandersman, A., Clary, E. G., Forbush, J., Weinberger, S. G., Coyne, S. M., & Duffy, J. L. (2006). Community organizing and advocacy: Increasing the quality and quantity of mentoring programs. *Journal of Community Psychology*, 34(6), 781–799.

Weiss-Gal, I., & Gal, J. (2009). Realizing rights in social work. *The Social Service Review*, 83(2), 267–291.

Wildman, P. (n.d.). *Welcome to the ALS virtual advocacy community*. ALS Association. Retrieved April 30, 2010, from: http://www.alsa.org/policy/article.

Willie, C. V. (2008). A perfect grassroots movement: The Montgomery bus boycott. In C. V. Willie, S. P. Ridini, & D. A. Willard (Eds.). *Grassroots social action: Lessons in power movement* (pp. 21–39). New York: Rowman & Littlefield, Publishers.

Wood, G. G., & Middleman, R. R. (1989). *The structural approach to direct practice in social work*. New York: Columbia University Press.

Zernike, K., & Thee-Brenan, M. (2010, April 15). Discontent's demography: Who backs the Tea Party. *The New York Times*, A1, A17.

13

Using Organizing: Acting in Concert

Goodbye Bill. I die like a true blue rebel. *Don't waste any time in mourning. Organize…* Could you arrange to have my body hauled to the state line to be buried? I don't want to be found dead in Utah.

Joe Hill, labor organizer, songwriter, martyr[1]

Community organizers … are passionate, because they believe that change is possible, and because they enjoy working with people. … although it is not an occupation that leads to great wealth, community organizers can make a living at it. … They do well by doing good.

Szakos and Szakos (2007, p. xi)

Community organizing involves connecting people in communities to change the status quo. Community organization brings together people in defined geographic or functional areas to protect and strengthen their social connectiveness, cohesion, and capacity. It can develop communities and mobilize people for change through social action. Community organization can be progressive or radically reactionary, like the Tea Bagger (aka Tea Party) movement (Barstow, 2010; Ferris, 2009; Kim, 2010; Raban, 2010). What distinguishes a progressive community organization and organizer is the pursuit of social justice in the organizing. Changing society is never easy, but this chapter, as has the previous chapters, will describe ways to mobilize the community, whether the focus of change is building community or promoting a social cause. This aim of this chapter is to convey what progressive community work is like today in terms of its goals, approaches, and preoccupations. But be forewarned: progressive community organizations and social actions pursuing social justice face greater obstacles and challenges from the conservative media and power holders than do reactionary and conservative organizations such as the Tea Party Bagger movement (Nichols, 2010; Raban, 2010). Efforts to appoint liberal Supreme Court justices (Baker, 2010), and the media and legislative pillorying of Association of Community Organizations for Reform, ACORN, with Congress passing laws defunding ACORN based on unproven charged made by deceitful radical conserveratives reveal the uneven playing field for progressive organizers (vanden Heuvel, 2010a, 2010b).

Organizing has a proud history. Traditionally, organizing emphasizes "mobilizing community residents to form their own identities, renew their interest in public life, and fight for their rights across a broad range of issues" (Kingsley, McNeely, & Gibson, 1997, p. 27). Organizing also entails economic and social analysis. Success comes from "strong people skills to bring people together and keep them inspired and working well; capable organization to assure that the work involved actually gets done; and strategic savvy in order to pick the right objectives and the right public actions to win them" (Shultz, 2002, p. 97).

Community organization and community practice methodologies have long been part of progressive social work's arsenal for change. They also are part of clinical and direct social work practice's responsibilities. They help the micro practitioners be part of activities such as building community capacity, identifying community assets, creating caring social connections, and joining with others to promote community cohesion and individual and group self-respect. Workers practicing on a micro and personal level can still be social change agents pursuing social justice and drawing attention to social injustices, and they should become knowledgeable about the problems clients share so that others trust their expertise and recommendations. Community intervention encompasses the ability to tap community strengths and the skills of including, linking, engaging, and empowering clients as citizens.

Community Organizing and Organizations

The Current Scene

Community practice has increased the status, if not the popularity, of our profession and workplaces. President Obama lists it on his résumé. Despite the increased efforts and successes of radical conservatives and the challenges to ACORN, progressive organizing and advocacy is robust. Even a list as impressive as MoveOn. org, Americans United for Separation of Church and State, Highlander Research and Education Center, Industrial Area Foundation, Neighborhood Assistance Corporation of America, Center for Community Change, Take Back the Land, and the National Low Income Housing Coalition does not scratch the surface of the inventory of progressive organizations.[2] As the epigram at the beginning of this chapter said, "They do well by doing good" (Szakos & Szakos, 2007, p. xi).

Community practice involves working beside people of varied backgrounds to create a culture of change, identify assets, link groups, and pursue social justice. Spirited community organizations make the crucial difference between a vital community and a stagnant one, between a community dominated by controlling vertical corporations and the moneyed class and a community run by and for the grassroots.

Community workers increasingly are celebrated as creators of social capital and sustainers of social communities.

The Earlier Scene

The contemporary community intervention activity is both a rebirth and continuation of the community-focused efforts of the 1960s with new auspices and rhetoric. The 1980s and 1990s were somewhat tranquil for progressive community action. Liberalism was in full retreat, if not in hiding. It was an era more characterized by public self-introspection and the pursuit of the material than the social good. The current activity, which ideally is not short-lived, is being motivated without the federal encouragement and fiscal subsidies provided by the earlier Economic Opportunity Act, Model Cities, and the range of New Frontiers and Great Society legislation. University of Maryland social work professor Mark Battle, the former executive director of the National Association of Social Workers, called the 1960s the "first substantive federal-to-community-to-people program. . . . Its design and operation had facilitated . . . a flow of money from the federal government to the man on the street." From his vantage point as Administrator of Work Training Programs of the U.S. Department of Labor's Manpower Administration during this era, Battle concluded that the broadly based War on Poverty "enriched democracy" and gave "worth in the larger public mind to poor people" (Battle, n.d., para. 7, 15). The programs of the 1960s included the federally supported domestic programs of the Great Society and War on Poverty programs ranging from the Economic Opportunity Act's Community Action programs, Head Start, Job Corps, Neighborhood Youth Corp; Model Cities; Volunteers in Service to America (VISTA); Manpower Development and Training Act; Comprehensive Community Mental Health Act; and the Peace Corps abroad. There are remnants today of that heady time in Head Start and over 1,000 surviving Community Action Agencies across the nation.[3] However, despite today's Great Recession, there is little government support for community intervention and social justice for the increasing numbers of poor and marginalized.

Community Building

Minkler (1997) defines community building as "an orientation to community that is strength based rather than need based and stresses the identification, nurturing, and celebration of community assets" (pp. 5–6). Fabricant and Fisher (2002a, 2002b) call community building the most significant social service work of the 21st century. They view it as a process based on principles of reciprocity, respect, inclusiveness, and accountability. Some authors equate community building with community empowerment. It matters less what the process is called, as long as it facilitates collective change (Checkoway, 1997) and empowers "disadvantaged citizens to more effectively define and advance their own life chances" (Turner, 1998, p. ix). Many of the activities listed in Box 13.1 relate to community building, engaging a community to improve itself.

Two distinguishing features of community building are (a) collaboration, to tap the strengths of both displaced and well-placed citizens (Martinez-Brawley, 2000), and (b) engagement by the community itself, in contrast to the use of peripatetic professional organizers (Minkler, 1997) or remote social service providers. When professionals are involved, ideally they partner with community groups rather than dominate them (Turner, 2009).

Usually community-building initiatives have four elements:

- Focus on specific, geographically defined target areas
- Planning based on a recognition of community assets and available resources as well as needs (see Assets Inventory and Mapping in chapters 5 and 6)
- Community participation in the governance, planning, and implementation of development activities
- Comprehensive development, including an attempt to integrate economic, physical, and human development activities (Chaskin, Joseph, & Chipenda-Dansokho, 1997, p. 435; also see Foster-Fishman, Cantillon, Pierce, & Van Egeren, 2007; Frisch & Servon, 2006; Geoghean & Powell, 2006; Heenan, 2004; Steeves & Blevins, 2005)

This requires community practitioners to "work across multiple systems simultaneously"

BOX 13.1.   Current Modus Operandi

Different groups are coming together to improve their communities, at least from their perspectives. Ordinary residents use groups and community organizing to make themselves heard in local and regional decision making, with and some without mandates requiring resident-driven planning. Sometimes shouting from their side and their opponents drowns out rational discourse. Some are true grassroots groups; others are Astroturf organizations (groups that are presented as grassroots organizations but are often sponsored by corporate interests and lobbyists) and Potemkin organizations (false-front organizations designed to appear larger than they actually are). No single ideology or approach prevails. Web sites, media stories, and professional articles are filled with write-ups of community change success and failure. Some community organizing concepts are:

coalitions
collaboratives
community development
community organizing
community revitalization
comprehensive initiatives
constituency building
cultural strategies
empowerment zones
faith-based groups
healthy cities

holistic approach
interorganizational networks
internet and networking
local regeneration
neighborhood issues
participatory planning
partnerships
resident involvement
social entrepreneurship
sustainable development

(Mulroy & Matsuoka, 2000, p. 229). Community capacity building uses established or new organizations. Community building helps the socially marginalized by surrounding them with a potent village that it takes to nurture and sustain humankind. It is about social cohesion, social infrastructure, and social capital. These have inherent civic and political repercussions.

Warren (2001), emphasizes, however, that building social capital "at the level of local community institutions":

may not be sufficient, if those community institutions remain detached from our political system. What has largely been overlooked in the debates about social capital is the growing disconnection between politics and what remains of American community life. . . . The political efficacy of turn-of-the-century political parties and twentieth-century cross-class federations both promoted civil participation and benefited from it. . . . Revitalizing democracy, then, requires community building, but also something more: creating institutional links between strong communities and our political system. (p. 19)

Johannesen (1997) holds that vital social development is not possible without political development and action. Social development inherently involves a redistribution of political control and capacity needed to accompany economic redistribution. Wakefield and Poland (2005) "suggests that social capital cannot be conceived in isolation from economic and political structures. Social capital . . . needs to be placed in its economic and political context, while recognizing that social organization—not just social connection—'have impact on personal lives'" (p. 2828). These are the empowerment and social integration functions of social work. Social development, social participation, and community building are inherently political (van Deth, 1997).

Saul Alinsky's biography summarized in Box 13.2 illustrates the political nature of organizing.

A Well-Known Example of Comprehensive Community Building

Infamous since the 1950s for widespread blight, the South Bronx was a place that Presidents Carter and Reagan visited to wring their hands.

BOX 13.2.	Saul Alinsky and Grassroots Organizing

Saul Alinsky (1909–1972), son of an Orthodox Jewish Russian tailor, studied sociology at the University of Chicago. Alinsky married a social worker. His career started as a youth street worker concerned with the social milieu of delinquents. Alinsky, who hated to see fellow humans pushed around, demonstrated that (a) mass-based organizing can be accomplished with unsophisticated people and (b) organizing skills can be taught. He has inspired thousands of organizing projects by both progressives and now even the radical right.

Alinsky's classic books, *Reveille for Radicals* and *Rules for Radicals,* serve as a social activist's bible. They details Alinsky's philosophy, theory, leadership building techniques, and nonviolent conflict and disruptive tactics for social action.

Alinsky's approach was to develop and work with talented indigenous leaders and build mass people's organizations, gaining recognition for local leaders and power for the organization so that dominant employers in the community, such as Eastman Kodak, would negotiate with them. He believed that change can come about through the use of real and perceived power. In the 1940s, Alinsky organized the Back of the (Stock) Yards, a working-class Polish area in Chicago, in part by uniting labor unions and Catholic functionaries—groups that historically had been at odds. He convinced them that it was in their self-interest to coalesce. His forte was strategic thinking coupled with spontaneous, disruptive tactics. He was a master of gaining the support of and resources from influential people. Marshall Field III, a department store heir to a fortune; Catholic Bishop Bernard Shiel; and Kathryn Lewis, daughter of United Mine Workers union leader John L. Lewis, helped establish the Industrial Areas Foundation (IAF) to support Alinsky's work in furthering democracy. Gordon Sherman used Midas Muffler money to help Alinsky launch a training institute.

Alinsky is remembered as a fighter for the disenfranchised and someone who put democracy into action. He still inspires and guides both reactionary and progressive community organizers. For an Alinsky biography, see Horwitt (1989).

Then, in 1977, some impoverished families rehabbed three abandoned apartment buildings slated for demolition. 'Following this restoration, each apartment was sold for $250 to those who had invested 600 hours of labor in restoring the building. . . . In addition, the families created a grassroots self-help organization known as the Banana Kelly Community Improvement Association" (Abatena, 1997, p. 28).

Major resurrection started in 1986 with new housing built by community development corporations (CDCs), which gave themselves names such as Mid-Bronx Desperadoes (Grogan & Proscio, 2001). Still, the schools and other services remained pathetic. Much of the later progress is due to Anita Miller, a leader who convinced the Surdna Foundation to underwrite massive changes: "A one-time banker . . . Miller had been intimately involved with South Bronx CDCs as a program officer at the Ford Foundation and later as program director at the Local Initiatives Support Corporation. Well connected to everyone who mattered in both the public and private sectors, Anita Miller not only recognized the paradox [of physical renaissance with inadequate human supports] but was bursting to do something about it" (Schorr, 1997, pp. 329–330).

Collaborative community building does not always go smoothly or solve every problem (Meyer, 2002), but the South Bronx as an environment now has new resources (day care, senior services, retail services) and is more livable. Successful community builders must function well in their local community ecosystem and be cognizant of the interstices between it and larger societal institutions (Bowen & Richman, 2002, p. 68).

Patch Approach as Micro Community Building

In the 1970s, Britain developed the *patch approach* as a system of community assistance that deploys teams of human service workers to defined neighborhood-sized geographic catchment areas or *patches* (Payne, 2000, 2002). Fieldworkers, case managers who often lived in their assigned patches as settlers, supported and built "on the resources of informal networks of kin and neighbors" and joined with other local organizations and institutions "to solve both

individual and community problems" (Adams & Krauth, 1995, p. 89). In other words, the patch approach makes use of natural helpers and community networks. Creating a patch team is a decentralized but organized way of providing flexible personal social services to people in an immediate geographic area. However, a locality-based patch can be a rather large patch (a field?) since it often includes 4,000 to 20,000 people (Martinez-Brawley & Delevan, 1993, pp. 171, 181). The patch can be specialized and focused on a particular clientele or general and broad-based (Martinez-Brawley & Delevan, 1993, p. 9). We will discuss the patch approach again in Chapter 14.

A Case example

In 2000 a community development worker was working in the City of Whitehorse, Australia, Box Hill Central Business District (CBD) Youth Services Team to reduce drug-related problems (Rogers & Anderson, 2007). The community development worker established links with business and retail proprietors, shopping center managers, police, community representatives, youth agency representatives, ward councilors, and council staff. Meetings were held throughout the community that focused on relevant topics of concern, with particular emphasis on the public drug consumption by youths in the Box Hill neighborhood. The community worker assisted in efforts to increase drug treatment services in the area, to educate security staff at local businesses regarding appropriate interactions, to increase use of youth centers, and to implement proactive design measures. In addition, this worker helped lead efforts in an education project designed to combat misconceptions about the neighborhood. The project reportedly was successful. The authors assert "the importance of fostering relationships and creating opportunities for open dialogue between key stakeholders probably has universal application" (Rogers & Anderson, 2007, p. 95).

Communities of Solutions

Successes seldom involve the entire rural or metropolitan community. Community builders know to focus on the "community of solution" (see Assets Inventory and Mapping in chapters 5 and 6), a concept that means that boundaries are defined by problem, actors, and solvers. A community of solution is not bounded by jurisdictional lines of governmental and voluntary agencies. It can function at any level, even internationally. In health and social services, a typical community of solution involves those organizations and people who want to address an identified problem, perhaps an alliance that gets together because the problem affects everyone in the group (see the above example). As nursing professors Allender and Spradley (2001) note, "Recently communities of solution have formed in many cities to attack the spread of HIV infection. Public health agencies, social service groups, schools, and media personnel have banded together to create public awareness of the dangers present and to promote preventive behaviors" (p. 5).

The community undertakings demonstrate that, despite the shameful national neglect of the poor and their hardscrabble neighborhoods, an array of professions has become involved in meaningful local work and partnerships. These undertakings also demonstrate that community building is an antipoverty effort.

Asset-Based Community Building

Assets, resources, and strengths have become a central revitalization focus for low-income and inner-city neighborhoods. After banks and insurance companies refused to do business in desperately poor neighborhoods, activists secured the passage and enforcement of the Community Reinvestment Act to stop this practice of "redlining." Prior to the mortgage and lending crisis that sparked the Great Recession, the long-term results of the implementation of this law led to more interest in tangible personal and community assets. Activists and other change agents became equally intrigued by tangible and intangible assets and the talents of people in impoverished neighborhoods, as demonstrated by Philadelphia's Mural Arts Program (http://www.muralarts.org/whoweare/). The potential for political influence, social capital, and the ability to build relationships are inherent in community building.

Asset assessment is part of good patch analysis. The patch approach looks for the social networks in the patch, establishes communication between groups and between agencies, and assesses structural and personal assets. Full use of the opportunities and resources available to a

community requires a broad, inclusive understanding of the community's assets.

The following are five ways in which assets play a role in urban and rural community practice:

1. Asset building
2. Asset claiming
3. Asset identifying and mobilizing
4. Individual leadership assets
5. Cultural assets

Our abbreviated discussion here is an introduction to a multifaceted practice approach and a chance to see what these efforts reveal about community and community building. Many professionals find the emphasis on intangible assets such as strengths and resiliency to be a better way of working with communities rather than limiting the attention to only problems and deficiencies (Ammerman & Parks, 1998). The community from a strengths perspective builds on what it has (Delgado, forthcoming). Asset inventories and mapping were discussed in the assessment chapters. Once identified, these assets become tools in community building.

Asset Building

Asset-building programs develop tangible assets such as housing, small business ventures, and savings accounts. They have the potential to change impoverished communities in many ways. Michael Sherraden of the Center for Social Development at the George Warren Brown School of Social Work, Washington University, has long advocated an assets-building approach for the poor (McKernan & Sherraden, 2008; Sherraden, 1991). He holds that asset building with the poor will reduce their dependency on tenuous welfare transfers and provide them with stakes in the community. Community practitioners will need to be familiar with the range and success rates of programs in order to further broad progress. Those engaged in direct practice will want to be aware of opportunities as they help families navigate the path to dignity and economic security.

Habitat for Humanity. This well-known nonprofit organization, based in Georgia, is a self-help, sweat-equity program in which volunteers help families build their own houses and houses for others like themselves. Each family usually puts 300 to 500 hours of labor into their own house as it is built to receive a no-interest mortgage. The idea for Habitat for Humanity International came from minister Clarence Jordan. The organization was founded in 1976 by Millard Fuller, a business partner of Morris Dees, founder of the Southern Poverty Law Center (Walls, 1993). Former President Jimmy Carter's volunteer work with the organization gives it invaluable publicity. The Habitat for Humanity organization has built 150,000 sound homes in 3,000 communities (see http://www.habitat.org). Former corporate executives work side by side with church groups and low-income families, and the interaction that occurs between different people is a strength of the program.

Microenterprise. There are reportedly over 2 million microenterprises in the United States funded by microenterprise programs (http://www.microenterpriseworks.org). Microenterprises targeted at the poor are small businesses that range from a self-employed street vendor or seamstress to a small shop owner. Their size may be only 1 (no one but the owner) up to 50 employees (*What is a Microenterprise,* n.d.). The concept of microenterprises as a way to encourage financial independence started abroad. Economics Professor and 2006 Noble Laureate Muhammad Yunus in 1979 established the Grameen (rural) Bank in Bangladesh with the objectives of eliminating the exploitation of the poor by moneylenders; creating opportunities for self-employment for unemployed people in rural Bangladesh; bringing the disadvantaged, mostly women, into organizational formats they can understand and manage themselves; and creating a cycle of "low income, injection of credit, investment, more income, more savings, more investment, more income" (Banking for the poor, Grameen Bank, 2010). This concept has hundreds of variations in the United States (Banerjee, 2001; http://www.microenterpriseworks.org/).

Individual Development Accounts. Robert Friedman (2002) of the Corporation for Enterprise Development puts it this way: "To work for, earn, and own an asset gives one a stake in one's own future. The very process leading to ownership builds the capital, competence, and connections to keep people reaching toward and building dynamic and promising futures" (p. 1). For years, Sherraden and his colleagues have promoted individual development accounts (IDAs), an asset-based policy innovation (Sherraden, 1991). The model encourages the poor to get in the habit of saving, even $25 to $30 a month, by matching their savings for the first few years. The saving are for home ownership, an education, and basically community stakes.

Asset Claiming

Asset claiming can be for individuals, families, categories of workers, or populations. It was discussed in Chapter 1. Social workers have an obligation to help eligible households to obtain the various forms of community mutual support and to identify sources of income, such as the earned income tax credit and child tax credits (Weiss-Gal & Gal, 2009). Just as importantly, social workers can explain to the general public how such supplements and tax reductions lift people out of poverty.

Living Wage Movement. The living wage movement is a response to the growing imbalance of America's productivity, with workers getting relatively less and owners significantly more. Economic inequality has ballooned over the past half century, as discussed in Chapter 4. Many global corporations not only fail to share their resources with workers but also fiercely fight any attempts to promote economic democracy. Nevertheless, working people continue to claim a right to fairness in their economic relationships with their employers. Such sentiments have launched community-organizing campaigns to secure a living wage. A living wage differs from the substandard federal minimum wage that will keep a family of three below the meager federal poverty standard; rather, it is a wage that meets the designated standard of living (http://www.universallivingwage.org/). The federal government has been unconscionably slow in raising the minimum wage, and therefore organizers have looked for leverage to help workers who are paid under city contracts or under large government contracts to for-profit firms. The living wage movement has largely been locally based.

The first policy agreement to pay a living wage was negotiated in 1994 with Mayor Kurt Schmoke in Baltimore, Maryland, by a coalition of labor (led by the American Federation of State, County, and Municipal Employees) and community groups (led by Baltimoreans United in Leadership Development, the Industrial Areas Foundation, and the Solidarity Sponsoring Committee). It required city service contractors and government suppliers to raise the pay of 4,000 low-wage workers (Uchitelle, 1996). The agreement resulted in resetting the starting wage for such workers to $2.65 above the minimum wage. Similar ordinances have been passed in a number of political jurisdictions (Gertner, 2006). In 2007, Maryland passed the nation's first statewide living wage law after Maryland's voters endorsed a living wage in the 2006 election (http://www.progressivemaryland.org/page.php?id=148). The economist Robert Kuttner described the movement as "the most interesting (and under-reported) grassroots enterprise to emerge since the civil rights movement . . . signaling a resurgence of local activism around pocketbook issues" (as quoted by ACORN, n.d., The Living wage movement, para. 1).

Historical Fairness Claims. A second area of assets claiming is grounded in historical fairness and restitution claims for past injustices and atrocities. They relate to specific populations such as the Amerindians, who were subjected to genocide, ethnic cleansing, and an apartheid reservation system, and are still owed money by the U.S. government and have had their property exploited under government trusteeship. The issues of genocide and ethnic cleansing buttressing the Amerindians' claims as well as the claims of African-Americans rooted in slavery and the racism of the Jim Crow era (Gates, 2010) were discussed in Chapter 1. Now that Japanese-Americans who were interned in camps during World War II have received federal compensation and European workers are being reimbursed by corporations for forced (slave) labor during the same war, there is a precedent for Amerindians and African-Americans to receive the promised but never-delivered assets.

Individual Leadership Assets

Community leadership is decisive for a vital community (Foster-Fishman, Cantillon, Pierce, & Van Egeren, 2007; Gambone, Yu, Lewis-Charp, Sipe, & Lacoe, 2006; Hannah, 2006; Ohmer, 2008). Individual leaders, "even idiosyncratic ones," are more likely than plans or ideologies to yield change, according to The Rensselaerville Institute (The Rensselaerville Institute, n.d.). Leadership identification and development are critical organizing tasks in assets inventory, development, and management. There are many ways to solicit and refine individual assets (Lazarri, Ford, & Haughey, 1996; Rodriquez, 1998). Citizen participation in community activities allows identification of actual and potential leaders. There are many grassroots leadership training organizations, including the venerable Industrial Areas Foundation (IAF) headquartered in Chicago (http://www.industrialareasfoundation.org/index.html) and the southern Appalachian Highlander Research and Education Center (http://www.highlandercenter.org/). Online training resources are readily available, generally at no cost, from organizations such as the W. K. Kellogg Foundation (Monteiro-Tribble, n.d.) and Americans United for Separation of Church and State (http://www.au.org/take-action/activist/).

There are potential and undiscovered leaders in almost every community. Maggie Kuhn, founder of the Gray Panthers and an advocate for the elderly, didn't emerge as a leader until she attained senior citizen status. Women are often an untapped resource. Despite the wealth of personal assets in communities, most usually are not applied to social goals, because people are scattered and undirected. An individual may embody valuable assets such as knowing the community and being nurturing of others but lack confidence. Gathering these people together, orienting them, and creating situations for empowerment are key tasks. Any training, whether in workshops or workbooks, must be a complement to participation in the community. Community participation allows emergence of potential leaders, networking, and building social capital. The community practitioner needs to develop "winnable" projects with the community and potential leaders. The community practitioner can help nurture confidence and greater community empowerment with social action and community projects that are successful.

This is not to say that only potential leaders count. Each individual has strengths and weaknesses, assets,[4] and practitioners can connect people and their assets through networking to increase community and individual empowerment, community cohesion, and social capital.

To identify potential and current community leaders, community builders can use key informants with reputational assessments: Who cares about the issue? Who has had problems with the issue, if anyone? Who knows and is known on the issue? Whom would you turn to for advice on the issue (or generally)? The names are inventoried and eco-mapped for social networks. The names most often mentioned and those with network centrality are the most promising potential leaders.

Leadership assets include personal qualities like being trustworthy and having emotional maturity, intelligence, and honesty and skills like raising money. Organizer Si Kahn writes about cultivating, supporting, and spotting community leaders: a leader is "someone who helps show us the directions we want to go and who helps us go in those directions" (1991, p. 21).

Cultural Assets

A function of culture, any culture, is to provide people with an integrated system of tools, symbols, language, and beliefs to understand and relate to the physical and social world (Jenks, 2005). It gives its adherents a sense of community, identity, and history and the ability to construct a reality. Culture provides intangible and tangible assets. A community's culture contains many assets, and sometimes liabilities.

Communities can create and enrich cultural assets that will contribute to their social solidarity. An example is Philadelphia's Mural Arts Program (http://www.muralarts.org/whoweare/). Its mission is to unite "artists and communities through a collaborative process, rooted in the traditions of mural-making, to create art that transforms public spaces and individual lives." Since the Mural Arts Program began in 1984 as a component of the Philadelphia Anti-Graffiti Network, under the direction of muralist Jane Golden, it has produced over 2,800 murals and involved over 20,000 underserved youth in neighborhoods throughout Philadelphia. The Anti-Graffiti Network reached out to graffiti writers to redirect their energies from destructive graffiti writing to constructive mural painting. Mural-making provided a support structure for the youths to develop their artistic skills and empowered them to take an active role in beautifying their communities. Mural projects often include stabilization of abandoned lots and revitalization of open spaces. Today's Mural Arts Program, a nonprofit organization, is an innovative and successful public/private partnership. Community participants include block captains, neighborhood associations, public schools, community development corporations, local nonprofits, and city agencies.

Using Community Assets

To establish and use a successful assets program, we must make a regular practice of finding out who knows what and who knows whom: assets inventorying and mapping. We must be on the lookout for knowledge linkages (Fesenmaier & Contractor, 2001) and social–emotional linkages between individuals, groups, associations, and social institutions. An important element of community building is networking in and to a community.

We also must be on the lookout for the unattached. Social and organizational networks are much more powerful when reinforced by emotional bonds. Faceless or neglected individuals need to be connected to fellow human beings. For this reason, along with practical considerations, the late Maggie Kuhn, organizer of the Gray Panthers, promoted the concept of the "healthy block." It makes sense for people to care about and look after each other in times of crisis. If neighbors would spare a little time to become familiar with the needs of those in the immediate neighborhood, we could move beyond neighborhood crime watches and into true community.

Organizing

Relationships and Belief Bonding. A born organizer, the late Senator Paul Wellstone was "famous for talking not just to the customers of the cafes he loved to frequent, but for going into the kitchen, talking up the dishwashers and fry cooks, urging them not only to vote for him but also to demand more for themselves. He befriended U.S. Capitol security guards and brought them home to dinner" (Smith & Lopez, 2002, p. 1). He formed relationships. Twenty thousand people celebrated his life at his memorial service life. Having an affinity and respect for people is crucial.

Building relationships is a necessary first step in "belief bonding" with the constituency: creating a belief that together, the community practitioner and the groups composing the constituency, the initiator, client, change agent, action, and support systems, can effect change. Organizers must also gain the trust of strangers and create a climate where people want to mobilize themselves. Alinsky holds that only the people can build a people's organization for change (Alinsky, 1969, p. 74).

Besides attending community events, organizers spend much informal time with the relevant constituencies. The relationships begin with the participant-observer techniques discussed in the assessment chapters. They patiently gather information in casual ways. The community

practitioner reaches out to individuals and key informants, expressing interest and listening to their concerns and narratives. When groups wish to reach out, the organizer can propose house meetings, events held in homes for base-building purposes, usually involving around eight people. Organizers talk to new people every day.

Organizers look for ways to bond. Food and beverages (a potluck or even a cocktail party) serve to create a relaxed environment and to advance one-on-one recruitment to the cause. Cesar Chavez, the eminent National Farm Workers Association leader, agricultural workers union builder, and civil rights leader, timed his visits to the homes of farm laborers, the *campesinos*, at mealtime. Eating together was a means of bonding and leveling the social relationship: by feeding him, the workers felt like they had done something for the leader and were not just takers (Box 13.3).

The organizers who created the Solidarity Sponsoring Campaign, an association for low-wage workers in Baltimore, were keenly aware of the need to establish trust. On cold nights, social worker Kerry Miciotto set up a stand on the street and served hot tea to janitors and

---

| BOX 13.3. | The Recruitment of Cesar Chavez |

Legendary community organizer and poor people's advocate Fred Ross was trained by Alinsky's Industrial Area Foundation and employed by the Community Organization Society, a Mexican-American civil rights, social justice, and community-building organization founded by Chicano veterans after World War II. He went to the Chavez home in the *Sal Si Puedes* (roughly translated as *escape if you can* or *get out if you can*) section of San Jose, California, three nights in a row to ask the couple to sponsor a house meeting in their home. Ross first won the trust of Helen Chavez. At the meeting—over the babble of babies and children—soft-spoken Ross had to capture the attention of Cesar Chavez (then a 25-year-old veteran and laborer with a history of participating in farm labor strikes) and his *pachucos* (tough-guy) friends and neighbors as they sat on old couches that "sagged audibly under the weight of too many people" (Ferriss & Sandoval, 1997, pp. 37–39). Ross described neighborhood problems and

his organization's success in the firing and jailing of Los Angeles police officers who had nearly killed seven young *pachucos zoot-suiters*. Thinking back, Chavez recalls, "I knew about the Bloody Christmas case, and so did everyone else in that room. . . . Fred did such a good job of explaining how poor people could build power that I could taste it. I could really feel it. I thought, Gee, it's like digging a hole; there was nothing complicated about it" (p. 43). Ross got Chavez to attend another organizing meeting with him that very night. Within months, Chavez was recruiting strangers himself through house meetings and canvassing and then a mass meeting. This made him "nervous to the point of illness, afraid no one would come," but since he had organized well, a slow trickle eventually swelled to a crowd of over four hundred (p. 51). The man—with an eighth-grade education—was a success. Chavez made history as a farm labor union and civil rights leader.

other workers as they came and went from office buildings.

A member of ACORN takes the discussion beyond trust: "When you set up a meeting for poor people, make sure to provide transportation and food. The hungriest people are who you want at an action" (Brooks, 2001, p. 73).

Gestures that say "we are listening to you" build relationships. Chavez successfully recruited farm workers with a simple procedure: After passing around self-addressed three-by-five cards with space on the back for the worker's name and address, Chavez asked a question that each person could answer on the card: "What do you consider to be a just hourly wage?" His method of surveying farm workers was an instant hit—because these workers were being consulted for the first time. As one worker said, "It's like letting us vote . . . on what we think" (Levy, 1975, p. xxi). Likewise, ACORN organizers visited 500 workfare sites in Los Angeles and asked workers about their concerns (Brooks, 2001, p. 72).

Clearly, successful organizing involves analysis of relationships, not just "banners, literature, and personalities" (Robinson & Hanna, 1994, p. 80). Robinson and Hanna (1994) describe the careful listening and probing that occur in such meetings: "The focus is on discovering the core motivational drives: Why did the person do what they did; why does the person feel this way; why is the person concerned about this issue? Childhood experiences, pivotal life events, and watershed personal decisions often figure in. The answers to these questions will reveal the person's value system" (p. 85). Chavez had a habit of bumming cigarettes and rides off *campesinos* for the same reasons: it created a reciprocity obligation and it also provided an opportunity to get to know the farm workers on a personal level.

Make Each Person Count

Groups and actions work best when they tap the strengths of each participant. In Steinbeck's fictionalized story of a 1930s apple pickers' strike in California, he describes two organizers' efforts to use a crisis as an opportunity and to make each person count. Mac, an experienced organizer, and Jim, the acolyte, are preparing to help a young migrant deliver her baby in a Hooverville. There is no medical attention available (Steinbeck, 1963, pp. 40–43):[5]

[Mac] "They won't help us. We got to do it ourselves. . . . . Christ, we got to stand by our own people. Nobody else will. . . . You guys know how to work together."

. . .

A change was in the air. The apathy was gone … Four cans of water was [*sic*] put on to boil; and cloth began to appear. Every man seemed to have something to add to the pile.…

And after the successful delivery of the infant with assistance from some of the women and men:

[Jim]-) "I never knew you worked in a hospital…."
[Mac] "I never did…."
[Jim] "You acted sure enough,…."
(Mac) "Well, Christ Almighty, I had to! We got to use whatever material comes to us…"
.…
[Jim] "You didn't need all that cloth. Why did you tell London to burn it?"
-[Mac] "Look, Jim. Don't you see? Every man who gave part of his clothes felt the work was his own. They all feel responsible for that baby. It's theirs, because something from them went to it. To give back the cloth would cut them out. There's no better way to make men feel part of a movement than to have them give something to it."

Organizers like Mac and Jim get to know their people and give them something to do in the movement or activity. They make it their business to know who plays the piano, who likes taking minutes, who is happiest without assigned responsibilities so she can "choose" to set up or clean up. The organizer uses the process to bond the members, too.

Reflecting the Community

The issues you choose to focus on must be of interest to the community. This is an imperative of ethical and critical community practice—community self-determination, empowerment, and conscientisation—as well as a tactical requirement. Butcher (2007) states that a core of critical community practice is "a commitment *to working for social justice through empowering disadvantaged, excluded and oppressed communities to take more control over the conditions of their lives*" (emphasis original) (p. 17). Among Alinsky's (2006) rules for organizing social actions are "[n]ever go outside the experience of your people" and "[w]henever possible go outside of the experience of the enemy." Going beyond the community can most often result in either disinterest or confusion. SNCC leader Bob Moses (Moses & Cobb, Jr., 2001, p. 85) recalls how, as civil rights organizers framed the community's everyday issues, they had to slowly and deliberately "search out where [consensus] was lodged beneath layer after layer of other concerns".

Leaders also should also reflect the community. Though more indigenous leaders often are being hired as organizers, the average organizer usually does not match the neighborhood culturally or demographically. Organizers need not be from the community, but they must be viewed as one of the community. In building bonds and developing leadership, organizers find ways to bolster the self-confidence that leads to leadership (Banks, 2007). Pointing out skills and competencies of individuals to their peers in an even-handed manner helps later, during situations when people have to rely on each other's strengths. Alinsky (1969, pp. 64–79) believes the only viable and enduring leadership for a people's organization will come from the community. Organizers also need to realistically assess who will be good leaders and will work well in trying circumstances and who will not.

(Mac) London's with us. He's the natural leader. . . . Leadership has to come from the men. (Steinbeck, 1963, p. 43)

Leadership Development. For new practitioners, it can be hard to bond with people, build things together, construct solutions together, and then let leadership proceed on their own. Yet, almost as soon as the joining process and the building of social capital begin, the worker must begin to trust in people's strengths and leadership (Foster-Fishman, Cantillon, Pierce, & Van Egeren, 2007; Itzhaky, 2003). The excerpts below, from a community worker's diary, make vivid such emotions.

Tonight the first meeting of the neighborhood action group (Operation Upgrade) is to take place at 8:00 P.M. in the Methodist Church. I didn't want the group to lean too heavily on me, or foster the idea that what they needed all the time was a professional to rescue them. I told the [seven-person] Steering Committee two weeks ago to decide if they wanted me to come to the neighborhood meeting, and if they decided, they would have to invite me. This has really been a troublesome, trying day for me. I kept hoping they would

have strength and confidence enough to handle it without me. Each time the phone rang today, I hoped it would be an invitation. At 4:30 P.M., Mr. Halley came to tell me the Steering Committee had decided to let me rest for tonight. They will invite me at a later date. He thanked me for my help and promised a report soon.

....

Who do these people think they are? I gave them the idea, coached them, and met with the Steering Committee, and now they think they can handle a meeting without me (Cohen, 1971, pp. 341–342).

Widening the Circle of Participation. Building internal relationships and a support network is necessary but not sufficient. Expand the networks and look for linkages with other networks. This is where the assets mapping, networking, and coalition skills are applied. Members are encouraged to bring others to important meetings and events. Members make lists of the people they pledge to bring to meetings or into the action system. Members, new and old, need to feel involved and valued before they can turn difficulty into determination. Here, as in many contexts, it is prudent to learn what members want from an experience and to be there for them. The bottom line is that organizers try to expand the number of supporters and allies who will support the cause. Turning to Alinsky (2006) again, "a good tactic is one that your people enjoy." When new people are brought in and old people are retained, as Max from **In Dubious Battle** advised above, give them interesting and exciting things to do.

Focus, Focus

Alinsky (1969, 1971, 2006) advocated that the target system be defined, preferably as simply and as personally as possible. A specific villain is not a law of nature but must be created and defined. Ganz (2003), an associate of Chavez, urged worker to focus their resources:

- Concentrate resources at the point they will do the most good.
- Act at the moment when the group's chances of success are greatest.
- Undertake activities consistent with the group's capacities.

BOX 13.4.	Social Action Planning Checklist

- Has everything been done to make the target system's perception of the action system powerful? Power is in the target system's perception. The action system needs to appear big and bad. According to Alinsky, power goes to two poles: to the money and to the people. If the action system doesn't have money, it needs to have or appear to have the people.
- Does the target system understand how the target system behaves? Are the target system's vulnerabilities assessed? Does the action system understand the target system's rules so that it can make it live by them—or, at the least, call attention to their violation?
- Has the target system been personalized and focused so the action system can identify it?

- Are the tactics understood by, acceptable to, and enjoyable or exciting to the action system and unpredictable to and outside the experience of the target system?
- Have tactics that are unpredictable and embarrassing to the target system been designed? Has the media been alerted as to when these tactics will be used? Who will be the action system's voice and face?
- Are the tactics action-oriented, exciting, understandable by the action system, and quickly doable?

Adapted primarily from Alinsky (1969, 1971, 2006).

Box 13.4 provides additional guidelines to planning social action.

Formulating Strategies: Key Elements

People drawn to social action want action rather than planning; they tend to "ride to the sound of the gun." However, before action, planning must occur if the action is to be anything but noise. Before action, assessment, field analysis, mapping, and networking are required. The problem-solving systems, especially the target, change agent, action, and support systems, must be identified and developed. Assets must be assessed and the field analyzed. The targets must be specific and broad, and vague goals must be SMARRT. Once SMARRT objectives are formulated, winning strategies and action plans can be developed.

Working with Conflict. "Change means movement. Movement means friction," explained Alinsky (1971, p. 21). Change in the status quo usually entails conflict, except in the very rare instances when all parties agree with both ends and means (Messinger, 2006). "A people's Organization is a conflict group. . . . Its sole reason for coming into being is to wage war against all evils which cause suffering and unhappiness," wrote Alinsky (1969, p. 132). Some organizers plan and use conflict to train and

develop leadership and develop community identity and cohesion. They want "to rub raw the sores of discontent" and get people's ire up when the privileged make statements of the "Brownie, you're doing a heck of a job" variety that President George W. Bush made to the Federal Emergency management Agency direct Michael D. Brown on September 2, 2005 during the Hurricane Katrina disaster. Alinsky proved that even though have-nots lack power and money, their numbers can allow them to start and stop many things. Putting one's body on the line to face police dogs is one example, but leaders speak more of justice, education, pressure, and action than of outright physical confrontation with targets. Simply moving one's body to the right place at the right time and bringing along 10 friends is also people power; rallies can draw thousands of people. And thousands of people means television. And being on TV is empowering (Cohen, 2009).

Conflict and Consensus. Some organizers, such as Mizrahi (2002), suggest that we "assume the principle of least contest" (p. 6), escalating or antagonizing only to the degree needed. Least contest preserves resources for another day. Consensus is held as the optimal tactical approach in that it holds the potential to aggregate resources and bring together a range of key decision makers (Heenan, 2004; Jacobson, 2007). If conflict is not to be perpetual, consensus needs to be reached at some point in a contest (Jacobson, 2007). Conflict is a tactic that needs to be well thought out in terms of the potential for success, and not used just the fun of it. Eichler (1995), a proponent of the collaborative approach, describes consensus organizing as "a yearning for partnerships—a desire by all the parties to succeed and a sense that everyone has to pull together in order to succeed" (p. 257). Once the target comes to the table, there is a presumption of consensus between the action system and the target. Some groups make decisions mainly in consensus mode (e.g., Amerindians, Quakers), and it is the best way to mobilize them into action. However, it should not be used as an excuse or cover for defeat. Consensus is possible only when there are some overlapping interests. See Chapter 10 for the discussion of bargaining.

Consensus and conflict orientations are not diametrically opposed. Eichler (1995) concedes that consensus building does not work when key partners refuse to participate and will not be brought to the table. Beck and Eichler (2000) believe "organizers and community practitioners should learn both techniques so that the issue can guide the strategy" (p. 98). Consensus builders argue for a commonality focus and believe that building on what unites is more strategic and lasting. Those who support identity politics remind us to start where people are, that an initial spotlight on uniqueness and differences with its attendant discrimination and alienation will lead people to broader social concerns (Guinier & Torres, 2002).

Community practitioners inevitably reach moments when they have to decide whether to include or fight the power elites in the community. It is important to be aware of both options and use either when effective. Social workers need to engage in far more organizing and social action, using whatever mode works best for those they serve.

Organizing

The Change Systems Once the community practitioner and community residents, the initiator and client systems, have decided what should be done, the SMARRT objectives and the target system, they must think realistically about the support, change agent, and action systems. The composition and size of the change agent,

support, and action system must be determined and the systems established and operationalized. Here the data from the assets inventory and mapping and the field analysis are useful. Key questions are:

- Who the necessary allies and the desirable allies for the action and support systems?
- How can they be recruited and networked?
- Is there a wider supportive group who might provide resources but not direct action?
- What resources and budget are needed (talent, leadership, social capital, and physical resources such as space, equipment, parking, and communications)?
- What are the action system's internal resources and assets and what assets will be necessary from a support system?
- How can the external resource holders be recruited and networked?
- What organizations and tactics will be necessary to implement the action plan?

Change Systems Composition. Organizations and people, the constituents, composing the various change systems need not belong to the client system or the initiating organization; they can be all those who identify with the change goals, objectives, and cause and who benefit if the goals are attained. The field assessment of driving forces should identify the supporting organizations that will support the change. The field analysis and community assessments also can identify the restraining forces and opponents to change.

When developing an action plan, it is a good idea to make lists of who, on key issues, are already with (driving forces), possibly with, or probably against the goals and social change (restraining forces). For example, a neighborhood organization dedicated to increasing and enforcing gun control might come up with this list of players:

Potential constituents (change agent, action systems; driving forces): mothers (parallel to MADD), siblings, other students (parallel to SADD), peace churches and organizations, local chapters of Million Mom March, handgun control groups

Potential allies (support, action systems; driving forces): emergency room personnel, community leaders in high-crime areas, socially concerned faith-based organizations, police

Potential opponents (target systems; restraining forces): National Rifle Association chapters, gun dealers, pawnshop owners, hunters, farmers, gun-owning county council members, Tea Bagger supporters, U.S. Supreme Court

Any interested person or task group should be brought into the change agent and action systems and become driving forces for change, even if training is necessary for some constituents to be effective. Certain allies would be particularly valuable—in this case, doctors and nurses from emergency rooms overburdened by the victims of gun violence. This element makes us ask who can be enlisted to act or form a coalition and whether we can outwit our opposition, neutralize them, or take them out of the field.

Target Systems. Selecting appropriate targets combines assessment and organizing skills. Alinsky urges that the targets be personalized (Alinsky, 1969, 1971, 2006; Cohen, 2009). "Pick the target, freeze it, personalize it, and polarize it" (Alinsky, 2006). Alinsky provides the sound advice that in complex communities there needs to be a clearly identified villain to rail against. The Tea Bagger supporters in the 2010 political campaign selected Speaker of the House Nancy Pelosi for this role.[6] Targets should be vulnerable, even if they are not the most significant restraining forces to change. The target should be a personification, not something general and abstract such as a community's discrimination practices or a major corporation or City Hall. Use the mayor, the CEO of a health insurance company, or, at the least, a specific health insurance company. This is the tactic in organizing where opponents are made to feel the heat so that they will see the light.

Themba (1999, p. 95) recommends asking the following key questions in choosing the target:

- Who or what specific institutions have the power to solve the problem and grant the demands?

- Who must be influenced before the real power holders can be influenced?
- What are the strengths and weaknesses of each potential target? Which are the most vulnerable?
- Which targets are appointed, which are elected, and by whom, when, and how?
- How are they influenced (as by voters, consumers, taxpayers, investors, shaming, etc.)?
- What is their self-interest in this issue?
- Who may have jurisdiction if the issue is redefined (e.g., turned a tobacco advertising issue into a fair business practice issue, a public health issue, a child welfare issue)?
- Can the decision-makers be influenced to be made driving forces, or at least, not restraining forces to change?

Tactics. The tactics used must fit the nature and character of the change agent, action, and support systems and the vulnerability of the target system. If a new group or organization, a new change agent or action system, is eager for a victory, the community practitioner can find a "fixed fight"—a sure winner—to build confidence. Greater care and judgment must be exercised to avoid premature losing struggles or change efforts that produce no change. Our late colleague, friend, and long-time activist Edward Dutton, a great participant in noble losing causes and some winning ones, was fond of the expression: "Any blow that doesn't kill, strengthens." Only martyrs seek to lose contests and then to die strong. In social change, it is better to win.

In a first fight, the community practitioner must be careful lest the victory comes too rapidly and too easily. If the struggle is too easily settled, a false sense of power can develop and there may not be adequate time to develop leadership and action system bonding and cohesion.

Self-determination, empowerment, and informed consent require that the change agent and the action systems, the people who will be on the line, be central in designing the action plan tactics. Social action tactics range from public information approaches (leafleting, informational pickets, letters to the editor, blogging, holding candlelight vigils) to direct action tactics (boycotting, obstructing, sit-ins, strikes).

The group will enjoy coming up with imaginative tactics and the media will relish them. Alinsky said, "People hunger for drama and adventure, for a breath of life in a dreary, drab existence" (1972, pp. 120–121). Alinsky (1969, 2, 2006) also advised us never to go outside the experience of the action system and always try to surprise the targets. Create confusion and fear, and be unpredictable. As power often is in the perception, try to appear stronger and conceal your actual strength, if possible. Remember, a good tactic is one that the action system enjoys. Happy warriors are better fighters than miserable martyrs. Hands-on exercises are preparatory, creative, and mobilizing. Organizing is serious and yet fun-loving tradition. Experience has shown that participants must enjoy and be challenged by the tactics. However, a concrete win, the social change, is the reason for social action, not moral victories and fun.

Debriefing sessions after an action encourage participant responsibility and creativity and help cultivate leadership. They evaluate the action to date, the objective accomplishments, and any changes in the field, and start the process for the next phase of the change effort: where do we go from here? Evaluation looks at whether the effort was successful, at what price, and the next steps that will be used to influence decision makers.

Using a SMARRT Strategy Chart and Field Analysis

Given the complexity of large-scale change, incrementalism (breaking problems into small, manageable steps) is reasonable. A strategy chart with the SMARRT objectives and sub-objectives, similar to a critical path analysis, is an assessment tool whose simplicity and versatility make it a helpful planning process for seeing the terrain and for mapping out a route to change. It can be used in community and organizational projects. Box 13.5 gives an example. It can be coupled with a field analysis chart.

Illustrative Exercises

1. What could make a prospective leader feel good? What are opportunities and assignments that will let the person achieve something—build self-esteem through accomplishments.
2. Research the biography and social change efforts of Jane Addams, Emily Greene Balch, Ron V. Dellums, Dorothy Height, and Jeannette Rankin. Do they share anything in common?

Community Coordination

Coordination involves assembling resources, synchronizing activities, providing order, and encouraging teamwork of individuals, groups, and organizations to connect as a system or network. Coordination is network building and management (see Chapter 10). The community practitioner must pay attention to coordinating all the elements of the change system, except the target system. Coordination concentrates and focuses assets, resources, and the change systems.

Coordination Through Information

Network and people can be connected by countless means: the Internet, communication technology, Twitter,[7] word of mouth, telephone and virtual networks, posters, newsletters, leaflets and handbills, and face-to-face meetings, among other methods. Their purpose is to convey information about expected network members' behaviors. Community education involves targeted outreach to and coordination of (a) diverse lay audiences who are able to respond to alerts and advice and (b) opinion leaders who help diffuse information. Box 13.6 illustrates spontaneous communication in a city. We discussed communication education more fully in Chapter 11.

Community Participation: Putting Community at the Center

Progressive community practitioners believe that a small group of decision makers from distant governments and large, vertical and global companies ought not to run communities because these vertically related decision makers rarely have the best interests of the community central to their deliberations. Critical community practice, as discussed in chapters 2 and 4

BOX 13.5. Strategy Chart

Midwest Academy Strategy Chart: After choosing the issue, fill in this chart as a guide to developing strategy. Be specific. List all the possibilities.

Goals	Organizational Considerations	Constituents, Allies, Opponents	Targets	Tactics
1. List long-term objectives of campaign.	List the resources that the action system brings to the campaign. Resources, assets required: tangible as money, personnel, volunteers, other in-kind, and intangible	Who cares enough about the issue to become part of action or support systems? Whose problem is it? Who gains if win? What are the risks? Power over target? Organization of action system?	Primary Target Always a person or specific people, never an abstraction.	For each target, list the tactics that the action system can best use to make its power felt.
2. State intermediate goals for this issue campaign. What constitutes victory? How will the campaign: • Win concrete improvement in people's lives? • Give people a sense of their own power? • Alter the relations of power?	List the specific ways that action system can be strengthened by the campaign: Expanded leadership, increased leadership experience, expanded membership base, new constituencies, fundraising	Who are the opponents and the target? What will losing cost them? Resources in opposition? Power and power sources?	Secondary targets, Target's support system? Power holders over them? Action system power over them?	Tactics: In context? Creative and flexible? Directed and focused? Makes sense to action system? Backed by specific power?
3. What short-term or partial victories can be won as steps toward the long-term goal?				Tactics include: Social marketing Public information as by informational pickets Public hearings Media blitzes Strikes and disruptions. Civil actions Other (be specific)

Source: Bobo, K., Kendall, J., & Max, S. (2001, p. 33), *Organizing for Change,* c. 2001 by Seven Locks Press. Adapted and used with permission.

BOX 13.6.	Community Support and Organizing

In 1993, hate activities in Billings, Montana, reached a crescendo. Ku Klux Klan (KKK) fliers were distributed in public places and mailboxes, the Jewish cemetery was desecrated, the home of an Amerindian family was painted with swastikas, and a cinder brick was thrown through the bedroom window of a six-year-old boy displaying a Hanukkah menorah. Billings was not intimidated by the hate; it acted together as a community. Coordination was spontaneous. The police chief urged citizens to respond nonviolently before the violence escalated any further. Religious groups from every denomination sponsored marches and candlelight vigils. The local labor council passed a resolution against racism, anti-Semitism, and homophobia and held a "Stand Together Billings" rally to urge community adoption of an anti-hate proclamation. The local Painters Union's members painted over the racist graffiti. The local newspaper printed full-page menorahs that were subsequently displayed in nearly 10,000 homes and businesses. The community made an unmistakable declaration: "Not in our town; we are a decent community." Since then, no serious acts of hate violence have been reported in Billings. Billings exercised social control through mutual support and social justice.

Source: http://www.pbs.org/niot/about/niot1.html, 5/27/2010.

and in the introduction, considers citizen participation, participation of the marginalized, community self-determination, and community empowerment to be fundamental to democracy and social justice. This tradition stresses democracy, public and client participation in decision making, and multi-stakeholder accountability. The goal of community participation is broad involvement of citizens in all phases of the improvement process until residents own and sustain it. This usually requires benefits to flow from engagement: tangible benefits such as a job and a better life, and intangible benefits such as inclusion and empowerment (Butcher, Banks, Henderson, with Robertson, 2007; Orsini, 2006; Shaw, Gallant, Riley-Jacome, & Spokane, 2006; Wakefield & Poland, 2005). Community residents want to influence their environments—not just carry out someone else's ideas—and have "partnership arrangements as a way of giving local people a major say over what happens in the area" (McArthur, 1995, p. 66). If not control, in terms of planning, service creation, governance, or evaluation, beneficiaries, as a minimum, should have peer representation (Masilela & Meyer, 1998). There should be larger numbers and more types of consumers in any collaborative or consortium.

The dearth of community/grassroots involvement in decisions regarding what happens to communities has given credibility and momentum to the reactionary and homogenously white Tea *Bagger* movement. It has feasted on America's growing sense of powerlessness, alienation, and estrangement (Barstow, 2010; Kim, 2010; Raban, 2010; Zernike & Thee-Brenan, 2010).

Mutual engagement with and participation by service users and the citizenry is more than a goal; it is our professional obligation to do what is necessary to involve a diversity of community members (Daley & Marsiglia, 2000, p. 83). Henderson (2007) contends that community practice is about stimulating, engaging, and achieving active community participation and engaging individuals and groups in the participatory process. Butcher (2007, p. 17) reinforces his colleagues position: the core of critical community practice is "a commitment *to working for social justice through empowering disadvantaged, excluded and oppressed communities to take more control over the conditions of their lives* [emphasis original]". We must get beyond our own professional fields, our own circles, our group's opinions, and 'rounding up the usual suspects.' It must be done to improve the quality of information, build social capital, and because it is just.

Miley, O'Melia, and DuBois (1998) recommend three factors to increase the likelihood of successful participation on the part of consumers:

1. A clear directive for consumers' participation by the sponsoring organization or authority

2. A power base from which to assert consumers' rights to participate
3. Recognition of consumers' legitimacy as spokespersons (pp. 379–380)

Points two and three speak to the need for clients and consumers to organize and develop a power base independent from the sponsoring authority.

In contrast, a low-income community can be set up for failure when residents are expected to (a) understand jargon and talk and act like the traditional spokespeople, (b) donate considerable time as unpaid volunteers, with the accompanying expenses and income loss, and (c) keep things going without resources after professionals complete their project, the sponsoring authority withdraws support, and the community organization more or less is set adrift (Lewis, Lewis, & Rachelefsky, 1996).

Box 13.7 suggests ways to avoid paternalism. If the marginalized are included, don't re-marginalize them. Do their views count? Involving people in task forces or coalitions and sustaining their participation is not an easy task, but forming a representative group and enlarging the sphere of participation are worthwhile challenges.

Ensuring True Representation. When the 1960s and 1970s Great Society, War on Poverty, and model cities programs, and the more contemporary empowerment-zone programs, expanded and looked for indigenous leadership, self-anointed leaders often pushed themselves forward.

Not surprisingly, a search for indigenous community leadership attracts the upwardly mobile and often ersatz leaders instead of the marginalized. This is a participation challenge: while hustlers and the upwardly mobile may not be the most representative people, at least they are from the neighborhood and may be more indigenous than the Astroturf leaders the power structure historically cultivated.

As Kahn (1970) reminds us from that era, "leaders require followers." Actually, a leader is someone whom others follow. A community-building task is developing indigenous leaders to replace the Astroturf leaders ordained by the power holders. In recruiting community representation, a community practitioner will:

1. Consult with members of communities, key informants, about whom they would appoint.
2. Ask current clients, client representatives, and other key informants whom they look to for advice and help with decisions.
3. Identify the most widely admired community members by the community members from the assets inventory, power analysis, and community assessment. Use community segmentation to ensure the range of community diversity is covered.
4. Survey agency critics to assess if they should be added to the community leadership. It is better to have them in the tent than outside yelling. Don't limit participation to the passive and the sycophants; they are unlike to mobilize a community.

BOX 13.7.	**Connecting and Dissimilarity**

As human service professionals, we support social processes that create community and embrace differences. Altruism researchers believe that humans can have personal and group identities and still include others. We can extend the clan. According to Oliner and Oliner (1995), expressions of communal care grow out of eight processes:

Promoting attachments with those in our immediate settings:

1. Bonding
2. Empathizing
3. Learning caring norms

4. Practicing care and assuming personal responsibility

Promoting caring relationships with those outside our immediate settings and groups:

5. Diversifying
6. Networking
7. Resolving conflicts
8. Establishing global connections

Source: Excerpts from *Toward a Caring Society* (pp. 6–7), by Pearl M. Oliner and Samuel P. Oliner, 1995, Westport, CT: Praeger Publishers. Copyright 1995 by Pearl M. Oliner and Samuel P. Oliner. Reproduced with permission of Greenwood Publishing Group, Inc.

BOX 13.8.	Guidelines for Critical Community Practitioners and Community Involvement

- Identify and know your own values, agendas, interests, and goals and those of the people you are working with, and distinguish between the two.
- Own your own role and power; recognize the skills and information you have and never assume that others share it.
- Recognize that it is essential to enable people's involvement, social self-determination, and empowerment for community work; these cannot be taken for granted in the pursuit of other laudable goals.
- Build on the skills and experience that people have.
- Give people the opportunity to work out their own objectives and forms for involvement and social self-determination, and be aware of the danger of unintentionally imposing your own goals and objectives.

- Make realistic assessments with people of what is actually achievable in any given situation, what the possible outcomes are, and what the costs may be, so that people can make a truly informed decision about what they want to do.
- Be sensitive to the fears and uncertainties people have.
- Appreciate and respond to people's need for self-confidence and assertiveness in working with you.
- Recognize and fulfill your modeling and teaching responsibilities.

Source: Croft and Beresford (1988, pp. 278–279). Copyright *Community Development Journal*. Used with permission of Oxford University Press and the authors. Supplemented with Butcher, Banks, & Henderson, with Robertson (2007).

5. As names are suggested, critically assess whether they bring a new perspective from an underrepresented community segment and whether they have a following in that segment. Again, leaders have followers.

Box 13.8 presents additional guidelines for critical community practice.

Illustrative Exercise

The purpose is to involve all stakeholders, especially the powerless, in community building during a time when communities are under severe strain. The City has allocated your agency $200,000 of stimulus money to form an advisory council to advise the City on youth programming cutbacks strategies during the Great Recession. The council is to have representation from youth service programs, youth groups, the youth community, and other relevant community segments with "an interest in the youth community" (the mayor's words). It looks like an onerous community-building task—spending scarce resources to form a community advisory council to advise on how not to spend money. What kinds of individuals, groups, and organizations will you contact? Be specific as to the segments of people (by organization type, group,

and position or status within the group). How will you determine the leaders of the different segments?

Innovative Change Philosophies

Some organizing approaches to change require new constructions of reality. Cultural activism, multicultural organizing, feminist organizing, and the Freirean approach are examples. These approaches share common elements: (a) a strong oral tradition, (b) self- and group realization, (c) cognitive liberation, and (d) the resilience and expressive power of people. *Cognitive liberation* (Ash, 1972; McAdam, 1982) means freedom from prevailing dogma and openness to new possibilities—that other species can be treated unjustly, for instance, or that God is feminine. Like Lee's (1994) empowerment practice and critical community practice, cognitive liberation requires recognition of the collective history, the social realities of class, gender, and sexual orientation, and ethnicity, and that all relations are political. *Resilience* embodies the human capacity for laughter and the ability to rebound from adversity and tragedy (Felkins, 2002, p. 55; Irving & Young, 2002, p. 25). With deconstruction and critical analysis comes reconstruction. Self-expression can serve the purpose of liberation and rebellion, as with the Chicano *corridos,* the music of the history, heroes, and villains of local communities in the United States and Mexico. Folk music has long served this purpose.

Cultural Activism

Scottish patriot Andrew Fletcher once wrote, "If one were permitted to make all the ballads, one need not care who should make the laws of a nation" (Cultural Environment Movement, 1999). Thus, cultural activism can arise from any population; for example, francophones who want to preserve French cuisine and language in Canada, the Mexican-American's *corridos,* and the urban rappers. Artists and other culture workers use cultural symbols in their organizing.

Cultural activism is a means to dramatize and expose injustice and strengthen those who struggle by connecting them to their history. The past is prelude to the present and future. Lee (1994) points out that cultural history can serve as a personal as well as a social change strategy by instilling political consciousness and political unity. Organizers consider how to challenge the dominant view and to connect disregarded people in vision and action, as Luis Valdez (1996) did with *El Teatro Campesino* with plays such as *Quinta Temporada* during the National Farm Workers Association strikes.

Tactics vary: it can be song, visual and performing arts, or the Philadelphia murals. Cultural activism creates opposition to pervasive but invisible consciousness shaping and subtle education. Why is there a business but not a labor section in the newspaper? (Hofrichter, 1993, p. 88). Why is there a society section but not a people section? People are overwhelmed by corporate-controlled culture inundating them from the media, and the change agent helps people analyze links between communication, power, and politics. "I watch soap operas," said Paulo Freire, "and I learn a lot by criticizing them. . . I fight with [television], if you can understand. A commercial rarely catches me unawares" (as cited in Gadotti, 1994, p. 78).

To create concrete applications, we must become attuned to others' experiential realities. Kahn (1997) urges social workers to reach people through "cultural work," which he defines as "the conscious and strategic use of culture, craft and art to achieve political goals . . . The power of culture can also be an antidote to people's racialized and gendered inertia, to their inability to see beyond their own eyes. . . . Cultural work can transform consciousness, can perform the acts of political education that, combined with community organizing, make social change transformational" (p. 128).

Woody Guthrie, Pete Seeger, and Bruce Springsteen's protest music can inspire and unite. *We Shall Overcome,* a gospel song by 19th-century black minister Charles Albert Tindley, was adapted by Pete Seeger to become the civil rights movement's anthem and then a worldwide protest and resistance anthem. It was sung at the fall of the Berlin Wall and in South Africa with the end of apartheid. It has even been sung at Tea Bagger rallies.

Multicultural Organizing. "Disenfranchised, abandoned, and underserved communities of color need organizers . . . [to help] these communities establish and reestablish dignity and opportunity," Rivera and Erlich declared (1998, p. 256). Other subjugated groups in liberation struggles also need new ways to engage, inspire, and unleash the imagination. Since transformation can be visceral and emotional, old organizing approaches may not work. Intellectual education methods "aren't always adequate to deal with a transformative process, particularly one which challenges racism, sexism, homophobia, anti-Semitism, and other barriers that divide people from each other," asserts Kahn (1997, p. 128). Glugoski, Reisch, and Rivera (1994) recommend that we "identify similarities as well as differences shared by all groups" (p. 85) and "adopt the role of an active listener interested in discovering the people's world through dialogue" (p. 90). To do so requires in-depth exploring of least one facet of another's world.

Care must be exercised to go beyond divisive identity politics (Appiah, 2005). Salcido (1993) urges culturally appropriate interactions, such as the interactions that occur when Anglos reach out to Latinos and Latinos to African-Americans. Cultural labeling can also hide differences within cultures or may have limited relevance. How much, for instance, does a native-born African-American social worker know about West Indians and African-born blacks? What do they share beyond discrimination and skin color? They do not share a common language other than English or a common history. What unites Hispanics beyond language and perhaps religion? Do Mexican-Americans, Cuban-Americans, and Bolivian-Americans share the same culture? And what unites Asian-Americans after millenniums of conflict in Asia? Muslim cultures embrace Bosnians, Iraqis, Iranians, Nigerians, and Indonesians, among many, many others. The glue that bonds these groups in America may be discrimination rather than shared culture.

Cultural labels are, at best, a starting point in assessment and organizing, not a place to end. The better acquainted we become with cultures other than our own, the more commonalties we see. This is reason enough to learn about the cultures for community building—to build from what we share.

Feminist Organizing

Social issues that affect women differently than men because of different social roles and power include day care and rape and sexual assault. Providing quality day care and eliminating sexual assault should be gender-neutral goals, but unfortunately they are not; they are presented as "women's issues," as if no men are involved in childbirth, abuse, or rape (Goodman, 2010). Action such as "taking back the night," defending abortion clinics, and guaranteeing fairness to prospective lesbian and gay adoptive parents are presented as feminist.

There are differences in *feminist* organizing, as distinct from *women* organizing. Feminist organizing is a philosophy that guides tactics. Mizrahi (2007) concluded after a qualitative study of 48 women that women organizers were less likely to stereotype, make a greater use of interpersonal relationships, and are more tenacious than are male organizers. Two related themes emerged regarding participants' styles: a developmental approach that focused on the relationship between the self/individual and the group/collective, and a holistic approach connecting the issues to the women's lives.

Mizrahi and Lombe (2007) in a subsequent study found the gender alone did not overcome all differences. While feminism for the feminist organizers did define both identity and style of organizing, it was not enough to unite all women. They recognized, to varying degrees, that the complexity of identity was nested also in race, class, age, and sexual orientation and how each of these are positioned and interact to influence the women's perception of reality and the salience of issues to them. The challenge for women organizers, indeed all organizers, and their stakeholders is to acknowledge the complexity of the multilayered entities that define identity. It is not possible to organize around a single, albeit a singularly significant, trait.

Most feminist organizing (Bricker-Jenkins & Lockett, 1995; Hyde, 2001; Peterson & Lieberman, 2001; Weil, 2001) theorists agree with Mizrahi and Lombe (2007). Gutierrez and Lewis's (1994) philosophy about feminist organizing "involves both the rational and nonrational elements of human experiences, with emotions, spirituality, and artistic expression used as tactics for unifying women and expressing issues. Involvement in social change is considered organic, not an adjunct, to women's lives" (p. 31). The practice of caring about others is not inherently female; both genders exhibit it when encouraged and socialized to do so. Unfortunately, cruelty and meanness are not gender-bound, either, as recent harassment incidents indicate (Clifford, 2009; Eckholm & Zezima, 2010).

Freirean Approach. Indigent and indigenous communities are the focus of this approach. To get a sense of the political world as Paulo Freire saw it, imagine the Southern Hemisphere with a giant mouth—forced open—into which the North pours its culture. Then imagine the poor and illiterate, prohibited from resisting, while the dominant in their own country demand passivity and the educated force-feed knowledge down their throats. Box 13.9 and 13.10 illustrates Freire organizing ideology.

Freire thought that everything was political and that humans had critical curiosity ready to be triggered in a situation of learning among equals. Freire (1994) viewed popular education as informal interchange with people discovering they are capable of knowing (pp. 46–47). Education, he believed, triggers reflection and action (praxis) and social transformation. Like critical community practice and empowerment

BOX 13.9.	Paulo Freire and Liberation

Born in 1921 in Recife, Brazil, Paulo Freire (in Portuguese, pronounced Pall-ou FRAY-ree) studied law, but became a teacher. His philosophy was to relate education to a social context and to avoid "banking"—where students are empty vessels into which teachers pour their accumulated knowledge and maintain external authority. Interested in illiterates, who would benefit from social transformation, Freire started working in cultural circles, exploring liberating themes and words (hunger rather than food) that related to problems lived by the group.

What a track record he had! In northeast Brazil, he taught 300 adults to read and write in 45 days. At Con Edison in New York, he used an inner-city vocabulary to teach functional illiterates to read at a sixth- to seventh-grade level in 13 weeks. He wrote books such as *Pedagogy of the Oppressed* that still sell worldwide. Exiled from his own country for 15 years, the good-natured Freire made common cause with others, including social workers who admired his bottom-up change model. During his career, he held government positions in education and worked for diverse institutions—the Institute of Cultural Action in Geneva, Harvard University, and the World Council of Churches.

With a goal of political transformation, Freire modeled quiet ways to liberate the oppressed. An optimist, he experimented his entire life with ways to enable people to break out of passivity and silent subjugation.

Sources: Based on Associated Press (1997), Cashmore & Rojek (1999), and Gadotti (1994).

social work practice, Freire's empowerment education, according to Wallerstein (1993), "offers a three-stage method. The first step is listening for the key issues and emotional concerns of community people. . . . The second step is promoting participatory dialogue about these concerns. The third step is taking action about the concerns that are discussed" (p. 222).

As a person who was able to politicize as he taught literacy, Freire grew in influence as organizers looked for role models that not only respected oppressed and discounted peoples but also immersed themselves in their world. Among the U.S. models were social worker Dorothy Day, who established Catholic Worker hospitality houses, and Myles Horton of the Highlander Center in Tennessee (Horton & Freire, 1990).

Additional tenets of Freire's philosophy that are relevant to community practice include the following:

- Basing informal education on everyday experience (Castelloe & Watson, 1999, pp. 73–76; Gadotti, 1994, pp. 18–19)

BOX 13.10.	Dialogue: A "Space of Possibility"

Members of popular (populist) groups and illiterate people looked up to Paulo Freire for having studied. In the following excerpt from his book, *Pedagogy of Hope* (1994), Freire recalls the dialogue that occurred at one of his meetings:

[Freire] "And why couldn't your parents send you to school?"
[Audience member] "Because they were peasants like us."
"And what is 'being a peasant'?"
"It's not having an education . . . not owning anything . . . working from sun to sun . . . having no rights . . . having no hope."

"And why doesn't a peasant have any of this?"
"The will of God."
"And who is God?"
"The Father of us all."
"And who is a father here this evening?"
Almost all raised their hands, and said they were.
[Freire] picked out one of them and asked him, "How many children do you have?"
"Three."
"Would you be willing to sacrifice two of them, and make them suffer so that the other one could go to school and have a good life, in Recife? . . ."
"No!"

- Giving up the superiority of being more learned (Carroll & Minkler, 2000, p. 28; Freire, 1994, pp. 46–47)
- Becoming humble to empower someone else (Blackburn, 2000, p. 13; Freire, 1994, pp. 22–27; Glugoski, Reisch & Rivera, 1994, p. 90)
- Facing and overcoming limit situations (i.e., concrete realities) (Freire, 1994, pp. 205–207; Sachs & Newdom, 1999, p. 98)
- Bringing forth social, political, and critical consciousness (Gadotti, 1994, pp. 147–149; Reisch, Wenocur, & Sherman, 1981)

Narration

Narration is used to tell us something about people, their worldview, and their needs. Narration is a dimension and a tool of cultural activism, multicultural organizing, feminist organizing, and Freirean popular education. Narrative deals with meaning, myth, metaphor, dialogue, and culture transmittal. A narrative can lament or celebrate an individual, a group, a community, a tribe, or a quest. It can exemplify shared experience and convey respect for roots. It can crystallize professional values and highlight whether we do what we say we value—practice what we preach (Walz, 1991). A narrative can be in the form of stories, rap, a Chicano *corridos*, or Merle Haggard's *Tulare Dust/They're Tearin' the Labor Camps Down*, a lament to the Dust Bowl migrants. The message may be overt or covert, such as resistance to oppression or the injustices of the economic system. Davis (2002) contrasts self-narratives that are personal with movement narratives that are oppositional and subversive—that is, war stories that help form collective recognition and identities (pp. 22–26).

Clinicians can use narrative therapy, which holds that "people can continually and actively re-author their lives" (Freedman & Combs, 1996, pp. 15–16). Community practitioners can shape or direct narrative to help people come together, achieve something, overcome a difficulty or change, or regain self-respect. Oral histories, a form of narrative, can reveal journeys from accommodation to self-determination and effective resistance. In interviews he conducted,

Couto (1993) found "common elements in the stories such as a member of the community looking at a dominant person in the eye and the art of challenging a dominant person without incurring retaliation" (p. 70). If the conventions of daily life in society so dominate us that we are unable to challenge, as some theorists believe, then narratives provide a means of liberation from conventionality and passivity (Loeb, 1999, p. 212). Thus, narratives offer "new possibilities for staging a resistance to the damaging effects of social, cultural, and political dominant narratives and for inviting subjects to write for themselves more empowering, less subjugated narratives" [italics added] (Wyile & Paré, 2001, p. 171).

Narratives have potency at the macro level. A narrative both reveals the story of its narrator and is useful in identifying others with like experiences. The telling of the stories provides ways to build solidarity, from folk tales to the confessions at Alcoholics Anonymous meetings. Professionals can elicit, hear, and steer narratives to encourage empowerment and liberation. Persuasive arguments embedded in a story form can be an effective springboard for internal transformation of an organization, declared Denning (2001), and for gaining support from external constituencies, according to Heugens (2002). Community practitioners can use narratives to help people make a leap in understanding, to encourage groups to bridge their differences, to create confederations, and to forward causes. Social movements are created and sustained by "bundles of narratives" (Fine, 2002). Davis (2002) said, "Through stories, participants, actual and potential, are called . . . to identify and empathize with real protagonists, to be repelled by antagonists, to enter into and feel morally involved in configurations of events that specify injustice and prefigure change. . . . [Key] events— be they sit-ins, nuclear accidents, or court decisions—are interpreted and made the basis for action through stories. . . . [Storytelling] specifies valued endpoints and stimulates creative participation" (pp. 24–27).

Narrative also allows movements to reach those who cannot read. Song stories, *corridos*, and folk and protest songs have often served this purpose. Mexican revolutionary leader *subcomandante* Marcos (2001) wrote about values in free verse, which is more easily memorized than most expository political statements: "Zapatismo poses the question[s]: 'What is it that has excluded me?' [and] 'What is it that has isolated me?'" (p. 440). Marcos writes parables and updates old stories that can be related and discussed around a bonfire, part of normal social practices. Some poke fun at the weaknesses of the establishment ("The Parrot's Victory"), while others encourage acceptance of differences such as sexual orientation ("The Tale of the Little Seamstress"). Zapatistas use the Internet to spread their message, so they reach computer-literate sympathizers around the globe as well as illiterate indigenous people. Thus, the narration method can include the broad use of simplified stories to liberate and to combat oppression and to provide information, mental images, and coordinated messages (Themba, 1999, pp. 140–141).

At a psychological level, narratives allow the powerless to reframe their lives. Just as many individuals spend time in therapy ridding themselves of limiting personal scripts inculcated in them by others, so people in certain aggregates cope with social typing that limits them. Those who live in public housing deal with "pathological narratives" from outsiders. In response, residents tell defending stories and group enhancement stories (Salzer, 1998, pp. 578–579). Despite people's reluctance to forgo their defending stories, there need to be transforming possibilities in their group enhancement stories. As Woody Guthrie sang, it's not enough to simply tell the world about feeling bad. You must to declare that you "ain't gonna be treated this a-way."[8]

Telling or Hearing Stories Establishes Connections

Ultimately the storyteller should come to view himself or herself as a story *maker*. The Midwest Academy, in its training of social activists and community organizers, included a session on storytelling as an organizing tool. The focus is on the need to know people's life stories as a necessary step in developing leadership and framing issues (Ganz, 2001). In the same vein, both author and lecturer "gain new skills, meet new people, hear and heed new stories" (p. 214).

To recap, the narrative has been used in myriad ways to link disparate people and unify communities, build revolutions, or stop conflict between human groups. Narratives are used in social action to rally supporters, "rub raw the sores of discontent," and instill a common spirit. Caseworkers and clinicians can elicit client narratives and highlight them as they stage public issues. Through client narratives they can find common patterns of collective identity and a common sense of grievance and community discontent or achievement. Similarly, rural and urban practitioners can help get narratives disseminated, draw linkages with community problems and assets, and note commonalties of narratives that allow disparate groups to find common ground.

The Theme of Connecting

Community practitioners are networkers and connectors in the pursuit of community solidarity, community betterment, and social justice. The connecting is for all three: social problem resolution, building caring communities and citizens, and promoting social justice. They are inseparable. Communities built on caring and mutual support are needed now as much or more as anytime in our collective histories. The physician's quote in Chapter 4 needs to become a historical artifact: "American culture simply has never been based on caring about what happened to your neighbor" (Smith, 2009). Caring must be the core of community.

Discussion Exercises

1. *Which way of creating or better using assets (asset building, asset claiming, asset identification and mobilization, individual leadership assets, cultural assets) most interests you, and why? Do you have personal or professional experience with any of the described programs?*

2. *Is your agency engaged in community building? Does it give annual "hero awards" to those improving community life, to make the work of such people known to everyone?*

3. *Why are associations as important as individuals to social work practice? In your view, are communities "bowling alone" in the sense of disengagement or "bowling along" in the sense of building anew and muddling through? Look up Robert Putnam on the Internet to learn his views on civic participation and association (try American Prospect at http://www.prospect.org/cs/search?keyword=Putnam. http://www.movingideas.org/links/civiclinks.html).*

4. *Using the Internet and other resources, research government funding sources for community projects. Start with the U.S. Department of Housing and Urban Development's revitalization HOPE VI funds and the Community Outreach Partnership Centers.*

5. *Gina Johnson, age 45, has a job, a home, five dogs, and one cat. Young men have beaten her up. She videotapes drug transactions and prostitution and has worked for years to get more law enforcement on the streets. Finally, an undercover officer came but was killed—and she still feels guilty. Some see her as bold, others as prickly, some as reclusive. She has come to your community office wanting help with crime and in forming some type of action group. How can you learn more about Ms. Johnson as an individual in relationship to the neighborhood? How could she be an asset? A liability? What is your obligation to her?*

6. *Many people who die in storms live in manufactured housing. A proposed solution is to require trailer park owners to install huge storm cellars that can accommodate residents. Debate the issues (the costs that will be passed on to residents versus saving lives). If the trailer park population is divided over this issue, how can the positions be reconciled, or can they? Draft statements to give before a state legislative committee. How does it build community to consider the well-being of a portion of the populace? If the trailer park residents must hire experts, what associations might help with fundraising?*

7. *Role-play: You tell your governing board of a grant-making organization that you want to involve interested indigenous leaders, service users, and service providers in the grant-making decisions. Board members appropriately ask (a) how you will define and identify interested and indigenous stakeholders, and (b) why you want to line up those already interested rather than expand participation to include those who never participate but should be interested as they are affected by the grant-making. Respond.*

8. *If a homophobic act occurred in your community, explain how will you respond and help the community respond.*

Notes

1. From letter to Big Bill Hayward just before he was executed by a Utah firing squad.
2. For more complete listings see: http://www.starguide.org/orgs and http://www.CommonDreams.org.
3. http://www.communityactionpartnership.com/
4. See the discussions of assessment and assets inventory and mapping in the assessment chapters.
5. For a history of the California farm labor organizing efforts, see Cornfield (1995), Dunne, (1967), and Weber (1994).
6. For example, see the FOX Web site for any Tea Bagger posting during the 2010 campaign: http://www.foxnews.com/opinion
7. The 2010 flash riots by Philadelphia-area teenagers were coordinated by Facebook, tweets and cell phone networks.
8. "Going down the road feeling bad, Lord, Lord, An' I ain't gonna be treated this a-way." From Woody Guthrie's Dust Bowl migrant anthem, *Blowing Down That Old Dust Road*, April 1940, C. Hollis Music Inc., New York, 1960.

References

Abatena, H. (1997). The significance of planned community participation in problem solving and developing a viable community capability. *Journal of Community Practice*, 4(2), 13–34.

ACORN. (n.d.). *ACORN's living wage*. Retrieved May 31, 2010, from http://www.acorn.org/index.php?id=12341

Adams, P., & Krauth, K. (1995). Working with families and communities: The patch approach. In P. Adams & K. Nelson (Eds.), *Reinventing human services: Community and family-centered practice* (pp. 87–108). New York: Aldine de Gruyter.

Alinsky, S. D. (1969). *Reveille for radicals*. New York: Vintage.

Alinsky, S. D. (1971). *Rules for radicals: A pragmatic primer for realistic radicals*. New York: Vintage.

Alinsky, S. (2006, Winter). *Alinsky's rules for power: From rules for radicals*. Semcosh. . Retrieved September 8, 2010 from http://www.jasongooljar.com/AlinskyTactics.pdf

Allender, J. A., & Spradley, B. W. (2001). *Community health nursing*. Philadelphia: Lippincott.

Ammerman, A., & Parks, C. (1998). Preparing students for more effective community interventions: Assets assessment. *Family and Community Health*, 21(1), 32–45.

Appiah, K. A. (2005). *The ethics of identity*. Princeton, NJ: Princeton University Press.

Ash, R. (1972). *Social movements in America*. Chicago: Marham.

Associated Press (1997, May 4). Paulo Freire dies at 75; Brazilian literacy expert. *The Washington Post*, p. B8.

Baker, P. (2010, May 11). Liberals, in moderation. *The New York Times*. pp. A1, A15.

Banking for the poor: Grameen Bank. (2010, April 15). Retrieved May 14, 2010, from: http://www.grameen-info.org/

Banks, S. (2007). Becoming critical: Developing the community practitioner. In H. Butcher, S. Banks, & P. Henderson with J. Robertson. (Eds.), *Critical community practice* (pp. 133–152). Bristol, UK: The Policy Press.

Banerjee, M. M. (2001). Micro-enterprise training (MET) program: An innovative response to welfare reform. *Journal of Community Practice*, 9(4), 87-107.

Barstow, D., (2010, February 15). Tea Party lights fuse for rebellion on right. *The New York Times*. Retrieved February 17, 2010, from: http://www.nytimes.com/2010/02/16/us/politics/16teaparty.html

Battle, M. (n.d.). *Reflections: 1960's, Into the community, interview with Mark Battle*. Retrieved June 20, 2003, from: http://www.umbc.edu/socialwork/index.php?page=talking-with-mark-g-battle

Beck, E. L., & Eichler, M. (2000). Consensus organizing: A practice model for community building. *Journal of Community Practice*, 8(1), 87–102.

Blackburn, J. (2000). Understanding Paulo Freire: Reflections on the origins, concepts, and possible pitfalls of his educational approach. *Community Development Journal*, 35(1), 3–15.

Bobo, K., Kendall, J., & Max, S. (2001). *Organizing for social change* (3rd ed.). Santa Ana, CA: Seven Locks Press.

Bowen, G. L., & Richman, J. M. (2002). Schools in the context of communities. *Children and Schools*, 24(2), 67–71.

Bricker-Jenkins, M., & Lockett, P. W. (1995). Women: Direct practice. In R. Edwards (Ed.-in-Chief), *Encyclopedia of social work* (19th ed., pp. 2529–2539).

Washington, DC: National Association of Social Workers.

Brooks, F. (2001). Innovative organizing practices: ACORN's campaign in Los Angeles organizing workfare workers. *Journal of Community Practice*, 9(4), 68–85.

Butcher, H., Banks, S., & Henderson, P., with Robertson, J. (Eds.). (2007). *Critical community practice*. Bristol, UK: The Policy Press.

HButcher, H. (2007). Power and empowerment: The foundations of critical community practice. In H. Butcher, S. Banks, & P. Henderson with J. Robertson (Eds.), *Critical community practice* (pp. 17–33). Bristol, UK: The Policy Press.

Carroll, J., & Minkler, M. (2000). Freire's message for social workers: Looking back, looking ahead. *Journal of Community Practice*, 8(1), 21–36.

Cashmore, E., & Rojek, C. (1999). *Dictionary of cultural theorists*. New York: Oxford University Press.

Castelloe, P., & Watson, T. (1999). Participatory education as a community practice method: A case example from a comprehensive Head Start program. *Journal of Community Practice*, 6(1), 71–89.

Chaskin, R. J., Joseph, M. L., & Chipenda-Dansokho, S. (1997). Implementing comprehensive community development: Possibilities and limitations. *Social Work*, 42(5), 435–444.

Checkoway, B. (1997). Core concepts for community change. *Journal of Community Practice*, 4(1), 11–29.

Clifford, S. (2009, January 21). Teaching teenagers about harassment. *The New York Times*, p. B1.

Cohen, M. H. (1971). Community organization practice. In A. E. Fink (Ed.), *The field of social work* (6th ed., pp. 333–361). New York: Holt, Rinehart & Winston.

Cohen, N. (2009, August 23). Word for word: Saul Alinsky, know thine enemy. *New York Times*, p. wk5.

Cornfield, D. (Ed.) (1995). *Working people of California*. Berkeley, CA: University of California Press.

Couto, R. A. (1993). Narrative, free space, and political leadership in social movements. *Journal of Politics*, 55(1), 57–79.

Croft, S., & Beresford, P. (1988). Being on the receiving end: Lessons for community development and user involvement. *Community Development Journal*, 23(4), 273–279.

Cultural Environment Movement. (1999). *Who's telling these stories?* [Brochure]. Philadelphia, PA: Author.

Daley, J. M., & Marsiglia, F. F. (2000). Community participation: Old wine in new bottles? *Journal of Community Practice*, 8(1), 61–86.

Davis, J. E. (Ed.). (2002). *Stories of change: Narrative and social movements*. Albany: State University of New York Press.

Delgado, M. (forthcoming). *Assets management and community social work practice*. New York: Oxford University Press.

Denning, S. (2001). *The springboard: How storytelling ignites action in knowledge-era organizations*. Boston, MA: Butterworth-Heinemann.

Dunne, J. G. (1967). *Delano: The story of the California grape strike*. New York: Farrar, Straus & Giroux.

Eckholm, E., & Zezima, K. (2010, March 30). 6 teenagers are charged after classmate suicide. *The New York Times*, p. A14.

Eichler, M. (1995). Consensus organizing: Sharing power to gain power. *National Civic Review*, 84(3), 256–261.

Fabricant, M., & Fisher, R. (2002a). Agency-based community building in low-income neighborhoods: A praxis framework. *Journal of Community Practice*, 10(2), 1–22.

Fabricant, M., & Fisher, R. (2002b). *Settlement houses under siege: The struggle to sustain community organizations in New York City*. New York: Columbia University Press.

Felkins, P. K. (2002). *Community at work: Creating and celebrating community in organizational life*. Cresskill, NJ: Hampton.

Ferris, K. (2009, February 15.). Community organizing proves helpful–to GOP. *The Philadelphia Inquirer*, D1, D6.

Ferriss, S., & Sandoval, R. (1997). *The fight in the fields: Cesar Chavez and the farmworkers movement*. New York: Harcourt Brace.

Fesenmaier, J., & Contractor, N. (2001). The evolution of knowledge networks: An example for rural development. *Journal of the Community Development Society*, 32(1), 160–175.

Fine, G. A. (2002). The storied group: Social movements as "bundles of narratives." In J. E. Davis (Ed.), *Stories of change: Narrative and social movements*. Albany: State University of New York Press.

Foster-Fishman, P. G., Cantillon, D. Pierce, S. J., & Van Egeren, L. A. (2007). Building an active citizenry: the role of neighborhood problems, readiness, and capacity for change. *American Journal of Community Psychology*, 39, 91–106.

Freedman, J., & Combs, G. (1996). *Narrative therapy: The social construction of preferred realities*. New York: W. W. Norton.

Freire, P. (1994). Pedagogy of hope (with notes by A. M. A. Freire; R. R. Barr, Trans.). New York: Continuum Publishing Company.

Friedman, R. (2002, Summer). A call to ownership. *Assets: A quarterly update for innovators*, 1–12.

Frisch, M., & Servon, L. J., (2006). CDCs and the changing context for urban community development: A review of the field and the environment. *Community Development*, 37(4), 88–108.

Gadotti, M. (1994). *Reading Paulo Freire: His life and work*. Albany: State University of New York Press.

Gambone, M. A., Yu, H. C., Lewis-Charp, H., Sipe, C., Lacoe, J. (2006). Youth organizing, identity-support, and youth development agencies as avenues for involvement. *Journal of Community Practice*, 14(1), 235–253.

Ganz, M. (2001, August). *The power of story in social movements*. Paper presented at the annual meeting of the American Sociological Association, Anaheim, CA.

Ganz, M. (2003). Why David sometimes wins: Strategic capacity in social movements. In J. Goodwin & J. Jasper (Eds.) *Rethinking social movements: structure, meaning, and emotion (people, passion, and power)*. Lanham, MD: Rowman & Littlefield.

Gates, Jr., H. L. (2010, April 22). Ending the slavery blame-game. *The New York Times*, p. A27.

Geoghean, M., & Powell, F., (2006). Community development, partnership governance and dilemmas of professionalization: Profiling and assessing the case of Ireland. *British Journal of Social Work*, 36(5), 845–861.

Gertner, J. (2006, January 15). What is a living wage? *The New York Times Magazine*. Retrieved May 17, 2010, from: http://www.nytimes.com/2006/01/15/magazine/15wage.html?pagewanted=all

Glugoski, G., Reisch, M., & Rivera, F. G. (1994). A wholistic ethno-cultural paradigm: A new model for community organization teaching and practice. *Journal of Community Practice*, 1(1), 81–98.

Goodman, P. S. (2010, May 24). The new poor: Cuts to child care subsidy thwart more job seekers. *The New York Times*, p. A1.

Grogan, P. S., & Proscio, T. (2001). *Comeback cities: A blueprint for urban neighborhood revival*. Boulder, CO: Westview Press.

Guinier, L., & Torres, G. (2002). *The miner's canary: Enlisting race, resisting power, transforming democracy*. Cambridge, MA: Harvard University Press.

Gutierrez, L. M., & Lewis, E. A. (1994). Community organizing with women of color: A feminist approach. *Journal of Community Practice*, 1(2), 23–44.

Hannah, G. (2006). Maintaining product-process balance in community antipoverty initiatives. *Social Work*, 51(1), 9–17.

Henderson, P. (2007). Introduction. In H. Butcher, S. Banks, & P. Henderson with J. Robertson (Eds.),

Critical community practice (pp. 1-15). Bristol, UK: The Policy Press.

Heenan, D., (2004). Learning lessons from the past or re-visiting old mistakes: Social work and community development in Northern Ireland. *British Journal of Social Work*, 34(6), 793–809.

Heugens, P. P. M. A. R. (2002). Managing public affairs through storytelling. *Journal of Public Affairs,* 2(2), 57–70.

Hofrichter, R. (1993). *Toxic struggles: The theory and practice of environmental justice.* Philadelphia: New Society.

Horton, M., & Freire, P. (with Bell, B., Gaventa, J., & Peters, J.) (1990). *We make the world by walking: Conversations on education and social change.* Philadelphia: Temple University Press.

Horwitt, S. D. (1989). *Let them call me rebel: Saul Alinsky—his life and legacy.* New York: Vintage Books.

Hyde, C. (2001). Experiences of women activists: Implications for community organizing theory and practice. In J. E. Tropman, J. L. Erlich, & J. Rothman (Eds.), *Tactics and techniques of community intervention* (4th ed., pp. 75–84). Itasca, IL: F. E. Peacock.

Irving, A., & Young, T. (2002). Paradigm for pluralism: Mikhail Bakhtin and social work practice. *Social Work*, 47(1), 19–29.

Itzhaky, H. (2003) Developing empowerment and leadership: The case of immigrant women in Israel. *Affilia*, 18, 289–301.

Jacobson, M. (2007). Food matters. *Journal of Community Practice*, 15(3), 37–55.

Jenks, C. (2005). *Culture* (2nd ed.). New York: Routledge.

Johannesen, T. (1997). Social work as an international profession: Opportunities and challenges. In M. C. Hokenstad & J. Midgley (Eds.), *Issues in international social work: Global challenges for a new century* (pp. 146–158). Washington, DC: National Association of Social Workers Press.

Kahn, S. (1970). *How people get power: Organizing oppressed communities for action.* New York: McGraw-Hill.

Kahn, S. (1991). *Organizing: A guide for grassroots leaders.* Washington, DC: National Association of Social Workers Press.

Kahn, S. (1997). Leadership: Realizing concepts through creative process. *Journal of Community Practice*, 4(1), 109–136.

Kim, R. (2010, April 12). The Mad Tea Party. *The Nation*, Retrieved March 25, 2010, from: http://www.thenation.com/blog/mad-tea-party.

Kingsley, G. T., McNeely, J. B., & Gibson, J. O. (1997). *Community building: Coming of age.* Washington,

DC: Development Training Institute, Inc., and the Urban Institute.

Lazarri, M. M., Ford, H., & Haughey, K. J. (1996). Making a difference: Women of action in the community. *Social Work*, 41(2), 197–205.

Lee, J. A. B. (1994). *The empowerment approach to social work practice.* New York: Columbia University Press.

Levy, J. (1975). *Cesar Chavez: Autobiography of la causa.* New York: W. W. Norton.

Lewis, M. A., Lewis, C. E., & Rachelefsky, G. (1996). Organizing the community to target poor Latino children with asthma. *Journal of Asthma*, 33(5), 289–297.

Loeb, P. R. (1999). *Soul of a citizen: Living with conviction in a cynical time.* New York: St. Martin's Griffin.

Marcos, S. (2001). *Our word is our weapon.* New York: Seven Stories.

Martinez-Brawley, E., & Delevan, S. M. (1993). *Transferring technology in the personal social services.* Washington, DC: National Association of Social Workers Press.

Martinez-Brawley, E. E. (2000). *Close to home: Human services and the small community.* Washington, DC: National Association of Social Workers Press.

Masilela, C. O., & Meyer, W. A., III. (1998). The role of citizen participation in comprehensive planning: A personal view of the experience in Morgantown, West Virginia. *Small Town*, 29(3), 4–15.

McAdam, D. (1982). *Political process and the development of Black insurgency, 1930–1970.* Chicago: University of Chicago Press.

McArthur, A. (1995). The active involvement of local residents in strategic community partnerships. *Policy and Politics*, 23(1), 61–71.

McKernan, S-M., & Sherraden, M., (Eds.) (2008). *Asset building and low-income families.* Washington, DC: The Urban Institute Press.

Messinger, L. (2006). History at the table: Conflict in planning in a community in the rural American South. *American Journal of Community Psychology*, 37, 283–291.

Meyer, M. (2002). Review of "Civic Innovation in America." *Social Services Review*, 76(2), 341–343.

Miley, K. K., O'Melia, M., & DuBois, B. L. (1998). *Generalist social work practice: An empowering approach* (2nd ed.). Needham Heights, MA: Allyn & Bacon.

Minkler, M., Ed. (1997). *Community organizing and community building for health.* New Brunswick, NJ: Rutgers University Press.

Mizrahi, T. (2002). *Basic principles for organizing: Perspectives from practice.* Retrieved September 8,

2010, from http://www.hunter.cuny.edu/socwork/ecco/bpfo.htm

Mizrahi, T. (2007). Women's ways of organizing: Strengths and struggles of women activists over time. *Affilia*, 22(4), 39-55.

Mizrahi, T., & Lombe, M. (2007). Perspectives from women organizers. *Journal of Community Practice*, 14(3), 93–118.

Monteiro-Tribble, V. (n.d.). *Leadership development workbook for aspiring or current grassroots leaders*. Battle Creek, MI: The W.K. Kellogg Foundation. Retrieved May 15, 2010, from: http://www.racial-equitytools.org/resourcefiles/kellogg.pdf

Moses, R., & Cobb, C. E., Jr. (2001). *Radical equations: Math literacy and civil rights*. Boston, MA: Beacon Press.

Mulroy, E. A., & Matsuoka, J. K. (2000). The Native Hawaiian children's center: Changing methods from casework to community practice. In D. P. Fauri, S. P. Wernet, & F. E. Netting (Eds.), *Cases in macro social work practice* (pp. 228–242). Boston: Allyn & Bacon.

Nichols, J. (2010, April 4). Bad brew: What's become of Tea Party populism? *The Nation*, Retrieved April 4, 2010, from: http://www.thenation.com/blogs/thebeat/551668/bad_brew_what's_become_of_tea_party_populism?

Ohmer, M. L. (2008). The relationship between members' perceptions of their neighborhood organization and their involvement and perceived benefits from participation. *Journal of Community Psychology*, 36(7), 851–870.

Oliner, P. M., & Oliner, S. P. (1995). *Toward a caring society*. Westport, CT: Praeger.

Orsini, M. (2006). "Community run" to community based'? Exploring the dynamics of civil society-state transformation in urban Montreal. *Canadian Journal of Urban Research*, 15(1), 22–40.

Payne, M. (2000). *Teamwork in multiprofessional care*. Chicago: Lyceum.

Payne, M. (2002). The politics of systems theory within social work. *Journal of Social Work*, 2(3), 269–292.

Peterson, K. J., & Lieberman, A. A. (2001). *Building on women's strengths: A social work agenda for the twenty-first century* (2nd ed.). Binghamton, NY: Haworth Press.

Raban, J. (2010). At the Tea Party. *The New York Review of Books*. 57(5). Retrieved March 3, 2010, from: http://www.nybooks.com/articles/23723.

Reisch, M., Wenocur, S., & Sherman, W. (1981). Empowerment, conscientization, and animation as core social work skills. *Social Development Issues*, 5(2/3), 62–67.

Rivera, F. G., & Erlich, J. L. (1998). *Community organizing in a diverse society* (3rd ed.). Boston, MA: Allyn & Bacon.

Robinson, B., & Hanna, M. G. (1994). Lessons for academics from grassroots community organizing: A case study—The Industrial Areas Foundation. *Journal of Community Practice*, 1(4), 63–94.

Rodriquez, C. (1998). Activist stories: Culture and continuity in black women's narratives of grassroots community work. *Frontiers*, 19(2), 94–112.

Rogers, N., & Anderson, W. (2007). A community development approach to deal with public drug use in Box Hill. *Drug and Alcohol Review*, 26, 87–95.

Sachs, J., & Newdom, F. (1999). *Clinical work and social action: An integrative approach*. New York: Haworth Press.

Salcido, R. M. (1993, March). *A cross-cultural approach to understanding Latino barrio needs: A macro practice model*. Paper presented at Council of Social Work Education meeting, New York.

Salzer, M. S. (1998). Narrative approach to assessing interactions between society, community, and person. *Journal of Community Psychology*, 26(6), 569–580.

Schorr, L. B. (1997). *Common purpose: Strengthening families and neighborhoods to rebuild America*. New York: Anchor Books.

Shaw, B. A., Gallant, M. P., Riley-Jacome, M., & Spokane, L. S. (2006). Assessing sources of support for diabetes self-care in urban and rural underserved communities. *Journal of Community Health*, 31(5), 393–412.

Sherraden, M. (1991). *Assets and the poor: A new American welfare policy*. Armonk, NY: M. E. Sharpe.

Shultz, J. (2002). *The democracy owners' manual: A practical guide to changing the world*. New Brunswick, NJ: Rutgers University Press.

Smith, A. D. (2009). Obama's audience speaks first. *The New York Times*, p. A29.

Smith, D., & Lopez, P. (2002, October 26). A voice for the "little fellers." *Minneapolis Star Tribune*.

Steinbeck, J. (1963). *In dubious battle*. New York. Bantam Book.

Steves, L., & Blevins, T., (2005). From tragedy to triumph: A segue to community building for children and families. *Child Welfare*, 84(2), 311–322.

Szakos, K. L., & Szakos, J. (2007). *We make change: Community organizers talk about what they do – and why*. Nashville, TN: Vanderbuilt University Press.

Themba, M. N. (1999). *Making policy, making change: How communities are taking the law into their own hands*. Berkeley, CA: Chardon Press.

The Rensselaerville Institute: Theory of Change. Retrieved September 8, 2010, from http://www.rinstitute.org/theoryofchange.php

Turner, A. (2009). Bottom-up community development: Reality or rhetoric? The example of the Kingsmead Kabin in East London. *Community Development Journal, 44*(2), 230–247.

Turner, J. B. (1998). Foreword. In P. L. Ewalt, E. M. Freeman, & D. L. Poole (Eds.), *Community building: Renewal, well-being, and shared responsibility* (pp. ix–x). Washington, DC: National Association of Social Workers.

Uchitelle, L. (1996, April 9). Some cities pressuring employers to raise wages of working poor. *The New York Times*, p. A1, B7.

Valdez, L. (1996). *Quinta Temporada*. In S. Yogi. (Ed.). *Highway 99: A literary journey through California's Central Valley* (pp. 223–231). Berkeley, CA: Heyday Books in conjunction with the California Council for the Humanities.

vanden Heuvel, K. (2010, March 8). The rightwing witch hunt against ACORN. *The Nation*. Retrieved March 9, 2010, from: http://www.thenation.com/blogs/edcut/538559/the_rightwing_witch_hunt_against_acorn?

vanden Heuvel, K. (2010, April 19). Right-wing smear machine: They'll be back. *The Nation*. Retrieved April 20, 2010, from: http://www.thenation.com/blogs/edcut/553114/right_wing_smear_machine_they'll_be_back?

van Deth, J. W. (Ed.). (1997). *Private groups and public life: Social participation, voluntary associations, and political involvement in representative democracies*. London: Routledge.

Wakefield, S. E. L. & Poland, B. (2005). Family, friend or foe? Critical reflections on the relevance and role of social capital in health promotion and community development. *Social Science & Medicine, 60*, 2819–2832.

Wallerstein, N. (1993). Empowerment and health: The theory and practice of community change. *Community Development Journal, 28*(3), 218–227.

Walls, D. (1993). *The activist's almanac: The concerned citizen's guide to the leading advocacy organizations in America*. New York: Simon & Schuster.

Walz, T. (1991). *The unlikely celebrity: Bill Sackter's triumph over disability*. Carbondale: Southern Illinois University Press.

Warren, M. R. (2001). *Dry bones rattling: Community building to revitalize American democracy*. Princeton: Princeton University Press.

Weber, D. (1994). *Dark sweat, white gold: California farm workers, cotton, and the New Deal*. Berkeley, CA: University of California Press.

Weil, M. (2001). Women, community, and organizing. In J. E. Tropman, J. L. Erlich, & J. Rothman (Eds.), *Tactics and techniques of community intervention* (4th ed., pp. 204–220). Itasca, IL: F. E. Peacock.

Weiss-Gal, I., & Gal, J. (2009). Realizing rights in social work. *The Social Service Review, 83*(2), 267–291.

What is a Microenterprise? (n.d.). Retrieved May 14, 2010, from: http://www.gdrc.org/icm/micro/what-is.html

Wyile, H., & Paré, D. (2001). Whose story is it, anyway? An interdisciplinary approach to postmodernism, narrative, and therapy. *Mosaic, 34*(1), 153–172.

Zernike, K., & Thee-Brenan, M. (2010, April 15). Poll finds Tea Party backers wealthier and more educated. *The New York Times*, pp. A1, A17.

14

Community Social Casework

In the end, poverty, putridity and pestilence; work, wealth and worry; health, happiness and hell, all simmer down into village problems.

Martin H. Fischer, physician, philosopher

Never believe that a few caring people can't change the world. For, indeed, that's all who ever have.

Margaret Mead, feminist, humanist, cultural anthropologist

Independence… [is] middle-class blasphemy. We are all dependent on one another, every soul of us on earth.

George Bernard Shaw, playwright, socialist, Nobel Laureate for Literature

Mrs. J, a 30-year-old white woman, was referred to a family services agency (FSA) for help. She faces a variety of challenges. Her 42-year-old husband chronically physically and emotionally abuses her. Mrs. J was raised in the rural southwestern United States. She quit high school in her sophomore year because she was pregnant with her first child. She didn't return to school or obtain a high school equivalency certificate. The child, John, is now 14 years old. Mrs. J's current husband is not John's father, and this is a source of family conflict. John and Mr. J do not get along: Mr. J repeatedly physically and emotionally abuses the boy. John is routinely absent from school, he is disrespectful, and he is a member of a loose-knit gang of antisocial white youths who call themselves a skinhead militia. He generally is out of Mrs. J's control.

Mrs. J married Mr. J when she was 20 and pregnant with her second child. Mrs. J's second child, Sarey, is now 10. She is a good student and popular, and not yet in any serious trouble. She is Mr. J's daughter, and he adores her. Sarey worships John, and Mrs. J is worried that Sarey is picking up John's wild ways and will repeat her life story of an early pregnancy and motherhood, an unhappy marriage, or worse.

The family moved from another state to their current community about 6 months ago. They moved so

Mr. J could obtain work as an auto mechanic, his occupation. He has been working consistently since their move. He financially supports the family. John's biological father has no contact with John and provides neither financial nor emotional support.

Mrs. J. has not worked outside the home since her marriage. Prior to her marriage, she worked for about 3 years as a waitress. Her mother babysat John. Mrs. J met Mr. J at her waitress job. She has no other paid employment experience. She now wants to find a job so that she and John will be less financially dependent on Mr. J, but her desire for a job is a source of friction between her and her husband. Mr. J, a fundamentalist Christian, believes mothers should not work outside the home: it weakens the home and child-rearing, places women in the path of temptation, and reduces the authority of the father as head of the family. He believes that supporting the family is his Christian duty and that Mrs. J is responsible for the children's upbringing. He tells her she is doing a poor job raising the children and they are "going bad." How does she expect to both work outside the home and properly and morally bring up the children when she can't bring up the children now? She should, her husband believes, devote her energy to being a homemaker, wife, and mother, supervising the children. He does want John to get a job, however. John is not attending school regularly and is failing. A job will teach John responsibility. Their discussions on these matters generally result in violent arguments.

Mrs. J has neither close friends nor relatives in the new community and rarely gets out of the home except for household duties and church services. She does not have a primary social support system. Although a church member, Mr. J does not allow her to participate in any church activities alone. He is extremely jealous and distrustful. She feels socially isolated and marginalized, in adding to her marital and family problems.

Mrs. J was referred to the FSA by an emergency room doctor who treated her for an injury apparently caused by her husband's physical abuse. Mrs. J told the emergency room doctor that she fell, although the indications were that the injuries were from abuse. The physician made no police referral, because Mrs. J was insistent that it wasn't abuse. He had no time due to staff cutbacks to counsel her or do follow-up. The hospital had no social workers available. The doctor could only urge Mrs. J to go to FSA.

Mrs. J did go and told the FSA intake social worker about her violent arguments with Mr. J. She said she would like to figure out a way to either end Mr. J's abusive behavior toward John and her or to find a job and leave the home with her children. John has been threatening to leave home and live with his skinhead militia friends if the abuse continues. Mrs. J is afraid that John's violent friends will retaliate on Mr. J. For now, Mrs. J feels at a loss to do anything; she feels immobilized and isolated. She has no close friends or family supports in this community, no place to go, no social supports, no money of her own, no source of income other than Mr. J, and no idea where to turn for help.

What is Community Social Casework?

Mrs. J, like many clients, is caught in a morass of social conditions requiring many community resources and social supports and her own capacity and strengths to improve her life. Unfortunately, the community resources that still exist after the cutbacks of the Great Recession are not usually organized in ways conducive to easy access and use by Mrs. J and people with multiple challenges. Often, people like Mrs. J, and the social workers they turn to, are ignorant of the social reasons for their problems and the community resources available to address them. They are also often naïve about the importance of primary and secondary resources.

The social worker, out of fear of venturing into the community, frequently retreats to a biopsychological problem construction and intervention, leading to a mental illness diagnosis. For successful use of the community as a social support, the client and social worker have the tasks of community assessment to locate potential resources and then use community skills to network and manage with primary, secondary, and tertiary resources and social supports. The social worker needs to be a community social caseworker.

Community social casework draws from a rich heritage and antecedents of pre-psychotherapeutic social casework (Richmond, 1917, 1922). The International Association of Schools of Social Work (IASSW) and the International Federation of Social Workers (IFSW) drew from this heritage in their joint definition of social work intervention:

The social work profession promotes social change, problem solving in human relationships and the empowerment and liberation of people to enhance well-being. Utilising theories of human behaviour and social systems, social work intervenes at the points where people interact with their environments. Principles of human rights and social justice are fundamental to social work…. . Social work in its various forms addresses the multiple, complex transactions between people and their environments…. . Social work bases its methodology on a systematic body of evidence-based knowledge derived from research and practice evaluation, including local and indigenous knowledge specific to its context. It recognises the complexity of interactions between human beings and their environment, and the capacity of people both to be affected by and to alter the multiple influences upon them, including bio-psychosocial factors. The social work profession draws on theories of human development and behaviour and social systems to analyse complex situations and to facilitate individual, organisational, social and cultural changes. (IFSW, 2010)

Community social casework recognizes that most social supports are provided by a community's primary and secondary groups rather than by formal tertiary social agencies and social services providers, regardless of the community's ethnicity (Adams & Nelson, 1995; Barber, 1991; Garcia, 2005; Gordon & Donald, 1993; Karabanow, 1999; Lindsey, Browne, Thompson, Hawley, Graham, Weisbart, Harrington, &

Kotch, 2008; Mason, 2009; McLeod, Bywaters, Tanner, & Hirsch, 2008; Payne, 2000, 2002; Phillips, Bernard, Phillipson, & Ogg, 2000; Smale, 1995; Tsai, 2006; Uttal, 2006). Community social casework views the community as (a) a source of resources for addressing and resolving concerns and (b) the locus of problem-perpetuating interactions. Social workers should work with and within the community and the family and other secondary groups rather than attempting to substitute for them. Community social casework accepts that professionals are not at the center of helping systems. Others do most of the caring and managing: families, kin, neighborhood networks, informal groups, and formal organizations such as churches and schools. Effectiveness depends on how well the professional caregiver interacts with the whole complex of formal and informal elements to strengthen a community's capacity to care for its members and address shared needs and concerns (Adams & Nelson, 1995, p. 6).

Community social casework heavily draws from the now antiquated British model of casework, with its community emphasis and network analysis and patch approach (Adams & Krauth, 1995; Gordon & Donald, 1993; Payne, 2000, 2002; Rogers & Anderson, 2007). The patch approach focuses on neighborhood-sized geographic catchment areas, or *patches*, where the resources of informal networks of kin and neighbors are used and built upon to address individual and community problems (Adams & Krauth, 1995, p. 89; Adams & Nelson, 1995). The patch is generally the neighborhood, but it can be a geographic area with a population for a sufficient resource base of assets (see Chapter 13). The patch approach localizes and integrates services at a neighborhood level without overly "clientizing" the client. *Clientizing* means making the client dependent on the caseworker—or therapist—and social agencies. Patch work is inherent in good community social casework. It is a unitary practice approach recognizing the integrality of social supports, social problems, and client problems. It acknowledges a need for client involvement in the neighborhood and the community's formal, informal, and political organizations and processes. This is vital to solving both client and community problems. Community social caseworkers use a patch approach to weave together clients into primary social supports, a neighborhood's secondary social supports, and a community's more formal tertiary social supports.

Community social casework stresses what Sheppard (1991) calls indirect helping as "activities that the worker undertakes on *behalf* [italics added] of the client to further mutually agreed upon goals" (p. 3). Indirect helping is work with others designed to influence a client's behavior and/or circumstances. Sheppard's British conception of indirect practice differs from the more typical U.S. conception of indirect helping put forth by Taylor and Roberts (1985, p. 18), which equates indirect helping or practice with community organization and administration using a direct-indirect practice dichotomy along a micro–macro continuum. The community social casework model of indirect practice is client-focused and views community practice as indispensable in casework. Casework requires understanding, modifying, and using the community to mold and pursue case objectives. It assesses, modifies, and uses a client's social and cultural context. Community social casework is radical because it goes back to the profession's roots.

Community social caseworkers continue the development of the comprehensive case management model discussed in the first edition of this text. We since have discarded the case management label as antiquated. Case management has been co-opted by agencies and has lost its original community flavor and social work roots. The social work mission has become confused with its organizational and institutional contexts. Management controls the worker's relationship with clients, often to the detriment of both workers, as professionals, and service users.

We propose several unifying themes underlying community social casework:

- All people have the capacity to change and improve their lives.
- Individual lives are entwined with and inseparable from their social environment.
- Social networks and organizational infrastructure affect professional practice.
- Strengthening community helps to solve individual and community problems.

- Community is cardinal in current views of personhood and nationhood.
- Knowledge of the larger world is empowering.
- Collective, as well as individual, activity is of value.
- At every system level, there are myriad ways to exert influence.
- Collective and individual social involvement and action builds social capital and reduces social marginalization.
- Collective and individual social involvement and action is empowering.

Our model of community social casework understands, as do Swartz (1995), Raheim (1995), Smale (1995), Lee (1994), and Butcher and his colleagues (Butcher, Banks, & Henderson with Robertson, 2007), that *all* social work is political and must be directed toward enhancing client empowerment. It is political because it is concerned with the power distribution in communities. Change in an ecological model must involve community as well as individual change. The client must be involved in the community (Warren-Adamson & Lightburn, 2006). Although it uses social marking skills and market analysis, this model rejects the commercial rhetoric and constructions of practice as products and clients as consumers and customers. Client community involvement is an instrumental action toward efficiency and effectiveness in addressing client problems, it is empowering, and it helps build community cohesion and social capital. It is a normative action because it is right, as well as a client right and a community citizen responsibility. Client community involvement is a contribution to the reciprocity obligation. Interventions either preserve or change the status quo for clients. Everything in treatment, intervention, and social services programs can be presented to promote client consciousness, change, and empowerment. There is no objectivity or professionalism in maintaining a socially marginalized client's status quo. A social worker has a responsibility to demystify and help clients understand (a) the processes of services, (b) their regulatory functions, and (c) how services and the client's status promote the status quo. The scarcity of social welfare and community resources and an extreme concentration of resources and wealth in the upper strata of society pit various client and community needs, client groups, community constituents, and service providers against each other. This is heightened by the elite's current infatuation with globalization, the market model, and the privatization and commercialization of education, health, corrections and the justice system, and social welfare services. It is a professional responsibility and part of their empowerment to radicalize clients and communities and help them understand the political nature of social welfare. Hidden injuries of class and caste should be revealed. The social worker needs to take sides when people are wronged, if the professional value of social justice is to be meaningful.

Community social work, by its many labels, recognizes clients as partners and necessarily active participants in any change processes, and not as passive recipients of services. Community social casework is a unitary and holistic practice approach. The change partnership of client and professional with community civic structures allows and provides the client with opportunities to reciprocate the community for service, recognizes client strengths, enables clients to contribute to building community strength and cohesion, and promotes both client and community empowerment.

Community social casework differs from community-based clinical practice, although community social casework can be community-based practice. Community-based practice is a laudable approach to practice that shares with community social casework the goal of integrating practice physically and socially into the fabric of a community in order to reach those parts of the community unlikely to use traditional services. It also shares the objective of making communities healthier and recognizes that community and individual welfare are inseparable (Lightburn & Sessions, 2006). The major difference between the two is the community-based clinical practice emphasis on situs and a lesser community obligation for the practitioner and client. Community-based practice is located in the community. Community social casework's situs is secondary to fulfilling the functions of community social casework. It can be downtown or community-based, so long as it is community social casework.

Community Social Case Work Knowledge, Skill, and Tasks

Case Management Skills

Individual clients like Mrs. J face resource management and coordination challenges. The community social caseworker and client's tasks include case management tasks. The disparate and unorganized but potentially available client strengths, community resources, and primary and secondary group supports need to be accessed, organized into a system, and managed. Community social casework uses the logic of management by objectives in managing interventions. It is a client-centered, client-level, service-coordinated, goal-oriented approach to service integration. Fundamental management skills of community social casework include (a) planning; (b) organizing and managing the services system; (c) directing and controlling; (d) advocacy, negotiation, brokerage, and contracting with other service providers; (e) reporting; and (f) evaluating the service system's effectiveness (Dinerman, 1992; Morrow-Howell, 1992; Rubin, 1987; Washington, 1974; Wolk, Sullivan, & Hartmann, 1994).

Social Casework Skills

Community social casework incorporates the range of direct service knowledge and skills characteristic of and necessary to a social casework and clinical social work practice case plan: client assessment, developing case theory, establishing case and intervention SMARRT objectives, contracting with the client on SMARRT objectives, implementing and monitoring interventions, teaching and modeling of intervention skills for a client and others in the action system to use, and the evaluation with the client and other significant stakeholders of objectives' success. Modeling and teaching are essential casework intervention tasks. The intent of teaching the knowledge and demonstrating and modeling the skills to clients is to enable clients to do their own assessment, development, and management. Clients who are better able to develop and manage their own social support systems will be better able to manage their lives. Modeling and teaching improves the client's self-efficacy and promotes client empowerment (Pecukonis & Wenocur, 1994). Clients will need the skills to manage their lives long after the social caseworker is gone. These skills ought to be common to all direct service practice.

Community Practice Skills

Community social casework recognizes the social component and context of the client's condition and problems and uses formal and informal community resources in the intervention. Community practice skills of community social casework are set forth in Box 14.1. Most have been discussed extensively elsewhere in this text. The community social work approach emphasizes primary and secondary networks as much as tertiary resources. A good understanding of the local community, including the client's personal community, is fundamental. Different communities have different patterns of behavior,

---

BOX 14.1.	**Community Social Casework Tasks**

- Interpersonal communication (verbal, written, nonverbal), self-awareness, and oral and visual physical presentation of self
- Outreach to reach potential clients and potential primary social supports
- Client assessment, SMARRT objective setting, and case theory building
- Ethnography
- Community, patch, and network assessment
- Network development, management, and consultation

- Client advocacy, brokering, negotiation, and contracting
- Direct casework
- Teaching and modeling community social casework skills for client
- Reassessment and evaluation
- Problem staging, public education, social advocacy, and social marketing
- Monitoring quality

power, and resources, and learning this requires community assessment skills.

Community Assessment and Patch Analysis

The foundation for all community practice is community and network assessment and analysis, eco-mapping, and patch analysis. All have been discussed elsewhere in this text, so we will not review them at length here. Patch analysis is a specific form of community analysis particularly useful to community social casework. Its intensive neighborhood- and client-centered micro community assessment provides an inventory of a neighborhood's primary, secondary, and tertiary resources and the networking requirements that are potentially most available to a client population. True patch work involves both worker and clients in the community (Adams & Krauth, 1995; Payne, 2000, 2002; Rogers & Anderson, 2007).

Ethnography

Community social casework, patch analysis, and the patch approach require ethnographic skills, with the worker functioning as participant-observer. A community social caseworker both observes and participates with a client in the client's community. Ethnography is "associated with some distinctive methodological ideas, . . . the importance of understanding the perspectives of the people under study, . . . observing their activities in everyday life, rather than relying solely on their accounts of this behavior or experimental simulations of it" (Hammersley & Atkinson, 1983, p. ix). Ethnography's concern is with events, relationships, and, most significantly, the meaning of these to their participants. People interpret stimuli and events, and these interpretations, continually under revision as events unfold, shape their actions. The same physical stimulus and events can mean different things to different people and to the same person at different times. The community social caseworker needs to appreciate these meanings. We have discussed the use of ethnography in case study assessment in Chapters 5 and 6.

Community, patch, and network analysis and eco-mapping are not ends but only means to developing client supports, achieving community integration, and reaching case objectives. These skills will need to be accompanied by the skills necessary to create, access, and integrate clients into primary social supports and a community's secondary and tertiary social support systems. Negotiating, brokering, bargaining, and client advocacy skills enable networking, exchange, and social support to occur. Advocacy, as Payne (2000, p. 323) asserts, goes beyond arguing and includes social action on behalf of and with the client. Advocacy promotes client community empowerment and humanizing the client into full citizenship status. Full citizenship status compels, as Warren-Adamson and Lightburn (2006) point out, that clients and patients become involved community activists.

Community social casework skills are client-centered but recognize the community as pivotal to client welfare. Community problem staging and advocacy for resources development are used to translate clients' private troubles into public concerns. Social marketing and social activism for services and community change are part of a complete community social caseworker's repertoire. Again, these are done *with* and not just for clients.

Community Social Casework Protocol

1. Preliminary Community Assessment and Patch Analysisc

A requisite step in any community social casework protocol is a preliminary community and patch analysis. The analysis is to get the basic lay of the community: resources and requirements, values and norms, and behavior patterns. The assessment is baseline and preliminary and must be refined for each client and client grouping.

2. Assessment, Refinement of Community and Patch Analysis, and Establishing SMARRT Objectives

Client assessment, refinement of a community assessment and patch analysis, and establishing SMARRT objectives are interdependent components. SMARRT objectives are specific, measurable, acceptable, realistic, results-oriented, and time-specific (see Chapter 1 for the SMARRT format). SMARRT objectives are stated in outcome, behavioral, and measurable language. Their realism and viability depend on the available resources and a client's strengths. The resources necessary to assist a client to achieve SMARRT objectives are contingent on the specific SMARRT objectives selected. Conversely, the availability of resources will expand or constrain the capacity to realize specific SMARRT objectives. The SMARRT formatted objectives guide the social worker and client in their resource assessment, development, coordination, and management.

A community social casework process uses marketing's outside-inside philosophy, beginning with an assessment of the client's conception and meaning of the problems and objectives rather than a preconceived agency boilerplate diagnosis. Assessment calls on the caseworker's ethnographic and assets inventorying skills. It is mutual, a task performed conjointly with a client, and involves understanding a client's construction and meanings of problems and social ecology, determining a client's strengths and resources, establishing SMARRT objectives, and refining the community and patch analysis to be client-focused and to assess its resources relative to the SMARRT objectives (Bisman, 1994, pp. 111–176). Assessment must recognize that a client's situation is unique, multifaceted, and community-bound.

Assessment results in a theory of the case. The case theory explains a client's situation and organizes case information to provide a map, a plan, of intervention to accomplish the SMARRT objectives (Bisman, 1994, pp. 111–121, Bisman & Hardcastle, 1999, pp. 44–62, 151–162). Overly reductionist and simplistic case theory with narrow views of cause and effect should be avoided. The causes of any problem lie in a range of complex individual and social phenomena. Solutions will probably also require an array of personal, primary, and community resources appropriately coordinated and managed.

The first assessment and case-theory-building phase leads to belief bonding, mutual understanding and agreement between caseworker and client, and a shared construction and understanding of problems and SMARRT objectives. Joint agreement by casework and client on an assessment and a case plan is critical to its success if a plan requires the caseworker and client to work together to achieve a plan's SMARRT objectives. As yet, we know of no social work methodologies that can achieve SMARRT objectives without the client's consent and participation.

Application of SMARRT Criteria to Mrs. J's Case Plan

Mrs. J can have a series of related goals such as the following: (a) to establish and maintain a physically and emotionally safe home for herself and her family; (b) to financially support herself and her children at her current income level and be financially independent of her husband; (c) for John and Sarey to achieve grade-level school performance, graduate from high school, and not engage in antisocial activities; (d) for the family to become socially integrated into the community and develop social support networks.

Each of these objectives can be stated in a SMARRT format. In establishing the objectives, Mrs. J and her caseworker need to complete a community assessment and patch analysis to establish her potential social support resources, develop information for networking and community integration, and locate and assess secondary and tertiary resources potentially available and their requirements for networking and exchange. Potential interventions necessary to achieve each essential objective and any requisite sequencing and requirements of the change agent system are elaborated in the case theory. Mrs. J and her family are components of the change agent system. If the resources and interventions are not available, objectives will be modified to fall within the constraints of potentially available resources.

The first objective, to establish and maintain a physically and emotionally safe home for herself and her family, can be operationalized and evaluated by the SMARRT criteria:

1. **Specific:** Establishing a physically and emotionally safe home, one absent of physically and emotionally traumatic behavior in interactions between family members, is a specific criterion. It is an outside-inside approach focusing on the client's concept of needs and not on a specific intervention or product offered by the caseworker. "Physically and emotionally safe" and "traumatic behavior" will have to be conceptualized and operationally defined in language meaningful

to Mrs. J, her husband, and the children, with a shared understanding if not acceptance of the meanings. Interventions can range from a combination of family therapies, from expansion of the family's social support networks to relieve and alter internal dynamics, to the extreme of Mrs. J and the children's leaving the home. Objectives such as Mrs. J's employment and John's school performance and social support networks can be made equally specific and measureable. The objective doesn't dictate a specific intervention but guides, along with the case theory, in selecting interventions most likely to achieve the objective. It is the objective, not the intervention, that is the critical first step.

2. **Measurable**: Physical and emotional trauma and their absence can be measured by observations and the judgment of Mrs. J, the children, and the caseworker, as well as by medical measurements. Measurements need to avoid spurious precision and incoherent meaning for the J family. The phenomena of concern are the physically and emotionally abusive interactions experienced by Mrs. J, John, Sarey, and perhaps even Mr. J. The critical features of any measurement process are its truthfulness, and its meaning and usefulness to the family.

3. **Acceptable**: The objective needs to be acceptable to Mrs. J, the J family, and anyone voluntarily providing resources and cooperation in the change effort. Mr. J will need to accept the objective and its measurement if he remains a part of the household. Acceptance by all participants of the objectives and subsequent interventions is decisive, unless the caseworker has the ability to coerce compliance with an objective and to compel the provision of resources and behavior. This will apply to any changes in John's behavior as well as Mr. J.

4. **Realistic**: The caseworker and Mrs. J need to assess the potential of any intervention and resources available to establish and maintain a physically and emotionally safe home. If it is projected that Mr. J will leave the home, then an alternative physical and safe living arrangement will have to be established or a way for the family to remain in the house without Mr. J. The criterion that objectives must be realistic assesses the probability, given the potential resources and strengths of the interventions, that the objectives can be accomplished. If Mrs. J and the caseworker project that none of the options can be accomplished, unfortunately this objective will need to be recast.

5. **Results-oriented**: The objective is changes in Mrs. J's and Mr. J's behaviors, lifestyles, and social interactions rather than a process of treatments and interventions. Interventions and networks are used because of their theoretical potential to achieve the objectives. The objectives are outcomes, not the means used to produce outcomes. It is not the *doing*, but the *achievements*. The value of the casework and networks is how well they achieve an absence of physically and emotionally traumatic behavior in interactions between family members. Their value doesn't rest on adherence to a model of a process or techniques used.

6. **Time-specific**: The caseworker and Mrs. J will need to arrive at a specific projected time for a safe home to be established. The projected time is based on their assessment of the potential resources, including the J family's strengths and the power of the available intervention technologies. As Mrs. J is new to the community, without many social supports in the community and with low economic skills, the time needed to achieve the specific target will be longer than if these social supports were more available immediately or if Mrs. J had a greater and more recent employment history. The time frame can be modified with unfolding circumstances, but a realistic time-specific target is needed to guide the intervention and provide a basis for reassessment. Without a time-specific objective, Mrs. J might indefinitely remain in an abusive situation and be involved in an ineffective intervention.

The other case objectives need similar SMARRT formatting.

Assessments and theory construction rest on basic and abstract assumptions of the nature of client behavior and the importance of the client's community and social ecology.

The Nature of Client Behavior. The *biopsychomedical reductionist models* of behavior generally hold that dysfunctional behavior results from biological and emotional pathologies, whether due to genetic content or faulty early socialization. Psychological theories such as psychoanalytic psychology fall within this set of models. Treatment involves altering the client's emotional content separately from the social context. Interventions applied to intrapsychic content frequently are called psychotherapies.

Community social casework rejects these models as overly reductionist, limited in explanatory ability, and naïve. The biopsychomedical reductionist models make community social casework a largely irrelevant intervention. Intervention is centered on the client's disease, pathology and physiology, and psychological deficits and aberrations. The models emphasizing therapy and treatments rather than social resources development and management don't hold community social casework's assumptions central or necessary to successful client treatment. Treatment compliance, biopsychological condition management, and providing services to compensate for client deficiencies are the major features of any social intervention. If a biopsychomedical model is used by Mrs. J's caseworker, social and community influences, constraints, and primary, secondary, and tertiary social supports and resources are unlikely to be pursued. Instead, intervention will focus on pathology in the family.

Educational models see problems in client behavior and in management of social relations and the social environment as learned inappropriate behavior. If learned behavior, it can be unlearned and functionally appropriate behavior can be learned. Interventions address unlearning inappropriate behavior and learning and substituting socially appropriate behaviors. Operant and behavioral theories reflect these models. The educational models require, in treatment based on social learning theory, that the caseworker demonstrate or teach (generally by operant conditioning, cognition, or a combination of the two) the functional behaviors. Community social casework also rejects these models as an overly reductionist and simplistic view of human behavior that ignores the fundamental and multiple impact of many different social variables on behavior.

Psychosocial models posit that a client's behavior and management of the environment are functions of the individual's psychological content in interaction with a social context. Interventions confront the psychological content in its social context and the social context's impact on the psychological content and behavior. These models emphasize social variables and conditions that are useful to community social casework.

Biopsychosocial models of human behavior promote a more complex view of client behavior as a function of the client's biological and psychological content in a social context. Behavior is the result of a complex interaction of biological, psychological, and social factors and forces. Behavior has social elements. Poverty and limited social environments, social marginalization and isolation, abuse, and limited interpersonal and social skills all affect behavior. All components need to be considered in the case theory and intervention. As with the psychosocial models, intervention must address the context as well as the content of behavior. It can include providing education and improving management skills as well as altering a client's environment. This model is the most comprehensive and adaptable to community social casework.

Obviously, this classification schema of the models of human behavior, like biopsychomedical reductionist models, suffers from oversimplification. Empirically, the models rarely exist or are applied in some kind of pure form. However, a social worker's selection of a model of human behavior has implications for case theory and implementing an intervention plan. Community social casework is more compatible with the social models with their strong social content and context.

The Conception of the Community, the Social Resources, and the Task Environment

We have emphasized in this text the importance of community as a major force in shaping and limiting the behavior and the lives of people. Community social casework holds to this *systems approach* to the community and the individual. A system's elements must be coordinated and share some common purposes (Churchman, 1965, p. 29; von Bertalanffy, 1967; Payne, 2002). A client's physical and social environment can be a cornucopia of potential social supports and resources, but the resources don't exist as a system until they are coordinated and integrated. Each potential resource may have no or limited interest in a specific client's life. An employment agency's interest is limited to employment. A landlord's concern for a client may be limited to the client's ability to rent space without damaging it. Each service vendor and resource provider can achieve its limited objective without much interaction, coordination, compatibility, or meeting a client's objectives. An individual client may need a support system in this turbulent and complex environment; it is not as important for any unit in the set's survival or functioning to support an individual client. Reciprocity between the client and the support system is necessary if the system is to endure. A community social caseworker's and the client's tasks are to create and manage a client-centered support system from a set of sometimes indifferent and often competing resource suppliers.

The model of behavior used by the community social caseworker and Mrs. J will guide the assessment and provide a basis for constructing its case theory. A limited biopsychomedical model or educational model will direct information gathering and assessment to focus on family members as individuals and their interaction. Explanations of causation and projections of interventions and solutions will center on these same units. If more expansive models are used, although family members and their interactions are still assessed, the impact, limitations, and opportunities provided by the social environment are basic to developing a case theory and plan.

3. Determine Resources Necessary and Required to Achieve Goals and Objectives

Once the objectives have tentatively been established and SMARRT formatted, the necessary resources to achieve the objectives need to be determined, located, and acquired. The community assessment, patch analysis, and assets inventory and mapping are made specific to the case.

A. Assess the Client Strengths, the Client's Primary Support Systems, and the Community Social Caseworker's Resources Relative to the Resources Required to Achieve the SMARRT Objectives. The first potential source of resources, and the first with responsibility to help achieve the case plan's SMARRT objectives, are the client and the client's primary systems. The sociologist and communitarian Etzioni (1993) contends, "*First, people have a moral responsibility to help themselves*

as best they can" (p. 144, italics original). All people have an obligation, no matter how disadvantaged or handicapped, to be responsible for themselves as best they can and to the maximum extent of their capacity. This is the fundamental basis of empowerment, self-efficacy, and self-determination. Etzioni continues, "*The second line of responsibility lies with those closest to the person, including kin, friends, neighborhood, and other community members*" (p. 144, italics original).

Self-responsibility comes first and is linked directly with autonomy, empowerment, self-efficacy, and self-determination. To not consider the client as a primary source of strength and responsibility promotes powerlessness and dependency. Primary group responsibility comes second. Primary support groups provide the most help. This is where reciprocity and interdependence, rather than dependency, are most balanced and the client is least vulnerable. Mutual support is best given and received under conditions of mutual obligation and responsibility. Community and network cohesion, as well as primary group efficacy, are enhanced, trust is facilitated, and interdependence is promoted with primary group reciprocity. The client and community social caseworker should seek, whenever possible, to strengthen primary structures and build or rebuild primary support networks. These networks help the client reintegrate into the community, reduce the social and emotional isolation, and provide some buffering from the stresses of larger social institutions. A client's primary system includes immediate family, friends, and other personal support networks that can be called on to support and assist a client in fulfilling the case plan. As the protections, the safety nets, of the welfare state are eliminated or reduced with the Great Recession, devolution and reformulation of the welfare state, an individualistic ideology, and the social environment becomes more competitive and demanding, primary and secondary support systems are more important to clients.

Community, patch, network, and assets assessment are useful to determine, locate, and appraise actual and potential primary and secondary social support networks and systems. The social supports are largely unique to each client, and a case plan should be individualized accordingly. These should be explored and developed prior to referral to tertiary systems.

The community social caseworker recognizes and helps Mrs. J understand her own and her family's assets and strengths. Strengths include recognizing a problematic situation for herself and her family, wanting to change the situation, and wanting to reduce her dependency on Mr. J. Although she has not worked outside the home for several years, she has worked. She wants to preserve the family and strengthen her relationship with Mr. J by altering the nature of the relationship. Leaving Mr. J is the option of choice only if the abuse and the nature of their relationship are unchanged. Even without a more thorough assessment of Mrs. J's current and potential intellectual and social capacities, it is clear she has many strengths. By recognizing and acting on these strengths, Mrs. J will increase her sense of self-efficacy and empowerment.

Mr. J's strengths are also considered in developing the case theory. Although he has abused Mrs. J and John, he has been a consistent provider and feels strongly about his responsibilities as the breadwinner. He wants the children to be responsible citizens. He doesn't want a family breakup or the loss of Sarey's affections. Like Mrs. J, he wants change, although they do not agree on the specific change needed. These are strengths to use in beginning the case theory and plan.

B. Assess the Differences Between the Client, Community Social Caseworker and Agency Resources Available, and the Resources Required to Achieve the Case Plan's Goals and Objectives. Community, patch, assets, and network assessment will need to locate potential social supports for the family to achieve their objectives and the requirements of the supports for networking. The community resources needed, including secondary and tertiary resources needed from the set of social agencies, is determined by any deficit of client resources and strengths and community social caseworker's and host agency's resources compared to the resources required to achieve the case plan's SMARRT objectives. If the community social caseworker and the client possess all the required resources, or if the client has the necessary network assessment and management skills, there is no need for additional resource

development and networking by the community social caseworker. However, the basic biopsychosocial model assumes that behavior is a function of social factors. It is unlikely that all resources will be contained within the family unit. These resource deficits determine the required secondary and tertiary resources and guide social support network construction. The client and community social caseworker should look to resources from the larger community only when the client, the client's primary groups, and the community social caseworker and the host agency do not possess them. The client participates in the assessments, development, and management of the networks to the maximum extent of the client's capacity.

If Mrs. J and her family have either the resources or the knowledge and skills to assess employment resources, to manage John's and Sarey's socialization and education, to establish any needed social support system, and to manage their relationship, there is little need for the caseworker to do it. However, it appears that supportive primary and formal tertiary services in addition to family resources are needed. Members of the J family, especially Mrs. J, are socially isolated and marginalized. She is also becoming more marginal within the family. Mr. J has only his job and the church. Mrs. J's social network is her immediate family and to a very limited extent the church. The children have family, church, school, and their peer groups, although in John's case the support is not positive. Social supports are needed for a range of intervention efforts to achieve the SMARRT objectives.

4. Assess the Community to Locate Needed Resources and Their Exchange Requirements

Etzioni (1993) holds that the third imperative for support beyond the client and primary groups is the community. "As a rule every community ought to be expected to take care of its own. . . . Last but not least, *societies (which are nothing but communities of communities) must help those communities whose ability to help their members is severely limited*" (p. 146, italics original).

The community and the society or state imperatives of responsibility come into operation after the client and the primary support systems. Responsibility works outward, with personal, primary, neighborhood, and community responsibility explored before state responsibility. The community social caseworker recognizes that public education, social marketing, and staging of social problems often are necessary to help the community and state recognize their responsibilities.

After the client and the community social caseworker have assessed the resources they and the primary groups possess relative to the case plan's goals and objectives, the location, the domains, and reciprocity requirements of the additional required resources indicated by the community, assets, and patch analysis are reviewed. The basic questions of this protocol's phase are: (a) What are the additional resources needed? (b) Where are the resources located? and (c) How can the resources be secured? The assessment using community, assets, and patch assessment, networking, and market research methodologies discussed elsewhere appraises the agencies and community structures with the resources, the social prices of the resources, and the networking and reciprocity requirements.

The community social caseworker and Mrs. J assess the community resources needed to achieve the case SMARRT objectives. These resources will allow Mrs. J and her family to create a new social environment and community of interaction. The ability of Mrs. J to access the resources of agencies and organizations providing family counseling, education, and job training and placement is critical. Client advocacy and preparing the family for the exchanges is required. Before embarking on intervention, the community social caseworker determines how legal aid and a possible safe haven can be established for Mrs. J and the children, if needed.

Mrs. J will need to explore social supports (the more primary groups and also the secondary organizations such as churches, neighborhood associations, and PTAs) to reduce her social marginalization and emotional isolation. She will also need to develop an understanding of how her husband's conception—and her prior conception—of a woman's role is a political construction contributing to her marginalization. Although Mrs. J is new to the community, she shares her social isolation and a lack of appropriate primary and secondary social support networks with many clients. John needs tutoring assistance and an alternative secondary social support group to replace the skinhead militia gang he is now using for social support.

5. Evaluate the Case Plan's Goals and Objectives Relative to the Total Resources Available From the Client, the Client's Social Support Networks and Potential Networks, the Community Social Caseworker, and the Community

If the currently and potentially available resources are not appropriate and adequate to meet the case plan's SMARRT objectives, the objectives will need to be modified to fit within available resources if additional appropriate resources can't be developed. It should be done by an incremental modification, not a wholesale discarding of the original objectives. The client and community social caseworker may want to pursue the original goals and objectives with a subsequent case plan after some more preliminary objectives are achieved, or the client can independently pursue the objectives after developing greater self-case-management skills.

Community social caseworkers should not assume that resources are unavailable simply because the community social caseworker doesn't have contacts with the domain (the holder) of the desired resource. The task, as discussed in Chapter 10, is to assess and establish the linkage or chain of contacts between the client and the needed resource. When resources are not available or potentially available, the task is community development and staging to establish a community-shared perception of need for and to develop essential resources.

6. Negotiate Exchanges and Link the Client with the Resource Domains

After needed resources are identified and located and their holder's exchange preferences are determined, the next task is to make the exchanges and obtain the resources with the client. This establishes a client-centered network. This protocol entails marketing the client or community social caseworker's assets and resources to a trading partner or resource holder. It requires brokering, negotiating, linking the client to social supports, and the community social caseworker's use of power (Dinerman, 1992; Hagen, 1994; Levine & Fleming, 1985).

Community social caseworkers need to understand and use power in their networking. Power has been discussed here in the theories of community practice. The crucial consideration in power is in the perception and the willingness to use it when necessary (Alinsky, 2006). A source of power inherent in a case plan is derived from the client as a potential resource to another service provider (Dinerman, 1992, pp. 5–6). The client may bring resources such as vouchers and third-party payments. A client and community social caseworker, or both, can help the trading partners achieve their goals. Both exchange and learning theory, discussed earlier, tell us that a trading partner, the holder of the resources needed by the client, is more likely to engage in exchanges when its needs are met and the exchanges are perceived as fair.

The community social caseworker also should possess and use the power derived from the expertise and skill in assessment, system development and management, and bargaining and client advocacy discussed earlier. Negotiation and bargaining is advocacy for the client or case. Advocacy can cause strains in network relationships, but the strains are minimized if the negotiations are cast in a win–win or non–zero–sum construction and viewed as fair by all participants. Advocacy calls for professional judgment as to when to engage in it and skill in how to advocate within a collaborative relationship with other network professionals.

The community social caseworker negotiates for needed resources and prepares Mrs. J to be a resource in exchanges and to be her own advocate. She affects the quality of services received by what she contributes to the resource provider in exchanges. Mrs. J and other family members are resources to the other units in the network if they can help other network units achieve their objectives. Mrs. J will need to demonstrate that she is indeed a resource by advocating and reciprocating appropriately. For example, training agencies, to be successful, need

trainable clients who can and will be employed. As Mrs. J learns what she can bring to the exchange and how she can reciprocate, her self-efficacy, sense of power, and social capital increase.

7. Monitor the Network and the Exchanges for Fair Exchanges

Networks as systems do not automatically maintain themselves (Churchman, 1965, p. 33). They require managing, monitoring and intelligence, and maintenance to ensure that the negotiated fair exchanges occur and that all network parties fulfill their bargains. Without attention, a network as a system will undergo entropy. *Entropy*, an enduring property of systems according to systems theorists (Churchman, 1965; von Bertalanffy, 1967), is a tendency of systems to deteriorate and become disorganized and random. Entropy in a client-centered system or network occurs when network units, often including the client, no longer engage in the agreed-upon resource exchanges necessary to achieve the objectives and the system or network drifts apart.

Monitoring and evaluating by Mrs. J and the community social caseworker address the contributions of network service and resource providers and Mrs. J's participation in the exchanges. For exchanges to be fair, all parties in a network have to uphold their part of a contract. Mrs. J needs to reciprocate appropriately.

8. Teach and Model the Networking Protocols to the Client so the Client Can Assess, Construct, and Manage a Social Support and Resources Networks (Client Empowerment)

Client empowerment is an ethical obligation and intrinsic practice objective. A practice task is to teach and model its knowledge, skills, and behaviors so clients can assess, develop, access, and manage their social support systems and mediating structures. Clients' empowerment is enhanced as their capacity to control their own lives increases.

Social learning theory ((Bandura, 1977, 1982, 1986, 1989, 1997; Payne, 2006; Thyer & Hudson, 1986/1987) states that personal and environmental influences are bidirectional, interactional, and interdependent. Over time they become self-reinforcing, with less need for external stimuli and reinforcements. Client involvement in developing and implementing a case plan allows the client to learn and a community social caseworker to teach and model (Becker, 2009; Kunkel, 1975, pp. 51–76; Pecukonis & Wenocur, 1994; Weiser & Silver, 1981). As clients learn and use appropriate community practice skills—community assessment, bargaining, negotiation and self-advocacy, construction of client-centered networks and systems, systems management and monitoring—their sense of efficacy should increase and dependency on community social caseworkers decrease.

Mrs. J is empowered when she recognizes her assets and learns to access and negotiate with social and community resources. The resources include job training, educational and social supports for her children, or financial and emotional supports from the children's fathers. As Mrs. J's skills in assessment, bargaining, negotiation, advocacy, and management increase, her dependency on the community social caseworker deceases. Equally important is Mrs. J's need to increase her knowledge and skills to access, negotiate, manage, and reciprocate with the range of social supports required in any healthy, functional life. The community social caseworker recognizes that an integral part of community social casework is modeling and teaching skills to Mrs. J.

Effectiveness of Community Social Casework

As yet there have been no studies of community social casework's effectiveness as a coherent model in this country. The literature assessing the effectiveness and efficacy of case management (Cheung, Stevenson, & Leung, 1991; Kantor, 1991; Polinsky, Fred, & Ganz, 1991; Rife, First, Greenlee, Miller, & Feichter, 1991; Rubin, 1992), a subset of the community social casework model, and other model components is promising and generally presents a positive picture (Bond, McGrew, & Fekete, 1995; Gordon & Donald, 1993; Karabanow, 1999; Payne, 2000, 2002; Phillips, Bernard, Phillipson, & Ogg, 2000).

Washington and his colleagues (Washington, 1974: Washington, Karman, & Friedlob, 1974) concluded, as a result of their seminal and most extensive case management social research and development, that the model of case management used can achieve outcomes beyond client satisfaction. The models of choice moved toward a community social casework model. Effectiveness was associated with the manager's assessment, negotiation, and broker skills. It was also associated with available funds to purchase needed services. Case management is not particularly effective in overcoming the limitations of a resource-starved task environment. Community social casework can have similar difficulties in this era of devolution and declining public support for social services if it relies on tertiary services. However, its emphasis on primary and secondary social supports is promising. Research on community social casework's emphasis on client involvement in the community and in activism and self-advocacy is affirmative. Positive results have been found with mental health patients (Becker, 2009; Boettcher, Jakes, & Sigal, 2008); youths, especially high-risk youths (Delgado & Staples, 2008; Nicotera, 2008; Paterson & Panessa, 2008; Pearrow, 2008; Wandersman, Clary, Forbush, Weinberger, Coyne, & Duffy, 2006); public assistance recipients (Brooks & Brown, 2005; Gray, 2005); and other challenges (Dowrick & Yuen, 2006; Itzhaky, 2003) with patch work (Rogers & Anderson, 2007), client community involvement, and activism.

Summary: A Community Social Casework Model

Community social casework requires the knowledge and skills explicated in this text. It rests on several assumptions regarding the client and the community:

1. The community is the context of an individual's behavior. It provides both opportunities and limits, and behavior can only be understood in this context.
   (a) People live in communities and often are beset by a range of living and environmental management problems or social isolation.

(b) Human behavior is not solely the province of an individual's biopsychological capacity and content.

(c) Regardless of the model of human behavior used, social coping needs are real and must be addressed if a person is to function more effectively in the community and to become empowered.

(d) Human problems and coping needs are usually embedded in their social marginality to and isolation from community supports.

2. Community social casework's objectives are to improve a client's social context and assist the client in managing the social context to improve social functioning.

(a) The community is the situs of a client's life, not the service center, social agency, or therapist's office. Intervention should occur in the community.

(b) While clients vary in their individual capacity to cope with and manage their social context, all clients have usable strengths and must be involved in the assessment, case theory building, planning, management, and implementation of interventions.

(c) All communities potentially have strengths, with primary and secondary supports, if not tertiary supports.

If the client and community propositions are valid, a reasonable case model is:

1. Case objectives are behavioral and measurable and formulated in a SMARRT format.
2. Case objectives, the dependent variable, are client behavior and social functioning, and the independent and intervening variables are the client's community and support systems, including the community social caseworker and the service system.
3. A case plan's strength is in its emphasis on specified objectives stated in behavioral and measurable terms and a shared clarity of objectives with the client, the community social caseworker, and other critical resource providers in the service delivery and social support networks. A fundamental generic goal of community social casework is to integrate clients into a supportive social environment.

4. Community social casework's strength lies in its flexibility, which allows the community social caseworker and client to use an array of possible primary, secondary, and tertiary supports to achieve objectives and integrate clients into the community rather than limiting interventions to specific agency services. Clients must be activists in the case plan.

5. Community social casework's service protocol flow requires that the community social caseworker understand a client's construction of reality and the client's community or social context, and be able to help a client perceive and define realistic objectives in a given social context.

6. The community social caseworker's network management for a client depends on the client's capacity, knowledge, and skills to function in the social context.

7. A fundamental goal of all intervention is client empowerment. Empowerment occurs in a social context. Therefore, community social caseworkers need knowledge and skill in client, community, patch, and organizational assessment; negotiating, bargaining, contracting, and advocacy; and social support networks development and management, as well as the capacity to model and teach clients these skills. Self-management as self-control is the essence of empowerment. Clients must be activists in the case plan and community for client empowerment and reciprocity. For empowerment, clients need to develop community practice skills.

References

Adams, P., & Krauth, K. (1995). Working with families and communities: The patch approach. In P. Adams & K. Nelson (Eds.), *Reinventing human services: Community and family-centered practice* (pp. 87–108). New York: Aldine de Gruyter.

Adams, P., & Nelson, K. (Eds.). (1995). *Reinventing human services: Community and family-centered practice.* New York: Aldine de Gruyter.

Alinsky, S. (2006, Winter). *Alinsky's rules for power: From rules for radicals.* Semcosh. Retrieved September 8, 2010 from http://www.jasongooljar.com/AlinskyTactics.pdf

Bandura, A. (1977). *Social learning theory.* Englewood Cliffs, NJ: Prentice Hall.

Bandura, A. (1982). Self-efficacy mechanism in human agency. *American Psychologist*, 37, 122–147.

Bandura, A. (1986). *Social foundations of thought and action*. Englewood Cliffs, NJ: Prentice Hall.

Bandura, A. (1989). Social cognitive theory. *Annals of Child Development*, 6, 1–60.

Bandura, A. (1997). *Self-efficacy: The exercise of control*. New York: W. H. Freeman & Co.

Barber, J. G. (1991). *Beyond casework*. Basingstoke, UK: Macmillan.

Becker, S. M. (2009). Psychosocial care for women survivors of the tsunami disaster in India. *American Journal of Public Health*, 99(4), 654–658.

Bisman, C. (1994). *Social work practice: Cases and principles*. Pacific Grove, CA: Brooks/Cole.

Bisman, C., & Hardcastle, D. (1999). *Integrating research into practice: A model for effective social work*. Pacific Grove, CA: Brooks/Cole, Wadsworth.

Boettcher, R. E., Jakes, L., & Sigal, L. M. (2008). An evaluation of a community collaboration approach to psychosocial rehabilitation. *Journal of Community Practice*, 16(2), 165–181.

Bond, G. R., McGrew, J. H., & Fekete, D. M. (1995). Assertive outreach for frequent users of psychiatric hospitals: A meta-analysis. *Journal of Mental Health Administration*, 22(1), 4–16.

Brooks, F., & Brown, E. (2005). A program evaluation of Los Angeles ACORN's welfare case advocacy. *Journal of Human Behavior in the Social Environment*, 12(2-3), 185–203.

Butcher, H., Banks, S., & Henderson, P., with Robertson, J. (Eds.). (2007). *Critical community practice*. Bristol, UK: The Policy Press.

Cheung, K-F. M., Stevenson, K. M., & Leung, P. (1991). Competency-based evaluation of case management skills in child sexual abuse intervention. *Child Welfare*, 70, 425–435.

Churchman, C. W. (1965). *The systems approach*. New York: Dell.

Delgado, M., & Staples, L. (2008). *Youth-led community organizing: Theory and action*. New York: Oxford University Press.

Dinerman, M. (1992). Managing the mazes: Case management and service delivery. *Administration in Social Work*, 16, 1–9.

Dowrick, P. W., & Yuen, J.W. L. (2006). Literacy for the community, by the community. *Journal of Prevention & Intervention in the Community*, 32(1), 81–96.

Etzioni, A. (1993). *The spirit of community: Rights, responsibilities and the communitarian agenda*. New York: Crown.

Garcia, C. (2005). Buscando trabajo: Social networking among immigrants from Mexico to the Unites States. *Hispanic Journal of Behavioral Sciences*, 27(1), 3–22.

Gordon, D. S., & Donald, S. (1993). *Community social work: Older people and informal care, a romantic illusion*. Aldershot Hants, UK: Ashgate.

Gray, K. A. (2005). Women who succeeded in leaving public assistance for a living-wage job. *Qualitative Social Work*, 4, 309–326.

Hagen, J. L. (1994). JOBS and case management: Developments in 10 states. *Social Work*, 39, 197–205.

Hammersley, M., & Atkinson, P. (1983). *Ethnography: Principles in practice*. New York: Tavistock.

IFSW (2010). *Joint definition of social work: Adopted July 2000*. Retrieved June 21, 2010, from: http://www.ifsw.org/f38000022.html.

Itzhaky, H. (2003) Developing empowerment and leadership: The case of immigrant women in Israel. *Affilia*, 18, 289–301.

Kantor, J. S. (1991). Integrating case management and psychiatric hospitalization. *Health and Social Work*, 16, 34–42.

Karabanow, J. (1999). Creating community: A case study of a Montreal street kid agency. *Community Development Journal*, 3(4), 318–327.

Kunkel, J. H. (1975). *Behavior, social problems, and change: A social learning approach*. Englewood Cliffs, NJ: Prentice Hall.

Lee, J. A. B. (1994). *The empowerment approach to social work practice*. New York: Columbia University Press.

Levine, I. S., & Fleming, M. (1985). *Human resources development: Issues in case management*. Baltimore: Maryland Mental Health Administration, Center for Rehabilitation and Manpower Services, Community Support Project.

Lightburn, A., & Sessions, P. (Eds.). (2006). *Handbook of community-based clinical practice*. New York: Oxford University Press.

Lindsey, M. A., Browne, D. C., Thompson, R., Hawley, K. M., Graham, J. C., Weisbart, C., Harrington, D., & Kotch, J. B. (2008). Caregiver mental health, neighborhood, and social network influences on mental health needs among African American children. *Social Work Research*, 32(2), 79–89.

Mason, M. (2009). Social network characteristics of urban adolescents in brief substance abuse treatment. *Journal of Child & Adolescent Substance Abuse*, 18, 72–84.

McLeod, E., Bywaters, P., Tanner, D., & Hirsch, M. (2008). For the sake of their health: Older service users' requirements for social care to facilitate access to social networks following hospital discharge. *British Journal of Social Work*, 38, 73–90.

Morrow-Howell, N. (1992). Clinical case management: The hallmark of gerontological social work. *Journal of Gerontological Social Work*, 18, 119–131.

Nicotera, N. (2008). Building skills for civic engagement: Children as agents of neighborhood change. *Journal of Community Practice*, 16(2), 221–242.

Paterson, B. L.m & Panessa, C. (2008). Engagement as an ethical imperative in harm reduction involving at-risk youth. *International Journal of Drug Policy*, 19, 24–32.

Payne, M. (2000). *Teamwork in multiprofessional care.* Chicago: Lyceum.

Payne, M. (2002). The politics of systems theory within social work. *Journal of Social Work*, 2(3), 269–292.

Payne, M. (2006). Modern social work theory, (3rd ed.). Chicago, IL: Lyceum.

Pearrow, M. M. (2008). A Critical examination of an urban-based youth empowerment strategy: The teen empowerment program. *Journal of Community Practice*, 16(4), 509–525.

Pecukonis, E. V., & Wenocur, S. (1994). Perceptions of self and collective efficacy in community organization theory and practice. *Journal of Community Practice*, 1, 5–21.

Phillips, J., Bernard, M., Phillipson, C., & Ogg, J. (2000). Social support in later life: A study of three areas. *British Journal of Social Work*, 30(60), 837–859.

Polinsky, M. L., Fred, C., & Ganz, P. A. (1991). Quantitative and qualitative assessment of a case management program for cancer patients. *Health and Social Work*, 16, 176–183.

Raheim, S. (1995). Self-employment training and family development: An integrated strategy for family empowerment. In P. Adams & K. Nelson (Eds.), *Reinventing human services: Community and family-centered practice* (pp. 127–143). New York: Aldine de Gruyter.

Richmond, M. E. (1917). *Social diagnosis.* New York: Russell Sage Foundation.

Richmond, M. E. (1922). *What is social casework? An introductory description.* New York: Russell Sage Foundation.

Rife, J. C., First, R. J., Greenlee, R. W., Miller, L. D., & Feichter, M. A. (1991). Case management with homeless mentally ill people. *Health and Social Work*, 16, 58–66.

Rogers, N., & Anderson, W. (2007). A community development approach to deal with public drug use in Box Hill. *Drug and Alcohol Review*, 26, 87–95.

Rubin, A. (1987). Case management. In A. Minahan (Ed.), *Encyclopedia of social work* (Vol. I, 18th ed., pp. 212–222). Silver Spring, MD: National Association of Social Workers.

Rubin, A. (1992). Is case management effective for people with serious mental illness? A research review. *Health and Social Work*, 17, 138–150.

Sheppard, M. (1991). *Mental health work in the community: Theory and practice in social work and community psychiatric nursing.* London, UK: Falmer.

Smale, G. G. (1995). Integrating community and individual practice: A new paradigm for practice. In P. Adams & K. Nelson (Eds.), *Reinventing human services: Community and family-centered practice* (pp. 59–80). New York: Aldine de Gruyter.

Swartz, S. (1995). Community and risk in social service work. *Journal of Progressive Human Services*, 61(1), 73–92.

Taylor, S. H., & Roberts, R. W. (Eds.) (1985). *Theory and practice of community social work.* New York: Columbia University Press.

Thyer, B. A., & Hudson, W. W. (1986/1987). Progress in behavioral social work: An introduction. *Journal of Social Service Research*, 10, 1–6.

Tsai, J. H-C. (2006). Xenophobia, ethnic community, and immigrant youths' friendship network formation. *Adolescence*, 41(162), 285–298.

Uttal, L. (2006). Community caregiving and community consciousness: Immigrant Latinas developing communities through social service programs. *Community Development*, 37(4), 53–70.

von Bertalanffy, L. (1967). *Robots, men and mind.* New York: Braziller.

Wandersman, A., Clary, E. G., Forbush, J., Weinberger, S. G., Coyne, S. M., & Duffy, J. L. (2006). Community organizing and advocacy: Increasing the quality and quantity of mentoring programs. *Journal of Community Psychology*, 34(6), 781–799.

Warren-Adamson, C., & Lightburn, A. (2006). Developing a community-based model for integrated family centered practice. In A. Lightburn & P. P. Sessions (Eds.), *Handbook of community-based clinical practice* (pp. 261–289). New York: Oxford University Press.

Washington, R. O. (Ed.) (1974). *A strategy for service integration: Case management.* East Cleveland, OH: East Cleveland Community Human Service Center.

Washington, R. O., Karman, M., & Friedlob, F. (1974). *Second year evaluation: Report of the East Cleveland community human service center.* Cleveland, OH: Case Western Reserve University, School of Applied Social Sciences, Human Services Design Laboratory.

Weiser, S., & Silver, M. (1981). Community work and social learning theory. *Social Work*, 26, 146–150.

Wolk, J. L., Sullivan, W. P., & Hartmann, D. J. (1994). The managerial nature of case management. *Social Work*, 39, 154–159.

Subject Index

Author Index